Understanding India

The Evolution Of Indian Consciousness

Abraham Jacob

Printed in India

ISBN: 978-93-6045-107-3

First Printing, 2024

The Write Order

A division of Nasadiya Technologies Private Ltd.

Koramangala, Bangalore

Karnataka-560029

THE WRITE ORDER PUBLICATIONS.

www.thewriteorder.com

Edited by Sakshi Tiwari

Typeset by Parinkumar Nirmal

Book Cover designed by Nikhil Kamath

Publishing Consultant: Anagha Somanakoppa

TABLE OF CONTENTS

PREFACE

I do not claim to be an expert on Indian history or Indian philosophy. I am emboldened by the fact that Bertrand Russell, when he wrote his monumental 'History of Western Philosophy,' quite humbly accepted that he was no expert on any of the philosophers he was writing about, with the exception of Leibniz. Likewise, my only excuse is that I have been truly mystified by what we as a people are today. Therefore, I went in search of an answer. It led to a study of Indian history, Indian philosophy, and the evolution of Hinduism. I have tried to present in narrative form what I discovered. The presumption is that what I found would be useful for not only those with similar interests but also those who may not have had the time or inclination to do a detailed study. I also hope that the narrative is both interesting and stimulating.

Being no expert and on a journey of discovery, I obviously had to depend on the knowledge of others. Further, being no Sanskrit scholar, I had to depend on the translations I could lay my hands on. The debt to some of the greats cannot be avoided. For most of the information in chapters one and two, I am indebted to Dr. Radhakrishnan. For my knowledge of the Rig Veda and the Laws of Manu, I am indebted to Doniger Wendy and also to her work, 'Hindus: An Alternate History.' On Indian philosophy, I depended on R. Paligandla's 'Fundamentals of Indian Philosophy,' along with Dr. Radhakrishnan's monumental work, 'Indian Philosophy,' and Monier Williams' 'Indian Wisdom.' Much of my chapter on the evolution of the gods is taken from Diana L. Eck's 'India: A Religious

Geography.' The story of the Shudra is largely from Ram Charan Sharma's 'The Shudra in Ancient India.' My knowledge of the Arthashastra is from L.N. Rangaragan's translation. The quotations from the Bhagavad Gita are from Stoner Miller's translation.

I have been fascinated by the books of Robert Calasso. Both 'Ka' and 'Ardour' have made a deep impression on me. Nirad Choudhry has been, for me, the most intuitive historian of India's past, and I cannot help but admit the impact of the works of Dr. Romila Thapar. Yet, like most Indians, I started with A.L. Basham's 'The Wonder That Was India' and Nehru's 'Discovery of India.' Indian thinking is so complex that it is very difficult to reduce it to a linear narrative; thus, I speak in different voices to convey the diverse interpretations possible, often with an apology. In this context, among modern writers, it is Devdutt Pattanaik who best conveys this complexity.

Abraham Jacob,

November, 2018

CHAPTER 1

INTRODUCTION

Clouds gather and thicken as we try to peer into our past. Mists fill the landscape, and only from myths and legends can we discern the ideas that shaped our consciousness. No concrete picture emerges of our past, as so little history has been written and even less has survived.

The Harappan civilization, which left ruins that speak of a very advanced civilization with modern drainage and sewage systems and a highly regimented lifestyle, speaks for itself but is mute in all other senses. Their language, tantalizingly depicted in seals, symbols, and texts, has evaded human intelligence's attempts to decipher it. The collapse of the Harappan civilization, without any real continuation in any other civilization, is unique. In all other civilizations, the decay and fall of civilization was always a stepping stone for something new, often better. The Harappan civilization, instead, seems to have just decayed and got buried in the desert sands from which it originated, leaving no trace of migration of its people nor the transmission of their ideas to any other people. It seems to have come from nowhere, got buried, and disappeared. How long that 'shrunken visage' lay in the silent desert is also a matter of conjecture.

Indian philosophy has always spoken of the futility of human life, and the Harappan civilization, in its ruins, stares back at us as if into dark spaces and unknown reality. The real, what actually happened, is no longer available to us, and the people who lived in ancient India thought likewise—that what is important is the present, the past—a memory that fades, corrupted by new ones while the mind grapples with eternal questions of existentialism. That is why historians say Indians were essentially spiritual people.

The opacity that faces the Indian historian does not end with the problems of origin but continues until the arrival of the Muslims as conquerors. There has been an aversion to history as something written down. Like the continued mystery of the Harappan Civilization, all of Indian history tantalizes with what it could have been, held together by memory, myth, and legend.

While history is said to determine the nature of a people, we have so little history that we have created our persona from memory, modified by the present. The dead are burned, and their ashes merge with Mother Earth; even their memory is only a quintessence of what they were, an idea, not the story of real flesh and blood. The present, therefore, creates the past.

Long ago, a British historian, more to provoke than to state a fact, asserted that India was not a civilized country and had no culture. He claimed that Hindu culture, if it existed at all, was available to such a minuscule minority of its population that calling it the culture of the nation would be misleading. Even Hinduism, claimed by Indians to be their religion, is so variously and differently practiced across the country that calling it the same religion would also stretch its meaning. He then asserted that the only common ethos running across the country was its poverty—dirty, ugly, and demeaning. From the slums of the cities to the villages of India, the only common factor is abject poverty, which leads to ugliness, brutality, cruelty, and a life that invariably has to be amoral. It is neither bright nor joyful but is everywhere dark, gloomy, and dirty.

There is much that is pertinent in the criticism for anyone wanting to understand Indian culture. The language of India, Sanskrit, the language of the sacred texts and all learning, was not known even to the educated and was, in fact, the preserve of the few who claimed the priestly order and to whom it had been entrusted. Thus, all the music, science, dance, and humanistic treatises written in Sanskrit were available only to a very select few and were not part of the common culture. For most of Indian history, it was also a crime to teach and, in fact, even to hear the language, except by those to whom it had been entrusted.

Our philosophical tradition that grew out of the Vedas is so deeply metaphysical that very few even try to understand it. We dress differently from north to south and from east to west; we eat different foods, speak different languages, and worship different gods; we are even different in color and size. The Japanese have a common language, the samurai tradition, and Zen Buddhism; the Chinese have a common script and Confucianism and Taoism mixed with Buddhism; and the West has a common Greco-Roman tradition and Christianity. Meanwhile, we as a nation seem to have no common binding language or common racial memory. India has always been divided into various small states and empires and has never been ruled as a single nation, even during the time of the largest empire, that of the Mughals, or during the years of the might of Imperial Britannia.

In the end, we have no option but to accept the fact that the only common thread that runs through the fabric of Indian society is a common belief embedded in the religion that we call Hinduism. Even if Hinduism is more a way of life than a religion and its practices differ almost without recognition across the country, it is still the only thing that binds Indians culturally and the nation into a civilization. It has also been extremely powerful and corrosive, grinding everything in its path to its likeness. The truth of this can be seen in the corrosive power of 'Hinduism' to convert all new ideas and even revolutionary movements into its ever-extending umbrella of beliefs. Thus, Buddhism disappeared, and all revolutionary philosophies that originated in the country have been absorbed and laid to rest, to be discovered only by the scholar.

What it did to uncompromising religions like Christianity and Islam is most revealing. The ideas dominant in Hindu thought, like the caste system, have permeated both Christianity and Islam to such an extent that they have become an indictment of their own stated principles of equality and justice. Christians and Muslims became superstitious, believers in astrology, and accepted with abject submission the idea of Karma and the sanctity of the caste system. Christians have become idol worshippers, with icons and statues dominating their worship, while Muslims worship at the tombs of saints and fakirs. The church at Velankanni and the pilgrims who flock to that church are no longer distinguishable from those who visit Tirupati, as both wait in long queues and even crawl their way to the shrine and come out with bald heads, having donated their hair to their respective gods.

Consequently, if there is any cementing force binding all Indians together, it has to be Hinduism. The question then is, what is Hinduism? For it is certainly not the Hinduism of the Vedic people, which was open, questioning, and agnostic, nor the religion of the Harappan people, of which we know nothing. How do we even describe the spectrum of Hinduism as practiced today, an idolatrous religion that has fostered a thousand gods and allows for an endless variety of worship, where the idols are propitiated with offerings as diverse as flowers to arrack and from fish to human sacrifices and where the Ram Leela of North India and the Theyyam dance of the Dalits of Kerala are all accepted forms of celebration and worship? As the religion evolved, it invariably did so unevenly, with some regions being more amenable to change while others retracted into reactionary and conservative ideas. The educated, the wealthy, and the powerful, obviously held to traditional values, while others demanded change. Yet, across the centuries and across the length and breadth of the country, the belief in Karma and the practice of caste stratification are pervasive.

The historian sees in this evolution of religion the defining principles of our intellectual evolution. In that evolution lies the foundations of our identity, which we need to understand. That will be the scope of our study. However, the bafflement at what we have become never ceases. How did an open-questioning people become a nation of mute worshippers, and how did the people who created the Harappan civilization that boasted the best sewage system become a nation of open defecators? How did a person who said that the gods came later and scorned the claims of the gods, stating that with tapas and sacrifice, we could hold even the gods to ransom, become fatalistic and apathetic?

The components of our nationhood are made up of our religion and the core values we have accepted over the centuries—the caste system and the belief in Karma. They both lead to many attitudinal problems, yet they are the core of our being as Indians. That is our tragedy; we are a fragmented society, lost without Karma and rudderless without the caste system. Yet, any system is better than nothing; having nothing leads to chaos and anarchy, and that is where we are being led as we question the caste system, a clearly unjust and cruel system that no society can condone or accept.

Consequently, we are facing a social order devoid of any guiding principles and a vacuum with no order and no faith. The modern Indian is an anachronism caught in a time warp and suspended in no man's land. He lives in a world of Western institutions and ideas, which he neither accepts nor believes, and is therefore forced to meander through life with no convictions, being fatalistic and apathetic.

The Great Forgetting

Standing in Fort Kochi, overlooking the Kochi harbor and observing people going about their business or eating peanuts, one sees only blank faces, indifferent to where they are—the port that may have been Muziris, where traders from the West came thousands of years ago to trade and make it their home. There is no semblance of any awareness of the history that surrounds the place or the momentous events that happened and shaped our beings. The Bihari kid who playfully kicks stones at what was the site of Nalanda University likewise has no inkling of where he stands, literally, on hallowed ground. The racist Indians who bully Northeastern Indians as Chinese-looking have no idea that they themselves are descended from a Chinese tribe called the Yueh Ti, who created dynasties and became part of us. We lack awareness of our history and our bloodlines, staring blankly at the truths of history.

Our amnesia about our past is astounding and terribly unsettling. Before the arrival of the British, we, as a people, did not even know of the historical existence of Ashoka, the emperor. In fact, while there was a rumor about a man called Buddha, there was little record of his life or work, which had to be compiled from Sri Lankan and Tibetan records. While Egyptians also had to wait for the white men to reveal their past, they at least had the Pyramids to remind them of who they were. We Indians, however, had to wait for the Englishmen to excavate at the sites of Harappa and Mohenjo-Daro for us to be aware of the antiquity of our civilization. It has, however, revealed a past shrouded in mystery that we are still neither able to decipher nor link in an unbroken chain of history. What is worse is that so little of our history is known. There is a total blank between the time of the Harappans and the Mauryas, a blank until the Guptas, and a further blank until the arrival of the Muslims. In fact, the life of one of the most revered saints of Hinduism, Sankaracharya, who lived in the tenth century, is more like a myth, as so little of his life has been historically recorded. What is worse is that the little we know we owe to foreign visitors, especially the Chinese pilgrims like Huan Tsang and Fa Hein, Muslim writers like Ibn Battuta and Alberuni, and Jesuit preachers and adventurers like Marco Polo.

Did the elite, the educated, the dictators of faith, and the rulers of the country know any better? What did the elite of India, who claimed to rule and dictate the canons of faith, know of the past? They had the Ramayana and the Mahabharata, a mythical story of some forgotten past; they had the Vedas, the Vedantas, and treatises on mathematics, music, dance, language, and grammar; some science; and a lot of astrology. The only history they had was the Puranas, a mythical history of the fortune-telling of kingdoms and society, bereft of historical evidence and lacking sufficient coherence. A few great works, like the Arthashastra, were written and referred to, but a copy of it was first discovered in 1936. There may have been the Manusmrithis and some of the works of Kalidasa and other poets, but nothing like a corpus of work on which history could be written. Thus, even the elite were blind to their past.

A review of what we knew of ourselves when the British arrived would show how appallingly ignorant we were. Less than one percent of the population was literate. We were a nation steeped in poverty with local pockets of governance, and we were regional natives owing loyalty only to locally spoken languages. Our past was a blank slate, and the Brahmins were still chanting in an ancient language that almost no one understood, and we accepted diverse practices to propitiate our many gods. Something of the mythology of the Ramayana and the Mahabharata had percolated down to the people through the popular local renderings of the Ramayana in Tamil and in Awadhi, thanks to Kambar and Tulsidas, and also because of the local festivals of Ram Leelas, Katha-kali, storytelling, and dramas.

Indians, however, are neither aware of the ignorance of our past nor bothered. Even Nehru, when he tried to write a history of India, long after the pioneering work of the Orientalists, still had to call it 'The Discovery of India.' A stupor seemed to have gotten hold of our minds, and we sleepwalked into the modern era, blinking as we were conquered and subdued, blinded and abused, till we emerged as a somnambulistic nation searching for pride and honor.

The Brahmin, who was the custodian of all knowledge, appeared disinterested in a scientific study of history, for superstitions would better serve to retain his position of power. Consequently, only a Western-oriented history is available. The reaction against Western scholarship created a distorted legacy; consequently, the truth of our past keeps shifting with the changes in political power and accepted ideology. In an attempt to create a mythical unity in the religion called Hinduism, all that was part of the dissenting culture of the religion has been forcibly deleted and passed off as Western propaganda. The vastness of Hindu philosophy has been stunted, and the plurality of its thinking, its spread, and its contradictions swept under the carpet, as it were, to present an anemic and rigid religion devoid of ambiguity and romance.

The question then would be, Why did Indians not write history? Even more troubling would be the question, Why are Indians not aware of their total blindness to their past? Why is it that foreigners were prepared to dig in the desert, trek in the forests, and endure great pain merely to unravel the history of India's past while Indians themselves seemed oblivious to such a need? What is it about our national make-up that shuns the past and fears self-knowledge? The troubling fact is that not only do we shun the past, but we also try to destroy what remains of the past. When the British finally tried to do a detailed study of the past, they found that a large part of the records and monuments of the past had been deliberately destroyed, especially those pertaining to Buddha and Buddhist history. Stupas and Buddhist temples had been turned into Hindu temples and then made sacred so that no excavations would be done; rock edicts and pillars had been defaced, broken, and buried. The attempt, it would seem, was to obliterate the past. We have been an independent country for seventy years but have shown little determination to unravel the past or to ensure an open-minded look at our history instead of being buried in ignorance.

The Great, Unanswered Questions of Indian History

If a person did not know his parents, his origins, his place of birth, his language, his culture, and his heritage, he would almost surely become neurotic. Thus, we Indians, who have almost no knowledge of these, must also be neurotic people. Yet, we do not even seem to care. Is that perhaps a sign of a greater neurosis, as Freud would say? Have we merely suppressed and repressed our most traumatic memories? The inability or unwillingness to know ourselves results in the shutting out of the truth and the creation of superficial people who merely pretend to be whole and who act out a way of life with no conviction or confidence. Indians certainly exhibit these characteristics. Is it neurosis that paralyzes our soul and makes us inconsequential? However, the worst aspect of this apathy is that it allows us to accept stupid and false notions of our heritage because anything is better than being without any roots. In fact, a lack of a clear identity can even lead to schizophrenia. That may explain why we appear superficial, gaudy, and loud, lacking sophistication in culture and manners, upholding fanciful ideas without any regard for the truth; in fact, we are determined that the truth should never be known, lest the fanciful notions of our greatness be proved false.

While our ignorance may be an escape, there are many historical details that should interest us. They include, among many, the appearance and disappearance of the Harappan civilization. While there were similar vintage civilizations in Greece, Mesopotamia, and China, what is special about the Harappan civilization is that, as we know it, it was already a fully developed civilization with modern-level drainage and sewage systems and city planning on par with modern-day standards. What is even more surprising is the amnesia surrounding the life and times of Ashoka the Great. Despite the fact that he wrote rock edicts and erected pillars all over the country, speaking of his life and his philosophy, all of them were deliberately forgotten and discarded as rubbish. The rock edicts were defaced, and the pillars were broken down and used even as road rollers in the time of the Muslim rulers, before the Mughals. Ashoka, in his time, was supposed to have built 84,000 Buddhist temples; what happened to them? The Buddhist stupas and monasteries were vandalized, broken, and desecrated, and the stones were used to pave roads. How then could we ever be able to study history or respect it?

When Ashoka wrote his edicts, he mentioned the Cholas, the Pandyas, and the Kerala Putras, yet we have no knowledge of them until the Cholas, as a dynasty, seized power in the tenth century, while the Kerala Putras, we know next to nothing. The kingdom of King Solomon in Israel is recorded to have traded with the people of Malabar, and there was supposed to have been a Jewish settlement on the Malabar coast from the 6th century B.C.; what happened to them? An early kingdom, situated with its headquarters at present-day Kanchipuram, was called the Pallava Kingdom, which means Persian; how did the Persians come so far south and create a kingdom? No one seems to know. Anyone who has visited any country in Southeast Asia or stayed there for any length of time is struck by the pervading Indian ethos and the many Indian-inspired monuments. They date back to as early as the early Buddhists and before, to Hindu kings, we don't even know about. What is intriguing is how they got there, how they overpowered the local people culturally, and what sort of maritime knowledge led them there.

More baffling, perhaps, are some of the social and cultural facets of our past. The caste system was slowly imposed on the people of India and has now become a defining characteristic of us as a people, but it was resisted from the very beginning by all the intellectual and religious classes. The Sramanas and their varied philosophies of materialism and stoicism scorned such ideas. The Buddha and the Jains clearly fought against the imposition of the caste system, and at every stage of history, there was open rebellion against the caste system, with all reformers of the Bhakti movement denouncing it. Yet none of these made any difference as the caste took a stronger and stronger hold on the country. What can possibly explain such a phenomenon? India was at the forefront of science and mathematics during the 1st century. Why then did it neither grow nor result in the growth of a parallel technology? Why did the knowledge of hydraulics not even lead to the use of windmills? These are merely a few questions that immediately surface, but a deeper study of Indian history only raises more and more baffling questions.

Our Intellectual Heritage

Dr. Radhakrishnan starts his introduction to Indian philosophy with the claim that India, a land of plenty without the terrible extremes of climate, was not a battleground of continuous battles and was instead a sedate, tranquil place where the spirit was able to dwell on the question of the infinite. Thus, Indians did not have to deal with Plato's pronouncement not to allow 'one misfortune to befall us. Let us not become mislogues as some people become misanthropes, for no greater evil can befall men than to become haters of knowledge.' Thus, instead of thinking of itself as only a respite from the horrors of war, Indians thought had the luxury of continuous attention. The greatness of India is that it has held fast to this special heritage where thinking and spiritual action were always considered supreme. Indian thought was also the result, almost purely, of native thinking and had no need to borrow from any other source. The history of Indian thought, says Dr. Radhakrishnan, 'illustrates the endless quest of the mind, ever old, ever new…' The spiritual motive dominates life in India. The founders of philosophy strive for social-spiritual reformation of the country. Religion in India is not dogmatic. It only keeps pace with the progress in thought. In India, religion is hardly a dogma but a working hypothesis of human conduct, adapted to different stages of spiritual development.

It was only religious, says Dr. Radhakrishnan, to the extent that 'the problems of religion stimulate philosophical thought.' He then cites the progress made in philosophy from the Vedic hymns to the Upanishads and to Buddhism, summing it up by saying, 'The philosophic spirit has become the confident attitude of mind.' While the Samkhya is silent about God, Jaimini refers to God only to deny providence and his moral government of the world. The supremacy of religion and social tradition in life does not hamper the free pursuit of philosophy, says Dr. Radhakrishnan. The evidence speaks, he says, of a strong intellectual tradition that, in the search for truth, delved into logic, grammar, and the sciences—in fact, into everything that was interesting and relevant to the pursuit of truth. The attempt was to establish the nature of reality and the essence of self. In the quest, they realized that the mystical was very much part of the range of human intellect. Despite this focus on the subjective, Indian thought also delved deeply into the objective sciences like mathematics and astrology. They also developed their own science of logic and a detailed science of grammar. Dr. Radhakrishnan, however, accepts that the Indian mind did not produce any profound technology that could lead to an industrial revolution.

Indian philosophy was initially monistic and even non-dualism—a philosophy that sees no dualism in the universe, a form of monism that believes that a single type of matter pervades all existence. Consciousness, unlike the all-important 'I think, therefore I am,' is, in Indian philosophy, a very practical concept, taking into account modern psychological insights and including waking consciousness, dreaming (sleep) consciousness, and the totally blank state in deep sleep. All life is seen as relative; the waking state is only relatively different from the dream state. There is no absolutely real world—the dream world, the blank world, and the waking world of action are all parts of the same reality, Thus, we can even think of existence without outward action or the general experience of life. The reality of the human experience is therefore extremely complex. The empirical world seems bound in space and time and exhibits a correspondence to the laws of causality. Yet, cause, time, and space seem to contradict each other. They are relative terms and have no separate existence; they are devoid of human existence.

This perception of human life is what is termed 'Maya' in Indian Philosophy. The relationship is between the self, the apparent flux of time, and an attempt to pin it down so that it allows us to assume that all things have a cause and a reason. These assumptions are never provable. The infinite can never be expressed in finite terms, and the limited cannot manifest the unlimited. Even to say that the infinite degenerates into the finite to make itself manifest would be a contradiction in terms. What is changeless cannot be seen in the changing. All thought is only part of the relative and transient world, and therefore we can never hope to understand the infinite.

This limitation that Western philosophy took a long time to reckon with is not swept under in Indian philosophy but taken as a part and a condition that limits human thoughts, a truth that always remains in the background of all attempts to understand. When this is accepted, philosophy realizes that all we have is human existence and the reality of the self. There is no knower who knows; man can only try to know himself. This is the basis of the philosophy of Advaita, or non-dualism. There is no 'I' and the 'other,' or 'self,' or matter; they can be understood only in totality, as part of a single reality. The ultimate self remains unmoved in the theater of change and becoming. Change is an illusion; nothing is added and nothing is removed; all change is only the appearance of change. 'The truth of universal mobility is the immobile being,' said the ancient Indians.

To know the truth, we must first remove the layers of ignorance (avidya), the molds created by intellect. The purpose of philosophy and logic, as the ancient Indian philosophers and Wittgenstein said, is to expose the inadequacies of intellectual categories. They also claim, with Heisenberg, that to measure reality is to distort it. We need the higher power of 'abstract intellect' to enable us to 'feel' reality instead of dissecting it to learn its reality. When we realize that all reality is merely the projection of the mind, then we realize that there is nothing but 'being.' Only in the opposition of reality and unreality, negative and positive, do we create a tangible world. The universe is created by thought and sustained by thought; subject and object are merely moments in time. God is merely a fixed point from which thinking can begin. God is the inner reality through which the manifestations of the universe are made intelligible. God is the highest limit of our intellectual capacity, and the tragedy is that it is only a construction of our thoughts.

As the ancient sages looked at the world in the Rig Veda, they consciously accepted the validity of human experience. The 'Upanishads' quickly realized that reality cannot be comprehended by the intellect. This forced Buddhist philosophy to deny the world of appearances. Nagarjuna, however, maintained the truth of the central position of the Upanishads: that reality cannot be comprehended by intellect. Conflict arises only when a compromise is made to understand reality; the compromise then becomes the untruth that the limited intellect of men continues to attack, forgetting that the untruth was the compromise that made thinking possible. Positions differ, different schools emerge, and wrong conclusions are reached as each school tries to grab reality and claim to know the truth. In the end, they become self-contradictory. Thus, evolved the idea of "Darshana." This seeing is beyond mere intellect and involves both intuition, revelation, and grace. An insight, a flash of intuitive knowledge, a sudden revelation as though from some higher providence. In this flash of illumination, all intellectual skepticism is put aside, and a new insight is gained. The problem is that this insight can be defended only with an intellect that is fallible. Darshana is thus a 'spiritual perception, a whole new view revealed to the soul sense.' Such insight is not available to everyone. One needs an inquiring mind, freed from material desire, with the courage to go where logic leads, even to pitiless self-examination. Only with such an attitude would knowledge open its doors.

Dr. Radhakrishnan claims that reverence for the past is a national trait, that Indians tend to hold fast to their traditional faith, and that Indian culture has, in an essential sense, survived through the centuries. The old spirit is maintained, and only new names are given to old beliefs. This is what makes Indian society seem immobile. He also claims that the many systems of philosophy are merely the branches of the same tree of Indian philosophy. He sees history as Hegel did, as a general unfolding, where truth is unfolded bit by bit through successive systems. However, Prasthana Bheda opined that the many systems of philosophy only prevented men from falling into atheism, as the many interpretations of perception, reviewed almost endlessly, kept atheism at bay. While defenders of Nyaya, like Udayana, see Maya as truth, theists like Ramana see only in theism the ultimate truth. Indian philosophy thus encompasses many systems and is unafraid to accept even the seemingly dangerous, as long as it is backed by logic.

Dr. Radhakrishnan then defends Indian philosophy against some of its often-cited drawbacks. The criticism that Indian philosophy is pessimistic is answered by Dr. Radhakrishnan, who says that it is not pessimistic but only realistic, where 'Sath' indicates both reality and perfection. He then answers the charge that Indian philosophy is not openly logical but harps back on authority and revelation. Dr. Radhakrishnan admits that Indian thinking tends to accept the Vedas as revealed knowledge, and very often philosophy is only a defense of the Vedic position, accepting that the Vedas are too often canonized and accepted as dogma. Yet logic continues to be the standard by which all philosophies are judged. The criticism that Indian philosophy is largely unethical is answered by Dr. Radhakrishnan, who says that 'Dharma' has always been the most important part of Indian philosophy.

Dr. Radhakrishnan's defense appears to be too weak for the great failings of Indian philosophy. Indian philosophy is clearly other-worldly, as seen in the concept of Maya. It is also true that many of the basic concepts of Hinduism, like 'Karma' and the resultant caste system, despite regular challenges from the outside, retain their basic features and have largely remained unchanged. Further, despite the harsh challenges to Vedic rituals, they have survived to the present, with almost no change at all, with the priest chanting the same mantras for rituals celebrating birth to death, with the same words, in the same intonation, and around the same ritual altars, as sacrosanct and unchallenged. It is also true that Indian philosophy from the Vedas has concerned itself more with the concept of reality, between Maya and divine manifestation, between monism and dualism, and Advaitha. However, it may be an exaggeration to say that 'Dharma' was always a central concern, as morals are largely derived and never explicit. The Vedas do not teach ethics, only the proper rituals and mantras. It is only from the major epics that ethics have been derived. Unfortunately, the epics present a terribly ambiguous idea of ethics, which is always relative and conditioned by the concept of Karma. Manu and Kautilya also present such a relative concept of morality that the modern man, living in democracies where equality is an accepted norm, finds it, if nothing else, confusing.

The more generous presumption that Dr. Radhakrishnan makes is the acceptance that Indians are spiritual people. Indian philosophy and the greatness of the Indian cultural heritage are too often used to make sweeping statements about India as a whole and to hide its many limitations. All cultures are essentially elitist, but the problem with Indian culture and philosophy is that they were deliberately denied to the vast majority of Indians by the caste system. Based on the written record of the only literate people in India, where the vast majority, in fact, 99%, were illiterate even until the arrival of the British, to say we are a spiritual nation would be debatable, especially if we define 'spiritual' as that which is opposed to the materialistic.

The philosophy was available only to a minuscule minority who were literate, and their thinking has had little impact on the rest of India. Popular movements like the 'Bhakti movement' and the earlier challenges of Buddha and Mahavira were relevant, but the fact that their religions have almost vanished from India shows that there was an orthodoxy so powerful that even where they lost ground for some moments in history, they always came back with a vengeance. The Bhakti movement, which should have killed the caste system, faded away, leaving caste even stronger.

Dr. Radhakrishnan's claim that the founders of the philosophical systems sought socio-spiritual reformation may be true, but the more relevant question is why they failed to change the socio-religious conditions of the people. His claim that Indian religion is only a working hypothesis and not dogma is also difficult to accept. Hinduism has fossilized into rigid ritualism, and the philosophical content is rejected as too arid. In fact, the most pertinent question facing the Indian historian is why we, as people, have spurned the open-minded philosophy of the past and accepted unthinking devotion, not even of the Bhakti kind but of the bargaining kind. The answer lies not in the interpretations of historians but in what millions of Indians did for generations, slowly changing customs and beliefs, controlled by power and social dominance. It also ground arid philosophies and brought them closer to their hearts, rejecting the merely intellectual. The rest is the result of the quirks of history. We are also invariably the result of the random throw of dice, of those who came and those who went, of natural calamities, even of continental shifts, the ice age, and the flood. Yet we have evolved as a recognizable type, not in the whole, but at least in parts.

CHAPTER 2

THE FOUNDATION: THE SRUTHIS

The universal Indian belief is that we first verbalized our thoughts in the sacred texts called the Vedas. It is believed among Indians that the Vedas were not merely outpourings of wonder but divine revelation. It is believed that in the mists of time, the gods themselves whispered the secrets contained in the Vedas to a select band of sages. It was then passed down verbally from father to son for centuries, always ensuring that not a word, not a syllable, nor the intonation of sounds was ever incorrect. As literature, they are poems of wonder and delight. They are also songs of praise and cries for help that turn into prayers and expressions of thankfulness. The later Vedas were more specifically associated with mantras associated with sacrifices and rituals. Together, they formed the Vedas, which were initially only three, but a fourth was soon added.

It is difficult to discern a consistent philosophy or even a clear pattern of thinking in the Vedas, and it was left to later thinkers to make sense of the apparently random thoughts that were compressed into the Vedas. These later commentaries and interpretations were authored by some of the most revered sages of ancient India and are called Vedantas, literally meaning the end of the Vedas. They are also called the Upanishads. With the Upanishads, an attempt is made to systematize Vedic thought, bringing with it a discernible philosophy that includes epistemology and metaphysics. Being the initial outpourings of a people, they had not yet evolved a moral code or social ethics. What emerges is a view of the universe that is largely agnostic, where even the ultimate reality is unknowable, at best formless, and without attributes. Yet the Vedas exhibit a curiosity and an acceptance of ignorance that is rarely exhibited in Indian thought thereafter.

While there is no doubt about the antiquity of the Vedas, they were written down much later, maybe as late as the 1st century C.E., with a great deal of interpolations and additions. They were written in Sanskrit, which then became a sacred language and ceased to evolve. The words of the Vedas became sacrosanct and had only to be repeated. The meaning was soon forgotten; even two thousand years later, the same words, in the same tone, are recited daily by millions of Indians across the country every morning and at every important ritual and ceremony. The impact of the Vedas on the thinking of Indians as a whole seems negligible, while all religious and philosophical thought has originated almost entirely from them. They have remained sacred and beyond the reach of the common man, only to be intoned during rituals by priests for devotees who rarely understand.

The Vedas

All Hindu thought traces its origins to the Vedas. They hold that the Vedas are revealed knowledge, 'Sruti,' as heard and consequently, Divine. All subsequent thought not only owes but also acknowledges a debt to the Vedas. In fact, a system of thought was considered orthodox and acceptable only if it recognized the divine nature of the Vedas. The word "Veda" literally means knowledge. Thus, there is no knowledge without the Vedas.

Later thinkers have made what may appear as artificial divisions to properly understand the Vedas. They have divided them into Samhitas and Mantras and into Brahmanas and Aryankas. The Vedas themselves are four in number: Rig-Veda, Yajur-Veda, Sama-Veda, and Atharva-Veda. According to the Vishnu Purana, they were given to the great rishis and consisted of a hundred thousand verses. Veda Vyasa, to whom it was first given, was then supposed to have entrusted the Rig Veda to Pali, the Yajur Veda to Vaisampayana, the Sama Veda to Jaimini, and the Atharva Veda to Sumanta.

To most early thinkers, the Vedas were the sum of all knowledge. Yet, the great Sankaracharya defined the Vedas only as "The knowledge of supernatural methods for the achievement of a desired object and avoidance of the undesirable." This is something that Nirad Chaudhri was also later to assert: that the Vedas are essentially a worldly treatise, a program to adjust and live in harmony in the harsh conditions of human life.

The Vedas are essentially songs to be recited as part of different rituals and sacrificial performances. Each has the 'Samhita,' or reason for which it is used, and an actual 'Mantra' to be recited. The 'Brahmanas' mostly contain details of the process and detailed descriptions of each sacrificial rite and how it is to be performed. As people forgot the original purpose, it was necessary to explain the significance of the rites, thus the necessity of the 'Aryankas.'

The Aryankas were called 'Forest Texts' as they were the result of the thinking of people who had left the Aryan fold to venture out into unknown territory, trying to understand their rituals. They were later elaborated, chapter by chapter, as the Upanishads or Vedanta, the end or culmination of the Vedas. In the oral tradition, there was therefore a ritual and an explanation, but when the Vedas were finally written down, only the original revelations were included, while the explanation became the Upanishads, treated with a different level of sacredness as they were human interpretations.

The recitation of the Vedas was always considered sacrosanct, as it had a spiritual value beyond its application in a ritual, as the sounds of the chants were supposed to be magical. A large part of the original Vedas and the Aryankas have been lost over the centuries. There were also many interpolations by many later gurus included. In fact, originally, the Vedas were called 'Trayi' meaning three, and the fourth Veda, the Atharva Veda, was itself clearly a later-day addition.

With a proliferation of interpretations and commentaries, a system of thought was developed called 'Mimamsa,' which believed that the Vedas were only meant as verses to be recited during religious rites and that all the other parts of the Veda that did not specifically deal with rituals should be considered redundant. The parts specifically dealing with rituals are now called 'Karma Kanda,' while those that deal with philosophy are called 'Jnana Kanda.' The Upanishads are thus part of the Jnana Kanda.

This division was essentially an artificial one that was not to be taken rigidly, nor was it actually true when the Vedas are seen in a more holistic manner, where ritual and meaning are too often irretrievably mixed. The Vedas, especially the Rig Veda, are man's first utterance as he looks up in awe at the universe, the power of the sun, the wind, fire, and water. It is a poetic response of human consciousness to their desperate need to know and how to relate to all they see around them.

Many of the hymns are hymns of praise and attempt to explain creation and the purpose of human life. In the famous Rig Veda hymn of creation, it asks:

"Who knows, who ever told, from whence this vast creation rose?
No gods had then been born; who then can e'er the truth disclose?"

One sees a great sense of wonderment and an equal dose of humility that is balanced by their desperate need to know.

Vedic Reality

As seen in the creation hymn, the Vedas as a whole seem to have an agnostic view, where God may not exist, and any attempt to describe or explain ultimate reality seems impossible. All that man can know is the reality of his own existence.

The Vedas are plagued with doubts as to whether the Cosmos really exists as an absolute reality or if it is only the manifestation of Brahman, an illusion and a reality that encompasses realities beyond human comprehension. Brahman is both Suguna (all in all) and Nirguna, as in nothingness. However, the Vedas seem to accept the manifested world as the only reality and think it prudent to accept that there is nothing beyond the material world, which itself is nothing but the manifestation of Brahman.

The creation story enumerates how Brahman created the rest of the world through his will. Brahman brought everything to be, as he desired: "Let us be many." The Vedas state, "Breath is Brahman (ka), pleasure is Brahman (kha), and the ether is also Brahman," in an attempt to explain the all-encompassing nature of Brahman.

In the 'Chandogya Upanishad,' in a story, the son is taught the truth that there is no difference between the individual soul and Brahman because essentially there is no life without Brahman. It is in this context that the later growth of the pantheon of gods becomes both an inversion of the Vedas and a rejection of the abstract nature of its philosophy—a philosophy that provides no consolation for ravaged mankind and sees nature as indifferent to human suffering and merely as an abstract principle.

The greatest of the hymns is in the Rig Veda (Mandala X-129), where the hymn to creation says:

"In the beginning, there was neither nought nor aught.
There was neither sky nor atmosphere above.
What then shrouded all this teeming universe?
In the receptacle of what was it contained?

There was neither death nor immortality.
Only the existent one breathed calmly; self-contained.
Nought else was there.

Then first came darkness hid in darkness, gloom in gloom.
Next all waters, all chaos indiscreet.
In which the one lay void, shrouded in nothingness.
Then turning inwards, he by self-developed force.
Of inner fervor and intense abstraction grew.
And I in him, desire, the primal germ of mind.
Arose, which learned men, profoundly searching, say.
Is the first subtle bond, connecting, entity.
With nullity. This ray that kindled dormant life.
Where was it then? Before? Or was it found above?

Who knows? Who can declare?
How and from what has sprung this universe? The gods.
Themselves are subsequent to its development.
Who, then, can penetrate the secret of its rise?
Whether it was framed or not, made or not made; he only.
Who, in the highest heaven sits, the omniscient Lord.
Assuredly knows all or haply knows he not."

The Vedas clearly accept the impossibility of knowing what existed before existence, where it was contained, and the matter that was used to create the universe. All that they accept is that there must have existed something uncreated, appearing like the void, something neither mortal nor immortal. The Vedas then bring all creation down to something man can understand: desire. The Vedas claim that even in the eternal being, it was a growing desire that forced the need for creation; a form of desire generated the heat required for the passage from 'nullity' to created matter. How this happened, we may never know, says the Vedas, and maybe the 'ultimate one' may know, but it is also possible that even God does not know.

Having accepted defeat in knowing the origins of creation, they turn next to the mystery of time. Thus, in a beautiful hymn to time (53 Atharva Veda XIX), they say:

"Time, like a brilliant steed with seven rays,
And a thousand eyes, imperishable,
Full of fecundity, moves all things onward.
On him ascend the learned and the wise.
His rolling wheels are all the worlds; his axle
Is immortality.
He is all future worlds.
Past and future issue out of time.
Through time, the eye perceives: mind, breath, and name.
In him are comprehended.
When time arrives, the monarch who has conquered
This world, the highest world; the holy worlds.
Yea, all the worlds.
And ever marches on upon thy shining car."

This is an appreciation of time that the West was not to have until the seventeenth century, when Immanuel Kant saw through the many assumptions of Western Philosophy. It is only with this concept of time that we can even imagine the past or anticipate the future; time is a necessary condition of our consciousness. The pity is that this stupendous discovery is not elaborated on even in the Upanishads.

Finally, they turn to the wonders and beauty of the created world. There are beautiful hymns to night and dawn where men were clearly astonished and ecstatic as they surveyed the immensity of creation. There is a beautiful hymn to Ushas, the Goddess of Dawn, that says,

'Hail, ruddy Ushas, golden goddess, borne
Upon thy shining car, thou comest
A lovely maiden, by her mother, decked
Thou art forever young.'

The paradox is clear: man grows old and dies, but the dawn is forever beautiful and young. Nature, like the gods, is forever, and they remain young and beautiful.

The Evolution of Gods

Initially, the Vedic hymns were all hymns of praise and songs to Mitra, the sun; Varuna, the God of the night sky; Dyu and Prithvi, the Sky and Earth; and Agni, the God of fire. However, even in the Vedas, we begin to see a slow evolution of the gods, transforming mere natural forces by slow sublimation into gods. At the sight of the immensity of the universe, the Vedas speak of it as Aditi, the infinite. Yaksha calls Aditi the mother of all gods. The Rig Veda also calls Aditi 'the mother of all gods' and even says, "Aditi is mother, father, son, all gods, and five classes of beings." The rishis soon divided eternal space into dyloka, the heavens; triloka, the Earth; and antarikloka, the intermediate space between the two. Surya is the Sun God, and the God of heaven is Indra. Vayu (air) is the God of intermediate space, and Agni (fire) is the God of the Earth. Then comes the multiplication; the three gods are multiplied and become thirty-three. They are the eight Vasus, the eleven Rudras, the twelve Adityas, and Dyu, the sky, and Prithvi, the Earth. This is then multiplied by their many aspects and manifestations. However, the Vedas still maintained that these were only artificial divisions and that the ultimate reality was only one. What they were accepting was that the Divine is too complex to describe or assign a nature, and therefore, all that man can do is worship God's many manifestations.

The pre-Vedic God Mitra soon becomes Aditya and Surya, the Sun God. Mitra was also the God of light and Varun was the God of the blue sky. It was only in the later Vedic hymns that Vishnu appears; he first appears as one who strides the universe in three steps, making him synonymous with the sun. The God that the Vedas especially sang of was Indra, the God of the wind. He was the God who was thanked for all human comforts, making him the first, a sort of personal God. Agni, the God of the Earth, is also the ruler of all sacrifices. Thus, the famous Vedic hymn says, "O Agni, thou art the giver of joy, the domestic guide of men, messenger, and inviter of gods." Agni was also worshiped as Rudra. Despite their apparent devotion, the Vedas at another level saw gods only as equal to men, and it was believed that in ancient times there were men who achieved such perfect knowledge that they could challenge the gods. The sages also claimed that they were in communion with the gods.

The oneness of God is also stressed in the Rig Veda, and it specifically says, "The wise call him Indra, Agni, and Varuna, but the great divinity of God is one." And in the Hamsavati hymn, the same idea is repeated more poetically when it says, "As light, he dwells in the luminous sky; as Vasu (air), he dwells in mid-space; and as Hotr, he dwells in the sacrificial fire... As the supreme entity, he exists, as 'Ita' and he exists everywhere. He is the father of all but known by many names." Yet separate hymns are also sung to the many gods. The initial hymns in the Rig Veda are invocations to the gods as great, powerful, and beautiful. Yet as they go on, they begin to entreat the gods to help and protect them. To Varun, the Vedas say,

"The mighty Varun ....
.... This boundless Earth is his
His, the vast sky, whose depth no mortal e'er can fathom.
Both oceans find a place within his body yet
In a small pool, he lies contained...."

It was to the God Indra that the Aryans prayed for protection and help in war and in life. Thus, to Indra and the God of fire, they say,

"Indra, twin brother of God of fire
When thou was born, thy mother Aditi
Gave thee ....
Of mountain growing Soma – source of life ....
The eye of living and terrestrial things
Immortal Indra, unrelenting foe
Of drought and darkness, infinitely wise
Terrific crusher of thine enemies
Heroic, irresistible in might
Wall of defense to us, thy worshippers ...."

To the Vedic people, Agni was both the Sun as the ultimate God and his other manifestation as Fire. It was to fire and to Agni, as God, that the Aryans were most devoted. He was their guide who lit a path for them through the jungles, a light in darkness, and the source of all warmth and heat. To Agni, they say,

"Agni, thou art a sage; a priest, a king
Protector, father of sacrifice …
One in thy essence, but mortals see thee
Displaying thine eternal triple form
As fire on Earth, a lighting in the air
As the sun in heaven ….
Purge us from the taint of sin,
….and when we die
deal mercifully with us on the pyre
burning our bodies with their load of guilt
but bearing our eternal part on high."

Strangely, we also see a concept of sin and forgiveness in the later Vedas, and the universal invocations of the Vedas are then infused with personal desires. Agni becomes the first God to be treated as a personal God.

Vedic Thought

While there is no formal attempt to philosophize in the Vedas, taken as a whole, they do reveal a trend of thinking that could have created a very cogent system of thought. Yet, the Vedas were also an attempt to analyze the knowledge gained, theologically, metaphysically, and psychologically. The hymns indicate an attempt to understand reality intuitively, and the result is often intense devotion and worship. They saw the universe as Parama-Purusha, in which all is embodied. They tried to understand creation and almost gave up, saying, "Only the gods know, and who knows if even the gods know." They created a logic for cosmic causality in the law of karma, a law of cause and effect, and then came up with the theory that even as 'Brahman' sacrificed himself to create the world, humans must continue to make sacrifices to sustain the universe.

The Vedas did not preach any morality, for they say, "At that time, there was neither aught or naught" and add, "There was neither death nor immortality." They blamed their inability to see the truth and ultimate reality by saying, "The sages in their minds realize that the bird (the all-pervasive god) is covered up by Maya." The individual soul is deluded by Maya because, even in manifesting himself, 'Maya' is still necessarily an aspect of supreme reality. To explain how men are deluded, they claim that what we apparently perceive is merely a manifestation of God; the mortal is merely a reflection of the immortal; the physical and the soul are also one. The individual soul is part of cosmic eternity.

From such a position, it is difficult to explain how so much ritualism finally crept into Vedic practices. The ritual aspects of the Vedas, which were later to become permanent and overshadow the intellectual element of the Vedas, were based on the belief that Parama-Purusha sacrificed himself to create the universe. Thus, the 'rishis' saw the cosmic dance that sustained the universe as nothing more than the performance of a great sacrifice. The Vedic saints, even then, saw the eternal truths of life as beyond the possibility of reason and therefore looked to repetitive rituals as the embodiment of human submission to the harmony of the universe.

The Format and Scope

The Rig Veda consists of 1,017 hymns grouped into ten mandalas. Most of the early Vedas are entirely composed in verse, while the Yajur Veda-Veda is entirely a prose work. The Yajur Veda-Veda is basically a work that deals with rituals for the attainment of desires and all forms of protection from harm. The Sama Veda is again in verse and deals mainly with the sequencing of rituals, largely based on the systems described in the Rig Veda. The Atharva Veda has twenty sections; it is not about sacrifices but contains magic spells to drive away diseases, cause injury to one's enemies, and mantras that can bring prosperity and ensure a person's peace of mind. They also contain the fourteen mantras used in marriages and all the burial hymns, all borrowed from the Rig Veda. In the fifteenth book, however, there is an attempt to praise and conceptualize the supreme God and the beginning of a religious consciousness. The Rig Veda, which is in verse, also has many hymns praising Indra, Agni, Soma, Vishnu, Surya, Varuna, and joyful salutations to many other deities.

The Vedas tended to see gods in human form yet gave them reverence for the gods. They also knew that the universe could be explained in a mechanistic manner without the need for gods. It was the awareness of something beyond human perception, a feeling of a residual something that they could not explain, that prompted the Vedic sagas to look upwards. The Vedas have a duality in their approach to the gods. In one story, Vala hides his cows in a cave, and Indra kills him and recovers the cows. Here, cows are treated as light, the light of knowledge. The second is of King Vatra, who blocks the flow of a river, and Indra kills Vatra to release the water. This is a sacrifice—the killing of Vatra—to bring down water to humankind. In both stories, the objects of veneration, the river and the cow, were merely symbols of light and knowledge. Water also has to be seen as a life-sustaining element. It was an attempt to combine our world and the higher worlds and an attempt to mythologize what was not clear to human reason: that all human life is sustained at a certain level by the intervention of the gods. In all these stories, killing is also seen as a sacrifice that leads to knowledge and creates a bridge to the world of the gods.

While the Vedas praise the power of sacrifice, knowledge is the other option. In the Vedas, sacrifice is represented by the bull, while knowledge is the horse. The 'Aswins,' the keepers of the horse, are also the keepers of knowledge. In a similar way, 'Soma' is connected to rituals, while 'Madhu' is connected to knowledge. The impression that the Vedas create is that the world of Samsara and Karma is best dealt with by sacrifices, while the world of Jnana is only for intellectuals, as they are too high for ordinary mortals. In fact, Jnana is also seen as dangerous. The story goes that Indra confided some knowledge to the sage Dadhyac and told him to keep it secret, and that if he told the secret to anyone, his head would burst. Thus, the Aswins who wanted that knowledge presented Dadhyac with a horse's head, and it was to that head that he gave the 'Aswins' the knowledge they desired. Yet, the Vedas say that only through Jnana would the soul attain everlasting bliss. Despite the acceptance of a certain fatalism, taken as a whole, the Vedas do not indicate any pessimism or any yearning to be rid of the human body. Life is not seen as miserable but assumes that happiness and contentment are possible with the Vedas as a guide.

The Atharva Veda, however, is gloomier and deals largely with black magic. It seems to suggest a totally different approach to life, and it is this parallel thought process of the Atharva Veda that runs through the history of Indian thought not only as a powerful alternative but also as a counterbalance to mere Jnana and sacrifice to the gods. It represents an alternate power, which, during periods of stress and turmoil, led to Agama and Tantric philosophies, emphasizing the importance given to mantras and darker ritual practices. While the Rig Veda deals with the higher needs of man, the Atharva Veda seems to look at his more basic desires and fears. All in all, the Vedas saw human life as good and worth the effort, yet they also saw it only as a stepping stone to a higher form of life.

The Rituals

The Aryan religion was a religion of sacrifice, but the need for killing in a sacrifice was a matter that created a great sense of guilt. Sacrifice, in a sense, was also a re-enactment of human life, where man has to kill to live, and the whole universe of living things is sustained by such killing. The taking of life was a very troubling thing for the Vedic sages, yet sacrifice was central to ensuring the harmony of the universe. That is why sacrifice is pre-phased with a great deal of ritual. It was an attempt to sanctify and purify the soul of the devotee. Sacrifice was the food that kept the universe in good health. It was also a memorial to the first sacrifice that 'Prajapati,' the creator, performed, where, out of his dying body, he created the universe. Thus, as a devotee sacrifices, he must be pure of heart, and his sacrifice must also be an atonement for the killing of innocent life. The ritual of sacrifice had thus to be perfect in setting, in intent, and in purity of heart so that the taking of life is forgiven for the greater good. It also had a selfish purpose; it was an invitation to the gods to attend and, in attending, become indebted to the person who sacrifices.

The Vedic sacrifice is like a commercial transaction, where the worshiper makes a sacrifice in exchange for a reward from the gods. As the sweet smell of the sacrifice reaches the gods, their hearts are so delighted that they grant man the boon he seeks. The Vedas, however, always saw the two sides to man's longings, one in worship and sacrifice, where it is the gods that are propitiated, and the other in the search for magic, a purely human endeavor, to counter the total arbitrariness of human life. That is the reason seen in the Rig Veda and the Atharva Veda. In all sacrifices, Agni is treated as the mouth of the gods. The item to be presented depended on the nature of the wish and the particular food that God is known to appreciate. However, soma, honey, and milk were the constant items. Every sacrifice was personal and required the construction of new altars. Every sacrifice was to be a fresh offering and a personal statement; there were no temples or houses of God during Vedic times, and no cult of worship either. Idols were not recognized, even if some were known.

Sacrifices were grouped into regular, periodical, and special. The Agnihotra (fire offering) was to be performed daily. There were new and full-moon sacrifices. There was also a sacrifice of the first fruit. In the case of animal sacrifice, mantras were recited, seeking forgiveness for killing, before the actual sacrifice was performed. The Soma sacrifice was the most important of all sacrifices. It was performed only by kings and the wealthy, and the common people were merely spectators. There was also a warning that those who could not afford to perform a proper sacrifice should not, as a badly conducted sacrifice was worse than no sacrifice and that it would also taint them by their failure. There are also five daily rituals, which include the sacrifice of all beings, guests, etc. At every stage, from birth to death, special rituals governed Vedic society. This is what later created the priestly class and made it grow, as they were the custodians of the mantras, and each ritual required mantras, a special arrangement of the altar, and a number of priests, each with a special function.

While the Vedic people were initially transfixed by the power of the sun, fire, and death and sang hymns of praise and pleas for help to these gods, soon a greater abstraction entered their thinking. The first attempt to see creation as a whole was in the 'Purusha Sukta Hymn,' where Purusha is seen as the eternal all-pervading spirit. The hymn talks of:

"Thousand-headed was Purusha…
Purusa is all ….
He is the lord of immortality
He grows on sacrificial food."

So great is Purusha that only one-fourth of him is required to create the entire universe, as 'in all directions he spread.' It was an attempt to see all creation as arising from a single source. Purusha is seen as all the universe and beyond. The result was a most complex creation myth where Purusha is transcendent and beyond his creation. This would lead to the inevitable question: how is the infinite also finite? How can the infinite be part of creation? The transcendent nature of Purusa, as the famous Nasadiyasuka hymn says, consists of the fact that before him, "Non-being, then existed, nor being." Thus, he is neither a being nor a non-being, and his origin and nature remain a mystery. They assert, "Who knows for certain," and then to distinguish Purusha from the gods worshiped, they say, "The gods were born after this world of creation," and add, "Then who can know whence it has risen? /…he who surveys the highest heaven, /He only knows, or perhaps he may not know." Purusha is thus beyond the gods, and his nature and origin are unknowable. He is indescribable, indeterminate yet absolute. Thus, the Vedas make a clear attempt towards a monism that inevitably becomes increasingly complicated.

While the original Vedas are three in number, the truth is that the Rig Veda is the only real Veda. The Sama Veda merely poetically transforms many of the verses of the Rig Veda into chants and songs. In fact, the Sama Veda is the first attempt by Indians to create music and write down a melody. However, only 75 of the 1549 verses in the Veda are original; the others are merely transforming the verses in the Rig Veda into music. Similarly, the Yajur Veda only reduces the Rig Veda verses into mantras to be used in rituals. It can, therefore, be said that the Rig Veda is the Veda, and the others are merely improvizations of the themes raised in the Rig Veda.

The Society of the Vedas

There is no indication of any social stratification in the Vedas. In fact, the Vedic sages seem so concerned with greater things that humans, as part of society, were the least of their concerns. At that time, Aryan society was still a close-knit and homogeneous society, where everyone was a brother and a relative, with only some specialization in the work they did. Society then grew in complexity and size, requiring some hierarchy and social organization, and a system of social segregation had to be invented. Yet, open-minded thinkers, even of succeeding ages, refused to see caste as divinely ordained, and the tolerance of Mahavira and Buddha to all castes is testimony to such thinking.

Consequently, only by sanctifying the concept of caste could it be imposed without too much resistance. Thus, what seems an anomaly in the Rig Veda, a hymn in the Mandala 90x asserting the origins of caste from the creation of man, was clearly an interpolation resorted to by later defenders of orthodoxy. It says,

"All creatures are one-fourth of him, three-fourths
And that which is immortal in the sky
From him, called Purusha, was born Viraj.
And Viraj was Purusha.
Whose gods and holy men made their oblation?
With Purusha as the victim, they performed
A sacrifice. When they divided him,
The Brahmin was his mouth, the kingly soldier.
were his arms, the husbandmen his thighs
The service Shudra issued from his feet."

With this hymn, the Orthodox claimed that caste was divinely ordained. It was then used to chain society into a heartless system that continued for centuries, and its effects are potently visible even today. In the process, it destroyed the unsullied greatness of the Vedas with the petty sadism of the caste system. Without this hymn, there would not have been any reference to caste in the Rig Veda. Its interpolation was a conscious attempt to justify the caste system as existing from the dawn of time and therefore no one was to blame. In the study of the Artharva Veda, we will also see how local beliefs were accepted and how the purity of the Rig Veda was further compromised.

The Later Vedas—The Atharva Veda

A distinction is made between the first three Vedas and the fourth, the 'Atharva Veda,' because it was not originally in the canon of the recognized Vedas. Early thinkers referred only to the Vedas as being three in number. Furthermore, the Atharva Veda was clearly written much after the other Vedas. It was also not accepted into the orthodox canon for a long time. However, what is significant to us is that the Atharva Veda marked a clear departure from the ethos of the earlier Vedas. It was clearly the result of new influences on the Vedic mind.

The Atharva Veda was to set a pattern for all the later assimilation of new influences that were to color the thinking of Indians through the centuries. As new ideas and new belief systems were encountered and assimilated, new scriptures were written, with epics like the Ramayana and Mahabharata being the blending pot in which new ideas were first presented in story form. This churning of new ideas, new beliefs, and new gods continued until the last known Purana was written. It clearly showed that whoever presided over the orthodoxy of beliefs was either coerced into accepting new ideas or was so open to new ideas that they welcomed and incorporated. Yet, the story of Indian thinking was never a cakewalk for anyone but a persistent war of attrition between the forces of orthodoxy and the large sea of conflicting ideas.

While the Rig Veda was an intense outpouring of delight, wonder, and reverential awe at the majesty of the universe, by the time the sages wrote the later Vedas, they had to deal with the very real problems of living in an alien land, among alien people, and in a harsh environment. Their earlier belief that sacrifice and rituals were for the furtherance of the harmony of the universe and a belief in a give-and-take between them and the gods was clearly a belief of a people at peace with themselves. Things had changed, and every day, new challenges had to be faced. As they moved into the heart of the land they called Bharat, they were confronted with an alien people, an alien culture, and a settled belief system that was perhaps much deeper and more complex than theirs. They may have even been challenged to prove the efficacy of their own beliefs. The Aryans had to take on the challenge posed by the alien religion. They, therefore, had to create a religion that would allow them to survive in their harsh new surroundings. With the Atharva Veda, we see a change where religion becomes magic and the focus is on magical mantras, some even diabolical.

That is how India becomes a superstitious nation, says Dr. Radhakrishnan, and its people become believers in witchcraft and black magic, a nation of amulet and token wearers, of mantras, tantric, and evil sacrifices. All right-thinking people should condemn that text, says Dr. Radhakrishnan, the most eminent scholar of Indian philosophy and one who cannot be charged with being biased against Indian philosophy or Indian tradition. He claims that the Atharva Veda, which he calls 'the weird religion,' was actually, in what it represents, an even older tradition than the Rig Veda, even if what has come to us was written down much later. He claims that the Aryans were not to blame for the Atharva Veda equates Aryan thinking to the Rig Veda and blames the Atharva Veda on the Aryan interaction with the local people, who had a long association with religions that had many of the negative elements of the Atharva Veda. It was the result of the Aryan attempt to be inclusive so as to attract and hold the local population by incorporating their beliefs. It is difficult to believe that the openly questioning Aryan people of the Rig Veda, who saw in man divine possibilities, would accept such a lame, negative, and fatalistic set of beliefs to merely include the locals. The new beliefs were not merely tolerated until a more rational attitude was developed but were legitimized by the writing of the Atharva Veda, which then had to be treated as divine revelation. This was clearly more than a compromise. Either a large percentage of Aryans were themselves lured by the local creeds, or the Aryans accepted that their power was not only real but also seductive, to have accepted and to create a sacred scripture around it.

The Rig Veda speaks of a time when the Aryans were in open conflict with the local people, while the Atharva Veda speaks of a time when conflicts had ceased and the two peoples were trying to live in harmony through a negotiated compromise. "This spirit of accommodation is what elevated the religion of the primitive tribes but degraded the Vedic religion by introducing into it sorcery and witchcraft, the worship of spirits and stars, trees and mountains," says Radhakrishnan. As a result, Bloomfield says, "Even witchcraft became a part of Hindu religion; it had penetrated and become intimately blended with the holiest Vedic rites." This is what gives Hinduism its 'miscellaneous character,' says Dr. Radhakrishnan, and he adds, "such is the revenge which the weak of the world have on the strong." The problem, says Radhakrishnan, was that from the beginning, the Aryan religion was expansive, self-developing, and tolerant. It went on accommodating itself to the new forces it met. To say this, however, also means that the Aryans had no core faith, nothing non-negotiable, and that they had no great respect for their own forefathers, who preached a very rational, questioning religion. Radhakrishnan rationalizes by saying, "He (the Aryan) did not possess the pride of the fanatic, that his religion was the one true religion." Such humility is fine if it is supported by rationality, not a weak acceptance of all superstitions. Radhakrishnan makes amends by saying, "They forgot that intolerance was sometimes a virtue."

"The religion of the Atharva Veda is that of primitive man, to whom the world is full of shapeless ghosts and spirits of death," says Radhakrishnan. A religion of men who trembled before thunder and rain and were clueless in the face of sickness and death. They thus saw the world as 'crowded with goblins... dissatisfied spirits that could be appeased only with bloody sacrifices, human and animal'... 'a weird, repulsive world of darkly scowling demons…' While the Rig Veda gods were 'approached with reverent faith, love, and confidence,' the new religion was 'rather a kind of cringing fear, at powers whose wrath is to be deprecated and whose favor curried.' The mantras, which earlier were an instrument of devotion, became a tool of superstition to wring favors from a reluctant God, where even magic was permissible. It became 'a religion of magic, with its childish reliance on sorcery and witchcraft.' Where earlier, great sages and ascetics could obtain mastery over nature, the religion now allowed ordinary men to 'participate in divine power through the hidden power of magic.' Discipline and knowledge were thus brushed aside as stupid men participated in magic without discipline or knowledge of its consequences, with the result that magic and mysticism soon became confused.

The Atharva Veda gives a genealogy of demons and gods that included the worship of 'Kata (time), Kama (love), and Skamba (support), called indiscriminately Prajapathi, Purusa, and Brahman.' Rudra is the Lord of animals and is also Pasupathi, the Lord of cattle. Prana is the life force, which was part of the concept of vital forces and with which Kundalini and esoteric sex became the basis of Tantric philosophy. A place called Naraka (hell) was also invented. In this state, everything becomes permissible, and the Veda only tries to make a distinction between black magic and white (or good) magic, where magic used for hostile purposes is called Angirasas. Because of the compromises with so many elements alien to the original Vedic thought, it took some time for the Atharva Veda to be accepted as part of the sacred canon.

Dr. Radhakrishnan contrasts the simplicity of the Rig Veda with the "coldness and artificiality" of the later Atharva Veda. Following the acceptance of the Atharva Veda as part of the religious canon, Dr. Radhakrishnan says that the religion developed lethargy, and 'the priest becomes the Lord.' He describes the religion of the Atharva Veda as 'mechanical sacerdotalism.' The truly religious spirit could not survive in the stifling atmosphere of ritual and sacrifice. Religion becomes a 'dreary repetition of petty requests for the good life' and a complicated set of sacrificial rites. The poetic fire and heartiness of the Vedic hymns are no more. Prayer becomes a mere repetition of mantras, 'which nobody could understand.' Sacrifice became a way to gain Earthly profit, not heavenly bliss, 'a rigid soul-deadening, commercialistic creed based on a contractual motive in the place of simple devout religion.' The increasing dominance of the idea of sacrifice helped to exalt the position of the priests. Selfishness, with its longing for power, prestige, and enjoyment, pressed its way in and dimmed the luster of the original idea. There are priests who seriously declare that they can bring death to the person who actively employs them, though they should have had the moral sense to know that such an act is forbidden. As Radhakrishna puts it, the Atharva-Veda was what brought about the change from the self-motivated rituals of the Rig Veda to the temple and to the priest-oriented sacrifices and consequently to the rise of 'Brahmanism.'

The result, according to Radhakrishnan, is that "morality was dismissed as altogether irrelevant." However, he adds that "the Brahmin was neither wicked nor stupid." Radhakrishnan excuses them by suggesting that they had a sense of their calling, and if they erred, it was because they were fettered by tradition and their thoughts were paralyzed by the conventions of the time. Yet, the fact that none objected and that they had the most to gain from this herd-like mentality and superstitious belief makes them clearly blameworthy, even if one does not call them downright scoundrels. In the nature of things, a professional priesthood is always demoralizing, says Radhakrishnan. While the Rishis, unblended by passion, wrote the hymns in the Rig Vedas, which thus transmit only truths as the poet hears, were inspired and revelatory, even when they attribute them to the effects of Soma. While in the Rig Veda, speech as 'vak' is divine, now when the spoken word becomes rigid and fixed, it loses all its spirit.

It was with the Atharva Veda that a separate caste of priests was created. Along with that, the Varna separation, which had all along been a mere social segregation, now becomes religious and is supported by the theory of Karma. As a result, says Dr. Radhakrishnan, the exclusiveness born of pride becomes the basis of caste. It tended to suppress free thought and retard the progress of speculation. The Shudras were excluded from the highest religion. Mutual contempt increased. 'The Brahmanas have no view on the afterlife; instead, he who sacrifices obtains perpetual prosperity... Particular sacrifices enable us to reach the spheres of particular gods. The more sacrifices one has offered, the more ethereal the body he obtains.' While the Rig Veda sees the sinner as nothing and the virtuous as immortal, in the 'Brahmanas,' all are merely reborn to be compensated for their deeds. 'A man is born into the world that he has made.' Dr. Radhakrishnan ends by saying, 'In spite of suggestions of a higher ethics and religion, it must be said that the age was, on the whole, one of Pharisaism, in which people were more anxious about the completion of their sacrifices than the perfection of their souls.'

Dr. Radhakrishnan has been quoted at length to show how, even at this distant date, a rational mind, reviewing the Atharva Veda, is shocked by the compromises made and the level to which a pristine religion could descend. No Westerner would have made such a scathing criticism. Dr. Radhakrishnan sees almost no redeeming feature in the descent of Vedic religion when it accepted the arcane and fear-infested religion of the Atharva Veda. In fact, there is little doubt that the decay of Vedic religion was due to this compromise. The free, questioning religion of the Vedas then gives way to a superstitious, ritual, and mantra-dominated religion that soon led to black magic and a clear shift from the search for truth, sublimity, transcendence, and spiritual fulfillment to a religion that merely promised physical comforts and wealth, oblivious to any transcendental goal. The Vedic yearnings for higher truths of the Rig Veda are soon engulfed by the darkness of human desire, and along with it comes deceit and compromises.

While Dr. Radhakrishnan sees the Aryan as noble and the natives as some sort of primitive tribals, the fact that it was the Aryan who bent low to compromise says a lot about the natives. While Aryan beliefs have a certain innocence and purity about them, they lack subtlety; they have not gone beyond wonder to create a theology. If the local people were the descendants of the Harappan civilization, they already had a very regimented society and perhaps a very complex religion that had evolved along with the growth of its civilization. This meant that religion was an integral part of society, not merely a personal quest for the truth. Consequently, it may have had a social order based on the stratification of society, with a separate priestly class. The Aryan, as an independent worshiper, stood no chance against an organized hierarchy. Even where the sages of the Aryans stood together on principles, they were clearly intrigued by the complexity of the local religion. While truth is a great ideal, comfort, protection, and wealth were clearly more important to the common man. The average Aryan must have thus approached the local priests for the secrets of their religion, which they might have offered to share with them for a place in the hierarchy of their society. Soon they were writing texts that became sacrosanct and creating a priestly order that, until then, did not exist in the society of the cattle herders who made up the Aryan society.

This was also understandable, as all ancient religions that grew out of the Mesopotamian and Nile River civilizations, be it the Assyrians or the Egyptians, developed a priestly class and some class distinction, especially of the priest, warrior, and peasant. Their religion also grew from an initial belief in a mother goddess to some sort of divine hierarchy, with most accepting a supreme God. Their worship was shrouded in mystery, with their secrets known only to the priests. Apart from sacrifices, there were typical human inducements presented to the gods in terms of music, dance, beautiful dancers, and virgin hostesses. These civilizations had gone beyond the acceptance of the infinity of time and the universe to a more personal problem, existentialism. They knew that nothing could be done about the essential nature of human life, its mortality, and therefore sought only the best way to lead a comfortable life. Thus, religion created rituals to please the rain gods for rain, to appease the wind gods that caused storms and fire that burned, and to sweep them away. The priests claimed that the gods were angry and then created a method to appease them. That was the great trick played by the priestly class. They continued to rule because men did not have the guts to question the priests for proof, as daily tragedies were sufficient reminders of what the gods could do. Consequently, the descent of the Vedic religion of the Rig Veda into the religion of the Atharva Veda was, in many ways, only a natural progression. Yet, like Dr. Radhakrishnan, one nostalgically wishes that the Aryan had more faith in his rationality and had steered his religion towards 'jnana' instead of accepting that fear and mystery are fundamental to religion.

Meaning of the Vedas

There is perhaps no greater lover of India's ancient literature than Robert Calasso. In his book, 'Ka,' he established himself as one of the foremost scholars of ancient India. Yet in 'Ka,' he only dealt with the mythology of the Vedic people. It is in his new book, 'Ardour,' that he tries to understand the origins of Indian thought and their relevance for the modern world. All his writings on the Indian past are suffused with the incandescent light of his love for all things ancient India.

He starts by claiming that the ancient Indians were unique and that, unlike any other ancient society, including the Greeks, they have remained a mystery to the modern mind, like a dream blotted out by wakefulness. They left no monuments, no records, no castles, or even a history—nothing, only a memory contained in verses that have survived to the present day. The Aryans disdained history in a way unparalleled in human history. Their only interest was to know. Thus, in their verses, they did not record their conquests and triumphs, only their knowledge. Similarly, there is no mention of time or the passage of time, leaving the Vedas and their verses without context, existing in a vacuum, almost unreal, and therefore also eternal.

Even kings had no palaces or safe places. The only thing they valued was the altar that had to be constructed for the sacrifice. As the Aryans descended from the mountains to the plains of the seven rivers, their God was Agni, who later became Indra—the fire that burned a path for them as they traveled through the virgin jungles of the plains. It was Agni who helped them subdue the land. They moved eastwards without a permanent dwelling place—only the temporary settlement of nomads, forever searching for new pastures. Thus, there were no palaces, no forts, and no castles.

Yet, while they never boasted of the empire they created or the lands they subdued, they boasted of a language they perfected: Sanskrit, which itself means perfect. Their main aim was to have a perfect language to express the knowledge that they so remarkably attained. Their reluctance to leave behind traces of their lives mirrored their devotion to sacrifice, which, at the end, had to be obliterated without a trace. After the fire had consumed the sacrifice, even the ashes had to be ceremonially cast away into the waters. The Aryan saw himself not only as a wanderer on Earth but through the milky-way. Life was transient, with no permanent resting place.

It was in the realm of sacrifice that the Brahmin was supreme. Yet, power was always split between the doer and the maintainer, the temporal and the spiritual. One of the first things they discovered was duality—the duality between action and thought, symbolized by the distinction between the Brahmin and the Kshatriya. In the sacrifice, the Brahmin was supreme because the knowledge of sacrifice was first given to the Saptarishis, the seven seers.

Another important aspect of sacrifice is that the benefits accrued only to those who participated. Thus, not only did the Kshatriya need sacrifice, but everyone wanted to be invited, even the gods; nothing was worse than being excluded. This cemented the link between the people and the final act of the sacrifice, the drinking of Soma. After the sacrifice was the feast and the reveling. This is what created a special people, a people who claimed to know. In their uniqueness, they saw the cementing of this duality in Soma, the ultimate elixir of life and the object of all desire.

In mythology, Soma abducts Tara, the wife of Braspathi. As Soma abducts Tara, the Brahmin loses his cool and forgets his functions, and soon, the Kshatriya and the Brahmin have only one goal: the search for Soma. Without Soma, there is no purpose in life. In fact, in the quest, all will have to give up all that is peripheral to seek the ultimate experience of human life, beyond ritual and even knowledge—Soma. The paradox, however, is that while all are seeking him, all that Soma wants is a woman. Soma is what makes the Aryan alert, acute, and alive, but at the back of Soma is the shadow of a woman, a dark sensual reality that is perhaps the fountainhead of all life.

The Aryans were, in no way, gentle people—no lotus eaters but fierce warriors who annihilated their enemies, burned their fortresses, plundered their cities, and slaughtered their people. They saw themselves as the storming sons of Rudra, accompanied by their chariots and their thunderbolts, 'laden with songs and spears,' and the 'Earth shakes at their approach.' Yet, it is not their deeds that they sing about but their awakening. An awakening to knowledge that Agni allows by leading them and by lighting their "pada" (path) While the Asura kept Agni to themselves, the gods shared it with the Aryans, who were then able to multiply its power manifold. The worshippers of Agni, with Soma to guide them, do not seek power; only rapture, rapture that allows them to see the infinite as an ever-expanding circle of light that illuminates consciousness, leading men to the gods.

To know is thus to burn, as is the pouring of milk into the sacrificial fire. The sacrifice is the outward manifestation of the inner transformation that takes place within when 'Satya' (the truth) and 'Shraddha' (faith) become the internal fires that interact. Atman was first alone, but Indra had a female companion, Viraj. It is the coitus between Indra and Viraj that creates consciousness, the realization of being. The Atma is self-existing but indistinguishable, thus 'Nirguna' (without qualities), and can come into being only through desire and manifest only through the eternal coitus with Viraj. At another level, there is the eternal loneliness of Atma, split from a part of himself that was taken to form a woman, which makes him always aware of an emptiness and a sense of bereavement that can be soothed only by union with the other half. As the Vedas say, there is no pleasure to match that union in coitus, for it leads Atma back to when he was whole, when he can return to his original form as 'purusha.' The full Atma is thus the shape of an Atma in a tight embrace with a woman. In man's need to be whole, he has a choice: to seek in a woman, 'Katayana' or 'Maitreyi,' a companion in sacrifice and life, or a woman wedded to the world with all her feminine charms.

The Brahmanas

Calasso bemoans the fact that the Brahmanas have been the most neglected of the ancient texts. It deals with the actual ritual.

It is neither in the form of a story nor is it couched in poetry. It is in prose, and perhaps it is with the Brahmanas that the prose form originated. The Brahmanas are the only authoritative text that deals with sacrifice; it is, in fact, a manual for sacrifices, explaining both the theology and the spirit behind them. However, the concentration on ritual resulted in the spirit behind the ritual being lost. Brahmanism, 'laden with gesture' and based on the underlying assumption of the supreme importance of liturgical gesture, inevitably led to the predominance and importance of gesture for its own sake. At that stage, the ritual was more important than thought itself. It was assumed that the flavor and aura created by ritual could not be reduced to metaphysics. Anyone moved by a church service held in an awe-inspiring cathedral where the sound of the organ and the choir singing evokes some much-remembered tune, with the rays of the sun slanting to enter through the tinted glasses of the cathedral windows along with the smoke of incense and the ringing of bells, can understand why ritual plays such a great part in any belief system. It would, however, be opinionated to merely see the Brahmanas as empty rituals, while the Upanishads alone have all the meaning. The Vedic people invested so much meaning into every ritual and gesture that, like some elaborate dance, it conveyed so much of the thinking and the spirituality of the Aryans.

The Rig Veda

The Rig Veda was not so much heard as seen by the rishis. They saw the hymns in the same way as they saw the trees and the rivers. The first of them were the Saptarishis, the seven stars in the Big Bear. At the heart of the symbol lay a great epistemological paradox: they were between the unmanifested and the manifested, like gods and men at the same time, so that they could see what normal men cannot. The Vedic hymns thus bring 'asat,' the unmanifested, to be manifested, creating 'sat.' They also bring 'pranas,' the breath of life, to non-living things. In the same way as creation was 'tapas,' the concentration of all energy into a desire to create, it is the convergence of all energy in the mind that creates an incandescence of illumination. Tapas, as Ardour, thus comes before thought. However, all acts of creation, such as sacrifice, are inevitably accompanied by pain and death. Creation is inseparable from ultimate death. Brahma creates and allows creation to attain a certain level of order, but there always lurks the figure of Shiva, a reminder that all that is created is doomed to death. By treating all creation as manifestation, the Vedic people allowed for the possibility that all is, after all, only in the mind. Thus, all attachment and hatred are the result of false emotions. Yet, man can live in a world without ultimate purpose only when fueled by desire; it is only desire that can smother the feelings of despair, even momentarily. Thus, Viswamitra, who, in his anger, wanted to destroy the three worlds, was mollified with the offer of two hundred cows and two chariots for his Soma sacrifice.

The Meaning of Sacrifice

So awesome is the responsibility involved in sacrifice, and to explain its horrors, Bhrgu, the son of Varuna, is made to go through a historical review of the horrors of the natural world, where every plant and animal is only fodder and food for some other animals, and killing and being killed are the natural order of things. Such violence would only end in the annihilation of the world. Yet, without killing and eating, life would also cease. It is to elevate eating to an accepted level that the Vedic people invented sacrifice. Thus, even the gods depend on sacrifice for their survival. To justify sacrifice, an elaborate set of rules had to be invented. It starts with the idea that fire demands to be fed, where the natural desire of fire is to consume even men. Thus, man can either feed the fire or become fodder for the fire. That is the essence of sacrifice.

The Vedic Indians saw sacrifice as an attempt to give back to fire what was due to fire. According to them, all matter becomes alive by imbibing fire from the sun. Thus, plants and animals are actually made of fire, which, in a sacrifice, is returned to fire. Yet, even this subtle philosophical twist of logic was not enough for man's conscience, for they knew that they themselves were, in an earlier time, sacrificial animals in the chain of nature's killing. It was only in his mind that he developed tools and became a predator. He thus saw in himself a betrayal of his earlier camaraderie with all animals. To justify this betrayal, he had to use many symbolic and mythological explanations. The ritual, therefore, demands that the sacrificer adequately apologize to the animal that is being sacrificed, for it is also his kin, a member of the family. Yet, even this is not enough, so they blame the gods who placed a post as something intrinsic to the division of life, and the impulse to kill is also passed on to Savitr, at whose bidding man makes the final act of killing. The post then becomes the most potent symbol of sacrifice. Animals that earlier walked on two feet, like men, now have to crouch on four legs to enter the post. By becoming four-footed animals, they lose their similarity to men and become sacrificial animals. Yet, a certain affinity remains.

As part of the explanation and justification, the Vedas explain how man became a naked ape. They claim that the gods flayed man to cover the cow with his skin. This makes the cow always fearful of men, thinking he may demand his skin back. That is why man must not approach a cow without his clothes; he must always be clothed, preferably in white linen. This nakedness makes him prone to pain, and his clothes make him look artificial, like an outcast among animals. Even though man is always in pain as he has no covering to protect himself, killing the cow or any animal is also always sacrilegious. The eating of flesh then becomes, like sex, a guilty pleasure. Life itself becomes a wound that never heals. This leads to the deception of sacrifice, the disguise for greed.

The greatness of sacrifice is in the name itself, 'Yagnavalka,' where 'Yagna' means sacrifice and 'valka' is a difficult root to decipher, thus serving as a reminder of the ultimate unknowable. All life is from the sun, and all knowledge, 'to know,' is also 'to burn.' Knowledge comes from 'tapas,' a form of internal fire; thus, the belief is that false knowledge can set the mind aflame and break it into splinters. The need to achieve true knowledge is always paramount. As human life evolved, the elements of sacrifice changed; at first, it was only the grass, then the cereals, and only later did it rise to living beings. It, however, retained at all times the intrinsic belief that sacrifice has to be made of 'satya' (truth) and 'shraddha' (faith). Sacrifice is always a transformation from the physical to the realm of the mind. Yet, Vedic men admitted that truth was alien to men; it was a quality of the gods to which sacrifice hoped to elevate men. Truth is the sacrifice offered, and shraddha, the faith, is the fire. It is by offering our feeble understanding of truth to fire that our knowledge and our values are tested.

At another level, Indra, the flaming one, who later became Indra, the king of the gods, is also truth, and Indra contains within himself his female part, 'Viraj.' It is in their eternal embrace that consciousness is created. The entire capacity to think is thus an erotic activity within the mind. It is also the mind that can create 'abhaya,' peace and freedom from fear. Sacrifice is to gain peace of mind and a state of fearlessness. The other side of sacrifice is the fear of death and the need to escape. The Brahmin, who is the mind of sacrifice, is thus seen as both vulnerable and untouchable. He carries with him the sins of the world. On him hangs the smell of carrion and the smell of the smoke of sacrifice, and only with the aid of Soma can he dispel the odiousness of sacrifice.

Creation as the Origin of Sacrifice

The creator Prajapati, who, in the act of creation, actually dissipates himself and becomes powerless, or, as the myth puts it, his power is usurped by his own sons. In the process of annihilation, the secret of creation dies with Prajapati. The creator, who is Ka, remains an unanswered question, Ka. In giving God a name, we recognize our inability to comprehend the creator and our cowardice in accepting something less. The eternal first cause remains unknowable, except through creation. Put another way, creation was an attempt to know himself. He who is eternal and timeless, in the act of creation, set in motion, as it were, the flux of time. The other idea is the idea of creation as the result of desire or will. Only a being with desire would want to create. Thus, the Satapathi Brahmans often talk of desire. Yet, even in creation, he could only manifest his qualities, which, like him, are eternal and infinite. Consequently, the first of creation are the seven essential elements, 'the vital breaths,' that, like the creator, are formless and eternal. As creation is a manifestation of himself, he loses himself in creation; it is no longer possible to distinguish the creator from the created. The secondary creations are the result of the copulation between the Earth and the sky. Creation is also the first sacrifice, as Prajapati dissipates himself in a sacrifice for the sake of creation.

The second creation of Prajapati is 'Vac,' or speech. When his mind is impregnated with 'Vac,' he produces the eight 'Vasus.' As desire continues, the eleven drops of seed that fall on the ground become the eleven Rudras, and the next twelve drops create the 'Adityas,' the great gods of light. Then the other gods and Vac itself become the 34th God. The seven rishis, the Saptarishis, then join together to take human form. This is also where 'asat,' non-matter, becomes 'sat,' matter, and Indhu breathes the breath of life into them. Since they cannot act alone, they join together to create the senses. Thus, 'asat,' which has no qualities, takes on the qualities associated with 'sat,' and their combination in different ways creates all matter.

Prajapati has to sacrifice to create; thus, it is Prajapati's eyes, swollen with desire, that fall off to cause creation. Consequently, all Vedic rituals are forms of sacrifice that involve loss, death, or killing. Sacrifice and all rituals are a reminder to men of the great sacrifice that started all of creation. Agni is the light that consumes. Prajapati, in his eternal form, does not know what to create, and creation is thus a series of trials and errors, a form of evolution. With creation comes the inevitable end of creation, which is death. Creation, bringing death, causes so much fear that it causes 'Vac' almost to erupt from Prajapati. It is the same 'Vac' that allows man to reason away his fears and takes him away from the path of violence and killing, so intrinsic to life and to the idea of symbolic sacrifice. The self-expressing 'Vac' and 'svaha,' made up of 'sva' greatness and 'aha' pertaining to him, become the invocation that must accompany all rituals. 'Svaha' is also reflection and thinking and is what leads to the creation of the third person in the self, the mediator between the mind and the self. This is what leads to the possibility of an internal dialogue that we call thinking—a separation of 'I' from the self.

Creation also results in the simultaneous operation of time. Prajapati then sees his own creation, the sky or dawn, Ushas, and falls in love with her and couples with her. However, the gods see it as an outrage to their sister. Further, the union fails to bring forth fruit, as the seed falls on the ground and the gods emerge from it again as though born a second time. While Prajapati is both their creator and their father, the gods do not trust him. They, therefore, try to get rid of him, especially now that creation has enfeebled him to the point of extinction. Consequently, all sacrifice thereafter is tinted with guilt and anger, and that ambiguity is retained in all rituals.

Prajapati and Mrtyu or Death

As Prajapati creates, he is overcome by exhaustion, to the point of death. This is the eternal connection between creation and death. The period without creation is endless, and Nirguna, without any discernible qualities, means that creation, by bringing something into existence, also invariably means its own death. Death is the inevitable end of all creation. As Prajapati lay exhausted, he had to contend with the hungry, open mouths of his sons, waiting to devour him. Out of this great fear, Prajapati bursts out in 'Vac' (speech), a female being that was always part of him, now released out of terror and fear. In the beginning, it was nothing; only after Prajapati massages his body and a white liquid forms on his body and a voice from within tells him to offer it as a sacrifice does it become greatness, 'sva,' and speech, 'aha.' Speech then becomes the defense against the terror of death, and all sacrifice is the commemoration of that great fear. 'Svaha' is also consciousness. Out of creation, a reflexive action causes the birth of consciousness and speech.

The first symbolic sacrifice was 'Agnihotra,' a ritual that assumes danger and the passing of time, both harbingers of death. Creation stirs Prajapati to desire his own creation, his own daughter, Ushas, and he couples with her. The gods, however, see it as the ravaging of their sister and realize that if they do not do something, Prajapati may turn next against them. So, they plan to kill him, but the arrow they send at him only wounds him and tears out flesh from his side. This flesh then becomes the highest element of the sacrifice, as the gods use it as their sacrificial material. Consequently, sacrifice is always part anger and part propitiation. Sacrifice is the propitiation of a wound that is caused, and in healing it, a guilty act is condoned. There is also the acceptance that life is always the result of a grave crime and therefore living things are always in debt and guilty; they bear the burden of something like the original sin. Since the guilty needed an intermediary, the post of officiating priest was created as a buffer between men and the gods. The priest, in a way, enters the sacrifice, taking the guilt of the people and therefore is always in danger. He must prepare himself, be purified, and, as a symbol of his purity, wear only white clothes. It is dangerous but essential, and it is the acceptance of that role that makes the Brahmin arrogant, even to question the gods. Shiva swallowed poison to save the gods; the Brahmin, in the same way, is man's intermediary and therefore is required to eat the remains of the sacrifice. It is a 'prasitra,' the sacred remains.

While creation brought death, desire intensified vision and reduced this mystery to words. Prajapati is the infinite unspoken, and the eternal problem of sacrifice is its inexpressibility. Creation, caused by desire, leads to sexual reproduction, which is the beginning of death. Kama, like a parasite, eats away at creation; desire is a hunger that is satisfied only with eating and killing, resulting in death. This problem is symbolized in the sacrifice of 'Sri,' the splendor of creation, which is also feminine, but the gods immediately try to grab 'Sri' and molest her, and only some parts are salvaged. The result of sacrifice is thus never complete and is always a process that starts in pain and ends in pain. Prajapati's pain leads to 'Ka' or happiness. The purpose of all sacrifice is to lead man from pain to happiness. To gain 'Ka,' 'Ista' is offered, and 'istika,' the bricks that make the altar, take their name from 'ista.' Happiness is also 'Sri,' splendor, and 'sukha,' but 'suk' is attached to 'ka,' the passage of time, and only when 'suk' is released does the priest breathe. But once he starts breathing, he will inevitably die.

The Sacrifice

The Vedic people saw most of their higher concepts in sexual imagery. The altar is shaped like a beautiful woman, flaring at the ends and narrow at the center. The 'Vedi' or altar is female, while Agni, the fire, is male. Every sacrifice is a covert sexual act. As Prajapati spilled his seed merely at the sight of Vac and later, the sight of Ushas, overcomes him with sexual tension, the gods are always prone to sexual excitement. Thus, the altar must be beautiful enough to entice the gods and as close as possible to the shape of a naked woman to excite them. In fact, in the course of the sacrifice, the spouse of the supplicant is asked to make suggestive glances at the priest and at specific moments, she is even required to expose her right thigh in an invitation to kindle Eros. The sacrificer encourages his spouse to betray him to entice Agni. Yet, this behavior is also considered impure, and therefore, after each glance, ghee is offered to Agni to purify the sacrifice, while the wife, being the guilty party, is not allowed to look at the ghee as it is offered. The sacrifice is also done in secret, like the sexual act, and others are not to look on except through the door, which is made for God. The culmination of the sacrifice is the cry, 'May Agni conduct you to the gods,' a cry in orgasm.

While sacrifice had a high purpose, the Vedic people did not deny the power of Eros and accepted that eroticism was at the core of all desire. The overwhelming power of Eros is explained in the young bride's willingness to leave the safety and comfort of her home to join her husband in expectation of erotic bliss. The Vedic people saw in marriage not the end of virginity but only a new erotic state, for they presumed that the maiden had already been ravaged twice, first by Soma, the imaginative underworld of thoughts, and then by Ghandahara, the wicked genie of erotic fantasies and dreams. She leaves her room, the scene of so much ravaging, with the words, "Leave here, this woman; she has a husband." Let her leave the room of her dreams, for she now has the real thing. Marriage, however, does not still fulfill her erotic dreams—not even ten children. The Vedas thus advise society to ensure that women have 'inside her ten children and let her husband be her eleventh.'

The Purpose of Sacrifice

Man has many desires and searches for fulfillment, but to achieve them requires patience, perseverance, and a barricade from the world. In Vedic culture, the hut (sadas) is thus the first symbolic structure in which he prepares his sacrifice—a place apart. Preparation involves wakefulness, for to enter a rite is to enter into truth. Man is untruth; only the gods are truth. Thus, before he enters the sacrificial hut, he has to clean himself with water, the thunderbolt that can carve out the mountains, with the plea, 'take my evil from me.' The ritual is full of symbolism.

The night before the sacrifice, the supplicant must separate himself from the world and sleep alone in a hut prepared for the sacrifice. He must fast to eat before the gods will be mean. He must lie on the ground, not on a bed, ever ready to serve the gods for whom the higher place is reserved.

The sacrifice itself is the yoking of fire and water. The way to combine them is through coitus, but in their forced attraction, there is always tension—too much water or too much fire would quench the fire or evaporate the water. They must remain in the correct proportions and at the correct distance to raise the erotic tension to its limit, which alone results in a perfect sacrifice. As Shiva disrupted the sacrifice of Dhasha, all around were gods and asuras, ready to disrupt the sacrifice.

To confuse them, there are moments of silence when the ritual turns inward and becomes mental. To ensure that contamination does not take place, the vessels in the sacrifice are, at intervals, brought close to the fire to purify them and to drive back intruders.

The task of the fire is to point the way, and the altar is a beautiful woman of perfect proportions, whose nakedness entices the gods to come to the sacrifice. All sacrifice presumes the need to expiate some guilt, and therefore a certain tension is inevitable—a mixture of guilt and terror. The purpose of sacrifice is to move from untruth to truth. Yet truth is an unnatural state for man and therefore unstable until the sacrifice is brought inward into the mind of the supplicant.

The fire and the embers then become symbolic; the fire becomes the word and the eyes become the embers. However, to the woman, the sacrifice remains coitus—the vagina is the flame and sparks, the pleasure. There is, however, a deep pathos in all Vedic sacrifice, as all must end in the last rite of death. All the symbolism vanishes, and the logs are merely logs, and the embers are merely birth and death. No more words are left as their tongues fail them, accepting that only silence remains.

The Ends of Sacrifice

All sacrifices aim to lead humans from darkness to light. The prayer is, "Lead me from non-being to being." Human beings are half in the light and half in darkness, evolving creatures still dark and full of death. All sacrifice is an attempt to enter the light and achieve immortality. It is a journey from the familiar to the unfamiliar, an attempt to be different and to distinguish themselves. Thus, the hut, the preparation, and the need to cordon off the altar, along with the requirement for secrecy, as enemies and jealous individuals are always ready to disrupt and plunder the benefits of sacrifice.

Sacrifice is intended to gain benefits and is therefore a very selfish activity. Embedded in the Indian psyche is the attitude of never sharing knowledge or the secrets of sacrifice. Every sacrifice is also an acceptance of a debt—a debt to Prajapati for creation. While sacrifice is an attempt to dominate, a lurking sense of guilt and the realization of weakness always remain. The sacrifice attempts to imitate the gods, and as 'Vac' gave Prajapati a voice, men depend on their poets to provide them with the right formula and the right hymns. The poet, from the 'vipra,' the tension between terror and excitement, shivers with transcendental glory, and out of it, he utters the hymns that are the right words and the right tone.

The Libation

Libation is the act of pouring a liquid into the fire and is perhaps the most universal gesture of ritual throughout the world. The ritual is central to religious ceremonies and has two basic parts. The first is the need to appease the gods, and the second is a pact with the Sun, whom the Vedic people saw as the agent of death. The Sun, in its avatar as fire, before it was controlled, destroyed and killed everything in its path.

The actual libation is a bribe to the gods, an appeasement, a 'tyaga,' a sacrifice. According to the Prajapati myth, creation required man to continue the sacrifice the gods had started to sustain what had been created. The basic minimum length of sacrifice was 'sattra,' lasting at least a thousand years. Since men are too weak and incompetent, the gods reduced it to a year, with the marching of a thousand cows. However, even this was too much for men, and therefore it was reduced further and further until it became 'Agnihotra,' the pouring of milk into fire. It was the essence and intrinsic purpose of sacrifice, the 'arrowhead' of all sacrifices.

At the most basic level, it is a personal rite with no priest or even the spouse. It is performed at the break of day and at sunset to appease the sun, symbolizing the taming of fire. It is a compromise made with the sun to evade death. At the most basic level, libation is the linking of two basic elements: fire and liquid, representing speech (vac) and manas, the mind. The word for libation comes from the root 'graha,' which means to grasp the divine. The ritual is, in effect, an attempt to grasp the truth of divinity.

The Residue

At the end of the sacrifice, after the gods have eaten, what remains is the residue. The importance of the residue was highlighted in the very first sacrifice. After the gods had eaten and risen up to the heavens, what remained turned into Sesha, the endless snake on which the universe itself exists and on whom Vishnu rests. As Vishnu rests on Sesha, a lotus blooms from his navel, and Brahma appears in the lotus. The residue is thus endless and eternal, something that the gods themselves did not realize.

In the story of Rudra's omission from the sacrifice of the gods, Rudra threatens to destroy their sacrifice. He is then invited, but after the sacrifice, the gods ascend to heaven, while Rudra is left behind, almost as part of the residue. His continued presence is a source of great anxiety for the gods, as they fear the power he might gain. The residue thus becomes the unexpected, the unplanned, and the uncertainty at the heart of all human endeavors. Thus, the reason Rudra remains behind is never explained. A similar story is told of how Shiva was not invited to Dhasha's sacrifice and how Shiva threatens to destroy the sacrifice with greater consequences as his wife dies. Even though the gods mollify him, Sati becomes the residue that men began to worship. The residue is the uncertainty that exists at the heart of the most elaborately planned sacrifice. Historically, it also attests to the Aryan disdain for the local gods and the unexpected way they emerged as powerful gods.

The residue, as the leftover from the first sacrifice, is creation itself. This residue then transformed itself into 'sesa,' the snake on whom Vishnu sleeps, Ananta, the endless. Thus, it is the residue that somehow keeps creation alive and is eternal and co-existent with God. In explaining the theory of Karma and man's endless voyage through endless lives, it is claimed that no life is complete in itself, as an 'amsa' or 'sesa,' a residue, is always left behind. To consume the 'sesa,' man is born again and again until he approaches his ultimate 'atman,' gradually reducing the residue. In another sense, 'sesa,' the residue, is also the acceptance that no theology can explain everything and therefore the need to tolerate other creeds. While in Hinduism it meant the acceptance of other gods, to Buddha, 'Sesa,' is left over because of human desire, as man is never satisfied with his life. He is never able to satisfy all his desires in one life, and it is his desire that brings him back to Earth, to satisfy some desire, one more chance to experience all that was missed. To Buddha, desire is at the root of all human tragedy and 'nirvana' is a state where all desire has been burned away. Such a state alone has no residue; that is his idea of 'sunyata,' the void. To achieve the void was, according to Buddha, the ultimate purpose of life.

King Soma

The consumption of Soma is the purpose of sacrifice, as it was in the first sacrifice the gods undertook. Calasso claims that thousands of pages in the Brahmans are devoted to Soma and that all the hymns in the ninth circle of the Rig Veda are devoted to Soma. Such is the importance that these people gave to Soma that they had only two gods, Agni and Soma. Symbolically, the sun was fire, and Soma was the fire within, the expanding consciousness. Even Indra, as he feels great, asks, 'Have I drunk Soma?' He is also the first of the gods to sing the praises of Soma and to attribute to Soma all his powers and daring deeds. Yet, one day, the gods refuse Indra Soma. Indra, the God of the Warriors, being excluded meant that the Kshatriya were being reduced in status. Thus began the conflict between the Brahmin and the Kshatriya, and Indra then tried to drink Soma by force, beginning the endless pursuit of Soma.

To the indologists, Soma was some sort of plant to be crushed and the juice drunk. But despite a continuous search, no such plant has been found, and they soon lost interest, concentrating on the literal translation of the Vedas. Calasso, however, says that Tapas and Soma are the most important ideas in the Vedas and are so central to the thinking of the Vedic people that we must try to understand what Soma meant. Tapas, the inner fire, is what caused creation, and Soma is the divine spark that alone makes human life worth living. Soma has an illustrious parentage; his father was one of the Saptarishis, Aditi, and the father of the Lunar Dynasty. Aditi sat in Tapas for a thousand years before a white liquid began to flow down his eyes, immediately illuminating every corner of the universe. However, after Soma was born, he was caged in with no freedom to fly or roam. Even while contained, Soma's eye fell on Tara, the wife of Brihaspati, the chief priest of the gods. Soma then abducted her and had intercourse with her, leading to a war in Heaven. The symbolism is complicated and mixed. Soma is what gives life meaning, yet Soma himself is driven by lust for a woman. Man seeks the spark that makes life bearable yet as he consumes Soma, the magic elixir of life, he is driven by lust and sex. As they admit, it is desire that causes creation, and man will eternally seek that spark.

The consumption of Soma leads to 'Buddhi,' the seat of all wisdom. Soma is the only God of the Brahmin, and the abduction of Tara by Soma was a double shame; it was as though God himself was rubbing their nose in the mud. The Brahmin thereafter is not a benevolent and happy person, for while driven to seek Soma, he always fears that his wife is being ravaged. Yet, without Soma, there is no Brahmin, for Soma is the essence of all things. It is so radiant and intoxicating that even Indra, when denied, forcibly drank it. Yet Soma is a dangerous God, and Indra almost died drinking it without dilution and filtration; it was only the Sautramani rite that was able to revive him.

Soma is like some primeval substance that even God had to have. Yet, it is not only a heady substance but a beguiling one, creating Maya, Suprani, and Kadru. Suprani is also Vac, which is imprecise without the help of Kadru. Words have no meaning; only usage gives them meaning. Thus, Gayathri, in the shape of a big bird, has to snatch Soma from the air, sealed in two golden cups. It is only through tapas and offerings of ghee that Soma is finally opened. The third element required to open Soma is 'shraddha,' or faith, for Soma is also the truth, and men are unfit to handle the truth. Even the priest, as he pours ghee to open up Soma, does so with a golden thread tied to his fingers, so that Soma would only touch the pure gold, not his impure hands.

Soma was the king and the ultimate treasure. Yet, it was not a thing that could be described but was known only by its effects. Men sought it as though their lives depended on it. Soma was the peak of enlightenment and the ultimate pleasure. Even the gods fought for it, traded it, and even prostituted themselves to get it, yet it was never clear what it was. Like the impossible need to know and the height of pleasure, it is the ultimate desire of men, impossible to describe or explain. It was brought to Earth on the beak of the great bird Garuda as a ransom for his mother Vinata, and it is the beauty of the greatest hymns that allowed it to ascend to heaven. It was then guarded by the snake nymph. Soma is a force in the mind, the light in the water, and a vehicle of transport to heaven and beyond. The Vedic people saw the universe as a skin that was spread over the firmament, and to drink of Soma was to get to the other side, to see the worlds beyond our known universe, to see the great unknown, the unmanifested.

All is permitted in the quest for Soma: trade, compromise, and even prostitution. The cost in wealth lost, health, the scars, the pain, and even war—it is worth everything else. It causes creation to vibrate with tension, 'vipra.' It is the flow of time that has no shame, no tradition, no loyalties, and only total freedom. It is what lovers see—only the existence of their loved one. She is beautiful and irresistible, an Apsara who strolls into the sacrificial arena, and all the gods walk away in pursuit of her. She is the other side of ceremony and established truth—the irresistibly beautiful, the unknown, the seductive, and the dangerous. In fact, at the mere sight of Urvashi, the gods Varuna and Mitra spilled their seed, and the result was the rishis, Vasistha, and Agastya. As they were dragged away from the sacrifice, they cursed Urvashi to live among men and for their pleasure, but when she came down and saw the dark and handsome men, she actually preferred them to the gods. The effect of Soma is the recognition of the beautiful, a filling of the soul with delight even at the cost of all other comforts.

The story of Urvashi and Pururavas is meant to explain what Soma means but is itself shrouded in ambiguity. Urvashi does not overwhelm Pururavas with her beauty but becomes his charioteer so that she can always be with him, always in love but never consummated. It was this companionship that she found most seductive; an eroticism that reached for the stars but remained unconsummated. Pururavas' love is related to apprehension and fear, as though of falling into a hole, a hallucination, and a dream. Urvashi, however, makes herself known when she realizes that he may go mad and says, "It is I who made the hole appear." They then make a covenant: he can have her three times a day, even without her consent; the only condition is that he must never appear fully naked before her. They then live happily for some time with two beautiful lambs attached to the posts of their bed, but one day, Urvashi wakes up to find her beloved lambs gone. In her anxiety, she wakes Pururavas up, who, in his rush to do her bidding, gets up without his clothes. When he returned with the lambs, Urvashi had disappeared. Desire must always be something prohibited, forever alluring, and once all mystery is lost, eroticism descends to mere lust.

Why never naked, and why lambs? There is no answer. Her disappearance is attributed to abduction by the Ghandahara, yet Urvashi explains that the highest satisfaction is essentially transient and says, "I slipped away like the first dawn; I am like the wind; you can't hold me." Separation from you is death, says Pururavas. This softens Urvashi's heart, and she proposes a new agreement: he can have her once a year or become a Ghandahara and share her with all the other Ghandahara. The search for true love is always transient and even deceiving, and all that we can have is the fire, perhaps an erotic fire that must, in the end, take the place of love, a fire that creates, illuminates, warms, and even thrills the mind with 'vipra.'

Manas (The Mind)

The mind as Manas is actually a term that denotes a much higher concept, the idea of consciousness. The Vedic people saw it as the one who comes forward, as though from afar, and awakens and recedes as we slumber. Consciousness is the waking of some sleeping God that could make man the equal of the gods. The mind is as marvelous as the gods; it can imagine anything. It is, like the Rishis in a state of eternal contemplation, a situation between 'asat' and 'sat,' between the manifested and the unmanifested. So, absolute is the power of the mind that the Vedic people said in their prayer, "May that which the mind conceives be propitious to me." Yet the absoluteness of the mind does not make it omnipotent. Even before creation, God was conscious; thus, consciousness is not omnipotence. Instead, the Vedas say the mind was with God, for creation presupposes consciousness. In the state of non-existence, 'manas' consciousness was the first creation. The mind is like God before creation, never sure whether it exists or not. The mind, like Prajapati himself, dissolves after creation and is forever unsure of its very existence. So important and perplexing is the idea of 'Manas' to the Vedic writers that the term 'Manas' occurs as many as a hundred and sixteen times in the Rig Veda.

Mind and Speech

Vac, as speech, is the next great idea in the Vedas, but without consciousness, there can be no intelligible speech. Yet, without speech, the mind is also powerless to express itself. The Vedas, therefore, see Prajapathi along with 'Vac' and 'Manas' as gods. 'Vak' is so important because, without speech, there can be no sacrifice and perhaps no gods. The supremacy of consciousness over vac is mythologically stated by the fact that the Asuras opted for speech while the gods took refuge in consciousness, or 'manas.' Speech is never complete and is always flawed as it tries to translate thoughts. While all Western philosophy has been an attempt to capture the external and internalize it, Indian thinking is rooted in the internal, with a very early realization that the external is nothing but a manifestation, greatly, if not wholly, determined by internal perception.

The Ancients made clear the role of the mind in thinking but also went beyond mere thinking. As in the case of Prajapati, who seduces Vac, Vac is seductive, but it is the mind that is corrupted. The realization that thinking can be corrupted by various external factors was why the Ancients insisted on the rigor that is to be found in Sanskrit grammar. Speech, the Vedas tell us, was not born normally but by tearing the womb in which it was conceived and therefore always bears the marks of that traumatic birth. The paramount need to unite speech, thought, and consciousness is emphasized in all the rituals and is intrinsic to sacrifice. Yagna (sacrifice), when it saw Vac, was so enamored by it that it immediately wanted to couple with it; thus, seduced, Vac became a tool of Yagna. Words lost their independence and became a tool of desire. Ritual is the solidification of thought, and all ritually religious people betray a fear and cowardice of the power of Manas, its uncontrollability, and its unpredictability.

Atman

The duality of body and mind is seen as a man who eats and a man who watches the man who eats, for a long time indistinguishable. It is the process of self-realization, created by the dialogue between 'Aham' and Atman, the 'I' and the self. The Atman is the image that appears in the pupil of the eye, the only image that the 'I,' 'Aham' is aware of. This discovery comes only later in the Brahmans, in the teachings of Buddha, and in the writings of Sankara. While Western philosophy saw the discovery of the self, the third person in the mind, as a destructive idea, corrupting all thought and perception, Indians saw it as the precondition to all understanding.

The impact of this discovery is told in the story of Sanatkumar and his pupil, Narada. Narada, proud of his knowledge, tells his master that he knows all the Vedas, all the sacred texts, and all the philosophical writings. Sanatkumar then asks him if he knows his Atman, which deflates him completely. As Calasso puts it, 'the immense Vedic expanse, brim-full of gods and powers, was suddenly reduced to a narrow gap.' To the later Vedic writers, all knowledge is seen as objectified and dated, while 'Vac' continued to be more than just knowledge but free to go anywhere to seek the truth. However, they also realized the truth that 'Manas' is the originator of all thought. To this trinity of Manas, Vac, and knowledge, there is Atman, the all-seeing ghost in the machine. It is 'Manas' that perceives and gives direction to Atman. Thus, 'Manas' has to deal with 'sankalpa' or intention, something more than awareness or consciousness. However much a person knows, if he is not aware of Atma, he does not exist.

Beyond Awareness: The Essence of Meditation

Beyond mere awareness is meditation, 'dhyana.' All existence is a deep meditation from which 'vijnana' or understanding emerges. However, to men in their mortal coil, knowledge and understanding are useless without 'bala' or courage, the greatest virtue. Without 'bala,' knowledge is of no use; it lacks the strength to push itself or to defend itself. Even hope, which the Vedic people equated with 'pranas,' the breath of life itself, goes only along with 'shraddha,' or faith. Ritual without faith, they say, is useless. The final requirement is 'joy,' the overflow and abundance of life that provide the semblance of infinite possibilities. Sacrifice is thus to be taken up only with that sense of overflow and abundance, with joy in the heart. Only such a sacrifice is pleasing to the gods.

Yet the Vedic seers were no fools; they saw through the short-lived joy of human life in all its ambiguity as 'sukka' and 'soka,' similar-sounding words but poles apart, joy and sadness. Udakkla Arumi also teaches his son, Svetaketu, who brims with the arrogance of knowledge, that 'sat,' existence, is Prajapathi, and it is 'tegas,' incandescent light, and not Agni, who was the first 'Anna,' food, or 'vac,' who is merely his daughter. Existence is the transition from non-being to being, where water, 'appas,' and food, 'anna,' sustain existent beings.

The next big issue is: how then to raise tegas? It is by tapas, they say, 'By the power of tapas/The one born/Empty and clad in emptiness.' The idea of the void is not seen in the early Vedas and is therefore a later realization. Adour and tapas create Kama, which is the first seed of consciousness. From desire comes thought. The Vedic people, who had tried to disentangle the knots of speech, realized that thinking was nothing but the understanding of the underlying relationships between things, that life is but a network of connections, and that all things are inter-connected. Yet, they also realized that we can only know that which is manifested, while the large bulk of creation lies beyond human intelligence, unknown and unknowable. They also keenly felt the essential uncertainty at the heart of all human knowledge.

Wakefulness

Long before Thoreau, the Vedas claimed that to be godlike, one must be fully awake. The difference between the gods and men was that the gods do not need to sleep and are always awake. This is also central to the teachings of the Buddha, for 'Budh' is to be awake, to pay attention. To be awake is central to the idea of being alive. The gods do not sleep and are forever vigilant so that no one comes to steal their Soma. Similarly, only by being fully awake can man hope to taste Soma. In fact, the gods try all their tricks to keep men in a state of sleep and to lull them from thoughts of Soma. To be awake is so important that the Vedas insist that in every gesture or ritual, the mind must be purposeful, not mechanical and meaningless. The mind must be fully awake so that no gesture or word is ever casual or automatic. Without such total involvement, the sacrifice becomes useless. Thus, Soma says to the person who is fully awake, 'in your friendship, I feel at home.'

Even Nirvana, gained through good deeds, is merely the crumpling of immortality. In contrast, wakefulness allows man to achieve infinite perception, the closest thing to Godliness. Wakefulness leads to a more intense Tapas, 'more divine, calm, and more ardent.' External sacrifices then turn inward and become a fire in the heart and mind, the final and invisible sacrifice. The first step to achieve this is the daily study of the Vedas, which eventually turns inwards, becoming an intense inner dialogue where all that has been learned, seen, and heard becomes fodder for the inner fire.

A man who is fully awake has an internal fire burning in continuous tapas, a state even the gods cannot surpass. In such a state, the Vedas say, 'even if he studies his lessons, stretched out on a soft bed, oiled and adorned and completely full,' he is still burned by tapas, 'up to the tips of his fingernails.' All creation is caused by such an inner fire. To be conscious is to be awake; that alone is the sensation of being alive. Thus, 'Vajra,' the lightning of the gods, is connected to the root word, 'Vegeo,' which means to be awake. The Rishis treated breath before the flesh and desire before the body. It was the Rishis who first felt and were dazzled by this wakefulness, the realization of consciousness.

The Vedas emphatically answered the question of whether consciousness was part of evolution with a resounding no. They asserted that nothing in nature could have led to consciousness. Wakefulness is a new birth. The first birth is the realization of being conscious, while the second birth is when a man tries to understand what it means to be alive. This realization leads man to question his very existence. Thus, in the beginning, the Brahman existed alone; the gods only gradually woke. The gods became gods when they woke up to their consciousness. To become aware of what one is thinking is to become Brahman. Men who are not awake are no better than cattle and can be lumped together as the herd, people whom the gods play with.

The Aryan civilization, according to Calasso, was rooted in a singular idea—a recognition expressed as "the arrow that buried itself within us and penetrated deeper and deeper into our brains in every gesture we made, until, ultimately, it became our only thought." This idea acknowledged that "the universe is a secondary and derivative fact." The Vedic Indians almost seemed to suggest that everything we are might be a mind in a jar, with only the mind and its thoughts being real while everything else is derived. When this realization struck, it felt as though a saber had swept down from the sky, cutting off their hands. Suddenly, the impetus was gone, distracted by something that made everything else hollow.

To the Vedic Indian, the conviction that only the mind mattered and nature was merely an opinion imposed itself more profoundly than on anyone else. They realized that all they had was the naked sensation of consciousness.

The Meaning of Life

To the Vedic people, life appeared to be meaningless, and only ardor and sexual desire made it tolerable. They believed that all creation stemmed from desire, and despite their continuous search, they could only identify it in the realm of sexuality. Since creation was evidently the result of sexual desire, they pondered the purpose of its continuation. Presuming that the perpetuation of creation relied on keeping the fires of desire burning, they considered desire to be the foundation of life—a driving force that gives life meaning. Man could find the spark to live in ardor, whether in the form of sexual desire or the exhilaration of the mind caused by knowledge. Without Soma, there would be no life, no desire, and no sense of achievement. For them, worldly conquests and success held little significance; what truly mattered was uncovering the source of desire—the essence of life. Soma, to them, was the ultimate source of desire, the kindler of intellect, and the very spark of divinity.

The Origin of the Sanyasi

The concept of the sanyasi is absent in the Rig Veda; it first emerges in the later Vedas. Initially perceived as an extreme form of renunciation, the idea of the 'naked fakir,' as Winston Churchill referred to Gandhi, evolved gradually and faced societal disdain. The Upanishads, critical of renunciation, preferred the term 'tyaga,' or sacrifice, emphasizing detachment from life while remaining engaged in the world as the highest form of sacrifice.

The evolution of the sanyasi concept mirrored societal changes and provided the rationale for this transformation. Born from the unmanifested in darkness ('tamas' or ignorance), humans strive to manifest in the light ('sat'). However, as this emergence involves transitioning from darkness ('Mrtyu,' or death), death remains an integral part of life. Advancement, then, becomes an effort to dispel darkness and overcome death.

The sanyasi, in this context, symbolically sacrifices his outer self in a ritualistic 'purusamedu,' or human sacrifice, before embarking on his quest. Turning away from society, he liberates himself from its conventions, beliefs, rituals, and even the duties of an 'agnihotri.' Simultaneously, all the external sacrifices and rituals meant for the world must be internalized. The sanyasi carries out these unseen sacrifices within his body and mind, maintaining an internal fire in his heart and mind, akin to the life of a Brahmin. Similar to the Brahmin's ongoing pursuit of knowledge, the sanyasi must keep an inner fire burning to bring forth knowledge from the darkness.

The Churning for Amrutha

The gods and asuras were once mortal, and the war between them resulted in a massive loss of life for the Devas. While the Asuras also perished, their chief priest, Kavya Usanas, learned the secret of 'sanjeevini,' the science of resurrection, from Rudra. Through this knowledge, the Asuras were revived, bearing the wounds of death. In their mutual pursuit of immortality, both groups agreed to cooperate.

The endeavor involved churning the entire universe, using Mount Mandara as the pivot, the giant turtle 'Akupara' as the fulcrum, and the snake Vasuki as the rope. As the Asuras were the firstborn, they held the head of the snake, while the gods held the tail. The churning transformed the universe into pulp, giving rise to the sun, the moon, Shiva, the Apsaras, and all the jewels of the world. However, the sought-after Amrutha did not appear. Instead, a sticky mass of dark material emerged, containing the concentrated poison of all worlds.

To proceed, it became imperative to dispose of the poison. Vishnu, recognizing Shiva as 'the first of everything,' requests that he handle it. Shiva ingests the entire poisonous mess, resulting in his neck turning blue due to the potency of the poison. The splendid blue color resembles that of peacock feathers and is bright and luminescent.

'Kalakuta,' the poison that emerges from the churning, is the residual substance formed from hatred, jealousy, rape, and murder—the fruits of desire. Yet, it also symbolizes that true knowledge is not possible without the ability to sublimate evil. To know, understand, and then sublimate is the only path to true knowledge. Shiva can swallow that poison because he is all-compassionate; only with compassion and tolerance can evil be overcome.

Even then, the gods get to taste Amrutha only because Vishnu transforms himself into Mohini, the irresistible Apsara, to distract the Asuras. However, after everyone partakes, Indra hides Amrutha again. Now that the Asuras have also become immortal, they begin to feel the lack of 'Vac.' The gods then use it as a pretext to send Vac to them, a 'Trojan horse' in their midst. The Asuras fall for Vac, but she betrays them and returns to the gods. Thus, the Vedas compare the mere recitation of the Vedas to the knowledge of the Asuras, while true knowledge is much deeper, something that the gods saw in 'Saraswati,' the way of the gods.

A Religion of Humility

It is interesting when one tries to summarize the thinking of the Vedic people that what we see is a strange or very pleasing innocence and humility in the presence of nature. They accept their animal origins and have a genuine affinity for all animals, long before killing itself became a taboo. The universe is sustained by sacrifice, a form of cosmic necessity where killing at some level is inevitable. What the Vedic people did was to ritualize it and give it meaning, elevating it to a religious requirement. To make the gods guilty, the sacrifice is offered to the gods. Yet, sacrifice, at its heart, is a mystery, which even the gods approach with extreme caution. Thus, there is a need to be particularly exact in all its aspects and stages.

While at one level it is directed to the gods, at another it is to sustain creation itself and finally to bring the devotee from darkness into the light. It is essentially a quest for knowledge that is beyond mere human intellect, requiring the flash of divine light. A more interesting idea is that of desire. They saw all creation as the result of desire and realized that life has meaning only when there is the vital ardor to live; it is the lust to live that sustains creation. To keep men on the edge with ardor was thus the real goal of life. Long before Sartre, they realized that 'ennui' or spiritual boredom was the greatest killer of human life.

The Vedic religion was a virile religion of bold adventure and deep thinking. To live life to the fullest and to participate in society was central to Vedic religion; thus, the later spread of the culture of renunciation was anathema to Vedic thinking. It was not Buddha's philosophy that was wrong but the glorification of renunciation. The greatest thought that struck them like an arrow was the fact that thinking and consciousness were the only reality, and all else may be just derivatives and 'Maya.' That was at the core of their philosophy.

CHAPTER 3

THE UPANISHADS

The Upanishads may perhaps be the first philosophical treatise in human history. The Vedas were clearly old but were enigmatic and more in the nature of abstract worship. The Upanishads are both an interpretation of the Vedas and an attempt to formulate a philosophy. As far as Indian thought is concerned, the Upanishads are the fountainhead of all further thinking. The history of Indian thought is largely a continuous appraisal of the Upanishads, and even where new thinking was opposed to the Upanishads, the Upanishads continued to be the focal point from which a departure could take place. Vedic thought had no worldwide following, and it was Buddhism, pervaded with the philosophy of the Upanishads, that made the philosophy of the Upanishads universal. The Upanishads, however, continued to be otherworldly and were an attempt to see reality beyond the mist of Maya, the real beyond the apparently real. Yet, in the canons of Hindu thought, it ranks only as a sastra, a second string, in the thread of sacrosanct texts, after the Vedas, which were considered divine revelations, and behind Smriti, the heard revelations of Manu and the great sages. The Upanishads are the beginning of the Shastras, the beginning of written texts. They represent the thoughts of the greatest sages of India, and their texts are considered just short of divine.

The origins of the Upanishads can be found in the Vedas themselves, with a distinction being made between the 'Brahmanas' and the 'Aryankas.' As though by natural progression, the physical rituals of the Vedas were internalized as meditation. This was, in a way, forced, as the Aryan left the comfort of his society to venture into new countries, very often places that were still forests. Without the guidance of the Sages of society, these forest dwellers were forced to explain their rituals, at least to themselves. This was the origin of the 'Aryankas,' also known as the 'forest texts.' They were seen by the first authors of the Upanishads as the 'bhandus' or the connections between ritual and knowledge that supported them. The 'Chandogya Upanishad' starts with the eternal sound, 'om,' the belief that with sacrifice, man is now equal to the gods as he too can sound the eternal sound. This confidence led him to internalize sacrifice, where he was no longer pleasing some God nor even sustaining the universe with the smell of burnt offerings but entering into himself to seek the God inside of him, the connection with the 'Brahman.' Thus, the Upanishads say, 'Ayam atma Brahman' that the self is Brahman and again, 'Tat Tum Asi,' you are that.

Dr. Radhakrishnan explains the meaning of the word Upanishads as made up of 'Upa' (near), 'ni' (down), and 'sad' (to sit), thus meaning teachings that were heard while sitting down before a Guru. It was what was communicated only between the Guru and his pupil, a 'rahasyam,' a mystery only to be revealed to the initiated. A father was also permitted to transfer such knowledge only to the eldest son, as it was part of the Vedas, a divine revelation. Over time, the Upanishads also became 'sanatana,' eternal and timeless. Even if it was only the wisdom of sages, it was the sages who seemed to have had a direct vision of the truth, beyond mere human perception and human reflection. It was as though God himself had blown the spirit of knowledge into the ears of the sages, who then saw truth in a flash of inspiration.

The Vedanta originally meant the Upanishads because the Upanishads were the end of the Vedas, the conclusion, the summation, the culmination, and the final interpretation. It was the quintessential wisdom of the Vedas. The Upanishads are said to be compiled in ten books, but Sankaracharya says there are eleven, and he comments on the Isa, Kena, Katha, Prasna, Mundaka,

Mandukya, Taittiriya, Aitareya, Chandoga, Brhad-Arayanka, and Svetasvatara. He also mentions Kaitaki, Jabala, Mahanarayana, and Paingala, together with Maitrayaniya and Maitri. Ramanuja also accepts all of them and includes Subala and Culika, and he also mentions Garba and Jabala as Maha Upanishads. There are also some Upanishads that are accepted as part of the canon but are essentially only religious and ritualistic, with little philosophical content, and belong more to the Puranas and the Tantras than to the Vedas.

It is clear that the early Upanishads predate the Buddha and may have been written sometime between 800 and 600 B.C. However, it cannot preclude the fact that Mahavira and Buddha may have been contemporaries of some of the sages who wrote the later Upanishads. The ideas that the Upanishads used may also have been floating around in some philosophy and used to explain the Vedas retrospectively, which also cannot be precluded. The sages to whom the Upanishads are attributed include Aruni, Yajnavalka, Balaki, Svetaketu, and Sandilya. Over the years, an attempt was made to compress the Upanishads into a single treatise; the result was the Brahma Sutra.

The Vedas were ritualistic doctrines, made up of magic formulas, hymns, prayers, benedictions, and rules for sacrifices, while the 'Brahmanas' were more in the nature of doctrine to explain the significance of the rituals. Vedic literature is thus divided into mantras and brahmanas, the actual words and their supposed meaning. The Rig Veda is not mere commandments to priests but also an outpouring of wonder at the universe and hymns of praise to the various gods. The first gods that the Vedas recognized were Surya (sun), Soma (moon), Agni (fire), Dyaus (sky), Prithvi (Earth), Maruts (storm), Vayu (wind), Ap (water), and Ushas (dawn). Only later did Varuna become the God who coordinates the course of the sun and keeps the world in order. He is also the God who propounds the moral law and punishes sinners. Indra then becomes, like Zeus, the king of the gods. Agni is the mediator between God and men. He is a friend of the Grha-pati. Mitra is the God of light. While worship was due to many gods, the God of creation was only one, Praja-pati. According to the Vedas, there was really no Indra or any other; only he was the true one, says the Vedas. However, the hymns in the Rig Veda clearly say that the gods were later creations of no different origin than man.

The Vedas are also man's first attempt to tell the story of creation. It says, first, all was dark and full of water, and out of the power of tapas was creation initiated, as the dark abyss was not in itself capable of creation; it was only potential. It was the supreme Lord who breathed life into the abyss, "stretched like a woman in the throes of childbirth." The world is thus the creation and perhaps the projection of God, a vision of the eternal, yet only a fragment of the supreme being. The fact that the universe is a mere projection of the infinite reality of God means that what man sees is only a fragment of reality, and endless possibilities remain, always open to new meaning and deeper understanding. The real always lies behind the passing manifestations of phenomenal life. The Rig Veda mentions no concept of rebirth, except as it sees the universe itself as continuously evolving and changing in cycles of time, where creation and destruction are an endless cycle of death and transformation.

While the Rig Veda comprises hymns of praise and adoration that also contain sacred knowledge, the Atharva Veda, on the other hand, deals only with the conduct of rituals and sacrifices. The gods involved in the Atharva Veda were Prajapati and Parameswara, along with Kala (time), Kama (desire), and Skamba (the forces of evolution). The Atharva Veda also assumes the presence of many spiritual powers that have to be dealt with, including dark and demonic powers intent on nullifying the power of sacrifice. While the Rig Veda also dealt with sacrifices, with the Brahmanas, they also gave an interpretation. In the Atharva Veda, sacrifices and rituals are seen as the ultimate power, with the gods mere onlookers. Sacrifice became the force that upheld the universe. By not giving any importance to God, the Brahmanas of the Atharva Veda saw human life as an end in itself, where sacrifices allowed them to live a full and happy life. The Rig Vedic wonder and concern for the eternal are replaced with a practical concern for the present. The Aryankas of the Atharva Veda glorify sacrifices by adding a philosophical element extolling the power of sacrifice and its importance in life.

The Vedantas also follow the four divisions of Vedic literature: the Mantra, Samhita, Aryankas, and Brahmanas. In an older tradition, there were only Mantras and Brahmanas, while Aryankas and Upanishads belonged to the Brahmanas only. The Vedas clearly began only as Mantras. It was only during the transition from the oral to a written tradition that an attempt was made to understand the Vedas. The Upanishads were the result. While initially it merely placed the rituals in context, the questioning of the purpose and demand for an intellectual explanation came later. At first, the Brahmanas and Aryankas were actually an attempt to explain the Mantras. However, in trying to explain the mantras, they were faced with a deep problem. The language was old and often archaic, and the experience that was expressed was transcendental and spiritual, quite unamenable to logic and semantics. The Brahmanas, the original but partial attempt to explain, were part of the Vedas themselves and thus the predecessors of the Upanishads.

Mantras were initially regarded as the very essence of the Vedas; their rituals were the very basis of religion itself. The mantras were so integral to rituals that many asserted that they were valid and pertinent only in the context of a ritual. However, there were many mantras that seemed to stand alone, suggesting the possibility of something beyond rituals. While the Mantras were by and large only the verbal element in rituals and sacrifices, the Brahmanas were divided into Jnana-kanda (knowledge) and Karma-kanda (ritual). Knowledge, in Jnana-Kanda, is not intellectual knowledge alone but also refers to all spiritual realization that is intellectual in nature—a state of illumination that the Rishis called 'Swarg,' or the realm of light. Thus, the mantras and the rituals taken together gave human beings an experience of Swarg or heaven, an extension and sublimation of sense experience.

The Mantras claim their efficacy on the magical nature of vac, or the word; thus, racial memory had to preserve its original form. The Mantras were also seen as deeply spiritual, hence the term

'Mimamsa,' a deep exercise of the mind. The mantra was an attempt to fuse deep intellect with spiritual enlightenment. This duality led to the twin approaches to religion—faith and reasoning or 'Sraddha' and 'tarka,' as the Vedantas say. However, intellectual thought is also divided into 'Purva Mimamsa' and 'Uttara Mimamsa.' The 'Purva Mimamsa' became ultra-ritualistic, while the 'Uttara Mimamsa' tried to understand the reason behind the ritual. Yaksa, with his grammar and analysis of all words in the Vedas, propelled Vedic thought into the realm of semantics. Later ages tended to forget the logic and become more ritualistic. Thus, most of the later 'Brahmanas' do not even attempt an interpretation; they merely paraphrase the original mantras. The 'Brahmanas' became more of an attempt to systematize the rites and rituals than to explain them. This attitude led to the doctrine of faith, relegating open thinking and questioning to intellectuals alone.

To defend themselves, they elevated the Vedas to revelation, divine inspiration, and the words used as 'Vac' eternal and unchanging. The words are sacred because the experience described is transcendental and cannot normally be encased in human speech. The revealed 'Vac' thus has sanctity beyond tarka discussion. Even Yaksa finally says, "No one can claim to have perceived the truth if one is not a seer...." Thus began the closing of the Indian mind. The writing of the Upanishads was, however, never an uncontested activity but forced on the later-day sages by a demanding set of worshippers to make sense of that which had already become eternal and divine. Swami Gyanananda claims that the word 'Upanishads' was taken from the root (upa-near, ni-perfectly and sad, to attain or destroy), meaning to destroy and attain perfect knowledge. Sankara says only people who seek liberation and are fed up with the mere senses should take up the study of the Upanishads. The Upanishads are perfect knowledge and the essence of all the Vedas, yet clearly not meant for the common man.

The Aryankas, along with the Brahmanas, tended to be rooted in life, scorning the importance given to the Upanishads, stating that only monks who reject life take to the study of Upanishads. Vedic religion was thus divided, with one side stressing the importance of life while the other reinforced the need for a higher meaning—a search for truth. The Upanishads were a journey into the heart of knowledge, scorning the religion of empty rituals and proclaiming that God, who is all and in all, does not need men's sacrifices; what God seeks is man's heart and soul. Every homa (sacrifice) is, at heart, a svaha (ego) asserting itself as great. The Upanishads demand a return to the religion of the Rig Veda, where it states that "the self is the sacrifice, and the human soul is the fire." True sacrifice is the abandonment of ego when man approaches the search for knowledge with a profound sense of need. The deep intellect needed to interpret the Upanishads meant it was open to all castes and social classes. In fact, the story of Satyakama Jabala is interesting; even though he could not give his father's name, he was accepted and initiated, as his devotion to truth was all that mattered. They believed in the saying, "Tat Tvam Asi," that God is within.

Vedantic Evolution

The Upanishads, like all things great, had an eternal appeal and a fascination for all who called themselves intellectuals. Thus, their commentaries also became part of sacred literature. The later Vedantas were only commentaries on the Upanishads. While many commentaries have been written, three individuals, with their inclusive and incisive minds, created new sectarian philosophies. They are Sankaracharya, who created Advaita philosophy; Ramanuja, who modified this into a qualified dualism and Vishtadwaita; and Madhava, who together created the philosophy called Dwaita. The study of the Vedas, initially divided into 'Purva Mimamsa' that emphasized ritual and 'Uttara Mimamsa' that dealt with the underlying philosophy, soon had further divisions. Mimamsa commented on ritual, while Vedanta commented on the philosophy behind the rituals. The study of the Vedas, divided into the Samhitas, the Brahmanas, the Aryankas, and Mimamsa, soon had Vedantas for each segment.

Even the Brahmanas had their own rudimentary elements of ethics and morality that exhorted men to be kind, to love all nature, and to forbid theft, murder, greed, and jealousy, and the Aryankas were an attempt to transcend mere symbolism, paving the way for the Upanishads, the culmination of all Vedic introspection. The Vedas were the raw material for discussion in the Upanishads. In trying to explain the Vedas, scholars were caught in contradictions and complexities of thought, with each commentator trying to explain as best as he could. The Upanishads, being an interpretation, do not start with first principles nor do they proceed to create a philosophical system that is internally consistent. The Upanishads are not philosophy in the strict sense of a school of thought that justifies itself from first principles but are an attempt to understand and explain the Vedas. They have many limitations, yet certain basic concepts get clarified as the Upanishads delve into philosophical speculation. From the pantheistic beliefs of the Rig Veda to the monism of the later Vedantas, the Upanishads allowed philosophers to state their beliefs and clarify the scope of religion. The major concepts that evolved as a result of their introspection were the concepts of Brahman, Atma, and Moksha.

Yajnavalka, perhaps the greatest sage of the Upanishad era, went deep into himself and realized that the 'Brahman' is elusive, that it can be understood only in negation, by saying, "neti, neti," (not this, not this); even then, we don't reach anywhere near the real thing. Only by discarding all that it is not can we seek the 'Brahman' that remains. The problem is that in seeking the 'Brahman,' we have to discard all that we know until there are no words to describe what it is that we seek. Something without qualities, no fixed location, and timeless. Despite what appeared to be an abyss that they had reached, the quest was exhilarating, creating an intellectual ferment that was not to be repeated in Indian history. It was a time when kings became intellectuals, like Janaki, king of Videha, Pravahan, Jaivali, and the king of Kuru Panchala, and men like Sandilya, who were all obsessed with the need to understand 'Atma' and 'Brahman.' In fact, Yajnavalka was the personal philosopher of King Janaka, who sought to understand reality and famously said, "You can't hear hearing, the thinker thinking, or the seer seeing, who then hears and sees." This led to a deeper understanding of consciousness—that it is impossible for the perceiver to perceive himself. As these questions came fast and furiously, the contestants in the brahmodya contest had to come up with some answers. This forced Indians to think deeper into human consciousness, where they divided consciousness into wakefulness, sleep, dreaming, and deep sleep—different states of consciousness. It was from this that they evolved the idea of deep meditation, in an attempt to reach the core of being, in the hope of finding 'Brahman.'

Deep meditation was first explained by Yajnavalka in a carnal way as the temporary loss of self in an intense embrace of a woman. It is a moment when one loses oneself and all other senses as the two are joined as one. While the descent into the self is an attempt to reach the ultimate recesses of the mind, it also resulted in the realization that man is not merely the sum of his actions but is made up of his knowledge of the world and of himself. Yet man is also the sum of his desires and therefore, "A man who is free of desire is Brahman." It is not in renouncing the world that one is led to inner realization, but in transcending desire. Thus, Uddakala Aruni, one of the greatest sages of the 'Chandogya Upanishad,' continued as a family man. His advice to his son, Svetaketu, is central to the Upanishad: that man is essentially his physicality. He is what he is made of; the clay from which man is made will always cling to him. The mind is not pure intellect but is made up of the food we eat, the air we breathe, the water we drink, and all our desires. The Atma cannot escape being part physical and part spiritual. Thus, purifying Atman from all its physicality is not easy. The body is also Atma. Even the God Indra took ages to understand that as we delve deeper and deeper, shedding all human desire, the Atman at the core of consciousness is also unconsciousness, no different from death. Our physical nature is so a part of us that to remove it is death.

Svetasvatara Upanishad

While the early Upanishads dealt only with the Brahmana and the Mimamsa, explaining the method of the rituals and their meaning, soon there was a demand to explain a purpose beyond the idea of harmony. Men needed motivation for rituals, and perhaps more importantly, they were asking for something personal that could encase their lives and protect them. The later Upanishads, especially the 'Svetasvatra Upanishad,' were thus an attempt to create some sort of theology. It was necessary to stress the importance of the creator God, who, as Prajapati in the Rig Vedic, dies to create the universe. Thus, a new set of gods were created from the existing powers that were worshiped, like fire, the sun, and other natural powers.

They could not look to Brahman or Atma, as they were eternal and, in many ways, the essential elements of the universe. While earlier, the universe was seen as self-regulating and therefore not indebted to any celestial power, and sacrifice was merely meant to ensure the existing harmony, with the Artharva Veda, all sorts of supernatural powers had already been imagined.

As the Artharva Veda incorporated local beliefs, the most potent power was seen as Rudra. The 'Svetasvatra Upanishad,' written, as tradition has it, by 'the sage with the white mule,' accepts the incorporation of Rudra as a God, as Shiva, giving to him the supreme place as 'Brahma,' creator and sustainer of the universe. Yet, even now, the sages refuse God's full power but created the concept of 'Karma' where the universe and all living things are regulated by the law of karma. It entails the belief that human life, like all matter, has to decay, die, and be reborn in different shapes and contents, based on the laws of chemistry and physics.

In the case of human beings, the rebirth and the type of life a person has are entirely controlled by how he lived in his previous life. With this came the escape clause called 'Moksha,' the possibility of liberation from the cycle of life. Here again, Shiva was the power beyond Samsara, the cycle of life, and thus the one to whom man can seek solace from the inevitability of Karma.

This clearly created a yearning to worship God and to seek favors. It also created the idea that God can be personal. This resulted in the concept of 'Iswara,' a personal God and the subsequent proliferation of gods based on the infinite attributes of God. It also led, in time, to the creation of idols to represent the idea of God as a physical reality. While the Vedas saw God as 'Nirguna,' without attributes, they also assumed that it also meant that God was also 'saguna,' the embodiment of all qualities.

From this idea of a God who can be personal, it was only a small leap to think of God as constantly acting in the world and in the universe with a plan. To upstage the prominence of Shiva, the idea floated was of a God who took human form, as in an 'avatar' to ensure 'dharma,' protect the good, and punish the wicked even in this world. Thus, Lord Vishnu was introduced. The idea is not unique, as the Christians see Christ as the son of God, and even the Greeks have a myth of how the God Prometheus brought down fire to human beings.

Language

As the Vedas were initially only oral, there was great reverence for speech as 'Vac,' which is repeatedly celebrated in the Rig Veda.

However, the Vedas saw speech only as the fourth part of the actual process of verbal communication, which it says has steps, stages, and grades, some of which are secret, before they become speech. They understood the complexity of thought and its mysterious origins. In this intuitive or reasoned understanding of speech, the Indian sages were centuries ahead of Western thought. Some sages actually saw the initial three stages as divine gifts, as innate, imprinted in us from heaven. This was also an attempt to lay the groundwork for the divine origins of the sounds of the Vedas. The word 'Vac' was thus almost divine, and it had to be studied with all seriousness, especially while trying to understand the Vedas.

Language itself was divided into its elements, like sound and meaning. Siksa was first referred to in the 'Taittiriya Upanishad,' where it is divided into Varna (individual sounds), Svara (accent), Matra (quality), Bala (organs of pronunciation), Saman (delivery), and Santana (euphonic laws). In the study of words and sentences, there were other elements like 'Chandas' (meter), for which the sages of the Upanishads clearly relied on Pingala's 'Chanda Sutra.' There was also a fascination with meter, and the Vedas make elaborate use of it, so much so that they attribute to it mystical origins, something akin to the divine harmony of the spheres.

The most important element was the logic of language or 'Vyakarana' (grammar), which almost always meant the grammar of Panini. Yet, with the Vedas being older, there had to be earlier versions, and tradition talks of 64 grammars before Panini, especially those of Apisali and Kasakartsna. Panini perfected Sanskrit grammar to such an extent that his Vyakarana (grammar) remains the greatest Indian contribution and is widely acknowledged as the mother of all grammar. Panini was the father of Sanskrit grammar, but he had one important predecessor in Yaksa. Yaksa is placed around 700 B.C., and even he refers to earlier works. His 'Nirukta' is a book of twelve chapters where he lists the words used in the Veda as 'Nighantu,' semi-divine, and comments on them. The language of Yaksa's time was called Basha. There was great similarity between the speech of Yaksa's time and the actual language of the Vedas. Yet, many of the nouns used in the Vedas are now not traceable to their verb form. With Yaksa, words and their meaning became eternal and frozen forever, and even Panini had to work around them. Yet Yaksa's greatest contribution was to make the Vedas understandable and amenable to linguistic analysis.

Panini built on the work done by Yaska and was the most respected Indian of his era. His great work, 'Astadhyayi,' is perhaps the greatest work on grammar ever written. Indologists, without exception, accept that he was perhaps the greatest grammarian of all time. Panini is normally dated to about the 5th century B.C. He was born in what is now modern-day Lahore. So great is Panini's contribution that Hwuan Hsang says, "In the process of ages, the devas descended to Earth to spiritually guide men, and such was Panini—born with great intellectual gifts and added to them by an intense and persistent search for knowledge." Panini wrote in sutras and fossilized Sanskrit for the ages. As the story goes, he wrote his grammar, closed the book, and gave it to a king who kept it under lock and key—closed and untouchable. Not only was it closed and sealed, but only through the elaborate set of tools developed for study can an attempt be made to understand the Vedas.

The Philosophy

As the sages try to explain the Vedas, sometimes a clear but often confused and nebulous philosophy emerges. As they view with wonder all that has been created and the unique human gift of consciousness, man's place in the scheme of things begins to crystallize. The main idea that the Upanishads propagate is the distinctive idea of Atma and Brahman as both a duality and a unity within the individual self and the all-pervading reality of the universe. Sankaracharya, however, disagreed and finally repeated, "Thou art that," that the multiplicity of the universe was only a perception of phenomena, while the ultimate reality resides beyond phenomena and is essentially one. Ramanuja countered by saying God is separate, yet the soul and all matter exist only for his sake; thus, they have reality only in that which is eternal and can have no separate existence. Souls are and appear to be separate and different, but they can never be independent of God. The atma is migratory and an eternal entity, causing births and rebirths. Along with the idea of an eternal Atma came the belief in the earning of merits and the possibility of better births as rewards and punishment.

Brahman

As the Vedic people looked at the monotony of the universe and at human life, which seemed to be nothing more than endlessly being born and dying, where everything only changes in an endless cycle of seasons, coupled with pain, sorrow, and inevitable death, man longed for something permanent, eternal, and meaningful. All their hopes were pitched on the concept of Brahman, the very antithesis of endless change and becoming something unchanging and eternal. Thus, they said Brahman is eternal, unchanging, and imperishable.

"In the heart of all things,
the imperishable,
a self-luminous being is formless.
He dwells within and without."

The changing, finite universe and the eternal, unchanging Brahman are the duality that man perceives. Brahman is the soul of reality; Brahman is forever the same. Brahman is transcendent; he cannot be grasped, perceived, or described; he is the power that pervades all matter. The Upanishads, therefore, say:

"Brahman is he whom speech cannot express,
that which cannot be comprehended by the mind,
that which the eye cannot see,
that which does not draw breath."

And then emphatically assert that "Brahman is not the being who is worshiped by man." That is the punch line: man cannot fathom Brahman and therefore cannot even worship him. When men worship what they think is Brahman, they are clearly mistaken. The duality of the changing, dying, decaying, and the eternal and perfect are reconciled in Brahma, yet man can only see the flux and the transient; the infinite is merely a postulate.

The philosophy of the Upanishads is deep and anticipates a number of later traditions in Western philosophy. However, we first need to understand the term 'Brahman,' which is also used in the Vedas as 'sacred knowledge or utterance,' the ultimate reality and all manifestation, and as 'Vac' the word. In the Upanishads, the term 'brahman' is used according to its root 'brh,' which means to grow, to burst forth. Thus, Brahman is seen as creation, evolution, and change. Sankara uses the term with the root 'brahati,' which means eternal, the real, and the pure. To Madhava, Brahman denotes fullness, while in the Brahmanas, Brahman denotes ritual as the one who knows and controls the universe. In the Vedas, the Brahman was the one who had been taught the sacred knowledge, as the universal and the true, behind the façade with the capacity for true perception, beyond false and partial knowledge, to true knowledge.

Yet, one of the great themes of the Upanishads is that what we see and perceive is real because it is the manifestation of ultimate reality. The problem is that we see it in a particular way, only as the divine wants us to see and only as what He reveals to us. Thus, the religious experience is not subjective; it appears subjective because God cannot be known except as he reveals himself. The experience is real and depends on each human being's capacity to discern the presence of God.

Yet the real is not the actual. The Upanishads accept that it is not mere Maya either; it is not nothing, yet it is not everything. It accepts, like Descartes, that it is impossible not to be, and therefore the 'I' is real because we cannot live a rational life without assuming the reality of our being. From this assumption comes the belief that the phenomenal world, real or not, is all that we can perceive. Brahman is 'Satyasya Satyam,' the reality of the real. In 'Taittiriya Upanishad,' a son asks his father to explain nature. He explains that dead matter cannot create life, yet consciousness is more than mere life, so intellectual consciousness is Brahman. Through consciousness, man alone has the power to change himself and transcend his limitations. Consequently, the purpose of life is to achieve happiness or the delight of consciousness. Reality is Satyam (truth), Jnanam (consciousness), and Anantam (eternity). From this, it is also clear that mere evolution, as propounded by Darwin, cannot explain the creation of consciousness. Life, mind, and intelligence are different from mere matter. Life is not merely mechanical but also exhibits uncertainty. Life cannot be produced by lifeless particles, and the mind cannot be created by mere matter. The world was not created by mere chance, and there has to be an element of the eternal in consciousness.

The Upanishads propagate a philosophy close to the Hegelian idea of perfectibility. While the cosmic order is in a state of constant flux and unceasing change, life creates duality. The opposites, like the sexes, emerge out of this constant churning and lead to development, progress, and evolution. When the purpose of the universe is accomplished, duality will cease, and all will unite in a divine order. Like Hegel, the Upanishads seem to suggest divine intervention that continues to establish itself along a divine path that will lead to ultimate unity with God. Thus, the Linga (body) also has Buddhi, the mind, which is made up of Sattva, Rajas, and Tamas. Buddhi is the 'Sutaram,' the secret being of the individual.

While the Greeks saw logos (the word) as reason, the Vedas also speak of vac (word or sound) as light and supreme knowledge (Jyotish).

While God is not bound by our consciousness, all manifestation is an expression of God, and that manifestation is all that we are able to perceive. But God is neither bound nor limited by his manifestation. God is also capable of more manifestations. Manifestation is made up of Shiva and Shakti, wisdom and power. All that is manifested is Brahman. God, thus, cannot be understood through human consciousness, which can only perceive that which is manifested. The divine is much more and is absolute; the infinite is the creator of manifestation, all in one. The Absolute is made up of Brahman, the creator, Iswara, the world spirit, and 'Hiranya-garbha,' the world. This is the concept of 'tri-suparna,' which later came to be worshiped as Brahma, Vishnu, and Shiva. Thus, the absolute is not anything we know; we can describe it only negatively, as what we don't know. The mind, which is merely a created thing, cannot comprehend its maker, a thing too much beyond itself. However, just because we cannot comprehend the absolute does not mean it is not real or devoid of essence. It is 'Swaroopa,' the essence of all, Sat, Sit, and Ananda (being, consciousness, and bliss). Yet, in attempting to understand the absolute, the Upanishads end up speaking of it as 'suguna and Nirguna,' as having all qualities and also as a thing with no qualities, or being beyond qualities. It says that the Absolute, in the form of Iswara (the world spirit) and Hiranya-garbha (the world), is always present in the world to guide men. God is in the world and in the spirit of evolution and change.

The Atma

When the Vedic man looked inward into his own consciousness, he was again struck by duality. The world that he saw around him was transient and changing, yet in his thoughts and his feelings, there was a strange permanence—the permanence of consciousness. All of the transient universe is merely a theater for consciousness, which is still the center of chaos. "How can that be?" asked the Vedic sages.

To answer this apparent contradiction, the Upanishads created the concept of 'Atma,' the eternal, unchanging, non-transient, and eternal element of human life. Atma is not ego, which is changing and tortured by the lust of the flesh and the sorrows of mortality. It is pure consciousness, pure spirit, unborn, uncreated, and eternal. Atma is eternal yet a silent and passive witness—the unchanging consciousness in the midst of the flux of life. The question then was, how can there be two eternal beings, Atma and Brahman? At first, they said Brahman is the eternal matter and Atma is the eternal spirit, but the culmination of Upanishadic theology was what Sankaracharya said: "Tat Tvam Asi" (thou art that) and "Aham Brahma Asmi" (I am Brahma). Thus, Atma and Brahman are one. Atma is the self that lives within, a shrine of Brahman. "That is the truth," said the Upanishads.

In trying to explain Atma, the Upanishads create the contours of Indian Metaphysics. It asks the questions: how do we know, how reliable is what we know, and is it absolute? The Upanishads refuse to identify Atma merely with the self, as it is also part of the infinite. The sages accepted that Atma includes man's life and his intellect (Prana and Prajna). The Rig Veda speaks of it as eternal and includes the unborn and the immortal Atma. Thus, the self is not merely the present self but is part of the absolute. This, according to the Upanishads, is what gives depth and a certain legitimacy to man's subjective knowledge. In 'Chandogya Upanishad,' there is a story of how the gods approach Praja-pathi to explain Atma to them. Praja-pathi then explains by going deeper and deeper. He says Atma is the one who hungers and thirsts, who eats and sleeps, grows old, and dies. Yet consciousness seems to be alive even when we sleep. So, what is Atma? At its lowest level, it is what we perceive as a reflection in water, in a mirror, and in the eye of a beholder. Does this mean that if we were blind, we would cease to be? We also have the capacity to dream, to imagine, and to make plans for the future. We even have a life made up of mental states alone. We continue to be conscious, even when apparently unconscious; when we forget and are unconscious, the Atma still exists. Thus, the atma is clearly more than the personal consciousness of the self. Atma is not an object but causes knowing and is also the theater in which all experiences take place. It is neither objective nor purely subjective. Sankaracharya says of Atma,

"I am distinct from the body;
I have no senses...
I am without activity.
Changeless, eternal, formless, without taint,
forever free...
Like boundless ether, permeate
The universe within without abiding
Always…"

We are not alone, for the self is also a constant witness of our consciousness. The Upanishads say consciousness has many manifestations, like Vaisvana (the experience of the gross), Taijasa (the experience of the subtle), Prajna (the experience of the transcendental), and Turiya, the experience of the supreme self. While Atma is the individual self, Brahman is the universal soul, and until they unite, Atma cannot perceive the infinite. The same idea is repeated in the concept of Narayana, who is God, who lives in man, Nara. The immortal God has a mortal dwelling place in man, but great insight is required to realize that God is within.

Atma and Self

Centuries before Freud and Jung, the Upanishads saw both the duality, fragmentation, and ultimate fragility of the self. 'Jiva' or self is what has the breath of life. In this biological entity exists the Atman, soul, or psyche, which survives death and is impacted by Karma. The human personality is kept together by Vijnana or Buddha (all forms of knowledge). The ego pertains to the world of flux, but at the back is the universal consciousness or Atma. The human self is made up of Anna, Prana, Manas, Vijnana, and Ananda (flesh, breath, heart, mind, and bliss). The nature of the ego depends on how these five elements are combined and which predominates. It is memory that keeps the ego together, and we are what we have been and what we remember. Like Kant, the Upanishads say we receive information through our senses (Manas) while it is understood by our intellect (Vijnana), which then creates it into intuitive knowledge for ready action. This is the knowledge that corresponds to reality; all other knowledge is deductive. knowledge that the intellect gathers with difficulty, as true knowledge is always hidden and has to be unveiled. Such knowledge also has to be assimilated, like our understanding of cause and effect, for the world to appear logical and purposeful. It is a mistake to assume a duality between the knowing subject and the object known, for the knower is always a part of what he has assimilated, and it is only thus that he can know. There is no objectivity in knowledge; it is always particular and subjective. True knowledge is possible only as a result of revelation and assimilation. Indian thought then takes a great leap and says that true knowledge is an integrated activity of the soul. "Those who know become the truth." Knowledge and being are the same thing—inseparable aspects of a single reality. Duality is an aspect of the intellect, but the Atma, as Ananda, sees only unified knowledge. To objectify knowledge is to be alienated from knowledge. It is this alienation that leads to beliefs in right and wrong. Those who have only 'a-para vidya' can only know the rituals of the Vedas, but with 'para-vidya,' one soars above the empirical and achieves ultimate knowledge. The real is not attained by the force of intellect but has to be revealed. With pride of knowledge (panditya), one cannot see the truth; only with humility (Balya) and purity of intellect does truth emerge out of darkness; only then is truth known. Only through detachment from the world, its values, and honors is wisdom achieved. Then they say, The "self cannot be realized except by those whom the self chooses... It is the fruit of strenuous effort and divine Grace. We don't hold an idea; the idea holds us and we are possessed by it."

Maya: The Concept of Reality

Man is always tempted to discard this world of strife and worry and seek eternal bliss, but we cannot ascend into ultimate reality without contending with the unreal. Even truth is covered by untruth, and only with the help of God can we look beyond the unreal, the world of illusion or Maya. Often, we seem to think that only through indifference to the world will we gain spiritual consciousness, yet the Upanishads say we can ascend the ladder of consciousness only by first overcoming the unreal; we cannot merely reject Maya nor withdraw from it. The Upanishads, while appearing to suggest duality, never admit that there are different realities, only one beyond the other. The world that is known to the self is as real as that which is known only to Atma. What we perceive is a manifestation, and all manifestations have a cause. The world does not explain itself; it has to be understood through inquiry. What is finite, passing, and transient cannot exist by itself; it must be produced by some higher reality, perhaps something infinite, absolute, and real. The natural state of things is to be eternal, and it is the transient that has to be created.

The manifestation is real because God does not merely create the universe; he becomes the universe. Creation is an expression of God. The apparent contains within itself the source of its essence, its laws, and its evolution. God resides in his creation; that is why, in time, we will discover eternal truths even through the manifested, as in love and beauty. The absolute is not a mere abstraction, an unattainable idea, nor is it a void or something that Wittgenstein would say has to be passed in silence. The absolute is not a denial of manifestation but a transcendence. If the world were totally unreal, we would not be able to ascend from the unreal to the real. Ultimate reality resides even in the unreal, and that is what maintains the universal theater of cosmic life. The creator is like a poet or an artist, and his art reveals the mystery of life and the beauty and infinity of his creative powers. What is relative in this transient world points to the eternal and to the perfection of the absolute world.

While 'Prakriti' (all creation), is 'Maya,' the human self, which is mere creation, is taken in by Maya because of human ignorance. To accept the transient as real is to overlook the ultimate unity of the transient and the absolute, the real and the unreal. 'Rupa' is form, while 'a-rupa' is the form of the formless. The world that is manifest is, therefore, dependent on the absolute. The laws that we deduce from the mere study of manifestations are only the laws of possibilities, which conceal the full nature of reality. The world tends to delude us into thinking that what we perceive is all there is. Maya reveals not reality but only the way we perceive reality; it describes the world but does not take us any closer to its real meaning.

Moksha

Knowledge is of two kinds: lower and higher. Even the Vedas are only part of lower knowledge, while higher knowledge transcends the senses and results in a connection with the eternal source of knowledge. It is non-perceptual and intuitive. Rituals and sacrifices are merely the mechanical parts of worship. It is not intellect either but the intense love for knowledge that seeks truth with a burning ardor that can realize true knowledge. That is the only path to the realization of Brahman, helped by the cultivation of moral purity and the advice of a truly learned and wise Guru. But ultimately, it is grace that allows one to know the truth and understand it. Words cannot reveal it; the mind cannot comprehend it; only devotional worship, in a mind absorbed and a heart that has melted with love, can perceive Brahman. 'Moksha' is the realization that we are all part of Brahman. It must be realized in this life, not in some future life. We are like lions brought up by sheep, says Ramanuja, and have forgotten that we are lions but bleat and move around like submissive sheep; it is knowledge that will free us, for then we will realize that we are all Brahman, free and eternal. Philosophy, forced to use words to express itself, can never describe Brahman. It is never what we can say—always more, always deeper.

Jnana

As long as men treated the Upanishads with reverence, there was always a place for Jnana, or the path of knowledge. In fact, Sankaracharya says,

"Knowledge alone affects emancipation.
Fuel is essential to cooking.
So knowledge is delivery.
Knowledge alone dispenses ignorance.
As sunlight scatters darkness"

It was in the tradition of Jnana that the Upanishads were written. Out of it were born Indian religious thought and ethics. It was the slow disappearance of respect for Jnana and the closure of the Indian mind that led to the decay of Indian civilization.

Ethics

The ethics of the Upanishads are seen in the teachings of both Buddha and Jesus. Man, say the Upanishads, is a mix of mortal flesh and divine eternity. He is thus capable of the evils to which flesh is subject and yet can soar to become divine. The discord between these two elements is real and at the crux of the human situation.

Man has freedom, but like the birds that confine themselves to their nests, humans become Earthbound by their attachment to the pleasures of the flesh. Yet, it is not in renunciation of the world but only in the endeavor to overcome the world, to transcend the pleasures of the flesh and be released from enslavement to them, that salvation is possible. If one cannot reject the world totally, the next best is to accept everything in the world without prejudice, with love and tolerance. The world is not evil; it is our greed and lust that bring evil into the world. It is not an act that is evil but the intention behind the act. Acts do not proclaim themselves as good or evil; it is the mind that corrupts all action. When the mind is cleansed of evil and becomes pure, all acts are good. From the goodness of being, good acts will flow.

Another important tenet of the Upanishads is the acceptance of a social mandate. They say it is not enough for an individual to overcome the world, but that all enlightened souls have a duty to teach other men the way to salvation. The enlightened must enlighten and transform the character of all men and thereby change the course of human history in the direction of a divine plan.

The Upanishads are not otherworldly but insist on the need for ethical conduct. They presume free will and make man accountable for his actions. Life has to be a sacrifice, say the Upanishads. In a telling story, it is asked, if there is no animal for sacrifice, what should we do? Use fruits and flowers; if these are not there, use water. If nothing is available, the human heart is the best sacrifice, say the Upanishads. According to the Upanishads, the great virtues are three: dama (self-restraint), dana (self-sacrifice), and daya (compassion). All creation is evil, says the Upanishads; the gods have desire, men have greed, and the demons have anger. These are the things that have to be curbed. We will never achieve knowledge with our pride, position, or intellect. Only when we become children—instant and willing to see without pride and prejudice—will we be able to perceive the divine.

The Law of Karma

Karma is central to the Upanishads. Life is a ceaseless flux called 'Samsara,' and it is determined by laws of health, morals, and spirituality. The law of karma is not external but internal, created by our own self. The law of karma is dispassionate, neither tender nor cruel. A man merely becomes the sum of his actions. Yet his actions are determined by the level of his knowledge.

The endless births are necessary to allow each man to attain the knowledge of truth; till then, he will continue to be part of Samsara, the flux of life. Freedom from the shackles of time and flux can come only with perfect knowledge. Freedom is not a state we can wait for but the result of the perfecting of the mind. Once we have attained the knowledge of truth, our deeds no longer have power over us. The knower who attains true knowledge ceases to be stained by his deeds. That is also the message of the Geeta—that the moment one has attained true knowledge, one is one with God. Such a person no longer acts, for his acts are devoid of desire and hope of rewards; such a person then becomes a mere instrument in god's universal plan.

However, the attainment of true knowledge is not easy; that is why there may be a need for symbols and names, which can then be worshiped by ordinary people till the mind has been trained to meditate on higher things. The man who has attained knowledge of the eternal has still to live in this world with all the ailments that are part of mortal life; the difference is that he no longer views the terrors of mortal life as terrors but as mere episodes in the theater of his life. He lives in the flesh but is no longer limited or consumed by the needs of the flesh.

The Upanishads justify the need for religion by claiming that God is not easily known. There is both a mystery and a reserve about God. Man cannot even glimpse the reality of God unless he makes the effort to know God. Man has to accept responsibility for the truth, become a seeker, and suffer the dangers of the quest before he can know God. Religion is therefore justified as a way to prepare man for this arduous quest.

The main elements of religion are 'Shraddha' or faith and 'Upasana' or worship. In this, there are three stages: Sravana or hearing; Manana or reflection; and Nididhyasana or contemplation. This is where the Vedas and the Smrithis become useful, followed by sutras and then the words of sages and Gurus. But the final leap of faith has to be made by the individual through his own commitment and intellect. Mere contemplation or meditation without faith is useless. With the decline of faith, the spirit of inquiry increases, so the Upanishads insist that all inquiry should be rigorous and logical and never descend to mere speculation. Truth can only be taught to a point; gurus can only guide. The final step is always dependent on the individual.

Despite this rather dispassionate view of the human quest for knowledge, the Upanishads also accept the need to come down from high abstraction to symbols and names, to gods that can be seen by ordinary men, to help them take the first step towards a truer realization of the truth. Thus, the Bhakti movement is very much rooted in the Upanishads' teaching of attaching oneself to a personal God. God has to first become real before man is able to reach out to the abstraction that is the true nature of God. The supreme is often too high and requires too great an effort, so gods and symbols are the steps in the ladder to the appreciation of a higher consciousness. Religion is that ladder that helps the seeker tread a known path, rest along the way, till he reaches a greater and greater understanding of the truth. Like yoga, religion is a training that begins with the external, the body, and slowly moves upwards to the mind and spirit. The Upanishads see visions, voices, and other hallucinations as merely embarrassing episodes in man's quest for the ultimate. The ultimate is within; God is within us; heaven is a state of mind.

A Review

The great contributions of the Upanishads, unfortunately never taken forward nor recognized for their worth, include the realization that the 'self' is essentially fragmented—not only between body and mind but also within itself by desires and transcendental longings. They also understood the many levels of consciousness, the consequent differences in perception and the resultant differences in knowledge. Along with this was the realization that consciousness is an interactive process where the self has to grasp and devour what it perceives for any understanding. In the process, both the object of perception and the self that perceives are in a dance, changing the manifested world.

Where Indian philosophy is considered deep is when it talks of 'Brahma' and 'Atma,' and truly revolutionary when they see the universe as a manifestation of God. The problem is that, pushed deeper and deeper into negation, the Upanishads saw 'brahman' as the ultimate reality of the universe and 'Atma' as human consciousness, a partaker in the manifestation, making the universe explicit. Atma is thus inextricably linked to 'brahma' and cannot exist apart. Together, they create the visible universe. However, when asked to explain 'Brahma' or 'Atma,' the Upanishads can only try to explain by negation, "neti, neti." It can only be said that it is not anything we know. What we cannot know is thus given a name. Having named two unnameable entities, they then try to explain the manifested world. From the unknown can come only the unknown, so they say the perceivable universe is only 'Maya,' an illusion, a show presented for us by the unknowable. The universe is also essentially unknowable. They get caught in circles as 'brahma,' the unknowable, cannot have qualities and is therefore 'Nirguna.' Similarly, the 'Atma' that is reached by the most arduous meditation is also 'nothing.' The problem created the concept of 'sunya,' which even Buddha refuses to talk about. Sunya is more than zero and more like infinity, and anything that has sunya in it would end up as sunya. As infinity, plus, minus, multiplied or divided, remains infinite or nothing.

While the Upanishads can rightly claim to be the first to voice the idea of 'Ahimsa,' the fact that the Upanishads were not accessible to the vast majority of the common people meant that it remained only as an idea in the memory of some intellectuals. It was Jainism and Buddhism that actually propagated the idea of Ahimsa as an ethical ideal, along with ideas like 'moksha' and 'Karma' that, because of their mass appeal, became central to Indian consciousness. All others were copied from the Upanishads.

The Upanishads are the end of the Vedas, literally, for the Vedas are knowledge. After that, all that commentators like Sankara and Ramanuja can do is debate whether Brahma and Atma are separate or a single entity. Having described Brahma as infinite and Atma as also infinite and since there can be only one infinity, 'atma' has to be part of 'brahma.' This leaves man without an explanation or solace. The ultimate is unknowable. Perhaps this is what led to the scorn for jnana among the later saints, leading to the embrace of the practical problems of life. Anything to make life tolerable and pleasurable. In this conflict, we also see the differing emphasis on Shaivism and Vaishnavism. While Shaivism saw Shiva as 'Nirguna' and the universe as Maya, with the Bhagavata cult, Vishnu is shown as the God who cares and thus 'suguna.'

CHAPTER 4

THE AXIAL AGE AND THE GREAT CHURNING (900-200 B.C.)

It was Karl Jaspers, the German philosopher, who called the period from 900 B.C. to 200 B.C. the Axial Age. Gore Vidal wrote about it as fiction in his novel 'Creation,' while Karen Armstrong wrote of it in her magisterial work, 'The Great Transformation.' It is, therefore, not surprising that it was in the Axial Age that India also saw the greatest flowering of philosophy and religion. In the case of India, it was a great churning, out of which all the foundations of our thinking were created. While the Vedas were already in the racial memory of a certain group of people, it also caused the fermenting of the Vedas with a strong mixing of other ideas, both local and those that continued to flow into India through its northern frontiers and through maritime activity in the Indian Ocean. Like the mythical churning, the orthodoxy hoped to find nectar at the end of the churning, but it had to first deal with all the muck that floated to the surface. Worse were the evil and the poison that got mixed with the nectar. It was only after Lord Shiva swallowed the poison that nectar was finally available. Then they had to deal with the Asuras, who helped churn the milk. In many ways, that is how the orthodoxy saw the rise of Jainism and Buddhism and the many secular philosophies that flourished during this period. It was, however, a time when intellectual curiosity was at its peak and men had not been regimented into a stratified caste system that would stifle free thinking and social mobility.

Political and Social Turmoil in Ancient India

Political and social turmoil were constant features of the period. While the Vedic period is seen by scholars as having been sometime between 3000 and 2000 BC, the telling of the Epics may have taken place around 1500 B.C. However, historians see the writing of the Epics as much later, perhaps only between 150 and 400 A.D. By then, the Vedic hymns had lost their original power, and the Arya were no longer wandering nomads; instead, they were a people who sought permanent settlements while still wanting to push the frontiers of their influence, resulting in a great deal of reassessment of their initial philosophical positions.

The Epics were thus a concerted effort by the sages of the age to reassert the values of the Vedic age in a much more cosmopolitan society. It was also a period of great turmoil, as there were successive waves of invaders, from Alexander to the Persians and Chinese. In the meantime, Indian towns were slowly becoming city-states, and the impulse for empire-building was also becoming apparent. This led to an intellectual vibrancy without parallel in the history of India, with ideas from invading people mixing with the free-thinking ideas that had become common in the more cosmopolitan city-states.

Religion, irretrievably mixed with magic and faith, was challenged by philosophical skepticism. Men in settled societies had more time to review their lives, to see beyond the present, and to demand meaning—a pursuit that led to a belief in an endless cycle of births and deaths linked to a new idea of karma that made life and all human action, in fact, everything, fatalistic. The atmosphere was thus ripe for the rise of the most adventurous period in the history of intellectual thought in India.

The period saw the birth of Jainism and Buddhism and a wide variety of materialistic philosophies, from Stoicism to Epicureanism. While the Sceptics and Cynics looked on all attempts at philosophizing with amused detachment, it also produced philosophers like Sanjaya, the skeptic who repudiated all knowledge; Ajita Kusakambin, a materialist who saw all matter only as a combination of four elements; Puraka Kasyapa, who refused to accept that morality had any logical basis; and Makkala Gosala, who saw life as a tragedy, where man had absolutely no power over his destiny. Most of their philosophies rejected any appeal to authority and asserted that what we see is all there is, something that Western philosophy had to wait for David Hume to say in the 17th century.

Matter is all that exists and therefore, it was logical to assume that matter can think. Intelligence, they claimed, is merely the chemical product of the interactions of the four elements, a manner of thinking that is today being advocated by leading scientists. They were emphatic that there was no such thing as the soul, as it could only be part of the body, and since no one has seen a soul, it is only a figment of human imagination. Consequently, there is no soul that, after death, can enjoy the rewards of karma. They claimed that religion was nothing but madness, a mental disease. Nature has no respect for human life, and the universe is only a self-created entity. Religion is merely the response of humans to their perceived weakness and the consequent response of a coward, something that Sartre was to say in the 20th century. In their thinking, they were clearly centuries ahead of anything the West could boast of. Many were thus induced to accept the Epicurean ideal and say,

"While life is yours, live joyously;
None can escape death's searching eye;
When once this frame of ours they burn,
How shall it e'er again return?"

All concepts of virtue were seen as delusions, and morals were considered merely man-made. They laughed at the Buddhist view that all pleasure is mixed with pain, asking, "Just because a grain of rice has a husk, do we throw away the rice?" Wisdom, they insisted, tells us to enjoy the pleasure that is available and leave it to fate to deal with the pain if it is inevitable.

The greatest impact of such thinking was on the authority of the Vedas; thus, many philosophers started calling the writers of the Vedas madmen, cheats, and fools. They boldly asserted that the Vedas were written only so that Brahmins could make a living. "The three authors of the Vedas were buffoons, knaves, and demons," they said, specifically citing the case of the Ashvamedha Sacrifice, which they asserted was an obscene rite where the Queen had to lie with a horse.

The greatest of the materialists of the age was Carvakas, whose sastra is called 'Lokayata,' which proposed that only what can be perceived is real. He was also troubled by the dogmatism that had set into Vedic thinking, resulting in the original freedom of thought being lost and the Vedas being reduced to a religion of rituals. The period thus saw the creation of a great tradition of free thinking and an undying hatred of orthodoxy. Such philosophies saw an eternal division between the 'Sramanas' and the 'Brahmanas,' those who refuted the authority of the Vedas and those who saw in the Vedas alone the justification of all thinking. The great tragedy for Indian intellectual history was that later centuries saw the victory of the Brahmanas, with almost all dissident philosophies being buried along with their philosophers.

However, the powerful questioning that these materialistic philosophies created resulted in many positive intellectual responses that were centuries ahead of Western thinking. Thus, on the question of the soul, they asked, if consciousness is merely part of the body, how could it be conscious of itself? Consciousness cannot be a property of that which consciousness can be conscious of. If consciousness were a property of the body, then, like all qualities, it would be possible for others to see our consciousness, yet they can't. Finally, the body is something like a ship, a thing that has to be controlled. Who controls it, ask the Vedic scholars? Consciousness is the controller, they assert. They then take on the more basic argument that a materialist would ask: If man is only matter and part of nature, from where do moral ideas come? This led to the Kantian question: If perception is the only source of knowledge, what should we call the thinking process that uses induction, deduction, and logic to arrive at knowledge? They scorned the belief that anything that cannot be seen or measured cannot exist. One group, like the later-day Bishop Berkeley, asserted that only the mind and all it imagines are real.

Megasthenes (350–290 B.C.), the Greek ambassador to the Mauryan court, says that the Indian philosophical scene was divided between the Brahmins, who were part of the ruling class, and the 'Sramanas,' wandering monks who seemed to be rebelling against all authority and questioned all revered truths. Philosophers were initially divided into 'astikas' and 'nastikas,' those who recognized the authority of the Vedas and those who did not. While Nagarjuna says an 'astika' is doomed to hell, Manu only says a 'nastika' is one who challenges the authority of the Vedas. This division became, in time, synonymous with the later traditions of the 'Brahmanas' and 'Sramanas.' According to Tamil tradition, the Sramanas were made up of three sects: the Anuvadis, Ajivikas, and Jains. The Buddhists were seen as a separate group and called 'Sakhyas.' The main unifying theme of all the Sramana groups was a refusal to accept the authority of the Vedas, a disdain for the caste system, and a rebellion against all institutionalized religions, their overemphasis on rituals and sacrifices, and the lack of any accepted moral code. They were largely world negators who preached detachment from human life and even called for a renunciation of all human pleasures.

Akriyavadins: Purana Kassappa

The leader of the Akriyavadins was Purana Kassappa, who was perhaps a Brahmin. He was reported to have told the Mauryan king Ajatasatru that there was no merit or demerit in any human action and that he was quite free to do what he liked without fear of any retribution or loss of merit. He claimed that the soul was passive and beyond the mortal frame's capacity to alter or impact and is 'Niskriya' (uncreated), and therefore, beyond good or evil. He also refused to believe in the law of cause and effect and did not even believe that we could learn and acquire knowledge through the study of cause and effect, claiming that Jnana and Dassana, knowledge and insight, were not the result of any cause. He himself claimed to be always in possession of 'nanadassana' (introspective knowledge) through his capacity to tap into 'anantena jnanam' (infinite knowledge). While his philosophy has been dumped, the idea of innate knowledge has continued to creep into Indian thinking and is at the core of yoga, the attempt to see knowledge at the heart of consciousness.

Anuvadins (Pakadu Kaccayana) or Prakruddha Katyayana, were also one of the Sramana leaders. Knowledge about him, his sect, and his teachings is so scarce that very little of his system of thinking is known. Yet, tradition has it that he was a fierce teacher who did not even believe in any theory of creation or the existence of the gods. He claimed that seven things were never created: the Earth, water, fire, and air, and then added that uncreated things include pleasure, pain, and the human soul.

Makkhali Gosala: Ajivikas

With Gosala, the rebellious mendicant became a threat and posed a truly imposing challenge to the Brahmanas. He was from a low caste, and like Jesus, since his parents could find no place to deliver him as a baby child, he was born in a cattle-shed. He was initially a friend of Mahavira but in time, they parted company. Gosala was a notorious character; he claimed he was a mendicant not because he was holy but to make a living on alms. He was gross in behavior and contemptuous of others. He made both the Buddhists and Jains hate him and called his old friend, Mahavira, "a mercenary teacher, vending his wares like a merchant." He was a convinced determinist; he saw life as totally ordained and that man had neither free will nor any role to play in the cosmic order of the universe. He refused to accept the laws of causation and said all humans have to go through an almost endless cycle of births. Destiny is destiny, he said.

He did not believe in gods, temples, or sacrifices. He felt that the best that men can do is to enjoy life, so he included dancing and singing as part of his teachings on religious life. This aspect of his religion was used by the Brahmanas, Jains, and Buddhists to scorn him, claiming that it was blasphemy, yet all of them slowly incorporated music into their rituals as time passed. Yet, as per the Tamil treatise, 'Nilakeci,' Gosala exhorted his disciples to maintain a strict moral code, and many of his disciples practiced severe asceticism, systematized into a religious routine that included asceticism, austerity, comfort-loathing, and solitude. Gosala was most famous for saying that no spiritual development can ever take place through moral observance. He believed that human life is merely part of the cycle of matter in the universe, moving upward and downward in the chain of matter; man dies, his body becomes the fertilizer that feeds the trees that make them grow, etc. Souls have no power; they are merely the sum and product of their environment, class, and place. He believed in an atomistic theory, with all matter being made of Earth, water, fire, and air. He saw all humans as having some form of astral color, including black, blue-black, green, red, yellow, and white. Only those rare beings with white astral color, he claimed, were in a state of release from their mortal bodies. While Gosala had a detailed reincarnation theory, he also added the idea of 'Mandala moksha,' where some good souls who have attained Moksha are sent back to Samsara (the chain of life) to teach other human beings the way. While the sect originated in northern Punjab and had a presence in the whole of continental India for some time, it lasted longest in Tamil Nadu, where it was present till around the 13th century.

Another non-Brahmin teacher, Ajitha Kesakambalin, preached that there was no benefit in sacrifices or rituals and that no karma would attach to any human deed, good or bad. There is no afterlife and it is claimed that the present life is all there was. Like the Epicureans, he advised men to make the best of the present life, for there were no rewards for good living nor was there an afterlife.

Jainism

In some sense, Jainism is as old as Vedic Hinduism, as the Jains claim that during the Mahabharata war, the Jain order was already in existence and was led by their 22nd Thirthankara, Neminatha. Thus, 21 other Thirthankaras had already lived and died. Mahavira was the 24th Thirthankara, and the original Jain sect was called Sramana-sanga, and it was from this group that Buddhism later broke away, based on the teachings of Buddha. Mahavira was of royal descent, and tradition gives his birth as around 599 B.C. and his death as around 527 B.C. By the time Mahavira died (who was believed to be the last Thirthankara), there was a strong and well-organized religious group called the Jains. The Mauryan emperor Chandra Gupta, after his renunciation, was supposed to have followed Bhadrabahu with a band of Jains into Mysore, where they settled close to Shravanabelagola. A rock edict at Shravanabelagola commemorates this settlement and the visit of Chandra Gupta. The Jains found favor in many courts, flourished under many dynasties and settled almost throughout the country. In time, Jainism split into two groups: the Digambaras, who went naked, and the Svetambaras, who were clothed. A further division took place, affecting both groups, when idol worship, which was opposed by a group that wanted only the scriptures to be sacrosanct, had its way. This led to the breaking of the Digamnaras and the Svetambaras into two further groups, the Terapathis and the Samaiyas, respectively, who rejected all idol worship.

One of the great contributions of Jainism was the opening up of learning to a much larger group. Unlike the use of Vedic Sanskrit that the Brahmins regarded as a sacred language and so refused to teach it to others or part with Vedic knowledge, Jains used local languages as far as possible, giving a great fillip to Prakrit, which grew into modern-day Hindi and all the other north Indian languages. Mahavir preached in the Ardha-Magadhi, a mixed dialect. In fact, both early Kannada and Tamil literature owe much to Jainism. The Jain tradition, like Vedic Hinduism, was initially preserved through an oral tradition, and the first attempts to write them down were unfortunately lost; consequently, the earliest available Jain texts date back only to about 450 A.D.

A fundamental aspect of Jainism was its revolt against the culture of animal slaughter for sacrifices and rituals. Thus, the main tenet of Jainism is 'Ahimsa.' They claimed that the basic conflict in the world was the result of living and non-living things coming into conflict; this, they say, causes the continuous need for births and deaths. The conflict creates energy, and only when the energy is stopped and exhausted will the cycle of births be stopped. Their religion was based on the seven tattvas or truths. The first Tattva was that the soul is part of a living body, and the essence and character of the soul are consciousness. They claimed that the individuality of the soul remains despite the destruction of the body. The body is merely made up of the five elements: fire, water, Earth, and air. Animals are divided into four groups depending on whether they have two senses: three, four, or five. Since the soul is indestructible, every person is born with consciousness, which also has the capacity for full knowledge. Human knowledge is gradually attained from scriptures, from experience, and from the knowledge of others; the ultimate knowledge leads to knowledge of everything.

The second tattva is the presence of non-living things. They consist of matter of all kinds, which can be probed and analyzed to discover their composition, form, and nature. Matter is as real as the soul and is also eternal. Another form of 'Ajiva,' or non-life form, is dharma, which fills the universe like water in the sea (something akin to the medieval idea of ether that fills the universe). As a counterbalance to dharma, there is adharma. This substance also pervades the universe (Here, Jains use the words Dharma and Adharma, not in the Vedic sense of righteousness, for which their words are Punya and Papa). The next tattva is 'Akasa' or space, of which we can see only the 'Loka Akasa,' while space, void, and vacuum that we do not perceive are called 'aloka akasa.' The last non-living thing, 'ajiva,' is time or kala. Kala is separate, unmixable, and broken up into minutes, hours, and days. All Tattvas are, however, subject to the inevitable processes of the universe, which are seen as production, decay, and permanence.

Into this world of Tattva, the Jains entrusted a philosophy called 'Anekanta,' where a thing is and is not describable and indescribable, etc., where seemingly contradictory statements are shown as true: a man is a man; he is a father as he is a man; a father, a man, and a father, and so on. The Jains believed in a self-existing universe where there was no creator or supreme being. The soul was eternal and surrounded by fine matter called Karma. It invades the soul and affects the mind and emotions. Contact with karma causes the creation of a soul in a body. The soul is light; in fact, it is the lightest substance, but the karma that it attracts creates the heavy body, which emits colors ranging from darkness close to black, blue, gray, yellow, red, and white in ascending order of purity. The closer the bond with karma, the more it causes delusions. It also shrouds insight and true knowledge. Good karma, however, leads to clarity and good activities. By controlling mental and physical activity, the invasion of fresh karma can be avoided.

The Ethical Code

A Jain, like a Vedic Hindu, was basically a householder. He was governed not by rituals and sacrifices but by five inviolable commands:

1.Not to do harm to any living thing—the concept of Ahimsa.

2.To always speak the truth—Satya.

3.Not to commit theft—Asteya.

4.Not to commit adultery—Brahmacharya.

5.Not to covet or be greedy for worldly possessions—Aparigraha.

As far as Ahimsa was concerned, it was divided into (1) accidental, (2) occupational, (3) protective, and (4) intentional. A man is excused when he harms accidentally, as is a soldier who has to do his duty, and so is harm caused as the result of self-defense. Only when the violence is intentional is it wrong. However, with reference to Satya, there was no allowance. Not only must one always speak the truth, but one should not allow the spreading of lies, betray secrets, backbite, forge documents, or cheat in any way. The prohibition against theft was also complete; not only was one not supposed to steal, but one must not appropriate to themselves anything that does not belong to one. The Jains perceived adultery in a much wider sense and saw it as applicable even when one only has thoughts of lust and not limited merely to actual acts. Lastly, a Jain should be content with his worldly possessions and not continually crave for more.

This ethical code was meant to inculcate self-denial, self-control, and a capacity for renunciation. Only when this is achieved should they proceed to achieve the other positive attributes. The higher demands included meditation and contemplation, reduced physical wants for food and shelter, and finally, even for clothing. The aim was finally to achieve a life of meditation and an acceptance of physical austerity and asceticism. A Jain should learn to fast and to reduce all his physical needs. Right conduct would then lead to the right faith, which is what leads to the right knowledge. For the monk, the discipline was much harder; he had, in fact, to forgo all the comforts of the world, be immune to hunger, thirst, cold, heat, and pain, until nothing matters and the self is absorbed only in thought.

The Philosophical Foundation

While the philosophical systems of Ancient India were divided based on belief in the Vedas as astika and non-belief in the Vedas as nastika (almost synonymous with Brahmanas and Sramanas), there was also a further division in Sramana philosophy, where it was split into astika and nastika on the basis of a belief in God, a supreme being or a creator. Thus, all 'nastika' philosophies were essentially agnostic in nature, while 'astika' philosophies depended on the belief in a creator God. Yet, this appellation was ambiguous, as many of the Vedic philosophies were also agnostic in nature. The Samkhya school rejected any idea of creation, and in the two schools of Samkhya, Iswara was not God in the sense of a creator but was an ideal to be aimed at by men. Even in the Nyaya and Vaisheshika schools, while they talked of 'sristi' (creation), it was only the cosmos of elements that then led to creation, a part of natural evolution. In Purva Mimamsa, there is no mention of God. Even in Uttara Mimamsa (the Vedanta), the universe is only seen as a manifestation of the ultimate reality or Brahman. In Jainism, while there is no God or creator, they talk of the ultimate, the ideal, and karma as an all-pervading substance, accepting the Purva Mimamsa position on creation.

Jains, therefore, don't believe in a supreme God or Creator. The reason they revere their Tirthankara is that they believe that all souls are capable of destroying the chains of Samsara and destroying the power of invading karma and to become shining 'siddha-paramesthi,' with infinite perception, infinite knowledge, and infinite power, and to live in infinite bliss. Even at a lower stage, the 'arhat-paramesthin,' who is beyond human limitations, has overcome the world and is on the path to supreme realization. In fact, the Jains look up to these 'arhat-paramesthins' and 'siddha-paramesthins' who are sometimes returned to the world of men to teach people the right path. Such men are born to conquer the world with their tapas and knowledge. When they appear in any part of the world, even the animals recognize them, and that region blooms with peace and prosperity. They are worshiped by many names, including Mahadeva, Mahavishnu, and so on. With the arrival of each Tirthankara, the world becomes ripe for change, ready for an evolutionary jump into the next stage of human development. The Jains believe that the world exists almost eternally and merely goes through cycles of decay and regeneration.

The enduring appeal of Jainism is in their belief that human beings are capable of divine realization. They also make such perfection humanly possible by claiming that perfection is reached through stages of development. Apart from the highest level of 'siddha-paramesthins' and 'arhat-paramesthins,' humans start their journey to ultimate divinity in stages, as 'Acharya-paramesthins,' 'Upadhyaya-paramesthins,' and 'Sadhu-paramesthin.' In the first stage, they must rid themselves of all attachment to worldly things, apply Ahimsa in all their dealings, practice the three ratnas—right belief, right knowledge, and right conduct—and be free of base emotions like anger and ambition. In both the acharya and upadhyaya stages, they are not allowed to initiate others; they must limit themselves to the lay functions of building up the sanga, popularizing jina-dharma, and working to educate and instruct people. Even when a person reaches the 'Sadhu-paramesthin' stage, he still has no divine powers; he, however, becomes a role model to other men in their quest for salvation.

The Scriptures of the Jains

Even though they did not believe in God, they claimed that their scriptures, 'the Agamas,' were revealed by the omniscient one, 'Sarvajna,' and handed down to a succeeding generation of Tirthankaras. The Agamas are grouped into three: the Anga, made up of twelve books; the Purva, of fourteen books; and the Prakirna, of sixteen. The biographies of the Tirthankaras are also part of their holy canon, called Mahapuranas. The book containing the rules for a householder is in the science of the universe in Karananuyoga and all Jain philosophy in Dravyanuyoga. The Jain metaphysics admits no creator; the world is uncreated and eternal. All reality is in the process of birth, decay, and death, and the semblance of permanence is created by transitory things that appear and disappear continually. Identity and permanence are maintained through a continual process of evolution and change. More importantly, Jain philosophy sees reality in opposites: forces of affirmation and negation that are always in a dynamic matrix. They also see the elements of the universe as Jiva, Pudgala, Dharma, Adharma, and Akasa, which are treated as eternal elements. Of these, only pudgala (matter) has volume, a core of reality; the others are merely nebulous, like life or the soul. It is also interesting that long before Einstein, they also saw time as one of the elements or dimensions of the universe and of human perception.

Jain metaphysics sees all matter, Dravya (that which manifests itself), as having both Guna and Paryayas, which in Platonic terms can be termed form and essence, along with its manifested qualities. Its manifest qualities appear and disappear, while its Dravya (essence) is permanent. Dravya, however, has both Utpada and Vyaya in its appearance and disappearance, indicating the transitory nature of manifestation as the reflection of the permanent Gunas. Yet, Guna cannot exist without Dravya; only in the transitory is the essence manifested. However, unlike Plato, they do not see any fundamental difference between Guna and Paryayasm; they are only two aspects of the same thing, one manifested, the other eternal. In the case of Jiva (life forms), the Dravya represents knowledge, feelings, etc. that are carnal and exist independently of the eternal Guna of the soul. Only when the two are combined is consciousness created (Cettanna Dravya). Thus, Guna may be eternal but is affected by its Dravya, its human form, and only then can it live in the human world of Sukha and Dukha (pleasure and pain) and gain Jnana (knowledge). Since Jiva has to reside in a body (pudgala), Jain philosophy does not make an absolute distinction between matter and Gunas. While Samkhya philosophy sees the soul as residing in the body but not an actor in the world, the Jains see the soul as capable of knowing, of receiving pleasure, and also of acting to achieve its ends. In fact, Jains see the immaterial soul as capable of defining and changing the material body.

This association with matter is what makes the Jiva a Samsara Jiva, a product of the cycle of life and death. As an organism with five senses, man is at the top of the chain and is only one step away from divinity. It is because we are born of material parents that we have the karmana sharira (human body). Being part of Samsara, the pure soul is then tarnished by the pleasures and demands of the flesh. Its intrinsic purity is thus lost. Yet, there is no escape for mortal man except in the eternal principles of dharma and adharma. Dharma for Jains contains all the power that makes us capable of action and choice; adharma is the source of negation, the principle of rest and inaction. Only when man sees the inevitable loss of purity through a life of emotions will he be able to opt for a life of negation, which will then stop the further soiling of the soul. They, however, assert that change is an essential part of life, the result of the opposition of dharma and adharma. However, this moving theater of life would become apparent and manifest only if we had a concept of time. The world would end if there was no time. It is time alone that makes us aware of the changing nature of the essence of things, which, in a different way, is actually forever the same, for it is time alone that creates this impression of change and flux.

The Jiva attracts karma by the way it grows to love pleasure and existence; this soon becomes a bondage to the flesh that holds the Jiva down. Only when the Jiva realizes that its essential nature is distinct from the material will it try to untie the bonds that bind it inextricably to mortal life and its pleasures. The first step is to stop attracting karma. This can be done through a detachment from life and a concentration on the eternal. This is where yoga, as well as meditation, tapas, and austerity, helps. Almost as a consequence, when new karma is not added, the old karma is no longer able to sustain itself and crumples. This leads to the creation of the pure soul, the Paramatma. The Jains saw the soul as an embodiment of knowledge; it was the bonds of karma that prevented it from seeing clearly. Thus, the acquisition of knowledge is akin to an unveiling. This is done in many ways: through the knowledge of scriptures, through proper sensory perception, by imbibing the knowledge gained by others like gurus, through insight and vision, as a result of meditation and tapas and finally as a result of a total detachment from life, resulting in a state of Moksha where one is finally in a one-to-one relationship with ultimate reality.

Equality (Samaiya)

Jainism is often seen as the religion of Ahimsa and karma, yet the underlying principle on which these concepts are based is equality. Jainism's greatest thrust was equality; as all souls are equal and undifferentiated, it is only the absorption of karma that makes them different. It is this equality that sees and reveres the soul in every living thing and insists on respecting all life as sacred. All humans are the same; their differences are only the state of evolution they happen to be in. Consequently, every human soul, despite its apparent carnal defilement, is essentially pure and needs to be treated equally and respectfully. They also insist on the concept of 'maître,' or goodwill towards all men. Mahavira kept stressing the idea of equality, or samaiya, and further added to the concept of samaiya by claiming that it consisted of samya, samata, and sama (sameness, equality, and of the same essence).

Similarly, the concept of non-violence or Ahimsa was not only about not harming any living thing but was based on the mental attitude of tolerance for all creatures. This tolerance was insisted upon even when it pertained to the question of beliefs and faith. Jainism stresses that 'obstinate insistence on one's own belief or attitude is an enemy to the attitude of equality.' One must always respect the attitudes and beliefs of others. This attitude is perhaps the only way for men to exist peacefully. Jainism thus always takes a non-absolutist view of knowledge. It never considers any knowledge or belief as being the repository of absolute truth but believes that there is always room to tolerate opposing views.

Even the laws of karma were based on the principle of the equality of souls. All souls are equal and pure; it is only the absorption of karma that alters the soul. Every soul has the freedom to choose, and it is the self alone that determines what it will be. The past is designed by the self, the present is being acted out, and the future will be what we create. Karma attaches itself to souls that lack true knowledge; all karma is actually the result of ignorance. Yet, Jains also believe that karma is always present, in the past, in the present, and in the infinite; that is why there is a human predisposition to the attachment of karma. It is only this opposing tendency that then pulls the soul down and hinders the soul's journey towards purity. Thus, the human aim should be to rid itself of ignorance and seek a path towards ultimate knowledge.

In Jainism, religion is only a tool to help the soul discipline itself in its search for ultimate truth. The stages of knowledge acquisition are (1) knowledge of oneself and (2) the conquest of passions, attachments, and hatreds. Only after these can the soul concentrate on the search for real knowledge, where austerity and self-control would allow the soul to direct all its energies to the search for knowledge. Jainism believes that every soul has the capacity to achieve godhood and that there are infinite ways to truth. They, therefore, value all forms of knowledge as sacred. They welcomed the science of logic, accepted all new discoveries in science and had great regard for epistemology and metaphysics.

Buddhism

Siddhartha Gautama Buddha was born in Pataliputra, a small town on the foothills of the Himalayas, in the 6th century B.C. He was from the Sakya clan and was therefore also known as Sakya Muni, or the sage of the Sakyas. His early life was that of a prince, with all the pleasures of the flesh. Thus, it was his renunciation of both his princely claims and the comforts of a princely life that made him famous. His later attempts to live the life of an ascetic, to torture his flesh until he attained enlightenment, have become the stuff of legend. Yet what he actually realized and preached has over the years been corrupted, as it has become a major religion with its separate sects, rebels, and defenders. This transformation has been a great loss to the intellectual heritage of India and the world at large. Buddha was clearly one of the greatest philosophers and psychologists that ever lived. The problem is that, unlike Socrates, whom he so much resembled, his ideas did not form the basis of a philosophy or psychology; instead, they became a religion to be defended or opposed with the ferocity that only religious bigotry can produce. It thus lost the power to ignite new minds that would have taken his teachings to new horizons and created a far superior society to anything the West has been able to produce.

At the core of Buddhist teaching is that the Buddha was only a man and merely one of the many Buddhas who have been born and would continue to be born to take mankind forward. It was also based on the firm belief that no teaching of any Buddha was to be accepted as the ultimate truth but to be treated only as the truth for the time and allowed to evolve so that it would always be relevant. As the Buddhist saying goes, each baker must apply his knowledge so that the bread is always fresh. Buddha, like Socrates, wanted his followers to put everything he said to the test of logic and truth and never accept anything just because a Buddha had said so.

The greatness of Buddha is that he insisted on deep thought, followed by actual testing, a method that is essential to all philosophy and all the sciences. In the process, he insisted that unless one knows something personally, one would never be able to understand the subjectivity of one's reasoning and the extraneous factors that contribute to the creation of ideas. As it is said, "to study the way of the Buddha is to study oneself. To study oneself is to forget oneself. To forget oneself is to be enlightened about everything in the world. To be enlightened by everything is to surrender one's own body and mind.' Buddha finally realized that he could gain complete control of his body and mind only if he could rid himself completely of all passions, both of the mind and body.

Consequently, as Buddha meditated, the temptations he faced were quite different from those faced by Jesus. To the Indian mind, 'Mara' symbolized all the obstacles that prevent a human being from attaining enlightenment. Thus, Buddha had to first face Mara's army, which fires arrows at him and invent all forms of physical torture that are possible. When such a tactic fails, Mara then sends his daughters to entice him; they are the embodiment of all sexual passions and lust. "Come, taste the pleasures of the world," they say, and only when Buddha surmounted both of these temptations was he ready for enlightenment. The Indian tradition clearly acknowledges the reality of the many serious temptations of the flesh that man can easily succumb to and is aware that they can be determining factors in human choices. This was an understanding of human psychology, clearly ahead of its time. The significance of the subconscious is also highlighted, as it is said that Mara's daughters awaken in the Buddha, his dark repressed fears and erotic fantasies, and bring back fragments of his memory, doubts, pains, and sufferings, to confuse and unbalance him.

Man, Buddha said, is caught in the wheel of life, which he called 'Samsara,' and the conditions of the present life are determined by 'Karma,' where the human ego creates a chain of desires and lusts that cause suffering, resulting in the endless cycle of births. He said that all Dukkha (profound sadness) comes from the feelings of impermanence, imperfection, and dissatisfaction. traumatic contrast to the comfort of the womb, where humans begin their lives but are then expelled with great pain and trauma. This is also an insight that later psychologists were to hail as an ultimate truth. This, said Buddha, remains the first experience of the alien world they are born into, even if most people are not able to remember their birth. Once born, we are all subject to all forms of sickness, old age, and death. Life is transitory and meaningless. Within the context of a life without any higher purpose, man is inevitably condemned to live shallow and unsatisfying lives. This creates a sense of bewilderment, not knowing what we are or the purpose of our lives, and this, said Buddha, caused all human suffering. In this life, each man can only see himself as 'I,' and the 'I' becomes all-important, and man is so immersed in himself that he cannot see the bigger picture. Only in the rare moments when man momentarily loses consciousness does he become capable of seeing beauty and truth.

The History of Buddhism

The story of Buddha, part legend, part truth, is known to most people and needs no retelling. What is important is to understand what he actually taught, how it became a religion and what caused it to split into many fractions that caused its decline.

Legend has it that the first Buddhist council was held almost immediately after the death of Buddha in Rajgarh, the Magadhan capital. At the council, Upali, the chief disciple of Buddha, is supposed to have recited the 'Vinya Pataki' or the rules of the Sangha. Then Anadha, the favorite disciple of Buddha, recited the 'Sutta Pitaka,' a collection of all the sermons of Buddha. With these two recitations, the basic rules of Buddhism were laid. However, by the time of the second council, which was held only a hundred years after the death of the Buddha at Vaisali, divisions within the Sangha were evident. In fact, by the end of the council meeting, irreconcilable differences made a split inevitable, leading to two major fractions: the Sthaviravada, or Theravada fraction, whose name translates as those who believed in the teachings of the elders, and the Mahasanghikas, or the great community.

The third council is a historical fact, as there is a historical record of it and it was held at Pataliputra under the patronage of Emperor Ashoka himself. A great effort was made at this council to unite the warring factions, and in the end, the political power of the emperor was used to silence dissent, and all the rebelling fractions were expelled from the fold of the Sangha. As a result, the Sthaviravada school was declared the only orthodox school.

As Buddhism became a major religion under the patronage of Ashoka and grew far beyond its natural boundaries, it had to deal with the compulsions of political power. In fact, Ashoka was supposed to have built 180,000 Buddhist temples all over the country during his reign. While Buddha taught that he was only a man, within 500 years of his death, his divinity was enshrined as part of the theology of Buddhism. In the meantime, the places where his ashes had been deposited became stupas and monasteries, centers of worship and learning. As it had grown on the wings of political patronage, it soon also had to deal with its enemies who had attained political power. They thus had to face persecution at the hands of kings like Pusyyamitra of the Sangha Dynasty and many other newly grown powers, which were backed by Hindu orthodoxy.

In the chaos and turbulence, the Mahasankigas, who had been expelled, made a return in a new form, as the 'Sarvativadinas,' especially in Mathura and Kashmir. This led to the first open split into the Mahayana and Hinayana sects, the greater and lesser vehicles.

The Hinayana tradition has been preserved in its original purity in Sri Lanka, where it took roots and became the undisputed religion of the people. The greater trade in the North West, to Persia, Greece, Rome, and other places, forced Buddhism to adapt to new ways of thinking, and one important imperative was the need to raise Buddhism to a religion with its own theology and its own God. This led to the growth of the Mahayana sect, which soon outstripped the Hinayana school in most parts of the country and the world.

Consequently, even by the 7th century, when Huan Tseing visited the country, he found almost no trace of Hinayana Buddhism and declared that it was extinct in India. A general decay had also taken place, with monasteries in ruin and only Nalanda University remaining intact.

As Buddhism went east, it had to deal with the predominance of followers of the Tantra philosophy. This led to the evolution of 'Vajrayana,' or the vehicle of the thunderbolt. The persecution continued and from the 6th century, especially in the reign of the Huna Kings, Miharakula and Suanka, fanatic Shaivite kings of Bengal, persecutions were clearly at the prompting of their Brahmin advisers. So persistent was the persecution that, by the 15th century, Buddhism was extinct in India. The last Buddhist text written in India was in the 15th century, after which there was only silence.

The Theology

By 500 B.C., a very large corpus of religious writing had already been composed. The 'Tripitakas' were composed around 500 B.C. and written down sometime in the 1st century B.C., consisting of thirty-two books that fell into three baskets, namely:

1.Discipline of monks: 'Vinaya'

2.Teachings and discourses: 'Sutta'

3.Special doctrines: 'Abhidharma'

They were also the foundation on which the later Dharmashastras were written. What is interesting is that much of the early literature of Buddhism has been totally lost in India but was rediscovered through Tibetan, Chinese, and Sri Lankan sources, retained in translations from original Indian sources. Very early in the history of Buddhism, there was keen interest in countries like China, where the greatness of Buddhism was immediately recognized, and Budhabadhra and Fa Hian translated many parts of the Vinaya into Mandarin, which are still available. Similarly, the Kasyapa school of Tripitaka survives only in Chinese translations. Thus, for much of Buddhist history, we have to go to foreign sources.

The original Buddhist literature was all written in Pali, and Pali, in a sense, became the sacred language of the Buddhists, and the literature was called the Pali Canon. This Canon has a further reason to be considered particularly sacred, as it was also called 'Buddha-Vacana' or the actual words spoken by the Buddha. To the Pali purist, Pali alone transmits the true thoughts of the Buddha. The Pali canon was initially an oral tradition, and once it was written down, Pali became a dead language and ceased to grow. Buddha himself encouraged his disciples to teach in the various local languages, and 'Prakrit' was the chosen language of Buddhism.

The original Pali Canon, when written down, consisted of as many as 84,000 sections, of which 82,000 were attributed to the Buddha himself. The actual authorship of the Pali Canon is not claimed by anyone in particular, as it is claimed to be a comprehensive and unanimously accepted canon. It was an all-embracing canon, but the goal of a Buddhist was not the observance of any set of rules but a change of heart and a new consciousness.

At a canonical level, the religion was based on beliefs that consisted of:

1.Buddha, the man, the master, and his personality.

2.Dhamma, or his message, doctrine, and discipline.

3.Sangha, the order, organization, and institution.

The new consciousness the religion attempted to create was based on:

1.Recalling all past experiences, including all past births.

2.The ability to see into a person, his aims, and his future.

3.Being aware of the impediments that lay in the way of full consciousness.

The canon further asserted that real learning comes from:

1.Knowledge and views of other great souls.

2.Knowledge that is arrived at through rational thinking.

3.Knowledge that comes from extending the teachings of Buddha and his thoughts.

The final aim of true Buddhism was to 'so behave that you make yourselves your own island, your own refuge, and seek no other refuge.' While the religion was totally open to new ideas and rational thought, it saw human life as one of suffering, and the aim of life was the ending of suffering. In such a life, knowledge was the only thing of value. But the validity of knowledge itself is transient and brief.

Buddhism attempted to find ways to bridge the void in human life—to reconcile human suffering and conflict—yet was always aware of its mortal state. Buddhist philosophy thus revolves around the concept of 'sunyata' or nothingness. The awareness of sunyata and the need to obliterate the subject-object relationship that causes all desire and pain. Long before Hegel, the Buddha said that each view can be made stronger by opposing it with its opposite view and that looking at the opposite view always adds strength.

The basic theology of Buddhism is made up of the four noble truths and the eightfold path. The four noble truths are the noble truth of sorrow, the noble truth of rising sorrow, the noble truth of stopping sorrow, and the noble truth of the noble way. Buddhism saw all life as 'dukkha' or sorrow. Man is born in sorrow and continues in sorrow through sickness, old age, and death, and only through the termination of the cycle of rebirths would sorrow come to an end. All sorrow comes from human desire, and only the eightfold path could allow it to be mitigated.

The eightfold path is made up of right views, right resolve, right speech, right conduct, right livelihood, right effort, right recollection, and right meditation. The cardinal element of the theology is the concept of desire, craving, or lust, which is part of self-consciousness and creates the idea of self, or the 'I' as opposed to 'the other,' which comprises the rest of the universe. In this concept, the existential purpose of 'I' is to satisfy its lusts, while the rest of the world is merely fodder to be devoured, processed, or experienced. This makes life essentially a tragedy because the self is never satiated by the fulfillment of its lusts; instead, it merely becomes a desperate pursuit of emptiness. Thus, the only flavor life has is sorrow, in the same way as the only flavor of the ocean, despite all its vastness, is saltiness.

The sense of despair is increased because life is all too transient. Like Heraclitus, Buddha saw change as the only constant and no man is the same from moment to moment. Yet, man seems to think that he is immortal when he is nothing but a collection of transient moments, transient feelings, perceptions, a state of mind and consciousness in a transient body.

There is no light in the night of Buddhist theology. Buddha ruled out the possibility of an eternal soul and asserted that even the universe is soulless and transient. He saw life as nothing more than a chain of inevitable circumstances. While not stated explicitly, the world of Buddhism implies a universe without a God and consequently without purpose. The only hope that man can have is to attain a state of 'nirvana,' a state of bliss, when one has attained the ultimate knowledge of the universe and everything becomes clear: there is nothing to hunger for, as all is only an illusion. Then, one enters into a state of absolute peace, a state of bliss, 'Nirvana.' One then becomes one with absolute consciousness, with no desire, free, and in bliss. In a universe always in a state of flux, Nirvana is the state of rest.

Mahayana: The Greater Vehicle

Buddha never claimed to be divine, yet just before his death, he was supposed to have imparted the three jewels of his doctrine to his close disciples, which they claimed were:

1.I go to the Buddha in refuge.

2.I go to the Dharma in refuge.

3.I go to the Sangha in refuge.

The idea that Buddha was a refuge for the devotee allowed the theoreticians to turn him into a God. It was then propagated that

Buddha, even in life, was in a state of nirvana, and his physical death broke the cycle of life and death, making him eternal. Thus, while Buddha taught that he was only a Buddha in a chain of Buddhas, his followers made him into the ultimate Buddha, a God. In the concept of the 'Bodhisattva,' he became not only a God as a universal principle but also a personal God. In fact, in defining the Bodhisattva, the similarity with the Christian concept of God is so striking that one has to presume that the Christians borrowed from the Buddhists, or it was the other way around, as the Mahayana doctrine crystallized only during the 1st and 2nd centuries C.E.

It talks of the Buddha as a man of sorrows who takes on the sorrows of the world and becomes a sacrifice for all. He is the ransom for the sorrows of the world. These are exactly the symbols with which Jesus is also described. In this way, Buddha becomes a personal God who looks down on humanity from his eternal abode and has compassion for men. A further refinement resulted in the creation of a duality in his nature, akin to the 'good cop, bad cop' idea. Buddha is 'Vajrapani,' or the stern Buddha who calls people to account for their lives, while Buddha as 'Maitreya' is the compassionate one, to whom man can reach out as a friend. In time, they also created a happy land where good men can go after their deaths, 'Sukhavati,' the heaven of Buddhism. Yet, in philosophy, Buddha was only the center of calm, the 'Sunya,' or void, the emptiness at the center of the universe.

Neither the term Mahayana nor Hinayana is found in the original Pali scriptures and is only found in Sanskrit texts of later origin. The term 'hina' means small and 'maha' means large, and the term 'yana' means a vehicle. Thus, 'hinayana' was the small vehicle, while 'mahayana' meant the large vehicle. The Hinayana was called a small vehicle as it limited itself to the words of Buddha, revealed only to his closest disciples. The incorporation of later thinking, along with the concept of 'Bodhisattva,' created the 'Mahayana' sect. Buddhism was particularly prone to dissensions because Buddha, in trying to verbalize certain very deep philosophical ideas, was inevitably ambiguous. It was very difficult to define terms like anitya, anatman, nirvana, or tathagata. The big problem was the definition of divinity and whether the soul ceased to be part of the wheel of life or remained a separate entity. The Hinayana group refused to discuss such issues on the plea that Buddha had not given any definitive answer. The Mahayana sect, on the contrary, claimed that Buddha, after he attained enlightenment, had said that the common people were not yet ready to receive the deeper truths of his philosophy and so imparted certain secret teachings only to them. They believed that human souls could become like Buddha and attain something akin to divinity. They, however, insisted that the realization of such eternal truths was possible only through intense training, including the renunciation of the self and the perfection of the self through the secret precepts taught by the Buddha. In this process, the final stage involves intense and deep meditation. The new teaching introduced the worship of the Buddha as a God and led to the deification of other legendary sages who had attained nirvana.

Hinayana: The Lesser Vehicle

It is in Sri Lanka that all the Hinayana scriptures have been preserved with fanatic devotion. Not only was Buddhism exported to Sri Lanka during the reign of Ashoka, but it was also there that the original Pali scriptures were first written down and translated. This was done as early as in the reign of Vattagamani, around 89 B.C. to 77 B.C. This effort was so important to the history of Buddhism that it later became the foundation on which the history of Buddhism was reconstructed in modern times. Even the fact that there was a king called Ashoka was known only through a study of Sri Lankan Buddhist records. The destruction of Buddhist records in India was so complete that even in the 5th century, Fa Heing, the Chinese pilgrim, could not find a copy of the 'Vinaya Pitaka' in India. The Vinaya Pitaka contained the rules of the sangha, while the Sutta Pitaka contained the sermons of Buddha, broken up further into Digha, the long sermons, Majjima, the medium-length sermons, Samyutta, the connected sermons, Angutta, the graduated sermons, and Khuddaka, the minor sermons. Apart from these, there were many commentaries, of which the most interesting is 'Milinda Pittha,' which is in the nature of a dialogue between the great Buddhist philosopher, Nagasena, and the Greek, Menander. For modern readers who are fortunate enough to study these original texts, the pervasive psychological content would come as a surprise. All sorrow is seen as the result of consciousness, especially consciousness of the self as a distinct and separate entity, and that human tragedy is the result of the unending desires of the self, lusts that merely satisfy the ego.

Madhyamikas

The Madhyamika school of Buddhism was an attempt to bridge the gap between the two main sects and was the brainchild of one of India's most important philosophers, Nagarjuna. Nagarjuna was born into a Brahmin family and was a true Brahmin, well-versed in all the Vedas and Upanishads, before he became a Buddhist. Very little is known about his life and what prompted him to become a Buddhist. What is important is the enormous contribution he made to Indian philosophy, particularly to Buddhist doctrine. The works attributed to him run into thousands of pages. If even a portion of all that is attributed to him were actually his, he must have been one of the greatest philosophers ever, as his philosophy runs through the entire gamut of philosophy from Plato to Wittgenstein. In an attempt to show that there is no great difference between the positions held by the two rival groups, he created a philosophy called 'sunyata' or emptiness, which claimed that even 'Bodhisattva' and 'nirvana' were only words used for easy understanding, to conceptualize deep concepts, and to help devotees climb the ladder of knowledge to the ultimate stage, when all words, definitions, and concepts disappear. As in the concept of 'Nirguna,' what Nagarjuna was saying was that in the end there is nothing, only the eternal void. All perceptions are unreal; all that we perceive is mere emptiness, or 'Sunyata.' However, conventional truth is related to a hearer and seeker, while absolute truth transcends self and knowledge so Nagarjuna asserted that as seekers, we have to accept that the emptiness of the universe is only apparent. He, like Parmenides, claimed that the cosmic flux was only a perception, for if the flux were real, then even Nirvana would be only a transitory experience. This would lead only to nihilism, where everything is neither eternal nor real. The Yogacara school latched on to this to say that the entire universe was nothing but the creation of the conscious mind, no more real than a dream.

Knowledge in the worldly sense has to have meaning to someone, whereas the ultimate truths are beyond self and knowing. It is divine, beyond human perspective, and best described as nothingness. This state of realization is not reached through knowledge. He abolished all transitory objects and all the phenomena of the world as unreal and said that truth is eternal, without form, neither created nor capable of decay. The world has neither cause nor effect, and all the objects of the phenomenal world are only apparent. Nirvana is that which is uncreated and eternal. He quotes Buddha, who said that to merely follow him is to take the easy path, which is ultimately the wrong path. The Buddha is what is eternal in the universe and all great sages share some of those eternal qualities; they only show what is not but can never convey what is, which the mortal human intellect is incapable of grasping.

Yogacaras

The next break came with the sect that called themselves the 'Yogacaras.' They accepted the philosophy of the Madhyamikas but compromised by saying that, in this temporal world, it is necessary to accept the reality of phenomena, as the deeper truths are too complicated for mortal men to comprehend. To the scholar alone, they prescribed the way of true knowledge, while for the lay followers, they prescribed the following of the precepts laid down by the Sangha, the way of the eightfold path and other practices that had been laid down by the Buddha. They also accepted the validity of mental images to the extent that they were important to each individual.

Vajrayana or Tantric Buddhism

By the 5th and 6th centuries A.D., the vitality and mental exuberance of Buddhist thinking had faded to a pale shadow of their former selves, and thinkers were picking at straws to keep the faith. Tantric mantras and rituals had always been part of Hindu belief and a part of the Atharva-Veda. Early Buddhism saw such beliefs as the ultimate sign of superstition and ignorance, and many of the early texts warn against falling prey to their spell. Yet, when Buddhism fell prey to doubts and became bereft of new ideas, a sizable group started to bring to Buddhism the very practices that they had abhorred. This group soon created a sect that expanded its philosophy to embrace tantric practices. The rites, rituals, and strange tantric practices became part of Buddhism, supported by the argument that mortal men need rites and rituals and a sense of power to entice them to live within a framework of beliefs. At the philosophical level, they accepted most of the Madhyamika theology and declared the phenomenal world as 'Maya.'

Because Buddha's teachings became a religion, there were soon three interpretations of what Buddha actually said and meant. These became the three schools of Buddhism: Hinayana, Mahayana, and the Vajrayana. 'Vajra' means diamond or the eternal way. It is also known as the 'Vehicle of the Thunderbolt.' Hinayana incorporates all the basic teachings of Buddha, and Mahayana is what it became to accommodate the needs of being a worldwide religion, while 'Vajra' was only meant for the initiated. In the early years, however, the teachings of Buddha were the preserve of his disciples, who tried to live like him as ascetics and wandering pilgrims, living on alms. Their purpose was tranquility, through meditation and a renunciation of the world. With the help of kings like Asoka, they got temples and monasteries to live in and, in the process, lost touch with the reality of human suffering. Buddha had warned against such a tendency and had wanted the monks to go forth among the people, to know the problems of the poor, the sick, and the old, and to have compassion for the world at large. Mahayana was an attempt at this inclusiveness, so that Buddhism was not merely a religion of the ascetic but for all men, where the sufferings of the world could be overcome with compassion. Vajrayana was only for the initiated and those who could forsake the world in a desperate search for eternal truth. Vajrayana, as the diamond way, established itself only in Tibet, where their ancient religion of Padmasambhava used Buddhism to subdue, not annihilate, forces of evil. Vajrayana does not reject any aspect of human life but believes in the possibility of converting all human experience into a life-enhancing experience. Anger can become intelligence and ignorance can transform into compassion. So contradictory seemed the teachings of this philosophy that it was termed 'crazy wisdom.' Buddhism was brought to Tibet by Santiraksita, who was also a tantric and thus Tibetan Buddhism is tantric and sometimes called Siddha Buddhism. Through Tantra, a person's worst failings are turned into energy for good. Thus, Siddha does not scorn pleasure but recognizes the energy created by desire. In fact, a Lama said that if one's thoughts towards dharma were of the same intensity as those towards love, one would become a Buddha. Vajrayana asserts that any religion that preaches the renunciation of human pleasures is denying the reality of life. It even sees sexual intercourse as a pleasant spiritual exercise that can lead to higher goals, beyond pleasure, to the realization of emptiness. But Tantra, without its higher purpose, can destroy a person, so the tantric is told that once you start, you must reach the end, for Tantra is a porcupine, which once you catch, the thorns could trouble you. The tantric is also told: go into the world, see everything, experience everything, and then turn them all into positive energy. Even negative emotions contain some truth that can be distilled. Yet the central theme of Tantra is that no person should practice it until he is totally pure in spirit. Vajrayana also introduced the feminine aspect to the godhead, 'Taras,' who are feminine Goddesses. The sexual union then became a metaphor for higher consciousness. One important aspect of Vajrayana Buddhism was its adherence to meditation or 'Sadhana,' where a person tries to enter into the realm of the eternal. Vajrayana Buddhism retains much of its basic character as a psycho-analytical and philosophical religion. Thus, what Jung said of the universal consciousness is basic to Buddhism: that the representation of Buddha as a God is only a representation of a universal archetype. Their gods are represented in a range extending from the gentle and peaceful to the sexy and terrifying. While modern man still fears death and tries to sanitize death, Padmasambhava, the great Buddhist scholar, on leaving his home in a palace, took up residence in the charnel grounds with half-rotting corpses and said, There is no difference between a palace and a charnel ground; it is the mind that matters. Fear of death freezes us, and all life then becomes an attempt to cheat death, being dead even in life, by seeking asceticism, life-denial, and penance instead of enjoying life.

Zen Buddhism

When Buddhism spread to China, it encountered Taoism, and the result was Zen Buddhism. Zen Buddhism takes one aspect of Buddha's teaching and makes it central to their system of belief: that only the present exists. All Zen teaching is an attempt to awaken human beings to the present moment. It scorns religious ritual and intellectual analysis, saying that nothing would be gained from such practices—only the present matters. All good actions come from the heart, with no concern for recognition, rewards, or achievements. The mind must not be attached to anything; only then will action be free. Freedom comes only when one ceases to run after things and is not bogged down by concepts of right and wrong. One has to empty oneself of self and all preconceived notions. The Japanese Zen masters took Buddhist ideas and turned them into poetry like:

"Fifty-three years This clumsy ox has managed. Now, barefoot stalks The void—what nonsense." (Sekishitu)

When only the present exists and life is only a dream, there is no fear of death.

While Buddha himself did not commit himself to any opinion on what happens after death, Buddhists believe in reincarnation, not of some eternal soul but from one birth to another based on accumulated Karma. The new life is not a continuation but a new birth, refined and modulated by the experiences of past lives. The gap between one life and the next, the Tibetan Buddhists call Bardo. The Tibetan Book of the Dead deals with this stage as the beginning of life itself. They see in the fear of death uncertainty, paranoia, manic depression, and schizophrenia—all forms of the loss of the functional and productive self. After that, the physical disintegration of the body is only the dissolution of matter. It is, in many ways, the most exotic version, but it also hides a deep understanding of the human psyche. It deals with many problems in life. The problem with knowledge is that, by itself, it is not a cure. A half-empty glass will not be filled unless someone actually fills it. Buddha's answer was to forsake the world and enter a world of the mind through meditation. He agreed that knowledge was only the first step and that it was never going to satisfy the soul. However, the deeper one is able to go into meditation, the less real the world would become, and so would the pains and sufferings of the world. At the deepest level, one may even glimpse the serenity at the center of the wheel of life.

The Social Conscience

Buddha realized what modern psychoanalysts had discovered the hard way: that all human illness is the result of dissatisfaction with the self, stemming from inferiority, repressed emotions, and poor self-esteem. Buddha, therefore, said, "First, learn to love yourself." We become filled with anger and frustration when we do not acknowledge the wounds in ourselves; we then blame others for those wounds. Buddha said all beings are capable of tenderness, and once we are reconciled to ourselves, we can easily be compassionate to others. The enemy is within, in our own ego, and once we have realized it, we will not need to seek enemies outside. Compassion, however, is not merely good intentions, said Buddha. It is not through our righteousness that we will be able to empathize with others but through spontaneous compassion.

Shanti Devi, an 8th-century teacher, put it best when she said, *"We should be a bridge that others travel over, like moonlight that cools the passion... like the sun that illuminates the darkness of ignorance."*

Long before Sartre and the Existentialists, Buddha said that all human experience only creates a great emptiness in the soul, the experience of 'Sunyata' or nothingness. This is also the result of the realization of the transitoriness of life—the fact that there is nothing in life that is permanent, that there is nothing that we can hold or possess. Life is nothing and is like the reflection of the moon on the water, the sound of an echo, or like dreams and visions that vanish when we wake. Humans merely pervert reality by giving it false meaning and deceiving themselves with absurd presumptions. They then mistake a rope for a snake. Since there is nothing permanent, life can only be experienced as it unfolds—no past, no future, only the present. The final understanding is to know that all life is but a dream, an empty charade. This view of life was brought to its logical conclusion by the great Buddhist philosopher Nagarjuna, who showed that any preconceived notion of reality can be proved to be wrong and self-contradictory. He saw the external world as a conjecture of the mind, conjured on the basis of stored memory and totally dependent on stored ideas and concepts.

There is something almost sublime about the morality of Buddhism, which has at its heart the concepts of love and pity. Pity, which means friendliness and benevolence. Consequently, there can be no deception, ill-will, or desire for evil. Instead, all men should be filled with unrestrained love and boundless goodwill. It preaches that instead of hoarding material wealth, men should show charity, love, goodness, and goodwill to all living creatures, as this would give more returns in the future and become a man's true treasure. Buddha said, "Brethren, love one another and care for the sick as you would care for me." Buddha urged the importance of truth and true speech and insisted on a prohibition on all forms of false speech and conduct. He said that the basic rule should be love, mutual trust, and respect. He advised husbands to treat their wives with respect and with love. Similar are the rules for parents, children, employers, and employees. In all relationships, he urged gentleness of speech, affection, and a sense of brotherhood. However, the Jataka tales also advise all people to be shrewd and cautious in their daily lives.

The Contribution of Buddhism and Jainism to Indian Consciousness

The very greatness of Buddhism as a philosophy was unfortunately also the reason why it left such a small impact on Indian consciousness. The philosophy of negation, renunciation, and withdrawal from life was too harsh a religion for the average Indian. It may have been a solace in times of extreme turbulence and social unrest but it was clearly a kill-joy in an age of prosperity and material wealth. Further, the idea of an immaterial nirvana, a belief that all life is but a magic show and a passing one at that, with no consequences, was not a religion for the common man. The deeper concepts of 'sunyata' and of the nothingness at the center of things—no phenomena and no essence—were also too abstract, even for the philosophically inclined.

Ahimsa

However, Buddhism and Jainism affected Indian life in such a dramatic way that it was never the same again, forever stamped by a new ethos. It transformed Hinduism and changed the thinking of its people forever. The first important idea was 'Ahimsa' or the belief in the sacredness of all life. Even if Ahimsa is mentioned in the Upanishads, it was Jainism and Buddhism that propagated the idea. This led to a total change in the system of religious rituals. Vedic Hinduism was essentially a religion of homa sacrifices, where animals of all kinds were sacrificed and eaten. The blood of animals and the smell of burnt offerings were hallmarks of Vedic Hinduism. With the Buddhists and Jains preaching respect for all life, rituals gradually turned from 'Homas' or burnt offerings to pujas, where flowers and non-living things were presented to the gods. With this change came an aversion to eating meat and the propagation of the doctrine of vegetarianism. These practices have become so ingrained in the Indian psyche that we now reject the idea that we were once animal sacrificers and animal eaters. Yet, it is important to realize that much of Buddhist philosophy was actually a take-off from trends started in the Vedantas. Thus, the internalization of sacrifices within the human soul, with the mind as the fire and the body as the sacrificial platform, was an idea already current. The abhorrence of animal sacrifice was also taking place, where the gradual refinement from human sacrifice by slow descent to the horse, cattle, and then to rice and barley was accepted as inevitable. Karma-Marga, or the path of sacrifice, was also giving way to Jnana-Marga, the way of knowledge, giving rise to the many schools of philosophical thought and the rise of yoga and meditation.

Karma

Karma has become part of all religions in India, and even Buddhists admit that the theory of karma was preached even before the birth of Buddha. Yet, there is no mention of karma in the Vedas, and it makes its appearance only in the early Upanishads. It started as a theory of the transmigration of souls, but with the incorporation of the theory of Karma, Hinduism lost most of its open-questioning nature, its basic mysticism, and its naturalness and became rooted in this one philosophical truth. The power of sacrifice that sustained the universe and the gods suddenly lost all relevance. Karma is based on the concept of desire, which man alone, among animals, is capable of feeling. As it was said, "as is his desire, so is his resolve; as is his resolve, so is his action." This attachment to the flesh and its desires grounded man to his mortal flesh and only when rid of desire is he free from his mortal coil. In such a world, bad actions draw man downward into lower forms of life. Consequently, man's life is determined by his past, and each life is a punishment and a reward. All life is a sum total of past deeds and a matter of chance in the present life, not dependent on man's actions or goodness in the present life. The Buddhists took this doctrine and made desire the root of all human suffering. Consequently, only when human action is devoid of desire is it free from Karma. This is what Lord Krishna taught in the Gita. Buddhism enumerates all kinds of acts that impact karma and how some affect the present, others the future, breaking them into physical acts, verbal faults, and mental perversions. Yet, Buddhism also refutes the existence of the soul and the possibility of karmic influence. Despite the doctrinal complexity and hair-splitting, the bare tenets of Buddhism passed into the Indian consciousness. a belief that we get the life we deserve, determined by the accumulation of past karma, with little hope for change. The belief in a personal God who can deliver us was a sop that was added to console man in the face of extreme human tragedies—a consolation, not a remedy. To the Jains, karma is the result of the body's impact on the soul. The impact caused by attachment to the pleasures of the flesh and an identification with the ego produces anger, pride, desire, and all the evils of human lust. This attachment engenders false beliefs and affects the soul by hiding true knowledge, preventing us from seeing the truth. We are then fooled by pleasure and the varied show of human life.

They believed that the universe is self-created and eternal and that souls are also self-created and eternal. However, the individual Atma is merely a biological entity and cannot outlive the death of the mortal body. All things have an atma, say the Jains, but their definition of the atma was more like Plato's idea of the essence of phenomena. The impact on karma is decided not by the act but by the intention behind the act. Thus, good intentions, even when they lead to disastrous results, do not taint, while bad intentions blacken even good results. Their pessimism is best seen in their refusal to accept the possibility of any change in karma and in seeing the human soul as utterly alone in the world, with only itself to blame for all that happens.

Nirvana

The concept of Nirvana, which is the central piece of Buddhist doctrine, is also the most difficult concept to understand. At the lowest level, it is seen as Aristotle's means, where human desires and goals are channeled through a middle path leading to a tranquil and serene life. At the doctrinal level, it means the repudiation of all desire and the denial of everything pertaining to the flesh. It assumes that this stage will be automatically reached when the soul is exposed to true knowledge, when the absolute meaninglessness of human life becomes transparently clear. Thus, desire is not merely to be denied but transcended, and that is when one gets into a state of bliss, where there is no conflict and no pain. That is Nirvana.

The problem arises when this concept is confronted with the theories of Karma and Samsara or the wheel of life. Since Buddhism denies the existence of a soul that outlives biological life, what can be the purpose of all human knowledge that leads to

Nirvana? What is Nirvana after death? This was a question that the Buddha refused to answer, as he claimed that human terminology would not be able to define or describe such a state. Consequently, once the state of Nirvana is reached, it results in the merging of consciousness and the unconscious as life inches towards the void and to nothingness. This is the great betrayal, as it were, that the greatest hope of mankind is to achieve a state of non-existence and nothingness. Yet Nirvana is seen as the highest good, a form of immortality, a state from which there is no death, no rebirth, and no decay. It is the final liberation of the human soul from the cycle of life. To explain this almost incomprehensible idea, Buddhists use the analogy of fire: it exists as long as there are things to be burned, but when all matter is burned, where has the fire gone? Similarly, when all human desire is burned and the self is also burned, there is nothing left except the memory of fire. But where does the fire go? Who knows? Even Buddha is silent. The final irony is that Buddhist Nirvana is also nothingness, extinction, and the void.

This apparent desperation at the heart of the concept of Nirvana arises because of Buddha's concept of self or Atma. The Upanishads had seen liberation from desire as the door to the realization of the true self and to a connection to the universal soul. As the individual discovers his true self and his true nature, the desires of the flesh fade away. By connecting it to the universal self, it becomes eternal and moves through the cycles of death into life.

To the Buddha, such an idea was absurd, for he said that if the ideas of self as 'I' and 'mine' remain and they only lead to desires and selfish preoccupations, deliverance is possible. He, therefore, said that as long as man accepts the notion of Atma, he identifies himself with the body he occupies. Thus, total deliverance is possible only when the self or soul is abolished. To explain what such a state would be like, he said that if one can imagine a soul, it is also possible to imagine a non-soul. That then becomes Nirvana, for only when the soul loses itself do all pain and desires cease. The concept on which this is based is the idea of 'niratma,' the state of being devoid of Atma, where Atma is seen only as an idea that has no independent existence. This is central to the 'Vijnanavada' school and the 'Sunyata' school of Buddhism, which denies the existence of the external world and maintains that there is nothing that is real. Man, merely out of his ignorance, thinks he perceives the world. It is through meditation on the concept of 'sunyata' that the world and all ideas of self vanish into the void, along with all notions of 'I' and 'mine.'

The Sangha

The Sangha or the community of Buddhists was something that evolved with time and was very much a part of the doctrine of Buddhism. A grouping of people in a Sangha often led to the building of monasteries and temples where the members could live together to study and worship as a group. The first rule of the Sangha was that anyone could join the Sangha; neither sex nor caste was a bar. However, full membership required the novice to have studied all the sacred texts and all other Buddhist literature, apart from a willingness to accept the discipline of the Sangha.

The second rule was that the membership of a Sangha was not necessarily a lifetime vocation but could be taken up for any length of time when one was particularly in need of solace, during a period of personal suffering, or during some life crisis and then go back to the world when the person had recovered sufficiently. They had to take a solemn vow to obey all the rules of the Sangha. The vows included a vow of celibacy and the three jewels of the Sangha, a vow against all false speech, Ahimsa, and the taking of any intoxicants, and against lavish living and frivolous pastimes. Vegetarianism was soon added. There was, however, no vow of obedience. This was in keeping with the Buddhist doctrine that each person is to think for himself. The Sangha was administered by the elders, but in effect, it was a democratically run organization. It propagated the four cardinal virtues: love, pity, joy, and serenity, and the avoidance of all impurities in thought and deed.

Yet the most interesting aspect of Sangha life was the insistence on deliberate consciousness. The Sangha taught that all Buddhists must be conscious at all times. They must be conscious of what they are doing, what they are thinking and feeling, their state of mind and the emotions that flood through their minds. All forms of distraction and carelessness were considered a lack of consideration. This is such a unique aspect of Buddhism that no other religion has even copied. The precept is so tough to follow that no other religion has been prepared to accept it or attempted a similar insistence. Yet, it was out of the concept of the Sangha that the idea of temples originated, along with some form of education and, most of all, the concept of the sannyasi.

The Rise and Fall of Buddhism in India

The greatness of Buddhism is recognized worldwide, yet like everything that is too good, it was much ahead of its time. The Buddha preached a religion of enlightenment through conscious and rational thought and, in the process, saw the universe as modern scientists see it: existing, perhaps expanding, and subject to cycles of growth and decay. He saw no truth in fundamentalism and advised his disciples to continue the search for truth. He gave no credence to the idea of a creator God or a judgmental God but saw life as an end in itself. His only problem was that he found no solution to the tragic waste of human life, no meaning, and no end. Yet between Buddhism and Jainism, they carved a separate identity, impacting the consciousness and religious thought of all Indians. That much Buddhist and Jain thought has been usurped by mainstream Hinduism and that Buddhism has more or less disappeared from India while the Jains appear only as a different type of Hindu is what we need to study.

In the initial years after the death of Buddha and perhaps due to the push given by Emperor Ashoka, Buddhism not only spread throughout India but also to all of Asia, from Japan and China to Indochina and Sri Lanka. The building of temples and stupas spread the Sangha culture far and wide. It also gave them a permanent base from which to teach and spread their religion, and it was the later pillaging and destruction of the Buddhist temples that finally spelled their doom. Ashoka also ensured a semblance of discipline among the Shangase, and his calling of the third council helped stem the tide of dissidence for some time and gave Buddhism a structure and a creed. In its massive expansion, Buddhism became institutionalized, powerful, and rich. This was an inevitable recipe for internal struggles for power and patronage, apart from the growing fundamentalism of the custodians of the true faith. It was, therefore, inevitable that divisions would arise and leaders would break away, creating new sects with peculiar beliefs, very often with little resemblance to the teachings of Buddha.

Almost immediately after the death of Buddha, the internal simmering of jealousy and petty slights came to the fore. Those who were seen as favorites of Buddha were targeted. Even in his own lifetime, his disciples like Devadatta were already jealous of Buddha's fame and respect, and some like Upanabda and Sadvarigikas were already rebelling against the rules of Vinaya made by the Buddha. Yet Buddha, being quite tolerant of mere breaches of organizational issues, may not have bothered, but with his death, such breaches became matters of discipline that affected the functioning of each mutt and Sangha. This was further accentuated by the Buddha not nominating a successor, leading to an immediate challenge to any authority that tried to assume leadership. This also led to a demand for a review of all organizational rules and even of beliefs and practices. In an attempt to stem the tide of growing rebellion Mahakasyapa, the most revered of Buddha's disciples called for a mahasabha to recite the teachings of the Buddha. This rehearsal of Buddha's teachings, instead of being the unifying factor that it was supposed to be, led to a clear division among the monks. Monks like Purama and Govapathi rebelled, claiming that what was being recited was not what they had actually heard from the Buddha. This group, supported by monks who had opposed Buddha even in his own lifetime and jealous of the rise of the favorites of Buddha like Mahakasypa, Upali, and Anantha enforced a breach.

The Breaking of the Shanga

According to Tibetan sources, within 100 years of the death of Buddha, the Pali monks from the eastern region were already rebelling against the rules of the Vinaya. While the main group of monks decided against these Vrijra monks, it led to a breakaway group who called themselves the 'the Mahasanghikas' who claimed that their aim was to modernize and improve the teachings of Buddha, thus isolating the 'Theravadins' or the traditionalists. Yet we do not even know the real reasons for much of what happened, as so few of the early Buddhist records have been preserved in India, and even what we know is from Tibetan, Sinhalese, and Chinese sources, where the continued reverence for the Buddhist scriptures caused them to be preserved. However, we know that even at the first council at Rajgir, the disciple Paruna stayed away, obviously unhappy with the leadership of the Sangha. He and his close associates soon broke away and formed a sect that was called the 'Mahasaskas,' who came with their own version of the 'Vinaya.' This group soon had a following in Sri Lanka. The weakening of the leadership resulted in further splintering, and many new sects, each with their own leaders, were formed, including the Sarvativadinas, the Harmavata, the Vasuputiyas, the Kasypithas, the Darmaputikas, the Sankarativadins, the Sathasiddhis, and many other schools. Many differed only in minor points yet the situation was ripe for sectarianism as each group mustered enough strength to survive as a separate group. This also indicates the spread and strength of Buddhism and the inevitable arrogance that such strength fostered. All the early sects were, by later definition, Hinayana sects, yet there was a move among them to deify the Buddha with the concept of 'Bodhisattva.'

The Spread and Dissipation

While Buddhism was splitting and splintering all across India, it began its gradual ascendancy across the borders of India, across the seas, and into many countries abroad. Buddhism reached Sri Lanka almost immediately after its birth in India, and there it retained loyalty to its original teaching, and the orthodox form of 'Theravada Buddhism' remains intact to the present day. The island also became a refuge and a sanctuary for all persecuted Buddhists from India and the repository of all the ancient Buddhist literature, which was not only preserved but studied with growing reverence.

In Burma, Buddhism was eroded by the intrusion of Tantric Buddhism that spread from the eastern borders of India; yet, the Theravada school of Buddhism retained its prominence. China too became a refuge for embattled Buddhism, where, from the beginning, it was seen as something special, prompting pilgrims like Huang Tseng, Fa Heian, and many others to make the arduous journey across the Himalayas to reach the land of Buddha and to read from the original texts. China has retained many of the original texts in translation and kept adding and propagating them for many centuries after their decay in India. Japanese and Korean Buddhism grew out of their association with China and soon developed their own special forms of Buddhism, especially Zen Buddhism, which focused on meditation and mental balance for a serene life. Tibet, like Sri Lanka, was a fortress, protecting it and allowing it to grow with distinctive scriptures and practices.

Causes of Buddhism's Disappearance in India

The disappearance of Buddhism from India is not documented in any history. Its disappearance is, however, a historical fact that stares starkly at our face. Even to conjure up causes for its disappearance would be a very detailed exercise, which is not the scope of the present study. What, however, is clear is that there were some very major reasons, like the loss of political patronage after the death of Ashoka when support waned and sporadic acts of intimidation and suppression were resorted to by upstart kings. By the 7th century, Buddhism had almost no support in North India and had been driven south of the Vindhyas, mainly to Karnataka and Tamil Nadu. Even there, the rise of foreign powers like the Pallavas, the Chalukyas, and the Shatavanas brought with them a more uncompromising form of Hinduism. Thus, by around the 13th century A.D., we see the final dying gasps of Buddhism even in the south.

The second major reason was the internal dissensions within the religion that resulted in the splitting of the once homogenous religion into many warring sects that were dispersed over the geographical landmass of India and therefore easy to break apart separately. However, even more important may have been the destruction and desecration of the temples and stupas and the forcible eviction of their members from their sanghas and monasteries. With the institutional base from which to grow having been destroyed, they became wandering mendicants, easy prey to destruction and submission. Without an institutional center to consolidate their teachings and without the ready-made students who became monks and teachers, willing propagators of the religion, they lost control over their fold and their ability to invigorate them or prevent the dissipation of their members. The end was inevitable, especially in the face of a resurgent Hinduism that did not spare the sword in its attempt to regain dominance.

The Ashes of Buddhism

Buddhism died in most parts of India by the 13th century, but it is the greatness of Buddhism that Hinduism, later and right up to modern times, is nothing but a reinterpretation of Buddhism within the larger school of Hindu thought. In a final attempt to swallow Buddhism, they even made the Buddha the ninth avatar of Lord Vishnu. The main tenets of Hinduism that are recognizable today, like the theories of karma, Ahimsa, and vegetarianism, the scorn for animal sacrifice, Tantra, Yoga, meditation, and temple worship, have all been imported from Buddhism.

The great Tibetan sage Padmasambhava is supposed to have prophesized that:

"when the iron bird flies
and the horses run on wheels,
the Tibetan people will be scattered
like ants across the world
and Dharma will come
to the land of the red man."

When Buddhism began to fade, it was Christianity that took its place, a religion started in Israel but adopted by the 'red men,' the Europeans.

The Sunyata that has been Left Behind

The extinction of Buddhism in India left an emptiness that has been impossible to fill. While it died in India, it went on, as legend says, to become an everlasting star in the sky, a reminder of what could have been. Buddhism not only taught us the concept of emptiness and of the void, 'sunyata,' but also insisted on the courage to face that emptiness and the need to go beyond. While Sankara and many other Indian philosophers placed similar concepts before us, it was, we thought, only clever arguments, never to be taken seriously. Buddhism, even as a religion, took it seriously and proposed that we live with it. an existential proposal, long before men were ready to contemplate such a heady idea.

Its insistence on deliberate consciousness was not just the Socratic "know thyself," but the demand that we be aware of every moment, every thought, and every emotion, at all times, was so revolutionary an idea that even today, we are afraid of its implications. Imagine what a nation we would have been if we had been brave enough to confront these absolutes, the void, and the essence of consciousness. Not mere world beaters but the inheritors of the future.

While Buddhism disappeared from India as a religion, it won a greater victory in the hearts of the people. It became part of the consciousness of all Indians. The other-worldly spirituality of the Indian ethos is also built around Buddhist ideas. Its ideas pervaded the psyche to the extent that all Indian thinking has since been built around ideas like Ahimsa, Moksha, and Maya. While these concepts entered the consciousness of the Indian psyche, as in the case of all complicated ideas, what was assimilated was a very simplistic version of the original ideas.

In the case of nirvana, the idea is normally treated with scorn as an absurd Buddhist idea, and the term merely means a state of bliss. 'Karma' has been totally reworked by orthodox Hinduism and made fatalistic and the justification for the division and sanctity of the caste system. It has become so important and integral to Hinduism that it can be said to be its central pillar and the pervading ethos of Hinduism. 'Ahimsa' has a more troubled history; it led to the decline of animal sacrifices and the rise of vegetarianism among the Brahmins. The privileges of caste, which Karma justifies, have trampled any hope that all life would be treated as sacred. In fact, it led to an anomaly where some animals are treated with far more respect than human life itself.

However, the most visible impact of Buddhism may not be ideas but the saffron-robed monks who gave way to the same-colored sannyasis and the acceptance of asceticism as a way of life, distinct and in rebellion to the Vedic idea of the householder. The other was the rise of temples and temple worship, along with the general acceptance of monasteries and the monastic way of life. In an effort to beat the Buddhists in their own game, Hindus began to organize themselves and create centers of learning that became the great mutts scattered all over the country.

One final word needs to be said: while Hinduism claims to be tolerant because it adapts to other ideas, that seems to be true of anything Indian. Thus, Buddhism, which started as something pristine and transparent, soon adapted to all Indian religious beliefs and practices and became, in time, especially with Mahayana Buddhism, a little different from Hinduism. In the same way, the pristine, questioning religion of the Aryans in the Rig Veda became, in time, pervaded with the ethos of the Atharva Veda. There seems to be a much stronger religious tradition, perhaps indigenous to our geography and culture, that tames anything that tries to be different.

The Philosophic Culture of Ancient India

One of the problems that western readers face when studying Indian philosophy is what seems to be a lack of logical rigor in Indian thought. This impression results from the unawareness of the actual philosophies of India, which include Nyaya and Yoga, and the many ancient systems of thinking. This misconception is based on the belief that Indian philosophy is synonymous with Indian religious thinking, comprising Hinduism, Buddhism, and Jainism.

Furthermore, it was not a lack of logical rigor but the realization that human intellect alone can never fathom the mysteries of the universe. Beyond a certain point, it inevitably becomes mystical and must appeal to divine grace for insight. This makes Indian thinking appear mystical. Another reason is that Indian philosophy does not see its role as an objective search for truth. Instead, it views itself as an inevitable religious role, a mode through which man betters himself and transforms his life. It is essentially a quest for values to live by, not a mere search for truth, even when value is treated as the ultimate truth. There is already a view that this life can never be perfect, and therefore, there is a need to transcend it. It is a personal quest for deliverance that makes Indian philosophy cosmic in nature, losing focus on the mere requirements of human life, the need for ethics and morals, and losing its roots in a social setting. It thus appears unethical and, at best, amoral. Even where ethical values are proposed, they are relative, and their application appears ambiguous.

While the abiding impression of Hinduism is of the plethora of gods, Indian philosophy has always tended to believe in monotheism. All the gods are mere representations of the unrepresentable, and to assist the less intellectually gifted, always be aware that the supreme being, as Praja-pathi or Viswakarma (the creator), is only one. This is the truth, say the sages; Agni, Yama, etc. are only different names of God. Yet, at an even higher level, man is seen as equal to the gods, as part of Aditi (the boundless). This takes man beyond the realm of morals, and the Rig Veda hymn of creation says,

"Then there was neither aught nor naught
...nor death was there, nor deathlessness."

They also, while talking of creation, questions the very idea of creation and says,

"who knows, who ever told, from whence
This vast creation rose?
No gods had been born – who then
Can e'er the truth disclose?"

Thus, at the highest levels of Indian thought, there is no creator, and gods were not yet born, making it clear that the gods are a creation of the human mind. Indian thought also refused to see the material world as real but saw it as 'Maya,' a manifestation of Brahma. However, at the other extreme, they see Brahma as Nirguna, as without quality, and as nothing. The universe and all material things are thus real in one sense and yet only a theatrical show, with the manifestation of Brahman at the other end. Brahman is everything—the ultimate truth—and the self and Brahman are one. God created the universe by transforming himself into the universe; thus, he is everything. Yet it is also an illusion, a mere manifestation, or something merely perceived.

Another reason for the seeming lack of rigor is that the ancient Indians had already realized that first principles cannot be deduced by logic. Thus, even their acceptance of Brahman as creator, who manifests himself, was only the acceptance of the need for a first mover, a creator. Brahman cannot be defined; the knower and known are one; knowledge, in the end, is to know oneself as part of the whole. This goes against the grain of all western thought, which says there is no object without a subject. Indian thought instead says that as long as 'I,' the empirical ego, sees objects, 'I' is only a distinct Atma, but when 'I' sees 'I' as part of Brahman, 'I' becomes Brahman.

The theory of karma appears to western minds as fatalistic and therefore a religion that denies free will. The Indian reply is that karma is not fatalistic nor does it reduce the options available for human choice. In fact, it is a theory that embodies the idea of the total freedom of the self. It is the self alone that creates karma and thus becomes bound by it. The self has all the power to decide what karma it will accumulate. It is a philosophy that sees humans as totally free to imprison themselves in their prison. Our freedom is compromised only by our free use of free will. For those who see the endless cycle of births and deaths as absurd and want to break the cycle, there is a problem. To overcome that problem, the Geetha gives a basically Buddhist answer: act without motive or desire and without seeking any benefit from any action; then one is free of karma, a principle also at the heart of Zen Buddhism. Essentially, the prescription is to act without desire. Western thinkers claim that desire, as will, is what drives all action; how then can one act without desire? The answer given is that one has to seek a desire beyond human desires; seek the desire for moksha that would be motive enough not to desire anything from a human act.

CHAPTER 5

THE SMRITHIS AND THE SHASTRAS

If there are three books that defined ancient India, they are the Laws of Manu, the Arthashastra, and the Kamasutra. The paucity of literature is itself a defining aspect of ancient India; so little has come down to us. However, it was not the result of any wanton destruction, but for the simple reason that so little was written. One reason for the paucity was the overwhelming preference for the oral tradition; the other had to be a complacence with the oral tradition and the fear of knowledge proliferation. Knowledge was passed on only from father to son in a closed society of the knowledgeable. Written books were a defiance against tradition and the result of having overcome the fear that the knowledge they contained could be used against the authors. Interestingly, therefore, the two books that matter are not books of knowledge but of rules to be followed, and in the case of the third book, the Kamasutra, the author was perhaps using the book to show off a knowledge he freely gave that was neither religious nor political and therefore not dangerous. These books define Ancient India, especially because there are no others; yet, they also say a great deal about the society for which they were produced. We will, therefore, study these books, except the Kamasutra, which is too specialized, and anyway, most people would claim that sexuality has little to do with the greater questions of religion and philosophy and only has a marginal impact on our consciousness. They are wrong, but we will, however, concentrate on the Laws of Manu and Arthashastra. However, the most important of the shastras was undoubtedly the Dharma Shastras. The Dharma shastras were written by some of the most revered sages, of which the Manusmrithis is the most revered. As many as six major Dharma shastras were written and many more minor ones. The lack of history and literature is compounded by the fact that every thinker, wanting to advertise his entry into the world of religious thinking, had to write commentaries on the Dharma shastras. Consequently, the study of the Dharma shastras is a universe in itself, and it would be presumptuous to deal with it in an off-hand manner. Thus, only an attempt is being made to indicate the content and parameters of the Dharma shastras with the insights of the great indologist Robert Lingat as our guide.

Dharma shastras: The Evolution of a Legal Consciousness

In trying to understand the Indian legal system, its origins, and its evolution, we are fortunate that the great indologist Robert Lingat had done the job so admirably many years ago. Robert Lingat was not only a great indologist but also one who specialized in the sources of law in the Indian legal system. When the British came to India, they were not able to get hold of a compendium of Indian law or anything resembling a legal code. In the meantime, almost eight hundred years of different levels of Muslim rule had caused a great deal of Islamic law to pervade the practice of law in the country. There was also a major problem: the ultimate power in any legal system, to have national validity, had to be a sovereign power or a king. With the disintegration of empires resulting from invasion and conquest, most parts of the country had been under Muslim rule, with no authority acceptable to all. There was no final appellate authority. The British, keen to understand and recognize the validity of the Indian system, were also at a loss to find enough legal history to create a system with a compendium of precedents and case law. They were therefore forced to introduce principles of the British legal system, which became a new layer of the judicial system, making the British legal system the last resort of a litigant. In this rather nebulous state of the legal system, Robert Lingat had to find some coherence. To create a sense of continuity and coherence, he went back to the foundations of the Indian legal system in the Vedas to understand the legal system, the hierarchy of laws, and the place of custom in law.

Dharma

He found that there was really no concept of law in the western sense. Law, as understood in India, evolved from the concept of Dharma, which was something transcendental, to maintain, sustain, and support the universe. A concept based on the idea that the universe is sustained by harmony and mankind has a duty to maintain it. In Vedic times, this harmony was maintained by sacrifices. It was a concept that did not account for man's duty to society or his role in it. It was focused on personal salvation, where society and its place had not been defined. As society became more complicated with the rise of cities and empires, Indian intellectuals realized that life was not only about spiritual merit. In trying to understand and regulate social life, they developed a philosophy that accepted that humans had certain basic needs and that dharma by itself was not enough. Thus, the concepts of Artha, translated as wealth and material comforts, and Kama, the pleasures of the flesh, were developed. Ancient Indian intellectuals recognized that an optimal combination of all three was essential for a healthy life and accepted all of them as essential. They then created a hierarchy of the sources of Dharma, recognizing three major sources: the Vedas, tradition/good custom, and the code of Manu and of Yajnavalkya. The Vedas were accepted as the ultimate source of Dharma, superseding all other codes or customs, and only where the Vedas are silent are the other codes to be used as arbiters.

The ultimate power of the Vedas rested on the belief that they were the result of divine revelation. The second source of Dharma is the Smrithis, including the code of Manu, considered partly revealed, as Manu was both God and the first human. His code, 'smriti,' as he calls it, connotes the idea of remembered rules, just one step below the Vedas. At the next level are the Dharma Sutras, then customs and traditions, and the way good people lived in more religious times. These 'Sad-achara' and 'Sista-achara,' are the conduct and practices that lead to religious merit and instructions on good conduct by virtuous persons or a system of ethics. Good customs can also be decided by the parisad (assembly) and samiti (gathering), giving local bodies a powerful say in the behavior of their members. The importance of good men, sages, and the like is emphasized by the saying, "One man without sin is better able to decide what is wrong than a thousand fools." Customs complemented the sutras.

The Principles

It is important to realize that Vedic rituals came first, and the idea of Dharma came much later. The Sutras challenge the supremacy of rituals and attempt to highlight the vanity of useless rituals. To that extent, the Dharma shastras were the beginning of an intellectual exploration of human life and man's place in society. However, no moral code or ethics evolved, as human conduct was invariably linked to the stages of life and to the duties of the separate Varnas and, therefore, relatives.

The first principle of the Shastras is the division of life into four ashrams (stages) and then the division of all people into four Varnas and their permissible actions. The division of people into the three Varnas laid down the duties for each caste. At the Vedic and Sutra stages, it was not only a division of people into Varnas but also into occupations. The Brahmins, Kshatriya, Vaishya, and Shudras were, however, also a presumed hierarchy. As the Manu legend says, the Brahmin was created from the mouth of Purusha, the Kshatriya from his arm, the Vaishya from his thigh, and the Shudra from his feet.

The Shastras say the Brahmin should devote himself to learning, teaching, and performing sacrifices and should always be ready to protect the Vedas. The Kshatriya's main function is the use of power to protect the people and fight foreign aggression; the Vaishya was to cultivate the soil, breed and tend cattle, and engage in business, while the Shudra was to serve the higher Varnas. Only the three upper castes were to have access to the Vedas and mantras. While there is temporal power in the form of a king, the Brahmin's only Soma is Lord (the Lord of sacrifice). The Kshatriya gets his vocation from the word 'kshastra,' which means virtue. It is his responsibility to protect the people, and with that comes the power to punish. To ensure proper devotion to caste duties, the Shastras emphasized that proper devotion to one's dharma leads to merits that ensure being born into a higher caste and that it was better to do one's caste duties badly than to presume to perform the duties of a higher caste.

The present life is the result of past lives and is 'Karma.' While Varna was a broad division based on hierarchy, Jati was the real division into castes. The theory was that Jatis were born out of a mixture of Varnas, where unequal unions produced Jatis. The

Vedas use the term Varna as a term denoting the Aryan race and distinguishing them from the Dasyu, who were dark-skinned. The original rules and the basis of the later division into rigid castes are not clear from the Vedas or the later Sutras and may have been the result of a need to retain a pure bloodline. Further, the supremacy of the Brahmin, as later acknowledged, was not an easy victory. In the years immediately following the writing of the Vedas, there was intense conflict between the Brahmin and the Kshatriya. Similarly, the privileges that were appropriated by each caste were the result of a battle of attrition and steady evolution.

While there was some laxity in the actual implementation of the caste system, the general rule that the lower caste cannot presume to usurp the functions reserved for the higher caste was clear, whereas the need for the higher castes, sometimes, to condescend to lower functions was accepted. Initially, the conflict was only between the three upper castes who were part of the Arya culture. The Shudra, who was clearly not, was excluded from all Aryan religious and social functions. This prohibition was total, and he was not allowed even to hear the Vedas or mantras. However, by the time the Dharma shastras were written, there was an attempt to bring the Shudra into the fold. The laxity in the rules of marriage, which allowed a second marriage of a Brahmin to a lower caste, allowed for the upgrading of the status of mixed marriages, especially where merit was clearly apparent. The rigor and intolerance that are seen today were a later development.

The four stages of life were the Brahmacharya, the Grahasta, the Vanaprastha, and finally the stage of the ascetic, who was, for all practical purposes, dead to the world. While these were the four stages, the Vedas only insist on the Grahasta phase as mandatory. The Vedas say that any man who performs adequately as a Grahasta cannot fail to reach heaven. Even Manu stresses the superiority of the Grahasta. The ascetic way of life was actually frowned upon and seen as threatening the gods, as penance and austerity could result in man attaining God-like powers. It was also an avenue open to the Shudra and, therefore, an open challenge to the rigid system.

Rules of Conduct

The rules of conduct revolved around the need for ritual sacrifices, the need to retain purity, and the honor to be accorded to guests. In fact, there were a plethora of rules regarding the treatment of guests. Of the sacrifices, the Shraddha for the dead was especially detailed. Every breach of duty leads to punishment and may even lead to excommunication from the caste. There was also a concept of penance for all sins, except the murder of a Brahmin or Guru, for which no penance was considered sufficient. Yet, almost all sins were forgivable; as it is said, anyone who recites the Gayathri mantra at sunrise 1008 times is freed of all sins. Marriage and the forms of marriage, along with what is permitted, take up a large part of the Sutras, as there is a deep-felt need to retain the purity of the bloodline. There is a code of conduct even in war and for all exercises of Kshatriya power. The Brahmin is also sacred in his person, and captivity, chaining, and bodily harm to a Brahmin are prohibited. The Shastras have a concept of confession and lay down rules even for the conduct of inquiry.

The Dharma Shastras

The origin of the Dharma shastras is semi-mythical but not connected to the Vedas. They are not philosophical but secular advice to a king on how to rule his country. Only those who could learn all the Vedas and Vedantas by heart could become priests. Those who could remember only parts could take up specializations in science, grammar, astronomy, mathematics, etc. The most important and respected of the Dharma Shastras is 'Manu-Smriti,' the code of Manu. William Jones first translated it in 1792, then George Buhler in 1886.

Manu starts with the creation of the world and how he received the Shastras from Brahma himself. He then recounts how the Shastras were given to six Manus, down the ages as dharma keeps declining over the yugas. He then tells of how the Varnas were created. Manu also claims that the Dharma Shastras were received from

Brahma, who ordered the sage Bhrgu to recite them and retain them in memory forever.

While the Manusmrithis has already been dealt with, merely to recapitulate, the first book is a mere introduction. The second explains the role of the Brahmacharya; the third is devoted entirely to the dharma of the householder. It includes the types of marriages and the respect due to women. Manu elaborates on one's responsibility toward a guest and finally details the ceremony for the dead. He enumerates the duties of the Brahmin, which revolve around the study and teaching of the Vedas. He deals with the need for charity and the rules for dealing with food and how it is to be eaten. Book V lists the foods that are prohibited for Brahmins. Meat is permitted only as part of a religious sacrifice. Book V ends with the duties of women. Book VI deals with the life of the mendicant monk. From Book VII, Manu deals with Raja-Dharma or the duties of a king: his choice of ministers and ambassadors, the protection of the realm, how the kingdom is to be divided among chiefs, into towns and villages, and also the salary to be paid to civil servants. Book VIII and IX deal with private litigation, the composition of tribunals, the protection of the weak, women and children, and the handicapped. Book IX expounds on the duties of husband and wife, and especially the need to watch women and keep them under control. Book X deals with the mixing of Varnas and the sins involving the loss of caste. It also deals with confession, penance, and austerities. Finally, it explains the purpose and methods of sacrifice and sacred learning and ends by advocating the pursuit of knowledge as the best vocation for the Brahmin. Manu Smriti is clearly an attempt by later Brahmins to pass off their heritage and customs as God-given and was written in an attempt to ensure its power and hold over posterity.

There have been many versions of the Manu-Smriti, but the oldest appears to be that of Bhrgu. It is difficult to date the Manu-Smriti, but all available evidence suggests the 2nd century B.C. to the 2nd century A.D. There are other Dharma shastras attributed to Yajna Valka, one of the most famous sages of the Vedic period. Two versions are attributed to Narada; others include Brihaspati and

Katyayana. The attempt to interpret these shastras and make them relevant to succeeding ages has been a continuing endeavor, with each generation producing its own commentaries.

Interpretations

Over the years, a large volume of commentaries has been written by many sages. They tried to explain, contextualize, and create a system so that the injunctions that had ceased to have any immediate meaning were seen in context or sublimated to a mystical level. Much of it was based on common sense and semantic analysis; the singular should include the plural, and male should include female, etc. They also tried to establish a hierarchy where the rules of dharma ranked higher than the rules of Artha and the needs of karma. In case of a dispute between commentaries, Pitambara says Manu should be considered supreme. Vijnaneswara, however, resorts to syntax and accepts an injunction as long as there are no contradictions. Concepts of jurisprudence and commonsense were the basis of interpretation, establishing, for example, that possession was in most cases a valid basis for a claim. It precludes minors and those of unsound mind from entering into agreements or becoming a plaintiff. It states that the loss of judicial remedy does not mean the right itself is lost. It enjoins those who are in possession of property illegally to at least ensure profitable use of land. It recognizes the contradictions in rules relating to marriage, especially between the Brahmins of the north and south, where marrying one's maternal uncle's daughter was prevalent in the south but considered incest in the north. They allowed custom as a valid principle and insisted that rules be understood in a context. That customs permitted by men of great learning, wisdom, and goodness for special reasons be honored. What strikes the modern reader is the diversity of rules, customs, and practices that were accepted. They range from marriage rules to rules of inheritance and land ownership. These commentaries led to different schools of thought and constant review and debate. The tragedy is that this tradition of comment, dissent, and evolution has slowly been stifled by orthodoxy.

Dharma and Custom

Accepting custom as valid appears to be a contradiction because it is assumed that the rules of Dharma should decide the validity of custom and not the other way around. The law, from the Vedas to Manu Smriti, was not based on the will of the majority but was proclaimed as divine revelation, so where was the scope for custom? Custom is purely social and in the nature of an agreement between men. The law, to be respected, cannot be merely social but has to be transcendental. To Manu, good custom was only the old Aryan traditions that were considered essential for the preservation and growth of the Aryan fold. Similarly, as Nietzsche said of the Vedas, it was the code for a race that wanted to excel. Yet it was really relevant only in the land of the Aryans, which was defined as between the two divine rivers, Sarasvati and Drishadvati. The spread of Aryans outside Arya-Desh made compromises necessary, but it also defeated the original aims of the pure Aryan. The acceptance in new and alien areas of different customs led to the theory of consensus. The compromises related mainly to marriage prohibitions, eating meat, and social associations. As Manu said, different Yugas require different Dharma. Humanity had lost its original innocence and had to accept a changing world. The writers of the Shastras were thus merely accepting the reality of Kali Yug. The justification was an inevitable compromise.

Another, perhaps cynical view, was the claim that the rules of Dharma are often in conflict with the needs of Karma and Artha and therefore need modification. While the rules of Dharma were supreme, they impacted only Karma and the next life and were not absolute in human behavior. Thus, men were allowed to choose based on the pros and cons to ensure a harmonious life, even at the cost of some loss of merit in the next. While they accepted that "what is odious to the world" was bad, perfect wisdom was only to be expected among Vedic saints. Yet, the commentaries make clear that customs cannot override clear injunctions of Dharma about life and purity. In the end, they say, wisdom cannot be taught; it is innate, and it would be unfair to castigate ordinary men because they follow custom. Brihaspati finally says, "For such practices, these people incur neither penance nor secular punishment." However, customs were only tolerated, not legitimized. Out of the plethora of customs grew the study of the law. The precepts of Dharma were eternal, while secular law had to consider customs and traditions. Indian law took these customs into a growing tradition of legal precepts, while Dharma remained relevant only to personal salvation.

Kingship

Indian Dharma sees kingship as divine ordination and believes that no society is viable without a king. The king is a semi-deity, and his functions fall within the scope of Dharma. Consequently, a king has to be worthy, a Kshatriya, a warrior, and a protector of his people. He has to be from a good family known for their virtues. Kingship is called Kshatra, the royal right, whereas Dharma is harmony and interdependence. While the king is entitled to act as he likes, he gains merit only insofar as he acts within the dictates of Dharma. He is the custodian of his people's happiness, including spiritual happiness. Dharma requires the king to act only for the good of all his subjects, and when he fails to protect them, the people are entitled to seek change.

The main weapon of the king is Danda (the rod) or punishment. Yet Dharma enjoins him to act justly. The Shastras admit the dangers of unlimited power and caution the king to use power judiciously. The duties of a king are akin to a sacrifice—a sacred duty. All his acts are sanctified by Vedic doctrine, which differentiates between Dharma and Kshatra, the spiritual and the temporal. While the king cannot be judged when his reign is rooted in Dharma, it is his duty to ensure that the people are protected. Due to the problems of unlimited power, the king is advised to have a counselor from among the best-educated and wise Brahmins. The Purohita's (the king's counselor) main role is to see that the king performs his religious duties and be an advisor on politics, economics, and statecraft.

The Shastras also proclaim the Brahmin as sacred. Even the lowest and least educated Brahmins are to be honored. He is never to be beaten, chained, or imprisoned. Even a person who threatens a Brahmin will fall into hell a hundred times, say the Shastras. To protect himself and annihilate his enemies, the Brahmin is even allowed to practice magic, charms, and incantations. The Brahmin is not taxable, and his person, his goods, and his possessions are sacred, and he cannot be molested. Where the Brahmin is respected, the kingdom will prosper, say the Shastras. Yet this acceptance of Brahmin dominance in things spiritual came about, if legend is to be believed, only after a long and bloody conflict with the Kshatriyas. Yet, the Shastras make it clear that the Brahmin is not to be honored because of his Varna or birth but because of his devotion to the study of the Vedas, and that is also what makes him qualified to teach and to advise. The duties of the king are spelled out as 1] Protection of his people, prevention of disorder, and neglect. 2) Punishment and penance for the guilty 3) Ensure peace and order and 4) Peace between his subjects. The king also has legislative powers as distinct from mere executive power, and there can be no question about the legality of a king's order. The king is, however, not expected to override principles that were considered divine. His law can be imposed with force where necessary, entirely on the prerogative of the king. The king, as an upholder of Dharma, is exempt from personal sin. Public wrongs, however, must be punished or expiated with penance. Stigma and guilt are washed clean, as long as the king's decision is followed, be it the payment of a fine or the performance of penance. Chastisement was considered its own purification.

Law and Litigation

The laws regarding private rights, loss, and redressal in Dharma are called Prakirna, or 'scattered, diverse, and miscellaneous' rules. Criminal law is different and is treated with a great deal more seriousness, where a magistrate appointed by the king or a commission of inquiry seeks out wrongdoers and punishes them. Private litigation is an area where the king is not to interfere, even where he has a desire for wealth. This is a very important prohibition, as many European monarchs grew rich by benefiting from private disputes, including inheritance. Private wrongs include the failure of children to look after their parents, cheating, mixing of Varnas, ill-treating ascetics, etc. And these were also areas where the king was not supposed to interfere. Katyana divides these types of legal issues into three groups, starting with aparadhas (offenses), including exposing secrets, waging war, abuses, misappropriation, acts contrary to public morality, becoming suddenly rich, or as we call it today, wealth disproportionate to one's known sources of income, attacking another man's wife, and so on. A second list is made up of chalas (abuses), for which a list is also given. Private wrongs that affect the kingdom are seen as 'thorns in the king's path,' and therefore the king has a right to interfere and eradicate them. If a 'thorn' appears to be serious, the king could inquire into it himself, while the lesser ones he could leave to tribunals set up for the purpose, where magistrates well versed in Dharma Shastras would adjudicate.

A cognizable private breach requires it to be a breach of a known and existing law and must involve injury and a plaintiff. Every case, therefore, presupposes an injury; there can be no case without a proven injury. There must be a plaintiff, and the plaintiff must act in his own interest alone. The injury must be apparent and real, not imaginary or invisible. The king would interfere only where public order was threatened. In Dharma, even criminal cases tend to be converted into torts, so punishments are almost always pecuniary. An injury could be to a person or to goods. However, the Shastras rarely care to make an absolute distinction between private and public wrongs. The hierarchy of jurisdiction was made up of shrenis (or guilds), pugas, gramas, and kulas. In effect, an appeal would always lie with a higher court. However, until an appeal was preferred, all these courts functioned independently and were considered self-sufficient. The Sabbas were permanent, and there were circuit courts. A permanent court was run by a magistrate with the royal seal. Kulas were self-regulatory guilds and were not considered part of the hierarchy of the judiciary.

The king dealt with dharma and was the supreme judge, guided by Smriti counselors. The king's court consisted of three judges appointed by the king, preferably Brahmins. The president of the forum pronounces judgment, which the king is bound to accept. The king could have his own view, but the duty of the judges is to make the king see the rightness of their judgment. Based on Vedic interpretation, justice was also seen as a form of sacrifice with the proper persons and the proper procedure, where the officiating judge, like a priest, is entitled to his fees. While in the domain of the king, there are no restraints, in the realm of justice, he is an arbitrator and therefore has to be just; it is no longer kshastra or danda, it is justice, where Dharma alone is supreme. The Shastras enjoin the king to ensure judicial rigor in all matters of justice and insist that he must reconcile the demands of justice with the concern for equity. The final order of the king is beyond debate; as always, the king only does his duty to ensure order and peace; he is performing a sacrifice. Yet, the Shastras do not allow a judgment to have precedent-setting value; each case has to be settled on its own merits, taking into account the nature of the case and the situation in the country. Nothing is static, not even justice. The Shastras make it clear that even justice is contextual.

To the sages, justice was what was legal; as such, a judgment had to be, by its intrinsic nature, legal. Yet, much of Indian law is based on custom but insists that where a statute or law exists, it will always precede custom. There is no real legal authority as such, and the law floats as it were through the Smrithis, the Shastras, and customs without any semblance of unity, where legal practices combine with customs and precedence, giving it the dubious advantage of maximum flexibility. It was also extremely practical, as it ensured that the law was never static by prohibiting any creation of precedent. The law was ever-conscious of the condition of the state and the condition of its people, their compulsions and their essential human weaknesses, and refused to be rigid.

The Legacy

The Dharma Shastras and the evolution of a judicial system were an acceptance of two important imperatives. A supreme secular power may not always be available, and therefore justice and human rights must depend on a higher doctrine, the concept of

Dharma. Secondly, even where secular power is available, it would not be all-pervasive, and therefore justice must be administered in a decentralized manner. The karmic separation of society into castes meant that each caste had its own dharma, and to a large extent, they were supposed to ensure justice through self-management. This was also delegated to the guilds and occupational groupings. The administration of justice, thus, was caste-based and decentralized. The apparent lack of rule of law today is largely the result of the non-evolution of a pervasive legal and judicial system and the fact that it is almost impossible to rule such a large country except by the decentralization that the sages in the past resorted to. It was caste alone that ensured a semblance of order, and without it, the state is tottering as it is forced to impose an equity it does not believe in.

As in all things that a society tends to inherit, all that was demanding and exacting has been conveniently forgotten, and all that remains are the parts that were most questionable. Thus, our legal system has forgotten the rigor that any honest practice of law must entail and is now oblivious to the fact that justice is to be a religious sacrifice where what is at stake is dharma itself. What it has inherited with glee is the apparent subjectivity of judgments, forgetting that such subjectivity was only permitted in the exercise of a holy function, where the judge was to be beyond worldly inducements. Today's judges seem to think that being subjective is a right and that there are no higher truths to which all judgments are subject. They usurp the roles of the legislature and executive and consider themselves above the law. This sense of omnipotence comes from the fact that our forefathers did not lay down an absolute system of justice but accepted custom and context, believing in the honesty of judges. The mere lack of a definitive legal text seems to be enough for judges to run amok in their own courts, only to be castigated by the appellate courts. This travesty of blame and counter-blame has become the hallmark of our judicial system.

The Laws of Manu: Manusmriti

The Laws of Manu, also known as 'Manu Smriti,' is perhaps the single most important book for Indians, even if many may not know much about it today. If Hinduism is considered a way of life more than a religion, the customs and the very way of life of all Indians were determined by the laws written in this book. Wendy Doniger, in her introduction to the translation of the book, quotes Apastamba to indicate the amoral nature of the contents, stating, "Right and wrong do not go about saying, 'Here we are.'" She also quotes Nietzsche, who said that Manu was not writing a moral code but attempting to create a masterly people, for whom the law becomes unconscious. That, he says, is the purpose of every holy lie.

It appears that Manu was not merely creating a law for a static society but for a society that had ambitions of becoming a great society and its people a master race. It was a law for growth, not static complacence. 'Manusmrithis,' as his work is called, assumes the position of a sacred text, as a 'Smriti,' representing sacred learning and referred to as remembered knowledge, part of the consciousness of the race, a heritage, and therefore above all merely written texts and treated as revealed knowledge.

The other term used to describe the work is 'Manava Dharmashastras,' implying that they are the 'Dharmic' laws of Manu, suggesting that they were not merely rules or laws but the very foundation of cosmic order, as Dharma in Sanskrit meant the laws that sustain the universe. Manu is both the 'wise one' and the Indian Adam, the first man. Yet, in its present form, the work is clearly the result of contributions from many authors over a lengthy period.

Manu is always ambivalent; he deals with the law with seriousness, but when addressing the importance of life and the order of things, and when dealing with women, marriage, life, and death, he is not only serious but exhibits reverence. Yet he is also able to say, "A man should abandon this foul-smelling, tormented, impermanent dwelling place of living beings, filled with urine and excrement, pervaded by old age and sorrow, infested by sickness, and polluted by passion, with bones for beams, sinews for cords, flesh and blood for plaster, and skin for the roof."

Feminists may find him objectionable as he says, "Good looks do not matter to them, nor do they care about youth. 'A man!' they say and they enjoy sex with him, whether he is good-looking or ugly. By running after men like whores... fickle-minded... (they exhibit) a natural lack of affection... (and are) unfaithful to their husbands." Yet, the same Manu also says, "A woman's mouth, a girl's breast, a child's prayer, the smoke of sacrifice, are always pure." The Manu who created the idea of impure orifices states that all orifices above the navel are pure, while those below, because through them defilements escape from the body, are impure.

Today, we think that the laws of Manu apply to all Hindus, at least, but that is a question that Manu himself opposes. Like Nietzsche, he seems to think that it was only for a select band—perhaps a special priesthood—and those who wanted to excel and become great. Its main focus was, therefore, purity through fire sacrifices.

Unlike the present belief that a good Hindu should be a vegetarian, Manu seems to think that there is a hierarchy even in what we eat. Humans eat animals, animals eat plants, plants eat water, and so on. Thus, to Manu, meat-eating was natural to man, and he says, "those that do not move are food for those who move... those who have no fangs are food for those who have hands ..." In the primitive world, one's food was one's enemy, and eating it was, therefore, a triumph. The highest class of animals, men, are the ultimate eaters. By offering these animals as sacrifices to the universe, they could control the power even of the gods, who partake of such sacrificial meat. Done correctly, it is what keeps the cosmos in order.

Manu clearly saw every class of animals and plants as food for a higher class, and the later idea of Ahimsa was only an attempt to break this cycle of violence, which, to Manu, was the natural order of things. Even in the Vedas, it is clearly said, "Meat is indeed the best kind of food." This natural order of things that the later orthodoxy turned into vegetarianism is a very striking example of the reversal of Vedic values. The reversal was linked to renunciation and Ahimsa, for which vegetarianism became the new sign of purity. This philosophical idea, propagated by Jains and Buddhists, was the means by which one was to be liberated from the natural cycle of violence, which alone would stop the cycle of endless births.

In many ways, Hinduism as a religion begins with Manu. The Vedas were too abstract and high-flown for most people and were also treated as some form of sacred revelation, given to man at the beginning, at the dawn of time, and therefore sacred and not to be dissected or critically examined. What Manu tries to do is be a bridge between the Vedas and real life, as well as bring down Vedic principles to something of everyday value. Vedic religion was based on sacrifice and killing, and consequently, killing in a sacrifice was neither sinful nor wrong. Yet, later, religious leaders began to see the idea of sacrifice almost as embarrassing. Manu was thus only the beginning of a chain of philosophical writers whose aim was to bring the Vedas down to the people and yet keep them relevant for the changing times. As in all religions, the timeless canons of revealed religion had to be continuously explained and, in the process, changed and manipulated for the benefit of the ruling class and for the stability of society.

While one of the obvious problems moderns face while reading Manu is the terrible subjectivity of his moral code, Manu is also capable of flights of greatness when he tries to suppress any rigidity in the application of the laws; he says, "The root of religion is the entire Vedas," not merely seeing a part of it. Manu was against a narrow interpretation of the moral code. He seems to be saying, caste be damned, the real law is that "a man should do all of what he does, diligently, and do whatever his mind and heart delight in, and whatever activity satisfies him inwardly, and when he is doing it, he should do it zealously... and whenever he perceives that his self is full of joy, something of pure light that seems to make him entirely at peace... When he longs with his soul to know something and is not ashamed when he does it, and his self is satisfied by it, that has the mark of the quality of lucidity." This statement is like a motto for both greatness and freedom, yet if any one text ensured the freezing and stratification of society into castes, it was the code of Manu.

The Genesis

The code begins with an explanation of its origins. The great sages of the age approached Manu while he was in meditation and asked him to explain the duties of the four castes. Manu then explains, "The Lord, who is self-existent and unmanifested, caused the universe to become manifest." He emitted his semen on the waters, and out of water was born the egg. The Lord is the first cause, unmanifested eternal, the essence of what is real and unreal. He emitted man, who is known in the world as Brahma. The Lord (Brahma) dwelt with the egg for a whole year and divided it into mind and heart, "the essence of what is real and unreal," and from the mind and heart came the sense of 'I,' the controlling consciousness of self, and he gave him five senses to sense the world. By mingling the subtle parts of the six boundless energies with the minute parts of his own self, he made living beings. In the case of man, it took on a human form called the body. The Lord then emitted a host of gods whose life breathes and whose essence is ritual, the everlasting sacrifice. He then created the oceans, the rivers, and all that we see from his inner heat; he created speech, sexual pleasure, desire, and anger. He gave man the sense of right and wrong and yoked him with pairs of happiness and unhappiness and all the opposites. Out of his mouth, he created the priest; from his arms, the ruler; from his thigh, the commoner; and from his feet, the servant. He divided his body into two; one half became a woman, the other a man. Manu then claims that the first man emitted by the Lord was himself. It was Manu who then created the ten great sages, like Arti, Angiras, Vasistha, Bhrgu, and Narada. He then emitted seven other Manus and then the rest of all creation, including nymphs and demons. And at his command, the great souls made the universe move by its innate laws. All souls were also conditioned by their innate activities. The other six Manus were born of the self-existent (Brahman). Then day and night came, and the ages came into being. First, the age of the gods (12,000 years), then of Manu (12,000 x 72 years). During the life of the many Manus, "religion would be brought down because of theft, lying, and deceit; religion would fade away, foot by foot." The first man would be great and healthy, but soon sickness will come, and man will grow smaller. Man's duties will also change with the changing times. The best among men live by intelligence; the best know their duties and know the Vedas. A priest is born to guard the treasure of religion. Therefore, the priest should only study and teach the Vedas, and only he. The universe is neither eternal nor real; humans perceive only what is made manifest by the creator. Even the gods are only part of creation. Though only a manifestation, the universe is subject to laws of creation that tend to decay, as are all things in nature. Even if it was a later interpolation, the Smrithis make clear that the separation of Varnas and the specific Varnic duties are part of the unchanging laws of nature.

The Essence of Religion

Manu says that religion is what is learned by learned men, good men who have neither hatred nor passion. In human life, desire is the controlling emotion, the equivalent of Schopenhauer's 'will'; without it, even the Vedas and rituals would not exist. Desire creates intention, and intention creates sacrifice. Not a single thing is done on Earth without desire. The root of religion is the whole of the Vedas and the customs of good people. The Vedas are divine, while all other teachings are merely tradition. Manu then says, "Any twice-born who disregards these two roots of religion because he believes in logic should be excommunicated by virtuous people as an atheist and a reviler of the Vedas." Manu limits the need for absolute devotion to religion to those "who are not attached to pleasure or profit." The land of the Vedas is defined as the land that lies between the Saraswati River and the Drishadvati Rivers. Others, he says, should learn their own religion from their own priests. Between the Himalayas and the Vindhyas, from the western sea to the sea in the east, is the land of the Arya. It is important to realize that his religion was an exclusive religion and not meant for everyone. Having defined Arya-Desh and having divided men into their basic occupations, he then prescribes the main sacrifices that a twice-born must perform.

The offering of fire for the embryo The birth rites The ceremonial hair was cut. The tying of the belt of rushes The study of the Vedas—by vows along with sons, triple learning, and great sacrifice, makes the body fit for ultimate reality. The birth rite is performed before the umbilical cord is cut, and the child is given honey and gold along with the recitation of the Vedas. Manu says that the initiation for a priest should be in the eighth year after conception, but those who seek to master the splendors of the Vedas can do it in the fifth year. The time prescribed can be much later for all ceremonies in the case of lower castes, including when they can learn the Vedas. A priest may never mix with the lower castes. He must eat his food facing east for long life, south for fame, west for good fortune, and north for truth. He must cup his hands together in homage to the Vedas.

In Chapter 2, he deals with the life of the Bramachari and the basic rules. He starts by saying that a man should always respect food and eat without criticizing. For a woman, the honor of serving her husband is equal to serving the living Guru. A learned man should always try to control his sensory powers because desire is never extinguished by enjoyment. The sun must be worshiped in the morning until it rises. This dispels the guilt of the night. A student should seek a teacher who not only knows the Vedas but who has curbed all his sensual appetites. He must always respect his superior, stand up when a senior comes in, and never sit on a chair or bed occupied by someone senior. Greetings should be with the words, "May you have a long life." Never teach the Veda to the undeserving, and anyone who acquires the Vedas without permission is a thief. The Guru, his wife, and his son are sacred. Yet one should always be careful in the presence of women, 'for the nature of women is to corrupt men.'

Marriage

The duties of the householder are prescribed in chapter-3. The period of study of the Vedas is 36 years, but with the permission of his Guru, he may marry. Manu then lists the types of marriages that are legal. A man who cohabits with a servant woman has no redemption. There are eight proper forms of marriage. When a father adorns his daughter and gives her to a chosen bridegroom, it is called Brahma. A man who takes a girl out of desire is a demon, and such marriages are called centaur marriages. The worst is a man who sleeps with a sleeping or drunk woman. A proper marriage that results in the birth of a son frees seven generations of ancestors. He also seems to accept the common belief and says, "A male child is born when the semen of man is greater than that of woman." He also adds, "Where women are not revered, all rites are fruitless," and "there is unwavering good fortune in a family where the husband is always satisfied by his wife," "If the woman is radiant, the whole family is radiant." However, a man at this stage must set aside time for study and always remember the gods and his ancestors in his daily rituals. Food must always be offered to the gods and guests. The treatment of guests is sacred, and Manu elaborates on it at great length. He then deals at length with the ceremony for the dead and even enumerates who should be invited, how people are to be fed and how to dispose of the leftovers.

Chapter 4 continues on the duties of the householder. He may make a living through legal and moral means, even begging for alms. Farming, Manu says, is traditionally called a 'deadly' mode of life, but even this occupation is permitted. He then says that 'contentment is the very root of happiness.' A man should not pursue wealth addictively. One should also not be addicted to any sensory object. Manu also makes certain strange demands: no eating naked, no bathing when totally naked, and so on. One should not eat with one's wife or watch her as she eats. One should not look at a naked woman, blow fire out of the mouth or warm the feet by the fire. One should never throw urine, excrement, or poisonous things into a river. An intelligent man who spots a rainbow in the sky should not show it to anyone. He should not uselessly run around trying to do things. He should not eat food on his lap or from broken vessels. He should not use second-hand shoes, clothes, garland, or a water pot. A man should not lie down when his feet are still wet. A king, not from the ruling class, makes his kingdom worse than a whorehouse. These commands are enumerated only to illustrate the irrational nature of some of his demands; no logic is given, as though their rationale is obvious.

When the Vedas are recited, it should be clear, but it should never be recited before servants, in a cremation ground, when there is a storm, or in the vicinity of a corpse. The Rig Veda is for gods; the Yajur Veda is for humans; and the Sama Veda is for ancestors. A man who hopes to do well should never despise a ruler, a snake, or a priest. One must strive for good fortune till the very end, never thinking it is too difficult. All things that result in one being under another person's control are unhappiness, and everything under one's control is happiness. One must always do what one does with zealous devotion. One should seek pleasure in the truth. But one should never be addicted to gifts. "An intelligent man should unfailingly respect all restrictions but must not regard all restrictions as obligatory." A man who gives will get in return. The meaning of everything is decided by speech. Speech is the root of everything. A man who robs speech robs everything. Here again, his laws are more in the nature of proverbs than a systematic moral code and devoid of any structure or hierarchy. However, he has great respect for knowledge and sincerity in his work.

Food and Evil

In Chapter 5, Manu gives his final laws on the duties of a householder, and in doing so, he tries to answer the question: if the Vedas are so powerful, why then are we not able to fight death with the Vedas? Manu's reply is, yes, the Vedas can even defeat death, but death triumphs because man, in his study of the Vedas, invariably corrupts it. He then explains the things that tend to corrupt the purity of the Vedas, including the eating of forbidden foods. He starts with garlic and scallions, onions and mushrooms, sesame seeds, cakes and flour, butter and sugar, rice, milk, sugar, cow's milk within ten days of calving, milk of a camel or cow in heat, carnivorous birds, whole-hoofed animals, goose, sparrow, parrot crane, birds that eat fish, etc. He says a man who eats meat is a meat eater, and one who eats fish is a fish-eater but he does not prohibit the eating of either. Wild birds are permitted to be eaten even by priests and are also used for sacrifice. He also says, "You may eat meat that has been consecrated by the sprinkling of water." He then says categorically, "the Lord of creatures fashioned all the universe to feed the breath of life, and everything moving and stationary is food for the breath of life." He adds, "Eating meat is the right thing to do for sacrifice; this is traditionally known as the rule of gods," "The twice-born should, however, not eat meat against the rules," "Killing in a sacrifice is not killing"; however, one should not commit unnecessary violence. Yet he is no believer in the absolute power of sacrifice but says, even, 'the Ashvamedha sacrifice' is only as good as a man who does not eat meat at all. This is because meat-eating is a perpetuation of the cycle of life and death and one who wants to go beyond this cycle of life and death must stop eating meat. The ambiguity of Manu's laws is what is frustrating. He permits the eating of meat, saying all things are created only to ensure the breath of life and then says that not eating meat is better than the Ashvamedha sacrifice. It is this ambiguity that has led to a similar ambivalence in moral doctrine.

Purification

Manu then elaborates on the rules for cleaning a dead body, the pollution caused by dead bodies, and the purification rites. Then he explains, "God made three purifiers for priests: what is not seen, what is washed by water, and what is approved by the word of a priest." He insists that the hands of the artisan are always clean. A woman's mouth is always clean. Even the meat of a wild animal caught by a dog is not polluted. Only the orifices below the navel are unclean. To be clean, one must have one cloth for the penis, three for the anus, ten for the left hand, and seven for both hands. Washing with water always cleans.

Women

He is skeptical about the nature of women and says that, from the time a woman is a girl to the time she dies, she must never be allowed to act independently. Her father is her husband, and when the husband is dead, her sons must control her. She should, however, always be cheerful and keep all her utensils clean. "A virtuous wife should constantly serve her husband like a God, even if he behaves badly, freely indulges his lust and is devoid of any good qualities. She must obey her husband in all things and has no authority to make sacrifices. She should never displease her husband. A woman who is unfaithful to her husband would be reborn in the womb of a jackal and would be 'tormented by diseases born of her evil.'" It is clear that these are not moral injunctions but laws to ensure the subjugation of women and rules that ensure the stability of society, as he saw it.

The Life of a Hermit

Chapter 6 deals with the rules related to the period of life when a man should leave his home and live in the forest and devote his life to contemplation, leaving behind his cares as a Grahasta. This is to be done only when a man has seen the children of his children. He should, according to Manu, spend a third of his life as a hermit. A time when he cares nothing for living or dying. He should become philosophical and think about the meaning of life. His main activity should be meditation. He ends the section by saying, "Twice-born men in all stages of life must constantly and carefully fulfill their ten-point duty," which are "patience, forgiveness, self-control, not stealing, purification, mastery of sensory powers, wisdom, learning, truth, and lack of anger."

The Duties of a King

In Chapters 7 and 8, Manu depicts the king as a divine instrument of God. A nation without a king is portrayed as a barbaric place where the law of the jungle prevails, with big fish devouring small fish. At the people's request, the gods 'emitted a king,' created from the elements of Indra, Yama, the Sun, Fire, Varuna, the moon, and Kubera, the Lord of wealth. The king embodies both life and death, fortune and wealth. He wields absolute power, and individuals must obey him or face his wrath and authority. The king serves as the source of all justice, administering punishment through his rod to ensure peace and order. Only the king's rod of punishment guarantees morality and order since there is scarcely a man who remains unpolluted. However, the king must be just, adhering to fair standards. Manu's priority is evident: maintaining order is paramount, and the fear of the rod of punishment is essential for this. Being a king is no easy task, and similar to Kautilya, Manu expects the king to work tirelessly from morning to night in the interest of his state and people. The king should surround himself with honest and unpolluted priests for counsel. He must strive to gain knowledge of the soul and 'work day and night to conquer his sensory powers.' Additionally, the king must endeavor to overcome ten great vices, including hunting, gambling, sleeping, gossip, women, drunkenness, music, singing, dancing, and aimless wandering—all resulting from the pleasure of the senses. He must also avoid slander, violence, malice, envy, resentment, and acts of anger. Conquering greed is another imperative for a king. Accepting good counsel and appointing only hardworking and honest individuals to govern the country are crucial aspects of the king's responsibilities. When selecting ambassadors, the king should choose well-educated, perceptive individuals with an understanding of facial and body language, along with being well-born, skilled, and honest. A likable, good-looking, and eloquent demeanor is also desirable. The king should show reverence to priests. Manu even prescribes a code for war and outlines the king's personal role in it. The king's primary duty is to safeguard the kingdom from enemies and ensure the well-being of his people. Manu, akin to Kautilya, proposes a management method involving division and delegation. He also theorizes on the aims of diplomacy and how to treat defeated kings and conquered people. Finally, he discusses how a king should relax from his duties and identifies legitimate pleasures.

The King's Justice

Chapter 8 is finally a chapter that deals with law and justice. There are times when it soars on high principles, but there are also moments when it is caustic, misanthropic, and downright reactionary. It reaches new heights when Manu emphasizes that the king should try cases on the basis of eternal justice. He also asserts that no person should enter a court of law with dishonest intentions, as justice is destroyed by injustice and truth by falsehood. When justice is protected, it, in turn, protects. Justice is a loyal friend that follows you faithfully even after death, as everything else is lost with the body. Manu clearly wants people to realize the sanctity of the court of law and perceives justice as the highest aim of humanity. Thus, when the king is unable to sit as a judge, he insists that only virtuous Brahmins who know the Vedas and are learned should preside as judges.

Yet Manu is also extremely practical and almost cynical about the human capacity for truth. He emphasizes that the judge should not only listen to what is said but must also observe body language, read facial expressions, and discern the tone of voice. According to Manu, "the inner mind and heart are grasped by facial expressions, involuntary movements, gait, gesture, speech, and changes in the eyes and mouth."

Manu expresses disdain for habitual litigants, stating that if a litigant fails to appear when called, the case should be closed. Additionally, if a plaintiff refuses to speak, Manu suggests subjecting them to corporal punishment. He further asserts that certain witnesses are clearly unreliable, including those with a stake in the case, individuals known to be corrupt, old men, children, and drunks, as well as those who can be manipulated due to hunger or thirst. Manu recommends that women should only be witnesses in cases involving other women. In situations where there are no other witnesses, a child, woman, or old man may give evidence, but their testimony is never to be taken as absolutely true.

Manu also underscores that a person of unsound mind has no place in a court of law. He emphasizes the duty of a witness to tell the truth as plainly as possible. Manu invokes the gods to punish all those who give false evidence, stating, "Evil doers think no one is looking, but the gods are looking right at them." He exacerbates the punishment for false testimony by asserting, "Whatever merit you have acquired since your birth, all of that will go to the dogs if you speak untruth."

Like in modern contract law, Manu makes it clear that a contract is not legal when made by unauthorized persons, such as drunks, those in pain, children, and old men. Any contract that goes against existing law is also void. Yet, similar to Kautilya, Manu has a criminal code that is distinctly relative. Punishment is contingent on the caste of the person involved. It is consistently more severe, and sometimes outright barbaric, when a lower-caste person commits a crime against an upper-caste individual. Conversely, when the same crime is committed by an upper-caste person against a lower-caste individual, it is typically settled with a fine. For instance, if a lower-caste man injures an upper-caste person in any part of the body, that same part of the body should be cut off. Even sitting on the seat of a higher-caste person could result in the cutting off of the buttocks. If he uses his hand to grab any part of an upper-caste person's body, his hands should be cut off. The same principle applies to cases of sexual misconduct and rape, where a servant who cohabits with a twice-born woman, even with consent, would have his sexual member cut off. This may explain the barbaric attitude of upper-caste men, even today, when dealing with presumed insults by lower castes.

No violence should be tolerated by the king. One who commits violence should be regarded as the worst evildoer. A king who allows violence without the sternest punishment is inviting violence and war. In fact, according to Manu, killing any person who carries a weapon is not a crime. While Manu expresses modern concerns about punishment for those who destroy plants and trees, he is also explicit that non-believers cannot be tolerated. He suggests that a king should 'energetically restrain' the irreligious through three means: imprisonment, chains, and various corporal punishments. However, a king should never kill a priest, regardless of his crime. Manu understands that religious beliefs sustain all other beliefs, and allowing skepticism would open the floodgates to all forms of sedition.

Women and Marriage

Chapter 9 is mainly dedicated to the role of women and vividly portrays Manu as a male chauvinist and a misogynist. He begins by asserting, "Men must make their women dependent day and night. A woman is not fit for independence. Her father guards her in childhood, her husband guards her in her youth, and her sons guard her in old age." Manu deems female independence so perilous that he blames a father who does not give away a mature girl and a husband who does not provide enough sexual activity. Even a weak man, according to Manu, has a duty to zealously guard a woman from addiction and bad company. Where force is insufficient, a man should ensure that his wife stays busy with housework, shopping, and ceremonies. He claims that women are so unprincipled that only absolute authority can keep them in check, stating, "Good looks do not matter to them, nor do they care about youth; any man, they say, and enjoy sex with him." Manu appears to think that women are obsessed with sex and that it is all they think about. He says women lack 'natural affection,' are unfaithful, full of lust, anger, crookedness, malicious nature, and bad conduct. They are fickle-minded and run after men 'like whores.' Understanding their nature, men have no option but to be strict with them. Manu considers a married woman who thinks differently from her husband as dangerous. Thus, having a good wife is synonymous with good fortune, as children and sexual satisfaction depend on a wife. Manu curses all unfaithful women to be reborn in the wombs of jackals. However, he also gives mythical importance to women, stating that because a man enters a woman and creates life through her, she is called Jaya (victor), and the product of her womb is Jayate (victory). Since a man can be reborn only through a woman, women must remain vessels of purity. Manu concludes by saying, "A man is only as good as his wife, himself, and his progeny."

Manu approves of a practice where, if a bride loses her husband-to-be, the brother-in-law can sleep with her to produce progeny. He asserts that a marriage where the defects of a girl are not disclosed in advance is void. A woman should wait eight years if a husband goes on a journey and does not return, while a man must wait only a year for a woman who hates him. A woman who drinks, is violent, or is wasteful can be discarded at any time. Manu allows men to have more than one wife, even from lower castes, insisting only on seniority being given to the woman of the highest caste. He also states that a father is bound to give his daughter in marriage only to a man of good qualities and that it is better for a girl to die a spinster in her father's house than to marry a man of bad character. A woman can choose her own husband if her father does not fulfill his duty even after three years of her maturity; however, when she does so, she is not entitled to take anything from her father or brothers. When a man chooses a bride, he must pay her money. Manu prescribes the age difference for marriage, saying the best age is for a thirty-year-old man and a twelve-year-old girl and a man of twenty-four with a girl of eight. If a man pays bride money and marries a girl, thereafter, even his brother can marry her if she agrees.

Manu then deals with the division of property and says a son's right is only to the property of his father, and in this, a daughter has an equal right. However, a mother's property should normally go only to the daughter. He also discusses the role of brothers in the family and elaborates on illegitimate children. Suddenly, he closes his rules on family life and returns to the duty of the king. Like Plato, he not only wants to ban all gambling but also finds bards and traveling actors dangerous, suggesting they could be thieves. Manu advocates for strong action against people who make false promises. Killers, especially priest killers, are not to be tolerated, nor are liquor drinkers. He also condemns bribe-takers and suggests, like Kautilya, that the king must have a secret service to apprise him of what goes on in his kingdom. The king must never spare the 'danda' against evildoers and should build prisons to keep them away from society.

Caste and its Rules

In Chapter 10, Manu revisits the topic of caste and its rules. He begins by emphasizing that a Brahmin must study the Vedas and proclaim it. Manu asserts that the priest is thrice born, while the other two castes are only twice born, and the servant has had only one birth. To maintain caste, a child must be born to a woman who was a virgin when she married, and caste is retained only if both husband and wife belong to the same caste.

Manu then details how to treat children born from different castes. Children born to high-caste fathers through Shudra women are to be considered outcastes. Various caste combinations, such as a Kshatriya father and Brahmin woman producing the charioteer caste, are outlined. Confused classes resulting from the union between a servant-woman and the commoner, royal, or priestly classes are deemed unfit and untouchable. Manu describes outcastes as those 'born against the grain' and attributes the downfall of warrior peoples like the Cholas, Kambojas, Greeks, Scythians, Persians, and Chinese to their failure to follow the Vedas, leading them to be 'sunk into the rank of servants.'

Manu suggests that a son born of an Aryan father and a non-Aryan woman can become Aryan if he exhibits Aryan qualities. However, the child of an Aryan mother and a non-Aryan father is always considered non-Aryan. Yet, Manu also states that when comparing an Aryan who carries out the innate activities of an Aryan and an Aryan who carries out the innate activities of a non-Aryan, the creator declared, "The two are neither equal nor non-equal," indicating that occupation alone does not define a person's worth.

Regarding priests, Manu allows a starving priest trying to earn a living to glean corn from the field. However, both a priest and a ruler should never lend money. Manu clarifies that a servant (Shudra) has no right to rituals, but he can improve himself by imitating the actions of good men. This dictum has led lower castes to mimic higher castes in dress, eating habits, and cultural practices, though without any rise in their caste status. Manu's intent was an attitude of mind defining the Aryan, not just the imitation of dress and practices.

In Chapter 11, Manu discusses various ethical principles. He states that a man who takes another's wife solely for sexual pleasure will not have children from such a union considered his own. He condemns a man who gives to others while neglecting his own family members as a cheat. Manu asserts that actions aimed at securing benefits in the afterlife, at the expense of those dependent on the individual, will have adverse consequences. He emphasizes that one's duties in the present life are more important than potential consequences in another life. Aware of the implications of the Karma theory leading to an attitude of renunciation, Manu emphasizes that the present life holds paramount significance.

Manu lays out certain principles for priests. A priest should never beg from a servant, and a king should never harm a priest, kill him, or seize his property. A priest who possesses knowledge of the Vedas can take matters into his own hands and doesn't need to wait for the king to act. He can use 'his manly power' and the use of mantras to avenge himself against his enemies, as 'speech is the weapon of the priest.' A priest is absolved of guilt by announcing his own wrongdoing, while others are subject to a series of prescribed punishments and penances. Manu warns that a priest who drinks corrupts the Vedas within himself. He concludes by stating, "A priest who retains the Rig Veda in his memory incurs no guilt at all, even if he destroys the three worlds or eats food taken from anyone. Anyone who, with a concentrated mind, recites three times the collection of Rig Veda, Yajur Veda, or Sama Veda, together with sacred texts, is freed from all evils."

In Chapter 12, Manu explores the consequences of sin, asserting that birth on various descending scales of life is the result of sin. However, unintentional sins can be cleansed by reciting the Vedas. On the other hand, intentional sins will be punished with deformity and specific marks on the body. Manu proceeds to enumerate various sins, starting with incest, cow killing without sacrifice, adultery, selling oneself, abandoning one's Guru and parents, corrupting a virgin, breaking a vow, living off one's wife, and using magic spells. Other offenses include having sex with a drunken woman, killing a woman, and killing a servant.

Specific penalties are detailed, such as a man who violates his Guru's marriage bed having to cut off his own penis and a man who kills a cow being required to follow a cow for three months. Additionally, a person engaging in sex in a moving cart pulled by a cow is instructed to bathe with clothes on.

With Chapter 12, Manu concludes on a high note of general principles, particularly addressing the fruits of karma. He states that all acts originating from the 'mind and heart' result in bad fruits. The undesirable actions of the mind and heart through speech include lies, abuse, and slander, while the bad fruits of the body involve violence, adultery, and other sexual wrongs. A virtuous man who has the 'triple rod' of control over his speech and body and can thoroughly suppress his lust and anger, along with being a knower of truth, will experience happiness and no unhappiness.

Manu emphasizes that life is determined by three forces: lucidity, energy, and darkness. The power of darkness is ignorance, leading to confusion and sensuality. Energy is passion that can result in anger, violence, and lust, while lucidity is the power leading to the Vedas, knowledge, and contentment. The Vedas create the inner heat necessary to suppress the senses. Pleasure is associated with darkness, profit with energy, and religion with lucidity. People of lucidity become gods, while others may descend to lower forms of life based on their actions. Those committing great crimes will experience many hells, and a priest killer may be reborn in the womb of a dog. Manu also highlights the connection between indulgence in sexual acts and the weakening of a man. All actions, according to Manu, have consequences, and the recitation of the Veda generates an inner heat that can conquer anything, leading to immortality. When a Vedic knower uses his knowledge for the benefit of the world, he becomes equal to the gods and is already detached from the world of the senses.

The Vedas are the eternal eye of the gods. A person who knows the Vedas is fit for any job, from king to General. However, there are levels to Vedic knowledge; it can be read, learned by heart, and put into practice. Those who put it into practice are the highest practitioners of the Vedas. This is often forgotten, with more emphasis being given to rituals and mantras. The Vedas create inner heat through which all guilt is destroyed, and when such sacrifices are combined with knowledge, a person becomes immortal.

Manu concludes by asserting that the laws of Manu will always be supreme, above all other laws. However, he acknowledges that an assembly of knowledgeable men who know the Vedas is competent to create new laws. He further states that a thousand ignorant people in an assembly may be unfit to create laws, while even one good man with a thorough knowledge of the Vedas is competent and sufficient to make new laws.

Manu: Impact and Legacy

Any reading of Manusmriti makes it clear that it is neither a philosophical nor a religious text. Manu presents no consistent philosophy and makes no attempt to justify anything. Similarly, in the creation myth, he does not take any recourse to the gods to justify himself. The work is not a moral or ethical discourse, and he makes no attempt to define morality or the need for ethics. It is an amoral treatise that focuses on laws to be obeyed, making them appear unquestionable and self-evident. However, his laws have had a lasting and profound impact on Indian society. In fact, the reason many people see Hinduism as a way of life is that Manu actually advocated a way of life, and it is in following Manu's prescriptions that Indians have become what they are. The laws of Manu created a people wedded to certain practices, establishing a way of life. From the division of life into stages, starting with the stage of brahmachari to that of a householder, or Grihastha, and finally to that of a sanyasi, Manu ensured an enduring model for all Indians to follow, which persists to the present day. By prescribing the duties at each stage of life, a pattern for Indian life was set forever.

His rules regarding caste, marriage, the role of the king, and all his other rules have been accepted without debate and have become part of our cultural ethos. While Manu saw the proliferation of castes as the result of inter-caste marriages, all parts of the caste soon became frozen and ridden with prejudices when they had to deal with aliens. This resulted in inhumane practices justified merely to sustain minor degrees of superiority. Yet the acceptance of Manu's laws was not the result of unanimity or majority acceptance, but because they were the only comprehensive set of laws available and because all teachers down the ages have been those who have studied these Laws. Since the masses were so illiterate, the educated were treated like gods, and their words were holy writ. The combination of these factors ensured that 'Manusmriti' would not only survive but become the bedrock on which the stability of society depended.

Kautilya: The Arthashastra (Translated by L.N. Rangarajan, 1957)

In summing up, two trends stand out about the history and scope of Manu's laws. While he insisted on the sanctity of his laws by bringing in the gods and treating them as the originators of the law, with the Vedas for support, he was clear that his laws may, in the future, be changed by good men of knowledge. While insisting on the sanctity of the laws, he left room for evolution. However, good men from Buddha to Ramanuja and from Basava to Guru Nanak have tried to change their laws only to be faced with the stone wall of Hindu orthodoxy. His laws, even today, appear only as a skeleton of basic principles that, by and large, are amoral and without malice to any group. While he created the caste system, he did not preach ostracization or caste violence. Similarly, most of his laws were open-ended, leaving room for society to compromise and allowing for integration. It was society that made the Laws of Manu rigid beyond his wildest dreams and blamed it on him. The Arthashastra is such a monumental work in the intellectual life of India that it is difficult to do justice to it in a work that merely tries to reckon its influence on the Indian consciousness. In creating an Indian consciousness, the towering shadow of 'Manusmriti,' so overshadows Arthashastra that it merely attests to the power of Manusmriti. 'Arthashastra' accepts much of what Manusmriti says, and that is what has gone into the psyche of the Indian people, not Kautilya's greater magnanimity, his tolerance, his stress on merit and competence, or his concern for economic and social well-being. Kautilya's Arthashastra is perhaps one of the first books to be written in India. The importance of the book lies in the fact that it is both a treatise on statecraft and a study of the economy. While these were the avowed aims, it also happens to be a book on law and the basis of the rule of law. Kautilya also gives us a very clear image of his age, its vibrancy, and the sense of optimism, something so rare that it is rarely met with again in Indian history. While the Arthashastra may not be the blueprint for what India was to become, it tells us the state from which we have descended. Even though a full copy of the Arthashastra was found only in 1904 in Mysore by Dr. Shamasastry, the Arthashastra has been quoted and referred to almost throughout Indian history. It has been one of the living sources of Indian intellectual heritage. The Arthashastra is mainly a treatise on kingship, the governing of a state, the need for proper economic management, and a dynamic foreign policy. Written almost at the beginning of Indian intellectual consciousness, it is one of the defining sources of the Indian conscience and its intellectual pillar. By dealing with justice, the law, and social organizations, the Arthashastra is a seminal treatise on law and justice and the foundation of the Indian concept of justice. We will, however, deal with Arthashastra more for its impact on the Indian psyche and the part it played in the development of Indian ethics and jurisprudence than its impact on government, war, and diplomacy. A reading of the Arthashastra gives us an impression of a huge and elaborate state, highly centralized and governed, to the smallest detail, by a large bureaucracy and a highly efficient system of law. So detailed and elaborate are the descriptions that many are forced to assume that Kautilya was only describing an imaginary kingdom. Yet they are too realistic to be imaginary. This has also prompted people to doubt the authorship of Kautilya, and consequently, the dating of the text has also been a problem. Yet the Arthashastra has always been a text to be quoted and defined for all subsequent thinking. To a great extent, along with the Vedas, the Manusmriti, and the other Shastras, the Arthashastra is one of the four pillars of Indian intellectual heritage, almost sacred in its antiquity and pervasive in its impact. Human needs are defined as made up of Dharma, Artha, Kama, and Moksha, and Arthashastra deals with all aspects of Artha, 'the wealth of a nation,' and of the science of political, social, and economic management. It also implicitly deals with the underlying human values that are considered important and, to that extent, have become the values that define us as Indians.

The Kautilyan Social Order

Kautilya accepts most of what Manu says in his code as given. Thus, the society that Kautilya describes is divided into Aryans and non-Aryans and further divided into the Varnas. The hierarchy is also clear, with the Brahmin at the top, the Kshatriya as rulers, the Vaishya in business and commerce, and the Shudras as the servants. This system determines all social life. Kautilya, however, makes a distinction even among Brahmins and says the Brahmin who is an expert in the Vedas is supreme and is called 'Srotriya,' who alone should be selected for special consideration by all rulers.

Kautilya recognizes the presence of Ashrams and Ascetics, including Vishalas, Pashandas, Sakyas, and Ajvikas. He also talks about a group of people who, through evil deeds, are thrown out of the Aryan community and accept the presence of Chandalas, Mellachas, and other untouchables. He accepts, without comment, Manu's four stages of life.

The religion that Kautilya describes is clearly Brahmanism. However, he also talks about temples, holy places, and pilgrimages. Vedic Hinduism was not a temple-based religion, so Kautilya describes a much later version of Hinduism that had already incorporated the temples of Buddhism and the idea of holy places. Kautilya also speaks of many gods not mentioned in the Vedas, including Aparajita, Jayanta, Shiva, Sri, Madira, Brahma, Indira, Yama, etc., along with Ashwins, Asuras, and Sagas. There is also a belief in black magic, charms, mantras, and sorcery, suggesting knowledge of the Atharvaveda.

The Practical Kautilya

Where Manu was clear that meat-eating should only be an exception, normally as part of a sacrifice, Kautilya assumes a large meat-eating population, where even dried fish and meat have become part of the everyday meal. He also indicates oil and other ingredients required for the preparation of meat and fish dishes. While Manu was scandalized by the drinking habit and spoke against the dangers of alcohol and drunkenness, Kautilya not only accepts drinking as a necessary part of life but also allows the running of bars and liquor parlors as a source of revenue for the state. In fact, he nationalizes the production and distribution of liquor and has a clear licensing policy for liquor bars and hotels. He also, unashamedly, uses them as part of his network of spies. Similarly, where Manu could not even think of sex except as part of marriage and the marriage contract and as a sacred bond, Kautilya accepts the need for prostitutes, allowing a scale of ascending classes of prostitutes, depending on their perceived value. They were also used by Kautilya as part of his pervasive network of spies.

Kautilya did not have much of an opinion of the business class or of human motives in general. He assumed that people would cheat and take advantage of the simple whenever they got a chance, and wealth would slip away from the foolish man. Kautilya had no faith in traders and was convinced that they would always try to make money at the cost of the consumer. He was therefore strict on the use of proper weights and measures. So cynical was Kautilya about human character that he said a woman who overweeps for a dead husband may have killed him. For administrative purposes, the country was divided into cities and villages. Other castes could dwell only outside the villages, and beyond it was the forest, which was used for recreational activities like hunting and for wood and mining.

Women and Sex

To Kautilya, as in the case of Manu, women were basically for the begetting of sons. Thus, concealing a woman's fertile cycle and not having sex during the period were considered as crimes. A woman who did not beget a son even after eight years could be divorced. The importance of legal progeny made virginity an important attribute, and the deflowering of a virgin was considered a major crime. Incest was considered unthinkable, and the punishment was the mutilation of the sex organs. Homosexuality and sexual penetration anywhere except in the vagina were considered serious offenses. While it was important that both the husband and wife fulfill their conjugal duties, all forms of adultery were considered serious crimes. While Kautilya makes it possible for women to own property, he endorses Manu's view that women should always be under the control of men: father, husband, and son. A woman cannot drink or socialize without the approval of her husband.

Women could not normally enter into a contract and were not considered suitable witnesses except, as Manu says, when there were no other witnesses.

Kautilya's Social Conscience

Kautilya accepts that the labor force is made up of people with varying degrees of freedom. At the bottom were slaves, then bonded labor, unpaid labor, casual labor, piece-rate workers, and those with regular wages. Kautilya insisted on laws for the regulation of labor and the payment of wages. Kautilya also talks about the weaker sections of society that need to be helped and protected, especially the protection of children. Slaves less than eight years old were not to be forced to do any work. He knew that people would be harassed by officials, so he lists forty types of corrupt practices that officials are likely to indulge in. He also identifies thirteen types of people who are invariably dishonest and need to be watched, from the village head to judges, magistrates, counterfeiters, and black magic practitioners. So sacrosanct is the king's duty to ensure order that if a theft is not solved and the criminal is apprehended, the king is required to compensate for the loss from his own treasury.

Kautilya's Philosophical Foundations

Kautilya accepts Manu's four Varnas and the four stages of life. He accepts Manu's belief that the main duty of men was to worship the gods, ancestors, and guests, emphasizing the value of the daily personal rituals and sacrifices mentioned in the Vedas. However, he sees dharma as Ahimsa and Sathyam, made up of ritual cleanliness, freedom from malice, and tolerance. He also accepts that each varna must follow their own dharma. However, while Manu does not have a hierarchy of vices, Kautilya sees anger as the greatest vice. Anger has no limit, so anger is justified only when the purpose is to put down sin—righteous anger. Anger makes one the object of hatred, and being hated is worse than humiliation, says Kautilya. The second great sin is excessive and uncontrolled desire. Having self-control is a great virtue, says Kautilya.

Law and Justice

"It is the power of punishment that protects the world." The judge is thus called 'Dharma shastras,' the upholder of justice. The basic foundation of the law is for all Varnas to follow their dharma; beyond that is custom, and where there is still a need for rules, the king may promulgate written laws. Kautilya, like Manu, gives the king the final power and makes him the final judge. He can appoint judges and must put in place a system in the districts, sub-districts, and provincial headquarters to administer justice.

Kautilya also lays down the rules for the conduct of judges. They should be impartial and earn the trust and loyalty of the people. He lists a set of don'ts:

- They should not threaten or intimidate.
- They should not abuse a person in court.
- They should not fail to ensure proper questioning.
- They should not lead the witness.
- They should never decide without proper evidence.
- They should never unnecessarily delay cases.
- They should not misrepresent facts, etc.

The basis of all law is Dharma, the law of truth, and this must be revealed through proper evidence, which is produced by witnesses and decided by customs and royal edicts. Apart from these, the punishment for each crime laid down by Manu was to be followed, and judges were not to deviate from them. The basic tenets of law that Kautilya proposed are quite general. The judges must act as agents of gods. No Brahmin, ascetic, woman, minor, sick, old, or helpless should be witnesses. No suit is to be dismissed on the basis of jurisdiction or the passage of time. No case can be filed a second time for the same offense.

Kautilya also lists a detailed procedure where the accused can file a counter and rejoinder. Unlike our modern system of uncontrolled delays, Kautilya makes it clear that defendants would be given only seven days to submit a counter, and the maximum, even in the most complicated cases and for genuine personal problems, was six weeks. After that, the case is to be dropped.

Kautilya also makes clear that a wife, father, and relatives are not to be produced as witnesses. The manner in which an oath of honesty is taken depends on a person's caste. A Brahmin is merely told to tell the truth; a Kshatriya is warned to tell the truth. The Shudra is threatened with punishment. However, Kautilya only recommends a fine for perjury. He also recognizes the problem of unreliable witnesses and contradictory evidence and says that an eyewitness who comes forward voluntarily and who is clear and straightforward is the best witness.

To Kautilya, one of the most important parts of law relates to the laws of marriage and marriage bonds. Caste purity has to be maintained for which only marriages between persons of the same Varna are recognized. He accepts the descending order of marriages between Brahmins and lower women and so on, as already pronounced by Manu. He also accepts the types of legal marriages as envisaged by Manu: eight types, starting with Brahma, where a father gives away a bride, and Paisacha, where a woman is abducted while she is sleeping or drunk; in between is the love marriage called Gandharva, where a man and bride agree to marriage. The others are Prajapatra, where marriage is solemnized with proper rituals but without the consent of the father; Aarsha, where whatever the form of marriage, it is later regularized by the husband presenting two cows to the father; Daiva, giving a girl to the officiating priest inside the sacrificial altar; Aasura, where a girl is given in exchange for bride money; and Rakshaa, where a girl is abducted by force.

Kautilya makes it clear that the bride's money must go to her parents. No marriage can be dissolved once a boy child has been born. It is the duty of a father to get his daughter married within three months of her reaching puberty. After three years of puberty, she is free to marry any person from her own Varna. A girl is considered marriageable at the age of twelve. A man can have sex with her if seven menstrual cycles have passed. A bride must, however, be a virgin. While admitting a man's conjugal rights, he says that once a woman has given birth to a boy child, a man may not force her to have sex. He makes no prohibition on widow remarriage. While Kautilya expects a man to discipline his wife, he prohibits excessive abuse or violence; the maximum is three slaps on her behind with a hand, rope, or cane. A woman abusing a man is unthinkable and will cause her to be subjected to the maximum punishment. Flirtations between man and woman, not married to each other, are prohibited, as is giving refuge to another man's wife, and adultery is presumed if a woman goes on a journey with another man, meets a man in a distant place, or accompanies a man other than those permitted by law/custom. Divorce is not permitted in the case of valid and proper marriages, as in the first four types of marriage; in the others, hatred and the wife's misconduct can be the causes of divorce. A detailed code of punishment for all forms of marital crimes is also listed by Kautilya.

Criminal Code

Kautilya lays down a detailed criminal procedure, starting with an arrest on suspicion, and lays down the valid reasons for suspicion for crimes as diverse as the fraudulent claim of Varna to possession of evil weapons, those overly curious about other women, those moving stealthily in the dark, low castes who conceal their caste, those that show fear at the sight of authority, etc. Kautilya explains what to look for in a case of burglary and also how to arrest and interrogate a suspect. He also proposes a postmortem examination and what to look for. Like a modern thinker, he talks about motive and even the methods of torture to get at the truth. Kautilya is extremely knowledgeable about human behavior, motives, and the tools of detection, interrogation, and psychological profiling of criminals.

In his law of defamation, Kautilya is interesting; he asserts that to say, "Your eyes are beautiful" to a blind person is sarcastic defamation, which should attract the highest punishment. To call a person mad, a leper, or impotent is aggravated defamation.

Sexual crimes include the defloration of a virgin and all forms of rape, including sex with a prostitute against her will. Certain forms of sex are also forbidden. Sex with a Guru's wife, with ascetics, all forms of incest, sex between Varnas, sex with any member of the royal family, a woman with a slave, and Aryas with outcastes. Unnatural sex is also prohibited, as is bestiality.

The Legacy of Arthashastra

It is difficult to overstate the significance of the 'Arthashastra.' Even though a reading of it today might leave one wondering what is so great about it, one must realize that the work was undertaken in the 4th century B.C. Comparing it with the knowledge available in the world at that time reveals the gigantic scope and depth of the thinking involved. Even classical Greece did not produce anything comparable to Arthashastra. While they had poets like Homer, historians like Herodotus, and philosophers like Socrates and Plato around the same time, Greece never produced anything like the Arthashastra, which is both a political treatise on statecraft, a theory on warfare and diplomacy, and an economic treatise, all in one. It was only with Machiavelli in the 15th century that the West had a treatise on politics and Statecraft. They had to wait for the arrival of Hobbes in the 17th century for a political theory. Economics as a serious subject of study came to its own only with Adam Smith in the 18th century. The greatness of Arthashastra is that it anticipates and precedes all of these Western thinkers and their ideas and has within it all the ideas and later theories in politics and economics. The West is yet to assign to Arthashastra the place it deserves in the intellectual history of the world.

However, India's first prime minister, Jawaharlal Nehru, was one of the first to realize its true greatness. He wrote about it in almost all his major writings. In 'Glimpses of World History,' he writes to his daughter about the importance and greatness of Arthashastra and the thinking of Kautilya. He then devotes a significant amount of space in his 'Discovery of India,' where he rightly says that historians tend to compare Kautilya to Machiavelli, but what is important is to realize that Kautilya was far ahead in time and superior in intellect.

In Arthashastra, Kautilya compares the state of nature to a place where the 'law of the fishes' prevails, where the big fish eat the small. Such a situation was so unbearable to the people that they got together and asked 'Manu' to become their king so that he could bring law and order to society. He thus anticipates Hobbes' idea of the law of the jungle, savage and brutish, and even looks forward to Rousseau's idea of a 'social contract.'

While Arthashastra is by and large amoral, it has a very exalted view of the role of kingship and the role of the State. Kautilya was much ahead of his time in seeing a need for a separation of the state and religion, and he does not normally mix the two. He has a very tolerant view of philosophical ideas, religious beliefs, and their adherence. Arthashastra also assumes that the king must rule only for the benefit of the people, as distinct from the western notion of the 'divine right of Kings.' He accepted the right of the people to dispose of their king when he ceases to work for their good, an idea that Cromwell had to so torturously come to before disposing of King Charles. He even anticipates Clausewitz when he says that war should only be a continuation of state policy. Kautilya was also one of the first to realize that war for the mere grabbing of land or for personal aggrandizement was wasteful. War must be undertaken only to remove obstacles in the path to a nation's economic and social goals and not treated as an end in itself. He advocated the idea of the 'balance of power,' an idea that Talleyrand was later to claim as his great idea. Finally, in his 'Mandela' concept, he saw the truth in the saying that 'my enemy's enemy is my friend.'

Summarizing the Greatness of Arthashastra

Kautilya's ideas on statecraft and their association with economic well-being are least appreciated, even though they are perhaps his greatest and deepest thoughts. He saw the state's role mainly as encouraging economic growth, facilitating trade, and, to ensure this, stressing the state's vital role in infrastructure building. He advocated an active role by the state to encourage economic growth, treating it as the state's primary function. He was among the first to realize that economic power is what makes a country truly great, and military might can only be sustained by economic strength. In his economic thinking, he foresaw the possibility of abuse and wanted the state to control infrastructure, waterways, mining, and the exploitation of mineral and forest wealth, with protection wherever necessary. In this aspect, he can be considered one of the first environmentalists.

We have not delved into the main focus of 'Arthashastra,' the duties of a king, the management of a kingdom, including the purpose of diplomacy, and the tactics and strategies of war, as these are predominant themes meant for those interested in statecraft. 'Arthashastra,' as one of the first intellectual creations of ancient India, holds added importance by revealing what society was like in ancient India. Understanding how we became what we are and why we think the way we do requires knowing who we were. The study of Arthashastra shows us what we were and painfully tells us that we have become people entirely different from those Kautilya describes. Arthashastra does not explain who we are because there is no rational evolution from the world of Arthashastra that would clarify what we have become. In fact, the world of Kautilya and the Harappan civilization seem entirely alien to what we have become. The only element of his society that resonates with our present society is the caste system, which, in the years after Kautilya, has hardened and become both intolerant and violent in ways Kautilya could not have foreseen. Otherwise, the world he describes is alien to us. It was a world where life was lived abundantly, where drinking and gambling were not only permitted but sponsored by the state, as was prostitution with its many grades of class and cost. It was a world wedded to the rule of law, where Dharma was the king's main priority. It was a rational society that believed in the proper use of all assets, and people had an almost reverential regard for nature. It was an extremely regimented society but with an almost religious respect for freedom of speech and belief—a society where every form of belief and way of life was respected and tolerated.

CHAPTER 6

THE EPICS

If the Atharvaveda was the initial attempt at creating a complex religion, unifying elements from local traditions, the Epics represent the final blending and an attempt to reconcile the conflict between two distinct civilizations. While the Epics narrate events long before the actual dominance of the Aryans in India, they were written down long after the time of Buddha, Mahavira, and many of the great material philosophers. They must have circulated in oral form for many centuries, shaping the consciousness of the people who lived in Bharath. If the Atharvaveda corrupted the Aryan tradition, the Epics aimed to give mythology a traditional lineage based on the foundation of the Vedas. Consequently, while the Purusha sacrifice had to be interpolated into the Rig Veda to justify caste stratification, the caste system is an accepted norm in the Epics. Yet, the Epics accept sages like Vyasa, an avarna, and openly acknowledge the nebulous status of Krishna. While the Pandavas are half-gods and the Kauravas have a fisherwoman as their ancestor, Karna, a poor charioteer's son, is shunned, and Ekalevya, a tribal, is cursed by Dronacharya. It is thus a story of events long before society had been stratified into castes, a retelling of the main stories with large-scale interpolations to justify the caste system while also serving as an instrument for the sanctification of local gods.

The Story of the Epics

The Ramayana stands as the quintessential epic for most of South Asia, akin to the Iliad for the West. It narrates the internal conflict within Aryavasta, leading to the banishment of Ram, the rightful king. Stripped of power, he, along with his brother Lakshman and wife Sita, is forced to dwell in the jungle. Sita is abducted by the powerful King Ravana, prompting Ram to form alliances with local beings, including a monkey civilization. In an ignoble act, he kills Vali, their king, by shooting him in the back. The loyal Hanuman becomes his formidable ally. With the help of the monkeys, Ram defeats Ravana and reclaims his wife. However, upon their return, doubts about Sita's purity arise. Conscious of his role as king above suspicion, Ram exiles Sita to the jungle. The narrative reflects internal family conflicts and diversity among the people and acknowledges the presence of an older Vedic civilization represented by Asuras like Ravan and Bali. Despite Ram's success, their return home lacks unanimous approval, hinting at fears of contamination and the loss of Aryan purity. Yet it may also symbolize the profound sacrifices made to appeal to local sentiments.

The Mahabharata unfolds as an internal quarrel between brothers, engulfing the entire world in a cosmic conflict resembling a world war. However, it asserts that the apparent brothers share various parentages. While the Pandavas boast divine lineage, the Kauravas inherit the mixed blood of local sages. Krishna, serving as mediator and relative, is a cowherd, and both he and many of his kin are described as black, including Draupadi, the Pandavas' wife. The narrative features anomalies, such as the Brahmin Drona fighting as a Kshatriya, the royal Karna raised as a charioteer, and the tribal Ekalavya recognized as the greatest archer.

Throughout the war, adharma prevails with deceit, women participating in battle, and covert killings. Despite these actions being justified in the name of contingency, the ultimate outcome is total annihilation. This raises the question: What is the true aim of the Epic? Perhaps it suggests that society, blended with the pure and impure, renders the concept of dharma unattainable. The acceptance of Krishna's philosophy, asserting that all is 'Maya'—where actions and the world are not real but mere manifestations—prevails. Essentially, the Epic serves to sanctify Krishna as a deity, omnipotent, omniscient, and the embodiment of Karma.

The Context

Dr. Radhakrishnan asserts that during a significant intellectual upheaval in the East, particularly in the Brahminical homeland, the West was immersed in war and faced incursions by invading armies. The Vedas had to acknowledge these invading hordes and the necessity to assimilate them into the Vedic fold. This process led to the dilution of many Vedic tenets. Another challenge emerged as the Aryans sought to subjugate the resistant native population. The Vedas contain numerous references to dark-hued people, with their hero, Krishna, bravely opposing the might of Indra. These cattle-breeding communities persisted in resisting Aryan dominance. Consequently, the Aryans had to adapt to the beliefs of the natives, employing a 'stoop to conquer' strategy. In this context, many Upanishads superimpose Vedic symbols onto non-Vedic beliefs.

In resolving this conflict, accepting some of the local gods became an apparent solution. The most formidable among them were Lord Shiva and Krishna, deified as Pasupata and Bhagavata, respectively, along with incorporating certain Tantric beliefs. The Epics, as a response, aimed to integrate local legends into the orthodox tradition, creating a new synthesis through storytelling. In this narrative approach, local heroes and beliefs became part of the overarching story, attempting to bridge the gap between diverse traditions.

The 'Mahabharata' deals with events that predate the Vedas, but its actual writing occurred after the spread of Jainism and Buddhism, both of which are referenced in many places. The long dominance of the oral tradition allowed the Mahabharata to expand in size from 24,000 to 600,000 verses when finally transcribed. This growth facilitated the gradual interposition of new beliefs and legends. Thus, according to Dr. Radhakrishnan, it bears "on its face the unsatisfactory alliance between folksongs and the superstitions of the new communities and the religious spirit of the Aryan." Vyasa made the best of this situation, writing a colossal poem that incorporated the floating mass of epic tradition, hero worship, and the dressing up of new gods of uncertain origin and doubtful morality.

In this transformation, Krishna is portrayed as a historical character and, instead of being the enemy of Indra, is now seen as an avatar of Vishnu, essentially the personification of Indra. The Mahabharata personalizes the divine, previously seen only as Prajapathi in the Vedas, into many separate gods. The Epics justify theistic beliefs, elevating Vishnu and Shiva to the rank of supreme gods. A great effort is made to combine the absolutism of the Vedas with the new theistic religion, and it shows. Despite the lack of deep philosophy or consistency, the overwhelming impact of the Mahabharata led many to consider it the fifth Veda. This success is attributed to its familiarity with local people and the fact that it was one of the first texts permitted for them to hear.

While the Mahabharata is more complex, the Ramayana is the older text. Whereas the Mahabharata delves into internal turmoil after the Aryans dominated the Indo-Gangetic plain, the Ramayana commences with their migration to the Gangetic plain, exploring the Aryan people's ongoing interactions, especially to the south. The Mahabharata primarily narrates a tale of internal conflict, while the Ramayana focuses on engagement with alien people.

The Ramayana envisions India as populated by Asuras, Rakshasas, and speaking animals. This portrayal likely refers to the local people, initially perceived by the Aryans as no better than animals. However, the Ramayana demonstrates that these individuals possess their own culture and perhaps a superior religious consciousness. Caste does not seem synonymous with the Aryan, as the Asuras are as well-versed in the Vedas as they are, and Ravan is depicted as the son of a Brahmin who knows the Vedas by heart. Even the power of religion is divided among many contesting groups, such as Pasurama, a local Brahmin, and individuals like Viswamitra, local sages of ambiguous caste.

The Epics narrate the stories of powerful men who were hermits, asuras, and rebels. Consequently, the Epics attempt to comprehend the Aryan's position in relation to local people, who are both intellectually superior and deeply divided in various ways. This division extends to their beliefs, where some are considered to come from a similar tradition that values the Vedas. In essence, the Epics strive, through storytelling, to create a religion and mythology that are relevant to all.

Dr. Radhakrishnan is convinced that it was the Vedic beliefs that were diluted, not the local people who condescended to accept certain Aryan ideas while imposing their religious beliefs on the Aryan. The fact that Vyasa was said to be the son of a fisherwoman and not twice born as the Aryans claimed suggests that it was the local people who compromised, not the Aryan. Alternatively, the Aryans might have been forced to accept a local sage to write the common creed, an abject surrender to the might, intellect, and determination of the local people. Yet, this still leaves unexplained why the local people accepted Sanskrit as the language of religion and the Vedas as revealed knowledge.

The 'Ramayana' is more of an epic poem than a religious treatise. It attempts to incorporate a more pantheistic religion than what is seen in the Mahabharata. Almost all native beliefs, cults, and heroes are accommodated. Thus, Kama and Kubera, Karthikeya, Ganga, Lakshmi, and Uma, the wives of Vishnu and Shiva, all join the pantheon of gods. Sesha, the snake, Hanuman the monkey, Jambavan the bear, Garuda, and Jatayu, different eagles, and Nandi the bull are recognized, and even the worship of snakes, trees, and rivers is accommodated, with Rama becoming an avatar of Vishnu.

In an effort to counter the Buddhist slant towards monastic life, the Ramayana glorifies domestic life and its virtues. It ridicules Jainism, portraying people as "clothed in air like madmen." In the Mahabharata, a person says he was born a jackal because he was an atheist who gloried in logic and reason, rejecting the philosophy of the material philosophers and reinforcing the belief in karma and devotion to personal gods.

The Mahabharata witnesses the fading of Indra and the rise of Krishna, symbolizing the defeat of Vedic orthodoxy by the Vishnu cult. Yama retains his place and is now Dharmaraja, the judge and lord of Karma. Agni and Surya remain, and Prajapathi is untouched. An attempt is made to unify the apparent polytheism into a trinity, as in the Narayana, the unification of creator and destroyer, Vishnu and Brahma. The Brahman of the Upanishads now has a human face as Iswara. A modification takes place in the Vedic religion as it slowly becomes the more recognizable Hinduism of later times, with Shakti, Pasupata, and Shiva, along with temples, idols, pilgrimage sites, and sacred places, all becoming part of the synthetic religion.

Durga worship is accepted when Krishna tells Arjuna to pay obeisance to Durga, soon becoming the wife of Shiva, addressed as Uma. Shakti worship must have been a powerful religion of the natives, which the Aryans slowly adopted by making her the wife of Rudra, who, as a verse says, "I bend the bow of Rudra to cut off the evil-doing hater of Brahman," thus making her a consort and a champion of Vedic Hinduism. In the 'Mahabharata,' we also see the metamorphosis of Pasupata into Lord Shiva, along with the entire theology of Pasupata, of 'Pati' as the cause, Karana, who creates, maintains, and destroys, who is also the manifestation of Karya, Vidya, and Kala, and the soul of man, or pasu. The belief in the five elements, five qualities, five senses, and five organs of action is also affirmed. They also introduced 'Vidhi' as the rules of logic, yoga, the discipline required, and 'Dukhanta' as the end of misery.

The Rise of Vaishnavism

The religious doctrine that predominates in the Mahabharata is that of Vasudeva-Krishna, a cult that slowly evolved into Vaishnavism. It also led to a form of monotheism and the rise of the Bhakti cult, which identified Krishna with Vishnu. These changes could not have taken place without serious opposition and great anguish, as the Rig Veda had portrayed the same Krishna as the leader of a black-hued tribe of cattle breeders who challenged the might of

Indra. The anti-Vedic nature of the cult was also criticized by the Vedantas; yet, by around 300 B.C., the Krishna-Vishnu Cult had so captivated the imagination of the people that it had not only become the leading cult but had elevated Krishna and Vishnu to the level of the highest of the gods.

The deification of Vishnu is told in the story of Narada, who visits Badarikashrama to meet Nara and Narayana and finds Narayana performing religious rites. Narada then asks, "Why do you, a great God, require worship?" Narayana replies, "I am worshiping the eternal spirit, which is the only original substance." Narada is then told that Krishna is the cause of all consciousness. The Vedanta, however, found it difficult to accept this theory as it was at variance with the Vedic account of creation.

The deification of Krishna also introduced the concept of monotheism, with him as the ultimate God. He evolved in the Vedas from Bhaga, considered the font of blessings and the God of boons and blessings. He is then identified with Vishnu, the God of the Three Strides, the great helper of the gods against the Asuras. Vishnu is not only a God but the ultimate God, to whom even the gods go for help. In an older tradition, he is a tribal chief who assisted the Aryans when they first attempted to settle in India and is also a non-Aryan chief waiting with 10,000 warriors to fight Indra. The same tradition makes Krishna the chief of the Yadavas, a race of Kshatriyas. Thus, the worshippers of Krishna were only slowly inducted into the Aryan fold, initially only as Bharatas.

While the Mahabharata sees the gradual deification of Krishna, there must have been loud protests from orthodox Vedic scholars. Thus, Bhishma is made to say, "Whoever says Krishna is a mere man is of dull intellect." By the time the Mahabharata was written, there was a great need to unify various opinions and religious cults that had fragmented the Vedic religion, and a hero was needed to rally the people into a unified religion. They found him in Krishna.

It is interesting that the orthodox latched on to the tradition of Krishna and the Gopis and gave up the revulsion they had for the licentious playboy by saying, "The violation of religious laws by gods and the daring acts of the glorious do not bring any stain, as fire is not stained by feeding on impure substance." The Bhagavata religion, also known as 'Pancharatra,' was an 'Agama' scorned by the Vedic Pandits but soon absorbed into mainstream Hinduism. It classified its knowledge system into Gnana, Yoga, Kriya, and Karya or Samskara (knowledge, discipline, construction, and rituals). Everything is in Krishna and Vishnu; they are the source of all substance and attributes. With the rise of Krishna worship, the Vedic religion of sacrifice gave way to the worship of images, temples, and the concept of Bhakti.

Krishna worship was a religion of individual devotion, of complete surrender to God, who helps anyone who falls at his feet. The contradiction of a God who forgives sins when even Yudhistra had to undergo punishment is made possible by the introduction of Lakshmi, who cannot harm and who, as Vishnu's wife, intercedes on behalf of human frailty. Soon, even Karmic stains could be removed by total devotion to Vishnu. The female devotees of Vishnu speak of total surrender to the heavenly bridegroom and of becoming harlots for God. This led, in the south, to the Bhakti movement with the Alwars of the 6th century. Their songs became the Veda of Vaishnavism and, in later years, were treated as the greatest commentary on the Epics.

The childhood stories of Krishna and Balarama's drinking indicate a non-Aryan heritage. In fact, the followers of Bhagavata were initially not allowed to follow the Vedic rituals. Vaishnavism was also totally against caste divisions, and the Kirata tribe of Hunas was said to have been purified merely by their devotion to Vishnu. The 'Agamas,' the original Vaishnavites, also refuted the Vedic rituals for the dead and opposed the doctrine of Samkara. They refused to acknowledge the Agnihotra and Joytistoma, yet in the Mahabharata, it is said that Bhrigu, the purest of Brahmins, was a devotee of Bhagavata. It was in its evolution into Pancharatra that Vaishnavism adopted the vertical mark on the head and the worship of images, defining them as a separate sect. While the Vedas were soon to become a non-negotiable element in Hinduism, it is clear that initially, the locals questioned even the doctrines and rituals of the Vedas.

While the Ramayana is a continuation of the worship of Vishnu as an avatar, it soon led to the deification of Ram as a God. This is where the ethics of the Epics get muddied. While Ram is 'Mariyada Purusothom,' even he is sometimes hasty, as when he cuts off Shambuka's head, and downright ignoble when he shoots Vali in the back. While this is no more than what Yudhistra does in the Mahabharata, even Ram's normally righteous behavior is not accepted by Sita or Lakshman, who seem to say that he is a God, not a human. That is where the problem starts, as the moral behavior of Ram is shown as inhuman and therefore is not a standard to be expected from mere mortals. When the ethics of Ram are seen as divine, mere mortals are not expected to follow him, as even the divine Sita and Lakshman are unable to follow him. This consequently justifies human compromises and the acceptance of contingency as only human. Thus, while Ram demands idealism in ethics, they make no dent in human behavior; instead, Ravan's lust, hatred, and hoarding mentality are what are accepted as human traits. In fact, in Ram's treatment of Sita, the impression created is that a demanding moral stance is perhaps evil, clearly cruel, and cold. Thus, the Ramayana ends up teaching no moral philosophy.

Justification in the Upanishads

Consequently, and as part of the writing of the Epics, it was necessary to create new commentaries to justify the evolution of faith. The later Upanishads show greater subtlety in logic and tend towards a new theism, where debates on the nature of God and creation are set aside, thereby creating a more dogmatic religion. The Bhakti cult introduced a monotheism based on a personal God who cares, forgives, and can be approached through prayer and worship. The elemental quality of God gives way to a personalized God, created in man's image. In fact, Deusser says, 'the Swetavatra Upanishad' is a monument to theism. 'Prakriti' is no longer an independent power but is controlled by God. Even 'Maya' is seen only as what God makes us capable of seeing. Along with this comes the concept of devotion, which requires man's total surrender to God as ultimate devotion. Sages like Jabala claimed that only extreme asceticism and the denial of all desire would purify the human soul. Similarly, the 'Kaivalya Upanishad' sees sanyasa and world renunciation as the only way to Moksha. Along with these changes, the Upanishads begin to justify the worship of symbols and images. Gnana is then relegated to a much lower order; as they say, God cannot be proved by logic and can be realized only by faith.

The Ethics of the Epics

The Mahabharata makes it clear that while truth and non-violence are important, they are relative and dependent on one's position in society and are relevant only in a specific context. It upholds the caste system and sees it as the bond that keeps society together. While the basic morality of the golden rule is upheld, it is relative to caste duties. It sees man's purpose in life as the pursuit of happiness and the avoidance of pain, but happiness is distinct from mere pleasure. Nothing finite can quench the thirst for the infinite, and true happiness is the state of calm that accepts pleasure and pain with equal composure. Instead of pleasure, the Mahabharata suggests a life of austerity, of tapas. Yet, it insists that man must first take care of his worldly commitments. The concern for social good becomes more pronounced in the later Upanishads as truth and non-violence become intrinsic values.

The love of humanity is a new focus, and the personal God understands human frailty and accepts the human capacity for repentance. Confession of wrongdoing and repentance, along with penance, become acceptable ideas. The harsh finality of Karma is moderated by God, who is the keeper of Karma and thus capable of modifying it. Three levels of karma are postulated: the karma that is activated at birth, the karma that is created by the immediate past life, and the karma of all previous lives. Man, by his actions, can modify the karmic stain of all earlier lives; only the karma he is born into is in the hands of God. This returns to man a little of his freedom and choice. The impersonal theory of Karma gives way to an idea of heaven and hell, of punishment for sins, and the possibility of going to Indra's heaven.

With these changes, the cosmology of the Vedas also undergoes a sea-change. The creation story is modified, and while the cosmic egg remains, manifestation is divided into Purusha and Prakriti, the two aspects of Brahman. Whether the infinite God can manifest himself in finite things and whether all is mere 'Maya' gives way to a clear acceptance of the world of the senses. The 'Mahabharata' speaks of the Gunas, qualities like Sattva, Rajas, and Tamas (goodness, passion, and darkness), and no longer is the 'atma' Nirguna, but composed of 'gunas,' and a human is defined by the nature of the mix. A good man has more Sattva, while a warrior has more Rajas and so on. Rajas is passion, Sattva is intelligence, and Tamas is ignorance. The concept of 'Maya' recedes as the Mahabharata accepts the reality of the five senses and the validity of sense perceptions. Yet, it also sees beyond the senses and says, "Seeing cannot take place without the aid of the mind."

The Bhagavad Gita (Translation by Barbara Stoler Miller)

There is an exaggerated reverence for the Gita, and to many people, the Gita represents the essence of Hinduism. Yet, the Gita is only an attempt to encompass a variety of views with one central theme. The result is great poetry but neither internally consistent nor rigorously thought. Scholars agree that it may have been orally transmitted around 200 B.C., but may have been written down in its present form only by about 200 A.D. Many believe that it was a separate piece of philosophical writing forming the core of the Bhagavata cult, which was then taken by the authors of the Mahabharata and interpolated between its narrative content. The links between the Bhagavata Purana and the Mahabharata are so profound that while Vyasa is said to have written the Mahapatra, Sukdeva, the son of Vyasa, is purported to have written the Bhagavata Purana.

The Gita reaffirms the central doctrine of Dharma as caste-based. Indian thinking has never looked at morals as God-given or provable from first principles but has always maintained that morality cannot be absolute and has meaning only in a context. Dharma is not morality but the relationships that sustain the universe; it is a sacred duty. Thus, right and wrong are never absolute but part of a patchwork of values and obligations within a Varna and in society as a whole.

The authority of the Vedas is not set aside, but the attitude suggests that the Vedas were valid for their own time and for a particular stage rather than as something universal and eternal. The Gita seems to say that Vedic rituals and sacrifices performed with any hope of gain tend to obstruct real spirituality. It, therefore, looks inward, and as in the Bhakti movement, the love of God becomes the supreme good. It is devotion to God and detachment from desires and worldly gain that are at the core of the Gita. The Gita favors the golden mean and scorns celibacy, fasting, and austerity as the madness of hermits and the spiritual suicide of saints who prefer darkness to sunlight and sorrow to joy. The Gita is down to

Earth and brings obscure philosophical ideas to the understanding of common people. The deep questioning of the Vedas gives way to the simple dualism of Purusha and Prakriti. What we see is Prakriti, while the manifestation of the divine is hidden in Purusha, a principle. This dualism is seen as two sides of the same principle. However, 'Purusha' is actually a mere spectator, while Prakriti is the actor. The Gita also accepts the theory of the Gunas and emphasizes yoga, or discipline, as the necessary condition for spiritual advancement.

In the Bhagavata cult, the Supreme Being is impersonal, but in the Gita, He is absolute and yet a personal God. The Gita is a discussion between the human Arjuna and the eternal God in Krishna. It starts with total dejection and a sense of futility in all human action and confusion about good and bad, with Arjuna questioning the killing of brothers, uncles, and Gurus for the sake of Dharma. Arjuna is thus unable to act, so he says,

"Krishna, I see my kinsmen
Gathered here, wanting war
My limbs sink,
My mouth is parched,
My body trembles,
The hair bristles on my flesh.
The magic bow slips,
From my hand, my skin burns ......
What joy is there for us, Krishna?
In killing Dhritarashtra's sons...
How can we ignore wisdom?
Of turning from this evil."

Even as Arjuna bemoans his dilemma, he accepts the great need for the regimentation of society where everyone knows his place and purpose. This acceptance of the caste system and the duties conjoined on each caste is a prerequisite for the later dialogue and so he says,

"When duty is lost
Chaos overwhelms the family

In overwhelming chaos, Krishna
Women of the family are corrupted
And when women are corrupted
Disorder is born in society."

One of the aims of the Epics is clearly to create a unified society. Thus, the need for family values and the duty of men to their families is stressed, as he says, "The sins of men who violate the family create disorder in society that undermines the constant laws of caste and family duty." Knowing the importance of Dharma and how social cohesion is sustained by a common belief in the caste system and the duties of each caste, Krishna knows that if everyone begins to question the very purpose of life, there will be chaos and death. Thus, he is brutally frank and asks,

"Why this cowardice?
In a time of crisis, Arjuna?
The coward is ignoble, shameful
Foreign to the ways of heaven."

To which Arjuna replies that he is confused by conflicting duties and the nebulous position of the ethics he had been taught: "The flaw of pity blights my very being. Conflicting sacred duties confounds my reason." Arjuna is talking about his duty, which seems to mean killing his relatives, which to him is a primary prohibition. Krishna is again brutal and clear, as he says,

"Learned men do not grieve
For the dead or the living.
Never have I not existed
Nor you, nor these kings
And never in the future
Shall we cease to exist."

God is eternal, so are men, says Krishna.

"Nothing of non-being comes to be
Nor does being cease to exist
Self is enduring
Indestructible and immeasurable."

Then comes the code of honor of a warrior, a passage that forever justifies the separate vocation of the separate castes and the need for vigorous action. In fact, total devotion and sincerity to one's duties are emphasized.

"Look to your duty
A battle of sacred duty
The doors of heaven open
For warriors who rejoice
If you are killed, you will win heaven
Diffuse and pointless are the ways
Irresolute men understand."

In advocating a determined course of duty, irrespective of consequences, Krishna also makes it clear that there is no other way for mortal men, as man is judged by his actions, not by his piety or sacrifices. Krishna thus attacks rituals and sacrifices as the refuge of proud men who selfishly think that their rituals will take them to heaven and says,

"Undiscerning men who delight
In the tenets of ritual love
Utter florid speech, proclaiming
'there is nothing else'
Driven by desire, they strive after heaven
obsessed with power and delights
Their reason lost in words.
Then comes the core of the Gita,
Be intent on action
Not on the fruits of action.
Avoid attraction to the fruits
And attachment to inaction.
Impartial to joy and suffering
Gain and loss, victory and defeat
Arm yourself to battle,
Lest you fall into evil
When one renounces all desires
And acts without craving
Possessiveness."

Action is both necessary and vital to human existence, and it is inaction that tends to lead the mind astray. Not only must one act but one must do so with all the vigor one is capable of. Action is a holy sacrifice, even if it is also what stains one's karma, so Krishna explains how action can be totally free of karmic stain. He says,

"Action imprisons the world
Unless it is done as a sacrifice.
Freed from attachment, Arjuna
Perform action as sacrifice.
All sacrifice comes from action
Surrender all action to me,
Fix your reason on your inner self
Without hope or possessiveness
I desire no fruit of action
And actions do not defile me."

Krishna also shows how action is also a form of inaction; action without hope of reward is actually a form of inaction.

"A man who sees inaction in action
And action in inaction
Has understanding among men.
One who does what must be done
Without concern for the fruits,
Is a man of renunciation and discipline.
Action is the means of the sage."

It will be seen from these early verses that the Gita tries to wean people from the mindless pursuit of rituals and sacrifice to the pursuit of a purposeful life. It sees rituals and sacrifices as mindless and selfish, made for personal and material benefits. However, the most important reason to shun rituals, says the Gita, is because they are obstacles to real spirituality—the search for truth and knowledge. In the Gita, there is blessedness only in action. It rejects the Buddhist and Jain ideas of renunciation, austerity, and withdrawal from human society. Instead, it asserts that man must live a life of action. Renunciation is achieved by the manner in which one acts. When we act without motive and with no hope of gain, action becomes a sacrifice. Similarly, action without hope, even of heaven, or action without any idea of virtue or morality, is a sacrifice. These ideas are powerfully proclaimed without any ambiguity. In fact, Krishna even says that only doubt and dithering are the real problems; action should be determined and clear. No action can defile; it is the love of inaction and not being ready to act that leads to evil.

Then Krishna starts on his second theme, 'surrender all action to me,' and goes on to say, "Men who always follow my thought, trusting it without finding fault, are freed, even by their action." He tells Arjuna, "I have passed through many births, and so have you; I know them all, but you do not, Arjuna." Lord Krishna then outlines the concept of Bhakti, but before its full disclosure, Krishna explains the importance of knowledge. He says,

"Sacrifice as knowledge is better
Then sacrifices with material objects
No purifier equals knowledge
An ignorant man is lost, faithless
And filled with self-doubt.
A soul that harbors doubt has no joy,
Not in this world or the next."

Then Krishna makes the point that the process of learning and knowledge are the same. This however, is what men need most to realize but rarely do.

"simpletons' separate philosophy
And discipline, but the learned do not
Applying one correctly, a man
Finds the fruit of both."

This idea that knowledge and the pursuit of knowledge are irretrievably intertwined, that it is the pursuit that matters, is very important, for ultimate knowledge may never be given to men. Even as Krishna sees knowledge as the most important pursuit, he also pleads for a society where there are equal opportunities for all. He says,

"Learned men see with an equal eye
A scholarly and dignified priest
A cow, an elephant, a dog
And even an outcast scavenger."

True knowledge, 'absolute joy beyond the senses,' can be attained only by absolute discipline, says Lord Krishna.

"The man of discipline, striving/With effort, purified of his sins / Perfected through many births /Finds a higher way."

And then says, "I will teach you the totality of knowledge," and explains that he is in all things,

"Composed of nature's qualities
My divine magic is hard to escape
Vice, deluded sinners are the men
Who fail to take refuge in me;
Their knowledge ruined by magic
They fall prey to demonic power.
Arjuna, four types of virtuous men
Are devoted to me
The tormented man, the seeker of wisdom
The suppliant, and the sage.
all noble, But I regard
The man of knowledge to be myself
He is the rare spirit who sees
'Krishna is all in all.'"

Lord Krishna bemoans the overdependence on sacrifices, which descends to magic when men 'fall prey to demonic powers,' where even the pursuit of knowledge is 'ruined by magic' and finds the true seeker of knowledge, the closest to the perfect man. Lord Krishna then deals with the concept of the divine.

"Men, without understanding, think that I am
Unmanifest nature becomes manifest.
They are ignorant of my higher existence.
My pure, unchanging absolute being.
I am unborn and inimitable."

The Vedic scholars had tried to comprehend nature, its cause, and its origin, whether it was created or self-existent. They finally came up with the idea of Maya, that all we see is an illusion created by the divine, a manifestation of the divine. To this, the skeptical asked, "How can the infinite be reduced to the finite? They are two totally different types of entities and such a manifestation would be a contradiction in terms." Lord Krishna thus claims to be both the manifested and the unmanifested, pure and unchanging, unborn and inimitable. All contradictions. He brushes aside all doubts by saying, "I am the amalgamation of all contradictions, the absolute being." He explains this with even greater ambiguity and says,

"At Brahma's break of day
All things emerge from an unmanifest nature.
When night falls, all sink.
Into unmanifest darkness.
Beyond this unmanifest nature
Is another unmanifest existence
A timeless being that does not perish
When all creatures perish.
It is called eternal unmanifest nature."

Lord Krishna seems to say that all nature disappears, becomes non-existent when darkness falls, which is clearly not true even if it refers to the day in God's eyes but then says that there is nature beyond the manifested, which is eternal. What is that? He explains by saying,

"The whole universe is pervaded.
By my unmanifest form
All creatures exist in me.
But I do not exist in them."

He says that he, the divine, eternal one, is manifest in all things, a contradiction in terms, to which he says, "They exist in me, but "I do not exist in them." I am what you see, but not limited to what you see; again, a circular logic."

"Sustaining them without being in them

gathering in my own nature
Again and again, I freely create
These actions do not bind me.
Deluded men despise me.
In the human form, I have assumed.
Ignorant of my higher existence."

He again puts rituals in their place and says that sacrifice is useless because,

"I am the rite, the sacrifice.
The libation for the dead, the healing herb
The sacred hymn, the clarified butter
The fire, the oblation.
I am the Lord of all sacrifices.
I am impartial to all creatures.
And no one is hateful or dear to me.
But men devoted to me are in me.
And I am in them.
Neither the multitude of gods
Nor do great sages know my origin.
I am the source of all.
I am self-abiding.
In the hearts of all creatures
I am their beginning.
Their middle and their end
I am Vishnu, striding among the sun gods.
I am Indra, king of the gods.
I am gracious Shiva
I am the beginning, the middle.
and the end of creations.
I am death, the destroyer.
I am the ritual chant."

He is all in all; Vishnu, Shiva, and Indra are merely names; sacrifices and rituals are merely a part of him. Lord Krishna is clearly trying to unify all the divergent theories about Godhood and to claim to be all in all. It was also an attempt to end the proliferation of gods by creating an inclusive, monotheistic religion while reducing the reliance on sacrifice. "I am impartial to all creatures," says Lord Krishna, discarding exclusiveness created by caste and untouchability. Like us, Arjun is not convinced, so he asks Lord Krishna to reveal his true self. At first, the Lord merely says, "You see all the universe. What else do you wish to see?" When Arjun is still unsatisfied, he gives Arjun 'a divine eye,' and what he sees is so truly awe-inspiring that it cannot be told in the first person and Sanjaya has to first introduce the vision to us as,

"It was a multiform, wondrous vision.
Everywhere was boundless divinity.
The light of a thousand suns."

Then Arjun himself says,

"I see the gods.
In your body
I see your boundless form.
Everywhere
I see you blazing.
Through the fiery rays
I see no beginning.
There is no middle and no end.
You alone
Fill the space.
Throngs of God enter you.
Some in their terror.
I lose my bearings.
And I find no refuge.
Be gracious, Lord of gods.
Shelter from the Universe
Tell me
Who are you?
In this terrible form?"

Lord Krishna explains,

"I am a time-grown old
Creating world destruction

Set in motion
To annihilate the world."
Now, at last, Arjuna is convinced and says,
Krishna, the universe
You are the original God.
The primordial spirit of man
The deepest treasure.
You are the God of Wind.
I bow in homage.
You are the father of the world.
Of all animate and inanimate things
I bow to you."

Then Lord Krishna tells Arjuna that he alone among men has had the unique privilege of seeing the Lord in his true form but no one else can or ever will.

"Not through sacred love,
Or sacrificial ritual,
Or study or charity,
Not by rites,
Or by terrible penance,
Can I be seen in this form?
In the world of men."

Thus, the mystery of divinity will always remain a mystery, but one thing is clear: there is only one God and he is Krishna. That rituals and sacrifices are useless and all may come to the Lord; caste and class are no bar; only faith and devotion to the Lord. To Arjun's question, "How should man seek the Lord?" he replies,

"Men reach me who worship
What is impressionable?
When they entrust reason to me,
Arjun, I will soon arise.
To rescue them."

He then outlines the qualities of a true devotee.

"One who bears hate for no creature

Is friendly, compassionate, and unselfish.
content always,
The world does not flee from him.
Nor does he flee from the world.
Free of delight, rage, and fear
And disgust
disinterested, pure, and skilled
Indifferent, untroubled
He does not rejoice in hate.
Impartial to foe and friend
Honor and contempt
Neutral to blame and praise."

That, says Lord Krishna, is a man most likely to find solace in the divine. The Bhagavad-Gita also accepts the reality of human flesh, and Krishna explains,

"Lucidity, passion, dark inertia,
These qualities are inherent in nature.
Bind the unchanging
Embodied self in the body
know that passion is emotion.
Born of craving and attachment
Know dark inertia born of ignorance.
Lucidity addicts one to joy.
From passion comes greed.
Most men, due to their nature, are
Bound by a hundred fetters of hope
Obsessed by desire and anger
They hoard wealth in stealthy ways.
To satisfy their desires."

The way to God, says Lord Krishna, is faith. "A man consists of his faith, and as his faith, so is he." Lord Krishna then says,

"There is no being on Earth.
Or among the gods in heaven
Free from the triad of qualities
They are born of nature."

Man, in human form, plagued by desire and hope, can never gain true knowledge nor be free from the bondage to flesh; only faith, total devotion to God and surrender lead to salvation. This philosophy of the Bhakti cult swept through the length and breadth of the country, creating a new Hindu ethos. Lord Krishna also promises to be there for all who are willing to give themselves totally to him.

"If I am in your thoughts, by my grace
You will transcend all dangers.
Make me your only refuge.
I free you from all evil."

Finally, there is the catch that confuses even Christians who are forced to accept St. Paul's concept of Grace. Lord Krishna uses the same concept and makes it clear that it is grace, not merit, that leads to salvation, for "no mortal can perform a service for me that I value more." The idea that God is not human and needs nothing from man is one of its important realizations. Sacrifices and rituals are therefore unnecessary, as they are all performed with selfish motives, for material and personal gain. The absorption in rituals also tends to blind people to the need for knowledge and truth. The Gita also sees the proliferation of gods as both silly and an attempt to divert human attention from the truth of divinity. Lord Krishna claims that all gods reside in him, forcing a better understanding of divinity and a belief in a single God. The Gita warms up the concept of divinity from the cold abstract idea of the Nirguna, the negative God propounded by the Vedas, to a personal God—warm, human, forgiving, and all-powerful. It also tries to bring together a society that had been splintered into Varnas and castes, including untouchables, into a single fold where the same God cares for all people irrespective of caste or class; all that is required is devotion.

Man is human, and his humanity makes him incapable of salvation by his own merit. Only total surrender to the will of God would cause God to extend His grace for his salvation. Man can redeem himself only through action, not through rituals or even by referring to the Vedas. He cannot gain his freedom by running away from life or by refusing to act. Action is a must; all that man can do is purify his action by detachment, to act without motive and with no hope of reward. To act virtuously and seek fulfillment in all action, treating all action as a sacrifice and a renunciation.

The problem is that Lord Krishna demands the impossible. He accepts that man is human and cannot escape his humanity—"there is no being free from the triad of qualities"—and then demands that man act without desire, which is a contradiction. No action can even be contemplated without purpose and the resultant benefits. Lord Krishna demands that man shed his humanity and be dead to his human self—no pleasure, no desire, no hope, and no fear. By asking for the impossible, even as he prescribes the correct way, it becomes irrelevant and unachievable.

I have quoted the Gita in some detail so that there is no doubt that we have not missed anything and to make it clear that there is nothing mysterious or secret about the Gita—no great hidden wisdom that only the initiated can fathom. While Lord Krishna gives us an almost infallible ethic, it is also both inhuman and actually meaningless. Indian thinking had begun with the idea that all creation was the result of desire. While the question as to why an all-powerful God would have the desire to create is asked and then brushed under the carpet, as it were, it was forgotten but now becomes a contradiction.

To claim that ultimate morality lies in the state of willessness is both the affirmation of the truths of Indian thinking and the total betrayal of the reality of human life. It is an affirmation of Indian thought in that it reaffirms the idea of 'Maya' and the world as a manifestation, thus unreal, or real only to the extent that each person makes it real. It is also an affirmation that life is driven by 'Karma,' where desire is what creates both life and death. Yet, it is the very antithesis of Bhagavata religion, which grew to counter the cold and nihilistic philosophy of Shaivite Advaitha, where all life is seen as 'Maya,' and only a regression into the mind, into a state of unconsciousness, is the answer. The state in which Lord Shiva normally is, meditating on the cold mountain snows of the Himalayas.

That seems to be exactly what Lord Krishna is now saying: that life is 'Maya' and that we should be dead to life and become as one without desire, or, as the Shaivaites say, be 'shava' without Shakti to manifest life. In fact, it is no different from the philosophy that the Buddha preached. This is a clear betrayal of human life, for it treats life as an illusion. 'Bhakti' rose mainly to reset this idea because even in the 'illusion' that is life, it is unfortunately beset with pain, sorrow, and tragedies that the human flesh is too weak to bear without consolation.

For an Avatar of Vishnu to now reject his purpose of being born is the greatest betrayal. In fact, apart from being a bitter betrayal, it is also immoral. It is a philosophy that does not care about what happens to the world or to others. One may burn an entire forest, and as long as it is done without desire, it is not just alright but great in leading to Nirvana. Killing relatives, stealing, betraying trust, and so on are all fine as long as they are done without desire. It is a morality that does not care about society, about pain, or about suffering. It is fine to pretend that all is an illusion, but as Schopenhauer asked, why is the pain so real? A morality without a social mandate and no personal accountability is not moral. Not having desire is death. Yet, the morality of the Gita demands that we be dead to the world and that the illusion of the world will go away if one shuts one's eyes to the world.

However, as in all religions, the people took only what was convenient and easy. Thus, rituals and sacrifices continue to this day without any change. Karma, as a fatalistic belief, and caste, as a permanent social segregation, have only been strengthened. Gods continue to proliferate, and the 'Mahabharata,' in which the Gita is the central religious tract, propagates the acceptance of more gods, apart from the worship of snakes, trees, and rivers. Lord Krishna's attempt at explaining the absolute, the infinite, as manifestation, a part of the infinite, confuses without explaining, thereby ending up promoting devotion instead of knowledge. With the Gita being the pinnacle of knowledge, all further inquiry into the nature of the divine became a delusion and an act of arrogance.

CHAPTER 7

INDIAN SYSTEM OF PHILOSOPHY

While the Vedas were being written, various teachings abounded in the cities and cosmopolitan centers of the Mauryan Empire. Jainism and Buddhism had become established religions, introducing along with their beliefs a way of life centered around monasteries and temples and idealizing a life of austerity—the way of the monk and sanyasi. The possibility of a life devoted to religion had the inevitable effect of producing a plethora of ideas and systems of thought. The 'Axial Age' was thus the beginning of a systematic pursuit of knowledge, and treatises in almost all disciplines of knowledge were written. The result was a series of philosophical systems. Many must have died natural deaths, but some have continued to provide distinctive ways of thinking that have their advocates and adherents to the present day. They are now treated as the special contribution of Indian thinking to the study of philosophy.

Many were used extensively in Buddhism and in the Upanishads, while many retain their secular tenor and can be studied as separate systems of philosophy. There always remains the elusive question of whether the Upanishads borrowed from secular philosophy or if all Indian philosophy had its origin in the writings of the Upanishads. The fact that there was a pre-Aryan culture and philosophy is not disputed, but what baffles the historian is how to fix its contours. The problem is also because it is difficult to determine the relative vintage of many of the philosophies and the actual dating of the oral tradition of the Upanishads.

Lokayata Mata (Materialism)

Ancient India was home to almost all possible systems of philosophy. From Stoics to Cynicism and Epicureanism, there were theists and atheists. It was a free and vibrant place where all forms of philosophy had a home. Unfortunately, almost all the writings of this multifaceted period have disappeared. All that remains are references to earlier philosophies in later works, by which a semblance of their philosophy can be gauged. Of the philosophies, what has come down in some detail is the materialism of Carvaka. Materialism was called 'lokayata-mata'—the way of the common people. While Carvaka was a disciple of the sage Brahaspati, he is credited with being the founder of materialistic philosophy. The actual writings of Carvaka have all disappeared; what remains is a work called 'Tattvopaplavasimha' by Jayavasi Bhatta.

Accordingly, according to this materialistic school, knowledge is only possible through the senses. All that cannot be perceived is therefore non-existent. They were like David Hume, radical empiricists. Sense perception, or Pratyaksha, was the only source of knowledge (Pramana). Instead of claiming, like Hume, that everything that appears to be independent of sense perception, like imagination and thoughts, is only the recollection and different combinations of sense perceptions, Carvaka claimed that the process called logic was made up of inference and thus analysis and deduction can only lead to false conclusions because they are not based on sense perception. His point was that a syllogism like,

"All men are mortal. Socrates is a man. Socrates is mortal."

This may be logical but is based on the premise that "all men are mortal," which has not been proved. Thus, all further inferences made from such a premise are faulty. Further, all inferences are based on past knowledge, yet we have no proof that the future will be the same as the past. How then can any inference be made from past experience to postulate the future? The final argument against inferences is that the conclusions that result are obvious from the premises, and therefore the conclusions give us no new information. That is, if all men are mortal, it is obvious that

Socrates, who is a man, is mortal.

The Lokayattas asserted what modern science has realized: that even scientific truths, which are based on perception and experiments, are only probabilities, valid only as long as no contradicting phenomenon is reported. There can be no general validity in moving from perception to universality, even if it is repeatedly true, because a general law has to be true for all time. However, without inference, no knowledge is possible. All our actions are based on presumed laws of cause and effect; we anticipate based on the past, and all history is only an attempt to discern patterns in the shifting sands of time. Life is possible only by generalizing and accepting the law of cause and effect.

Like David Hume, the Lokayatas say that since no one has seen God, heaven, or hell, there is no reason to believe they exist. All matter and all objects that we can see are the only reality. They also adhered to an atomistic theory, stating that all matter is made up of four elements: air, fire, water, and space. All matter is merely a combination of these four elements. Like modern doctors, they also deny any separate thing called the soul and claim that the mind, intellect, and emotions are the result of chemical action caused by the combination of the elements in different proportions. They deny God and creation and claim that matter is a combination of self-existent elements. To believe in a creator, they said, would force us to ask who created the creator. As the Rig Veda asks, "Who created the gods?" and finally concludes that the gods came later, meaning that men created the gods. To believe in creation would thus force us into infinite regression.

In a system without God, where matter is self-existent, death is also merely part of the endless churning of matter. The Lokayatas did not believe in heaven or an afterlife. Religion was only a business for priests to make a living, claimed Carvaka. Human wisdom lies in making the best of whatever position one is in, always attempting to maximize pleasure and avoid pain. Thus, pleasure that brings pain later should also be avoided. Enjoy while you can, says Carvaka, as death is the end; all that we have is this life, so make the best of it. There are no morals, and all is permissible in man's attempt to squeeze out whatever joy and pleasure he can get.

Samkhya

'Samkhya' may have its roots in the Vedas and is one of the oldest traditions in philosophy. The founder is normally recognized as Kapila, who is supposed to have written the Samkhya Sutra (the principles of Samkhya). However, what we have is only the 'Samkhya Karika,' which may have been written around 500 A.D. by Isvarkarna. Other works that have come down to us include the 'Samkhya Karika' of Bhagya, attributed to Gaudapada; Vachaspati Misra's 'Samkhya Kaumudi'; and Vijnanabhiksu's 'Samkhya Pravachana Bhashya.'

Samkhya means numbers and is a philosophy that attempts to be as exact and clear as numbers, a desire that has deep roots in Western philosophy, starting with Pythagoras and Descartes to Russell and Whitehead.

Kapila was an atheist who denied the existence of God. He demolished all the normal proofs of God. He claimed that God cannot be the first cause if He is also eternal and unchanging because God cannot remain unchanged when He acts (in creation) and interacts with creation. As is undisputed, nothing can act or interact with something else without being changed. As Heisenberg showed, even the act of observation causes change. Thus, if God exists unchanged, he cannot be both a creator and the controller of the Universe. The belief that God is good is also absurd, considering the amount of pain and suffering in the world. All attempts to create divinity based on absolute qualities like goodness, beauty, and truth are thus absurd.

Samkhya says if Purusha and Prakriti are eternal and indestructible, they could not have been created. Infinity cannot create another totally distinct infinity; it can only be part of infinity. That is why the Vedantas postulate that the universe is not a creation but a manifestation of God. To claim that God is perfect and then to claim that He is the creator is a contradiction, as a perfect thing can have no desire; it is perfect, complete, wanting nothing, whereas all creation assumes a desire for something.

Samkhya philosophy is a dualistic philosophy, similar to the philosophy of Plato. It sees all matter as divided between Prakirti (matter) and Purusha (spirit), almost the same division that Plato made between phenomena and essence. Unlike Plato, they insist that both are real and indispensable. They accepted the Lokayatas belief that matter, as Prakriti, is self-existent and therefore the first cause. They had an atomistic theory that starts with simple things, like a thread that can make cloth or milk that makes curd, and concluded that most things are formed from simpler substances and therefore there must be something like atoms that are the basic building blocks of all things. Everything that we see is thus only the different combination of these atoms. However, as they were not able to visualize how these atoms could also produce consciousness, they accepted that many complex products of the mind are different, postulating the existence of a different set of subtle elements, which could also be breakable into atoms that create the things of the mind. This reminds us of Descartes and his 'res cogita,' and modern thinkers who postulate something called 'memes.'

However, Prakriti, uncreated and eternal, pervades the universe. All that we see is an interaction between the atoms of Prakriti that appears to follow the principle of cause and effect. In their stable condition, they are the physical objects that we see all around us. Prakriti is defined as non-spiritual, inert, and unconscious. Their existence is manifested only by the conscious nature of Purusha (the spirit/self). Yet, it can be perceived only when it has certain qualities (Guna). Unlike Plato, who said that we can only see the form of things, not their essence, to Indian philosophers, the essence of things is made up of Gunas. Gunas are the building blocks that create the appearance of essence; consequently, 'essence' is not some other eternal absolute as Plato saw it but the manifestation of the gunas. In Samkhya philosophy, as well as in most Indian thinking, the Gunas are three in number: Satva, Rajas, and Tamas. Satva is seen as light, essence, and pure; Rajas as the capacity for motion, which gives it a place in space and time; and Tamas as the material quality made up of weight, hardness, shape, and feel. It is Guna that defines Prakriti and to which we give a name. It is defined by the combination of gunas, and once created, the combination of gunas becomes static and attains an equilibrium. In a dynamic state, it causes change, growth, and movement. The 'Gunas' are very similar to the Western philosophical concept of 'quality,' of Aristotle. The interesting aspect of Samkhya philosophy is its assertion that, once the Gunas combine to create an object, the Gunas are so transformed by the act of creation that it is no longer possible to break the object into its constituent Gunas. They become permanent and distinct objects. A tree cannot be broken down to make a monkey, and so on. The Gunas are thus transformed into a different entity.

The ultimate principle, God, or First Cause, is the dynamic equilibrium of the Gunas that existed prior to creation. When they existed in an unobjectified state—invisible, unrealized, passive—an eternal force with potential but no actuality. Once creation takes place, Prakriti is no longer stable; it has to evolve, change, grow, and decay. This perspective is very scientific and similar to the view of modern science. It also explains the cycle of creation, evolution, and death, followed by the endless cycle of births and deaths. Where it becomes a little fuzzy is when it claims that the transformation into a particular form or object is due to the predominance of one guna over others. Thus, where there is a predominance of Satva, it leads to the creation of the mind and intellect (mahat, buddhi). It is the mind that then makes the distinction between subject and object, resulting in consciousness and the creation of self as a separate ego, 'I' (Ahamkara). The ego is assisted by the five senses, the motor organs, and the intellect (Manas). However, since even the ego is made up of the Gunas, the capacity for subtle intellect or gross, base desires depends on the combination of the five elements and of the subtle elements, which Samkhya sees as the higher reaches of the same senses—subtle in touch and subtle color—while the basic senses are seen as the elemental colors, taste, smell, and touch. Higher intellectual, artistic, and spiritual capacities are created by the predominance of the subtle elements, while gross, sensual, and violent sensibilities are created by the predominance of the grosser elements. The problem is that the Gunas are an artificial division that has been postulated merely to explain the diversity of nature with no attempt to prove their existence. Similarly, the division of the elements into gross and subtle is more of a description than an explanation.

Samkhya philosophy, however, achieves a deep psychological insight when it says the self, as a combination of body and spirit, is made up of mind (mahat), ego (ahamkara), and manas (intellect). The Manas is part of antah-karana (internal being), more than intellect; it is the discerning moral and judgmental capacity of the mind and akin to Freud's 'superego.' Thus, Samkhya philosophy predates Freud's theories by many, many centuries. However, like modern doctors, they refuse to mystify the ego but claim that all the properties that 'antah-Karna' exhibit are created by mere physical entities, including the brain, the senses, the motor organs, and the nervous system—a conclusion that modern medicine and science are now advocating.

In their conceptualization of knowledge, they were also far ahead. They saw matter, Prakriti, as unconscious and non-existent until perceived by Purusha, the conscious element in the universe. It is consciousness that allows Prakriti to be manifested. Thus, like later-day Western philosophers, they claim that human beings are the creators of the visible world. For Samkhya philosophers, the world and all experience are never neutral or objective but the corrupted result of the interaction between the observer and the observed. It is always an interaction between Purusha and Prakriti. In fact, in a way, the self does not exist; it is only our capacity to conjure a manifestation of objects that makes us distinct from the 'other.' that allows us to become a distinct entity; we are alive only because of our capacity to see other objects. The self, according to Samkhya, is pure, unchanging, and merely a spectator. It is Prakriti that acts and is acted upon. Purusha (spirit/soul) is a passive witness (Saksin) to what happens. Thus, they claim that it is the ignorance of what Purusha means and how it exists that makes people assume that it is the soul that experiences pleasure, pain, and sorrow. The soul is untouched; it merely causes seeing and then merely exists as a witness (saksin). The problem with this absolute duality is that if Purusha (the soul) does not act, who does? Since Prakriti is a mere matter, how can it act or feel? The Gita elevates consciousness and demands that we become dead to ourselves, a dead Prakriti and an un-acting Purusha.

Descartes said, "I think, therefore I am," and the Samkhya philosophers also claim that if there is one thing that is irrefutable, it is the reality of our existence. We cannot deny existence without self-contradiction, as the question would then be, who then is denying existence? As Descartes said, even when I doubt, I only reinforce the reality of my existence. Yet, Samkhya differs from Descartes in that while Descartes still sees a duality between the 'I' and the body, Samkhya unites the 'I' and the body into a single piece, where the Purusha, or spirit, merely observes, while Prakriti thinks and acts. There is no distinction between the thinker and the actor because Purusha in Samkhya is non-existent, as it is never manifested and cannot be seen. Consequently, only Prakriti remains. This is to have the cake and eat it too. To explain consciousness, Purusha is postulated, but since the eternal soul cannot be seen or contaminated, Prakriti becomes the scapegoat. Yet, Prakriti by itself is unconscious.

That such a philosophy would get itself entangled in irreconcilable contradictions became obvious when they tried to explain purpose. They started by saying that matter (Prakriti), in its essential elements, is pre-existing and eternal. They take form based on the mixing of the elements. Yet Prakriti is purposeless and therefore has no reason to be creative. To explain this contradiction, it postulates that Prakriti takes shape only for Purusha to experience the world. Creation is, therefore, solely for Purusha, as Purusha alone has the consciousness to appreciate creation; thus, the powerless Purusha becomes a creator, a clear contradiction. In fact, Prakriti would remain invisible until Purusha made it manifest. Purusha (self/soul) is thus both consciousness, the purpose of all creation, and its creator. If the entire universe is created for Purusha, it raises the obvious question: what then is the purpose of the mortal life of eternal Purusha? Samkhya claims that the purpose is to refine men's gross nature; human life is an inching towards perfection. This is itself debatable, as it may be true that man tends to exhibit restlessness and does seek purpose; it may also be true that he seems to look up to some unknown divinity, yet there is no proof that perfection is an aim. Power, wealth, sex, happiness, and pleasure all seem more important than perfection. Only the fear of death makes him seek hope in a future life. Samkhya, however, sees perfection as the aim and Purusha, imprisoned in Prakriti, is keenly aware of the imperfections of the self and continuously seeks to evolve to a higher state of perfection. This is contradictory, as Samkhya also presupposes that Purusha does not act but is a mute spectator; how then can it cause evolution? To make it even more confusing, Samkhya says this conception that Purusha feels limited or imperfect is the result of a false identification with Prakriti. Thus, the liberation of Purusha is possible only when Purusha sees Prakriti as totally alien to itself, discards it, scorns it, and denies it. The realization that all Prakriti is unreal and only a manifestation and that Purusha is free to fly begs the question: what then is Prakriti and why is it necessary in the first place? Why does man to be first deluded for him to be liberated? If only a spectator, why this demonizing of Prakriti, which is incapable of consciousness on its own? Purusha creates the consciousness that manifests the universe only for us to realize that what we see is an illusion, that it never acts and is never tainted, yet without Purusha, there is neither Prakriti nor the universe. Why the illusion of morality when Purusha is incorruptible? Perfection is clearly nonsense, as Purusha has always been perfect, and Prakriti is merely common, dead matter.

Samkhya contradicts itself again when it claims that there is no one self but many selves. Then it says that each person is unique because he is a unique combination, a distinct self. The later Advaita Vedanta also contradicts this belief by claiming that the soul (Atma) and the divine are one; it is the ego, the self as a conscious ego, that separates us from the divine. The plurality of souls also calls into question the claim that the soul is as all-pervading as the elemental matter that pervades the whole universe. Samkhya explains itself only with an analogy, claiming that Purusha and Prakriti are like a lame man and a blind man and can progress only together, yet are separate and distinct. Even as an analogy, it is poor, as the lame man is carried by the blind man; the blind man cannot claim he is not acting and the lame man cannot claim he is not directing; therefore, both must accept responsibility.

Samkhya Epistemology

Samkhya believes, like the empiricists, that knowledge can be gained only through the senses. However, similar to Descartes and Kant, they realized that perception becomes knowledge only through an intellectual process of cognition and recognition. Thus, Samkhya also believes in inference—the process of logical reasoning—and even in authority, as long as the manner in which the knowledge is arrived at can be accepted as logical. Sense perceptions are received by Prakriti, which is unconscious; thus, only the mind and intellect, attributes created by Purusha, can generate knowledge. Prakriti perceives in darkness, and only with the help of the light provided by Purusha is knowledge possible. This is also contradictory, as Samkhya asserts that Prakriti and Purusha are separate and different entities. How do they interact to create Manas and Mahat? "A ghost in the machine," as Gilbert Ryle would assert.

The two levels of knowledge, as recognized by Samkhya, are pure sensation and perception. Pure sensation is undifferentiated and has an impact but no clarity, thus not resulting in knowledge or understanding. It is like the experience of a newborn baby, who is clearly aware of sounds, figures, and actions but is unable to discern them. Perception arises, similar to our acquisition of language by our ability to label experience into meaningful categories. Out of these arise our ideas of cause and effect, which lead to our ability to propound universal laws. From our perception, we conclude that we have the tools necessary for perception, even if we are not able to see how our eyes see or how it works. It prompts us to believe that it is our eyes or some other tool that we have that sees. From these, we make universal laws and common-sense rules to guide our daily lives.

Samkhya accepts transcendent knowledge and believes that the Vedas are examples of transcendental knowledge. It is the mind that creates knowledge out of sensations, creating patterns, formulating the idea of reasons, and postulating causes and effects. Like Hegel, they believe in the perfectibility of knowledge; they see each perception as limited and variable, and only through repeated and varied experiences does knowledge gain depth and inch towards truth. Since each person perceives differently, Samkhya accepts the existence of multiple standards of perception leading to different ideas of knowledge and truth.

Jnana and Salvation

Samkhya asserts that the self, as Purusha, is eternal and uncreated, pure consciousness, and therefore neither tarnished nor in need of salvation. The problem lies in its association with Prakriti, which acts out of ignorance. This ignorance is not about science and philosophy but about the true nature of the self (Purusha). All life is an endeavor to make the knowledge of oneself evident. All bondage to the needs and lusts of the body results from ignorance. Knowledge liberates the self from ego, mind, and intellect, leading it to its eternal and pure nature. However, Purusha cannot be improved or perfected because it is already perfect; what is required is a realization of its eternal perfection. The intellect, through Samkhya philosophy, can help individuals reach this realization. Such knowledge allows us to control our desires and master our passions. The self is always free, and salvation is not to be sought in the afterlife but through the realization of its perfection in this present life. Once a person masters his passions and controls his lust, he has already broken the bonds of karma.

The problem with Samkhya is that it leaves us confused about the nature of Purusha, and consequently, all that it asserts and propounds appears as a contradiction. What is the purpose of Purusha if it neither acts, guides, nor teaches? If Purusha is already perfect and eternal, why is it attached to a mortal body? What is the purpose of activating consciousness in dead matter? If the universe is eternal and self-existing, creation can have no purpose, and therefore, Purusha also has no purpose. It is merely an eternal aspect of the elements, and they change and evolve mechanically with no purpose, making all philosophy and morality a waste of time.

Yoga

Yoga, as a school of philosophy, attempts to address the very questions that Samkhya fails to answer. Yoga posits that, in addition to individual Purusha, there must be a supreme Purusha. This supreme Purusha is considered supreme and separate. However, yoga asserts that, despite being supreme, this ultimate Purusha is not the sole eternal reality. Other Purushas also exist, which are perfect and eternal. This assertion leads to a contradiction, as infinity is infinite and all its parts are infinite; there can be no other infinity. Another concession made by yoga is assuming that the eternal Purusha is God or Iswara. Yet Patanjali himself did not believe that yoga necessitates the acknowledgment of God. Yoga encounters yet another contradiction when claiming that the lesser Purushas are in a state of lower perfection and that their purpose is to attain higher levels of perfection. This is contradictory, as perfection is perfect and cannot be improved.

Yoga, as both a discipline and a philosophy, is believed to be pre-Vedic and perhaps part of the heritage passed down by the Harappan civilization. This belief is based on the discovery of a figure resembling Shiva, seated in the lotus position, surrounded by animals, with horn-like features resembling a trident behind the head. Upon seeing this figure, Stuart Piggott, an authority on Indian prehistory, remarked, "There can be no doubt that we have here the prototype of the greatest God, Shiva as Lord of Beasts and Prince of Yogis." While this may be true, authoritative knowledge of yoga as a philosophy has reached us primarily through the "Yoga Sutras," credited to Patanjali. Many treatises have followed, including Vyasa's "Yoga Bhasa," Bhojaraja's "Yoga Sutra Vritti," and Vijnanabhiksu's "Yoga Sara Samgraha." There is reason to believe that yoga existed as a philosophy, as even Samkhya philosophy refers to yoga as the discipline to achieve self-knowledge. Yoga was subsequently accepted into the Vedic canon as an orthodox system of inquiry. Yet Patanjali was clear that yoga does not require devotion to God and can serve both atheists and the God-fearing. The practice of yoga assumes much of the Samkhya philosophy to be true, using yoga to gain the knowledge that would liberate

Purusha from Prakriti. When the self can perceive the splendor of the universal self, it's all-pervading glory, the things of the world and its attachments fade away. This necessitates complete control of both sense organs and internal organs, along with total mastery of buddhi, ahamkara, and manas (intellect, ego, and mind). The goal of yoga is to control all bodily functions until they become practically nonexistent.

To attain such control, yoga teaches four paths or 'Padas.' They are: 'Samadhi Pada,' where a student is taught the aims and methods of yoga and the control of the internal organs. The second is 'Sadhanapada,' which is philosophical and, like the Buddhist way, analyzes the cause and nature of human suffering and explains how the taint of karma is transferred to the soul by attachments of the flesh. The third part is 'Vibhutipada,' which deals with psychology and explains the paranormal and what lies behind appearance. The fourth path is 'Kaivalyapada,' an attempt to explain how human beings can free themselves of Karma, realize their universal and eternal selves, become free, absolutely free, and attain moksha.

Yoga philosophy delves into the nitty-gritty of how this is to be achieved by what Patanjali calls 'Ashtanga-Yoga' or the eight-limbed yoga, a technique that involves eight steps. This includes the initial preparation, including mental exercises and the practice of moral virtues like cleanliness, truthfulness, non-violence, and detachment from greed and covetousness, until one achieves a state of general contentment. These practices are called the five 'Angas' of yoga: Yama, Niyama, Asana, Pranayama, and Pratyahara (detachment, internal purity, discipline, control of internal organs, and detachment from all senses). The first two detach the self from the desires of the flesh, while the next two desensitize the organs of the senses from the lusts of the mortal body. Once this is done, the soul is totally isolated from the body and no longer distracted by the world. The soul is then ready for true meditation. At this stage, it must rid itself of all beliefs, desires, emotions, and feelings. Only a pure soul can intuitively grasp eternal truths. It is reached through dharana, dhyana (preparedness and meditation), and samadhi, the final door that opens to deliverance or moksha.

The problem with yoga is that it makes the stages of concentration so difficult that when the student fails, he can always be termed a person who did not try hard enough. The stages start with 'Dharana,' where the student is asked to calm his mind so that the rapid flux of thought is gradually stilled. The mind then begins to concentrate less and less, till the mind is almost blank. In this stage, all unintentional thoughts have ceased, and meditation is possible. At the Pratyaya stage, the total capacity of the mind is concentrated on a single issue. This is a stage when great insights are obtained about life, purpose, meaning, and truth. It is also a stage when any subject can be mastered. The last stage, Samadhi, is possible only when all thoughts disappear, and one becomes conscious only of one's consciousness when the mind is detached from the body. In the Dhyana stage, while great insights are possible, they are always in the nature of subject and object; in the Samadhi stage, the duality between subject and object disappears, and the self is no longer egotistical but merges with the object to create absolute knowledge.

Patanjali claims that all matter is made up of 'rupa and swarupa,' the outward form and its essence. During the first two stages of meditation, only the 'rupa' of things is seen. Only in the final stage does one see the essence of all things. The stages cause a gradual withdrawal of the ego from perception until only the essence of things remains. The tainted glasses of ego, prejudice, beliefs, and emotions are removed, and we are able to see the universe as it really is. Unaffected by subjectivity, we see the real, the eternal, and the pure. Patanjali arranges these three stages into a system and calls it 'Samyama.' Based on these stages, he divides knowledge into Sabda, Artha, and Jnana. Sabda (sound) is based on the sensation of sound, while 'Artha' is its meaning. 'Jnana' is beyond subjective knowledge and results when the selfless soul intuitively sees truth in a flash of illumination. Yogic knowledge is, therefore, neither common sense nor scientific knowledge. It is not based on logic or inference but on direct illumination. It cannot be cross-checked or corrected and it cannot be modified by mere human knowledge or by the use of logic.

Patanjali thus makes it impossible to refute his philosophy. As Karl Popper said, any theory can be taken as true only if it can be falsified. By such criteria, Patanjali's yoga is mere mysticism. Further, yoga seems to have no Earthly purpose because its aim is to attain a state of selflessness, a state of non-existence. Even Advaita only attempts to make us aware of the unity of all creation, whereas yoga proposes a state of nothingness. What is the aim of yoga, which eliminates even consciousness? While Plato was skeptical about the human capacity to see beyond forms to the essential, Kant had clearly said that we are limited to the world of phenomena and that 'Nouma' is beyond human perception. Yoga says no man can perceive the essence of things except in a state of total oneness with creation, but like the dead that go to heaven, no one can come back to tell us what they have seen. Yoga makes the ultimate experience beyond logic and intellect and something to be grasped intuitively, thus precluding all possibility of explanation or analysis. The yogic experience is not only unreal, but it is also beyond logical explanation. Being an experience devoid of self, it is also devoid of expressibility.

Vaisesika (The Philosophy of the Concrete)

The Vaisesika philosophy starts as a common-sense philosophy with no high metaphysics or epistemology, accepting the world as we perceive it. It merely enumerates all perceptions with proper names and descriptions. It is very similar to British Empiricism. However, along the way, it gets complicated, mixing the concrete with the abstract. It is an atomistic theory that claims all matter is made up of irreducible atoms. However, unlike the Greek atomists, Vaisesika does not see atoms as having only one form but as dependent on the element to which they belong. Like other Indian philosophies, it sees the universe as composed of basic elements—water, air, Earth, and fire—each with different atoms. The human soul is also made up of these elements. Atoms are inert, justifying a God who is the first mover of atoms and creation. Vaisesika thus makes God supreme. While Kanada, the father of Vaisesika philosophy, was ambivalent about God and claimed that God exists merely by the authority of the Vedas, his later disciples accepted God as part of their canon. The anomaly that if atoms are eternal, God could not have created them is explained by saying that they are co-existent and eternal. God is not so much a creator as a designer who manifests the universe and can also destroy it. God gives intelligence to a dumb system. They are also scientific in postulating a universe that is created and destroyed in cosmic cycles of time.

The plurality of the universe is made up of five material elements and four non-material elements, making a total of nine different kinds of atoms. The problem is that the non-substantial elements, like space, time, soul, and mind, cannot be perceived; they can only be inferred and are thus almost unknowable. By treating all as atoms, the insubstantial, imagined, and abstract are treated on par with matter that can be seen, touched, and analyzed. To explain the presence of things that are not material, they postulate a separate category not made of matter, like space, time, soul, and mind. Space and time have to be real because humans can indicate direction, distance, and pinpoint a position in space, and time separates the past from the present and the future.

While the soul, as Atman, is all-pervading, consciousness is not an essential attribute of the soul; it only appears to be. The mind (manas) is made of a separate type of atom, but unlike matter, it cannot be combined with other creations. These atoms cannot be perceived; they are only inferred. Vaisesika disagrees with modern biologists who see the mind as merely biological and claim that it is a separate substance through which alone consciousness arises and through which alone our senses make meaningful perception. Like all atoms, they are eternal and can neither be created nor destroyed. All composite matter can be destroyed, reducing them to their basic atoms, while the atoms of the soul are unbreakable and remain distinct.

Vaisesika also assigns 'Guna' (quality) to all substances, such as color, taste, smell, touch, sound, and magnitude, which Aristotle would call primary qualities. They also include pleasure, pain, desire, and even moral goodness and moral badness, as is inherent in matter. Vaisesika thus mixes objective qualities with subjective and infused qualities. They claim that all substances are capable of motion or action and assert that while Guna is passive, karma creates the dynamism that makes it capable of movement. Since karma is an acquired quality, the soul and mind are also mobile, even if they cannot be perceived but are only inferred through thoughts, agitation, or harmony. An important quality is sameness and difference, which leads to the particular and the generic. Vaisesika asserts that there is nothing real about a generic term; it is only a word, not a particular thing. They warn conceptualists against the tendency to proceed from the particular to extrapolate nonexistent universal truths. Vaisesika insists on dividing all generalizations into different levels, like horses, animals, living things, etc., in ascending order, insisting that it is the particular that is clear and true and that all generalizations are merely words.

The concept of 'Samajaya' is unique to Vaisesika, where a distinction is made between things that are joined together with different atoms and those that are made with the same atoms. The different atoms go back to their original state, whereas similar atoms remain the same even when some atoms are taken away;

only size varies. Thus, water in a pot can be separated, but water remains water. 'Samyoga' is temporary while 'Samajaya' is eternal. This theory precludes permanent change through chemical reactions, the ascending order of elements in the periodic table, or the uniqueness of crystal formation that Schrodinger so eloquently speaks of. It also fails to appreciate that fire, water, air, and Earth are mere chemical combinations, not elements.

Vaisesika differentiates existence as previous non-existence, subsequent non-existence, absolute non-existence, and mutual non-existence. It sees total non-existence as absurd. Even to negate, they assert, assumes the presence of something; nothing can be negated from nothing. Mutual exclusion merely means that a flower is not a table; that particularization negates generality. Flowers and tables are things, but when they are differentiated, they mutually annihilate and change from a mere combination of atoms to something particular. Vaisesika epistemology is common-sensical and accepts knowledge as the result of sense perception modulated by the mind that separates it into categories, creating discernible knowledge. They accept inference as a sound source of knowledge. They claim that the qualities of an object are its own and not induced by the subject. While pretending to be a common-sense philosophy, it accepts the Samkhya idea of moksha and claims that men are bound by their ignorance. That it is Prakriti that enslaves the soul with human desires and that, once the soul realizes its true nature, the soul can liberate itself. However, their atomistic theory postulates that when the soul is liberated, it disintegrates into its atoms, becoming Nirguna, matter without qualities. This makes the human soul useless and meaningless. Thus, what starts as common-sense materialism ends, through logical progression, as another abstract philosophy.

Nyaya

Nyaya is perhaps one of the oldest systems of philosophy, yet it is perhaps the only Indian system that has a rigorous method and a proper system of logic. However, to modern readers, Nyaya is a muddled attempt at logical thinking. It suffers from many internal contradictions and far too many unsupported assumptions. Despite these apparent failings, Nyaya is an Indian philosophy that is amenable to formulation into a respectable course of study. Gautama is reckoned as the founder of this school. His treatise on philosophy is called 'Nyaya-sutras.' Since then, many others have been added to the literature of Nyaya. Its distinctive features came from Gangensa in 1200 A.D., who wrote 'Tattva Chintamani.' Consequently, Gangesa is considered the father of modern Nyaya philosophy.

Nyaya is a down-to-Earth philosophy that can best be described as 'realistic pragmatism.' It accepts atomistic pluralism, saying that there are many kinds of atoms. They claim that the existence of the universe can be explained logically without recourse to God or a creator. Nyaya, like all sciences, loves to make itself appear respectable by breaking up everything into many categories and classes. Thus, it is a philosophy of 'Padartha,' meaningful categories. It divides knowledge into sixteen categories, which include:

- Pramana — the way to know things objectively.
- Prameya — things that can be known objectively.
- Samsaya — doubt.
- Prayojana — purpose.
- Distanta — undisputed facts.
- Siddhanta— a theory.
- Avayava — a system of logic.
- Tarka — a system of discussion.

- Vadu — argument.

They also include the frivolous, like Jalpa, which represents arguing for argument's sake, and Vitanda — arguments that merely establish one's cleverness. Like modern linguists, they then divide statements into facts, premises, and assumptions. An attempt to digress, divert, and mislead is called Chala, and 'Jatiis' is the use of incorrect analogies. Their system to analyze an argument, which is called 'Nigrahasthana,' is like a template that allows one to see where one went wrong.

Nyaya epistemology says that knowledge is created by the contact between self and non-self, subject and object, perhaps through truism. All knowledge is only phenomenological. Knowledge is the light in a lamp; it not only allows us to see objects but also to see where the light is and the level of light that it emits. It illuminates not only objects but also itself. Like Aristotle, Nyaya philosophers see truth as a correspondence to reality. Since objects are real, truth is the extent to which we see things as they really are. However, unlike Aristotle, they are not particularly scientific but claim that knowledge of the real can be gained by four methods: perception, inference, comparison, and testimony. According to them, invalid reasoning is the result of poor memory, doubt, and hypothetical reasoning. Doubt is the result of an error in perception, where one sees things that don't exist. Hypothetical reasoning is wasteful because it can only confirm what we already know and cannot give us new information.

Like Kant, Nyaya accepts that perception is a two-stage process: raw sensation and its subsequent interaction with the mind, which produces understanding, classification, and recognition. They also accept that these two stages are so instantaneous that they appear to be inseparable. Thus, perception, 'Vaisesika,' is made up of 'Nirvikalpa' and 'Savikalpa' (indeterminate and determinate). They then divide perception into 'Laukika' and 'Maukika.' ordinary and extraordinary perceptions, and into internal and external perceptions. We perceive external things with our sense organs but can understand and feel them only through our mind. Nyaya goes back to Plato's concept of form and essence by saying that, to recognize an object, we have first to create an idea of the essential nature of such objects, say horses or tables, so that we recognize them despite differences in color and size and so on. What they mean by extraordinary perception is the complex association of smell, sound, and taste, as when the poet Emily Dickinson says,

"There is certain slant of light
In the winter afternoons,
That oppresses with the weight
Of Cathedral-tunes."

Where light oppresses and tunes have weight. How this is relevant to objective knowledge is not clear. The last form of perception, according to Nyaya, is intuitive knowledge, as, for example, a yoga meditator has insight as though in a flash, without mind nor reasoning.

By inference, Nyaya means the entire system of logical thought. To aid in proper reasoning, like Aristotle, they came up with a form of a syllogism. However, unlike Western logic, where the attempt is to make a foolproof mathematical model with symbols and then transfer them into propositions, Nyaya is more concerned with the actual correctness of each premise that goes into the syllogism. Their attempt is to weed out false premises, unsupported premises, partial truths, and conditional truths. They were thus closer to 20th-century linguistic philosophers than to mainstream Western philosophy. Nyaya also sees comparison and differentiation as ways to gain knowledge. It also accepts testimony as valid knowledge. The only distinction they make is to identify the accepted sources of authority. In matters of science, the scientist is accepted as an authority and so on. They also make a distinction between what can be perceived and what cannot. Thus, there is human (laukika) knowledge and divine (vaidika) knowledge. Where human knowledge cannot reach, they accept the authority of the Vedas, divine revelation.

The Nyaya metaphysics accepts almost every possible source of information as a valid source of knowledge. Thus, the senses, the body, the mind, and the intellect are all sources of knowledge.

Additionally, pleasure, pain, and suffering are also sources of knowledge. It acknowledges rebirth, essence, existence and non-existence, and even quality and motion as capable of imparting knowledge. Nyaya also accepts the Vaisesika division of all atoms into the four elements: fire, water, Earth, and air. All non-physical attributes like feeling, willingness, emotions, and purpose are seen as aspects of the self. They see the self as distinct from the body and accept the body/soul duality. The self is not 'manas,' yet it is not pure consciousness either, as in its human form, it is attached to the body and limited by its mortal prison. Nyaya complicates it further by saying that consciousness is not the attribute of self (soul/atma), which in its absolute nature is beyond mere consciousness, but in humans, it is only an attribute of self because it is imprisoned. The self cannot be perceived; it can only be inferred.

Gautama, the founder of Nyaya, may have implied a belief in God, but he did not elaborate. In time, there was a 'Nyaya-Vaisesika' school that incorporated a belief in God as part of its philosophy. They saw God in a sort of middle way, not as a creator but as a designer and the one who directs and sustains creation. Atoms, they assert, are the building blocks, uncreated and eternal; God only makes immobile atoms move and thus causes creation. God also gives direction and purpose to creation, thus coming up against the Samkhya argument that an all-powerful, eternal, and perfect God could have no reason to create.

Nyaya accepts Karma as the unseen (adrusta) power that determines all that happens; it is the unseen cause of all actions. It is unconscious and dumb; it acts as per the eternal laws of cause and effect. Since karma is unconscious, it is God who guides its operation. The aim of Nyaya is to liberate the human soul. Yet such liberation is possible only through the cessation of all desire and hope. This, they claim, can be achieved in stages, starting with the reading of scriptures (Vedas) and then understanding them, then moving deeper into real knowledge through yogic meditation. However, Nyaya is clear that liberation is only possible through actual experience and transformation, not by second-hand knowledge, and that such insight is given only by the grace of God.

The Concerns of Indian Philosophy

The main concern of Indian philosophy was the problem of perception. They readily accepted that human perception can never enter into the reality of things. This realization led to questioning reality itself. In desperation, faced with the possibility that nothing exists, as everything could be only in the mind, they came up with the concept of Maya. Yet, Maya makes human life nothing more than a joke, a phantom show where the sun is the lantern. The escape was to accept a creator who, like some master puppeteer, allows us to see or perform a magic show to keep us engaged. The universe is thus merely the manifestation of God. The immediate question that arose was: how can the infinite and the eternal manifest themselves in the transitory and the finite?

As in the case of Western philosophy, faced with the impossibility of certain knowledge, Indian philosophy also decided that logical rigor is all that can be accepted from philosophy. The role of philosophy is to define and ensure the correct and proper stating of valid propositions, followed by logical progression that leads to acceptable conclusions. Unlike Kant, they were honest enough not to accept the possibility of categorical imperatives. Instead, in desperation, they returned to the Vedas as divine revelation, which is an even worse form of slavery. The second reaction was to accept all perceptions as valid. Like the existentialists, with true knowledge being impossible, human perception became the main focus of philosophy. As was inevitable, this led to subjectivity, a lack of authority, and finally to relativism.

Sati and the Shakta Shrines

In the meantime, Daksha's daughter marries Shiva, but Daksha insults Shiva, for which Sati burns herself in the fire of her own tapas. On seeing Sati burn, Shiva takes her body onto his shoulders. As Shiva wanders about in his anger, Vishnu quickly shoots arrows at his body, resulting in different parts of her body falling in different places, which then became holy shrines. The saying then arose that whoever worships Mother Goddess at these locations will find nothing unattainable. As primeval man was the original sacrifice, a symbolic woman is sacrificed, and the places where her body falls become 'Pithas.' Thus began the glorification of Goddesses. 'Shumba,' who falls in love with Chandrika, is told that he has to defeat her in battle to marry her. He then dies at her hands, creating a concept of devotion based on a combination of hatred and love. In a famous story, the Asura Mahisha becomes very powerful through tapas and gets a boon that he can die only at the hands of a woman, the idea being that he was already so powerful that being killed by a woman was impossible. It is said that the gods then created Durga to entice Mahisha and kill him. Mahisha lusts for Durga, who is portrayed as extraordinarily beautiful. However, Durga subdues him by dancing naked before him, exhausting all his lust. Many see in this the symbolic sexual victory of women as Durga places her feet on the defenseless Mahisha. This is also the image of Kali dancing on the corpse of Shiva with a drawn sword as she stretches her tongue to lick the blood of the dead corpses at her feet. Remember, the dog that licks the sacrifice is unclean, and the licking tongue of dogs is associated with the yoni, which is insatiable. These stories were written to show that women were equal to men and that the gods had to deal with goddesses as equals. The imagery clearly suggests a sexual battle in which women are the victors.

Tantra

Tantra was also supposed to have developed from certain esoteric aspects of Buddhism that first surfaced in North India, perhaps Kashmir, and became a powerful religious cult by the 10th century, with its strongest hold in Central and Southern India. It was a religion of power and the attainment of power in this world, not in the next. Tantra promises release, akin to moksha in this world, through the magical powers of Siddhis and through a life of pleasure (bhogas). It preaches that one does not have to do good deeds and wait for the next birth to enjoy the benefits of good karma and that happiness is in our own hands. Tantra came in different forms for different needs. Those who sought knowledge had Bhukti-Mukti for those who sought release from life, Moksa-Mukti for those who sought enjoyment, and Bhoga-Mukti for those who sought enjoyment. It also had its Bhakti version, the Vedanta version, and the ritual version. To make it acceptable to the orthodox, it was divided into the left-hand version, which transgressed all orthodox rules and caste restrictions and included blood rituals, death, and sex, and the right-hand version, where the practices were orthodox, even if the religion was radical.

While the orthodoxy later denied Shiva's involvement in Tantra, the Tantrics, through their Puranas, claimed Shiva as their teacher and patron. Shiva is shown teaching the doctrine to save sinners in Kali Yug, where all forms of sin multiply. They claim that it was created by sages who were denied the Vedas but were saved by Shiva. The Vaishnava Tantrics claim that when Vishnu saw great sages being cursed and kept out of the pale of the Vedas, he sent Shiva to help Kapala, Pashupata, and Varma write new (left-hand) text. The orthodox replied that the sages were evil and the gods merely sided with them to delude the gullible and that Shiva would not possibly teach heresies. Others claim that heresy was necessary as a way to bridge the gap between the orthodox and total unbelievers and that Shiva knew the practices of certain people who could not do without meat and wine and therefore invented Tantra to bring them into the fold. Since Shudras and others were not permitted the Vedic rituals and mantras, Shiva was using a step-by-step method to raise them to the understanding of true religion. He uses the natural things of human life—food, sex, and wine—to teach the meaning of higher things. The orthodox were finally brought around by the realization that, in Kali Yug, only a religion that recognizes human evil can provide a suitable remedy.

Tantra is based on the acceptance of the five needs of man: madya (wine), mamsa (meat), mudra (parched grain like barley, wheat, and rice), and maithuna (sex). Instead of the fire and the purifying products of the cow, Tantra emphasizes the five jewels: semen, urine, feces, blood, and phlegm. Tantra was a direct challenge to orthodox beliefs, and human sexuality was worshiped, with the power of the yoni emphasized. However, to make it acceptable to the orthodox, continuous efforts were made to sublimate these crude practices into symbolic practices with an intellectual philosophy. Abhinavagupta, a sage from Kashmir (975–1025), treated all practices as meditative exercises, where the expansion of the mind was the goal. Many began to see tantric practices as symbolic and shunned the physical practices while accepting the philosophy; others lived an orthodox life and practiced tantric rituals in secret. A long chain of teachers even claimed that Tantra was merely a myth, never practiced, only imagined. As in the case of idols for people who cannot imagine the true greatness of God, who exists everywhere, Tantra merely provides physicality for those who cannot understand the abstract nature of religious rituals. Even the sexual embrace is nothing but the physical manifestation of a sacrifice, which, properly done, raises human consciousness. These apologies for the crudity of Tantric practices did not stop the practice of Tantra in all its gruesome detail from continuing in many parts of the country, along with witchcraft and human sacrifice.

Tantra's major contribution was that it allowed women full participation in religion and legitimized human sexuality. Yet, the greatest social purpose of Tantra was to bring the pariah and chandalas into the fold. Thus, Tantra from the beginning involved low-castes, and the mode of worship and behavior was a copy of low-caste behavior, legitimizing not only their caste but also their ways. In fact, the Tantra argues that there are only two castes: male and female. Tantra rituals also claim that Shiva was a pariah, while others claim that he loves to frolic with pariah women. In fact, in the Chola bronzes, Shiva is depicted with bells on his feet, bells that pariahs had to wear on their feet to warn caste Hindus of their presence. Shiva as Bhairava is also always depicted accompanied by a dog, a pariah among animals. The eating of meat, which Tantra allowed, was slowly accepted with certain prescribed penance. While many forms of meat eating were permitted, eating while in dire need and unknowingly was readily forgiven, and meat placed inside a tantric circle was automatically purified.

The power of the Tantra cult is best seen in the number of temples dedicated to Shiva in his Tantra manifestation. The Kailasanatha temple in Ellora, in fact, shows in stone what the Tantrics did in their rituals. The great temples at Khajuraho show the sexual aspects of Tantra. At Konark, while the main sculpture is of Lord Narasimha and Durga with the Sun God, the smaller sculptures portray the erotic. Many Yogini temples were also built during the period from the 8th to the 12th centuries. It is also claimed that many of these temples were actually built by Chandalas. The strange irony is that when the Muslims invaded the country, they destroyed many temples but left these tantric and erotic temples untouched. Tantra is thus literally preserved in stone, while the religion associated with it has gone underground—a religion of black magic, witches, and evil. Along with it came the legitimacy of the Shudra and the Chandalas and the return of the suppression of women and the prohibition of meat eating.

Tantra as Philosophy and Religion

One is in a serious quandary when trying to place 'Tantra' in its proper context. It is difficult to call it a philosophy, despite many attempts to give a rationale for its practices. It cannot be called a religion as it refuses to accept the transcendental. Yet, it is so widely practiced that not acknowledging it as part of religion and our special understanding of the world would be to deny a pervasive tradition. It has some connection to the Atharva Veda, even if the Veda is a much more polished doctrine and set of rituals. However, its acceptance of mantra as both white and black magic accommodates at least the rationale of Tantric practices. While no specific justification of Tantra is accommodated in the sacred canons, its claim to be part of the Shiva Puranas and the Shakti Puranas automatically gains credence, at least among Shiva and Shakti worshippers. It also seems part of a much older tradition that forced Aryan purity to be tested while reasserting the claims of local religion. That it finally faded away into an abhorred but prevalent practice shows both good sense and the power of Orthodoxy.

Looking at Tantra today, it appears to be an attempt to repudiate the sanctity of the Vedas and all accepted theories of Vedic religion and its practices. Thus, 'Mahanirvana Tantra' says, "Those who believe that the Lord lives in images made of clay, stone, metal, wood, or so forth and wear themselves out with asceticism without true knowledge—they never find release. Unless they have the knowledge of ultimate reality—how can they be cured?" Instead, Tantra claims that they could transform men into gods, thus invalidating the Brahmanical world of the Vedas and Shastras. It would appear to be a pre-Aryan philosophy, and the image of a man in a yogic posture surrounded by animals, found in the Mohenjo-daro excavations, seems to suggest that a form of Tantra was already in existence. It is also a strangely Goddess-oriented religion, with Shiva merely as the patron, which again suggests a linkage to the early worship of Mother Goddesses in Samaria and other Mesopotamian regions. Tantra thus has a very ancient claim, being mentioned in Shiva Puranas and repeated in later Puranas of 'Shakta' and the Goddess Shakti. While Tantric practices became an important alternative to orthodox religion in the early years of the first century A.D., it is normally accepted that a sage called Lakulisha (the Lord of the Club) founded a sect called 'Pashupatas,' who worshiped Shiva as the God of animals. By 381 B.C., they claim that they already had eleven generations of teachers who followed the teachings of Lakulisha. Even the 'Mahabharata' refers to the cult. The Aryan religion tried to condemn them, and the

'Kurma Purana' is a major tirade against the group. However, by the time the 'Linga Purana' was written, their doctrines had become orthodox beliefs.

The Tantrics initially scandalized the Aryan orthodoxy as they lived on cremation grounds, and their rituals included offerings of blood, meat, alcohol, and sexual fluids. They even practiced ritual intercourse, where caste was no bar. Their major treatise, 'Pashupata Sutra,' advises followers to go around like chandalas, behaving in the most uncouth manner so that people will ill-treat them. This was based on a theory that Lukalisha propagated reverse karma. The concept claimed that when people ill-treat them for their outward behavior, when actually they were very good people, they get the good karma from those who ill-treat them, while all their bad karma is transferred to those who ill-treat them. As a group, the Pashupatas carried a skull-headed staff and a begging bowl made of a skull. They matted their hair and had long beards, covered with the ash of the dead. This was, in fact, the attire prescribed in the Manusmriti for Brahmin killing. They were thus claiming to be Brahmin killers, of whom Shiva was their prime example. Their use of skulls made people call them Kapalikas (skull bearers). The story goes that one day when Brahma met Shiva, his fifth head made some noise, at which Shiva cut it off, but the head got stuck on Shiva's hand and would not fall off. Thus, Shiva went around with a skull on his hand. This story echoes the old Vedic myth that Rudra cut off Prajapathi's head because he committed incest with his daughter, Usha (Dawn). Another story says that one day Vishnu and Brahma were arguing as to who was the greatest when a flame-like Linga appeared in the shape of a three-eyed person adorned with snakes. Brahma immediately claimed that it was his son. Whereupon, Rudra got angry and created Bhairava, the terrible one, and commanded him to punish Brahma. Bhairava immediately beheads Brahma, and Shiva tells Bhairava to carry the skull and wander the Earth with a maiden whom he creates called Brahmacide (Brahma-hattya), begging for alms and teaching people the way to remove the sin of killing Brahmins. They clearly hoped to do away with Brahmanism and the call to fight the new religion of the Aryans without any fear of consequences. Initially,

Bhairava appears as a replacement for Shiva, and in some stories that repeat the story of Daksha's sacrifice, Bhairava is the person who wrecks the sacrifice. Thus, Lord Shiva commits a crime, expressly to create a cure for Brahmicide. He could have easily gotten rid of the skull, but he delays it so that humans are taught a new doctrine of salvation. He lets Brahma be attached to him to finally get rid of Brahmanism. This was also a counter-attack on Indra for becoming Vishnu. Shiva thus becomes a personal God who loves mankind and bears their sins, but to orthodox Brahmanism, Shiva is a heretic, and Daksha curses him and his followers to be pariahs beyond the pale of the Vedas. Nandi (Shiva's servant) retorts that Daksha and his followers are hypocrites, false Brahmins who would be reborn in Kali Yug as Shudras. Shiva is denied a part of the sacrifice of Daksha because he is a pariah. Shiva's reply is to attack their Brahmanism and call their faith hypocrisy.

A Modern Apology for Indian Philosophy

Indian philosophy blossomed in the Axial age, creating both secular philosophies and the deep thinking that went into the Upanishads. It was also the basis of the two major religions that came out of India: Buddhism and Jainism. There can be no doubt about the depth and spread of Indian philosophy. What, however, is a fact is that the questioning phase of the Axial age gave way to a dogmatic orthodoxy that negated the very spirit of nascent Indian philosophy. It was perhaps its very greatness that was its undoing, for subsequent thinkers found nothing more to add, and the orthodoxy could say that all that can be known has already been written down in the Vedas and the Upanishads. This put an end to speculation and, later, to the persecution of heresy. Even worse was the subsequent repudiation of many of the original ideas and the acceptance of crude practices, the justification of Tantra, the proliferation of gods, idol worship, and the belittling of Jnana.

In perhaps his best book, 'Being Different,' Rajiv Malhotra makes a plea for the recognition of the importance of Indian philosophical perception. Well-written and persuasive, he makes the point that Indian thought starts with radically different premises from those of Western philosophy. He sees Western philosophy as saturated with the assumptions that go with a belief in the Judeo-Christian religious system and tradition of thought. His main point is that all Judeo-Christian and even Islamic beliefs depend on history to justify their religions. They are also what he calls 'religions of revelation,' where God is supposed to have spoken through his prophets and his Son in the case of Christianity. Consequently, such religions depend on the veracity of historical events, like the virgin birth of Jesus, the death and resurrection of Christ, and whether Muhammad was divinely inspired. The tragedy for such religions is that when the historical facts they depend on are proved to be false or merely removed from an argument, they have no other basis to stand. Such religions also claim that the universe was created by God and therefore has a purpose, a beginning, and an end, and that God is the custodian of history. Consequently, man is to be judged, and on the final day, some will be saved while others will be sent to eternal hell.

Against such religions, rooted in history, Indian philosophy and belief systems are rooted in eternal concepts like the eternal soul and God as the amalgamation of the whole universe, not merely a figure in history. Based on such universal premises, Indian thought does not need history or even the external world to justify its belief systems. Instead, it demands a withdrawal inward, into the deepest recesses of the human mind, to the still center, away from the whirl, turmoil, and flux of human life, where the 'atma,' the human soul, merges with the 'Brahman,' the universal principle. From the outside flux and distractions of the world, it suggests an entry into the deepest reaches of human consciousness to discover the deepest secrets of life. It then allows man to enter the infinite ocean of deep knowledge to search for all the knowledge that he may need. While this opens to man an ocean of knowledge, unlimited by any belief system, the Judeo-Christian tradition starts with man in the Garden of Eden and his disobedience to God that sends him down to Earth, tainted forever with the 'mark of Cain,' and the original sin, unfit for heaven or even happiness in mortal life. Only the ransom paid by Christ on the cross would provide salvation, leading to a religion of strict moral policing and ritual demands, for there will be judgment on the last day. Indian thought, on the contrary, sees man not only as free but part of the very substance of God, and all Indian religious thinking is geared to facilitating the reunion of man with God, the Atma with Brahman. The second major point he makes is that Hindu religious thought is more scientific and sees the world and the universe more in the way modern science has finally been forced to see it. The ancient Indians saw the universe as uncreated and eternal, expanding and contracting in cycles of time. A world of evolved creatures, more in keeping with Darwin's theory of evolution. Instead of the certainty of the Judeo-Christian tradition, Hinduism accepted a certain level of uncertainty at the heart of the universe; thus, even in the 'Creation Hymn' in the Rig Veda, the actual act of creation is left unsaid except as a form of fable and the ultimate creator as unknown and perhaps unknowable. Ancient Indian thinking saw the universe only as 'Maya,' merely as the reflection of the divine and a manifestation of the Divine. It accepts the possibility that all we perceive is an 'illusion.' To make it understandable, they saw 'Shiva' as the representation of unmanifested consciousness, while his counterpart, 'Shakti,' is the manifestation of consciousness. The universe is merely a reflection of Shiva. It sees all matter as one and part of the divine, where each human being is part of the divine. Consequently, says Rajiv Malhotra, the Christian demand to love one's neighbor as oneself is, in Hindu thought, a self-evident need, for all men are of the same substance and part of the universal 'Brahman.' Not only is one's neighbor a part of us, he is also part of the divine. While this sounds great, the truth is that the same Indian mind created the 'Caste System,' which treated others not only as inferior but even as untouchable. One's brother and neighbor had no place in the evolving religion, which soon took roots in Indian thought until it became its defining accept.

As we review the foundations of Indian consciousness, there has never been a doubt about the depth and acute perceptions that are at the root of all Indian thinking. What again and again astounds us is the level to which it has descended and the fact that it did not have the vitality to withstand the corrupting influence of compromise and accommodation, which in the end eroded all its core values. In fact, we are astounded at the scientific nature of Indian perception, which modern science is today proving to be true. The acceptance of uncertainty at the heart of the universe and, therefore, the need to accept multiple explanations are also matters that place Indian thinking far ahead of its time. There is no doubt that Indian thinking was more scientific and that it was more prepared to accept multiple explanations for the origin of the universe and all phenomena. It is also true that at the heart of Indian philosophy, especially in 'Yoga,' there is the belief that ultimate reality resides in the unfettered stillness at the center of consciousness. Buddha, more than anyone else, stresses the inner recesses of consciousness as the seat of ultimate 'Nirvana.' However, he was also acute enough to see that at the heart of consciousness is 'sunyata' or total void, or utter emptiness. That is the problem. While it may be the greatness of Indian thinking to have been able to look inside and not depend on history or prophetic revelation to base its beliefs, the truth is that at the center of consciousness is only a void, an emptiness, 'sunyata.' Yet, that insight is extremely important for science, as it may soon prove that we are merely 'brains in a vat' and that the universe is merely a very sophisticated hologram, a manifestation created for us by some superior civilization. That would also be an affirmation of the acuteness of the perception of the ancient Indians. Consequently, like the idea of delving deeper and deeper into the human mind to seek truth, the idea of the universe as a manifestation of the divine does not help humans to live more meaningful lives. Human beings gain knowledge of the world only from their perception of the world; it is only by putting such knowledge to the test of mental systems like logic and causality and in the creation of patterns that knowledge is created. What then is the use of merely delving into the deepest recesses of the mind, where all one will find is the void, 'sunyata'? While meditation and the techniques of yoga may allow us access to the inner mind, no knowledge resides there. What we may gain is a reprieve from the hustle and bustle of real life and an inner peace that temporarily, at least, may ease the pain and tension of everyday life. The knowledge that the universe may be just a manifestation, while truly troubling, does not help guide us through life. In human life, the troubles of the flesh, like hunger, and of the mind, like psychological trauma, are all too real, and in fact, that is all that defines human life. Thus, to merely wish them away on the assumption that life is either unreal or a fantasy is no solution at all.

We can unequivocally agree that Indian thinking, in the beginning, was clearly superior to the Western tradition; it was more scientific, but that was also its weakness. As philosophers have told us time and again, mathematics is very logical, but it cannot tell us how to lead our lives, nor does it help us create values. Thus, while Indian thought was more scientific, it was also more arid as a guide to life; it was less capable of helping those seeking meaning in life and a purpose to channel their energies. While our meditation techniques allow us to access the inner mind, what would it tell us? Nothing but 'sunyata.' What use is the inner consciousness for telling us how to live our lives? It may release us temporarily from our human bonds and from the clasp of the ego and it may even give us a sense of elation at the perception of infinite emptiness, but it cannot guide our lives. In fact, while the capacity to enter into the inner recesses of the mind is one of the great feats of Indian thought, it can give us no knowledge. Knowledge comes from the senses, and it is Western science that realized that it is all that we have and so went on to refine perception with the aid of scientific tools and the scientific method, cutting out as much subjectivity as humanly possible, to arrive at knowledge.

The impossibility of the original Indian theological and philosophical position became apparent the moment the other-worldly philosophers had to deal with the real-life issues of hunger, heat, sickness, and death. While Buddha escaped into the inner world of 'sunyata,' most people were left with no comfort and demanded more. Thus, even the great Sankaracharya, whom the orthodox Brahmins called a Buddhist apostate, accepted the worship of 'ista devas' and felt that five was a fair number. Even before that, the Epics had brought down the gods to the level of humans, with their desires and needs, and they also seemed to justify human ideas of right and wrong. This led to a flood of worship, as temples and idols became the representations of heaven and the divine. This also led to the Bhakti cult and the concept of a personal God to be loved, who, in turn, protected and comforted his devotees. Consequently, the idea of the universe as uncreated and the idea of a creator who is likely to remain forever unknown, that all that we experience may be an illusion, was all right as mere philosophy, but as a creed, as a religion, as a source of solace and comfort, it was like the winter chill, only bearable for those who were properly prepared to endure its rigors. Consequently, the greatness of ancient Indian thought may be good as an intellectual argument claiming superior austerity and scientific clarity, but the truth is that the Indians themselves rejected such a philosophy and begged for something more personal, something to cling to in times of trouble and sorrow. The fact is that the Indians have lapped up the Judeo-Christian ideas of salvation, grace, and a personal God and merely claim that such ideas are also Indian.

Similarly, Rajiv Malhotra argues that the Indian concept of 'Karma' was a much deeper and more accurate system of rewards and punishments than the Christian and Islamic idea of heaven and hell and the possibility of eternal damnation. While Christians see man as steeped in sin from Adam and blighted by the 'original sin.' Indian thought saw man as an evolving being where many lives are necessary to refine a human being before he is able to see his own divinity. It is a system that adds the good and bad deeds in a sort of ledger for each human being, and every person has to pay for all their bad deeds and will receive just rewards for all their good deeds. No one is condemned on some sort of average of good or bad; even the best, like Yudhistra, had to go through hell for his little lie. There is no doubt that the Indian concept of Karma may be the most intuitive answer to man's desperate search for meaning. It is also a most just system. Yet, the most glaring problem about the idea is that humans do not remember their past, whereas the entire Karma theory is a system where one's quality of life, one's position in life, and even success and failure are determined by the actions in some past lives. Thus, a person does not know why they are punished nor why they seem born to win. Yet, this also is at the heart of the Karma theory, that action cannot be in the hope of gain, even in Karma. Thus, the central teaching of the Gita is that man ceases to accumulate karma the moment he ceases to profit from his action and when his actions are not prompted by any motive whatsoever. However, this also means that man has no motive to act in accordance with any principle, for all seems merely random. This is what creates what Westerners have seen as the fatalistic attitude of Indian thought. Later compromises, where there are gods and even personal gods, made Karma a negotiable idea, where faith, good deeds, and submission to God could wash out all bad Karma. This not only diluted the concept but also undermined its inexorable logic. Yet, like all good things about Ancient thinking, Indians themselves could not accept them as they were too logical for human life. Consequently, talking about concepts like Karma only shows how far we have descended from the lofty heights to which the Ancients had taken us in flights of logic. It is also a fact that Krishna's advice to Arjun to act without desire is inhuman, for it is desire that makes us human; consequently, there is an impossibility at the heart of the Karma theory that most Indians miss, the idea that man would never be free from the taint of karma, and thus we will be born and reborn, even as the universe renews itself in cycles of time.

CHAPTER 8

THE CASTE SYSTEM

Prof. Romilla Thapar confidently asserts that the Varna system, a rigid caste system, did not just descend from heaven, as the Purustha hymn in the Rig Veda and its repetition in Manusmriti would suggest. It was a slow process—an evolution that slowly hardened into the rigid caste system. The Aryans, as a distinct race or as speakers of a common language, were cattle herders and cattle breeders as they journeyed through India. Even as they entered India, they met with a settled society of city dwellers who had perfected working in bronze and in the making of pottery. There was also a vast population of unsettled people on the fringes and in the hills and forests. There were agriculturalists, hunters and gatherers, and subsistence farmers. They quickly took up agriculture and improved their capacity for crafts. Yet the Vedic people, used to herding, saw land mainly as pastures and fought to gain cattle and to protect their grazing lands. In such a situation, the warrior was a man who defended these rights and brought more of the same. Thus, a separate warrior class. However, there was an even more intelligent group that exploited the intrinsic religiosity in all humans with their hymns and special songs of worship and claimed that it was their songs that ensured victory in war and the protection of their lands. Thus rose the priestly class, which grew in strength and wealth from the share of the loot and from the gifts of grateful warriors and chiefs. They also benefited from the mandatory sacrifices they devised, which included milk, ghee, and different animals and soon included grains as they became farmers.

The unique feature of the caste system was the ability of the higher castes to claim lineage from the founding fathers. As the Vedic people entered India, they maintained their clan identity, which was said to be ten in number, made up of Puru, Druhya, Anu, Turvasa, Yadu, and some others. All Aryas have since claimed to descend from one of these clans. As they settled in inhabited areas, they created gramas, and when they settled in forest clearings, they called them aryanas. The kings came later; at first, there were the warrior leaders and the leaders of settlements. The leaders of Janas were called Rajans, yet a great deal of egalitarianism still continued to exist; the inevitable stratification came later. In time, there was a need to indicate who was older and more entitled to respect. The Rajans riding in chariots who protected the entire Jana and won land and cattle were clearly to be differentiated from the mere Vis, the people. The priests, to whom Dana and Daksina referred, the bards who wrote hymns and sang songs and the ritual experts who conducted the sacrifices and Yagnas had also to be distinguished. Thus evolved the three-layered society of Kshatriya, Brahmans, and Vaishya (the people). However, as the clans gathered more and more land, it became difficult to farm the land without help. This required the Arya to induct from the local population workers and helpers who were called Dasas and Shudras. They were needed only in the economic sphere and so were excluded from all social and religious activity.

A grouping of clans was called a Janapada, which was later called a Rastra. It is interesting to note that the word raja is from the root 'ra,' which means to give. The original role of the raja was to give and to sustain. Similarly, the root word for rastra is 'raj,' which means to shine; thus, the rashtrapati is one who nourishes and makes shine. Yet, from the beginning, there was always the feeling that they only looted and merely ate the produce of the Vis. In a strange chicken-and-egg-like story, the rajas became divine through the sacrifices done on their behalf, but they soon claimed they were divinely ordained. The raja was initially Indra but soon became a name for the landowner and finally for the elected rulers, who in time claimed hereditary status.

In many ways, the Vis was the Grahasta who created wealth for the upper castes. Thus, the religious offerings of bagha, bali, and sulka were the first forms of taxation. The Brahmin grew richer, more so as a result of gifts and grants from kings and other rich persons. At this stage, the Dasa and Shudra make an appearance as agricultural workers and servants. While later history treats them as a separate caste, they may have originally been separate tribes, and some of them, like the Balbutha and the Taruksa, were recorded to have given liberally to yagnas and sacrifices. Some of them were so strong that Indra's help had to be sought to subdue them. Yet, it was as a result of this conflict that the idea of 'us and them' evolved, between the Arya and the Mleccha, as well as between the Devas and Asuras and the gods to be worshiped. The fact that Aryanization of the South was a slow process with much fewer resources is seen by the fact that there are no intermediate castes—the twice-born Kshatriya and Vysha—in South India. It is also testimony to their later conversion and the hurried manner in which it was done.

Let us now go back to lineage, which started with clan ancestors and accommodated invading clans like the Sakayas and the Licchavis. With this came the idea of Gothra and the prohibition of marrying within the sagothara. This adoption of the Gothra idea is a little anomalous, as the Aryas also claimed to descend from the Vamshas, like Suryavamsha and Chandravamsha. However, what is clear is that the leaders quickly became the elite as they were instrumental in increasing their land holdings. The inclusion of the Shudra resulted in the distinction between the dvija (twice-born) and others. It was then necessary to create an interlocking system of rights and responsibilities, which soon solidified into a rigid caste system.

The Story of the Shudra

India, by and large, is a nation of Shudras, with more than 50% of Indians falling under the definition of Shudras. The upper castes, consisting of Brahmins, Kshatriyas, and Vaishyas, make up less than 30% of the population, while the Dalits and tribals account for the rest. From the Nairs of Kerala to the Yadavs of Bihar, from the Reddys of Andhra to the Gowdas of Karnataka, from the Thevars of Tamil Nadu to the Bhumihars, all are Shudras. Therefore, to understand Indians, it is more important to comprehend the evolution of Shudra consciousness than that of the Brahmin, which is what a study of Vedic literature and the practices of Hinduism as a religion would tell us.

The servitude, inferiority complex, and sense of victimhood that most Indians display originate from the indignities the Shudra, the largest component of Indian society, had to suffer. The history of the Shudra in India is a study of contempt, brutalities, and inhuman subjugation, which, while a little short of slavery, was in many ways more demeaning and dehumanizing. The fact that Shudra has survived to tell his tale and still claims to be a loyal Indian is nothing short of a miracle. The irony is that this was possible only because of the extension of hospitality to a caste even lower than them, the untouchables. It is the tragedy of Indian society that it was only by feeling superior to the untouchables that the Shudra was able to accept his own victimhood and, in the end, revel in his place in the caste system as an enforcer of caste rules, especially against the untouchables.

While historians have debated the origins of Aryan society in India, the Vedas make it clear that the people of the Vedas were called Aryans. They may have been a tribal people or just a people who spoke the Aryan language. The Vedas also use the term 'Arya' to refer to a noble race, as though of aristocrats. While there is still debate as to who they were and how and why they came to India, the Vedas make clear that they had to fight to enter and settle in what was ancient India. Numerous references from the beginnings of prayers to Indra for help to defeat the local people entrenched in forts, with their gold and their wealth, suggest this. It is also clear that the Aryans were a race of horsemen who knew how to build and use chariots, as these are repeatedly mentioned in the Vedas. They were cattle herders, and there are many references to cattle. India had an established race of people who dominated the land with their forts, lived in cities, and were also agriculturalists. They must have had a language of their own, but the actual language used by them is yet to be ascertained. The early Vedas make the Aryan people appear homogeneous, involved in various trades from cattle breeding, chariot making, and ironworking to rudimentary agriculture. There was no distinct class structure, and like the early Romans, in war, they all acted as soldiers, cooperating to create a rather egalitarian society with a simple democracy. As these homogenous people met and fought with the existing people of India, they had to differentiate themselves from their enemies. The name they gave to the natives they encountered was 'Dasyus.' Many references and prayers of thanks to Indra for destroying the Dasyus characterize them as unbelievers, 'A-Indra,' people without Indra. In many hymns, the Dasyus are described as dark, noseless, and bull-lipped, suggesting a Negroid race.

There are also references to 'Dasas.' who are often lumped together with 'Dasyus' as the enemies of the Aryas. Yet, the 'Dasas' appear to be slightly different from the Dasyus. The references suggest that the Dasas were not only different but may, in fact, have had some connection with the Aryans. The priests Atharvan and Varuna boast, "No Dasa, by his greatness, may violate the law that I will establish," clearly suggesting that the Dasa was part of the Aryan fold. References are also made that suggest that the Dasas were frequently treated as allies. There are indications that, even if they did not speak the same language, they understood each other. It is therefore possible that the Dasa, like the Aryans, were a migratory tribe that entered India perhaps some centuries before the Aryans, from the same area in Central Asia. While early Vedic literature makes it appear that the Aryans were a homogenous tribe who faced their enemies together, references to the Varna system are found in the 'Purusha Sukta' (hymn of man) in the Rig Veda. It is universally agreed that this hymn in the 10th book is a clear later interpolation, added as late as 800 B.C. The hymn claims that the Brahmin came from the mouth of Purusha, the Kshatriya from his arms, the Vaishya from his thighs, and the Shudra from his feet. However, till very late in Vedic history, there were only three Varnas, who had different roles but were considered equal in Aryan society. Everyone did their allotted work, and there was no clear ruling class or warrior caste like the Kshatriya. They all managed their fields and worked with their hands. There are mentions of slaves, a common feature of the ancient world, as conquered people were killed or reduced to slaves. However, there are more references to female slaves who did general housework, and Vedic literature does not give the impression that the early Aryans were major slave-owning people. Theirs was largely an egalitarian society. It is important to realize that the first mention of the 'Shudra' as a separate Varna is in the interpolation in the creation hymn. However, even before the appearance of any reference to the fourth Varna, there are references that suggest that the Shudras were a pre-existing tribe that lived in the region between Drsadvati and the Saraswati Rivers. Records from Alexander's advance party refer to a tribe called 'Sadrai,' who lived in modern-day Sind. In many later Vedic verses, there are references to the Shudras as enemies, like the references to the Dasyus and Dasas. By the time the Mahabharata was written, there were repeated mentions of Abhiras and Shudras. In fact, the Epics speak of Shudra as a kula. They are also referred to as existing prior to the Aryans and are mentioned along with Sakas, Tukharas, Pahlavas, Romakas, Chinas, and Hunas. It is interesting that they are not mentioned as indigenous people of India like the Dravidas and Pulindas. Their association with the Abhiras, who actually spoke an Aryan dialect, Abhiri, suggests that the Shudra may also have been of the same stock and merely earlier settlers in India, perhaps of an earlier wave of the same stock of people. The fact that they may be of the same stock is also attested to by certain references to the degradation of the Shudras as a result of their ungodly behavior, thus losing their place in the sacrificial rites. There is also a tradition that claims that the Shudras were originally Kshatriyas who were demoted because of the prolonged war between the Brahmins and Kshatriyas. This is based on a solitary instance in the Mahabharata that refers to 'Paijavana' as a Shudra king. While there are many references to the Kshatriya-Brahmin conflict, with heroes like Parasurama and Viswamitra, there is no indication that this conflict involved the loss of twice-born status. It was more of a dispute to regulate the monopoly of knowledge that the Brahmins claimed. In fact, Janaka, a Kshatriya, was a noted Upanishad scholar. The conflict also resulted in Viswamitra becoming a priest. The Sramana philosophies of Mahavira and Buddha were also part of this continuing conflict, with both Buddha and Mahavira supporting the Kshatriya claim to equal status in the knowledge hierarchy. The Shudra was also used as soldiers and in other military functions throughout Vedic history, leading to a claim of being Kshatriyas. It is also possible that the degradation of the Shudra was the result of their being on the wrong side of the conflict between the Brahmin and the Kshatriya.

The word 'Shudra' is normally said to be a combination of two root words, 'Suk' (grief) and 'dru' (to rush). While this does not denote any people, Buddha says that people who are capable of dreadful and mean conduct are called 'sudda.' This may be the origin of the derogatory connotation the word was to have and the demeaning status the Shudra came to represent. However, from the fact that the Dasa, a slave, and the Dasyus, probably a tribe, were all later to become Shudras, it is clear that the Shudra was not a homogenous group but the result of social churning caused by the influx of cultures and the consequent need for social integration. It was the result of the political and social domination of a group whose consolidation and domination took a considerable period of time. It was the result of the evolution of society to accommodate the various tribes, sects, and occupations into a single integrated society. While the origin of the Shudra is shrouded in mystery, the condition and treatment of the Shudra are well documented and leave no room for doubt.

The History of the Shudras

As has been seen, there is little mention of Shudras in the early

Vedas; it is only in the later Vedic literature that we see a division of society into four Varnas, with the status of Shudras placed at the bottom of the table. From all historical evidence, these references date to the early Buddhist era, some even after that, and as late as about 200 B.C.

By 1000 B.C., the Aryans, who entered India as hunters and herders of cattle, had settled down in villages and towns, developing a society with a certain basic division of labor. Thus, the initial social divisions. However, Aryan society had no system of land ownership; they owned only cattle. Thus, land was treated as common property, and those who wanted to cultivate the land had to do so themselves. The idea of Shudras as tillers of the soil was thus a later development. In the 'Mahabharata' and other early literature, there is even a reference to Prince Janaka plowing. With social stability, there was a need for artisans, especially chariot makers, metalworkers, carpenters, and so on, and in time, some of them became experts in their trade. Thus began the stratification of society. The deployment of slave labor to till the soil was seen only in the last stages of Vedic literature. The reduction of Shudras to low status was the result of a long process of consolidation by the upper classes. Initially, the arts and crafts, especially that of chariot making, were treated with great respect, and the ceremonial sacrifice was often called 'Silpa' or craft. In the early days of stratification, leaders of crafts were accepted as 'ratnas' (jewels) along with other important persons, and the Shudra was invited to the game of dice with the other Varnas. The 'Sabha Parvam' states that Shudras were invited to Yudhistra's coronation. Even 'Yajus' contain a prayer to confer brilliance on the worshipers, including the Shudra.

In time, small but significant prohibitions were applied to the Shudra. At first, he was barred from the Soma ceremony and the Vajrapeya (drink of strength) sacrifice. In the 'Taittiriya Brahmana,' he is excluded from the full-moon ceremonies. In later Vedic literature, he is excluded from the game of dice. In a slow process, the Shudra was soon excluded from all public life. The social status of the Shudra was still tolerable, and there was still no prohibition against the higher Varnas marrying Shudra women. King Bali was the son of Dirghatamas and a servant maid. Vyasa was the son of a fisherwoman, Vasishta, and a prostitute, and there are many other examples of such intermingling. There was, however, a tendency to treat Shudra women as objects of pleasure. The inevitable decline of their status was to follow. Yet the Shudra was clearly above the Chandala, who was already an object of contempt. It was the painting of the Shudra as ungodly and of bad moral fiber that led to his fall. After that, it was only a matter of time before he became an object of contempt.

In the early Vedic period, even though the Shudra was permitted only the householder's life, he was often allowed an education. Despite the prescription of a period of brahmachari for all priests, literacy was not widespread; thus, the Shudra's freedom to study would have been rarely used. In fact, the Taittiriya Brahmana, which says that the Rig Veda is meant for the Vaisya, the Yajur Veda for the Kshatriya, and the Sama Veda for the Brahmin, meant that the Atharva Deda was for the Shudra. Yet, by the later Vedic period, the exclusion of the Shudra from all formal education had begun. First, the Shudra was excluded from sacrifices and rituals on the plea that he was irreligious and then he was excluded from education by claiming that Upanayana is a must before any education can start, a Vedic ritual from which the Shudra was excluded.

The 'Rathaskara' and 'Taksaka' (chariot makers and metalworkers) were clearly part of Aryan society, and there are many early references to Shudras in many sacrifices and rituals. The exclusion came with the identification of Shudras as worshippers of alien gods. The Shudra is then called 'Pusan' because their God was Pusan or Pasupathy, a much-respected God of the Aryans, later degraded to the status of a God of the shepherds and cattle herders. The other gods were the Aswins, who were associated with milking and plowing. The only God other than Indra that the Vedas recognized was Rudra, who was also, in time, reduced to the God of the Shudras, as Rudra as Pasupathi was also a pre-Aryan God. Worshippers of such gods were called un-Aryan and un-Brahmin, and later Vedic literature talks of their being crushed. Shudras were then excluded from all sacrifices. Starting with the building of the fire altar (agnicayana) and the removal of fire, they were debarred from the Soma sacrifice and the agnihotra (sacrifice to fire), and finally, even the milk milked by a Shudra was barred for use in rituals. In later parts of Vedic literature, strict prohibitions about bodily contact with the Shudra were also enforced. An insurmountable barrier was raised between the Aryans and those who were soon to become the servant class. With this, all manner of craftsmen—the chariot maker, the ironworker, the carpenter, and all artisans—were excluded from the fold of the twice-born Aryan. The irony is that the justification for such exclusion was their purported worship of alien gods like Shiva, who later became the most powerful of gods, while his most loyal and ardent devotees remained outside the fold of orthodox religion.

The Degradation of the Shudras

It was with the writing of the Dharmashastras, around 300–600 B.C., that the degradation of the Shudra began. The early laws accepted social segregation based on Varna and saw the Shudra as the result of the mixing of Varnas, especially between higher Varnas and tribal women. By the time of the rise of the Mauryan Empire, society had become urbanized, requiring it to be divided into classes with specific functions and a hierarchy. However, we have little evidence of how the stratification of society actually took place, as the Brahmanical sources are clearly biased against the Shudras.

One factor was the growth of trade and commerce, which Kautilya wanted to control. The land was now extensively cultivated, leading to the creation of a surplus economy. This led to the institution of a standing army and a professional military class. With the overriding importance attached to rituals, a professional class of priests became a necessity. Cultivation required regular laborers, apart from slaves and serfs attached to the land; thus, the Shudra who tilled the land was degraded to the level of a serf, till they were regarded as fit only to serve the higher castes. Gone were the days when a prince like Janaka or Duryodhana could plough the land. The Dharmashastras, Manusmrithis, and all later Vedic literature relegate Shudras to a serving class, and all artisans are also degraded to the Shudra caste. Gautama, thus, gives Shudras the right to live by arts and crafts and mechanical arts. Shudra artisans continued to remain an honorable caste, as long as they were employed by kings and nobles for chariot making, the making of all forms of weapons, and as carpenters, builders, tailors, and garland makers. They were also weavers, smiths, and potters. These professions gave them a higher status and a freedom that the agricultural laborer did not have.

With social stratification, the institution of slavery also began to change. While in Vedic times, only women were normally treated as slaves, slaves were soon used as bonded labor in the fields, and this slowly spread to other professions, especially personal service like barbers, shoemakers, etc. While slaves were basically enemies captured in a war, a permanent class began to emerge. This was the final degradation of the Shudra. Beginning as agricultural labor, they soon became serfs, and their condition became that of a slave, into which class they slowly merged. By the time of the Smrithis, the Shudra had lost his place in the Aryan fold and had become a servant of the higher Varnas. With this came social discrimination and degradation. Gautama commands that the Shudra can only use garments, shoes, umbrellas, and other personal items that have been discarded by his master. Similarly, the Shudra was to be fed only with the leftovers from the master's table. They may not have starved, but all their dignity as productive human beings was taken away. The Dharmashastras even compel the Shudra to certain commitments, like working one day every month for the king and being a servant on call.

Apastamba explicitly says that no Shudra can be regarded as an Arya. The Buddhist text satirizes this attitude by telling stories about how, among the Kambojas and Havnas, the Aryas were treated as the dasas and dasis. The old ratna status, open to Shudras, is now withheld even from the Vaisyas, who were no longer appointed as counselors to the king. From Manu down to all the Dharmashastras, justice became relative to the Varna of the criminal, and the lower the caste, the higher the punishment. In a society obsessed with caste purity, the law against adultery was the most draconian and was ruthlessly applied to the Shudra. Further, the Shudra also became a class that could be beaten, tortured, and even killed by the higher castes with impurity. For the higher Varnas, the punishment was normally only a fine or a penance; the body of the Shudra alone ceased to be inviolable.

Social mixing became a crime, and food touched by a Shudra was unclean. Marriages between the higher Varnas and Shudras became impossible. The earlier provision that allowed three wives to a Brahmin, of whom one could be a Shudra, was now denied. Vasishta, however, says a black Shudra woman may, however, be a concubine and used for pleasure, thus reducing the Shudra woman to a mere object. Education, which was basically about Vedic literature, was prohibited in the Shudra. In the Dharmashastras, Vasishta declares that the Shudra is neither worthy of learning the law nor of being given advice on the provisions of the law. Not only was Shudra punished, but he did not know why. The Shudra was thus reduced to a non-entity and an object.

Shudras in Arthashastra

The Arthashastra gives us a quite clear picture of the Shudras under the Mauryan Empire. Even though the institutions described in Arthashastra appear more advanced than what is described by Megasthenes, the Asoka pillars and other inscriptions confirm the state of sophistication described by Kautilya. The state was all-powerful, and it was expanding into virgin territory. The Arthashastra uses the Dharmashastra's terminology to categorize the Shudra Varna as servants, allowed only to reside on the outer fringes of the towns unless they worked directly for the king. They were artisans, servants, and laborers in the erection of forts, in clearing new areas, in rehabilitation works, and so on. As agricultural laborers, they were treated like slaves or serfs. In Mauryan times, agricultural labor included sharecroppers, who were entitled to half of the produce and bonded laborers, who got only what their master gave. As artisans, they worked as weavers, miners, potters, and in the old profession of chariot making, the making of armor and weapons, mats, working with skins, shipbuilding, and all work that had to be done with the hands. While there was an attempt to form guilds, Kautilya clearly saw them as troublemakers and laid down many restrictions on such associations. They were very poorly paid and subjected to strict discipline to ensure servility, proper output, and quality.

Kautilya, however, debarred Shudras from all posts in the State. They were only used as spies in an elaborate espionage network, along with prostitutes and innkeepers. They were predominantly domestic servants to the higher castes, especially in towns and cities along with the Dasa and Dasi of the slave economy. They were weeded out of the army, where earlier they were quite prominent and could enter it only as servants of the Soldiers. Yet, Kautilya regarded an army of Shudras better than one composed of Brahmins. Shudras were still used in times of emergency while the legal position of Shudras continued to decline. Kautilya prohibited them from appearing as witnesses and could never testify against their masters. Kautilya also codified the social customs and prejudices and of the day, accepted justice as relative and damned the Shudra forever. Thus, while the Shudra had his hands cut off if he struck a person of a higher caste, the same crime by a higher caste merited only a much lesser punishment. A Shudra who committed adultery with a Brahmin woman was to be burnt alive, while for a similar crime the higher castes were more mildly treated. Kautilya maintains a strict distinction between Varnas, and only the Arya was a freeman. Even slaves could be freed if they were Aryans, thus an Aryan forced into slavery was 'aryavatam' (still an Aryan), while others were 'adasa' (slaves). Consequent on the size of the slave population, Kautilya made legal provisions for them while the Shudra alone had no protection under the law.

The Ashokan Edicts give the impression of equality before the law and impartiality in punishments; they, however, appear to have been merely idealistic proclamations, which society and custom denied the Shudra. The condition of the Shudra must have been quite bad, for Panini equates Shudras to Chandalas, who were not even part of the Varna system. Kautilya even vents his anger on the traveling monks and atheistic Ajivikas by calling them Shudras. To Kautilya, caste was sacrosanct, and he was determined to enforce it. In fact, Kautilya was so Varna-conscious that he says that a Brahmin forced by a king to teach the sacrificial rites to undeserving persons has the right to revolt against the king and mobilize even anatyas (aliens) to overthrow the king.

Manu and the Shudras

With the growth of empires, the Shudra also prospered, especially in crafts and artifacts. It was becoming clear to the Vaisya caste that Shudra was a better farmer. The growth of iron, bronze, and other metalworking resulted in the expansion of an export trade that made the Shudra rich and powerful. Additionally, a new industry in glass manufacturing was added. The growth of cities and the rise of powerful dynasties expanded the role of the Shudra manifold, leading to a belief among the upper castes that they had grown too big for their boots.

The Manusmrithis seem to be an attempt at putting an uppity caste in its place. By the time the Manusmrithis were actually written down, sometime between 200 and 400 A.D., there had been a great intermingling of Varnas and many incursions by invading clans of Parthians, Sakas, Humas, and the Yu Tchi. The victory of these tribes meant that alien dynasties, not acceptable to the Brahmanas or Kautilya, were in power. Since it was necessary to accommodate some of them, the backlash was to make the general rules of Varna and caste even stricter. Thus, Manu appears sometimes contradictory, reactionary in many aspects, and liberal in others.

Manu starts by bemoaning the crisis of purity created by the lax morals of the Kali age. He advocates the maintenance of caste purity as a matter of public policy, and kings were exhorted to punish defaulters. Brahmanism was thus born with Manu. Since society was forced to accept that the Kshatriya caste was open to every invading chieftain and his kin, it became even more important to maintain the high and pure status of the Brahmin.

Manu displays a new fanaticism about the Brahmin, his status, and his privileges. While he allows the manufacture of genealogy for foreign invaders, he insists that the Shudra is to serve the higher Varnas, especially the Brahmin.

In his attempt to reduce the economic clout of the Shudras, he legislates that Shudras cannot be custodians of money. The Brahmin is made the only person trustworthy enough to keep deposits of gold and other wealth. While other castes were allowed to partake in business, banking, and money lending, the Shudra was not allowed in such business and was also charged more interest than the Brahmin. Manu categorically legislated that the Shudra must not accumulate wealth. He even allowed a Brahmin to seize the goods of his Shudra slave. While modern apologists would claim that this was only applicable to slaves, the principle made a shudra's wealth always suspect and amenable to confiscation. To further demean him, Manu repeats Gautama's instructions that a Shudra should be given only leftover food, wear only old clothes, and sleep on discarded beds. Suspecting the Shudra of being capable of insubordination, Manu gives detailed rules for the hours of work, quality, and discipline that a Shudra must ensure.

Manu's anger against the influx of foreign invaders makes him say that no Aryans should live in a country ruled by a Shudra. He also makes it a rule that a Kshatriya Prince must consult a Brahmin about Vedic rites, and those who don't are automatically reduced to the status of a Shudra. The priesthood thus became an essential element in civil government, establishing Brahmin dominance in all functions. In the rules regarding witnesses, different warnings are to be given to different Varnas, and the Shudra is normally not allowed to be a witness. Manu, however, permits Shudras, slaves, women, children, and untouchables to give testimony in case no other witness is available. The king has to give priority based on Varna, and punishments are also relative to Varna. Yet Manu protects all women, and even a Shudra woman molested by a higher caste has legal rights. Manu, however, treats all Buddhists as Shudras to demean the religion. He also makes a distinction between the Shudra and the slave, who, despite his status, is entitled to own property. In fact, Manu treats a slave as a member of the family and advises the head of the family not to take personally the presumptions of a slave in his own house. The Shudra, however, is to be shown no such consideration.

Varna is all-important to Manu. Thus, he prescribes what each can wear, the names they can have, and the food they can eat. The food and vessels used by Shudra became polluting, and no one should eat the leftovers of a Shudra. The marriage prohibitions are repeated, yet Manu accepts the old custom of three wives for a Brahmin, but the Shudra woman cannot be the first wife. He is ambiguous about the status of mixed castes, whether to treat them as untouchables or as Shudras. The ban on Shudra education continues. In fact, anyone who teaches a shudra is forced to perform the sradha (purification) ceremony. He even insists that no one should give advice to a Shudra, and he cannot even witness a Vedic rite. Yet he allows the Shudra certain religious rights, if not rites. The Shudras were permitted to worship deities without mantras and were praised for behaving and accepting the habits of the higher castes but without the right to read the Vedas. This resulted in the aping of the Brahmin by the lower castes, from eating habits to family routines, that continues to this day.

These concessions were made by Manu to counter the growing influence of the Bhakti movement and Vaishnavism in general, where Vishnu worship promised salvation even to Shudras, women, and untouchables. It was also to counter the clout of foreign invaders who accepted Vaishnavism to legitimize their rule. The Puranas label all foreign invaders as Shudras and blame them for all the problems of Kali Yug, asserting that order was turned upside down when a king forced a Brahmin to give up his seat to a Shudra. Consequently, the succeeding age saw a hardening of attitudes; the 'Matsya Purana' prophecies that dharma would become lax and varnasrama (caste discipline) was destroyed. The 'Vajupurana' and 'Brahmananda Purana' see the end when Shudras act as Brahmins. Thus, in the 5th century A.D., a Pallava ruler, Simhavana, kills Buddhists, Jains, and Shudras and boasts that he is ever ready to save dharma from the sins of the Kali age.

The horror of foreign invaders killing Brahmins and seizing their wives is always kept before their eyes to instill the importance of Varna. To ensure that the Shudras do not grow too big, Manu even advises the king to ensure that Aryans are allowed to outnumber Shudras when new land is settled and to provide protection only to the Aryans.

Manu was dealing with what he saw as a social crisis: the rise of the Shudra, consequent on urbanization, increased trade, and agriculture, along with the rise of Sramana sects that opened an avenue for the Shudra to escape the caste system. There were clearly social and religious tensions that were just waiting to erupt, and Manu was trying his best to put a lid on all possible ways, religious, social, and through the might of the state. Caste becomes part of the religious equation, and Manu adds to it by claiming that the Brahmin is made up of Satva and Tejas, the Kshatriya of Rajas, and the Shudra and others of dark matter (tamas). Thus, the age was also the nadir of Shudra persecution. Yet, the Shudra grew in numbers as urban life and trade made the work of the artisan both economically and socially important. The religious ferment, leading to Bhakti and Vaishnavism, allowed the Shudra for the first time to participate in religion. Even though education remained closed, the new religious awakening led inevitably to some opening of education to the Shudra. The invasion of foreign tribes also allowed many Shudras to escape along with the new rulers into a nebulous Varna, which time could legitimize.

Shudra in the Age of the Puranas

By the time of the Puranas, between about 400 A.D. and 600 A.D., two divergent pulls stretched society in different directions. On the one hand, despite all efforts, society was diversifying rapidly, consequent to the intermingling of castes; on the other, a reactionary militancy rose to counter the seeming chaos in society. With kings unable to enforce Varna discipline or caste segregation, it was left to the priests, the pillars of orthodoxy, to frighten the people into submission with prophecies of doom that would inevitably overtake society if a return to orthodoxy was not ensured.

The Smrithis of Vishnu, Yagnavalka, Narada, Brahaspati, and Katyayana were all creations of the later Gupta period. The interpolations in the Vedas and the Epics justifying the new caste system were also the work of this era. These works reaffirm and reiterate the ideas of Manu and the Dharmashastras. The prohibitions of Manu and Kautilya were reinforced, and the Shudra, despite their increase in numbers and access to wealth, were still not allowed to own land. They continued to be servants but managed to become wage earners and artisans with their own guilds. The agricultural workers, tenants, and sharecroppers also became wage earners, as the law now required them to be paid wages, not merely food and shelter.

Yet the 'Santi Purana' repeats that the Shudra was created to be a servant of the upper castes. There is a reduction in slavery, but the conditions of the slave remained the same. The money market had substantially increased, and ownership of land descended from kings, through grants and gifts, to a land-owning class with hereditary rights, creating a landed gentry. Taxes and tax collection were introduced, with the Shudras also being taxed. The Shudra, being predominantly tenants and field workers, Hwan Tsang says that Shudras were of the agricultural class. The Shudra were slowly seen as peasants.

The Shudra dominance in art, crafts, metalwork, and steel continued to give them some sense of importance. The growth of guilds added to their power and importance, yet they continued to be demeaned with injunctions about the type of house they could stay in, the clothes they could wear, and that they could feed only on leftovers. They had no entry into the civil service, the judiciary, or the army, and their services were called upon only in emergencies. They could not act as witnesses, and the different warnings in court continued along with the relative punishments for different castes. The courts were still to give preference to cases of upper castes, and Shudras were subject to corporal punishment. A slow acceptance of equality existed before the law was evolving, especially in the case of murder. Yet, the 'Santhi Puranas' often treat the Shudra as enemies of the king. The Puranas also warn of the possibility of Shudras and Vaisyas joining together to get themselves Brahmin wives, while the 'Vaisatha Dharmashastras' depict the Shudra as hostile, boastful, violent, short-tempered, untruthful, extremely greedy, ungrateful, lazy, and impure, posing a danger to the king. The Shudras, who were actors, innkeepers, gamblers, and gaming housekeepers, were especially noted as dangerous. The clear antagonism of the ruling class left the Shudra feeling suffocated, with little prospects of upward mobility.

The 'Natya Sastra' advises that when speaking to Shudras, it should always be in a harsh tone and always in the nature of commands, addressed contemptuously. Different types of food are now prescribed; the Brahmin was prohibited from eating roots, onions, garlic, mushrooms, leeks, and village pig, while 'Brahaspathi Smriti' says laborers can eat the meat of the cow. Consequently, despite the Brahminical taboo on cow eating, people broke the taboo. The custom is related to the story of Manu's son, Vaisavatha, who ate the flesh of his guru's cow, upon which the sage Cyavana cursed him to become a Shudra. Beef eating has since been associated with Shudras, adding to their degradation.

Marriage prohibitions continued while the ceremonies for each caste varied. While a marriage among the high castes was solemnized by the holding of hands and the chanting of mantras, a Shudra marriage was only legalized through sexual intercourse. In fact, the Shudra woman was considered fit only as a sexual partner, not as a wife. At this stage, color distinctions are introduced: white for Brahmins, red for Kshatriyas, yellow for Vyasas, and black for Shudras. Black was his color, black his deeds, and black his character. Their position only became relatively better when a new class of people was recognized by the social order of the day, a caste that was so low that they were untouchables.

The Untouchables Accounted

There are early references to Chandalas, a word used to describe the aboriginal tribes. Even in Pali texts, the Chandalas were depicted as untouchables, where even contact with the air of a Chandalas' body was regarded as polluting. These tribes were hunters and fowlers and were initially used on cremation grounds to clean and remove dead bodies. They then became scavengers of all kinds. The recognition of the Chandalas as part of Aryan society was their doom, for they lost all freedom and dignity and were forced into a life of dirt, misery, and squalor. After being totally degraded, they were also morally condemned, equating them to persons of no virtue, persons without God, faith, or morals. Lack of faith, the worship of alien gods, and the idea of cleanliness were then used to condemn and demean them. While the degradation was historical, the reason for the concept of untouchability is not clear, as no literature justifies such a practice. A justification may have been found in the concept of ritual purity.

There was always a concept of Mellachas, of people beyond the pale of society, like tribals, hunters, and pagans, whom Aryan society did not permit into their midst. The irony is that it was by recognizing them as a separate social group that the Shudra began to be accepted into Aryan society. Vaishnavism must have had a great deal to do with the change, as well as the spread of the Sramana sects. While the trend of mixed marriages continued, harsh punishments were imposed, treating such Shudras on par with untouchables. Amara enumerates ten types of mixed marriages, while 'Anusasana Purana' enumerates fifteen. The Orthodox writers were so obsessed with these violations that they enumerated as many as eighty-seven ways in which a person could lose his caste. Their progeny was all treated as 'a-vaidya'—those who had departed from Aryan Dharma. Mostly, it was a child born of a Shudra father and a Vaishya mother. Such degraded Shudras were clubbed along with Dravidas, Kalingas, Pulindas, Sakas, Yavanas, and Kambojas. At this stage, the law books make a clear distinction between Shudras and untouchables, who are called 'antyavasayin' or 'antyaja.' Thus, as the ultimate punishment, a Shudra who lies down with a Chandala woman is reduced to her state. While the old contempt for the Shudra was difficult to overcome, the expansion of Aryan society forced it to deal with more and more people who were totally alien to their culture. The 'antyaja' group was so removed that they were not even allowed to live inside any village or town and had to live in their own cluster outside the main village. They were looked down upon as dog breeders and meat eaters, with a hint that they even ate dogs. Their religion was considered pagan and hideous. Thus, they were said to worship gods called Yaksas (Jakhas), whose temples were built on the bones of human skulls. They were characterized as impure, dishonest, passionate, greedy, and easily prone to anger. This resulted in the stricter enforcement of untouchability, and the 'Markandeya Purana' has a purification rite even for those who only look at an 'antyaja.' Yet, it also forced them to placate the Shudra to increase the numbers in their fold.

With the recognition of something worse than the Shudra, the Shudra found his place in society. In sharp contrast to Manu, the 'Santi Purana' now says all four Varnas must hear the Veda. Yet, in practice, the ban on Shudras hearing the Vedas continued even into the nineteenth century. However, the Shudra was allowed to hear the epics, including the Bhagavad-Gita, which advises the Shudra, instead of trying to understand the Vedas, to listen to the Mahabharata, which was permitted even for women. The 'Bhavishya Purana,' however, makes clear that they may listen to the Mahabharata but should not study it. This relaxation was how the religion called Hinduism was spread. The idea of a common religion was created through storytelling troupes that went from village to village, acting and retelling the story of the Epics, thus giving all Indians a common heritage and a semblance of an identity. This relaxation had far-reaching consequences, as it led surreptitiously to the spread of education among the Shudra and the subsequent rise of the Bhakti cult. Yet, in 'Mreehatika,' a judge reprimands Sakkara by saying, "A low-caste fellow, you are talking of the sense of the Vedas, yet your tongue has not fallen off." The relaxation also made local languages the medium for the spread of knowledge. The orthodox then tried to link the use of language to caste, and it was Magadhi that was reserved for the use of lower castes.

While religious rites were still restricted, the 'Santi Purana' requested that the three castes allow the Shudra the use of 'svadakara,' 'namaskara,' and 'mantra' and advocated that they help them to perform 'pakayajinas.' With this relaxation, the rites of penance were now available to the Shudra, a clear admission of his inclusion. In fact, in the Brihaspati Purana, the Shudra even allows the ear-boring and tonsure ceremonies. These were clearly inducements for the Shudra to become an upholder of Hindu beliefs and customs. However, his obligations were also codified. 'Vaijavapa Grhyasutra' even permitted certain rites without the accompanying mantras, including rites related to childbirth, birth ceremonies, parting of hair, naming, cereal eating, and tonsure ceremonies, making each new Shudra irrevocably linked to Hindu society. These also led to the concept of a pure shudra and an impure Shudra. Shudra marriages were still not recognized, and the ascetic life was also denied to the Shudra, as the Ramayana condemns the Shudra ascetic, Shambuka.

The inclusion of the Shudra resulted in greater prohibitions on the 'outcastes.' Outcastes were enumerated, and the social strictures were codified. The greater acceptance of the Shudra went hand in hand with the ostracization of the untouchables. As the Shudra became a member of Varna society, he began looking down on the untouchable, thus becoming a stakeholder in the propagation and maintenance of the caste society. The 13th and 17th centuries gave the Shudra the maximum access to religious rites, and their rights and privileges were also codified. Yet the Sraddha rites were still denied, despite the fact that priests happily accepted charity and gifts from the Shudra, an emerging wealthy class. While it was Buddhism that first accepted the Shudra, Vaishnavism forced open the doors to them. The Shudra could now seek salvation through devotion to Lord Krishna and Narayana; they had only to utter the name of the Lord to be liberated.

With Vaishnavism opening its doors to the Shudras, Saivism also became liberal towards the Shudra, while Tantra never discriminated against the Shudra. In the meantime, a tendency towards less ritualism and greater emphasis on good conduct helped the Shudra ease himself into the mainstream. With the concept of a good shudra, conduct became the yardstick for acceptability, leading to a competition to be 'good' to join mainstream. Theologians even preached the possibility of a Shudra of good conduct attaining Brahminhood at the next birth. Yet, at heart, there was a sinister motive: the Machiavellian idea that inclusiveness was a better way to control a divided society. Thus, while opening the doors to religious inclusiveness, it insisted on Varna duties where the 'good' Shudra was rewarded for his service to the higher Varnas. This inclusiveness extended Brahmanism to a much broader base, thereby strengthening society. It also led to greater prosperity for the Shudra, even if some may say that it was their greater prosperity that forced Brahmanism to open its doors to them. The improvements, however, were real. The wages and working conditions improved, artisan guilds were recognized, and the social rigors of Varna were relaxed. The tragedy was that, as a consequence, it became increasingly inhuman to the untouchables.

Limping into the Modern Age

While historians have coined the phrase 'Sanskritization of India,' this was not a uniform process. In fact, south of the Vindhyas, there are no intermediate castes like the Kshatriyas or Vaishyas. In Tamil Nadu, Kerala, Karnataka, Andhra, and even Maharashtra, except for Brahmins and Shudras, there are no other castes except the untouchables. Even the proportion of Brahmins in the southern states is much less than in the U.P. and other northern states. In this context, the superimposing of Brahmin supremacy on the southern states is itself a matter of surprise. While Agastya is supposed to have sensitized Tamil Nadu, the legend has it that Parasurama hand-picked sixteen Brahmin families to inhabit the newly created Kerala. This itself suggests a superimposition instead of a pervasive Sanskritization. In fact, the southern states may have continued without change until the Chola dynasty, when we see a form of caste system being practiced, and historians suggest that it was only in the time of the Vijayanagar Empire that a real thrust was given to caste stratification. Thus, Kerala, even today, celebrates the rule of an Asura king, Maha Bali. It may have been their small numbers that prompted them to allow marriages between close relatives in Tamil Nadu and the draconian caste prohibitions practiced in Kerala. It also means that while all people residing in the southern states, other than Brahmins, are today labeled as Shudras, their actual condition was different from that in North India, where they were deliberately suppressed. The Nair in Kerala and the Vellalar in Tamil Nadu have less of a caste complex than many other Shudra castes.

After the age of the Puranas, there was little improvement in the lot of the Shudra as the Muslims came into the country, first as conquerors and looters and later as empire builders. This forced orthodoxy into a shell from which it has yet to surface. While the work of great thinkers like Sankaracharya allowed Hinduism to unite against a common enemy, there was little thought of liberating the Shudra. There were many reform movements that sought to humanize the caste system, yet almost all of them failed to make a dent in the fabric of Hindu society, driven inward by fear and inferiority. Thus, the Shudra limped into the modern age, inhibited and illiterate, shackled by caste restrictions. The irony is that, having been accepted into the Varna fold, they became its greatest defenders, especially against the Dalits being allowed to enter the fold. It was the plight of the Dalit alone that made being a Shudra acceptable. Only the fact that they were superior to the Dalits made the Shudra feel relevant. Consequently, it was the Shudra who most demeaned the Dalit, and almost all the violence against the Dalit was by the Yadavs in the north, the Thevars against their Dalit brothers in the south and similar combinations elsewhere.

Untouchability: A Unique Indian Idea

Between 20 and 30% of all Indians are termed 'scheduled castes' and 'scheduled tribes,' a euphemism for untouchability. They are those whom Indian society has considered untouchable for more than a millennium. Yet it must be said that it was not an Aryan idea nor was it insisted upon in the Epics or Puranas. While Manu acknowledges their presence, he merely passes them off as chandeliers, and thus, even he cannot be charged with the crime of untouchability. It was society that gradually constructed this unique form of cruelty. It is difficult now to pinpoint the genius who thought up such a system, and it may have to be conceded that it may not have been the idea of any single person but must have evolved in the thinking of the orthodox leaders of Indian society to meet the changing circumstances that they faced. It then, like an unleashed monster, grew far beyond any evil genius's original intention to become the most monstrous social practice ever, combining humiliation and prohibitions and the thrusting down of a group of people into abject poverty, filth, and hopelessness. Once introduced, no one wanted to be accommodative, as it was in slavish obedience and the power of cruelty that society saw the possibility of order and harmony. To a large extent, it was done to placate the Shudra, the new entrant to society, that the Chandelas became the scapegoat. The Shudra was already the lowest of the lows, so how could anything be lower? It was this predicament that resulted in the evolution of the demeaning and cruel idea of untouchability.

As has been seen, the Shudra was accommodated into society between 400 and 800 A.D., and even that must have been a long, drawn-out process that extended to the new millennium. It must have started in urban centers where the Shudra was economically and socially powerful and where the Shudra had already elevated himself to the status of a craftsman, trader, and even as a cultivator and landowner, not a mere share-cropper. The higher classes were then left without servants, and worse still, the garbage must have accumulated everywhere, and the sewage system must have started stinking. This forced the leaders to invite the tribals and Chandelas to help them deal with the dirt, filth, and accumulating dead bodies. They were needed but equally despised and they looked on with a sense of revulsion for the type of work they did. The problem posed by the elevation of the Shudra was a lesson learned for posterity and they now decided that the new set of people who did the dirty work must forever remain in their position as scavengers and never be allowed into polite society. This was also a boon for the Shudra for suddenly, he too could have servants, in fact slaves, to do all his dirty work. Thus, the evil mechanism of untouchability that some evil genius thought up was something the Shudra was most interested in upholding. He almost voluntarily took up the job of ensuring that the Chandelas never rose beyond his place in the system. He became the enforcer of untouchability. The higher castes happily allocated to the Shudra the role of the executor of the social mandate to keep the Dalit in his place.

With the Shudra being accepted into society, it was the turn of the Chandelas to give up their freedom in the wild and to live on the fringes of villages and towns as laborers on call in their designated settlements. The appearance of the Chandelas in the vicinity of human populations made the Shudra conscious of his own position and did everything to show his difference from the Chandelas. The Shudra rejected all his former occupations, even as farmers, and became landlords who refused to farm their own lands but depended on Chandelas, who were now a form of bonded labor and slave. They aped the Brahmin in dress and styles of living and became paranoid about cleanliness, puritanical, and deeply class-conscious. To maintain their clear higher position, it was necessary to discipline the Chandelas into submission so that showing proper respect without any murmur would become instinctive. Thus, it was the Shudra who made the first set of rules that legitimized untouchability. However, to the higher castes, who did not deal with the Chandelas on a daily basis, their very existence was unthinkable. Thus, if to the Shudra, the Chandelas were untouchable, to the twice-born, they were not even to be seen. Thus began the descending prohibitions, more demeaning and brutal at every stage, till the Dalit had to have bells on his feet like cattle to warn the upper castes of his approach. He could never look directly at anyone in society and had to have his head down under all circumstances and to maintain a sufficient distance even when talking to any socially accepted person, until he was required to remain as much as fifty paces away from any twice-born. It was to be a life of the living dead, unheard and unseen, and if possible, non-existent.

The African slave had a truly brutish existence on the plantations of America but like the way the early Aryans dealt with their slaves, they were treated as human-beings and some even treated them as members of the family, whereas the untouchable in India were never even acknowledged as human or even existing. It is difficult to explain the idea of untouchability, for touching is in many ways the very essence of existence, but worse was that, in many circumstances, he was not even to be seen; he had actually to be non-existent. It was by making the Dalit non-human and almost non-existent that it was possible to inflict the sort of inhuman treatment that was meted out to him. No one claimed responsibility for such an inhuman idea and everyone blamed it as a social need that existed and was sacrosanct by its antiquity. In time, the karma theory was used to justify their position. God alone, it seemed, was to blame. The Dalit was merely being corrected for his past sins. It was all too deep for human understanding; only God could explain. Thus, social reformers who pleaded the case for the Shudra to enter society had nothing to say about the Dalit, the Chandelas, or the untouchable. It took even Mahatma Gandhi many years and the forceful rhetoric of Ambedkar for him to acknowledge the terrible crimes committed against such a large section of the Indian population. To his credit, once he was awakened to their existence, he made it his life's mission to end untouchability. It was only Western education and Christian charity that opened the eyes of Indians to the continuing holocaust in their midst.

The story of their slow emancipation in the 20th century, starting with the British and culminating in the abolishment of untouchability along with independence, is all part of a very recent history and needs no recounting. The truth, however, is that their place in Indian society is still so tenuous as to be schizophrenic. Their place is maddeningly nebulous, a powerful vote bank and yet a continuing reminder of the terrible violence at the heart of Indian society. They are a living reminder of the moral ambiguity that pervades Indian thinking. Consequently, when glib Indians talk of the greatness of India's past, the greatness of its religion and the glories of Sanskrit, it is the voice of the small vocal minority among the mere 20% of twice-born Indians and not the opinion of the vast majority that accounts for 70% of the country, made up of Shudras and Dalits. The consciousness of the vast majority only remembers in their bones the violence and cruelty and the perpetuation of institutionalized injustice at the very heart of Indian society, religion, and thinking.

The Practice

The idea of 'untouchability' is so revolting that no one has claimed responsibility for its introduction. While the prohibitions against the Shudra have been meticulously tabulated in Manusmriti and repeated in the Artha shastras and even find a place in the Brahma shastras, there is no record of any law that upholds, permits, or even describes 'untouchability.' Indian society has always polarized itself into separate compartments, and its leaders have always divided society to rule. The relative justice that Manu and Kautilya preached was nothing new but what ancient people all over the world had considered a truism and which the Romans made into a law, saying that there can be 'equality only among equals.' Polarization, segregation, and the total separation as to where each Varna lived made it possible to deal with each caste as a separate unit for the application of justice. While the Shudra was to live outside the towns and villages, it was the Dalit who had to do so once the Shudra was accommodated into society. Even the Brahmins had their own 'Agraharas,' not because they so loved each other but to preserve their customs and secrets from prying eyes. The orthodox enforcers of caste realized the truism that the idea of justice is always limited to their kind. Thus, experiments have shown that even monkeys get angry when one is given a cucumber while another is given a banana. Yet the monkey does not even care who gets what among humans. Similarly, by segregating human groups into tight compartments with no hope of mixing or upward mobility, each caste sought justice only within their own community. Even the horrific prohibitions of untouchability were accepted as long as they were uniformly applied to all in the community.

The fact that there were no written-down rules about untouchability meant variations in the way they were enforced and practiced across the country. Thus, while 'untouchability' was enforced across the country, along with all the prohibitions applicable to the Shudras—no mixing, no inter-caste marriages, no eating together, no social mixing of any kind—and the total prohibition of their presence in any religious function, each region developed its own minor variations. Thus, history tells us that the way untouchability was practiced in Kerala was perhaps the most severe. In Kerala, not only was the Dalit not to be touched, he was not even to be seen. He thus had to ring a bell as he approached a village or a town so as to warn the caste Hindus to take cover. It is said that Nair warriors would chop off the heads of any Dalit who had the temerity to raise his head in their presence. Lurid and more sexist was the demand that no Dalit woman could cover her breasts. In later periods, perhaps with the slow creeping of prudishness, they were allowed to cover it on payment of a 'breast tax.' A historical character was supposed to have been so incensed by this prohibition that when the tax collector came to demand the tax, she chopped off her breast and handed it over to him, leading to widespread condemnation and the eventual repeal of the tax. The law was merely what the leaders of orthodoxy demanded in each region, often with communities competing, to be the most draconian.

While untouchability was an inter-caste demand, like demands and rules enforced by each independent state, it was the squalor to which the Dalit was condemned to live that was most pitiable. Untouchability was a social demand, but poverty, dirt, illiteracy, malnutrition, and total exclusion from any medical service meant that they were condemned to a spiral of degradation. They became like zombies, the living dead, living only from day to day with neither hope nor grace. They had no resources to pull themselves out of the rut, as they were totally dependent on whatever work they were allotted and the payments made to them as thought fit by the upper castes, which were often in kind, not in cash. Their jungle brothers were actually better off, as they could live off the forest and were at least free. Instead, they had to live like animals in filth, almost always open to the full blast of the elements, with little shelter and less clothing. It was their lack of any education and total blackout of all cultural concepts that allowed them to remain sane, at least in an animal sense and not howl like King Lear when he stood half-naked in the storm and rain, challenging the elements to do their worst, for he was already unhinged and all he wanted was the peace of the grave.

There was great fear at the heart of Indian society. All violence and sadistic behavior are the result of fear. Thus, while politicians as a class are rarely cruel or sadistic to the bureaucrats who work under them, the bureaucrat himself is very often cruel and sadistic to his colleagues and juniors, caused by the fear that he may be upstaged. The great fear was a hangover from the days of the Aryan, who was outnumbered and had to fight for his place in the new home he established. While the fear of physical violence first prompted his violence, later it was the fear of being engulfed by the larger population of natives, whose culture appeared depraved, of a people who lived in squalor, totally without any saving graces of culture or religion. The prohibitions against the Shudra and later against the Dalit were an attempt to preserve their culture and way of life. Fear leads to violence, and the greater the fear, the greater the violence, which may explain the sadism and cruelty at the heart of the system of 'untouchability.' It also happened to be a great political and economic idea for it ensured the availability of a class of people to do all the dirty work who would never aspire to be anything else. A permanent class of slaves is always at the call of the higher castes.

Impact on Consciousness

It is very difficult to gauge the impact of untouchability on its victims. Almost no record exists of the actual response of the victims to their victimhood, and no one has written about their experience until very recently, when the absolute severity of untouchability had already been masked by legislation. Thus, the stories written today are reminiscences of past generations transmitted to the present generation of Dalits, who then see them through the lenses of a free and democratic society where the old traditions are viewed with unalloyed disgust and a strong sense of moral outrage, all of which may have been absent when they were actually slaves and treated like animals.

In fact, the present generation has no way to relive that experience within the social, religious, and historical context in which it actually happened. By and large, the Dalits were numbed into a fatalistic acceptance of their lives. By treating a person as an animal, a person soon becomes an animal, for that is the degrading impact of continued brutalization. The Dalit, who was refused any form of education and punished for any attempts to gain literacy, was forced to live by his instincts, not his intellect. He had no access to concepts like equality or justice; all he had was the present, the present of an animal that knows only hunger, pain, the impact of the elements like heat and rain, and the continuous life of squalor.

Like an animal, he was forced to accept them as inevitable and in the nature of things. Like the American Negro slaves, who saw their lives only within the framework of their social place, the Dalits were human only among themselves and in their ghettos. The regularity of punishment and the strict enforcement of the rules of untouchability made the Dalit a prisoner within the system. The world was what he got within the prison; there was no other world, and he had no concepts to imagine a different world. He was not recognized as a person within the law, and his body had no inviolability; he could be tortured and killed almost at the whim of the upper castes. Thousands were killed; more died of starvation, poor living conditions, and the brutal conditions of their working lives, often totally exposed to the elements; the rest died of sickness largely caused by malnutrition. Their life expectancy may not have been more than thirty. They had neither the time nor the ability to think; it was all a headlong squeezing of life till a mere husk remained in death. Very similar to the Holocaust victims of the German concentration camps, without hope, only a slow but sure melting away before actual death.

Their lack of education was used to dumb down superstition and fatalistic theories like the karma theory, which kept any possibility of questioning at bay. It was not God who was blind and silent but they deserved what they got. It was not man who was cruel but God. Thus, to a large extent, they accepted their fate and made what they could of their brutal existence, elevated by nothing but animal pleasures and the mere addiction to life.

It was only when the Dalit somehow got an education, often through Christian missionaries whose true aim was merely to convert him, that it became possible for him to imagine a different life, and then, and only then, did he realize that he was being brutalized and that it was not necessarily the way things should be. Then came independence and the abolishment of untouchability, which made the worst elements of untouchability, at least to many, a thing of the hoary past. Only then could he look back at his past with horror. Yet the horror is never real—not even the real recounting of experience but often the utter shame of acknowledging the most horrible indignities they suffered without protest. Like a rape victim, he is too ashamed of all that was done to him. A shame that demands justice and yet refuses to look the perpetrator in the eye. Thus, the horror does not result in a rebellion or an uncompromising demand for expiation, for every day, things seem to be getting better, and every day, the past is slowly being erased from memory and from the political conscience of the upper castes till the centuries of oppression cease to be even a memory, only a historical truth.

Brutality brutalizes the perpetrator more than the victim. The victim ceases to be human, while the brutalizer loses his humanity. In untouchability, man ceases to be human, and the longer the system extends itself, the less it has the capacity to brutalize. Repeated beatings only make men numb to further beatings. Repeated humiliations cease to humiliate. It merely transforms man into an animal. Thus, it is very difficult to evaluate the harm done to the Dalit and the consciousness that he is burdened with. There is no doubt that it must have created a sense of worthlessness and a fatalistic attitude toward life. All human endeavor appears meaningless; only entitlements mean anything. That may be why 'quotas' and all forms of affirmative action strike a chord with the Dalit. The possibility of raising himself by his bootstraps was impossible, and thus he cannot now fathom its possibility. The new world of opportunities, equality, and justice before the law all appeared like mirages, illusions that would soon dissolve into the brutality of the past. It will take time for the Dalit to become really human; he carries too much of the memory, not intellectually but in the contours of his mind and in the shape of his body, bent for centuries and thus perhaps crippled.

As far as the society that perpetrated such an atrocity is concerned, forgiveness is not possible, and therefore the attitude is one of brazen denial. Indian society, therefore, refuses to look at history with any sense of honesty and instead picks and chooses what appears to show us in a good light. The lack of honesty and the unwillingness to acknowledge our past atrocities have made us dishonest people in all aspects of life. Corruption in public life, the demand for relative justice, the lack of any respect for life, the lack of any inviolable dignity of human life, and the demand to be above the law are all the undigested remains of a consciousness that has yet to acknowledge its past with honesty so that it can move on, at least now, with a more humane philosophy.

A Defense of the Caste System

The caste system has been universally condemned, yet there has never been an open discussion on the subject. Even the most vociferous critics have merely condemned untouchability, including Mahatma Gandhi. The Government of India still caters to caste, be it in the Mandal Report or caste-based reservations. The encroachment of religion into a social problem makes the issue intractable. The Karma theory has been so inextricably linked to religion that it is not possible to discard caste without discarding Hinduism along with it. This problem has to be dealt with separately, but what is interesting is the defense of the caste system.

Nirad Chaudhuri, in his book 'The Continent of Circe,' says, "To the foreign reformers of Indian society and their Hindu imitators, please keep your tongues and pens off the caste system" and then adds, "If I could believe that the caste system was going to be destroyed, I would have added, Please do not pulverize a society that has no other force of cohesion into amorphous dust, but since there is no danger whatsoever to the caste system, I would only say, Don't make fools of yourselves." Nirad Chaudhuri feels that it is the caste system that keeps the country intact and that there is absolutely no threat to it.

He defends it by saying that it had never prevented talent from coming on top, with examples of the Nandas from the barber community, the Holkers from a goat herding community, and the Scindias, who were servants, all becoming Kings. He also mentions the Brahmins, who were great generals and bankers, not accepting that these examples are merely the exceptions that prove the rule. He also forgets that the caste system always accepted kings, whoever they were, and raised them to the list of twice-born. The Marathas being Shudras, an exception was made for Shivaji and his family, allowing them to wear the sacred thread, and Nair chieftains of Kerala were likewise promoted when they became Kings. He then even says, "The social immobility for which the caste system was made a scapegoat was really the result of stagnation created in the social life of the Hindu by Pax Britannia."

The absurdity of the defense by such an eminent person as Nirad Chaudhuri shows how difficult it is to change the caste system. Nirad Chaudhuri claims that the Aryans had "no other way in which to preserve their ethnic, social, and cultural personality from being submerged in the conglomeration with the native darks." It is only that "the Aryans in India carried the attitude to the logical extreme demanded by the dangerous conditions in which they were placed." He further claims that "nowhere and at no time did the caste system have a norm or finality. It remained elastic, and its expandability was seen in more than one direction. Such aboriginals as showed any capacity or desire for a superior kind of life were not denied admission into Hindu society. Some were admitted to one of the superior castes on the strength of their vocation or worldly power." His final praise of the system is that "in India, the caste system prevented not one kind of anarchy but many. Hindu society did not attempt to suppress the immense range of social, cultural, and economic diversities that history was creating for it in unending succession. On the contrary, it accepted them, gave each its place and niche, and brought into existence a living association of human groups of all sorts, which was a federation of its parts without trying to be any one thing. The caste system is the name given to this federation."

Even though caste is rightly seen as based on color since it grew out of the Varna division, the actual colors given to each caste are not normally known. It was white for the Brahmin, red for the Kshatriya, yellow for the Vaishya, and black for the Shudra. The original Vedic people may not have been biased toward any color and may have been purely symbolic. Thus, their gods, both Shiva and Krishna, were dark, and so was Draupadi. Parvathi was so dark that she was taunted by Shiva until she became Gauri. There are also many cases where Mahabharata kings fall in love with dark women whose beauty enthralls them. There are many passages, both in the Epics and in poems, about the beauty of dark women. The dark male was also seen as virile and handsome. However, modern Indians, as Nirad Chaudhuri says, "are all obsessed with a fair complexion and cannot see beauty in a person who is not fair." He makes it an indictment when he says, "The admiration for the aboriginal gradually died among the Hindus, keeping pace with the decay of their sensibilities and only their abhorrence remained. It was precisely the vitality and nobility that the Hindus went on losing."

Yet in the beginning, they even borrowed their myths and transformed them to be acceptable to the Vedic religion. When Rama comes to the kingdom of Guha, he has no hesitation in accepting his hospitality. All this is nothing, says Chaudhuri, compared to the Indian love of money. He will do anything for it, but it is always done in the name of Dharma; thus, Duryodhana, the archetype of adharma, quotes Dharma as he dies, quotes Dharma. He claims that religion alone keeps the Indian limited in his avarices and that secularism in a nation totally given to superstition is a travesty. He finally says, "No chivalry nor even a residue of compassion can be expected from a retrograde phenomenon." The aboriginal in his natural state was a self-assured person, but his contact with the superiority complex of the Aryan reduced him to a state of permanent rebellion that found relief only in conversion to other religions. Total and comprehensive industrialization is the only solution to the present fractured society, says Chaudhuri, and he adds, "The Hindu order in the present state has neither the energy, physical and mental, nor perhaps the intelligence to carry through the type of industrialization that is now contemplated."

Chaudhri makes many important observations that most people refuse to accept, especially that the nation of India is held together by the caste system. As he says, it was a federation of castes, with each caste running its own governments. Without such an understanding, only chaos would result. Consequently, when we tried to create a single nation, the problems of equity were insurmountable. Reservation created a sense of victimhood on the one hand, while the higher castes claimed entitlement. In the caste system, the relative position of the castes was rarely tested, as each caste kept to themselves and had at least a sense that they were determining their own lives. A grouping of unequal people cannot become a nation, and forcing such an amalgamation is fraught with serious problems. What is even more problematic is any attempt to create a uniform culture or even manners. Each caste is only aware of their own dharma, as it were, and how to behave within their caste group, aware of the prohibitions in any interaction with different castes. Once this is taken away and all are considered equal, society is suddenly bereft of any acceptable mode of interaction. One sees the other as arrogant, while the other sees him as uppity. In a society where the Shudra was to wear only handed-down clothes, a well-dressed Shudra becomes an affront. To an upper caste, an elderly Shudra needed not to be respected. When all are equal, respect for the elderly and the wise, even teachers and seniors in an organization, becomes a casualty. Yet, with such a breakdown of behavior, nothing new can be substituted; that is the tragedy, as education itself is tainted by caste consciousness.

CHAPTER 9

THE EVOLUTION OF HINDUISM

Dr. Romila Thapar confidently asserts, "Because identity is linked to religion, it can lead to the redefinition of a particular religion, more so in the case of one as amorphous as Hinduism. Such an identity tends to iron out diversity and insist on conformity, for it is only through a uniform acceptance of such a religion that it can best be used for political ends." It is natural, she says, that religions would try to increase their numbers by compromising if necessary or by widening the scope of the definition. Thus, Hinduism, seen as a largely 'Brahmana-dominated religion,' opened itself to accommodate all views, gods, and philosophies, with a 'plurality of doctrines' with a seeming absence of controversy, all this somehow integrated into a single religious fabric.

From the outside, it is a religion of deep religious thought, of the Advaita and Nyaya philosophies, and also a religion of idol worship and the proliferation of gods. This notion suppresses all textual contradictions and religious practices. At first, the distinction was between Brahmanas and Sramanas, those who accepted the authority of the Vedas and those who did not. As Patanjali says, their animosity was like that of a snake and a mongoose. The Brahmanas made a distinction between the 'twice-born' and all others but left belief in a deity a matter of personal choice. The focus was on sacrifice and rituals and the acceptance of Sanskrit as the language of religion. The Sramanas, on the other hand, accepted all people and classes and rejected caste segregation, social habits, and social hierarchy. The Sramanas had the numbers and for a very long time, it was Jainism and Buddhism that enticed most of the population.

The Brahmanas gained power mainly as a result of the large grants of land from kings and rulers, allowing them to develop Agraharas where intellectual indoctrination and militancy were developed. This was apart from the appropriation of the monasteries and temples of the Jains and Buddhists, who had to flee from persecution. They then incorporated local cults by Sanskritizing them and creating Puranas to accommodate their gods. While allowing them to add the locals to their fold, it also caused the gradual decline of the Sramana sects. The Bhakti cults, who were the inheritors of the Sramana philosophy, retained an attachment to their particular God and transcended caste. However, when Brahminism accommodated them, they merged them into the mainstream along with their caste. Thus, sects became castes, while their leaders became Brahmins. This trend started with the Krishna cult in Mathura and spread throughout the Hindi heartland. He was followed by Ram. The more aggressive groups were Shiva cults like the Vira Shivas, who broke from Brahmanism to create distinct sects. For long, these sects were treated with suspicion, and their existence did not mean acceptance. Their status changed only when they got powerful patrons to support them.

Idol worship was not contemplated in Vedic religion but soon became a distinguishable part of Hinduism. Sects and cults remained in geographically defined locations and were called 'Sampradaya,' or traditional beliefs. Different castes tended to create their own particularities. Dr. Thapar feels that the Epics were really the literature of the Vaishnavas and their growth depended on the popularization of the Epics and the Puranas. While changes were peaceful, it is a mistake to presume that the Hindu sects and cults were always non-violent. The Vira Shivas claimed to be warriors for Shiva, whose persecution of Sramana sects is testified to by Huang Tsang in Kashmir in the 7th century. Kalhana also mentions the destruction of Buddhist monasteries. There are also historical references to the killing of Buddhist monks by the Huna king, Miharakula. Even in Tamil Nadu, there were many incidents of Shiva sects attacking Jain establishments.

In Karnataka, the Vira Shivas and Lingayats attacked Jains and acquired large landed property. To the Vira Shivas, the Jain monasteries and their high standard of literacy were a constant irritation. In victory, the punishment was to treat all Sramana sects as untouchables. However, in the long run, they were all assimilated by including their gods as avatars, even the Buddha. The reason for this attitude of accommodation was the rise of guilds, specific to each occupation, like iron workers and weavers, who were sun worshippers, in Orissa. Each guild had the unstinted loyalty of its members. Be it fishermen, stone masons, or dancers, all worshiped their own gods. In fact, the Narada Smriti clearly gives guilds the power to make their own laws. Consequently, laws were called Sreni Dharma and even kings had to respect Jati Dharma. In time, these guilds became castes within the Brahminical system.

The modern definitions of Hinduism are the result of the semantic idea of religion being superimposed on a largely pluralistic religious consciousness, says Dr. Thapar, where differences are emphasized to create an identity. When Muslims first came to India with the hope of converts, what struck them was that Indian society had no concept of conversion, for birth and caste alone defined religion. Hinduism, as a term, was the definition of the 'other,' as it was a religion that they could not grasp intellectually or define. "The need for postulating a Hindu community became a requirement for political mobilization in the 19th century," and "conversion to Hinduism was invented, largely to bring in untouchables and tribals," says Dr. Thapar.

Historical Consciousness

While we bemoan the fact that there is so little written history, Dr. Romila Thapar argues that there are many levels of historical consciousness, and written histories are only its overt form. 'Embedded history,' as she calls it, is everywhere, from the Puranas to the Epics. They are like our subconscious and like our dreams, which have to be carefully deciphered. Thus, every nation seems to have a story about the flood. We too have one where Manu is told to build a ship in which he and the seven Rishis, who have all the knowledge of the world, remain safe until the flood is over, and Vishnu, in his fish avatar, saves man and human civilization. Manu is, however, only the seventh Manu, and the story assumes the washing away of many earlier cultures. Unlike in the Bible story, where Noah takes a pair of all animals, Manu takes with him only the seven Rishis, who have all the knowledge of the world. Knowledge is what is important because new generations are merely created from the body of Manu. Only knowledge was sacred, whereas to the Jew, it was creation that had to be saved, while God was always there to guide them. This sanctified the Vedas without recourse to any God. Thus, the Vedas can boldly assert that the gods came later. The second thing the story sanctifies is lineage, as all the succeeding generations are the progeny of the seven Rishis and Manu. The direct descendants of this group became the Brahmins. Yet, this story also suggests that it was a new beginning in a new place, a story of migration and new adventures. A story that alludes to the loss of old surroundings and family gods. It was a telling of the Aryan migration and may also explain the destruction of the Harappan civilization by the flood, the dispersal of the people, and the empty ruins.

As Dr. Thapar says, the important thing is how the story was transmitted down the ages. The problem with myths is that they are static; they do not tell a continuing story; there is no progression, no evolution, and no refining of values and ideas. The way in which the story changes only indicates the power of the dominant social classes in each epoch. When there are no new stories, the old ones are retold. As society grows more complex, new stories explain the way society has adjusted to the change. The story of the evil Vena, who kills all the Rishis, forces Manu to create a hero from his left thigh, Nisada, who proves inadequate to the task and is banished to the forest. Manu then creates Prithu, from his right arm, a righteous king who introduces cattle-herding and agriculture. Prithvi, therefore, lends him her name because of the great things he has done with the land. Vena, on the other hand, is evil and has stopped performing sacrifices. This paves the way for the Purusha sacrifice, which justifies the Varna system. The thigh produces only Nisada, the forest people, while from the arm arise the Kshatriya, the rulers and the warrior class, epitomized by Prithu.

Myths are the deepest level of embedded history, says Dr. Thapar. The Matsya Purana, where Vishnu takes the form of a fish to save the world, introduces gods, where earlier the Vedas alone held sway. The Purusha story is then interpolated into the Rig Veda to justify the caste system, making it God-given. Dr. Thapar, however, feels that the Varna was not linked to color or work but to lineage, as the Vish, the people at large, were all part of society, and there was no Shudra caste. In early stories, there were only two clans: the Suryavamsha and the Chandravamsha. As they encountered great kings who were hospitable, accepted their beliefs, and sacrificed to their gods, they were then eulogized in the Puranas because they were the necessary prop on which the Varna system depended. As Dr. Thapar says, the kings and heroes were a necessary part of the stability of the Varna system, as societies that force stratification require greater authority to maintain cohesion in society. The Brahmin maintained his status by being the sole performer of rituals and sacrifices.

The 'Itihasa Puranas' were thus the historical consciousness, written down as myth. The lack of historical rigor in Indian history is because the Itihasa were often a form of wish-fulfillment. They were used to justify the emergence of new gods. The first of these was the Vishnu Puranas, which became the model for all later Puranas. Yet it also gives us a glimpse of historical happenings, the Kshatriya lineage, and the rise of non-Kshatriya kings like the Nandas and even of Brahmins becoming kings like the Sungas and the Kanvas. We also have a record of lower Varna kings called Vratya-Dvijas, Shudras, and Mellachas. The fact that such kings are mentioned indicates the time taken for power to finally settle on the Brahmins and the Kshatriya. It was certainly not helped by the large and frequent invasions by foreign chiefs like the Greeks, the Sakas, the Parthians, and the Kushans, who were all called Vratya-Kshatriyas (degenerates). Another reason for the long-unsettled period was because people had the option to migrate from areas that were inhospitable and create their own societies. The Mahabharata mentions the kings linked to the Suryavamsha and the Chandravamsha, the Nandas, the Mauryas, the Sungas, the Kanvas, and the Andhras; they also name the invading kings as Indo-Greeks, Sakas, Kushanas, and the Kshatrapas.

In the later years, when religion became an emotive issue with the rise of the bhakti movement, many sectarian groups with their separate gods and goddesses had to be accommodated in the Puranas. The Jains and the Buddhists established themselves through their large corpus of writing, both in history and philosophy. Similarly, the separation into Vaishnavite and Shaivite groups, both competing for royal patronage, created flowery histories and powerful gods. The rise of local cults and foreign incursions meant more accommodation within the Varna; this also led to the concept of yagna and purification rites. The Puranas, which started as a means to deify the gods, ended up justifying sects, cults, and revolutionary movements. Dr. Thapar concludes by saying, "The Varna ordering of society, which never fully coincided with the clearly defined socio-economic stratification, became part of embedded history. Thus, history became a tool to sanctify religion and social norms and justify all the evil done in the name of religion."

A Concept of Time

When asked why Indians have no sense of history, the answer is that we burn our dead; we do not bury the dead for some later-day archaeologist to dig up and defile. The past is dead and must remain dead so that the present is not dragged down by the past. If this were true, it would have been, at least, a fresh perspective; instead, the lack of genuine history is merely used to justify every jingoistic and absurd interpretation of history. Dr. Thapar has a much more rational explanation. She says that while the West sees time as linear and therefore can talk of progress and even of perfectibility, Indians see time as circular and know that what has happened will happen again and again, in cycles of time, till the end of time. There is no concept of perfectibility, only of the inevitable collapse of all systems. It is this sense of cyclic time that makes all ideas of heaven, hell, and judgment rather puerile. It also led to the idea of Maya and the belief that all life is an illusion. This makes Dr.

Thapar say, "The argument is often made that because there was no distinction between myth and history in early Indian thought, resorting to history even today is irrelevant and meaningless to the Indian mind."

Daniel J. Boorstin, in his book 'Discoverers,' gives an even more basic reason why Indians did not write history. We have, over time, with scientists to guide us, assumed that time is an arrow that moves forward. Such an understanding of time demands that there be progress and, if nothing else, change to mark the passage of time. This is the reason we give so much importance to history. However, to people who see time only as a dimension, like space, with nothing progressive or changeable about it, and to people who believe that life never changes and seasons merely repeat themselves in an endless drama of monotony, history has no meaning. Where everything is merely the same, history has no meaning. History can have meaning only if there is a beginning, only if we believe in a 'D' day or the moment of the 'big bang' or in some creation story. Only from such a point can history begin. If one believes that the universe is eternal and creation and destruction are merely cycles, an endless mechanical drama, that each epoch ends and a new epoch begins, then what is the point of history?

History is a consciousness of change; the question, however, is what constitutes change. Even in a system of cycles, there is change and progression; the difference is that Indians see change only as leading to inevitable collapse, not perfection. Indians see time in Kalpa, 4320 million years, and yugas, where the total time varies from Yuga to Yuga. The smallest cycle of time was a Kalpa, a day in the life of Brahma, and at the end of each Kalpa, all matter merely returns to Brahma for creation to begin again. Thus, the total annihilation at the end of the Mahabharata is not a tragedy; it is only the end of an epoch, after which life will begin anew. Cyclic time justifies the concept of Karma and Samsara, the transmigration of souls and of endless lives. All religious beliefs are therefore a challenge to the determination of Karma. That is why St. Augustine was so vitriolic in his attack on what he called the heathen belief in the cycles of time, for only in the arrow of time could there be a movement to the 'City of God,' the eternal city, the end of history and ultimate perfection.

In the myths, the gods live in sacred time. The problem is that in the Puranas, the writers start with cosmic time and then change the tense from eternal time to the present. The Vishnu Puranas, which are the template for all other Puranas, start with the flood and with Lord Vishnu descending to the Earth. Once this portion is over, the measurement of time changes radically, and cosmological time gives way to chronological time, with the genealogies of Manu and the heroics of the Kshatriyas till the end of the Mahabharata. Like the flood, the Mahabharata marks the end of a cycle, a Yuga. After the end of the Mahabharata, we enter the Kali Yug. A dark age without heroes, truth, or greatness. Historical time was forced on the Indian consciousness by entry into Kali Yug. It also became prudent to accept such a concept of time because the Jains and the Buddhists had started writing history, dating it to the death of the Buddha. They were then forced to accept the reality of human time. Like absolute monarchs like Ram, the later kings had to deal with taxes and land deals that happened in real-time. Yet, cosmological time refused to fade away. Even the Buddhists, in their attempt to show the Buddha as the Chakravarty, the mover of the eternal wheel, had to revert to cosmological time, as 84000 myriad lakh spans of time.

With the commencement of Kali Yug, time becomes linear, so that it can map the decline of Dharma and point to events foretold at the end of Kali Yug, the arrival of the last Avatar, the 'Kalki Avatar.' The Puranas tell us when to expect the Kalki Avatar and how to interpret the decline of Dharma. The signs are clearly foretold: the breakdown of caste, the rule of Mleccha kings, Shudras pretending to have high-class status, and the spread of wantonness among women. While a society's concept of time determines their consciousness, we too have accepted linear time and forgotten cosmic time. The problem, however, is that in the process, the past is forever frozen in time, refuses to merge with linear time and creates an ambivalence to truth and to any dispassionate study of history.

Tradition as Consciousness

Tradition, according to Dr. Thapar, is the patterns of social behavior historically acquired and transmitted as symbols. Tradition is what links the present to the past. However, culture can only be the beliefs of the dominant group in a society, and the creation of culture is always a dynamic process where the present continually changes the past, with an equally powerful impetus to pretend that the past was something carved in stone. Everyone has their own deep prejudices, oblivious to the mechanisms that create culture and tradition.

History is like a specimen frozen in a very delicate liquid. Thus, digging it up and even talking about and studying culture alters the very fine balance of the liquid in which the past is preserved. All study brings with it biases and preconceived notions that inevitably alter and recreate the past. Very often, what is projected as the traditions of the past are nothing but the projections of present-day thinkers with modern-day ideas imposed on the past.

While we take the caste system as sacrosanct, believing that Brahmins were always Brahmins, the Vedic texts speak of important Brahmins as Dasi Putras and Dirghatamas, among whom was Vyasha, the author of the Mahabharata, the son of a fisher-woman, while Ravan was a Brahmin. The later Puranas, in an attempt to glorify Vyasha's status, retell his birth and make his mother a celestial Apsara who abandons him to be brought up by fisher folk. The same trick is used to elevate the subsequent gods, and that is how Krishna, a cow herder, is made into the supreme Lord. This, says Dr. Thapar, is the simplistic device by which the dynamic and flexible past is made to appear static, graven in stone.

The origin of the many gods and sects gives a false homogeneity to Hinduism, which was really very elastic and accommodative. The classic manner in which this was done can be seen in the story of Shakuntala. In the Mahabharata, she is the natural child of an Apsara, Menaka, and the rishi Viswamitra, left as an orphan with Kanva. She accepts a Gandharva marriage on the condition that her son would be king. However, when she comes to the court to claim her son's right, the king, Dushanta, refuses to acknowledge her and calls her a whore, and her son a bastard. He only relents when a heavenly voice proclaims the child's parentage. This story, in the hands of Kalidasa, becomes a story of amnesia and a lost ring. It also reduces the bold and confident Shakuntala into a submissive woman of high caste who has no guts even to claim her rights but must wait for the appearance of the ring. The new story legitimizes the king and elevates Shakuntala to a high caste, thereby robbing her of her independence, making her a model of submissiveness.

The Epic Ramayana was actually a story contrasting the values of the court with the honest values of the forest, between orthodoxy, dissent, and independence. The hermit who renounces the court is also rejecting the social norms and values of the court, something that Sita emphasizes in her life. The power the hermits obtained through tapas and austerities made them independent, and orthodoxy was then meant only for the herd, the sheep. The hermits of the Epics did not live for austerity alone but enjoyed life to the full, having their fill of sex. They were an alternate source of power to whom the Pandavas go to in exile and with whom Ram stays when in the forest. The life of the hermit was thus an alternate way of life, always available, free from the rigid ways of society. Their power legitimized their dissent and way of life.

This dissent was made into a mass movement by the Buddhist Sanghas. Their dissent was remarkable because they not only dissented against orthodoxy but were able to gather a congregation made up of the various Varnas. This was the reason for the vicious attacks against them by orthodox Hindu groups. It was also the beginning of the closing of the Indian mind to all alternative narratives. In fact, the Jain poet Vimalasan, in his Ramayana, claims this to be the authentic version, where Brahmins are the villains while Ravana is the protector of the Buddhist shrines. By suppressing it and treating it as heresy, the next generation learns only a whitewashed version of the past. Power alone decided the past and what constituted the orthodox tradition. This also calls into question the much-touted Indian virtue of tolerance and non-violence. In our claims to tolerance and non-violence, what is denied is that the caste system and untouchability are the most vicious forms of intolerance and violence. History has tended to gloss over the suppression of all alternate sects and religions and is silent about the violence that was used to suppress them, thereby obliterating our brutal past.

There is, however, a wealth of evidence to support the view that the Shiva sects had vandalized Jain and Buddhist shrines, and sanctuaries were appropriated. A Jain temple in the Tirunelveli district was, in the 7th century, merely converted into a Shiva temple. Similarly, many Jain temples were desecrated by Sivaviras and Lingayats in Karnataka. A Jain temple dedicated to the five Jinas was converted into a Panchaligaswara Shiva temple. In Srisailam, there is a record of Virasiva chiefs beheading Svetambara Jains. Tolerance and non-violence were not always accepted by the adherents of Hinduism. Only a thorough and impartial inquiry into the past would reveal the true nature of Indian society and our real culture. Only then would we know that violence was an ever-present danger, lying just below the surface, waiting to erupt. An impartial study is also essential to appreciate the values that violence has taught us.

While Hinduism was breaking up into sects with narrow affinities, the Buddhists and Jains were adding to their numbers and becoming 'the other,' the enemy, leading to intolerance. It is also important to realize that much of the religious clout was material. The Jains and Buddhists had been gifted large tracts of land when they were in favor, which aggressive Hindu groups grabbed when they had the power. An inbuilt incentive for violence was thus created, which soon snowballed into an acceptable ethic. However, the blame cannot be thrust on all Indians, as it was still a land of many sects and beliefs, and many were truly non-violent and may have perished with no one to tell their story. The strange part was that, while mainstream orthodoxy was trying to stem internal dissension, the Muslims had entered India without any overt disapproval or concerted opposition. Even when the Somnath temple was sacked, the news was only that foreigners had attacked a Vaishnavite temple, not as a threat to Hinduism or to India.

In India, identity was created more by caste, custom, and language than by belief. Even when Sankaracharya tried to galvanize his group of believers, it was only to the Shaivite Brahmins that he appealed, leaving the vast majority of Indians out of the call. A virtue like tolerance was thus a variable virtue; it was at best a tolerance that permitted many sects to survive in their separate areas of influence. Hinduism, as a monolithic religion, or Hinduism as a homogeneous religion, without its warring sects, is a myth of recent origin. It was a reaction to Orientalism and an attempt to create a national identity in the face of scornful external perception. Hinduism, as is projected by some people, has no historical validity in truth. Hinduism is an evolving religion whose roots are best seen in the rise of separate sects. To pretend that either the Vedas or any other religious text from the Vedantas to the Manusmriti forms the basis of the religion as a whole would be fallacious. Culture is embedded in social reality, but unless it is studied with impartial honesty, only a political picture will emerge.

The Rise of Temples

Vedic Hinduism was not a temple-oriented religion. It was a personal religion with personal duties that, in time, became rituals and sacrifices. Each man was his own priest, and the home was his temple. He was a grihapati. The closest that Vedic religion came to dealing with others was when clan chiefs made large sacrifices and distributed gifts. In these gatherings, in gratitude, some sang the praises of the chief. The bard was thus the first priest. The Vedas are full of poetic utterances and hymns of praise.

When this ability was noticed, the rich and powerful understandably sought such bards to sing their praises. Thus, a band of professional priests and, with that, a priesthood arose. The availability of a body of sacred texts like the Vedas made the recitation of hymns all the easier for a professional group who could remember them. The texts then became not only sacred but secret, to be disclosed only to a closed group, the hereditary priesthood. The learning and memorizing of the Vedas became their prime and often their only occupation. The fact that they perfected their art is a tribute to their greatness.

However, religion continued as a personal affair, and chiefs and kings performed major sacrifices more as an economic exercise, where wealth was redistributed to Brahmins and other castes. The main beneficiaries were the Brahmins, who soon became wealthy and rich in land and assets. Their reluctance to till the land they owned led to the creation of a class of tenant farmers who became the Shudras.

Even with this slow evolution of a caste system, nothing really changed; dissenters were still free to forsake society and take to the forest or roam as mendicants and hermits, as begging monks, preaching some Sramana belief. The only real change took place when Jainism and Buddhism made their way of life a systematic religious practice with their Sanghas and their monasteries. The monastic life was the real revolutionary change that was to have drastic consequences for religion and social life. It was a direct threat to orthodox Hinduism.

The Orthodox then copied them, resulting in the evolution of temple worship. A king like Ashoka ordered the building of 84,000 temples. Soon, there was a race to build temples, and in this, the Jains and the Buddhists had an edge, as they were the first to get donations from their congregation. When the patronage changed with the return of Hindu kings, there was a desperate attempt to catch up, and the age of temple buildings finally arrived, never to cease.

The return of Hindu kings also meant a backlash when Jains and Buddhists were attacked, and their temples were desecrated or converted to Hindu temples. This process continued for quite some time. There is the great example of the Simhachalam temple in Visakhapatnam, which rose on the foundation of a Buddhist temple. In the 11th century, the temple was destroyed in a period of great political uncertainty and remained in ruins until the 13th century, when it was rebuilt as a Vaishnava temple. However, the temple had a strange Shaivite antecedent and had the image of Vara Narasimha Vishnu with a Shiva Linga. The story is told that when the builders were trying to break an existing Shiva Linga, it started to bleed, and the builders immediately sent men to Ramanuja for advice, who told them to stop the destruction. Thus, we have today a Vishnu idol with a half-broken Shiva Linga. Destruction was not only limited to Buddhist and Jain temples but also to the temples of competing sects.

Another reason for the growth of temple buildings was the rise of occupational guilds. With the growth of cities and the increase in trade, many occupational guilds, like silk weavers, goldsmiths, and others, became rich and economically powerful. To show their might, they began to build their own temples, which increased the sectarian divide. Their later absorption into the mainstream left indelible marks of their sectarian origins, which were very often unorthodox. These artisans had long been outside the mainstream of Vedic religion, as they were socially low in caste, yet it was these people who mobilized others to build temples with donations, grants, and collections. This also made carpenters, masons, and sculptors actively participate in temple building. As for Buddhist temples, many were built with contributions from rich women freed from the shackles of their submissive roles who had become wealthy in their own right. As Buddhism broke down caste walls, more and more castes took to temple buildings.

Copying the model of Buddhist and Jain stupas and monasteries, Hindu temples also began to grow. Even though they were still centered around a presiding deity, they began to take the shape of stupa architecture. It manifested the patron's wealth and showcased the talents of the shilpis, artists, and stone masons, who grew in size and diversity. Competition led to an increase in size and grandeur, becoming the center around which cities grew. It had a large Brahmin community for rituals and sacrifices and musicians, dancers, and devadasis. The temple had its own lands, its own elephants, cattle, and maintenance staff. Thus, as in the case of the court, the temples became centers of employment and power. It also became a center of music, arts, and crafts, a Brahmin power center to rival the power of the kings. Consequently, when temples were attacked, it was rarely for reasons of faith alone but for their wealth.

The Puranas

The Vedic philosophy was not religious. It was an open and questioning philosophy that honestly asked, "Who created the universe?" and answered by saying, "Not the gods," because they came later. With great humility and as a challenge, it says, "Who knows? Maybe the creator knows, or maybe even he does not know." Thus, asserting that the two assumptions all religions make are debatable: that there are gods and that there is a creator.

Instead of God and religion, they saw the universe as running on some mechanical principle. They viewed sacrifice to the gods as something akin to feeding the universe—the fuel that keeps the universe in motion. Thus, they claimed that even the gods are dependent on the sacrifices of human beings. They did not see much of a distinction between gods and men, except that the gods were immortal, and even that was because they were lucky to drink the elixir of life. To achieve God-like knowledge, man had only to drink 'soma.' However, the Vedas accept that man only rarely enjoys the comforts of Soma, while the gods are addicted to it. Thus, to the Vedic people, drug-induced transcendence was all that the gods possessed, only eternally.

Yet they were amazed and bewildered by the power of nature, by the sun that seemed so great that it not only lit up the Earth but also sustained it with its warmth. Man-made fires were the smaller equivalent of the sun, with the capacity to light up the night, warm them, and cook food. This capacity to burn and to cook, to destroy and to provide made fire a thing most marvelous. The wind and the mighty rivers also impressed them. Thus, Vedic men felt obliged to express their indebtedness and almost something of a devotion and awe at these powers. Most of the Vedic hymns were addressed to the Sun and to Agni (fire). Dawn, as Ushas, the hope-inspiring beginning of the day, was also worthy of praise.

Yet the Vedas cannot even be called pantheistic, as the hymns do not indicate a religious element but are largely hymns of wonder and praise, more like the poems of Wordsworth. Instead of being God-like, they saw in these powers of nature merely the manifestation of the power of sacrifice. They believed that these powers were kept alive by sacrifice. Thus, they say, Brahman sacrificed himself to create the world, and humans must continue to sacrifice to sustain it.

However agnostic the Vedas appear to be, and however mechanistic they saw the universe, there were also in the Vedas the beginnings of a consciousness of something beyond human life. The fact that there was much that seemed to have no explanation and much to fear, like death and pain, made the Vedas look beyond. In their thoughts expressed in their hymns, the ideas that were later to become ideologies were already present. First was the idea of something beyond human beings, which they called gods. Yet, as we have already seen, they at first only accepted Surya (sun), Mithra and Varuna, Vayu, Prithvi, and Agni (night, sky, Earth, and fire) as gods. Yet, they were also able to conceptualize that these powers were merely the manifestation of something greater; that represented the sum of all powers, those things that man could not understand. Thus, in the Rig Veda, they say, "The wise call him Indra, Agni, and Varuna, but the great divinity of God is one."

The Upanishads postulated the existence of Brahman, the all-powerful and eternal being, along with Atman, the divine element in all human beings. They also speculated on creation and said that all creation was merely the manifestation of Brahman and that Brahman was also beyond manifestation. What we see is merely the visible part of Brahman. God as a personal deity was never part of Vedic conceptualization. Brahman was too awesome, vast, and almost a basic mechanistic principle to be personal or reducible to human form. Consequently, there was no concept of sin or the idea of God as a punishing and rewarding agent. Sacrifices were made to sustain the universe, not for personal gain. However, we have seen how, in the later philosophy of the Epics, God becomes personal and is reduced to a symbol for worship. Indian religiosity is the history of the gradual decline from cosmic wonder to narrow sectarian beliefs. Let us, therefore, see how each of the major gods evolved and what created sectarian beliefs.

As we have seen in Chapter 1, Dr. Radhakrishnan saw the pure religion of the Aryans being corrupted through compromise with local beliefs. Thus, the general belief is to assume that all the corruption was due to local influence and to demonize the local people and their religion. The fact remains that as the Aryans entered the plains of India, they had nothing like a clear religion, and in the local people, they met a much superior civilization with a rich culture and tradition of learning. In fact, what has to be assumed is that they were no match for the learned natives, who surprised them with the depth and complexity of their religious beliefs. Thus, most of the sages and hermits in the Epics seem to be from some older civilization, and many are treated as Asuras, whom they admit are their elder brothers. It is also a mistake to assume that there was only one enemy, as it were, for the Aryan to overcome; there were also the people of the south who may have been Dravidians and the jungle people with their own animistic beliefs and Stone Age culture. What then happened was a three-way struggle to develop a religion acceptable to all. That is where the changes took place. If we assume that the native civilization was the successor of the Harappan civilization, it had to have been both highly advanced and based on a religion similar to what was practiced in the Mesopotamian region. The beliefs of the jungle people must have been a crude version of the religion of their much more advanced neighbors, contact with whom must have triggered their first ideas of religion. The writing of the Puranas was the first attempt at creating a discernible religion with its own cosmology, theology, and practices. It was an attempt to amalgamate many existing beliefs into one narrative, and the loose ends tend to show. It was the final written-down compromise that entered into the canon of sacred literature. They do not tell of the many versions that must have been orally circulated and rejected or the bloodshed and compromises that took place to ensure that a version was written down without being burned and its authors crucified.

The actual religion of the Puranas, and when and where it originated, is difficult to establish, but there can be no doubt that they included pre-Aryan beliefs and practices many centuries older than even Buddhism or the Upanishads. It was finally written down only when the believers had to justify their religion to newcomers, who had somehow become powerful. The Puranas were thus not even a true rendering of the original practices or beliefs but what had been compromised and made acceptable to a group that it targeted. Consequently, the Shiva Puranas were supposed to have been written by Vyasa's son, Sukadeva, and the Bhagavata Purana by Srila Vyasa Deva, bringing the writers of the Mahabharata to sanctify the Puranas. While Shiva and Krishna were standalone gods with their own followers, when the Puranas were written, they were seen in the context of Aryan beliefs and other existing beliefs that had already been sanctified. The belief in goddesses may have been even older, but when they had to be written down, at a time of patriarchy and in the context of the Aryan religion, the convoluted stories of Parvathi, Kali, and the other goddesses would be understood as interpolations. As many as eighteen Puranas have survived, from the Bhagavata Purana, which may be the oldest tradition, to the Devi Puranas. Many of them have their own cosmologies and theology. They also exhibit knowledge of the philosophical systems and advocate practices found in the Atharva Veda and the Tantric texts. In many ways, each was a comprehensive text for a specific cult or faith.

Lord Shiva

There is no mention of Shiva as a God in the Vedas or Upanishads. In fact, Shiva is seen in the Vedas as the enemy of Indra. However, even the Vedas attribute an almost heroic status to Shiva, who led forces against the Aryas, requiring them to call on Indra to help them fight Shiva. Shiva is seen as the leader of a people devoted to cattle breeding.

In time, Shiva was worshiped as Rudra, as Bhava (being), as Sarva (the all), as Pasupathi (the Lord of Creatures), and finally as Maheswara, the great God. Yet he was not a Vedic God. This fact is clearly brought out by the story of Daksha's sacrifice, told in the Mahabharata. Daksha conducts a great sacrifice and invites all the gods but Shiva. Shiva takes this insult in stride, as he knows that the regular gods do not honor him. When his wife Sati feels offended and complains to Shiva, he shows his power by destroying Daksha's sacrifice and scattering the gods. Only when the gods return with folded hands, apologizing profusely, does Shiva restore the sacrifice. Shiva is not invited because, to Daksha, Shiva had no Varna or caste. He was an outsider who lived like a Chandala in the burning ghats and cremation grounds. He had no lineage, clan, or Varna; he was an outsider to Vedic society.

Even as Rudra, in the Vedas, is seen as the God of weapons, whose aid the Vedic people seek, he was treated with apprehension and entreated to keep his distance. He comes into his own only in the Epics and finally in the 'Shiva Purana' and 'Linga Purana.' By then, Shiva had become a mighty God, without beginning or end but still seen as an outsider, living 'in the wilderness of the burning ground,' as Appar, the Tamil poet, says. He was also a God who scorns sacrifice, the Yogi who resides in the mountains, the teacher of a deeper wisdom that relied more on Jnana than sacrifice. He lives in Kailash, beyond the Himalayas. He is also Neelakanta, the blue-throated one who saves both the gods and men by drinking the poison that threatens all creation. Yet he is still portrayed as the outsider, a Chandala in appearance who lives on cremation grounds with skulls that make up his necklace. He is also portrayed as dark-skinned, thus clearly not part of the Varna of the Vedas and is, in fact, an example of all that Manu's Varna ideology frowns on, the very antithesis of caste correctness.

As Shiva has no antecedents, we can know him only by where he lives. He is a mountain yogi, an ascetic God who is always in a state of intense meditation. He is a teacher of deep wisdom. When Sati is again reborn, she is also born in the mountains as Parvathi or Girija (the mountain born), the daughter of the Himalayas and his wife Mena. Thus, Shiva is the mountain God, and his home is Kailash, located on the western border of Tibet. Kailasha is also often seen as Mount Meru, the center of the world. Since he was a mountain God, almost every state has identified a mountain in their state as the residence of Shiva: Bhimshankar in Maharashtra, Tryambak in the Sahyadri, Mallikarjuna in SriSailam, and also in the mountains of Arunachala in Tamil Nadu. The story of how Varanasi became acquainted with Shiva is told in the Puranas. Parvathi's parents felt their daughter deserved better than the rigors of the mountains and pleaded with Shiva, who then agreed to settle in Varanasi and having chosen it, he called it Avimukta (the never-forsaken) and vowed to uphold the city at the tip of his trident. Yet, the Bhakti poet Appar insists that,

"All this is in vain, if you do not think;
The Lord is everywhere."

Shiva is today worshiped in the form of Linga, and the story goes that Shiva appeared spontaneously in a shaft of light, 'jyotirlinga,' in twelve separate places, which have become absolutely essential pilgrim centers for every devout Shaivite. In a greater effort to give credence to the story of the Linga, in 'The Shiva Purana,' a story is told that in the beginning, there was 'pralaya' (deluge), when there was neither day nor night, no Earth, no sea, only darkness. When only 'being' existed. It was 'Brahman,' the Formless, who took form as 'Sada-Shiva,' the eternal Shiva. Desiring a partner, he divides himself into two and becomes Shiva and Shakti. Shiva then created a place to stand, which he called Kasi, the luminous. Then Shiva-Shakti, between them, created a third being called Vishnu and entrusted to him the further creation of the world. Vishnu then entered into meditation, and as he slept upon the eternal waters, a being grew out of his navel; he was Brahma, the firstborn of creation. Then he woke up Vishnu and asked him, "Who are you?" Vishnu replied, "You are my child." Brahma refused to accept that and claimed to be the sole creator. As their arguments heated, a fiery shaft of light grew out of the cosmos and extended upwards. Vishnu and Brahma stopped arguing and tried to find out what the new phenomenon was. Vishnu, as a boar, dug his way to the ends of the Earth, while Brahma became a gander and flew upwards. They kept at it for thousands of years and yet could not reach the beginning or the end of the shaft of light. Then a mass of fire opened, and Shiva appeared in a form with five faces and ten arms, and both Brahma and Vishnu bowed down before Shiva, who manifested himself in the form of a fiery light. This story legitimizes the symbol of the Linga as the power of Shiva and as light, the light of knowledge. It also clearly subordinates Vishnu and Brahma, and Shiva, the outsider, had become the eternal and the origin of all beings, 'Sadashiva.'

This led to the higher philosophy of Advaita, where Shiva is also seen as Niskala, a being without qualities, as sheer light. Yet Shiva is also 'Sakala,' the being with all qualities. He is Nataraja, the dancer creating and destroying the universe, and 'Dakshinamurthi,' an ascetic and teacher. However, Shiva Purana makes a distinction; all other gods are mere Sakala, and Shiva alone is Niskala. It is mainly to emphasize the formless and eternal nature of their God that Shiva is worshiped as a symbol, the Linga. Apart from the common meaning of Linga as phallus, it actually means symbol, mark, or identity. Thus, the Linga is worshiped as a symbol, the shaft of light that denotes the merging of Shiva and Shakti. While idols of lingams are also worshiped, there are 'Suyambu Lingas,' self-manifested lingams.

Shiva: Jyotirlingas

The 'Shiva Puranas' list twelve Jyotirlingas. An inscription at Mahakala, one of the famous Shiva temples in Ujjain, reads:

- In Sourastra, Somnath
- In Shri Shaila, Mallikarjuna
- In Ujjain, Mahakala
- In Omkara, Mamaleshwara
- Paralli Vaidyanath
- In the South, Bhimashankar
- On the bridge, Rameswara
- In the pine forest, Nagesha
- In Varanasi, Visveshvara

- On the Gomathi, Tryambaka
- In the Himalayas, Kedara
- At the abode of Shiva, Grishnesha

Among these, Somnath is where Shiva is worshiped as the 'Moon's Lord' because Soma represents the moon. According to the story, the Moon married twenty-seven of Daksha's daughters but was in love with Rohini. Daksha cursed him to wane away. Upon the gods' advice, the moon sought Shiva's blessing. Soma worshiped Shiva in the form of an Earthen Linga. Shiva appeared to him and blessed him to wane only during the day for half a month and grow back to his lustrous glory. Shiva pledged to live in Prabhasa permanently, depicted with a crescent moon on his head. Philosophers see the waxing and waning moon as a metaphor for the Nishkala and Sakala aspects of Shiva. The word Kala is also translated as a fraction of the moon, giving special significance to Shivaratri, the darkest time of the moon.

Kedarnath is where Parvathi gains Shiva as her husband after much austerity. Despite her austerities, Shiva taunts her for being dark. She then does tapas and becomes Gowri, the white one. Despite this, when Shiva finally appears to her, he tests her by asking why anyone would want to marry Shiva, who has no proper lineage or clan. Parvathi answers, "Don't you know that Shiva is Brahman? He is unchanging, indescribable, and eternal, but assumes many shapes and forms for the welfare of his devotees." Shiva reveals himself and takes Parvathi as his bride. The mountain temple of Gowri is marked with the Hindi words, "The place of Mother Parthi's tapas." This is Gowri Kund, but the main Shiva temple is in Kedarnath, the northernmost location of the Jyotirlingas. The small temple is open only for a few months each year because of the terrible snows, but it also houses a Swayambu Linga. Legend has it that it was carved by Nara and Narayana when Shiva appeared to them in a sheer shaft of light. Kedarnath reinforces the outsider image of Shiva and the strange prejudice against the darkness of Parvathi. Both Shiva and Parvathi are dark, yet Parvathi becomes Gowri to marry Shiva, illustrating a complicated Indian association with color that can even affect the gods, and despite the gods being dark, a bias towards fairness persists.

Rameswaram, in the south, is the southernmost location of Jyotirlinga. It is told in the 'Skanda Purana' that Rama made an Earthen Linga at the beach in Rameswaram before leaving for Lanka and beseeched the blessing of Lord Shiva. Shiva appeared to him and blessed him. On their return from Lanka, Ram and Lakshman decide to consecrate a temple for Shiva, and Hanuman goes to the Himalayas to bring a rock for the Linga. However, since he took too long, Sita made a Linga with sand. When Hanuman returned and they wanted to replace the sand idol, Sita's sand idol could not be moved; it had become as hard as rock and totally grounded. Thus, there are two Lingas at Rameswaram: the rock Linga of Hanuman called 'Visvanath Linga' and Sita's Linga called 'Ramanatha Linga.' The miracles do not end there; Rama then digs a well with his bow, and the waters of the Ganga miraculously fill the well. Thus, once one reaches the Linga at Rameswaram, one does not have to go to Kasi for Ganga water. Mahakala, at Ujjain, is perhaps the most visited of all. Ujjain is also seen as the central point in India and therefore of the Earth. As the poet says,

"In heaven is the Taraka Linga
In the netherworld is Hatkeshwara
And here in this mortal world is Mahakala."

So prominent is Mahakala in Shiva mythology that the story goes that a devout Brahmin, who knew all the Vedas, was being attacked by Asuras. He made an Earthen linga and worshiped it. Next, when the Asuras attacked him, Shiva rose out of the Linga and burned them all to ash. This is clearly an attempt to bring Shiva into the mainstream of Vedic religion. The worship of a Brahmin who knows all the Vedas proves that Shiva is finally accepted as a true God, even by Veda-reading Brahmins.

There is Omkareshwara on the Narmada River. The mountain was shamed by Narmada, who told him that Mount Meru was higher and more glorious. Vindhya thus set up a linga and worshiped Shiva. When Shiva appeared, he agreed to dwell in the Vindhya forever. In fact, with this, Vindhya reached the sky, higher than any mountain, and it was only because of Agastya the Sage, who wanted to go south, that Vindhya bowed down to him and became a small mountain. Strangely, however, the Omkareshwara shrine has three parts, dedicated separately to Brahma, Vishnu, and Shiva. In fact, the word Omkara means all-inclusive, represented by the syllable "OM."

Vaidyanath in Bihar has a strange beginning, as it was established by Ravana through his tapas. He was a devotee of Shiva. The Shiva Linga at Gokarna on the Karnataka coast is also part of Ravana's penance. Finally, there is Sri Shaila in Andhra Pradesh, where legend has it that it was here that Shiva and Parvati came to be close to their son, Skanda, who lost out to Ganesha in a test of parental worship. Ganesha walked around Shiva and Parvathi, while Skanda tried to go around the Earth. Skanda then ran away, as far as possible, from them in anger, and the story has it that he settled in the Palani Hills in Tamil Nadu.

Apart from Shiva, worshiped as Jyotirlingas, Shiva is also worshiped as 'Panchabhuta,' the Lord of the five elements. Shiva thus has five faces and five syllables to be worshiped- Om Namah Shivaya. In Chidambaram, Shiva is worshiped as Nataraja, the celestial dancer, creator, and destroyer. In Kancheepuram, the site is special because Parvathi herself fashioned a lingam to worship Shiva. At Arunachala, in Tiruvannamalai, Shiva is worshiped as Dawn, a fiery shaft of fire. As the Tamil poet says, "The Lord of the gods."

"Whom Arumal and Vishnu could not find
is Lord of Annamalai."

In fact, Ramana Maharshi, one of the great Shiva devotees says,

"Silent you stand
O Shiva, as the hill Arunachala
Shining from heaven to Earth."

While there is much worship of Shiva as Suguna and Sakala, the greatest of the Shiva philosophers, Sankaracharya, sees Shiva and therefore God only as Nirguna and Niskala, one without qualities, the absolute, the indescribable, and beyond human conceptualization.

Lord Vishnu

We have seen that Lord Vishnu and Shiva may have been pre-Aryan gods and worshiped long before the Aryans arrived in India. We also know that their cults were very old, and their worshippers were large. In fact, the Aryans had no chance to impose their religion except by accepting them as supreme gods. Yet, Lord Krishna, like Shiva, was considered a local chief who waited with ten thousand warriors to fight the Aryans. Lord Vishnu was the God of the Bhagavata religion, and his final acceptance is seen in the Mahabharata, where he is treated as the supreme Lord, incarnated as Lord Krishna. In the Gita, he is also made the ultimate philosopher of the religion. It is the philosophy of action without desire, and it is Arjuna's vision as he looks into the mouth of Lord Krishna that becomes the overwhelming idea of God and his power. The devotees of each God make him out to be the most powerful and important God. Thus, Lord Vishnu is the eternal being who was sleeping on Ananta, the endless snake, during Pralaya. In him is contained all the universe, and out of his navel, a lotus rises, and out of it arises Brahma with his four faces; he is Lord Vishnu's agent for creation. Vishnu sleeps on the endless serpent with his consort, Shri, who massages his feet. Vishnu is thus the primal being and associated with water, the font of all creation. He is known as Narayana, the one who sleeps on water. The myth explains that Vishnu swallows all creation, and all that we know of reality is what lies inside Vishnu. Nammalvar, the great Bhakti poet, says,

"Lord of wonder
Long ago, you ate the seven worlds.
You disgorged them by your power.
You enter them,
Becoming all things.
Spread on open space
diffused through all,

Hidden, he pervades
Like life in a body
The radiant scriptures speak
Of the divine who ate them all."

The Vishnu legend thus tries to incorporate the philosophy of unmanifested Brahman, who is manifested but is not limited by the manifestation. Vishnu merely swallows all creation; thus, he is not limited by his creation. Yet, it could be argued that even what is inside an infinite being has to be infinite. In the Narada Purana, it says, "He alone is God Brahma, the creator of the universe, as well as Rudra, the destroyer." By including Rudra as a secondary God, Vaishnavites make Shiva subservient to Vishnu. Forgotten is Indra, but Rudra, the Vedic God, is resurrected to equate him to Shiva so that Vishnu is thus glorified. Vishnu is manifested in his Vyuha, which is five in number. They are Para, the transcendent one, with his consort Shri, who is Bhu, or Earth. He is the endless one resting on Ananta, who manifests the world. He descends to Earth as avatars. He is the God who dwells within 'antaryamin.' His images on Earth are called archas or image incarnations. These Vyuhas are separate and distinct, but like the holy trinity, there is one great being who merely 'takes' different forms. Dedicated to all his different forms, there are important temples. Believers in the Shri Vaishnava tradition speak of a total of 108 special places of Vishnu. To meet his devotees, Vishnu descends from Vaikundam, his home, to Earth, and it is believed that Vishnu, though omnipresent, his presence is specially felt, as though of a personal presence, in these special places. The famous Vishnu habitations are Srirangam on the Cauvery, Tirupati among the Tirumala hills, Kanchi and Melkote in the south, and Dwaraka, Mathura, Badrinath, and Ayodhya in the north. Srirangam is, in many ways, the center of the Vaishnava cult in south India. All the twelve Alwar poets speak of Srirangam, the home of Lord Ranganatha. The image of Lord Vishnu as Lord Ranganatha is said to have been placed by Lord Rama himself at Srirangam, bringing it all the way from his home in Ayodhya. Legend says that the temple rose from the sea at Brahma's tapas to the sun and that Surya was appointed the priest in the temple and from this line of kings was born Ram, thus the lineage of Suryavamsha. The story goes that Vibhishana, Ravana's brother, who helped Ram, returns to Ayodhya with Sita and is rewarded for his help with a gift from his ancestral family deity, Ranganatha. Vibhishana, while carrying it back to Lanka, rests on an island on the Cauvery River, but after his rest, when he tried to lift the idol, it would not budge. Ranganathan then tells Vibhishana that he would like to stay. Dharma Varman, the king, then consoles Vibhishana and tells him that he can instead build a great temple there. Thus rose the Srirangam temple. The deity in Srirangam is Vishnu reclining on Shesha the snake, known to Tamils as Namaperumal (our God). No one really knows how old the Padmanaswamy temple in Trivandrum really is. The present temple is supposed to have been built in 1050, even though a Tulu Brahmin, Divakara Muni, is supposed to have established it in 950 AD. Here, Vishnu, as the story goes, appeared as a little child to Divakara and he asked the boy to stay. The boy agreed on the condition that he would not be scolded. But one day, when the boy put the sacred Shaligrama stone in his mouth, Divakara could not help but scold him. He then disappeared and told Divakara that if he wanted to see him, he should go to the beach near the Anantha forest. There, the child assumed the shape of an immense, reclining Vishnu. Thus, the temple also portrays Vishnu in his sleeping pose.

When the Kali Age began and evil was rampant, Vishnu decided to be closer to his devotees. Thus, he asked Narada to recommend a place. He chose a place on the Swarnamukhi River, and Sesha the serpent lay down there and created the seven hills of Tirumala. The hills are in the shape of a sleeping serpent. Legend has it that Vishnu, in his Varaha avatara (boar), dug into the Earth to save Prithvi; the removed Earth then remained there, creating the present hills. But the Varaha image of Vishnu was so frightening that the gods requested that Vishnu take a more benign form; it is thus that he took the form of Venkateshwara. Thus, Vishnu, in Tirupati, is worshiped as Lord Venkateshwara. Sesha's tail is at Sri Shaila, the back at Ahobilam (associated with Vishnu as Narasimha), and Tirupati proper is where the seven-hooded head of Sesha is seen. Kalahasti is its mouth. At Tirupati, Venkateshwara Balaji is depicted in a unique form. He is depicted neither reclining nor standing, with four arms and his arms adorned with a Shiva-like cobra ornamentation. He beats a conch and holds a discus in his upper hands. He looks more like Shiva than any traditional image of Vishnu. The ambiguity was seen and appreciated by the Alwars, who sang hymns to Vishnu as Harihara, both Vishnu and Shiva. So ambiguous is the image that tradition has it that Ramanuja, to decide the true nature of the idol, put a flower on the idol and slept in the temple; when he woke up, the flower was on the Vishnu side, thus affirming that Balaji was Vishnu. The other aspect of Balaji is that he is portrayed as the boon giver. Consequently, in the Kali Age, people flocked to Balaji for boons. In the Vedas, Vishnu is known as the God of the three steps. The story of Bali, a great Asura, who, with his tapas, had gained great glory and was planning an ultimate 'Yagna,' to compete with the gods. To stop him from becoming greater than the gods, Vishnu took the form of a dwarf. As a guest at the Yajna, Bali asked the dwarf what he wanted as a gift; the dwarf replied that there were only three steps of land to do his rituals. Bali readily agreed; at that time, Vishnu showed his true form and, in two strides, covered the Earth and the heavens and could find no place for his third step. Bali offered his head and was thus pushed down into the netherworld. In his form as the striding God, Vishnu clearly takes over from the Sun God, who was earlier seen as the one who strides across the universe. The steps he takes on Earth have all been sanctified as Vishnu Padas, and great temples have grown there.

Earthbound and Transcendent

The significant aspect of Vishnu as a God was that he was the one most concerned with human welfare. Thus, he is the one who swallows the entire universe and sleeps on Ananta, the endless, yet he is also always available to human call. Thus, it is he who descends to the world in Avataras whenever men and the Earth are in trouble. He has already taken mortal form in nine avatars, beginning with:

1. Matsya is the fish that rescues 'Manu'—the man—from the flood.

2. Kurma, the Tortoise, was used as a fulcrum to churn and to create worlds.
3. Varaha is a boar who rescues the Earth when she is flung into the bottom of the sea.
4. Narasimha, Man-Lion, when Vishnu saves his devotee Prahalad.
5. Vamana, the dwarf who pushed Bali into the netherworld and saved the world for the gods.
6. Parasurama, who saves Brahmins from Kshatriyas.
7. Rama, who taught dharma to kings.
8. Krishna was born to cowherds to teach dharma to Kshatriyas.
9. Buddha, who deluded kings so that the Vedas could be re-established.

His last avatar is awaited, and it is predicted that it will be in the form of Kalki, ushering in a new age.

Shimhachalam, in Andhra Pradesh, is where there is a temple dedicated to Vishnu called Narasimha. The story goes that Prahalad, a devotee, was troubled by his father, the king Hiranyakashipu, who was an Asura and who thought it an insult that his son should worship Vishnu. Vishnu comes in the terrible form of Narasimha and kills Hiranyakashipu, but on Prahalad's request, he brings him back to life, gives him an opportunity to see the true form of Vishnu and thus becomes his devotee. The Narasimha avatar is clearly pre-Aryan and a Bhakti story, where even Asuras can worship Vishnu, and devotion alone is the criterion on which the Lord loves his followers, not caste, race, or varna. The idol at Simhachalam is also ambiguous, and there is a belief that it was earlier a Shiva temple. It also contains shrines for Lakshmi and the Bhakti poets, the Alvars, and Anda, sung in praise of all the gods represented. To affirm the nature of the deity, Ramanuja is supposed to have put Vibuthi (ash for Shiva) and Tulsi leaves, the puja for Vishnu, on the altar at night, and in the morning, the Tulsi was still on the altar, thus proving that it was a Vishnu idol.

While the Himalayas, especially Kailash and Kedarnath, are Shiva sanctuaries, and Shiva is clearly the God of the mountains, Vishnu has a place in Badrinath as Nara and Narayana, the human and divine soul, which is always associated with Vishnu because he is supposed to have performed austerities there. Here also, Urvashi was born out of Narayana's thigh. It was also here that the sage, Narada, performed tapas for a thousand celestial years to see the face of the supreme Lord. The Murti at Badrinath is thus the representation of the Lord in a pose of meditation. In the Mahabharata, the Pandavas journey from Badrinath to the hermitage of Badri-Vishala. Yet, even Badrinath is associated with Shiva, as the mountains around Badrinath are called Neelakanta. Here in Badrinath, religious beliefs seem to merge; the belief in Shiva and Vishnu, even Brahma and the other gods, all come together here, as though the gods are one and we merely call them by different names; they all reside at Badrinath. Devotees, when they reach Badrinath, recite and say, "in the Land of Narayana, at the sacred seat of Urvashi, in this temple of Shiva, Lord of Badri, and the feet of Narayana."

Lord Krishna

Krishna, along with Rama, is among the last of the great gods to be accommodated in the pantheon of deities. Accommodating Krishna required addressing a great deal of philosophical and religious ambiguity and anomalies. It was evidently a forced decision due to the significant gap between the common people's perception and the severe austerity of Advaita, as well as the high philosophy of the Vedas. It is now challenging to determine whether the acceptance of Krishna and Rama paved the way for the intense fervor of the Bhakti poets or if it was the other way around. Most likely, they were parallel streams that merged and contributed to the broadening of Hindu religion and philosophy.

The Krishna legend itself had much to reconcile. Krishna was born into a family of cowherds, even if it was the royal family of Dwaraka. Even in the Mahabharata, there is open scorn by the Kauravas and other kings toward Krishna's social position. From this humble background, Krishna not only becomes the avatar of Vishnu, but as he reveals himself to Arjuna, he is actually the supreme one, the beginning and a being without end, the one who holds the whole universe inside him, the father of all gods, including Shiva and Vishnu. There was so much to reconcile.

The Krishna legend also created a new type of God, where even as a child, Krishna reveals his divine powers. He sucks and kills the Rakshasa, who breast-feeds him, and Yashoda sees the whole universe in baby Krishna's mouth. Thus, Krishna is, even as a baby, a God with a separate cult following. Then there is his playful nature. The young Krishna and the playful Krishna bring forth the idea of God as lovable, not forbidding. His playful interactions with the Gopis add the final touch of human love and almost sexual desire to one's relationship with God.

The problem is that despite Krishna's clear lower-class status and the influx of lower-class devotees to Krishna, neither the caste system nor the karma theory were recast. In fact, in the Bhagwad-Gita, Krishna actually supports caste dharma. He seems only to humanize and deceive. Draupadi, his aunt, and Krishna himself are dark and are taunted for their color, yet no change takes place in the Varna theory of caste. Krishna is Arjuna's charioteer, yet Karna, adopted by a charioteer family, is scorned and denied even education in the same Mahabharata. Finally, while the Krishna legend brings God down to Earth as a child to be loved and as a man capable of human and even sexual love, the doctrine he preaches in the Bhagavad Gita is totally otherworldly, a doctrine of negation, so impossible to practice that most Bhakti poets give it a pass and concentrate only on his human side.

Krishna Worship

Based on the Krishna legend, the important worship centers of Lord Krishna are his birthplace, Mathura; his kingdom, Dwaraka, on the banks of the Yamuna, where he frolicked with the Gopis; and Vrindavan, the village in which Krishna grew up. The places where legend has it that he played are now pilgrim centers called Lilasthals. Finally, there is Govardhan, where Krishna is supposed to have been brought down from the Himalayas. Despite the widespread Krishna cult today, his worship was slow to begin and actually grew only during the early years of the Mughal Empire.

The establishment of Krishna as God and the pilgrimage to places associated with him were actually due to three scholar-devotees. The first was a Guru named Vallabha (1479–1531), a philosopher from South India, who journeyed to all the locations sacred to the memory of Lord Krishna. In his wanderings, Lord Krishna, as a child, appeared to him and revealed to him the correct devotional path, called Pushti Marg, the path of grace.

Another person who tried to reclaim the holy sites of Lord Krishna was Chaitanya (1486-1533). He was a Vaishnavite scholar who was appalled by the ascetic and dry philosophy of Advaitha. He had a loveless, non-human philosophy that he wanted to soften with the love of Lord Krishna. He saw Vishnu as a combined avatar of Krishna and Radha. Thus, Vishnu was not only human but also incorporated the feminine aspects as well. His disciples, Rupa Goswami and Santana Goswami, helped create a cult following for the Radha-Krishna movement.

Narayana Bhatta, a Tamil scholar whom people claim was the incarnation of the sage Narada, was born in Madurai in 1531. He claimed that Krishna appeared to him when he was only twelve. He journeyed to Braj, the holy places associated with Krishna, and helped to systematize the pilgrim path. These scholars brought to life the sacred landscape of Krishna's life. Soon, many Swayambhu (self-manifested) and Swarupa (real form) appearances were reported in places that then became major pilgrim centers. They include Vallabha, where Thirthas and Baitaks were established, holy to Lord Krishna. They also include Puri, Jagannath, and Haridwar. The last of the great Krishna sages was Vaithianath (1516–1586), who consolidated the Pushti Marg as the comprehensive compendium of Krishna worship, which was also linked to the landscape of Krishna pilgrimages.

Krishna in Braj

Dwaraka, the home of Krishna, clearly had to be the most important site for Krishna worship. However, as the Mahabharata says, Krishna himself, to punish his clan, the Yadavas, for becoming too haughty and unrestrained in their power, caused the ocean to swallow up Dwaraka. Close to Dwaraka is where Krishna is supposed to have died by the arrow of the hunter Jara, who mistook his foot for a deer. This location, about ten miles from the Somnath temple, is where a new Dwaraka has emerged. It is today a thriving pilgrim center. Here, the image of Krishna, jet black and four-armed, is similar to the idol at Mathura.

The second most important Krishna center is in the south, in Udupi. It is claimed that the Dwaraka idol was saved from the ocean and was being taken south when the ship carrying it was wrecked off the coast of Mangalore. The image was retrieved and erected at Udupi, cleaned, and sanctified by the great scholar Madhava himself. Madhava, though he traveled widely and claimed Badrinath as the best place to be, finally spent his last days in Udupi. There is a story that says that because the idol was inside the temple, many worshippers could not see the Lord. One such devotee, Kannadasa, sat outside and sang to the Lord. The Lord was so moved by his piety that he opened a crack in the wall so that he could be seen from outside. Today, the crack is covered with silver, but devotees can still see the idol from outside. Madhava, like Sankaracharya, established much math to propagate bhakti; in fact, eight are attributed to him.

To the people of the south, the great Krishna temple is Guruvayoor. The story goes that when Dwaraka was engulfed by the sea, Guru Brihaspati and Vayu begged the Lord that the waters be withdrawn so that the image of Krishna could be retrieved. When the sea withdrew and they went searching, they met Parasurama, one of the avatars of Vishnu, famous for having reclaimed the Malabar Coast from the sea, from Kanyakumari to Gokaran. When they found the image, Parasurama advised them to install it at the edge of a lake called Rudrathirtha. This has become known as Guruvayoor, and

Krishna is called Guruvayurappan. Its fame spread so much that it is now called the Dwaraka of the south. This temple was one of the temples where the Shudras agitated for temple entry in 1930 and was permitted in 1936. Yet, only Hindus are allowed, and Guruvayoor continues to be a center of Brahmanical orthodoxy.

The last of the four dhams is Puri, where Krishna is portrayed as Jagannatha. Jagannatha is black, block-like, with only a head and stump-like arms. He is depicted along with Balarama, who is painted white, and his sister Subhadra, who is painted yellow. This is again a unique representation. Legend has it that Krishna's body, after being burned, floated down from Dwaraka, around the Cape, and was found on the Orissa coast by tribals. There is also a tradition that says the locals worshiped a Goddess named Vimla, and in time, Subhadra, Jagannatha's sister, was seen as Vimla. Clearly, here again, an attempt is being made to establish universality, as per the Shastras: black is the color of the Shudra, yellow of the Vaisya, and white of the Arya. In making Krishna black, a powerful message of universality was being sent out. These legends of Krishna also show that his worship was pre-Aryan and part of a very old tradition in which later identifications were attached to existing gods. However, Puri, like Guruvayoor, has today become a center for Brahmin orthodoxy, not a place devoted to the all-encompassing love of Lord Krishna, born a Yadava. The Puri temple is still closed to non-Hindus, and only during the yearly Rath Yatra, when the idols are moved to their summer residence, do all people have a glimpse of the idols. Forgotten is the Lord Krishna, who breaks open a crack in the walls at Udupi so that all may see him.

Rama: The God

The Ramayana is the very centerpiece of Indian consciousness and can even be said to be the main cultural identity that unifies the entire Southeast Asian region. Yet, Rama has never become the God that Shiva, Vishnu, or Krishna have become, even though Mahatma Gandhi is supposed to have died saying, "Ram, Ram." While Rama is an avatar of Vishnu, he is seen more as an ideal king than as the supreme God. In fact, no claim is made for Rama as the supreme God. Rama himself is shown as a devotee of Shiva, thereby making a complex statement because he is also Lord Vishnu. While the Ramayana is clearly the older epic and, in its original form, predates Buddhism, Rama as a God is a very new phenomenon. Yet, if there is one story that unites India from north to south and east to west, it is the Ramayana. And unlike the Mahabharata, it has been retold in different parts of the country by poets of genius in their own languages. Thus, Kamban wrote his Tamil Ramayana in the 12th century, Krithivasan in Bengali in the 14th century, and Tulasidasa wrote his Awadhi version in the 16th century. These retellings made the story popular and led to Kathakali and Ram Lila plays, and theater productions of the Ramayana, symbolizing the religious conscience of India.

Rama, as God, was by and large the creation of Ramananda, a bhakti poet of the 16th century. His disciples, Kabir and Tulsidas, made Rama into a cult deity. In fact, till then, Hanuman, as the son of Lord Shiva, was worshiped as much, if not more, than Rama. As Rama was resurrected as God, the central locations in which the Ramayana is set became pilgrim spots. This included Ayodhya, which was supposed to be the birthplace of Rama. While there are Ayodhyas in Sri Lanka, Cambodia, and Indonesia, it was only recently that Ayodhya in India was discovered as Rama's birthplace. Yet, Ayodhya was important even during Buddha's time as the capital of the Kosala kingdom, and archaeologists claim that a town existed at the site even in the 7th century B.C. The place was, however, more famous in relation to Shiva and the city deity Nageshvarnathan, Lord of Nagas. In fact, even Rama devotees are told to bathe in the Shiva Nageshvaranatha temple to get the benefits of a pilgrimage to Ayodhya. Thus, unlike Krishna, Rama has not been able to dislodge old loyalties.

The second spot sacrosanct to Rama is Prayaga, the confluence of Ganga and Yamuna, where Rama, when in exile, stopped to rest at the Ashram of Bharadwaj. Other spots include the forest of Panchavati on the Narmada, near modern-day Nasik, where Sita was abducted, and Kishkindha, near modern-day Hospet in

Karnataka, on the banks of the Pampa, known as Tungabhadra in Karnataka. As Tulasidasa says, everywhere they went, the place became sanctified by their presence. Thus, Chitrakut in middle India, on the Godavari River, where the royal refugees had stayed with the Sage Atri, is also an important pilgrimage site. Wherever they went, they used to stay with sages in their hermit dwellings, with Bharadwaj in Prayaga, Atri in Chitrakoot, Agastya in Panchavati, and Sabari in Kishkindha. The final location sacred to the Ramayana is Rameswaram, where Rama stopped and built a bridge to Lanka but was also ambiguous as he stopped and prayed to Lord Shiva. Thus, Rameswaram is still called a Shivakshetra, as Rama himself prayed to Shiva for help.

The Goddess Cult

There were no goddesses in the Vedas, and it was long before gods were provided consorts, and even then, they were merely a feminine representation, not symbols of power. However, in time, goddesses proliferated, and there were goddesses everywhere. As a consequence, even India became Mother India, Bharat-Mata, and both 'Vande Mataram' and 'Jana Gana,' the national anthem, appealed to Bharat-Mata. The truth is that Goddess worship was much older than the Vedas. In fact, archaeologists claim that many artifacts found among the ruins of the Harappan civilization were actually mother goddesses. There is also no doubt that in every civilization, a matriarchal period precedes the dominance of men, a time when men worshiped goddesses. The post-Vedic period saw the rediscovery of goddesses and the slow acceptance of local beliefs that were incorporated into the pantheon of gods, mostly as consorts to existing gods and sharing their power. By the 10th century, when the later Puranas were written, the goddesses finally came into their own. Even the Epics respect the power of the goddesses, but it is really in the Puranas, like Bhagavata Purana, Devi Bhagavata Purana, Kalika Purana, Markandeya Purana, and others, that the Devi becomes powerful and then all-powerful.

Like the Puranas of Shiva and Vishnu, the Devi Puranas were written to establish the legitimacy of the goddesses, showing them as powerful in themselves, the better part of the gods, and finally as all-powerful and supreme. Thus, in the Bhagavata Purana, Shakti is shown as the great life force that animates all creation. Shiva is helpless without Shakti. In fact, Shiva becomes Shava (a corpse) without Shakti. In Devi Bhagavata Purana, Shakti is finally seen as the Supreme Reality; Brahman becomes Devi, the indescribable and ungraspable. She is all Sattva (purity), as Mahalakshmi, and both rajas (power and passion) and tamas (darkness) as Mahasar-aswathi. Where the Devi was only Prakriti, powerless without Purusa, the Devi now becomes all-powerful. Thus, in a story in Devi Purana, Lakshmi and Parvathi leave their husbands because they are boasters and braggarts. With their departure, Shiva and Vishnu become powerless and beg the other gods to ask them to return. Only with their return do the gods get back their power.

However, many ambivalent views continued to confuse the picture even about the goddesses, as they had been retrieved from local customs and part of an older and more primitive religion, along with the pantheon of universal gods. Thus, the writers of the Puranas are in a quandary as to whether to make them black or white. Devi, as Kali, is black, but as Gauri, she is made white by her tapas, as she is taunted by Shiva for being black. She is also the virgin goddess, as in Kanyakumari, and also the goddess of fertility. She is also the Goddess, Ganga, and Mother Earth herself, and Sita is her daughter, and even the Atharva Veda has a hymn to Mother Earth that says,

"Untrammelled in the midst of men, the Earth
May she spread wide for us, afford us Joy."

She is also the Goddess of forests and trees, as Panchavati. Her power is actually told in the story of the slaying of the bull, Mahisha. The bull was all-powerful and all the gods trembled before it. Then Devi took the weapons from the gods and slew the bull. The symbol of Devi is the trident of three points, almost the same as Shiva's trident. Finally, while orthodox religion became vegetarian and gods were worshiped with pujas, not sacrifices, Kali is still worshiped with the animal sacrifice of a goat, and her food still includes fish. In Mirzapur, U.P., there is a pilgrim site called

Vindhyachala, dedicated to the Vindhyavasini Devi. She is covered with marigold; next to it, and close by, is a temple to Ashtabhuja, the eight-armed one, and another to Kali, the black one. The Devi, in all her triple powers and embodiments, is worshiped here. In Devi Mahatmya, Parvathi, the mountain Goddess, produces Ambika (the mother), also known as Kaushiki (the glorious), but when she releases her mother's image and her luminous image, she becomes black and thereafter is known as Kalika. Shakti is thus black and white and her three-fold image is symbolized by the trident. She is worshiped as Mahalakshmi, Maha Saraswathi, and Maha Kali. At Ujjain, there is the Garha Kalika shrine dedicated to Kali, made famous by Kalidasa's devotion. Mahalakshmi, in Kolhapur, and Mookambika Devi, on the Konkan coast. She is worshiped in all her forms at Vaishno Devi in Kashmir and as Kamakhya Devi in Assam. In Puri, there is a temple honoring Vimla. In Krishna Jagannath and Kanchipuram, she is worshiped as the 'love-eyed' Goddess, Kamakshi. A very prominent temple dedicated to Devi is the Meenakshi temple in Madurai. Here the story goes that a king, after many rituals, got a child, but it was a girl with three breasts. While still perplexed, a divine voice advised the King to bring her up as the crown princess and that one breast would disappear when she met her Lord. She became a great conqueror and defeated all kings right up to Kailash, and there, when she met Shiva, her third breast disappeared and she married Shiva. The virgin, Meenakshi, thus becomes Shiva's wife and Shiva becomes Sundareswara, the beautiful Lord. Consequently, both the God and Goddess are worshiped at the Meenakshi temple. In Kanyakumari, the Goddess is worshiped as the virgin Goddess. Parvathi, as Shiva's consort, lives in the Himalayas. The Goddess is also Shakti in the form of Durga, Lakshmi, Saraswati, Savitri, and Radha.

Sati and her Body Parts

The sacrifice of Daksha and the death of Sati were made into legends to explain the spontaneous growth of the Kali cult all over India. The story goes that when Sati died, Shiva was so angry and inconsolable that he carried Sati in his arms and danced the dance of destruction. As he danced, the body parts of Sati broke off and fell in many parts of the country. This story is told in the Kalika Purana and Devi Purana. It is said that her parts fell in 108 places, and seven of them have become truly important pilgrimage centers. Her feet fell at Devikuta, where she is worshiped as Mahabaga; her thighs fell at Uddiyana, where she is called Katyayani; her yoni fell at Kamarupa, where she is worshiped as Kamakhya; her shoulders and neck fell at Purnagiri; and her navel in a location just east of Kamapura, where she is called Dikkaravasini; and her breasts at Jalandhara, where she is worshiped as Chandi. In all these places, Shiva is also present, and the Linga is also worshiped.

Sati's death in Daksha's sacrifice parallels the sacrifice of Brahman by the gods for the sustenance of the world. Thus, this story attempts to steal the thunder from the gods, as humans can also now perform Sati, the ultimate sacrifice. In the case of Sati, wherever her body parts fell, they became Shakti Peethas. Her elbow is at Ujjain, and her face is at Kashi, where she is known as Vishalakshi. Her heart fell in Vaidyanath; the same part is also claimed in Rajasthan, where there is a great temple to Ambaji. Her head is claimed by both Kangra on the Himalayan foothills and Kannur in Kerala. Yet, the most famous is Kamakhya Devi, in Kamapura, Assam, where her yoni fell, in the 'blue mountain,' Milaca, near Guwahati, where there is a stone image of the Goddess that remains miraculously moist. She is called Kamakhya because, as the story goes, Kama, the God of Love, tried to be fresh with her and she burned him alive, using Shiva's third eye, and he became a pile of ash. Kamakhya has a parallel in Chengannur, Kerala, where she is Bhagavati.

The Devi cult thus grew from first being mere consorts and then becoming gods in their own right, to Shakti, the power that resides in the gods, and finally to the ultimate source of the universe through the sacrifice of Sati. By spreading the Sati parts to 108 different places, all the local Goddesses like Menasha, Mariaman, and Kali were all accommodated. Thus, virginity, fertility, the rivers, and all the forest deities were also accommodated in the belief system. The interesting aspect is that as each new God or Goddess is accommodated, they are given supreme status in the Puranas. However, since all gods are considered supreme, in the end, the accommodation is merely an accommodation that rarely upsets the real scheme of beliefs, only that everyone's God is also legitimized.

Mother Ganga

No account of a Goddess would be complete without Ganga, a Goddess so powerful that her waters ensure eternal salvation. As the hymn says,

"This Ganga was sent out for the salvation
Of the world by Shiva, Lord
Of Lords, filled with sweet wine of compassion
Shiva having squeezed the essence of Yoga and Upanishads
Created this excellent river because of his mercy for all mankind."

The story goes that a great king, Sagara, was so illustrious that he performed the Ashvamedha sacrifice. However, the gods, fearful of the power he would gain thereby, stole his horse. Sagara then sent his sixty thousand sons to find the horse. They found it tied to the Ashram of the Sage Kapila. Thinking he must have stolen the horse, they rushed in while Kapila was meditating. This angered Kapila, who opened his eyes, killing all sixty thousand to ash.

Sagara then sent his grandson, Anshuman, to Kapila. Through his prayers and asceticism, he won Kapila's heart, who then told him that the sons of Sagara would be brought back to life if Ganga condescended to come down and wash their bodies. So, Anshuman's grandson, Bhagiratha, performed tapas to Lord Shiva, who finally agreed to help. However, Ganga, being so powerful, would have destroyed the entire Earth by falling directly down, so Lord Shiva caught her in the locks of his hair and tamed her before releasing her on Earth. The river, as it flowed over the ashes of the dead sons, brought them back to life.

By this precedent, Ganga has the power to quicken all the dead. Thus, all Hindus seek out the water of the Ganga to wash away their sins. The Puranas claim that the water of the Ganga is honeyed and even contains soma.

Unlike many new gods, Ganga is known even in the Rig Veda, where they sing to Ganga as,

"Froth from the midst of the flood they flow
Purifying, never sleeping, their leader the sea
Indra, the thunder, the bull has dug out their channels
Here may these Goddess water flow
Nectar they are, bright and pure."

In the early legend, Ganga is part of the story of Indra and his fight with Vritra, the serpent who had coiled around the vault where the waters of heaven were enclosed. By killing Vritra, Indra releases the waters of heaven for the enrichment of the Earth. As a result of this myth related to Ganga, all the major rivers of India have similar legends linking them to Ganga.

With the sanctification of the Ganga, the entire route of the Ganga has become a pilgrim center. Gomoh, the mouth of Ganga, is called the cow's mouth; then Gangotri, where Ganga becomes a river; and Haridwar, called Gangadhara, or the gate of the Ganga; then Prayaga, the meeting place of Ganga and Yamuna at Allahabad. As per legend, the ancient mythical river Saraswati is also supposed to meet the Ganga at Prayag. Finally, where the Ganga meets the sea in the Bay of Bengal, the whole Delta area is called Ganga Sagara. The prayer to Ganga in 'Ganga Lahari,' goes,

"Mother Ganga, may you water
Abundant blessing on the world
embodied goodness of the gods.
May your water, sublime wine of immortality
Soothe our troubled souls."

Ganga, is 'Mother Ganga,' embracing, soothing, enriching and forgiving. She is also the liquid Shakti of Lord Shiva. Thus, Jagannath in, 'Ganga Lahari,' says,

"I come to you as a child to his mother.
I come as an orphan
To you, moist with love
I come without refuge.

To you, giver of sacred rest
I come a fallen man.
To you, up-lifter of all,
I come, undone by disease.
To you, the perfect physician
I come, my heart dry with thirst.
To you, ocean of sweet wine
Do with me whatever you will."

A Synthesis

The study of Indian thought and consciousness reveals a belief in a spectrum of irreconcilable, contradictory, and conflicting. Yet, the reality of Indian consciousness is that all these were swallowed whole, and yet, there remains a semblance of separate identities. Identity in diversity is not just ironical; it is a contradiction in terms. It is like saying, fragmented to be whole. Yet, that is the truth.

To the eternal credit of Indians down the centuries, this was not the result of a mute acceptance of the irrational, the contradictory, and the inhumane. At every stage and in every age, Indians revolted, dissented, and threatened to secede from the family called Hinduism. The tragedy is that they failed to change the power structure, even as their protests were diluted by a passive acceptance of their point of view, which was thereafter relegated to the backstage of Hindu practices.

Thus, Hinduism, as we must call the amalgamation of Indian thought, changed from the austere, agnostic, questioning philosophy of the Vedas, through the Upanishads, the Shastras, and the Puranas, to a strange, multi-colored thinking that accommodated all forms of thought, from Advaita to Tantra, and saw God as an eternal principle, as well as the personal God of the Bhakti poets. It accommodated all local religious practices and incorporated the local gods as consorts, sons, and daughters of the already accepted gods like Shiva, Vishnu, and Brahma. It ceased to discriminate; the choice was left to believers as to who to worship and how.

What is amazing is the tragic descent of sensibilities. The Vedas talk of the Sages, who, through their meditative power, created knowledge, and through 'Vak,' the word, and through their poems and hymns, an original form of knowledge emerged. They merely looked at creation in wonder and asked, Who created all this? and were humble enough to say, Who knows? Yet they were arrogant enough to say, not the gods, because they came later. Man and his intellect were supreme.

The predominance of Sages and Hermits continues through the Epics. Thus, in the Ramayana, which depicts a period prior to 600 B.C., Rama, in his wanderings, always stays with ascetic hermits in their jungle Ashrams. Clearly, even as men were settling in towns and villages and taking to agriculture, there were still learned men who saw a greater validity in a life of thought. This group of traveling hermits and settled sages became a daily feature of life during and prior to the rise of the Mauryan Empire. The existence of these hermits indicates a reluctance to accept orthodoxy, an assertion that the truth is yet to be known.

The result was the growth of various philosophical schools, from Cynicism to the Stoics, Epicureans, and mere Materialists. Out of this churning grew two major religions: Jainism and Buddhism. These religions questioned the value of rituals, which the diluted Vedic religion had descended to with the incorporation of the Atharva Veda. They questioned the rationality of sacrifice and the ruthless killing of animals to please the gods.

More important was the fact that Jainism and Buddhism created Sangas and Mutts. A congregation of believers could now meet and discuss in mutts, while a monastery was where the more religious could retire to meditate and live a life beyond the mere rituals of daily life. These institutions were really radical, as they were the base from which schools and universities, like Nalanda, grew. Buddhism also moved away from Sanskrit and chose to deal with people in their own language. Prakrit was the spoken form of Sanskrit, and from it grew the many languages we know today.

The great weakness of Vedic Hinduism was that the Vedas were written in Sanskrit, which very few knew and even fewer could read, as the Grantha script had already become obsolete. Further, Vedic religion was not a temple-oriented religion but one that merely created a set of individual duties and rituals. It had no control over how people behaved or what they believed, dealing only with their ritual requirements.

The institutions of Buddhism were their greatest assets and also the source of their fragmentation and final disappearance. These institutions encouraged thought, which also resulted in dissent and conflict. The early Sangha tried to curb these rebellions through council meetings, but in the end, the inevitable happened: Buddhism broke into Hinayana and Mahayana and then broke into a dozen different sects, from Zen Buddhism to Tantra.

Vedic Hinduism, in its resurgence under Brahmanical empires, helped in suppressing Buddhism, persecuting its believers, and destroying their mutts and monasteries. The final disappearance of Buddhism in India was ironic; it was the result of Hindu orthodoxy accepting the Buddha as the ninth Avatar of Lord Vishnu and thus allowing die-hard Buddha loyalists to worship Buddha as Lord Vishnu, burying Buddhism as a separate religion.

Orthodox Hinduism, however, had to mutate into a new avatar to accommodate Jain and Buddhist beliefs. These were, however, against the grain of Vedic thought but very much in tune with the requirements of the new middle class that had begun to prosper during the last few centuries before the common era. These included the gradual limitation of animal sacrifice, the preference for a vegetarian diet, and the acceptance of Ahimsa as a tenet of belief.

With the beginning of the early centuries of the common era, much of the systematic dissent, as seen by major schools of philosophy and religions like Buddhism and Jainism, began to fade and remained separate and distinct, only in pockets. The rest of India came within the fold of orthodox Brahminical thought; however, the violence of the revolt from within was, if anything, even more aggressive.

Brahminical orthodoxy had by this time learned to deal with dissent and thus went more than halfway to accommodate divergent views. Initially, it meant only accepting strange new gods like Shiva, who was the antithesis of all that orthodox Brahmanism saw in God. He was dark, behaved like a Chandala, lived in the burning ghats, and adorned himself with a necklace of skulls. Even this God was accepted and, in time, became the supreme God. Finally, even great philosophers like Sankaracharya, despite his rather arid perception of God as Nirguna, were still Shivites.

The challenge from local deities was even more difficult to deal with, but in a massive exercise of writing down the Epics and the Puranas, they were all given legitimacy. As Rajiv Malhotra says in his book, 'Being Different,' "The Puranas were a vehicle for spreading Sanskrit beyond the elites and served as an ancient form of pop culture with spiritual messages embedded in fables and tales." In the process, Krishna, a Yadava born and brought up by cowherds, became the supreme Lord, swallowing, literally, all the other gods.

Krishna, a Shudra dark in complexion, was also accommodated without affecting the caste system or the theory of Karma. So too were the dark goddesses like Draupadi, Sita, and even Parvathi, who became Gauri, the fair one, to show that darkness was still not acceptable, even among gods. In the meantime, the agnostic questioning, supported by philosophic schools from Samkhya to Yoga to Nyaya, was slowly relegated to the classrooms for those who believed in Jnana as a way to salvation, while mainstream Hinduism morphed into a religion with many personal gods who could be worshiped by Bhakti alone. This eliminated the need for temples, rituals, or any serious theology.

On the other hand, temples continued to grow in sacred locations, like Jyotirlingas, Tirthas, Padas, and other sites made sacred by the Epics and the Puranas. With this development, pilgrimages became a way of seeking salvation, and as the Tirupati Venkateswara temple makes clear, in Kali Yug, when Jnana, truth, and even Dharma are under attack, people seek only material gains and comforts; the need is for a God who could grant boons.

While Buddhism disappeared as a result of internal fragmentation, Hinduism is totally fragmented, retaining the elusive appearance of something whole as a result of accepting fragmentation as a strategy. There is such a deep divide between the Hinduism of Jnana, the Vedas, the philosophical schools, and the Hinduism of everyday faith that it is impossible to see them as parts of the same entity. The abandonment of Jnana saw the exodus of those who could not live without reason. The Jnana Yogi, inevitably tolerant, could not cause the inevitable break; thus, the hybrid religion Hinduism was accepted by well-adjusted men, as they would the madness of the world.

The Philosophy

While most intellectuals see in the 'Upanishads' the pinnacle of Indian religious thinking and look down on the 'Puranas' as convoluted mythology meant for the credulous, a complete reading of the Puranas and a distillation of its thinking will show a very acute and pervasive understanding of all intellectual ideas.

Starting with the story of creation with Vishnu asleep on AdiShesha, the eternal snake, the ever-present consciousness has to be awakened for creation to begin. Yet, it starts not even with consciousness but with the unknowing birth of Brahma through Vishnu's navel. Even then, all he can produce is a lotus flower, white and almost immaterial. Even the creation of his sons only results in the senses required for sensual perception. It is only with the birth of Ushas, the dawn, that creation becomes self-sustaining, for it creates desire in Brahma. It is desire that manifests the unmanifested and forces nature to appear to have sensual perception. This focuses on two great ideas: that all life is the result of desire, thus justifying sexual attraction, which then leads to the greater idea that all thinking is a sexual fire in the mind, desire acting on curiosity. The second idea is that the subject becomes real only in the presence of the object, and the objective world has life only in the mind of a conscious subject. It is only perception that actualizes the material world, the world of 'Maya,' kept alive by desire.

In Shiva, we are given the very opposite view. Shiva is a realization that once humans become conscious and are driven by desire, it will be an endless pursuit of desire and lust that will end only in killing and death. It is an unsustainable system, except as an endless cycle. The escape from such an endless cycle is to turn desire inwards and forsake 'Maya,' the manifestation, and become self-contained with an inner fire that may, in human terms, be cold and even an annihilation of the objective world. It is this idea that Buddha clung to and was to make people say that Sankaracharya was a Buddhist because he highlighted the concept of a 'Nirguna' God and the world as 'Maya.' In creating desire, women are shown as the heart of desire and the symbol of creation. She is also the 'object' that manifests the objective world. With this, they introduce the ultimate philosophical concept that the world exists because there is a consciousness that sees the manifestation. The Purana writers thus also call Ushas 'Maya,' as she is also only an illusion in the mind of man.

However, Shiva's internal fire is not only an annihilation but can be projected outward for creation, as the Asuras learned. When they could not compete with the Devas, Shukra the Asura did tapas and when Shiva swallowed him to save the Devas, he escaped through Shiva's Linga. Once he comes out, he is all-powerful, even in a productive sense. The realization of nihilism at the heart of creation makes man God-like in knowledge and power. Similarly, Chandra, the Moon, as he loses his virility by being cursed by the gods for his partiality to Rohini, finds refuge in Shiva's locks and becomes virile again. Tapas and inward concentration, while an attempt to obliterate 'Maya' or manifestation, are also so powerful that they are unbeatable when used as power in life. While it is a corruption of its purpose, that is what Tantra, in combination with Yoga, attempts to do. In the story of Viswamitra, he ends his tapas only when the Apsara, Menka, forces his eyes to open and ends up copulating with her. In the Puranas, the Apsara are seen as water, from the word Apsa meaning water, that quenches the fire of tapas. Shiva himself is finally tempted by Parvathi only when she uses his own methods and, through her implacable determination, becomes his equal. Only when, as Kali, she sits on the phallus of Shiva does the world finally manifest. The idea that negation is also the power of creation is a very difficult concept.

Another group of stories in the Shiva Puranas deals with the final domestication of Shiva. Even the marriage to Parvathi does not make Shiva a family man. He refuses to allow his semen for procreation until his own sin of beheading Ganesh causes him to become a creator and, with it, establishes his fatherhood. Even then, he remains a resultant father and spouse. However, when he finally feels hunger, he has to go to Parvathi, and as she feeds him, she becomes Annapurna. Similarly, when he suddenly feels a desire for a Parvathi in the shape of a native woman, Parvathi creates a ruckus that he is unfaithful, and then Shiva becomes a hunter whom Parvathi falls for when Shiva is able to say, "We are now even." To the Vedic purist, Shiva is a very ambiguous God. In some stories, he is presented as the innocent God; he cannot discern caste or status; all are equal to him. He even fails very often to distinguish gender and has no sense of social correctness. He even offers Parvathi to Ravana because he is his devotee. The impression thus created is that Shiva is not a God for Earthlings who have to live with the compulsions of life, hunger, desire, and shelter apart from the need for meaning. The story of Kannapan and his devotion, leading to his sacrifice of his own eyes for Shiva, tells of the deeper and more intimate connection with Shiva, beyond the nihilistic philosophy, with an older native tradition, which the Vedic people merely accepted. The problem is that the stories humanize Shiva, but the philosophy does not correspond, as Shiva started as a God of negation for whom the world itself is unreal. Thus, only an inward regression would allow for any peace of mind. When he then becomes aware of human needs, he merely helps his wife and his devotees without any change in philosophy, leaving one confused as to how to deal with life and its problems. When Shiva, the eternal Yogi, becomes concerned with human problems, he becomes Sankara, the source of all joy. All that we get from the stories is that Shiva is 'Nirguna' while Parvathi is the manifestation. Shiva is renunciation, while Parvathi is the giver of all worldly comforts; yet, it is Shiva who swallows the poison of creation, as he is the only one who has overcome the world. His non-existence is eternal, while the world of Parvathi, of sensation, flesh, and blood, is impermanent, illusionary, and passing. Parvathi creates the world while Shiva guides us to the ultimate truth, yet one cannot exist without the other. The interesting thing is that while the Shiva tradition leaves us hanging in mid-air like Trisunka, it is the Vishnu tradition that tries to reconcile the material world with the world of Nirguna. In fact, it may have arisen due to the need to humanize religion. They start by accepting them as two sides of the same, a Purusha and a Prakriti; one cannot exist without the other, as Shiva is only 'Shava' without 'Shakti.' The idea is represented by

Mohini, neither a human nor an Apsara. Breathtakingly beautiful, neither male nor female. She entices, not to sexual union but to the greater truth at the heart of manifestation. It is the very beauty of Maya that forces us to look deeper. The problem is that it is man's capacity to visualize that creates 'Maya' and then trying to understand manifestation through one's intellect becomes a circular exercise. All that happens is that 'Maya' changes to adapt to the level of thinking that a man has reached. Thus, there can never be an objective reality, only a subjective one. Yet, there are different levels of understanding that the Vishnu tradition illustrates with the three stages of Vishnu, as Narayana; he is asleep, unaware of Maya, as Vishnu; he is beyond Maya, and as Avatars, he accepts 'Maya.' In a story, Narada goes to Vishnu to understand Maya; Vishnu says, "First, get me some water to drink." In searching for water, he is totally distracted by a beautiful girl he marries and with whom he has children and grandchildren, until one day a flood sweeps them all away. Heartbroken, he again appeals to Vishnu, who then reminds him that it was he who wanted to know what Maya meant. The basis of their thinking is that it is fine to know what Maya means but one can understand what it really means only by living it. The world is as beautiful as Mohini, but beauty, love, and the pleasures of life have meaning only in a finite life. An infinite life makes them meaningless. What is important is to be aware of Maya, even as we enjoy life. They consequently use the symbol of the weighing scale to push home the truth that in a plural universe, what is important is to understand the real value of life in the larger context of Maya. They contrast what they see as Brahma's view with that of Vishnu. Brahma, so caught up in the universe he creates (Brahmananda), tries to improve it, forgetting that it is all a manifestation and only Maya. This leads to the sprouting of his fifth head, the 'ego' that Shiva's knowledge destroys. Yet to merely accept Shiva's world is to return to the state of Narayana, a sleep of unawareness, which to human life is death. Vishnu's way is the way of 'Prakriti Marg,' which accepts life for what it is and sees life as the beautiful Mohini, so seductive as to entice even the gods. All that is needed is a weighing scale to weigh life in the balance of the eternity of Maya.

Raising the Barricades

With the writing of the Puranas, the orthodoxy seemed to have reached the end of their patience with the many concessions they had to make to please the common people, and then there was a halt, a silence that has not been broken to this day. No more accommodation and no more new gods. They seemed to be saying, thus far and no further, yet what the intellectual would say is that having completely destroyed the core of Vedic Hinduism, what more was there to destroy? Yet it is also a paradox that for many centuries, the religious leaders, despite rear-guard action from the orthodoxy, kept on compromising, going so far as to assist in the writing of Puranas to justify all the additions to their religion, and then, as though one morning they had enough, they clamped down on all further concessions and became rigid and intolerant of all further compromise, and put a total ban on dissent. They then entered a time described by Wendy Doniger in her book, 'Hindus: An Alternate History,' as 'the silencing of dissent.' The idea that the Hindu tradition of toleration suddenly stopped after the age of the Guptas is, however, an oversimplification, as she does not ask the question: who compromised and who suddenly became intolerant? That is one of the great unasked questions that the indologist helped to propagate.

The Hinduism that we have come to know has a checkered history and an interesting evolution. It began with nothing, only a questioning openness, and as it met with new people and new ideas, it incorporated them into its theology, making it appear comprehensive. The problem with compromises and the acceptance of divergent ideas is the appearance of inconsistency and incongruity. The attitude of the intellectual toward this aberration was to separate philosophy from practice. Thus, from the Upanishads on, the philosophy of the religion was austere, consistent, and rigid. In the face of the mob, they surrendered what was acceptable as worship and the nature and names of gods. They accepted the proliferation of gods and accepted that ordinary people need idols to worship. The philosophy behind the religion, however, remained a choice between Advaita and Dvaita, with God as Nirguna or Suguna and the reality of God as only one, while men were allowed to worship them in any name. The problem came only with the sharing of power between the custodians of religion and others. The fact that they not only survived but have retained power is the real story. How they did it is a very interesting and educational story. The important question is: who benefited?

Sanskrit and The Vedas

The 'Silencing of Dissent' started with 'Vak' or language. Sanskrit, as the language of religious rituals and magic, ensured that only the Sanskrit-educated Brahmin, who could understand it, would have access to and be able to interpret religion. Without any social power or the might of the king, the Brahmins thus ensured that all knowledge remained firmly in their hands. By treating Sanskrit as the language of religion, it became sacred and out of bounds, especially for the lower castes. The Kshatriya and Vaisya had better things to do and therefore made no attempt to enter the realm of knowledge. However, when the Kshatriya did, there was conflict on a colossal scale, with Brahmin heroes like Parasurama and Kshatriya heroes like Viswamitra almost bringing the world to an end. Yet, Sanskrit was never the language of daily life; Sanskrit was always, as the word means, perfect and artificial, while Prakriti, the language of daily use, was practical and natural. The Brahmin outlasted all his opponents because he had 'Vak' or language. He wrote history. Normally, history, we say, is written by the victors; in the Indian context, those who wrote history eventually triumphed, however much they may have suffered in the interim. They claimed it was 'Itihasa,' which actually happened, as though there was no alternate history to what they wrote. Consequently, as M.N. Srinivasan coined the phrase in 1952, the history of India has been a history of the process of Sanskritization. The question again is: who benefited from the imposition of Sanskrit?

Sanskrit was the language of the Aryans, a small group of alien settlers who were mere herders of cattle with little culture or complexity of religious beliefs. How did they thrust Sanskrit on a large, educated, and complex civilization that descended from the

Harappan people? Why did these people then accept the Vedas as revealed scriptures when they obviously had their own religion and systems of worship? This would suggest that the Aryans were great people and their Vedas astounded the local people, who, merely to get access to them, were prepared to learn Sanskrit. Yet, the later history of compromises shows that the local people were not only a massive force but also that their intellectual acumen was perhaps acute than that of the Aryan. Why then, did the local intelligentsia forsake their own language and accept Sanskrit?

The second major cause for the 'silencing of dissent,' which may sound contradictory and yet is at the core of Indian spirituality, is that Vedic religion started with nothing and thus could absorb and smother dissent by swallowing new ideas whole and forcing others into submission. The early Vedic hymns, especially the Rig Veda, portray a people who had no religion, who questioned the reality of the gods, and humbly accepted that it would be impossible to know if the universe was created or self-existent. Further, Vedic religion was based on sacrifice and the assumption that the gods and men depended on the smoke of sacrifice to exist. The harmony of the universe was maintained through sacrifice. To Vedic men, gods and asuras were merely like men, real only to the extent they depended on sacrifice. In fact, the anti-gods, the Asuras, had God-like power, implying that divinity and power were both acquired and not bequeathed. The anti-gods were brothers of the gods. The Vedic people believed that too much power would even corrupt the gods; thus, a foil was necessary. The gods were also not ethical in any sense; they merely had power. Such a religion was clearly waiting to be filled in, and history ensured the rest.

The Vedic Gods

The important Vedic gods were Agni, Soma, Indra, and Varuna. They were important because they were part of the Vedic sacrifice. Agni was the God of fire, the purifier, and the building of the altar was the foundation of all Vedic rituals. While fire burns, it is Soma, the liquid fire, that is the elixir of life. Indra is the killer of Vritra, the dragon, and the giver of rain, and Varuna is the sky God, the custodian of sacred rituals. Yet, within this seeming polytheism was a basic monotheism, where the Rig Veda asks, "Where did creation come from?" And asserts, "The gods came afterwards. He who looks down on it, in the highest heaven, only he knows." When the creator asks Indra, "Who am I?" Indra answers, "Just who you just said." Thus, to the question, "Who is ka?" the answer is, "Ka is who," like the Jehovah of the Jews who says, "I am who I am." While God was unknown, knowledge alone was God. Thus, the early texts say, "Do not inquire about the father or mother of a Brahmin; when you find knowledge in someone, that is his father and mother." Similarly, the Brahmanas tell of how, when Brahmins were performing a sacrifice at the River Saraswati, they saw Kavasha, son of Illusha, and drove him away to the desert; he sat and wrote poetry, and Saraswati surrounded him with water. So, the sages say, "The gods know him. Let us call him back." While this openness and humility means that even a sacrifice must accept greatness, knowledge, and poetic ability, the attitude changes to one of arrogance in the later Brahmanas, where they boast that their rituals can fix anything, including the gods. Yet, they were forced to revert to an attitude of compromise later, as the writing of the Puranas clearly shows.

Lord Shiva

If Sanskrit and the Vedas were not negotiable to the Aryans, Lord Shiva, the God of the native people, was also non-negotiable. Among the artifacts found at the sites of the Harappa civilization is what is called Seal 420. It depicts a man with horns surrounded by animals; "the lower limbs are bare and the phallus seemingly exposed." Shiva was thus clearly a pre-Aryan God of the native people. The Aryans, as they entered India, were immediately confronted with the God of the local people. In the Vedas, he is seen as leading his people against the Aryans. The Vedas also criticized 'those who worshiped the phallus.' They initially disapproved of Shiva, as he was a black God who lived like a Chandala, with ash all over his body, an antithesis of the Aryan gods, who were fair and clean. It is, however, clear from the Shiva Puranas that they were not able to make a dent in the local worship of Lord Shiva.

The story of Dhasha's sacrifice and his not inviting Shiva clearly indicate the attitude of the Aryans at one stage. But the power of Shiva makes them eat humble pie and, in an effort to woo him, they sent Durga, made dark in the womb, to be more pleasing. The later story of Ganga falling helplessly into the locks of Shiva's hair and the beheading of Ganesha as he presumes to prevent Shiva from going to Ganga show the victory of Shiva, the local God, over the Aryan gods. That was why Shiva was incorporated into the Aryan tradition. Shiva became the God of yogis, of cattle, and of animals, and they called him Pancha Mukha (the five-faced). The people worshiped Shiva as Pasupathi, the one who wears an 'animal skin' with a trident in his hand. The cult of Shiva was the first religious challenge that the Aryans had to face. In the appropriation of Shiva as a God, we see all the heartbreak, opposition, and rear-guard action that were to typify all further compromises. The violence with which he was opposed and his final victory made later compromises easier to make, even though a sense of unease never really disappeared. As the story of Dhasha's sacrifice tells us, the Shiva devotees were not beyond violence as Virabadhra and his goons destroyed Dhasha's sacrifice. The Aryans resisted Shiva as long as they could, and stories had to be manufactured, like his marriage to Parvathi as Gauri, the fair one, to create an impeccable lineage, and his marriage to Ganga, the Supreme River Goddess, to give him further legitimacy.

The Color Prejudice

From the beginning, Lord Shiva was always portrayed as dark. Lord Krishna is blue and dark. Thus, both the gods of Shaivism and Vaishnavism were dark. Add to that the wife of the Pandavas, Draupadi. Even as they prophesied the birth of Draupadi, as the woman who would be the death of Kshatriyas, she is called the Dark Woman. Because she was dark-skinned, Draupadi was portrayed as being born of fire. This makes her the patroness of the Brahmins, a slayer of Kshatriyas, born of fire. Yet, later, both orthodox Hindus and Brahmanism discarded her. She became a Goddess of the lower castes, Pariahs, and Muslims. Yet she is not alone; all mother goddesses appear dark; Matrikas and the most powerful of them, Maha Kali, are dark goddesses. The strange fact is that the colors black and blue have religious significance; thus, Krishna is dark, Shiva is Neelakanta (blue), Draupadi and Kali are black, yet in social matters, they don't seem to have made any difference because fair skin alone matters in Indian society. The black gods and goddesses were clearly part of an earlier tradition, and their worshippers were sacrificed when orthodoxy reasserted itself. It was, however, never a one-way absorption; it was a give-and-take between the Aryan and the local people. What made them insist on Shiva as a complete package but be prepared to sacrifice the ethnicity of their mother gods is a mystery.

Sacrifice to Asceticism

As the Vedas give way to the Epics, we see a significant change as sacrifice gives way to asceticism and the power of meditation (tapas). The Epics are full of heroes and villains who gain enormous powers through their asceticism. The ascetic and the idea of renunciation were, however, totally against the Aryan idea. Such ascetics belittled the value of life, and their power threatened the very core of Vedic religion. One only has to recall Ram's beheading of Shambuka to realize how great a crime it was. Yet, in time, the Atharva Veda incorporated many of the ascetic practices, and asceticism became an integral part of Vedic religion. The revulsion at the incorporation of the Atharva Veda into the corpus of the Vedas is yet to be forgiven by the more orthodox Hindus, including Dr. Radhakrishnan, who has only contempt for those who allowed it to be incorporated. Dr. Radhakrishnan also asserts that the Atharva Veda was part of an older tradition. Here again, the local people won.

The Varnas

When the Aryans encountered opposition to his dominance, they made only a distinction between them, Aryas and Dasyus. In an interpolation of 'The Purusha Sukta,' the idea of the four varnas is introduced, making the division of castes appear to have existed from time immemorial, whereas Vedic people had only three varnas. The term Vaisya was derived from the term for all, 'Vis,' and in the division into Brahmin, Kshatriya, and Vaisya, all of society was included. We also know that the Shudra was assimilated and recognized only after a long process, which resulted in the creation of the caste system, where the Aryan retained all three twice-born positions while the locals were accepted into the system on a case-by-case basis. The fact that the local people were larger in number and the Aryans were at their mercy raises the question of what prompted them to accept such a demeaning position.

Meat Eating

The Aryans were meat eaters, and even Manu, who says vegetarianism is good, still says it is natural for animals to eat plants; small animals to be eaten by bigger animals; those who have fangs would eat those without; and those with hands would eat those without. The point, however, is that it is this food chain that keeps life going; thus, to break the cycle of birth and death, one must stop eating. The Brahmans say what you eat, you become in the next world. Yet, animal sacrifice and eating were part of Vedic religion, only stipulating the correct way to sacrifice and eat with proper rituals. Manu even says meat is the best food. Even in the Brahmanas, they say a bull or cow should be killed when a guest arrives, and a cow should be sacrificed to Mitra and Varuna. Panini says, "One for whom a cow is killed is a guest." Even in the Dharmashastras, it says, "The meat of milk cows and oxen may be eaten." It was, however, a contentious issue; as Brahmana says, one who eats a cow would be reborn into something strange. The logic of the Brahmanas slowly became the norm, and sacrifice gradually came down. The Brahmanas say that in the beginning, the gods used man (Purusha) as a sacrifice; in stages, the power of sacrifice went into the horse, the bull, the goat, and finally into the produce of man's hands, like rice and wheat. It thus slowly accepted that sacrifice can be with almost anything. There can, however, be no doubt that this change was caused by the acceptance of the concept of 'Ahimsa' that both Mahavira and Buddha advocated.

The Sramanas

By the time of Mahavira and Buddha, the Aryan people may have penetrated a large section of Bharat and had found strong allies who accepted their cooperation with compromises to their faith. While the Aryan people accepted the local God Shiva and began to incorporate their religious practices into their Vedas, as in the Atharva Veda, they insisted on the non-negotiable position of the Vedas. While on the one hand, a large-scale integration was taking place, there was a 'Lakshman rekha' that could not be crossed; that was the acceptance of the Vedas as revealed texts. Yet, with the influx of Aryan ideas, the country saw the greatest intellectual ferment. It resulted in the many philosophies of India and the creation of two of the greatest religions in the world, Jainism and Buddhism. However, the new orthodoxy, made up of local converts and Aryan ideologues, branded them as Sramanas, almost an epithet for the Godless, because they did not accept the authority of the Vedas. The surprising fact is that they were not yet prepared to write the Atharva Veda and include it in the canon of the sacred. This contradiction continued. They fought the Jains and the Buddhists almost in a no-holds-barred contest for supremacy that saw Buddhism evicted from the country and Jainism a pale shadow of what it was. However, the moment they could claim victory, they appropriated some of the best ideas from Buddhism, including the concepts of Ahimsa, karma, and Nirvana.

The Supremacy of the Vedas

The Brahmanas say that evil originates in the gods and spreads downward to the anti-gods and then to men. The gods are responsible as they create evil, like delusion (moha), a stain (Kalmasha), and evil (papa), and then transfer them to men. The origin of sin is said to be the result of Indra getting drunk on Soma and, in his drunkenness, killing Vritra, a Dasyu Brahmin, who was an ally and thus incurring the curse of 'Brahmanicide.' To get it out of his system, Indra passes on one-third to the Earth, which is then promised fertility through plowing and cultivation; one-third to trees, who are told that when they are cut, they will grow new shoots; and one-third to women in return for pleasure during sex and the capacity to procreate. Thus, the Vedic people believed in original sin, but like the Greeks, they imputed it to the gods. Evil cannot be defeated, they say; it can only be kept away. Evil enters the world through the cosmic battle between gods and Asuras. However, by this time, man has Vak, making him creative and capable of competing with the gods through the merit of his hymns and through their knowledge of sacrifice. This frightened the gods. It is to ensure that men do not reach the gods that they let loose on men the evils of sleep, carelessness, hunger, love of dice, and the desire for women.

While sacrifice was one way to beat evil, the other was knowledge, as the gods themselves feared the power of knowledge that the Vedas represented. A person who knows, says the Brihadaranyaka Upanishad and venerates the truth has already passed into the flames and his mind, like lightning, leads him to the realms of Brahman. An even more interesting path is the story of King Janashruti, who, through his sacrifices, lit up the skies, but a passing goose says that is nothing because Raikva gathers all credit for himself. Hearing this, King Janashruti seeks Raikva and finds him under a cart, scratching his sores. The king offers him hundreds of cows and gold for his secret, but Raikva rejects them with contempt. Yet he agrees to tell him his secret when the king offers him his daughter. He despises cows and gold but loves women, and he claims that this is the way of the gleaner, who picks from the leftover harvest and on alms. The Vedic upholder looks in wonder at the success of this philosophy of Sramana ascetics, traveling monks, and hermits. This way also, in time, became an important part of Brahmanism—in fact, a required fourth stage in human life.

From these stories, it may be inferred that in their initial thrust into the country, the Aryans thought they could bulldoze their way through war and killing. They also accept, very definitely, that Brahmins were already existing in Bharat even before they came in. It was only by showing genuine repentance for their initial violence that they were able to get the local people to allow them passage and, later, cooperation. Consequently, even from the very beginning, the Aryan orthodoxy had to accept the Brahmin and his scheme of worship. In fact, the supremacy of the Brahmin may have been the price the egalitarian Aryans had to pay for their Vedas and their migration to be sanctified. It would be tragic to believe that the Brahmin, the elite of Indian society, sacrificed all the rest of the Indians to the Aryan overlordship merely so that their position would be secure. That is why their religion has been called 'Brahminism.'

Even by Force

History tells us that the Brahmins even resorted to force and violence to ensure the supremacy of Brahmanism. When Mahapadma Nanda, a barber's son, created a short-lived empire, Kautilya, with the help of Chandra Gupta Maurya, plotted his downfall. Again, after Asoka's reign, in 183 B.C., Pushyamitra, who was a commander in the army, deposed the Mauryas and established the Shunga dynasty. He also re-established the power of the Brahmins. Yet the best example of violence is the story of Shambuka in the Ramayana, a Shudra who, through tapas, was becoming a God. Ram, on his journey south, encounters him and asks him who he is, and he says he was born of a Shudra womb. Rama drew his sword and cut his head, even while he was still talking. Yet, other castes continued to attempt greatness through Tapas. The story of Trishanku is the best. When the Brahmans refused to attend his sacrifice, Viswamitra created a new Earth and heaven and was going to create new gods when the gods stopped him, leaving Trishanku suspended between Earth and heaven. This inspired Henry Wadsworth Longfellow to say:

Viswamitra the Magician
By his spells and incantations
Up to Indra's realms Elysium
Raised Trisanku, king of nations
Indra and the gods offended
Hurled him downward and descending
In the Air, he hung suspended
With their equal powers contended.

The story highlights the fact that local chiefs and intellectuals continued to challenge the supremacy of the Aryan and his ally, the Brahmin, for a very long time, and it saw many bloody battles. Ram is seen as irrevocably cutting short any attempt at an alternative power in religious belief with deliberate violence.

The Bhakti Deception

The Bhakti movement was an offshoot of the reading and popularization of the Bhagavad Gita as part of the Mahabharata, where a personal God is portrayed for the first time. Lord Krishna, who is dark-skinned, says that he is no respecter of persons and that all are welcome and equally dear to him. This is what made the lower castes finally seek solace in the Vedic and Brahmanical religions—the religion of Lord Krishna. In the south, it was spread by the Nayanars, devotees of Shiva, and the Alwars, devotees of Krishna-Vishnu. Most of them were from the low castes and included the great women poets Avvayar and Andal and the great Nammalvar and Manikkavasakar.

One of the great legends of the Bhakti Movement is the story of Kannappar, a pariah who, in his love for Shiva, offers his own eyes when he sees that the God's eye is bleeding, putting to shame the Brahmin's mere offerings of flowers. This also shows that Shiva worship was a long-standing local tradition, while the Brahmanical devotion to Shiva was perhaps only the acceptance of the inevitable, as his worship was pervasive among the people.

Consequent on the acceptance of the Bhakti saints, there was also a demand for access to temples by the lower castes. As A.K. Ramanujan says, Bhakti was actually a philosophy of devotion that showed that it was not caste, class, or wealth but love alone that mattered and that the Brahmin had much to learn from the lowest castes. Yet, nothing changed. The Bhakti poems, which circulated in oral form for years, were later converted into spiritual texts by the Brahmins, who wiped them clean of their lower caste flavor and added Brahmanical values. It was the price dissent had to pay to become acceptable. Ramanuja, the leader of Vaishnavism, preached equality but, in the end, refused to meddle with the caste system. So powerful was the caste system that Nammalvar, a Shudra, was portrayed by the orthodoxy as one who had refused breast milk from his Shudra mother, thereby proclaiming his higher status and denigrating the Shudra mother as contemptible.

While it was the Bhakti movement that finally allowed orthodox Hinduism to fight off the challenge of Jainism and Buddhism and perhaps even Christianity and Islam, having done its job, its origin and basis were denied, and caste-Hinduism reasserted itself. Thus, the worship of Varna and the continued contempt for the black Shudra are brought out in the story of Parvathi, who is dark. In the Matsya Purana, Shiva makes fun of her for being dark. She then does tapas to become fair. She finally gets her wish and becomes the golden-colored Gauri, the fair one. Even goddesses had to change color to be truly acceptable. Forgotten are Krishna, the dark one; Draupadi; and Shiva, as Neelakandan, who is black and behaves like a Chandala, living in graveyards with a necklace made of skulls.

The Victory

What Wendy Doniger calls the 'Silencing of Dissent' is actually the final victory of Orthodoxy over all its opponents. Initially, the Aryan met his match in the local Brahmin; he then made him his ally to fight Buddhism and Jainism. After being made the custodian of doctrine, the Brahmin furthered his power with the creation and consolidation of the caste system. He combined the Aryan Vedas and Aryan claims to royalty and created orthodoxy. Thus, with a united front, they then fought their later battles, both offensive and attrition. Once the final battle with the Bhakti sages was won, they were ready to raise the barricades. As the Muslims and the British could not be defeated, they had to pass the time until they destroyed themselves or left to return to the open field for the battle for the soul of India.

A Summation

Because Hinduism started with nothing, it was able to take on and absorb many new ideas and beliefs. Yet, as the process continued, it inevitably led to inconsistencies and incongruities. In the long history of compromises, what did not give way was the sanctity of the Vedas and the role of the priest. Perhaps more importantly, with every compromise, the stratification of society became even more rigid. In fact, every compromise, including the acceptance of full communities into the fold, was on the specific condition that, while the leaders and the rest would be accommodated, it was clearly on the basis of accepting to merge into the Hindu fold at the appropriate level of caste correctness.

While the acceptance of river gods and a monkey God appears outlandish, they were followed by Puranas that justified them, clearly showing a concerted effort to legitimize the compromises made. Compromises were thus scrutinized and either justified or rejected. Many ideas that were rejected have faded from memory, and since losers do not write history, they are also lost to history.

This attitude of accepting compromises led to the belief that Hinduism was a very accommodating, passive, and tolerant religion. But what has been seen tells us that the compromises were never willingly made but were thrust by superior might and accepted only to ensure survival. The legend of Shiva clearly proves this: Shiva and his devotees were too great to be subdued. The same can also be said of the Krishna cult.

However, a person who is forced to compromise at the cost of his own self-respect only waits for revenge; the anger merely builds up, ready to explode. This is what happened when Hinduism finally became the majority religion. It no longer had to bend; it was in a position to rule and to subdue all others. When this stage was reached, the leaders of the religion changed color, demanded obedience, and persecuted dissent. The obvious targets were the surviving Jains and Buddhists. When they were either destroyed or brought to heel, the next aim was the suppression of all internal dissent. The religion then turned militant, aggressive, and uncompromising. The tragedy was that just as it seemed that they had subdued all opposition, there came the Muslims, first as mere raiders, then as conquerors. Not only did they conquer and rule most of India, but they would not go away. What was worse was that, when they finally met their match, it was only the British who gained and then ruled India with the sort of comprehensiveness never seen in the history of the country. The consequent bottling up of emotions by an underdog in his own country was to remake Hinduism again in the 20th century.

CHAPTER 10

RELIGION AS HISTORY

No study of Indian thought is possible without reaching back to the origins, and that is where we encounter the Vedas and the Upanishads. It is almost taken as obvious that all Indian thought must have been influenced by the fountain from which it all began. Yet, any study of Indian thought tends to indicate the reverse. The Vedas were considered sacred and passed on from father to son as a family heirloom. Its sacredness meant that it was never dissected, discussed, or criticized. Consequently, the Vedas became a black book of secrets, more in the nature of untouchable knowledge that had no practical applications and was incapable of evolution. When it was finally written down, it was done in Sanskrit, which further killed any possibility of growth and evolution, as it was written down as though in stone, relevant for all times to come. It also made Sanskrit into a dead language; as the vehicle of the Vedas, it also became immutable and frozen in time, for any evolution would also affect the meaning of the Vedas.

The Vedas are the initial outpourings of wonder of a very acute race. While lapsing into eloquence at the beauty and in wonder at the marvels and mysteries of the universe, the tone is clearly one of curiosity and agnostic tolerance. There was clearly a yearning to know. In the later Vedas, for reasons now not known, an attitude of arrogant knowledge begins to appear. The Vedic writers then claim to know what sustains the universe and even the gods. They claim that it is the sacrifices that humans make for the universe. It is rituals and sacrifices, they asserted, that sustain the universe. This attitude turned into a belief in magical incantations, spells, and mystical rituals for health, wealth, protection, and even to cause harm. The same Vedic rituals are practiced even today with not even a change of word, sequence, or intonation, from the rituals for birth, marriage, and death to a wide variety of other occasions. Whatever the nuances of one's faith, the rituals have remained the same. This is the lasting legacy of the Vedas. Not its philosophy, not its open and questioning attitude and not its proud humility before the vastness of the universe, but rituals without meaning in a language even the priests no longer understand.

While all Hindu philosophy claims its roots in the Vedas and is by and large a refinement and development of ideas present in the Vedas, philosophy itself has meant little to Indians, mainly because so few were educated enough to understand and less were materially satisfied enough to devote their time to philosophy. The Vedic tradition led to Advaita and Dvaita and the many forms of qualified Advaita and modified Dvaita. However, all were too abstract and arid to enthuse the common man. Only with the Bhakti movement were ordinary people introduced to religion. When this happened, the Vedas and their agnostic attitude were all dumped in favor of all kinds of gods. It turned harsh, garish, and, in the end, materialistic, except for those who looked inward into themselves. The fact that so few do, that curiosity has been killed and that religion has become a contractual relationship with God, is the tragedy implicit in the history of Indian thought. The fact that what passes for religion today is only the recitation of magical mantras and a consumer-type belief in meditation and yoga has made the Vedas irrelevant and has become a relic of the past, a mere curiosity for historical research.

Sacred Literature as History

Experts in Indian sacred literature, such as Wenger Doniger and earlier Indologists, including Marx Muller, perceived ambiguities and contradictions in the sacred stories as confirmation that the sacred literature of India is beset with irreconcilable contradictions. They assumed that it was the trademark of the confused and fragmented thinking of ancient Indians. Robert Calasso, in his retelling of the sacred texts, suggests, without explicitly stating, that the sacred literature of India was actually a symbolized version of the history of Indian thought and beliefs. It tells the story of how Indian thought evolved and changed to fit with the changing times. In fact, the need to be current and relevant seemed to be their most important motive in all that they did. It, therefore, deals with the opposition they had to face and the impediments they had to overcome. It was inevitably a war of attrition and thus not a pretty story but one of persistence and endurance.

The Story of Creation

While the creation story can be seen merely as a creation narrative, historical elements immediately begin to creep in and overlap with the story. Thus, when Prajapathi had completed creation and was lying down exhausted, his sons, the gods, became fearful of his power and tried to get rid of him. They created Rudra from all the evil that also emerged as an inevitable part of creation, thereby admitting that evil was at the core of their intentions, even in the act of creation, as it was ultimately a product of desire. Rudra then shoots an arrow at Prajapathi, causing a wound on his side.

The fact that the gods were not all good is evident from their need to compete with the Asuras, their elder brothers. In fact, the Asuras were the actual gods of Avestha, and the gods' earlier deities were now cast in the mold of demons to be defeated by the new gods, the Devas. Thus, from the beginning, the Vedic people realized that their beliefs involved supplanting and, hopefully, improving upon their earlier beliefs. The religion that the Aryans brought to the country was a rebellion against their own older beliefs. In imposing their new religion, they were also attempting to extinguish an older and more legitimate religion, represented in this case by Prajapathi. The gradual disappearance of Prajapathi indicates their successful superimposition of their new faith, both forcibly and heartlessly.

The Birth of Vac

The Vedas depict vac, speech, consciousness, time, and death as co-existent with creation. It is desire and fear, stemming from the prospect of being killed by the gods, his sons, that compels Prajapathi to emit 'Vac' (speech), a feminine being living within him. In the historical sense, Vac represents the Aryan language, a language they brought with them. To the Aryans, being Godless meant not possessing 'Vac,' their sacred language.

When Prajapathi opens his eyes in exhaustion, he beholds his own daughter, 'Usha,' the beautiful dawn is so seductive that he immediately couples with her. The result is the creation of the gods, and if we are familiar with the earlier story, it is the creation for the second time of the same gods. The Aryan, captivated by the beauty of the dawn in his old homeland in the northern temperate zone, cannot help but think of it as the most beautiful, even in his new homeland, where the dawn is brief and hardly a thing of great beauty.

The Rishis

Alongside the gods, equal in stature, were the rishis—the original sages of the Aryan people. They were the creators of all the wisdom found in the Vedas, along with all the rituals. There must have been a period when their knowledge and rituals brought them happiness, but as times changed, new and alien beliefs and customs had to be confronted. In fact, trouble was brewing, and as the Aryans continued to explore their new home—a land alien to them—numerous challenges awaited them.

Shiva and Daksha

The initial challenge to orthodox Aryan beliefs manifested in the form of Shiva. Shiva was portrayed as dark, dirty, and uncouth, residing in a charnel house with a necklace of skulls around his neck, always covered in dust and oil. He stood in stark contrast to the Aryan model of cleanliness and purity. However, despite his unconventional appearance, Shiva appeared to be not just powerful but almost impossible to subdue.

The challenge Shiva presented to the Aryan belief system is illustrated in the story of Daksha's sacrifice. Daksha, the chief priest of the gods and the arch defender of orthodox beliefs, planned a grand sacrifice and invited all the gods and important figures except Shiva, a clear indication that Shiva represented something the orthodox would not accept. Shiva, confident in his identity and the loyalty of his devotees, was unfazed. However, his wife, Sati, was mortally offended, as Daksha was her father, and not inviting Shiva was a great dishonor. Sati saw it as an insult to her husband, whose ways she had adopted after abandoning her own.

This episode highlights the confrontation between Aryan orthodoxy and the powerful cults of the local people. Even at this stage, the Aryans were a divided people, as evidenced by high-ranking women like Sati embracing the local cult and preferring the religion of the local, dark-skinned people and their deity. Sati became a martyr for the new religion, and wherever her body parts fell, they became pilgrimage centers for the new faith.

The Aryan religion survived through compromise with local cults, involving a total capitulation, with Shiva eventually becoming the God of gods. Accommodating Shiva into their pantheon of gods was likely an anguishing process, leading to the creation of a new concept—the outsider, the Sanyasi. Vedic religion, rooted in personal cleanliness and purity, both physically and genetically, required the introduction of this new idea to justify Shiva as the renouncer—one who abdicates from social life and is no longer bound by societal norms or morality. As Nirad Chaudhri notes, the Aryans had two alternatives in dealing with the harsh conditions of India: to rise above it and preach a religion of cleanliness and purity, or to accept the unalterable fact of the heat and dirt and wallow in it. By accepting the unalterable conditions, the religion underwent significant changes but managed to retain some degree of purity by keeping the outsider outside the pale of human society, as though he lived in a different world, allowing the world of normal men to remain unchanged.

Shiva and Ganga

As the Aryans entered India from the northern mountains, crossing the Sindhu, they encountered the mighty Ganga—a river so powerful that it seemed impassable. The crossing of the Ganga became a potent symbol in narrating how the Aryans coped with the new land and its people. Ganga, the river that flows through the Milky Way, was brought down to Earth to offer humanity hope for salvation from sins and, in essence, from the clutches of death. However, the tremendous force of Ganga posed a threat to the entire Earth if she were to descend unchecked. Hence, a buffer had to be found.

Ganga is also identified with the Milky Way, where Agni and Indra are seen as mere sparks that shine intermittently. In the myth, the gods turn not to their own deities but to Shiva, the God of the indigenous people, acknowledging the need to pay obeisance to the Indian God to navigate the challenges of the land.

When Ganga is informed that Shiva will break her fall to the Earth, she inwardly scorns Shiva, confident that she will wash him away in her flood. This reflects the initial Aryan contempt for the indigenous black people and their seemingly crude religious beliefs. However, when Ganga falls onto Shiva's head, she becomes entangled in his hair, almost reduced to a placid lake. Even when Shiva eventually releases her, she trickles down from his hair as harmless and weak rivulets. This underscores the greatness of Shiva.

The story highlights the arrogance of the Aryans, who initially believed that the perceived barbaric black people would be easily vanquished by their might. However, the narrative reveals a transformation in their perception as they discover the locals to be not only their equals but often superior. The Aryans were compelled to accept Shiva as a deity, recognizing the importance of doing so to make headway in the country.

The heat of India alone could have impeded the Aryans' further march, but the cooling waters of the Ganga, according to legend, prevented Shiva from scorching the world. Consequently, Ganga and all rivers became integral parts of the Indian pantheon of gods.

Shiva and Parvathi

Having failed with Ganga, the Aryans were not satisfied. They plotted again to tame the ferocity and power of Shiva. Determined this time, they put a great deal of planning into deciding their next move. Thus, it was in the Himalayas that Parvati grew up, a rugged landscape that Shiva would appreciate. To make Parvathi acceptable to Shiva, while she was in the womb (of Meena), at night, when all were asleep, another Goddess stealthily entered Meena's womb and painted the fetus the color of night, black.

When Parvathi is old enough, she is sent to woo Shiva. When her initial efforts are rebuffed by Shiva, she turns to 'tapas' to win Shiva's love. Parvathi then practices the lifestyle of Shiva, an ascetic, a tapasvi, a rugged person who rejects all the comforts of the civilized world to become lovable in the sight of Shiva. Later, we are told that apart from the usual pastime of sex and dice, she was also capable of discussing the finer points of philosophy, astronomy, and theology. Parvathi was clearly groomed to be pleasing to Shiva, a 'Trojan horse,' yet programmed to be a worthy opponent for Shiva.

The Aryan gods needed Shiva because Brahma had already told them that only the son of Shiva would be able to kill Taraka, the mighty Asura, who was terrorizing the Aryan gods and causing total havoc. Here was an admission that even after taking care of the Shiva fraction of the opposition, there still remained more powerful fractions that had to be subdued before the Aryan religion and way of life could be imposed on the people.

When the Aryan gods were threatened, they realized that the only way to survive was to join forces with Shiva. Shiva's initial attitude, even toward a dark-hued Parvathi, shows that Shiva himself saw nothing enticing in the Aryan religion or their gods. On the other hand, the fact that Sati earlier and then Parvathi were attracted to Shiva showed the level of dissension they had to deal with within their own community. The blackness that Parvathi deliberately takes on may also suggest that large sections of the elite, especially among royalty and the priests, were already intermarrying into the local communities.

The fact that Parvathi was the 'Trojan horse' that the Aryan orthodoxy created to subvert the native religion is made clear by the fact that the gods had to make her artificially black to be enticing to Shiva or, more possibly, for Shiva not to suspect their designs. Further proof is that, despite her show of unconditional love, she still refuses to accept all that Shiva stands for and hopes to change him with her arguments while practicing tapas and acquiring learning apt for a companion of Shiva. Thus, she is jealous of her sister Ganga, whom she sees as always intertwined with Shiva, and also because, even despite all her efforts, she is not able to make Shiva spill his seed in her. Instead, Skanda is born from the seed spilled by Shiva, gobbled up by Agni and nurtured by the six stars in the Little Bear.

After Skanda is born, on the plea that Shiva made fun of her dark color, Parvathi does tapas and becomes Gauri, the white one, as white as a foreigner, thus betraying where her true loyalties lie.

The turbulence caused by the dissenting voice of Shiva, an alternate choice, forced the Vedic writers to look inward and evolve. Shiva, when he goes back to Tapas, is in a period of calm, but they accept that it is also a time when 'creation grows dull,' knowledge, and the world itself seems to lose its fragrance. Calasso puts it, 'Shiva is he who brings imbalance,' and the world can only absorb a tiny fraction of the turmoil he creates. The turbulence is shown in the terror created by Taraka, who is finally killed by Skanda, the son of Shiva, creating a fusion of Aryan and native thinking.

This is also shown in the life of Ganesha, the other son of Shiva. Ganesha, the son of Ganga, gets his head cut off when he tries to prevent his father from entering Ganga's room. Ganesha, the pure Aryan, as he is purely Parvathi's creation, is still not reconciled to the pollution caused by the copulation of Shiva and Ganga. But Shiva is able to cut off his head with a single blow, indicating the overwhelming power of the native tradition. Only by attaching Airavata's head, Shiva's loyal elephant, does Ganesha have a head. A God with an elephant head was clearly an aberration, a picture of incongruity, and a hopeless attempt at wholeness. This was exactly how the orthodoxy saw the attempt at a compromise and dilution of Aryan values. However, this incongruous God with an elephant head soon became a symbol of the diversity of Hindu thinking, and Ganesha became one of the most loved gods among all the gods.

The Ashvamedha Sacrifice

The Aryans, as a Vedic people, were not only transparent and honest about their beliefs but were also fully aware of the failures and compromises they were making. The ultimate Vedic sacrifice, the Ashvamedha sacrifice, was ostensibly to test the power of the king but also a test of the spread and acceptance of their Vedic faith. Every part of the sacrifice was symbolic, and every stage of the sacrifice was a test, a compromise, and a reaffirmation of their faith. The idea is clear: by letting loose a horse to roam unhindered for a year, the king was able to prove that he was the lord of all the land the horse had roamed. The return of the horse unharmed proved that all had accepted his suzerainty by conquest or compromise.

As the Aryans expanded into the country, they were in search of new land and new water resources. Their spreading out was also the result of desire—for conquest and to rule over the newly conquered people. Thus, the Ashvamedha horse was likened to the swollen eye of Prajapathi, so swollen and filled with desire that it fell off. The horse is desire, and the resultant creation is conquest. After conquest comes complaisance, a descent into the slack ways of the pagan people, and a slow acceptance of their way of life and their religion. There is, therefore, a need to reassert the importance of purity and the strict ways of the Aryan people, and the horse sacrifice was a testing of the state, as it were.

While the horse roams for a year, those celebrating the sacrifice sit together around a fire and retell the stories of their great heroes, their great deeds, and their past heritage. These must be the stories that finally came to be the Epics, the Ramayana, and the Mahabharata. Their storytelling was to recollect and reaffirm their way of life, their beliefs, and their religion. It was a time to regroup after the conquests, to reassess their practices and their beliefs, to make compromises where required, and to harden certain aspects of their religion and practices to ensure cohesion, all done in an effort to emerge stronger and more resolute.

The free roaming of the horse was to show the peaceful acceptance of the Aryan way. If compromises had to be made, they were made to ensure peace, and the horse and its guarding army also indicated a willingness to fight and to wage war if necessary to assert the suzerainty and power of the king. To test whether the acceptance of their way of life was genuine, it was necessary for those following the horse to question every Brahmin they met on the way and ask them what they knew of the horse's sacrifice. If the Brahmins showed ignorance of the significance of the Ashvamedha sacrifice, he was to be robbed. Thus, the real state of their acceptance of their way of life was tested. In the meantime, there was always the fear that the horse would not return. The fact that there were Brahmins who may not know their way suggests an older tradition with their own Brahmins.

The Ashvamedha sacrifice was to lead men from untruth to the truth, from non-being to being, from darkness to light. The fact that many forms of belief were still prevalent is shown by the fact that the sacrifice required the collection of a large variety of animals. The basic division that was made was between the wild animals and the domesticated animals. Clearly, the domesticated animals represented the group that had accepted their way of life. The wild animals were later let off before the actual sacrifice, indicating an unwillingness to use force in the case of religious practices and beliefs. Yet, it was also accepted that letting go of the wild animals actually affected the sanctity of the sacrifice. Therein lies the great emphasis that the Vedic people laid on compromises, to accept defeat symbolically while conquering the world. This is again demonstrated by the willingness of the Queen to expose herself before the crowd gathered for the sacrifice and to sleep with the dead horse, thus symbolically betraying her husband, the king. A young girl who walks beside the queen to the sacrifice and is symbolically made to represent the queen is then made available to all those in the Sabha, indicating the level to which the king was prepared to go to ensure the unity of his state. Interestingly, Manu, Chadrgya Upanishad, and Baudhayana's Dharmashastras all speak of 'Ahimsa' but not in the meaning that we have come to recognize in the word but as 'non-wounding.' It is also a word that comes from 'Satya,' the truth. While killing and conquest continued, truth itself was expected to emerge only through the process of dialogue, not by wounding the feelings of others but by accepting their concerns and by presenting a more comprehensive idea of the truth.

The Sabha

To explain the need and justification for religions to evolve, the Vedas tell of the discussion room, the Sabha, the hall in the palace or an important power center where the Rishis sit down to discuss. The Sabha, they tell us, has many doors, indicating the many different schools of thought that enter the Sabha for discussion and the many paths that would finally lead to a solution. This was most necessary in the time of cruel and bloody disputes when Vasistha, representing the Brahmin orthodoxy, had to take on Viswamitra, a Kshatriya but one who had more power than all the gods.

The importance of discussion is put across when they say, "Even when you think you risk losing your head, we are still responsible for the task of keeping thoughts moving and turning." True knowledge is represented by the God Varuna, the hidden God who guards the truth by keeping it hidden in the deep waters. Vasistha accepts, with envy mixed with fear, that Varuna processes the deeper truth. While thus laying the foundation for the need for change, they yet exalted the status of Vasistha, claiming that when the gods were performing the Soma sacrifice, Urvashi walked through the sacrificial clearing, and she was so seductive that Mitra and Varuna, simultaneously and spontaneously, spilled their seed. The seed was immediately collected in a bowl, from which Vasistha and Agastya emerged.

Vaisistha thus has an almost divine status as far as Vedic doctrine is concerned, and Viswamitra, even though a rishi himself, represented a revolt against that orthodoxy that had to be met, not with violence, which Viswamitra resorted to, but with compromise. The uniqueness of Vedic civilization was that, while other civilizations started with kings and dynasties, Vedic civilization was born from seven rishis. They also frankly admit their past atrocities as they tell all to remember that "let us remember, our children, your ancestors, those who call themselves Aryas, the noble ones, killed and enslaved the dark-skinned, nooseless, mean, and minute beings." Their journey into the heart of India also brought them closer to the sun God, Indra. The overpowering heat of the sun in central India was going to be a defining experience.

They accept that "unique among our ancients, they made themselves known exclusively through their language and their cult." They were fanatically attached to knowledge that they called 'Veda.' In fact, to them, the cow, women, and dawn were all really secret names for knowledge—an acceptance of the elusiveness and expansiveness of knowledge. As they traveled further and further from where they had imbibed Soma, the northern lands where the dawn was drawn out and the most beautiful spectacle, they were also moving away further and further from the place where their thoughts had meaning.

They also had no temples, as every sacrifice had to be fresh, in a new clearing with fresh items. Their religion never solidified bigotry but was always meant to be fresh and new. Even their knowledge was not written down or allowed to be dead on stone or paper but was seen as in a vision and as heard and remembered melodies, Sruti. There are a thousand and twenty-eight hymns in the Rig Vedas, but in none of them is a dwelling or city mentioned. To the Aryans, there was only one thought: what is Brahman and how to define the void?

The story of the gradual contamination of their thoughts is told in the story of Indra and his infatuation with Gautami's wife. For his indiscretion, Gautami tears out Indra's testicles. Gautami represents the new culture created by accepting Shiva into the fold and, with it, the idea of the ascetic. Even the ascetic, like the artist and poet, is inspired by a woman, a muse, and only when the temptation leads to desire and lust reaches a level of volcanic intensity and erupts in uncontrollable bursts does creation begin. Yagnavalka, however, warns all who presume knowledge that knowledge is a very dangerous thing, and Gargi, the most beautiful theologian ever, tries to break Yagnavalka's head by testing his knowledge. He, however, proves too good for her.

What comes out of his answers to her questions is that tradition and restrictions have no value and he says, "When I eat meat, I like it tender and juicy." And his final answer is to tell all gathered to hear them discuss that all the thousand gods are actually one; he is the Brahman in whom we are forced to face the void. God is thus even beyond the possibility of human ability to frame a question about him. To bring this idea down to Earth, he says, men faced with the void try to immerse themselves and disappear into the fullness or perhaps in the void of a woman, in a sexual embrace.

The idea that there are other ways to reach Godhead is told in the stories of the gods and the Rishis and of the Adityas and the Angiras. When they began to sacrifice together, it was only by cunning that the gods managed to be the first to get to Amrutha. However, what remained was good enough for the Angiras to travel to the heavens and conquer the skies; it turned into a turtle, which then became their vehicle of transport. Every sacrifice is, thus, an uncertain journey to an unknown destination. The Gayatri mantra and the Gayathri meters, along with 'Vac,' are merely the chariots that allow us to travel.

The unmanifested world is so infinite and vast that the manifested is only the residue of creation. Yet, Sesa, the residue, on whom Vishnu sleeps and where Brahma is no more than the bud of a lotus that grows out of Vishnu's navel, is also infinite. What we know is thus merely the trimmings of reality, the flakes and dust that fell off during creation. Agni is the light that makes things manifest to men; however, Agni, as knowledge, can never rest; Agni shines to lead men forward.

In one of the discussions held in the Sabha, Narada asks, "What is it to be immortal? To mortal men, who must perish in the body, do the great works of authors make them immortal? No," he answers, "they only become guests in our memory." Even the gods, fearing death, at first tried to hide in the Vedas. Thus, while the Vedas are the closest thing to immortality, nothing is Brahman; all knowledge is only an attempt to get closer and closer to Brahman. Uma (Parvathi), the mountain girl, even snubs Indra by telling him that he was rejoicing in a victory yet to be won. To men, even Maya is something to be grateful for.

Viswamitra is the first great dissenter. As he tries to press for Soma, Indra proclaims that he is 'prana,' the breath of life itself, the breath that resulted in the creation of the seven rishis. However, even the vision of the Saptarishis tells us only why things happened, not about what we cannot see or is not. The ancient ceremony of the Mahavrata is the celebration of 'varta,' the shadow of things. The shadow that follows every gesture. The concept also represents the aliens, the people bonded together in a cult with a vow, enemies who have no horses, who do not have language, the perfect Sanskrit.

Yet the attraction of these dark people to the Aryans was so great that every now and then, young people would disappear among these dark people and never return. They were the people of the jungle, the counterpoint to the 'gramma' way of life. These aliens were, however, also capable of great ferocity and violence that reminded the Aryans of the arrows of Rudra. They called themselves dogs. The Brahmin wanted to thrust down their way of life and their thoughts on them, as only through the acceptance of a common way of life would lasting peace be possible. Yet, there were many rebels attracted to their way of life, the esoteric, and hated the 'servitude and blindness in everything formulated within society.'

Viswamitra then explains that the esoteric is the vision of things as in themselves, without being clouded by the hardening of language, symbolized in rituals. He says that "it was I who celebrated the rites with the Varta," thus admitting that he was the one who tried to bring the natives to the Aryan way of life. They, however, unlike the Aryans, did not have a patron or a priest to officiate and their sacrifices were open to all. For the Brahmin, it was taken for granted as 'far off.' The Brahmin was concerned not only with the ritual but also with hiding all the traces of their rituals and leaving to the Varta only the castaways, the leftovers, and the unmentionables. Viswamitra is thus criticizing the descent into mere ritual without understanding the purpose and the step-motherly treatment of 'the other,' despite their being vital for the survival of the Aryan, where they participate while the rituals are not explained, thereby denying them full membership. knowledge of creation and the need to descend to a lower state. He then states an eternal truth: that knowledge makes man.

He adds that "whatever does not make one like the thought that has been thought is not full knowledge." This is why knowledge is dangerous, for real knowledge transforms, says Vasistha. The idea that conviction alone is knowledge is so basic to Vedic knowledge, yet it is so far from the reality of the Indian attitude toward knowledge.

The Churning for Amrutha

Even in the churning for Amrutha, we see the patterns of the old and the new being displayed without any attempt to claim the truth for any side. Thus, the story accepts that the Asuras were the elder brothers of the Devas and therefore held the head of the snake, Vasuki. Furthermore, the legend admits that they not only consumed Amrutha but were also the first keepers of Soma. In fact, the gods had to send Vac as a decoy to tempt the Asuras into parting with Soma. Their success, they accepted, was due to trickery. Thus, there is no belittling of the old; the three new gods only claim to be different.

Even in the slaying of Vrutra, the great dragon, through which the new gods become powerful, we are told that Vrutra was not evil but actually Brahman. The sacred texts thus merely tell us of a new beginning. Only after Indra slew Vrutra was he able to get Agni and Varuna out of darkness and into light. Thus, as Calasso says, "What is it that drew them out? It was the changing of tribal loyalties cautiously while remaining tied to each other." They also admit that initially, Indra was the crudest and most ignorant God; all he had was energy and thrust. It was only by drinking Soma that he showed knowledge and virtue. His attempts to wean the other gods to his side required Sarama, the she-dog, to lead him. Yet, even when Agni finally comes out, it is after great reluctance that he allows himself to be yoked to their one single idea and creed; he preferred the freedom to roam, to be mere light, to go wherever desire led.

Krishna and Bhakti

Krishna is the black one, a second type of Shiva, another dark figure that clearly represents the compromises the Aryans were forced to make. The acceptance of Krishna suggests a second stage in the process of consolidating their religion with compromises. Krishna arrives after a period of war and nomadic migration. The wars in the heavens had been settled, and as Calasso puts it, 'when many possibilities had been exhausted.' Yet accepting Krishna was no minor compromise, for as his mother looks into his mouth, she sees the whole universe spinning around inside. Later, Arjuna also sees it when he is finally allowed to see the true greatness of Krishna. Krishna was thus a late arrival, consolidating the contradictory theories and belief systems by being the ultimate God. What Krishna brought with him was bhakti, the love of the Gopis, innocent, honest, and without any need for ritual or liturgy. It was a religion founded on love, not theory or metaphysics. Thus, when Narada, the most acute of the Rishis, is with Krishna and Krishna develops a fever and becomes delirious, he tells Narada that only the dust from the feet of the Gopis would cure him. Not the Queen's, not that of leaders or the wise, but of the innocent Gopis. The Gopis, who love him without guile or pretense but wholeheartedly, who walk through the common lanes of life, burdened with simple lives, and are always in love with Krishna. Yet the love of the Gopis is a violation of all the conventions and rules of religion; it amounts, if nothing else, to the sin of adultery in the mind. Thus, Krishna is seen as 'Prakriya Dharma,' the breaker of the law, the law illegitimated.

Krishna and Arjuna

Krishna was not just a harbinger of change but the symbol of the end of an era and the beginning of a new one that rises from its ashes, as though from some sacrifice, a burning of all the old. Krishna was the dark one from a lower caste, yet not only the Gopis but all women, including the wives of kings, fell for the beauty of his persona, his physical beauty, and his charm. He was also the friend of Arjuna and the Pandavas, the last of the Luna line, a line that was to perish in the ensuing holocaust.

The first encounter with the past is with Agni, who has become powerless as Indra stands in his way. This is clearly an attempt to portray eternal truth held prisoner by orthodoxy. It is with the help of Krishna that Agni manages to reignite himself and burn an entire forest down. Indra looks on helplessly as Arjun and Krishna block his arrows. The fire then burns everything—all of the past. As the sacred texts tell us, only the four Vedas survived as they flew away from the fire as birds.

It is only by siding with Agni, against his own father, that Arjuna gets his magical Gentiva. As the fire subsides, the sacred texts tell us that 'kala,' time was in a hurry to put an end to and move on. Between them, Arjuna and Krishna defeated all the old gods, and only Agni and the Vedas remained. Arjuna, and by default, all the Pandavas, then marry Draupadi, whose skin is described as 'the dark, almost black skin of charred logs.' She was not just dark but very black, the very embodiment of the dark-skinned natives. Thus, even in the Mahabharata, the Pandavas had to accept the natives before their story could even be heroic. This adjustment to the native land and to an alien land continues almost endlessly in the Mahabharata.

While Draupadi loves Arjun most of all, it is Yudhisthira, the God Dharma himself, who is most enamored of Draupadi. Thus, when Arjun disturbs Yudhisthira and Draupadi, he has to go to the forest for twelve months, where he is exposed to the non-Aryan world. He then had to live as a woman because he had spurned Urvashi, who desired him but was also his mother. Here again, he is shown as being exposed to a new perspective. Thus, we see how Arjun, the arch Aryan hero, the son of Indra, spurns the old gods for a new understanding, expressed in Arjun's underwater copulation with Upali, the Naga princess. It was as though, Calasso says, "Dharma could not survive unless allied to the Nagas." The final knowledge is provided when Krishna allows him to see the whole universe—all the visible and invisible worlds in Krishna himself.

Arjuna then marries Subadhra, the dark sister of Krishna, who is also described as a beauty incarnate, but she was something else too. She was a propitious creature, a creature of time. Time opened up to her. Arjun then fights a hunter who beats him to pulp, but it is from him that he gets his greatest weapon, the severed head of Brahma. Thus, even with all his knowledge of the native ways and despite being the friend of the Native King and husband to two dark-hued women, he is still no match for the crude and basic knowledge of the hunter, a jungle dweller. The hunter not only severs Brahma's head but gives it to Arjun, who can then use it as the most powerful weapon in the war of Dharma. The old ways are clearly powerless, and it is time for change. Arjun then continues his journey of discovery, reaching higher and higher until he reaches the abode of Indra, his father. All the gods welcome him and fete him, and he is made to sit beside Indra, next to his throne. The texts then say that he looked at all the old gods, and Calasso says that the eyes he met had something vacuous and jaded about them, as they were no more than inset in stone. Even the beautiful and seductive Apsaras, with their swelling breasts and enticing thighs, seemed painted. Arjuna's rejection of the old thus has the approval of the old gods; in fact, their time has come to an end. Indra then gifts him his final weapon, the Vajra, the thunderbolt of Indra, indicating the passing of the Aryan legacy to a new order.

Janamejaya and Taksaka

The battle against the Nagas was led by King Janamejaya. He may have won the battle, but the Nagas were never totally defeated, as Taksaka survived the forest fire. Thus, even in victory, the Aryans, or orthodoxy, were actually losing ground to popular religion and customs. This is told in the story of how Janamejaya performs a victory sacrifice where a stray dog approaches but does not touch anything sacred. Janamejaya and his men beat the dog to a pulp. The dog then complains to its mother, Sarama, who was Lord Indra's own pet she-dog. All presume that the dog must have polluted the sacrifice, but what is clearly being told is that, even if it had polluted the sacrifice, it was no ordinary dog. In fact, it was a lesson against the illogical prejudices that the orthodoxy was continuing to harbor. It was a sign that attitudes needed to change, or, to put it another way, since things have gone so out of control where even a dog has to be treated as sacred, why bother? It was anyway beyond redemption. As in all previous yugas, the universe seems bent on destroying itself. The war with the snake people, the Nagas, was only the last straw. Sacrifices had become meaningless, and gestures no longer signified anything. As it is said, a day will come when it will be evident that 'the four Vedas did not exhaust every form of knowledge,' and gaps in knowledge had to be filled. Most importantly, people needed to know in a more understandable way. Thus, the Puranas were written.

Vyasa, the Author

The greatest of these stories is undoubtedly the Mahabharata, and the greatest of the ancient writers is its author, Vyasa. The antecedents of Vyasa, however, are not great. He was the illegitimate son of Satyavati, a fisherwoman, and a mendicant Brahmin. Symbolically and literally, he was a link to the past, being sired by a Brahmin, and his conception justified the future course taken, as his mother clearly projected the shift that the Vedic religion was taking and legitimizing. Yet, even his conception was legally and morally a taboo. In trying to create the disgust that an orthodox Brahmin would have had for such a conception, Calasso describes their mating as "the two bodies mingled with the puddles and scraps of food at the bottom of the boat," and he describes his mother as "dark, beautiful, dressed in rags. She gave off a subtle odor of fish and musk." It was from such conditions and from such a mother that Vyasa was born, to fill the gaps in the Vedas with the Mahabharata, soon acknowledged as the fifth Veda. In this context, it is also important to realize that all the heroes of the Mahabharata are his progeny, both the Pandavas and the Kauravas, as they were children of Ambika and Ambalika, whom he copulated with. To give some legitimacy, at least to the Pandavas, they were also shown as sons of the gods.

Satyavati and Bhishma

To add to the ignoble descent of the heroes, Satyavati, the mother of Vyasa, then becomes the wife of King Santanu, thus the grandmother of all the protagonists in the Mahabharata. It is Satyavati who forces Bhishma, the legitimate heir and ultimate product of the old order, to abdicate his rights in favor of the children of Satyavati and to give up his claim to the throne, remaining celibate for the rest of his life, a clear acceptance of impotence. He then becomes a witness to the destruction of the old order as he lies on a bed of arrows, unable to die before his time. His was the most tragic fate—to know and yet not be able to act, not out of fear or lack of capacity, but due to his own goodness of heart, and then to be made a witness to the destruction of all that he had stood for and all that he cherished. The poignancy with which the story of Bhishma is told indicates the anguish with which the orthodox gave up, inch by inch, their treasured beliefs, reluctantly accepting change.

Durvasa and Kunti

Durvasa is described as a portion, an 'amsa,' a splinter, a glowing coal of Shiva. He is perhaps the most terrible rishi that we meet in the sacred texts and was not like Yajnavalka, a scholar or a believer in knowledge but one whose power lay in his capacity to curse. Even the gods feared him, for when Airavata, Indra's elephant, rejected the garland offered to him by Durvasa, Sri, the splendor of the gods began to fade. No king or important person was therefore willing to deal with him or even to welcome him as a guest, as no one knew when he would suddenly get angry and start cursing, which curses even the gods could not undo.

Thus, when he went to the kingdom of the Kuntibhojas, the duty to look after him fell on Kunti, the teenage daughter of the king. She was so dutiful that she even held a boiling bowl on her back while it cooled as Durvasa ate at his leisure, and even the normally angry Durvasa was pleased to grant her the boon by which she could summon the gods to be her lovers. Durvasa represents both the power and danger posed by the native beliefs. Described as an emaciated mendicant in rags, he had the power even to summon the gods, not only for himself but to one whom he favored. Durvasa is both the 'amsa' of Shiva and a rishi. It was always a mixture of orthodoxy and some revolutionary idea that saw the gradual evolution of their religious thought.

Krishna, the New God

With the Mahabharata, Indians had a new God in whose mouth the whole universe whirled around. To make him acceptable, he was made the eighth avatar of Lord Vishnu. Yet, unlike in the past, when Vishnu had to come to reassert the power of Dharma, Krishna's mission was merely to speed up the end of a yuga. He seems merely bent on the destruction of the whole universe. Even in his destructive avatar, his person had to be elaborately white-washed for him to be acceptable. Thus, Durvasa, when he comes to the court of Krishna, is treated with utmost respect and courtesy and was made to feel so welcomed that Durvasa, as a parting gift, asks Krishna to paint himself with rice mess and Rukmani to paint herself with rice pudding so that they become fair, and then grants them the boon that Rukmani would always be fragrant and beautiful, and Krishna always loved. Thus, they are made white to satisfy the orthodox, while their original darkness was to placate the native sentiments. As Calasso puts it, the age of Krishna began when they no longer could sustain Vedic abstractions or explain the world or everything that had happened. In fact, in the Mahabharata, Vyasa tells Yudhishthira that ritual is dangerous, as any shortcoming in ritual or gesture is more harmful than not performing a ritual at all.

The Mahabharata, says Calasso, is throughout the story of Dharma being sick, weighed down by the impediments of history. This view is expressed in a different way by Yudhistra himself when he says, 'dharma is very subtle,' to justify their having Draupadi as a common wife. It was excessively subtle and difficult to follow, even for one who was the embodiment of Dharma itself. Yet, by the time of the Mahabharata, dharma was already jaded, and its meaning, especially that of death and liberation, was a distant memory. All the heroes of the Mahabharata are thus shown as illegitimate children and the progeny of the mixing of races and castes. It also presents the tragedy of those who try to go beyond their caste or fail to realize their place in society. Bhishma, a warrior, who, despite his clear caste duty to remain a warrior, becomes a renouncer; Drona, the Brahmin, who wants to be a warrior and a teacher of the martial arts; Karna, a warrior, brought up as a charioteer's son. Worst of all is the pervasive feeling that everyone has lost their taste for doing their duty; thus, Arjuna, the hero of the Mahabharata, is also called 'Bibhasta,' the one who feels self-loathing. The entire life of Arjuna in the Mahabharata is an attempt to escape his appointed role of prince and warrior, as shown by his escape to the jungle and his attempt to climb the mountains, right up to the gates of heaven and to the gods. These are all attempts to lead a life of recluse and to be a man in search of knowledge. Finally, the Gita's main message is that of Krishna goading Arjuna on to do his duty as a warrior. It is out of Arjuna's doubts and self-loathing that Krishna must establish the new order, and in this, Krishna says, "If the truth is lost to Arjuna, it is lost to the world."

A New Look at Consciousness

While the Vedas saw consciousness as Atman himself, in the world of doubt, self-loathing, and meaningless ritual, the sages of the new age saw only death, for it is consciousness that makes man aware of his own mortality. Consciousness is 'Nara and Narayana,' and the two have to coexist for one to be truly conscious. In the

Mahabharata, Krishna and Arjuna are Nara and Narayana. Thus, almost immediately after Krishna leaves the Pandavas, they begin to feel a sense of loss as though the light had suddenly gone out, only a perception of darkness all around, and as Calasso puts it in his quotation, it is as though 'a veil of dust fell upon their faces.'

The Meaning of the Mahabharata

The main feature that distinguishes the Mahabharata from all earlier sacred texts is its attempt to state a moral law. Thus, the dialogue between Krishna and Arjuna, termed the 'Bhagavad Gita,' is the new moral underpinnings of their religion. Yet, the story that the Mahabharata tells is a tale of many gods, many customs, and a great deal of moral ambiguity. Krishna, as the eighth avatar of Vishnu, is, for the first time, unable to actually bring back dharma to the world; instead, it is annihilation that he brings in his wake. The story is a story of defeat, even in victory. From satire, the story turns tragic—a tragedy on such a cosmic scale that all humanity is submerged in an all-encompassing holocaust. After the funeral rites for Pandu, Vyasa gives a speech in which he says, "The happy days are over. Tomorrow after tomorrow, each day will be worse. The Earth has lost its youth."The Bhagavad Gita is thus a moral code for an age that has already lost all ideas of true Dharma. Even as Krishna urges Arjuna to fight, the implicit message of the Mahabharata seems to be that, however great the provocation, peace is preferable to war, bloodshed, and devastation.

The End

In the end, the Pandavas and Draupadi are left alone, with only their faithful dog for company; even Krishna is gone. It is this group that then tries to climb up the mountains to the heavens. Draupadi falls first, followed one by one by the others until Arjuna also falls and Yudhistra is left alone with his dog. When they enter Heaven's gate, Indra himself welcomes Yudhistra but tells him that his dog is not permitted. Yudhistra refuses to enter heaven without his faithful dog, whereupon it is revealed that the dog was Lord Dharma himself. Thus, the Mahabharata ends on a note not to take things as they appear but to judge all things and ideas only after careful thought and without prejudice.

The Ramayana

The Ramayana was clearly the story of the spread of Aryanism to the south, right up to the island of Sri Lanka, not with a commanding army, except when finally confronted with the resistance of Ravana, but with the power of Dharma, as embodied in the person of Lord Ram. The troubles he encounters, the life he and his family had to live in the forest, and the loss of Sita are all symbolic of the difficulties that the spread of Aryanism entailed, the compromises that had to be made, the alliances that had to be affected by local powers, and the losses that they had to accept. The fact that Ram succeeded is told in the story of how the temple that he built even at Rameswaram is a miraculous and divine gift.

Ravana represented the final hurdle in the spread of Aryan control. Ravana was not just powerful; he was, in a sense, loved by his people and had a strong network of allies and kings. Ravana himself is portrayed as a great tapasi who had attained great power from the same gods, and his death at the hands of Lord Ram was actually a boon that he had secured. Many of his friends and relatives were also greatly empowered by Tapas, and his son, Indrajit, was one of only three people to ever master the three greatest astras: the Brahmastra, the Vaishnavastra, and the Phasuastra. The opposition was thus neither weak nor mean.

The overlapping story of Agastya and Parasurama as apostles to the south, to the Tamil country, and to Kerala tells of the missionary zeal with which the Aryans had spread out to cover the entire country in their way of thinking. They were prepared to go even to the ends of the country. In fact, the difficulty of crossing the Vindhyas is told in the legend of Agastya, who commands the Vindhyas to stop growing until he returns, and since he did not return, it became a stunted mountain. Parusarama's war with the Kshatriyas seems to suggest the total annihilation of the local population of Kerala, which then required it to be populated with sixty-four Brahmin families. The fact that there is no specific Kshatriya caste in Kerala seems to support the story to some extent. It also suggests that in some regions, the Aryans had to fight pitched battles before they could enter and become a force to be reckoned with.

The Agni-pariksha in the Ramayana, which Sita is made to undergo, was not a test of her chastity but a symbolic test of the acceptance of the compromises made in the Vedic religion to tempt the inhabitants of South India to accept the Aryan way. Clearly, when the proselytizing Brahmins came back from south India and presented the report card of their activities in the south, those who stayed behind and had become the orthodoxy must have seen in the compromises a clear betrayal of the core values of the Aryan way. It was to test, not so much the compromises per se, but whether it was done in good faith that they made Sita undergo an agni-pariksha. That she was a captive in an enemy household was accepted; what had to be tested was if she had betrayed her lord, the embodiment of Dharma, in this case, the core values of the Aryan way of life.

The Creation of a Common Religion

The sacred texts, right up to the Puranas and the Epics, clearly tell the story of the integration of the Aryan way with local traditions. The renderings of these encounters with an alien culture—the initial abhorrence and repulsive reaction, which later led to the acceptance of these alien ways—are a story told with a stiff upper lip, and for that reason, all the more tragic. As they enter India, they meet with the forces of Rudra and the local people they describe as black, nooseless, and without 'Vac.' Yet, in time, Rudra becomes Shiva, the God of gods, despite his dark skin and his uncouth appearance. From then on, it is a continuous series of compromises to adjust and accept the beliefs of the local people, at first from the sheer need for survival and later to lay claim to leadership. The descent from the worship of the martial qualities of their Aryan God, Indra, to the abject surrender to Shiva, whose praise, even when martial terms are used, is only symbolic, was steep.

Their aversion to the black natives is clear from their first description of them. This aversion continues as an undercurrent in their thoughts, despite their capitulation to the mightier forces of local belief. It surfaces in the story of how Ganesha tries to prevent Shiva from entering Ganga's room, where the idea of black Shiva copulating with the white Goddess Ganga still seems to cause a shiver of disgust. It was also told in the story of Dhasha's sacrifice, where he, the chief priest of the gods, refuses to invite Shiva. An insidious attempt to keep the local traditions from polluting their rituals and beliefs is a continuing theme in their stories, as the Aryans clearly did not accept the compromises they had to make with grace or meekly. Yet what appears inconceivable is the fact that it was their own intelligentsia that created the Puranas and stories to justify their compromises and to elevate the local gods and the local beliefs and practices into not only something acceptable but supreme. This abject surrender is not explained.

The most difficult part of the compromises was that every aspect of belief and ritual purity had to be given up, and all their cherished ideas in theology and philosophy had to leach away to accommodate the new beliefs. All that they achieved in their forceful rearguard action was to retain the Vedas as sacred texts and, with them, the mantras and liturgy that went with rituals and ceremonies. Their great achievement was, however, the stratification of the people of India on caste lines, even if it meant that the Dasa of today became the Brahmin of tomorrow, thus retaining their position to determine the social dynamics of the country. Further, despite accepting the black and dirty Shiva, they were able to underplay his behavior and retain the social importance of cleanliness and purity by making Shiva the God of the sanyasi, the renouncer of society and its rules. As a result of their rear-guard action, they were able to save the Vedas, the Mantras, the caste system, and the acceptance of purity and cleanliness, all associated with the white skin that became the dream color for all Indians. What they lost was credibility, a great way of thinking, an open, tolerant, questioning, and scientific religion that saw God as only the prime mover, without qualities, who, if eternal, cannot create a transitory universe, and therefore, all that we perceive is nothing but a manifestation of God. It was also the belief that since even God cannot create from nothing, we and all creation are only parts of God, "Tat tvam asi." While the Epics and Puranas clearly gave legitimacy to the incorporation of the native gods and local beliefs, there is an ever-present undercurrent of direct and often vitriolic attacks on the accommodations made to accept crude and illogical doctrines. The attack is couched in satire—not even of the subtle kind, but that which is often crude and disgust arousing. It would be absurd to presume that the acute ancient writers of these works were not intentional when depicting Shiva as black and dirty, Krishna as black and of low caste, and Draupadi as black, and all the heroes of the Mahabharata as bastards, with the origins of the lunar dynasty being attributed to Satyavathi, the fish-smelling daughter of a boatman, or in the incongruity of the depiction of Ganesha as a God with an elephant head. The Epics and Puranas thus cannot be taken as straightforward tales, especially to the Arya, who gloried in his heritage as a noble and pure race. In fact, it must have appeared truly amazing that the ordinary people, especially the natives, actually accepted these stories as the glorification of their gods.

There is an undercurrent of extreme bitterness in all that appears as compromises that were made to enfold the native population into their way of life. A white-hot rage coupled with impotence is normally reflected in satire in the Epics and, to a lesser extent, in the Puranas. To make a bitch, the embodiment of God, Dharma, cannot be anything but the overpowering disgust and revulsion overflowing into impotent rage. To suggest that the love of God was nothing more than the physical infatuation of the Gopis for Krishna must have been, at least to the intellectual class, a parody of religious seriousness. The fact that these were aberrations is clear from the fact that when Sankaracharya, in white hot rage, finally wanted to galvanize the Hindus to what he saw as the terrible decline in beliefs, he went back to the basic tenets of the Upanishads. He went on to beat the Hindu leadership into shape by advocating a religion that saw God as 'Nirguna' and all creation as merely 'Maya,' at best a manifestation of Brahman. These were exactly what the new leadership had denied while creating a religion of innumerable gods and, with it, blind and superstitious idol worship.

Hindu History

While many historians have looked at the sacred texts and the Puranas for clues about the history of India, always hoping to confirm such stories with historical facts to arrive at some possible interpretation, A.K. Mazumdar, a historian and Sanskrit scholar, published a book called The Hindu History in 1917, in which he asserted that all we need to know about ancient Indian history is fully written down in the sacred texts and the Puranas. Instead of bemoaning the lack of historical writing, he insists that the Puranas tell us all we need to know about the history of the people called the Aryas, who came from afar and finally made India their home. While there is no evidence to corroborate the story that Mazumdar makes out, he is happy to claim that a textual reading of the sacred texts and Puranas would tell us a clear story of the Aryas. A.K. Mazumdar claims that it is not only a valid history but an impartial one.

A.K. Mazumdar takes us back to 6000 B.C. and beyond to tell us the story of the Aryas. He claims that the Aryas, as a distinct people, emerged from Siberia and moved south when the temperatures in Siberia became unbearable. From the Puranas, he claims that the Aryas claim to be descendants of Indra, who had his home in Indralaya, a very cold place. As they moved south, they first made central Asia their home. He claims that they were essentially made up of eight extended families who then went their separate ways: one east to China, one northwest to Europe, one south to Persia, one southwest to Mesopotamia and further to Egypt and Greece. One group also made their way beyond Afghanistan to the northwestern regions of India, Kashmir, and even Tibet. He claims that these people were responsible for the ignition of civilization in Mesopotamia, Egypt, China, and the Indus Valley. Mazumdar claims that even after they spread out, they retained some of their tribal loyalties and, in fact, still seemed to refer disputes to their Pope, called Brahma, who may have remained in central Asia.

To strengthen his arguments, he claims that the Phoenicians who colonized the eastern seaboard of the Mediterranean were

Aryans, whose trading class was called Panis, from which the name Phoenicians was derived. After the initial migration, the Aryas merged with the local people and lost their original distinctiveness. The Indus Valley civilization was created by them, and they had a great deal of links both through trade and due to their affinity to the Assyrians in Mesopotamia as well as with the ancient Egyptians. The beginning of Kali Yug, around 3000 B.C., was a turning point for the Aryans, as they saw their culture being swamped by others. This was also due to another-worldly attitude of most of their best men, their Sages, and at one time, as many as thirty-three sages refused to marry. This trend was also seen among intellectual women, thus depleting the quality of the new generation of Aryans. It is from this time that Aryan philosophy was directed toward the importance of human existence and the insistence that salvation is only possible through active participation in life and not in renunciation. There was then another surge of migration from central Asia by an indignant group of Aryans, who then pushed their way through known regions in search of a new home. The sacred texts and the Puranas tell us the story of their journey and their subsequent successes and failures.

As they pushed eastwards, they were opposed by the Persians, who were called Asuras, as they were a puritanical sect who did not drink. The Aryans, who were migrating, were Suras, and they loved their drink, and they looked down on the Persians as Asuras, those without sura, drinks. To fight against the Asuras, the Aryans entered into a treaty of friendship with the Assyrians and their chief, Virtra. However, in an opportunistic moment, Indra, the leader of the Aryans, betrayed Virtra and killed him. This was to become an eternal blot on the honor of the Aryans, who valued honesty, hospitality, and most of all, the sanctity of their word. In the meantime, the original settlers, who had settled in the Indus Valley, the Sumerians, were harassed by Rudra, part of the first wave of Aryans, until they fled to other parts. The newcomers were led by Vishnu, a dwarf who was a crafty and mighty warrior and Indra. Vishnu got a foothold in the new region by pleading to the magnanimity of the mighty King of the region called Bali, in the guise of a mendicant. Having gotten a foothold, he infiltrated the region with his soldiers, took Bali by surprise and killed him.

Once he was in control, he sent out families with the promise of overlordship of all the new land they were able to occupy. Thus began the colonization of the Indus valley, then the Gangetic plains, and even Tibet and Bengal. The colonization of the south was entrusted to Agastya and Parasurama. The colonization of India was led by seven great sages called the Saptarishis. All high-class Indians claim descent from these sages. Mazumdar treats the sacred texts as secular history and claims that the Devas were not gods but superior persons who led the Aryans as they migrated into India and include Shiva, Indra, Vishnu, Durga, and so on. He maintains that the elevation of men as gods and the attempts to whitewash the sordid details of some of their doings were prompted by the ridicule that the Buddhists resorted to while attacking Aryan beliefs. Thus, while Agastya and Vasistha were born of a prostitute, Kumbha, when they wrote their story, they made Kumbha an Earthen pot in which the seeds of Varuna and Mithra were incubated.

India in Greece

To take Mazumdar seriously, one needs only to read a book called India in Greece, written by an acclaimed Greek scholar and indologist, E. Pococke, in 1851. He shows, with a multitude of examples (which makes his book full of references and therefore difficult to read), how all Greek mythology is actually nothing but a rewriting of Indian myths. Even Robert Calasso, in his book Marriage of Cadmus and Harmony, readily accepts that all the Grecian gods are shown, even in their own mythology, to have come from the east. Thus, even the basic mythology of how Zeus kills his father Cronos to become the supreme God is nothing but the Aryan myth of the war between the Devas and the Asuras. The Asuras were the earlier gods of the Aryans until they left Iran, and when the Devas became their new gods, it required them to show how the change took place.

The Victory of the Dasa

In some senses, the Aryanization of the country was not the victory of the Aryan but of the Dasa, the native population, who made the Aryan give up all his core values to accommodate the primitive and superstitious religion of the natives that included the practice of idol worship. Yet, to term the native religions only as something crude and primitive would be to deny their origins in the Harappan civilization and their roots in the most ancient civilization of all, the Mesopotamian civilization. Agastya, the apostle to the Tamil people, was a non-Brahmin, and as legend has it, he participated in the first Sangam, held in Samaria in 4000 B.C. There is very strong evidence, based on affinity, to suggest that the religion of the Harappan people was the same as the religion of Mesopotamia, which started with the cult of the mother Goddess and led to the worship of Baal, temple prostitution, and dance, apart from a tendency towards idol worship. At the other end was the imposition of Vedic religion, represented by Parasurama, who was a Brahmin but a rebel against the Brahmin policy of compromise, especially with temporal powers. The real tragedy was that, in fighting the Aryan invasion, the native went into his shell, as it were, and stopped evolving the tenets of his religion the way their brothers in the Middle East took to Judaism and later to Christianity and Islam, and even when they merely assisted the development of philosophy that relegated religion to the realm of myth, as in Greece and Rome. Similarly, the Aryans lost all that was good and progressive. In the end, what remained were the mantras of the Vedas, accepted as the common liturgy of all Indians, even if no one understood them, the supreme position of the Brahmin in the intellectual and religious realm, and the stratification of society on caste lines, along with a fatalistic belief in Karma.

Who Won?

Dr. A. K. Mazumdar has not been taken seriously by historians and has become a footnote in the history of India. However, that is a pity, for there is much that may be true. As we study the sacred texts and the final shape that Hinduism took by around 1000 C.E., certain aberrations stand out. Why did the Aryans compromise everything except Sanskrit and the Vedas, and why were the local people adamant about protecting their two important gods, Shiva, Vishnu, and Krishna, as their avatars?

The chronological timeline of the decay of the Harappan civilization and the entry of the Aryans into India also leaves a huge gap in history. Thus, it is very likely that there was an earlier migration of the Aryans around 3000 B.C. This would also explain the similarity and common origin of many of the European languages, where a migration in 1500 B.C. would be insufficient to explain the state of the Egyptian, Mesopotamian, and even Greek civilizations at that time.

The second reason to take him seriously is the fact that, as the Aryans entered India, he did not seem to have had a problem communicating. All the stories in the Puranas show both sides speaking to each other. This would suggest that a group of Indians were already speaking a version of Sanskrit. Further, many of the sages that the Aryans accepted were like Vyasa, products of local intermixing. The division into Asuras and Devas, where the Aryans accepted that the Asuras were their elder brothers, is perhaps the clinching fact. Then to portray many of the important Indian kings like Bali as Asura suggests that the earlier wave of Aryans had done so well that they were kings in many regions of India.

It would therefore appear that an earlier migration of Aryans had led to an intermixing with the Harappan people and the loss of their unique identity. The Harappan civilization, being a much more advanced one, must have forced the Aryans to accept at least some of their beliefs. In fact, it would appear that they even became priests. The fact that they were still speaking a version of Sanskrit shows that they had been able to force their language onto the remnants of the Harappan people, now bereft of any leadership. They must have also retained their memory of the Vedas and were thus happy to concede primacy to the Vedas.

In the compromises made, it was not the pure local who was at the forefront but the newly converted Aryan, who, in his enthusiasm for his new beliefs, was adamant that they be included in any compromise. The seductiveness of Shiva, domesticated through 'Nirguna' as a symbol of Aryan beliefs, and the more comforting image of Vishnu as the savior of mankind were, in the end, not so much a compromise but an inevitable requirement to make the Aryan beliefs into a tangible religion.

A pre-Aryan India is thus a misnomer. Yet, this was not the whole picture. There were clearly people south of the Vindhyas who may have had a totally different history. The fact that one of the stories in the Mahabharata stresses the fight of Arjun and Krishna against the Nagas suggests that even after the acceptance of Krishna, there were still other people who had a different history. The Pali tradition, along with the Buddha of Saka blood and the Jains, also suggests that the Aryan tradition was only one of the many splinter groups that survived the Harappan decay. In fact, the division between the 'Sramanas' and the 'Brahmanas' may have been more than religious and was also a division based on ethnicity. The apparent ease with which the later Aryans got adjusted was thanks to the presence of a small group of the 'elder brothers' who had formed a viable splinter group, happy to welcome new Aryans, so long as certain minimum requirements were met.

The Pre-Aryan Heritage

Mainstream Indian heritage and even Hinduism as a religion have been hijacked by the Aryan historical narrative, mainly because the Dravidian tradition has even less surviving historical evidence. Neither through monuments, written treatises, nor literary works is the Dravidian heritage available to us. According to history, the non-availability of records and archaeological evidence is as good as proof of their actual non-existence. Yet, the oral tradition and the stories told from racial memory claim that there were three Sangam periods before the one that is known to us through the oldest Tamil literature. Dravidian enthusiasts even suggest that the first Sangam period was actually in Samaria. While little historical evidence can be found to support such a belief, there are some interesting leads that may suggest a different narrative.

The seals found at the sites of the Harappan civilization are very similar to the finds in Mesopotamia, and the fertility cult seen in the figures of mother goddesses is also similar to the religious tradition in the Mesopotamian region. The only clear portrait figure of what appears to be an official or king found in Mohenjo-daro also resembles the Sumerian people, and the figure has a distinctive South Indian look. It is of a man with a snub nose and is of a semi-Negroid and Australoid type, very similar to the Dravidian ethnic type. While it may still be disputed, the general consensus is that the archaeological finds at the site of the Harappan civilization are the remains of a much older civilization that was clearly non-Aryan, and perhaps the people there were the ancestors of the Dravidian people.

Yet, the fact that there are no historical remains of civilization in the South leads to the inevitable question: how did they come from the Indus Valley to the South? There is a historical tradition that talks of continuous trade between the South and the Middle East, and through them to Greece and Rome. Even the Bible talks of King Solomon trading with the kingdoms in South India for teak and minerals for the building of his Temple. Since the common era, there has been a continuous record of trade and other forms of interchange between the Kingdoms of the South and the Gulf regions and through them, especially with the Roman Empire. Why was there this exchange with the South, and yet there are no indications of any such trade with the North, which was closer to the Gulf? Does this perhaps justify the existence of closer, and perhaps even more ethnic, links between the people of the Gulf region and the people of South India?

The obvious answer to the question of how the descendants of the Harappan civilization came to the South is that they were pushed out of their homes by some ecological disaster or by invading tribes, including the Aryans. The skeptic would still ask for evidence, and there is nothing so far from any archaeological search, not only of the pre-Aryan period but even of the early common era. The answer to this puzzle would be that, in dealing with the Harappan civilization, we are dealing with a unique civilization that refused to allow itself to be fossilized for future generations to dig up and misrepresent. Despite clear evidence from their buildings that they were a very advanced civilization, they left no written record and very little art. When they were uprooted and dispersed, they had no time to rebuild, as they were no longer a nation or state but refugees overwhelmed by their new surroundings. Before they could reinvent themselves, they also had to deal with the cultural dominance of the upstart Aryans.

A Review of the Historical Evidence

Professor X.S. Thani Nagayam has collected all the important papers written on the subject of the Dravidian civilization and published them as 'Tamil Culture and Civilization.' It gives the definitive position on many of the claims and counterclaims made by scholars on both sides of the divide: those who see present-day India as the cultural child of the Aryan heritage and those who claim that we are part of a much older culture that has been submerged by the more powerful Aryan culture.

Leonard Cottelli, in his work 'Lost Cities,' states that internal evidence from the Vedas itself indicates a rich and advanced civilization existing prior to the Aryan migration. The Vedic hymns speak of Indra as the destroyer of forts, and the Dravidians were said to have had as many as ninety forts. Indra is also called the destroyer of ancient castles. Then there is evidence of archaeological sites of the Harappan civilization that proves the existence of such forts and castles. Cottelli claims that the Harappan people were also an advanced religious society, and their word for God was 'ka,' and in Tamil and other Dravidian languages, the temple, the house of God, was called 'Ko-il.' The same word is seen even in the Vedas. He also claims that the Aryans only brought their barbaric animal sacrifices, which they called 'Homa' and 'yagna,' while the Dravidians had already gone far beyond such crude religious practices and had 'puja,' often only an offering of flowers, as their obeisance to their gods. He claims that Shiva and Uma were pre-existing Dravidian gods. An image of what appears to be Shiva with animals surrounding him and his power indicated by an erect phallus is also one of the archaeological finds from the Harappan sites. The fact that Shiva is also called 'Pasupathi,' God of animals, and the Shiva linga is worshiped as the 'Linga' is almost conclusive proof of Shiva being a pre-Aryan God.

Murray Emeneau and Thomas Burrow, in their study 'Linguistic Pre-History of India,' discount the belief that the Aryans were people of high culture. Instead, they claim that the Aryans were only nomads and cattle hustlers, whereas the local population was part of an advanced civilization. They also show how Dravidian languages influenced Sanskrit, perhaps more than Sanskrit was able to influence the local languages. Bishop Cadwell, in fact, claims that there is enough proof to link the Dravidian languages to the 'Scythian' branch of languages.

H. Heras, S.J., in his 'Studies in Proto-Indo-Mediterranean Culture,' cites comments made by Mr. Hewitt, saying, "The Dravidian races had covered the country with a network of strongly centralized and well-established governments and there is ample evidence to show that it was not Aryans who made India a great exporting country." Equating the Asuras to the local Dravidian population, it would be seen that even from the Aryan texts, they considered the Asuras as great builders, and even the Pandavas sought the help of Maya, an Asura architect, to build their altars. Further, even in the Brahmanas, it is said that the dark-skinned Brahmins were cleverer than the fair-skinned ones, clearly admitting that the local people were actually the more brilliant.

Professor Raichal Bannerji says, "The Aryans came to India in small numbers; they did not make any attempt at preserving the purity of their stock. In fact, many of the heroes of Aryan texts, like Vyasa and even the Pandavas and Krishna, were not Aryans; Vyasa was the son of Matsya, and the Pandavas descended from the Naga tribe." In a similar vein, Keith says, "Dravidian blood came more and more to prevail over Aryan."

E.H. Warmington, in his work 'The Commerce between the Roman Empire and India' says that there is evidence to suggest that there was an ongoing trade between the Roman Empire and the Kingdoms of south India, especially the kingdoms of the Cholas and the Cheras. The Chera kingdom was famous for its Muslim cloth and pearls. The Chola oral tradition has many references to collaboration with the Greeks in shipbuilding. In fact, the story of St. Thomas and his journey to India starts with the story that he met an Indian merchant who was looking for a master carpenter or builder to build a palace for a king. There is also a repeated story of an embassy from the Pandya kingdom having visited the Roman court of Augustus. The evidence of contacts and trade with the Roman Empire is supported by the discovery of Roman coins in Arikamedu, near Pondicherry. As R.E. Mortimer Wheeler says in his book 'Rome Beyond the Imperial Frontiers,' there have been more than twenty finds in many places in south India of Roman coins of the 1st and 2nd centuries. As it is, the coins of Augustus and Tiberius dominate, indicating that trade was at its peak during that time. Archaeological finds at sites in South India also include a large collection of Roman pottery and Roman glass from the 1st century. K.M. Panikkar also maintains that there was a maritime culture in the South Indian states stretching back beyond the common era. In fact, the Ragu Dynasty was actually called 'Assumadra Kshitiessanam,' rulers beyond the seas.

Heinrich Zimmer, in his great work 'The Art of Indian Asia,' stresses the similarity between the religion of Mohenjo-daro and South India, where the cult of the Goddess was predominant, whereas the worship of the Linga and the Yoni in the Aryan temples only dates to medieval times. Regarding its links to the Mediterranean, he cites the example of the fig tree as a revered plant in the Harappan civilization as well as the deification of the unicorn, otherwise unheard of in India. He claims that the cult of the mother goddesses was widely known from the Valleys of the Nile to Mesopotamia and the Indus. He claims that all art forms, from dance to music, were advanced in the Indus Valley civilization, and the same tradition is seen in the South Indian history of the arts, especially dance. Shiva, as a dancing God, is a Harappan motif that has a continuing history in South India as Nataraja and is also seen in the 1st-century bronzes, which, in fact, seem to mimic the style of the dancing girl and dancing God of the Indus Valley finds. Ritual dance is prominently mentioned in the Sangam works, says V.R. Ramachandra Dikshitar in his 'Studies in Tamil Dances.' Dance, as part of the worship of Vishnu, was called 'Kudam.' Shiva was the king of dance, and within his dance were both creation and destruction. Such a portrayal of Shiva is mainly seen in South India, linking it again to a continuous culture that began in the Indus Valley.

From P.T. Srinivasa Iyengar's 'Pre-Tamil Culture,' we also see how the color of many of the Aryan gods took their final hue. Murugan, the main God of the Tamils, was worshiped as the Red God, which is the color ascribed to Vishnu, while in the rural areas, Mullai was worshiped as the Black God, the same as Shiva. It is also interesting that it was in an attempt to describe Muruga that the theologians came up with the concept of 'formlessness' and beyond speech and to describe God as 'the nameless, formless one, worshiped by a thousand names in chant and dance,' which became central to the theology of the Upanishads. As Sir Charles Elliot says in his book 'Hinduism and Buddhism,' "The portrait of Shiva drawn by Tamil writers retains some features of the old Dravidian deity, who dances, who sports among men, and bewilders them by his puzzling disguises and transformations." Sir John Marshall finally says, "The pre-Aryan religion involved the cult of the bull and the snake, typical of Mediterranean cults." And as in the Mediterranean, the pre-Aryan religion was associated with the Goddess cult, phallic symbolism, and the devadasi cult. In fact, the Aryans buried their dead, and it was from the local inhabitants that they adopted the idea of cremation. In the end, Mortimer asserts that the only Aryan elements that have survived as a result of their contact with the local population are those elements of Vedic rites that are essentially social, such as marriage ceremonies.

An Alternate History

While there have been fanciful claims about Dravidian culture and civilization, we know that historical facts support the depth and extent of Dravidian culture to some extent. What is clear is that there was a civilization that had attained a very high level of social organization and artistic ability in continental India long before the arrival of the Aryans. Even if the Harappan civilization was not Dravidian, there was a clearly established, living, and deep-rooted culture with its arts, religion, and customs. It's possible that it was the Sangam period, which is celebrated in Tamil literature.

Consequently, when the Aryans arrived in India, they were not met only by opposing armies but also by a society with entrenched cultural practices and religious beliefs. Most historians accept that the Aryans were not some invading army that conquered India, but possibly only small groups of immigrants hoping to find a more congenial home. It would also be clear that the Aryans were more inclined to assimilate with the local people and accept their culture than to impose their crude way of life on a population that was so vast and extensive as to be impossible.

Yet, the Vedas clearly talk of conflict, of wars, of besieged forts, and of hundreds of castles. They also seem to suggest that even as mere raiding parties of cattle hustlers, they were much more successful than their numbers would have warranted. They had two advantages: the horse and the knowledge of how to forge weapons with iron. Their speed and the greater strength of their iron weapons gave them an edge over the local population that was still stuck in the Bronze Age.

However, even when they won battles, they did not have the strength nor the numbers to rule, as the stretches of territory were too large and the inhabitants too many and widespread. It was to deal with this problem that they devised or borrowed from the locals the idea of a stratified society on occupational lines, putting everybody in their place and reducing conflicts resulting from vertical ambitions. The system had inevitably had to be porous to allow new people, as they came into the fold, to find their place in society without too much heartbreak.

In the beginning, there was only the warrior and the rest of the people, 'the vas.' It was the confrontation with a more sophisticated religious order that forced the first compromise. The Epics and Puranas talk of a long and often bloody struggle between the Brahmin and the Kshatriya for domination. Since the Aryan was not a temple worshiper and his rituals did not require an intermediary like a priest, the Brahmin must have been a pre-existing institution that dealt with the more elaborate religion of a much more sophisticated civilization. Consequently, the battle for supremacy was not only between the warrior class and the Brahmin but also between two religious cultures.

Primitive people everywhere have a sense of some power beyond the human; thus, after victory in battle, almost all tribals have a form of thanksgiving where some animal is sacrificed as an appeasement or thanksgiving to the gods. This was all that the Aryans brought with them as a public religious ritual. However, when the fighting ceased and society was at relative peace, as the successful completion of the 'Ashvamedha sacrifice' was supposed to indicate that there was no power willing to challenge the king, society then needed to settle down to the business of living.

This is when other forms of sacrifice became part of religion and expanded into rituals for marriage, death, naming, atonement for wrongs, and so on, where a professional class of people called priests became necessary. This is when occupational stratification began to take on the contours of the caste system, emblematic of the Hindu religion. While Manu and the early writers of the religious texts make a big thing about racial purity, it is clear that it was only the fears of a society that was slowly losing all racial purity. The irony is that, in the end, the requirement was only really strict for the Brahmin, who was anyway more local than Aryan. It was not even related to respect or honor, as they accept Vyasa, the son of a fisherwoman, Parasurama, the apostle to Kerala, and Agastya, the apostle to Tamil people, as Brahmins. Not only was society irrevocably mixed, but even the custodians of the culture and religion were non-Aryans.

The Dravidian Influence

To the Aryans, it was clear that to conquer and assimilate, it was necessary to blend. The newcomers were thus forced to bend to the rule, if they actually ruled. Obviously, there were others, as the sacred texts themselves talk of non-Aryan kings and even saints and sages. History tells us that foreign tribes kept coming as invaders, including the Sakas, the Persians, the Greeks, and even Chinese tribes like the Yeuzhi, and many stayed on to create dynasties like the Sakas and Kanishkas. Their rulers were quickly accepted as legitimate kings, as long as they also accepted the cultural and religious practices of the local people, which clearly Aryanized to some extent. This also makes it clear that the force to be reckoned with was not the minuscule Aryan minority but the existence of a powerful orthodoxy that had forced even the Aryans to assimilate and now decided how invader kings and their tribes would be accommodated. By this time, the local population was a mixed race, and the acceptance of foreign rulers led to their slow assimilation through marriages and the acceptance of local customs, religions, and rituals. These assimilations also resulted in the acceptance of new gods and some foreign customs, legitimized by the Puranas with historical and mythological legitimacy.

What is not clear is who gave in more and who actually succeeded in imposing more of their culture. What is clear is the spread of Sanskrit as a language. It is the historical Sanskritization of the country that has led historians to presume that it was also the Aryanization of the country. To understand this, one has to realize that Sanskrit spread because it was the language of religion and learning. The powerful orthodoxy that controlled cultural and religious practices was really not Aryan but the Brahmanical class, local institutions, that allowed Aryan thinkers to join the fold. It was only to propagate orthodoxy that Sanskrit was accepted as the language of religion. The orthodoxy, looking at the large number of spoken languages, must have realized that without a common language, a common religion was impossible. In accepting Sanskrit, the orthodoxy was killing two birds, as it were, with one stone. It spread a common religion, not amenable to distortion by translation, and got the support of the local intelligentsia and the protection of a superior army. The compromise seemed to have required everyone to accept the supremacy of the Vedas, while all local gods and their different religious practices were also recognized and legitimized through the writings of the Epics and Puranas. While Shiva, Krishna, Murugan, and Hanuman were all added to the pantheon of gods, only the Vedas were chanted. In fact, not a single non-Vedic hymn, chant, or song was ever incorporated. That was the victory of the Aryan, or perhaps the superior intelligence of the orthodoxy that saw in the Vedas something eternal, transcending mere local customs. It was only the acceptance of a meaningless chant that, in no way, affected the content of one's belief.

The once transcendental religion of the Aryans, who even questioned the existence of God, thus accepted idol worship. What we don't know is the nature of the pre-Aryan religion and what was actually compromised. It is clear that the Aryan way of life was threatened as they tried to assimilate with the local population, but the question is, did the local population also feel threatened by the Aryan onslaught and, as a result, go into a shell, as it were, and become reactionary, no longer open and experimental? Was their reaction similar to what happened when they had to face the Muslims later and the British and their institutions even later? Were they fighting a defensive war to preserve their culture and religious beliefs, setting aside for a time the regular and periodical introspection and review of religious beliefs that the likes of Sankara and Ramanuja did as an ongoing tradition, even centuries later? Did it, as a result, become reactionary, stale, and putrid, refusing to change, innovate, or think about continuous religious relevance? Was that the reason for their lack of vitality and a resort to ritualism?

Yet, there was the Bhakti movement, which had its roots in an earlier tradition, clearly non-Aryan, where personal gods, devotion, piety, and ecstasy were part of the religious experience. However, it came too late, when mainstream Hinduism had already fossilized into a ritualistic religion, so that Bhakti became merely the songs that could also be sung, and their devotion, piety, and ecstatic reaction were merely an attitude that was also permitted. It is clear that, despite a certain grandeur about the Vedas, it was only the first expression of wonder, astonishment, and humility at the vastness of the universe and the enormous powers of the natural forces. It was the direct and therefore forceful poetry of a people learning to express themselves; their wonder and innocence have an agonizing directness. That was all it was, and more could not be expected from a nomadic people only used to cattle breeding and rudimentary agriculture.

The Upanishads

While accepting that the Vedas may have been almost entirely Aryan, in the Upanishads, we enter a different world. A world of acute distinctions, philosophical interpretations, and an attempt to justify rituals. While in the Vedas, gods were only the sun, moon, and natural forces like fire and the mighty rivers, in the Upanishads, we see a totally different conception of God. God as 'Saguna' and 'Nirguna,' all and nothing. The world and human life as 'Maya,' illusory, but through which alone ultimate reality could be understood. A depth of philosophy that had never been seen except in the most advanced of philosophies.

The natural progression of religious belief is normally from worship of natural forces like the sun, moon, and other natural forces to that of a mother Goddess. The Upanishads move directly from the innocent wonder of the Vedas to a very complicated and acute philosophy, proof of the interpolation of a more advanced religion and based on a tradition of thinking that had passed through many phases of thought. In fact, it is the product of a very advanced civilization. The Indus Valley civilization already had the worship of the mother Goddess and other fertility symbols, including Shiva with his erect Linga. With a heritage spanning more than two thousand years, local thought must have moved many degrees deeper into conceptual and religious thinking. From such a tradition, the Upanishads were a logical progression.

The Karma Theory

Like the Upanishads in general, the 'Karma Theory' is a very acute philosophical piece of theorizing, perhaps the greatest insight that man has ever been able to perceive about the nature of human life. It is so advanced in theory that even modern science has yet to fully catch up with its implications or grasp its fundamental greatness.

While the Greeks had also talked about the transmigration of the soul, it was only in India that the idea of a cycle of life, where one has to be born again and again in a never-ending cycle with progression and regression, where each life is a reward and a punishment and future lives are determined by the present life, was imprinted. The implications are stupendous, for it looks at life as modern scientists do, as spontaneous and lived entirely for itself. Evolution to a higher form is determined by the laws of evolution, and life is ever reaching a higher form of life. The 'Karma Theory' saw life as a process of refining, where all the bad has to be removed for life to move to a higher plane.

The Indian Sages saw it as the continuous refinement of life through a system of rewards and punishments, where a man can ascend through his good life to a higher level or descend through his evil deeds to a lower form of life. Life is eternal; only its form changes, determined by how we live our given lives. Cause and effect alone determine the future.

This idea is so advanced that the nomadic Aryan was clearly incapable of formulating such a theory. It had to have come from a very advanced civilization that had gone beyond the need for gods to a belief in a system that was self-sustaining, propelled by the laws of causality. As a conceptual idea, it could explain itself by the rigors of logic alone but added a certain religious connotation by claiming that someone up there was actually counting and keeping a record of our lives, where merits and demerits determine our future happiness. This was latched onto by the orthodoxy as the fundamental belief of Hinduism, as it helped to justify the caste system and to make people accept their given lot as God-given and non-negotiable.

Ahimsa

The concept of Ahimsa is also alien to primitive cultures where hunting and killing are normal and necessary. As Manu says, the big fish eating the small is the law of the world and the fundamental principle of life. Only a very advanced civilization, having seen the ecological implications, would accept the sacredness of all life. It is only a culture that understands the interconnectedness of life that would realize that all life is sacred. Consequently, the concept of Ahimsa must have originated in a very advanced civilization that may have seen great ecological disasters, not by some nomadic, wandering tribe. The Aryans, with their primitive ways of homa or Yagna, would have found it impossible to believe that the mighty Indra, a warrior, bloodthirsty and violent, would be satisfied with the mere offering of flowers.

The Epics and Puranas

The Epics and the Puranas introduced new gods and created a template for gods and their worship, which must have been Aryan in origin, as an entrenched society with its deep beliefs and traditions has no need for any justification or a genealogy to know their gods. It could only be the attempt of the Aryans to justify their acceptance of foreign gods. Further, the sometimes ironic and satiric tone of many of the stories in the Puranas suggests an outsider's take on the truth of the legends and myths. The very superficiality and lack of any internal consistency in many of the stories suggest that they were not written by people who had any deep faith in what was written but appear like a hurried attempt to create a plausible mythology acceptable to the mass, not the intellectual. Its attitude seems to be that this is what is claimed; you can take it or leave it. The real believers in Shiva and Vishnu addressed their lord in intense Bhakti poetry, not based on the comical stories of the Puranas.

The Pre-Existing Religious Thought

If we accept that the Vedas were conceived around 1000 to 1500 B.C. and written down only in the early years of the common era, it would be approximately 2000 years after the peak of the Indus Valley civilization. The local people thus had a 2000-year head start over the sages who dreamed up the Vedas. The society of people who worshiped mother goddesses and fertility cults had time to refine their philosophy and religion and, like the Egyptians, Mesopotamians, and Greeks, to fine-tune their philosophy and religious beliefs.

Thus, long before the Vedas were written down, teachers like Mahavira and Buddha were already roaming the Indian hills and plains. Theirs could not have been some spectacular new philosophy but the refinement of the philosophies that were already current. Indian philosophy was already so well-known that Alexander wanted to meet an Indian philosopher. In fact, all the known philosophies, from Stoicism to Epicureanism, were already being taught by Indian philosophers before the arrival of Buddha on the scene. In later years, when the Vedas had been imposed on those who accepted them, the main division among the philosophers was between those who accepted the authority of the Vedas and those who did not—the division into Brahmanas and the Sramanas. For a long time, Aryan orthodoxy was merely the acceptance of the divine origins of the Vedas; all else was negotiable. This attitude was what allowed them to accept new gods and new forms of worship, always insisting that the supremacy of the Vedas was non-negotiable.

The Dilution and Corruption of Beliefs

While the corruption and dilution of native religious beliefs can be laid at the doors of the uncivilized Aryans, who, in trying to assimilate with a much deeper, complex, and transcendental culture, had of necessity to simplify and, in the process, corrupt and trivialize existing beliefs, the question to be asked would be, why did the natives allow such a corruption to take place? Why did they allow the trivialization of their beliefs and allow idol worship and ritualism to engulf their much deeper religion? The answer may be power. The local people had ceased to have power. They had no empires or powerful dynasties to propagate their religion. The destruction of their main centers of power and learning had left them without a base or support, and their philosophers had been dispersed all over the land, leading to mere pockets of followers. This left them at the mercy of invading tribes from the Sakas to the Greeks, who, when they wanted to settle down, accepted the religion that was put up to them by the new orthodoxy, the Brahmanas, who attached themselves to all-powerful lords and claimed to be the custodians of all religious knowledge. The same people organized the writing of the Puranas, whose knowledge was second-hand and whose interests were more with the propagation of their caste and their continued status as the custodians of religious thought.

CHAPTER 11

CHRISTIANITY IN INDIA

There is a tradition that St. Thomas, a disciple of Jesus, came to the Malabar coast in the 1st century after traveling through Syria, Persia, and Northwestern India. This tradition is made credible by the presence of an entirely unique group of Christians in Kerala who call themselves St. Thomas Christians and claim that their ancestors were converted by St. Thomas himself. The problem, however, is what Nirad Choudhri said in his book, 'The Continent of Circe,' when presented with this claim: that if it is true, they have made no impact on the society or history of the people around them or the nation, and therefore their claim is irrelevant and to be ignored. Yet, it is not an empty claim. The situation in the world and especially in the Middle East during the 1st century C.E. was perhaps the most suitable for the journey that St. Thomas may have undertaken. The Roman Empire had given peace to a large part of the world, making traveling safer than ever before or after. Thus, the route St. Thomas is supposed to have taken, including the sea route to India, was both well-known and relatively safe. In 1983, while digging at the site of the old city of Pattinam, a huge cache of Roman coins dating back to the 1st century was found, clearly establishing that there was contact between that part of the country and the Roman world in the 1st century.

The presence of Christians in Kerala has also been attested to by many travelers over the centuries, including Pliny, the Greek historian, and Christian records from the 3rd century. Since the 10th century, the fact has been almost universally accepted, and

Marco Polo also attests to the fact. When the Portuguese came to the Malabar coast in the 15th century, they were met by a strong Christian community with a special, unique, and ancient tradition of Christianity, claiming spiritual descent from St. Thomas. They may not have been overly surprised because one of the motives of the Portuguese explorers was to meet up and join with Christians said to be living in the Africa of Prester John and the Christians in India, and to form a united front against the mighty onslaught of the Muslims. That Christianity predates the coming of the Portuguese is therefore beyond doubt.

The problem, however, is the lack of any clear historical evidence to prove the existence of Christianity as early as the 1st century. While there is no doubt about the fact that there were Christians after the 10th century, even this is attested only by travelers and visitors and not by archaeological finds or written records. No church record before the 13th century has been found. There is also no evidence of the Bible used or the liturgy used by the St. Thomas Christians to stand as a record of their religion before the arrival of the Portuguese. While there are records of continuous exchange between these Christians and their spiritual headquarters in Syria, their correspondence was isolated and limited to religious matters. Thus, when the Portuguese came to Kerala, they were accosted by a Christian sect that was still using an ancient Syrian liturgy that no one else seemed to understand. The Portuguese, being Catholics and fully conscious of the dangers of the Protestant heresy that had split Christianity in Europe, brought with them a sense of rivalry not only to India but to the entire east. Thus, the Spanish and Portuguese, who were the guardians of the Catholic faith, were always in conflict with the members of the Protestant nations like Holland and Britain wherever they met them. They were always ready to suspect the worst and saw in the indigenous Christianity shades of paganism and heresy that had to be rooted out. They therefore insisted on conformity with their religious practices and burned and destroyed all the relics, icons, and liturgy of the Kerala Christians. This, say apologists of the St. Thomas Christians, is the reason why the old records and proof of their religion are not available now. In fact, it was only after 100 years of Portuguese dominance that they began to realize that their religion had been suppressed, leading to a mini-reformation within the church that led to the breakup of the church into the Catholic, Orthodox, and Mar Thoma fractions in the 17th century.

The questions that immediately arise are: if Christianity was present in Kerala in the 1st century, why was it not more influential? Why was there no evangelizing, and why did they hide the light, as it were, in a bushel, as they were specifically told not to do by Jesus himself? The possible reason may be that in the 1st century, the Brahmin group that was supposed to have been converted to Christianity was a law unto themselves. Vedic Hinduism made no great distinction between beliefs, as it was an open, questioning religion where specific beliefs, especially about the nature of God and the ways to salvation, were open questions. Vedic religion before the Epics and the Puranas was not really a religion but a way of life. Its practices designated a special race and its rituals were meant to keep them as a separate race. As we have already seen, this led to a multiplicity of beliefs, from materialism to stoicism; all that the race demanded was a reverence for the Vedas as revealed knowledge. A group was never ostracized for their beliefs, only for practicing non-Aryan ways of life. Further, the Brahmin community of Kerala, as legend has it, was handpicked by Parasurama to populate and civilize the new land and were thus a small and close-knit family in a vast landscape of aliens. Thus, if seven Brahmin families had accepted the teaching of St. Thomas, as legend says, it would hardly have caused any flutter as long as they continued to practice Aryan rituals. The preaching of St. Thomas was also in no way revolutionary to knowledgeable Brahmins, for he merely claimed that God took human form as an avatar to rid the world of adharma and, in the process, was crucified by the demons of the Kali Yuga. This was no different from the story of the Ramayana or Krishna charitras. To Vedic Indians, God was undefinable, was both suguna and Nirguna, and thus could take any form, and all that St. Thomas seemed to be emphasizing was his suguna form as a personal and caring God. Thus, his message was not radical.

However, to remain within the Arya Dharma, the Vedic distinction between Varna and Avarna had to be maintained, and the rituals of the Arya had to be performed. Thus, despite the apparent conversion to a new religion, the converts and their descendants maintained their Vedic traditions. This also explains the lack of proselytizing and active evangelization. To pretend to have a better religion or belief or even a better intellectual tradition would have been presumptuous to their other brethren, and to preach to the Avarnas would be a shame. It would have also been presumptuous for others to tell them they were wrong, for all Aryans were considered good enough to decide for themselves and to have their own beliefs. Thus, while friendly attempts at persuasion may have taken place and some new converts may have joined the group through faith, marriage ties, or for political reasons, the new religious group expanded only through the multiplication of the original group of believers from generation to generation, minus some backsliders. They remained Brahmins in appearance and practices; the only difference was that they believed in a God who came as an avatar in the form of Jesus, as the embodiment of the 'suguna' aspect of a loving God.

As long as they did not disrupt society, there was no attempt to suppress them or even to treat them as different. In fact, Christian families were treated by kings with respect due to the upper caste, and they were entitled to positions of power, titles, and distinctions. Many worked as advisors, generals, and admirals. In the later part of the second millennia, when they were exposed as different, they too relaxed their appearance of being Brahmins, gave up the many taboos associated with being Brahmin and took up cultivation and active participation in administration and in the armed forces, reaching top positions in all fields. Consequently, they also had their own Kalari schools and were entitled to the pomp and ceremony associated with the nobility, like gilded umbrellas, elephants, escorts, and distinctive dress. This appreciation and honor made them, perhaps quite rightly, loath to give up all such privileges merely to become aggressive about their religion. Thus, their religion stayed at home and, like later-day Hindu orthodoxy, must have acquired an orthodoxy of its own.

The History and the Evidence

There is little hard evidence to prove the existence of Christianity in Kerala in the 1st century, even though the possibility of St. Thomas or some other missionary having come to Kerala and converted some people to Christianity is a distinct possibility. Further, the tradition of the existence of St. Thomas Christians in the 1st century is attested not only by a tradition in South India but also in the Church in the east. The western world had, for centuries, been thrilled by stories of Christians in Africa, of Prester John, of Christians in the land of the Queen of Sheba, and in far-off India. In fact, as already said, the Portuguese, in venturing to the east, were also in search of their fellow Christians, so as to join forces against Muslim might. There was also a claim in a work called 'Anjuvannam' that there were Jews living in Kochi from the 6th century B.C. and that St. Thomas was bold enough to cross the seas to come to Kerala because he expected to see his own fellow Jews in Kochi.

From the 3rd and 4th centuries, there is clear evidence of the presence of Christians and Christian establishments in Kerala. This is attested by letters and notes in the church archives and by church leaders like Bishop Ambrose, Gregory of Nazianzus, Bishop Jerome, Ephrem the Syrian, and Eusebius of Caesarea. There is even a claim that Pantaneas actually visited the Christians in Kerala in the 4th century. It is also a documented fact that Syrian missionaries were coming to Kerala from about the 4th century to serve the Christians in Kerala. It is most likely that the Christianity practiced was Nestorianism, which was then the dominant theology in the Eastern Empire, especially in Syria and Persia. A Syrian, called Thomas of Canna, was also supposed to have come to Kerala and established churches that were later called the Knanaya Churches. The recorded presence of Jews in 1st-century Kochi also makes the possibility of a similar group of Jewish Christians with Syrian connections quite likely. Much of the history of the Malabar Christians was thus neither written by Indians nor based on stories and legends present locally, as Indians were not history writers, but by visitors and in foreign documents. The most important of these are the recordings by Pliny, the Greek historian. They are also based on the record of works like 'The Acts of St. Thomas' and 'The Song of Thomas,' which were found in the Christian mission in Edessa, in Syria. St. Ephrem, of the 3rd C.E., says that St. Thomas was killed in India, and in a poem, he says (as spoken by the devil), 'I stirred the apostle to death; I slew him in India, overtaking him at Edessa.' There is evidence that the Church in Kerala was administered from Syria by the Patriarch of the Church of the East. There are even names that have come down to us, like Isoyabb II, who was Patriarch in 650 C.E., and Timothy I, in the 8th century. The headquarters of the Syrian Church were supposed to have been at Cranganore or Kodungallur, and visitors to India came through the ports of Murzris and Patinam. The Christians in Kerala were called St. Thomas Christians only after the arrival of the Portuguese; they were earlier merely called Mappilas or Nazaranis. Legend claims that St. Thomas established seven churches in India. An elitist version claims that he converted seven Brahmin families to Christianity. Another authority on the subject, Ramban Pather, however, claims that as many as 1600 people were converted by St. Thomas. The churches attributed to St. Thomas are Kollam, Niranam, Nilakal (Chayal), Kothamangalam, Chatukulangara, and Thiruvithancode, also called Arapalli (half church). It is also claimed that Niranam was the seat of the Metropolitan (head of the church), where originally there was a large Cathedral. The original cathedral was washed away in the great flood of 1341, which is a clearly recorded disaster in Chera history. Today, an old church that was built later, called St. Mary's Orthodox Church, stands in the location of the old cathedral and in the church are preserved many old relics and documents pertaining to the old Christian community. Kodanganallur or present-day Paravoor, was close to the port of Muziris and was the second-most important church. Kodungallur was where Chendamangalam, the home of the Paliath Achans, was; these Achans served as ministers and advisors to the Maharajas of Kochi. A Jewish song sings of the nobility of the Achans, who had donated land for the Jews and protected the Christian community. It is claimed that the first church in India was built by St. Thomas at Kottakavu, in Paravoor, in C.E. 52. There is a record of a church in this area being destroyed in the floods of 1676 and the Achan giving them new land to build a church. The ancient church at Kothamangalam was also destroyed over the years, and a new church was built in 1900 called the Syro-Malabar Catholic church. The church built by St. Thomas at Palayor was famed for its architecture, which was Indian in style. This was also a place where the Jews had reportedly been living for a long time before the arrival of St. Thomas. In the case of this church, there is also a record of an Italian priest seeking permission to rebuild the church in 1607. Close to this place is a place called the Jewish Hill, where the remains of an old synagogue were unEarthed, alongside which a Hindu temple presently stands. The Kollam port is mentioned by Pliny senior, and there is a record in copper plates of permission given to Nestorian priests to build a church by the Chera king, Raja Rajasekara Varma, along with certain privileges. It is also in Kollam that there exists some evidence of new converts being added to the fold, especially the Ezhavas for whom a special 'Tharisapalli Sasanam' was created. The Tharisapalli copper plates were given by the Chera ruler Sthanu Ravi Varman in 849 C.E. to the St. Thomas Christians to build a church along with some land. The Trivithamcode Arapply was also called Thomayan Koil, where today stands the St. Mary's Orthodox Church. There is also a claim that St. Thomas also built a church at Amalagiri, about 20 km from Nagercoil in C.E. 52.

The Jewish Tradition

There is another tradition that suggests almost all Syrian Christians were Jewish converts to Christianity. It is known that after the defeat of Israel in the 6th century B.C., there was an exodus of Jews, many as prisoners and others as exiles, to almost all parts of the known world. In fact, when Israel was again a nation, there were only two tribes, Judah and Benjamin, which has led to the story of the lost tribes of Israel. In this context, the claim that in the 6th century, a large group of Jews migrated to the Malabar coast may have some element of truth. The tribe that migrated was supposed to have been the Naphtali tribe. Even then, there was already a group of Jews on the Kerala coast, if tradition is to be believed. It is claimed that some Jews had come as traders during the reign of King Solomon, who had sent them to fetch material for building the temple in Jerusalem. They had then stayed on as traders with the Middle East and had established a base in an area close to the port of Muziris.

The story of St. Thomas's journey is then twisted to claim that St. Thomas was actually obeying Jesus's command to go 'to the ends of the world' to preach the gospel to the lost tribes of Israel instead of to the Gentiles. There may be a great deal of truth in this claim, as there is a persistent belief and claim that there were Jews in Kerala for centuries before Christ. This may also be the reason why St. Thomas was able to boldly travel to India, not to an alien land but to a known place where he would meet his own countrymen. Thus, if St. Thomas had actually converted the Jews, it might explain why they discarded their more orthodox practices and became indistinguishable from the local people. It may also explain the special privileges they got from the royalty from then on, as they were aliens outside the Varna system but clearly educated, and therefore, like all the invader kings who ruled in India, they were also absorbed into the system at a very high level.

The second wave of immigration took place around 50–55 C.E., when there was great persecution of Christians during the reigns of Caligula and Nero. This wave consisted mainly of Essene Jews.

After this initial migration, Bishop Dawood (David) of the Syrian church was supposed to have migrated with many of his congregation while escaping the persecution against the Arians and Nestorians around 300 C.E. There is then a claim that around 340 C.E., a group of Suraya Christians also migrated to Kerala and were known as Chaldeans. These people settled along the Konkan coast, up to Mangalore and beyond. They were a group that was seriously affected by the persecution of Christians during the time of Tippu Sultan in the 18th century. The proof of the Suraya migration is based on the claim that a cross with a Pahlavi inscription has been preserved in the church at Alangudi. A Persian cross was also supposed to have been installed by Mar Easo in the Kadamattom church.

The legend then says that the original Jewish settlers first settled on the island of Mali, off the coast of the port of Muziris. When this island was later washed away in a great flood, they moved further inland. These Jews had their own customs, and since they were foreigners and educated, the Chera kings gave them great respect and even allowed them to be a self-governing unit within the kingdom. It is claimed that their rituals and liturgy were based on the 'thaksa,' written by one of the first bishops of Jerusalem, Yacoob or Jacob, who was James, the brother of Jesus himself. This was incorporated into their 'holy Qurbana,' and that is why the Kerala Christians were called 'Jacobites.'

Language, Liturgy, and the Bible

One reason given for the lack of records is the problem of language. Till about the 9th century, there was no Malayalam language as we know it today. The language used was largely based on Tamil. Like the ancient Vedic Indians, the community may have resorted largely to an oral tradition based on memory and repetition. The first Syrian Bible was called 'Peshita' or the simple version, which was translated from the Hebrew original in the 2nd century by a priest called Essa or Ezra. However, evidence of the existence of a Syrian Bible is only from the 4th century, as recorded in the mission at Edessa. The consensus is that the Bible was accepted by all in the community by the 5th century and revered by all. The Latin Bible was produced only in 1857, and the writing of the Malayalam Bible is a story in itself. The educated among the Christians were ashamed that they had no Bible in their own tongue, and an effort was made by the community as a whole to translate the Bible, starting chapter by chapter of the New Testament. In the meantime, Ramban Philipose, along with some missionaries, was able to translate portions of the Bible by 1813, and a complete Bible by Benjamin Bailey was completed in 1829.

Modern History

There are clear records of Christianity in Kerala after the arrival of the Portuguese in 1498. With the arrival of the Portuguese, a sea change took place, as they allotted to themselves the role of being the head and arbiter of the church in India. The entire Christian community was brought under the umbrella of the Archbishop of Goa. The Syrian church initially welcomed the Portuguese as fellow Christians, even if what was sought to be imposed was at odds with their own practices.

To the Portuguese, it was clear from the beginning that they alone had the right to decide the correct practices and believed that they were the upholders of the true religion. They saw in the practices of the Syrian church vestiges of paganism and even heretical beliefs and thought it their responsibility to purge such practices and bring back Christianity to its pristine purity. Therefore, they thought nothing of the suppression of the beliefs and practices of the local church. The suppression was resisted, especially by the head of the Syrian church, the Metropolitan, Mar Jacob. When he died in 1527, the Portuguese aggressively tried to weed out what they thought were heretical beliefs and practices. When the next Metropolitan, Mar Abraham, also died in 1559, they sent the Archdeacon, George, who was next in line to become Metropolitan, to Portugal to be properly educated in matters of religion, leaving the Church without a head.

This was a great opportunity for the Portuguese to enter the vacuum thus created. In 1559, Alexio de Menzies, the Archbishop of Goa, convened a synod at Daimper and, through a bull, brought all the churches in Kerala under the control of the Archbishop of Goa. They then began purging the Syrian church of all its ancient rites and liturgy, collecting all their icons, relics, and books, and burning them. The purging continued until almost all ancient books and relics had been destroyed. The Syrian Bible, the 'Peshitta,' was also burnt. This was all done with the approval of the Vatican. They then introduced their Latin liturgy and made it mandatory for all churches to use only that liturgy, thus breaking the back of the Syrian church.

It took about 100 years for the simmering discontent to find a voice. Soon, like-minded churchmen got together to condemn the forceful suppression of their religion and their rites. Their opposition to Rome and to the Portuguese in India was confirmed by a vow taken by the dissidents at the site of a leaning cross near Cochin, which has become famous as the 'Koonan kurishu sathyam,' in 1653. This was done under the leadership of Archdeacon Thomas. However, the majority, led by Mar Thoma I, Mar Alexander Parambil, and Mar Alexander Kodavil, accepted the supremacy of the Church of Rome, represented by the Archbishop of Goa. This led to the breakup of the church in Kerala in 1661, with 116 churches remaining loyal to the Pope, while 32 churches broke away to return to their ancient roots, which they saw as different from what was being imposed by the Portuguese. This also led to a minor reformation in the church that brought the church closer to the Protestant version, which they saw as more akin to their original beliefs.

Christianity in the Modern Era

With the arrival of the Portuguese, Christianity in India became a proselytizing religion. While the Portuguese came to India as soldiers and conquerors, they were accompanied by an almost equal number of priests, monks, and other religious men who were, in many ways, more powerful than the warriors themselves. The thrust for proselytization was led by the Jesuits, who called themselves the Warriors of Jesus, a truly formidable force. They were warriors of Catholic Christianity who battled literally for the souls of men. Highly educated and deeply committed to their task of 'harvesting souls' for God, they soon learned the local languages and established schools and outreach posts even in the most remote parts of the country. The success of their efforts is now part of the historical record. Yet they were able to attract only the poor and the dispossessed, mostly among the marginal castes in the social hierarchy. Except in Goa, where through inter-marriage and power-sharing, a large number of upper-caste converts were added to the fold, elsewhere, from Kochi to Kollam and from Tuticorin to Pondicherry, new converts were made largely from the poorer sections of society. The Jesuits, who established many centers of learning and made attempts to translate the Bible into many different local languages, were, however, never disheartened nor did they slacken their pace of work but continued undaunted, even to the present day. Their contribution to education is undisputed, and even today, in many parts of the country, all that one has to do is claim that the school being run has some association with the Jesuit Fathers for it to become a prized education, so lasting has been the impression of the quality of education they have imparted over the years.

Thus, when the British landed in India, there was already a core group of Christians in many parts of the country. The rivalry with the Catholics was a great impetus for Protestant missionaries to come to India, not only to save the people from their pagan ways but also to protect them from the wiles of the Pope and his evil ministers. The British administrators, unlike the Portuguese, were more reluctant to mix administration with religion. Yet the fact that British domination of India was so much more widespread had its own impact. Consequently, a much larger contingent of missionaries could work all over the country, and they were able to establish missions from the hills in Tamil Nadu to the mountains of Assam. They worked in the mountains of Afghanistan to the tribal districts of Madhya Pradesh, everywhere, even where the British writ did not run. In numbers, the British may have been more successful than the Portuguese in converting locals to the new faith. Initially, the new religion had a great attraction to the upper classes and educated Bengalis who saw in Christianity the possibility of a new dawn for India as a whole, and large numbers embraced the new religion. Encouraged by this success, the British embarked on establishing more educational institutes and even established schools and colleges for the education of women. The British scaled up the initiative started by the Portuguese and created a large network of schools and colleges wherever they went. In addition to education, they also added health facilities, especially hospitals, clinics, and dispensaries.

After the initial success in Bengal, the British found it difficult to convert Indians, who reacted as though to an invasion and went into a shell, becoming reactionary, with their leaders making it clear that conversion was a form of betrayal of Indian civilization. Alternatives in the form of reform movements within Hinduism like Arya Samaj and Brahmo Samaj reduced the urge to convert. Thereafter, like the Portuguese, they were able to convert only the poor, the lowly, and the dispossessed. They, however, made a success of their missions in the tribal districts, especially in the North-Eastern Hills, where states like Mizoram became almost totally Christian. While unlike the Portuguese, the British did not encourage marriages with the local people, the inevitable mixing did take place, resulting in a new breed of Eurasians and Anglo-Indians who inevitably had to become Christians as they had lost all caste privileges. Their great contribution was clearly in education and health care, where there was a time when almost all private schools, colleges, and hospitals were mission-run. However, despite the herculean efforts of Christian missionaries of all sects, the dismal fact remains that even today, not more than 3 percent of the population are Christians. In a population of more than 1.2 billion, there are not more than 30 million Christians. Yet it must be acknowledged that their contribution to nation-building and their impact on the social consciousness of the people have been far greater than their numerical strength.

Ethnic Christianity

Due to the apparent Indianness of Christianity in ancient Kerala, it was not only tolerated but accepted as merely another form of Indian thinking. The fact that the early Kerala Christians did not rock the boat but instead accepted and continued to honor Indian customs and the caste system allowed them to prosper and create a community without any opposition from the rest of higher-class society. In fact, they continued to grow and be accepted as warriors and counselors, with appropriate honors and ceremonial paraphernalia. It was only the arrival of the Portuguese as conquerors and as a colonial power that exposed Kerala Christians as something alien. This exposure resulted from the Portuguese' attempt to absorb the Kerala church into its fold. The problem was that the leaders of the Kerala church, having been an ingrown church, were suddenly faced with people who claimed to be the custodians of the Christian doctrine and who had the power to demand obedience. The acceptance of the Roman

Catholic faith as the only Christian faith and the imposition of the idea of the inferiority of the native church saw most of the church leaders coerced into accepting the suzerainty of the Portuguese. This brought with it foreign customs, modes of dressing, and a new type of church architecture, all meant to discriminate against the natives. The Portuguese embodied the European ethos of Christianity, created during the centuries of Islamic domination, a mindset that led to the Crusades, which saw the need to crush Islam as a divine mandate. They saw India essentially as a pagan nation that needed to be saved. Thus, they burned all the existing liturgy, religious books, and even icons of the church in Kerala to create what they regarded as pristine Christianity instead of what they perceived as the local Indian Christianity of paganistic rituals. That ended the harmonious existence of the church in Kerala.

Yet, the Portuguese themselves were to rue their colossal mistake. While they were able to bulldoze an existing Christian community, when they tried to convert other Indians, they were faced with an almost wall-like resistance to their ideas. Thus, despite the bravery and hard work, especially of Jesuit missionaries, they had little success in converting Indians. Their success was limited to the lowest classes, especially the fisherfolk and the untouchables. It was here that we encountered the story of Roberto de Nobili (1577-1656). Nobili, who came to India as a Jesuit priest in 1605, was the son of an Italian nobleman. He first landed in Goa and then came to a small fishing village in Tamil Nadu, where he made his mission field. He then worked for many years among the fishermen, who were Paravas by caste. The village was actually the work of his predecessor, another Jesuit, Goncalo Fernandez, who had established a mission there in 1594. After great success among the fishermen, he came to Madurai, hoping to make converts among the upper castes. Despite his best efforts, they merely mocked him and his ways. By befriending some upper castes, especially a Brahmin scholar, Shiva Dharma, he learned that they thought of him and all Portuguese as low-class and their ways as barbaric. The fact that they worked and lived with untouchables also made them, in their eyes, untouchables. He slowly began to appreciate the Brahmin ideas of cleanliness and the distinction of castes. He realized that, to make his message acceptable, he had to first make himself acceptable. He thus transformed himself by dressing like a sanyasi, in saffron robes, bathing twice a day, and wearing only wooden sandals. He then became a vegetarian, gave up all wine and alcohol and took on the life of an ascetic, concerned only with prayer and learning. While these apparent idiosyncrasies raised the hackles of his superiors, he was finally able to get the Pope himself to rule in his favor, as it was seen merely as a way to better proselytize for the greater glory of the Church. He also immersed himself in the study of the Hindu scriptures, in the study of Sanskrit and Tamil, until he became an authority in Tamil, writing books about Tamil grammar and translating Sanskrit works. He soon gathered around his listeners, as a sage, and he was able to convert many upper-caste people. When he found a reluctance among Brahmins to associate with lower castes, he even established a church for Brahmins. To create a semblance of a continuation of old traditions, he began to use native words. It was he who first called the Bible a Vedam and the Church a Kovil. He completely Indianized the gospel with words, especially from Hindu scriptures. Following in his footsteps came John de Britto (1647–1693), the son of an aristocrat who became a Jesuit and came to India to preach the gospel. He landed up in Goa in 1673 and then immediately came to Tamil Nadu, to Madurai, the mission field of Nobili. He then moved to Sivaganga and to the Marwar region, where he preached the gospel, only to get into the bad books of the ruler, who had him deported from India. After spending some time in Portugal, he came back to India, fully aware of the risk he was taking. This time he followed the practice of Nobili, dressed as a sanyasi and lived the life of an ascetic Brahmin, avoiding all meat and wine. He also took to learning the language and all its literature. He took an Indian name by which he was thereafter known, Arul Anandar. He was so successful that he converted the Marvar prince. However, one of his wives was the daughter of the King of Ramnad, who was offended by the Prince for sending away his many wives, including his daughter, as a result of his conversion. He got Britto captured and executed on the coast of Oriyur. In time, the site of his execution became a pilgrimage site, and people claimed that the sand on the site turned red with his blood and remains so to this day. This sand is claimed to have miraculous healing powers. Even the Pope finally accepted his martyrdom, and de Britto was duly canonized in 1947. The last of the breed was Constanzo Beschi (1680-1742). Constantine Joseph Beschi, born on November 8, 1680, in Italy, became a Jesuit in 1698 and landed in Goa in 1710. He then went directly to Madurai. He followed the ways of his hero Nobili, dressed as an Indian sanyasi and behaved like a Brahmin. He was a scholar of great depth, studied Indian philosophy and religion and was a student of Tamil and Sanskrit. He became such an expert in the Tamil language and literature that he wrote its first dictionary and translated the Tirukkural into Latin. He then wrote Tamil poems and prose works, leading to his being called 'the father of Tamil prose.' He was soon recognized as a sage and he was called Viramanavar. He was also responsible for the building of many churches, including the Basilica called Poondi Martha, the Vyagula Martha church, and the Perianyagi Martha Shrine, all in and around the town of Thanjavur. However, the success of these radical and original Christian thinkers was short-lived. The arrogance of imperial power and the unabashed belief in the superiority of their cree led to the dumping of such practices and an attempt to thrust down Catholic ideas, embedded with the cultural prejudices of European superiority, down the throats of Indians, which only led to conflict and an aversion to Christianity as something both alien and corrupting. To think that Christianity in India, apart from the Syrian Christians of Kerala, was by and large an imported idea whose growth was dependent on foreign inputs is to belittle the contribution of the native trading in Christianity. In time, Christians in India evolved and created their institutions and even their saints. Thus, Father Chavara and a nun in Kerala are already on their way to sainthood. Furthermore, Father Chavara also created a brotherhood to rival the Jesuits. In fact, in many areas where the Jesuit movement seems to be in decay, it is the fraternity created by Father Chavara that is running schools, colleges, and hospitals with their brand of religious fervor. However, these are only small episodes in the network of missionary and social work that indigenous Christian groups are doing all over the country. From village-level medical services to specialized care for leprosy patients, from the foothills of Tibet to the remote villages in the Chambal valley, Christian work persists. The Indianization of Christianity is perhaps best exemplified by the life and work of India's own Francis of Assisi, Sadhu Sundar Singh. Sadhu Sundar Singh (1889–1929) was born sometime in 1889 in a devout Sikh family in a village close to Ludhiana. He came into contact with Christianity when he was sent to Ewing Christian High School in Ludhiana. There is clear evidence that he exhibited deep spiritual yearnings even as a youth, and he questioned both Sikh and Hindu teachers about religion, apart from reading everything that he could get his hands on. In the little that he wrote, he claims that he came to a point in his life when his desperate search for the meaning of true divinity seemed hopeless and he was wanting to throw himself in front of a train if no God appeared before him. It was then that, like Paul on the road to Damascus, he had a vision of Christ, who asked why he refused to accept him, who had died for his sins. That made him accept Christ as his God, and he converted to Christianity. The trouble with the life of Sadhu Sundar Singh is that his life has become the stuff of myth and legend. All sorts of miracles and grave adventures, his encounters with wild animals and poisonous snakes, his ability to talk to birds and animals, and his effortless curing of the sick have all become part of the folklore surrounding his life. Most of his journeys also seemed superhuman in terms of endurance and success. The problem is compounded by the fact that he wrote almost nothing of his own journeys or his adventures, and all his journeys were undertaken alone, so there was no one to corroborate the stories that were spread.

The Impact of Christianity

While millions of Indians were educated in Christian institutions throughout the country, and despite the fact that many of them would not have received an education except for those Christian institutions, very few converted to Christianity. Similarly, despite the fact that millions were treated in Christian hospitals, many would have died but for those Christian hospitals, very few converted to Christianity as a result. The fact that so few were converted must have been terribly disappointing to the Christian missionaries. Yet, this also showed that Christian work in education and health care was largely treated as ends in themselves. Despite almost seventy years of independence, these Christian institutions continue to play a major role in both sectors, which only shows how important they were to the nation in the initial years and how sustained the effort has been. The pioneering role played by the Christians has also caused many others, including Hindu missions, especially the Ramakrishna Mission, to start similar initiatives, which has only added to the social sector in the country.

In wanting to propagate their religion, the Christian missionaries had to learn the local languages, but they did not merely learn; they mastered them. The perfectionist trait of the Victorian missionaries was that they would not accept anything but the best. The result was that in trying to translate the Bible, which for them had to set the standard and become a hallmark of perfection, they not only mastered the local languages but added to them. While learning the local languages, they found that many had no written script at all; to them, they introduced scripts. Many had no grammar to speak of; for them, they created grammar that was accepted even by the pundits. Even in fully fledged languages, where nobody had earlier tried to list out all the words in use, to overcome that shortcoming, the missionaries created dictionaries in almost all the languages they had to deal with. Where nothing had to be done, they systematized the language, and in languages like Bengali, which till then was only written in verse, they introduced the prose form. In fact, to a large extent, the way languages are used in modern India, from Malayalam to Bengali, was actually created by these missionaries. In many languages, like even Assamese and many tribal languages, they actually created the languages that are in use today. The work they did to create working languages was such a massive undertaking and was therefore their greatest contribution to India, a debt that Indians would be most ungrateful to ignore.

While Christians number only thirty million in a population of more than 1.2 billion, it is not the numbers that count but the impact of the religion and its moral foundations. While it would be difficult to prove that Sankaracharya and Ramanuja were impelled by Christian doctrine, their philosophy was a timely reminder to Indians everywhere of the essential greatness of Vedic religion, at least they had forgotten. The Bhakti movement fully accepted the concept of a personal God and even added terms like salvation and grace to their idea of God, where final bliss was total surrender to God—all very important Christian ideas. The fact that the Arya Samaj and the Brahmo Samaj were greatly influenced by Christian philosophy is undisputed. Similarly, the ideals of the Ramakrishna Mission and Vivekananda's ideas of evangelism were clearly taken from Christian ideas.

English and Anglo-Indians

While Christians are a very small segment in an ocean of Hindus and Muslims, their impact in indirect ways has been spectacular. The main conduit by which Christian ideas came to India and stayed put was through the use of English as the language of education and later as an official language. The surreptitious ways in which language infiltrates into the mind have been pointed out by philosophers from Wittgenstein to Barthes, Baudrillard, and even Derrida. Thus, by the mere spread of English as a language, it brought with it Christian ideas, which then infiltrated into the native languages—concepts like justice, freedom, liberty, social justice, and even concepts like social responsibility and accountability. While few became Christians, the fact that millions studied in Christian institutions meant that they were exposed to Christian ideas of social justice, the concept of sin, social obligations, human rights, free speech, and even of a personal God. If nothing else, it produced a gentler attitude toward the treatment of all people in the rigid and harsh world of caste-ridden India.

Perhaps the most visible impact of Christianity, a visual reminder of their lasting legacy, is on the Anglo-Indians. They added color to the otherwise drab Indian lifestyle. They introduced Indians to Western music, especially the pop music of Elvis Presley and Jim Reeves. They taught Indians to dance and to party. They lightened up the otherwise uptight attitude of Indians. They brought a special culture to institutions like the railways and, to a large extent, were responsible for making participation in sports a glamorous affair. Perhaps their greatest contribution was a bright sense of optimism, even when their own lives were never a bed of roses, as they would say, "Smile, child, and the world smiles with you." It is, therefore, India's great loss that almost all of them have left for greener pastures in Australia, Canada, New Zealand, and the U.K.

CHAPTER 12

THE NEW MILLENNIUM

In the thousand years after the writing down of the Vedas, Indian religious thought had added a theology and a cosmology. The pristine thinking of the Aryans was now wedded to the deeper and more complex belief systems of the local people, and a discernible religion had taken shape, with some ethics and the theory of karma as its bedrock. It was the Epics that knitted the country together with a common mythical heritage. Meanwhile, society had been stratified into castes with clear social rules and prohibitions. By this time, even the idea of an untouchable caste had been legitimized.

Yet, all was not well as far as the orthodoxy was concerned. By the time of Sankaracharya, Jain and Buddhist thought had permeated society, and new religions like Christianity and Islam were also making converts. Thus, Sankara saw his role as that of a reformer, dealing with new challenges. For that, he borrowed from Buddhism the eightfold path and introduced the monastic system into Hinduism. Soon, Hindus were wearing saffron as a uniform. He also made Hinduism a competitive religion of debate and aggressive proselytization, for Sankara saw himself as a warrior of faith. This identification with a religion and the feeling that it was under threat was a new idea. However, once it was instilled in the minds of zealous believers, it was to become an idea that stayed. A story is told that the gods went to Shiva to complain that Vishnu had been born as Buddha; therefore, a champion was required for Hindus. Shiva thus consented and was born as Sankara to re-establish Vedic Dharma. The religion was under threat, and a warrior was needed.

Even at this time, the religious identification was primarily with the separate cults to which one belonged: Shaivite or Vaishnavite, Kali worshippers or Murugan and Mariaman worshippers. There was no such thing as Hinduism, even though the 'other' as Buddhist and Jain were slowly entering the Indian psyche.

An important element of social life was the total acceptance of the caste system in most urban centers and its percolation into most rural areas. On the other hand, the 'Shaiva Siddhanta' school, which followed the Bhakti cult of the Nayanars, only paid lip service to the Vedas, rejecting caste and welcoming all into their fold, teaching that the body was the true temple of Lord Shiva. It was, however, the battle between Shaivism and Vaishnavism that was to take center stage in the new millennium. The Shaivites saw a strange dualism that claimed that the soul was chained to the body, like a dog on a chain. The body, as Pashu, was controlled by Shiva's will, and all that we see is merely the illusion created by Shiva's will (Maya). While the aggressive missionary work of Sankara led to the revival of Shaivism, the subsequent revolt against Sankara was even more violent, as in the case of Madhava, who claimed that Sankara was the bastard son of an ogre named Maninar and a widow. Sankara then seduced the Brahmin wife of his host and converted through magic. He learned the sutras with Shiva's blessings, then joined the Buddhists and taught Buddhism in the guise of Vedanta. To stop him, the God Vayu was incarnated in Madhva. The other interesting development that took place in South India was when Vaishnavism attached itself to Lord Krishna as a child, a cult that grew around 900–1300 A.D. They then separated into the cat school (Thenkalai) in the south and the monkey school (Vadakalai) in north Tamil Nadu. The split was basically for control of temples, and some kings also aided the split. The Vijayanagara king supported the Thenkalai School, while the Tirupati temple supported the Vadakalai School. The Vadakalai school claimed that a personal God was like a mother monkey that always protected its young. The Tenkalai school countered by claiming that salvation was only possible through grace, as a mother cat picks up its young by the scruff of its neck. Both schools were, however, believers in Bhakti. While the Vadakalai school claimed to be made up of caste

Hindus, the Thenkalai school was scorned as the religion of the lower castes.

The Muslim Influence

Islam had entered Kerala as early as the 7th century, and by the end of the millennium, Muslim invaders were already wreaking havoc in the northwestern parts of the country. However, they were not yet a religious group that people took seriously, except in Kerala. The mystical aspect of Islam, Sufism, was different and had a following wherever Islam went. Therefore, it was inevitable that it would have an influence on Hinduism. In fact, Sufism is what distinguishes North Indian Bhakti from that of South India. Many Bhakti saints were influenced by Sufism. Most of them were low-caste Hindus, such as Ravi Dass, who was a leatherworker and an outcast. Others, like Dadu and Sena, were from the lowest caste. The greatest of them was Kabir, who came from a low caste of weavers. The story goes that his family were recent converts to Islam, yet Kabir was known to worship Shakti. After he became famous, many stories of his immaculate conception were spread. Like Moses, he was said to be born of a Brahmin mother, who set him afloat in a box to be adopted by a Muslim couple. When he grew up, Kabir became a disciple of the Hindu saint Ramananda (1370-1440). The Kabir Panthis claim that he remained celibate all his life, but others claim he married and had a son. The story goes that his wife, not having anything to eat, got provisions from a shopkeeper on the promise that she would sleep with him. When she did not go back to fulfill her bargain, Kabir carried her to the shopkeeper, whereupon the shopkeeper fell at Kabir's feet and became a sadhu. The story also highlights the terrible exploitation of lower-caste women. To Kabir, Sanskrit was 'like water in the well,' whereas languages spoken were like a flowing river. He therefore preached in the vernacular. With his Muslim background, he was fearless enough to say,

"If God wanted circumcision,
Why didn't you come out cut?
If circumcision makes you a Muslim,

What do you call your women?"

He also asked Hindus,

"If the thread makes you a Brahmin
What does the wife put on?"

He was tolerant in his outlook and amazed at religious intolerance. He said,

"Veda, Koran, Holiness, hell, woman, man.
It's all one skin and bone, one piss and shit, one blood, one meat."

He hated caste and its intolerance. So, when he became famous, he went into a prostitute's house, hugged her, and drank her water. The Brahmins laughed at him and said, "That's all a low caste is capable of." But Kabir was merely following the Pasupatha doctrine that the apparent evil in a good heart returns as good karma. To prove a point, Kabir was supposed to have made a buffalo recite the Vedas. He found the descendants of Ramanuja, who disregarded caste, becoming very casteist and not allowing the lower castes. So, Kabir made a buffalo recite the Vedas. He asked,

"Tell me where untouchability
Came from, since you believe in it
We eat by touching, we wash
By touching, from a touch
The world was born
So, who is untouched?"

Kabir was also a revolutionary and saw in religion a social mandate. He said the goal of religion is not mere nirvana but social and political freedom for all.

Lingayats and Total Rebellion

Ramanuja tried to create a more inclusive Hinduism, yet his descendants merely returned to Brahmanical practices. Thus, one of his followers, Basava (1106-1167), a Brahmin in the court of King Brijjala, saw in temples institutions of exploitation and a buttress for Brahmanical influence. He preached that our bodies are the real temples of God. His disciples called themselves Lingayats and Virashaivas, Shiva's heroes. He refused to acknowledge the need for worship and rejected all idol worship. "Our bodies are the only temple we can trust," said Basava. He asked,

"The Rich
Will make temples for Shiva
What shall I
A poor man do?
My legs are pillars,
My body the shrine
The head the cupola
Of gold."

Basava fought against caste restrictions and welcomed all into his fold. The Virashivas were aggressive social reformers. Yet, over time, even the Lingayats became part of mainstream Hinduism.

The Avatars and The Changing Hindu Consciousness

It is believed that Lord Vishnu is born among men whenever the Earth and humans are in danger. The early Avatars of the fish, tortoise, and boar were in the Krutha Yuga and not really important to the belief system. The first Avatar to really excite the imagination was that of the dwarf, a story we have already dealt with. In the Krishna legend, Krishna is born to Devaki, the wife of the king of Dwaraka, and along with him is born Kali, who is killed by Kamsa, thinking she was Devaki's daughter. She goes to heaven only to become the eternal Goddess Kali. With her, women were also elevated to the level of gods. Further, in the Krishna legend, he is a great lover of women. The Gopis leave their homes and their work to frolic with Krishna. Krishna also had as many as sixteen wives. Thus, the Krishna legend makes him human and love and sex are not only permissible but also good. The other social implication was that, being of the Yadava clan, the low castes established legitimacy, at least as Shudras. Buddha is also mentioned in the Mahabharata as a Vishnu avatar. In the battle between the gods and Asuras, the Asuras were winning, so the gods sought Vishnu's help, who was born as Buddha. Buddha then taught adharma and dissuaded the practice of sacrifices. The Asuras followed Buddha and became free thinkers, abandoning the Vedas and thus giving victory to the gods. Buddha was thus called 'the great deluder.' While Vedic Hinduism attacked Buddhism, in time, both Ahimsa and vegetarianism became part of Hinduism, and Buddhist thought was assimilated into the Upanishads.

A Permanent Antithesis

It was the legitimization of the Shudra and the acceptance of women into religion that started the Bhakti movement, which used the newly sanctified love of Krishna in human form to become a religion of intense love and free adoration of the gods. Yet, the intense love also led to the intense enmity between the sects. It all started with access to the Epics. For saints like Tulsidas and Kambar, Hindus had alternate renderings of the Ramayana available to all classes. Tulasidas (1543–1623) was the great Bhakti exponent of Vaishnavism. His 'Ramacharitamanas' has become part of the consciousness of North India, as they are acted out every year as Rama Lila. According to legend, to find out which text is most important, the Vedas and the Puranas were put on top of Tulasidas's Ramayana in a Shiva temple, and in the morning, the 'Ramacharitamanas' was found on top. In popular consciousness, the 'Ramacharitamanas' has remained the most important religious text. While Tulasidas respected caste, he showed great tolerance and compassion for tribals and Pariahs. In fact, in a story, he makes a crow live in the mouth of Ram. The crow, being a symbol of the lowest caste, is an uppity pariah, in contrast to Valmiki's depiction of the crow as an enemy.

Chandidas, a Bengali poet, claimed that he was a Brahmin village priest who was openly in love with the village washerwoman named Rami, for which he was dismissed from the priesthood. In protest, he did tapas and came back to life. Another Bengali poet, Chaitanya (1488–1553), sang kirtanas to Krishna, and his followers claim that he was, in a single incarnation, both Krishna and Radha. They preached a religion of free love where love, even with low-caste women and other men's wives, was not frowned upon as long as it was true love. In fact, Rupa Goswami talks of the passion that leads to devotion. Another Goswami added Tantra and erotic theology to Bhakti. Yet, in typical Indian hypocritic fashion, they make the Gopis an illusion, where only their shadows are frolicking with Krishna. Ramprasad, another Bengali poet, celebrates poverty, almost like Jesus, saying, "Blessed are the poor." Yet, Ram Prasad refuses to upset the apple cart of caste.

Tukaram was a Shudra, and his poems so angered the Brahmins that they made him throw them away in the river, but Tukaram prayed, and his poems came back floating to him. His poems denounce caste. As he puts it,

"I have come to your door
Like a dog looking for a home
O, kind one
Don't drive me away"

Mira Bai (1495–1547) was a woman poet who ran away when her people tried to force her to marry a prince. She lived the life of a mendicant, singing songs to Krishna and slowly becoming an acknowledged saint. She was against caste and wrote,

"The Bhil woman tasted them, plum after plum
And finally found one she could offer him
What kind of genteel breeding was this?
And hers was no ravishing beauty
Her family was poor, her caste quite low
Her clothes a matter of rags
Yet Ram took that fruit – that touched, spoiled fruit
For he knew that it stood for her love."

Reformers, saints, and poets all saw the injustice of caste; they all saw God as an entity beyond prejudices, yet their efforts have all been in vain.

Reformers and Saints

While the Vedic period saw Aryan ideals flourishing in a new landscape, expressed in poetry of amazement and delight, tinted with wonder, with a freedom they were never to know again. As the Aryans settled in the plains of the Ganges and ventured east and into the southern peninsula, they met not only physical opposition but also philosophical resistance to their simplistic ideas. The initial wonder had then turned into a system of thought in the Vedantas. In the process, it also caused a churning of ideas, resulting in a revolt against the sanctity of the Vedas when the Sramanas questioned the very place of the Vedas in any system of thought.

These essentially agnostic philosophers created a great diversity of thought, from Stoicism to Epicureanism and all forms of materialistic philosophy, deeply rooted in skepticism. Jainism and Buddhism were the immediate religious alternatives. These religions retained a large element of agnosticism with metaphysical concepts like Atma, Nirvana, and Sunyata that few actually understood. Their success was due to the social and community life that they encouraged. The building of temples, mutts, and monasteries, where a religious community could live, learn, teach, and grow. These religions also brought into the mainstream an aversion to animal sacrifices, resulting in a gradual reduction of homas and animal sacrifices for the gentler puja form of worship. It also spread the idea of vegetarianism as an offshoot of the concept of Ahimsa.

In a world without God, in a self-created universe, the human soul also became eternal, subject to the process of growth and decay, but in the specific case of the human soul, it was seen as part of an endless cycle propelled by Karma. The momentum created by these religions stopped as a result of internal dissensions and the breaking away of dissidents to form different sects. They then lacked the strength of a unified religion and became amenable to compromise at the right price. The decline and disappearance of Buddhism as a religion were one casualty.

The Gupta age was also, in some sense, the golden age of Hinduism or the Brahmanical religion that posed as true Hinduism. They had state support and, consequent on the persecution of Buddhists and Jains, had access to their temples and mutts without the need for any foundational work. The temples, usurped from the Buddhists and the Jains, became a powerful institutional base from which they launched themselves in their new avatar as a doctrinal religion. However, the golden age was short-lived, and after the reign of Harsha, India groped and figuratively limped into the dark ages, a period about which little is known and during which a different type of churning was taking place.

With defeated empires and local chieftains all vying for a place in the sun, each religion had to fend for itself. This world of naked opportunism resulted in the emergence of a more aggressive religious outlook, the growth of religious identities and, along with it, hatred. Positions were taken, and the identification with a sect caused antagonism for the 'other,' as religious identities got imprinted on the Indian consciousness.

Whatever character the Indian psyche has taken must have been created during these turbulent times when Hinduism began to take the shape we recognize today. The rear-guard action of Buddhism and Jainism to hold their own during these trying times had much to do with how Hinduism evolved. However, as the churning reached an interesting phase, a new religion entered the fray. The fact that Islam not only entered the country but did so in triumph over the many kingdoms of India meant that they were a religious force to be reckoned with. Instead of meeting this new religion head-on, Hinduism chose the path of outward submission and retreated into itself, assuming that it was only a temporary setback and that the Muslims would soon be driven out of India. But as it withdrew into itself and locked the door, as it were, it became suspicious and fearful, leading to a siege mentality that caused the further evolution of the religion to be guided by a hard and uncompromising attitude. It was forced on its backfoot, and the result was a clamping down on new ideas, a hardening of its attitude toward caste and a more rigid insistence on social stratification to ensure obedience and submission. It is within this context that we must study the ideas of the architects of Indian thought and consciousness.

The Bhakti movement created the single most enduring metamorphosis in Hinduism, making it finally resemble the Hinduism we know today. Until then, Vedic Hinduism, or Brahmanism, was primarily a religion of the elite, with minimal evangelizing to transform it into a national or people's religion. Sanskrit was restricted, and holy texts were prohibited for most people, preventing the religion from representing their beliefs or becoming part of national consciousness. Alongside Vedic rituals, people continued to worship various gods with offerings as diverse as fish and toddy.

The trigger for the Bhakti movement in southern India, especially in Tamil Nadu, and why it spread northwards are not clear. However, what is evident is that it resonated with the people, sending ripples across the country, fostering emotions of piety and instigating change until the beginning of the 19th century. The likely cause was the reduced political support for religions as major empires disintegrated after the 1st century A.D. and the nation fragmented into small local kingdoms immersed in chaos. With the decline of political power enforcing religious orthodoxy, the religion had to deal with the people directly. When facing the people, they observed the dominance of Buddhism and Jainism with their temples, mutts, and monasteries, influencing the common people through community-driven rituals and practices. Breaking this hold required the religion to reach out to the people and align with their beliefs.

It would be an overstatement to presume a concerted effort by a Brahminical strategic team to plan such a mass movement. The Bhakti movement had too many elements of a spontaneous movement to have been planned. Yet, in the end, the result was the creation of not only a many-faceted religion but also a victory for one religion and the development of a national consciousness.

With Mahayana Buddhism, Buddha became a God, and devotion

to Buddha became part of Buddhist religious culture. There is a tradition suggesting that Christian doctrine reached the Kerala coast by the 1st century A.D., introducing the concept of a personal God who loves, sacrifices, and takes care of his devotees to the Indian consciousness. By the 7th century, Islam had reached India, particularly the west coast of Kerala, making inroads into Indian beliefs. The idea of devotion to gods like Krishna as a doctrine of love and devotion was being enunciated, along with the concept of Vishnu Avatars, making God an active upholder of Dharma and a God who cares. It was a logical next step to see him as a personal God to whom man's human needs could be placed, even if it meant changing karma.

Whatever the reason, there was an outpouring of new faith based on devotion, especially in the south around the 6th century A.D., spreading across the country and reaching Bengal in the 15th century. Parallel to this movement was a more intellectual and orthodox movement leading to 'Mimamsa' and the creation of the three main systems of Vedanta by Adi Sankara, Ramanuja, and Madavachari. The coexistence and mutual influence of these movements, leading to a fusion that shaped Hinduism, is a crucial story for which we unfortunately lack authoritative history, relying on conjecture. One thing is clear: where there was peaceful coexistence of many religious beliefs and cults, this new religious fervor led to animosity, rivalry, and hatred. New identities were created that became mutually exclusive. It was both a great devotional upsurge and a great tragedy, starting as debates before kings to prove the greatness of respective beliefs and subsequently seeking the official support of the king. How these dynamics unfolded over the centuries is not well documented, as no proper records are currently available, with the victors inevitably writing history.

The Bhakti Movement in South India

As the Bhakti movement grew, it split into two distinct camps, with a clear divide between the worship of Shiva and Vishnu leading to separate schools of thought. The level of enmity between them is not entirely clear, but the fact that no effort was made for a compromise makes it evident that there was no love lost between them.

The Shaivite group was led by religious poets called 'Nayanars,' the devotional propagators of Shaivite Bhakti. It began with Thirunavakarasu, who was not a Brahmin but a Vellalar. He started as a Jain monk named Dharmasena but turned to Shaivism when the Jains could not cure him of a disease. The Jains were supposed to have tortured him for his apostasy, but in the end, his great devotion to Lord Shiva even made the king convert to Shaivism. This was a significant turning point in the rise of the Bhakti movement. The next great devotee was Nanasumdandar, a Brahmin who, as the story goes, got 8,000 Jains put to death after defeating them in a debate. Sundaramurthi, from a poor Brahmin family, and the celebrated Manikavasagar, who was supposed to have been a minister in the Pandian court, followed. Through his devotion to Lord Shiva, Manikavasagar was supposed to have performed many miracles and debated before the Sri Lankan king. All this shows that by this time, the Bhakti cult had not only found a following but also received royal recognition. Two of the Nayanars may have been women, with one supposed to have been a Pandian queen and the other, Karaikal Ammaiyar, who lived around the middle of the 6th century A.D.

The Vaishnavite group started with Poygai, Pudan, and Pey, from Kanchi, Mallai, and Mylapore, respectively. Then came Tirumalisai, from Chengalpet, who went through Buddhism and Jainism before finding solace in Lord Vishnu. The Vaishnavite poets were called 'Alvars,' and the next in line was Tirumangai, who may have lived in the 8th century A.D. After him comes Periyalvar, a Brahmin from Srivilliputhur, and finally, the only woman, Alvar, Andal. A Kerala ruler, Kulesekerar, was also supposed to have been a great

Bhakti poet.

The dating of the Bhakti movement in South India is also not easy, even though it is generally accepted that the Nayanars wrote their devotional poetry during the period between 500 A.D. and 800 A.D. and the Alvars between 600 and 900 A.D. The great work, Tiruvasagar, written by Manikavasagar, was composed around 800 A.D. However, many Tamil historians claim that the Bhakti movement was not something new but a tradition that already existed, even during the Sangam period when poets sang praises to local gods like Tirumal, Vaikai, and Murugan. The Sangam poets had also used the beauty of the landscape and the emotions of men to create a very expressive style of poetry, and the Bhakti poets were merely using the same tradition to express love for God in terms of human emotions and yearnings. By the 8th century, their poetry was being called 'thiruvaimozhi' or the sacred words. When orthodoxy intervened to absorb this tradition into its fold, they had to accept local religious practices and traditions along with the local gods. Thus, folk religion and local practices, with their own pantheon of gods, forced their way into mainstream Hinduism. From the beginning, theirs was a feminine submission to the gods. In the typical attitude of the Bhakti poets, they saw the gods, Shiva and Vishnu, as lovers for whom they pine. As Nammalvar says,

"Evening has come
But not the dark one
What shall I say?"

This attitude must have been accentuated by the devotion of the female poets. While many of the poets were Brahmins, there was also the celebration of the devotion of Kannapan, a low caste, whose apparently contaminated offering was preferred by Lord Shiva to the clean offerings of the Brahmin priest because of his greater love. There was clearly a questioning of the value of hierarchy, caste, and even gender in the poems of the Bhakti poets. While this gave great scope for the participation of the lower castes, it was all nullified when the movement was hijacked by the mainstream orthodoxy, which merely gave venerable lineage to the local gods through new Puranic stories and engulfed the movement in its own rigid and caste-ridden beliefs. The local gods were proclaimed to be the same Brahmanical gods, only with different names, and others became wives and sons of existing gods. Yet this symbolic purification came at a price: the continued oppression of the lower castes and the heavy contamination of Brahmanical ideas and rituals. The other paradox was that this intense love for God created intense hatred for all other religions and unleashed violence on a scale not seen before, with the first targets being the Buddhists and the Jains.

In the 'Bhagavata Purana,' Bhakti speaks of herself and says, "I was born in Dravida and grew up in Karnataka. I lived in Maharashtra and became old and weak in Gujarat, and in the Kali age, I was scattered by heretics and, on reaching Vrindavan, became young and beautiful again." While the Bhakti movement clearly spread far and wide and sustained itself for over five hundred years, what it stood for was never clear. It was an acceptance of a personal God to whom devotion was not only due but inevitable. It sought God both as a lover and as a source of solace in times of need. Clearly, the Nirguna of Advaita was not satisfying, yet the easy acceptance of unconditional love was not based on any internally consistent philosophy. It seemed to deny all the many tragedies of human life and never seemed to call the gods to account. What it actually did was allow for the incorporation of the local gods and local practices into the omnibus religion called Hinduism, but at a cost. At the cost of denying, or at least giving up on, the movement's main driving force, the equality of all men before God and therefore before men. It ended up being great poetry—something akin to the Psalms of the Jews but without their religious context.

While the Bhakti movement ended in poetry and empty piety, a parallel movement was taking place that was clearly intellectual and rooted in the philosophy of Vedanta. This was a movement that started with Adi Sankara, who wanted to provide a philosophical base on which Hinduism could claim to have a consistent philosophy and a creditable religious system of thought and practices.

Adi Sankaracharya

Sankaracharya, as he is called by his devotees, was perhaps the most acute Indian mind, not only of his age but perhaps in the history of India. His only competition can be found in the likes of Buddha and Nagarjuna. Yet his life was brief and filled with feverish activity, marked by a sharpness of aggression in thought rarely seen before or after. He saw his life as a mission to restore Hinduism, as he knew it, to its pristine glory and to demolish attacks against its doctrines and practices in the face of the growing appeal of other religious faiths. Yet, in his brutal honesty, he could only provide a God who was 'Nirguna,' without form or attributes, and a universe that was essentially only in the mind, Maya. Like all great thinkers, his metaphysics was clearly not meant for the masses, and even the more acute Hindus merely paid lip service to the master while continuing in their superstitions and meaningless rituals. He is, however, acknowledged as the propagator and establisher of the doctrine of Advaita, where divinity is seen as indivisible.

While Sankara is believed to have been born in Kerala, in the village of Kaladi, near Aluva, to Brahmin parents, there is very little authentic literature about his life. Many biographies have been written since the 14th century, yet most were written more than a thousand years after his death and are thus largely based on stories about him that were current at the time. Even his name is mentioned variously as Vaidya Sankara, Sankara Misra, and Sankaranandan. What all sources vouch for is that his life was brief, and he died when he was thirty-three. While Singeri records claim his birth in the 14th year of the reign of Emperor Vikramaditya, it is not clear which king this refers to, Chandra Gupta or some other king. The general consensus is that he was born around 733 to 746 A.D. in the reign of the Chalukya king, also called Vikramaditya, even though there are claims that he was born in 44 B.C. and died in 12 B.C. To this extent, the life of Sankara is the stuff of legend and not based on any authentic records that can be attested as true. While all Keralites assume and believe that he was born in Kerala, there is also a claim that he was born in Chidambaram, in Tamil Nadu.

His biographies speak of his taking up sanyas at an early age and leaving home early to study. As legend suggests, he reached near the river Narmada, where he found his guru, Govinda Bhagvatpada, with whom he studied the Vedas, Upanishads, and Brahma Shastras. Biographies also suggest that he then came into contact with Mimamsa philosophy through Kumarilla and Prabakara, famous proponents of Mimamsa. The emphasis in most of his biographies is on his extensive travels and his high-level debates with philosophers and scholars of all faiths, including Hindus of different schools, Buddhists, and Jains. His great claim to fame is that he founded many mutts and monasteries all over the country for the teaching and propagation of the Advaita philosophy. The Mutts he is claimed to have started are the ones at Singeri in Tamil Nadu, Sarasvati in Kanchi, and Thritha and Asramin in Dwaraka. Other claims also include Puri, Giri, Aranya, and Sangam. Through his travels, he gathered many disciples, like Sadananda, Brahmendra, and many others, who became mighty scholars in their own right. Legend has it that he died in Kedarnath at the age of thirty-two, yet there is also a tradition that places his death in Kanchipuram and even somewhere in Kerala.

Philosophy and Works

In his brief life, Sankara is supposed to have written more than 300 books and many commentaries on the sacred texts, with his classic commentary of the Brahma Sutras, called Brahma Sutra Bhasya, considered his masterpiece. He also wrote commentaries on the Bhagavad-Gita and many of the Upanishads. He is also supposed to have written many poetic pieces. Yet, much of the works attributed to him may have been written by his disciples and written much later. Further, there are works attributed to him that could not have been written by him at all. This makes any attempt at making a summary of his works and his thoughts very difficult. It is, however, accepted that he was the founder of Advaita Vedanta. Yet, Advaita was already one of the orthodox schools of thought founded by Bhadra Narayana; thus, Sankara's contribution was to make it systematic and, to his mind, free of contradictions. In dealing with Advaita as a philosophy, Sankara went beyond metaphysics to deal with what can best be termed meta-epistemology (Pramanas) or the means of attaining knowledge, as opposed to a mere critical look at knowledge.

The conclusion that he seemed to have reached is that knowledge is possible only through the systematic and verbal analysis of the Vedas and that the Vedas can be confirmed by the knowledge gained through direct experience. Sankara's main focus was on the need for absolute objectivity in the search for knowledge. Like Hume and Kant, he accepted that perception was the primary source of knowledge and that inference was the way to deeper knowledge. These, he said, were enough to lead us to a proper understanding of the world and its nature, as well as to what is good and what is harmful, with no recourse to the scriptures or any revealed sacred texts. It is only when we need to go beyond practical matters and deal with matters in the realm of metaphysics and ethics that it is necessary to consult the Vedas. While reading the sacred texts, he was especially critical of those who merely picked and chose verses from what they read, without reference to the context or the larger framework of an argument. He insisted that to understand a text, one must study the purpose, the conclusion, the repeated emphasis, and the unique message the text is trying to propound and accept only the totality of meaning that remains after all contradictions are removed. This is also an attribute of the Nyaya philosophical school of thought.

To Sankara, to worship was a contradiction in terms, for not to realize that we are all part of Brahman is to be deluded by dualism. However, he asserted that a proper understanding is possible only after one is purified through Ahimsa in body and mind. Religions and rituals are useful only to the extent that they prepare the mind for its inward journey into the soul. In essence, Advaita was the realization of the oneness of the soul (Atma) and Brahman. In his famous 'Atma Shatkam,' he says:

"I am consciousness, I am bliss, I am Shiva, I am Shiva.
Without hate, without infatuation, without craving, without greed
Without sin, without merit, without elation, without sorrow
Without mantra, without rituals, neither pilgrimage nor Vedas

Without fear, without death, without division, without Jati
Without form, without figure,
In everything I am.
Neither attached nor released
I am consciousness, I am bliss, I am Shiva, I am Shiva."

To Sankara, Moksha was to be achieved in this life, and it happens when man is liberated from his ties to life. It is a self-realization that there is nothing to seek, for we are already one with God. To achieve this, he saw yoga as a good means. Yet, like a truly modern rationalist, he did not see such realization in the concept of deep meditation, where the self is lost in contemplation of the infinite, but asserted that only through knowledge was realization fully achieved.

The main criticism of Sankara is that, while he is an ultra-rationalist and demands the same of others, when finally pushed, he still reverts to the sanctity of the Vedas as revealed and inspired truth. While there are similarities between Mahayana Buddhism and Sankara's philosophy, the main difference is that while the Buddhists deny the existence of the soul, Sankara insists that it exists. At the center of Advaita is the idea that Brahman is the only reality and all else is an illusion. The universe is only a manifestation of Brahman and has no existence of its own. We and our Atmas are also illusions and are only parts of Brahman. It is the consciousness of self that creates separateness; all selfish wants and the idea of 'I' and 'mine' treat all else as 'others.' Our carnal and selfish wants can never be satisfied because they are creations of the ignorant soul, which does not realize that the self and the universe are unreal. Only by the realization of the unreality and illusion that is life is the soul freed from its mortal attachments and from the bondage to the flesh. The realization of man's oneness with God is both bliss and the state of ultimate being.

While Sankara is claimed by the Shaivites as their patron philosopher, he actually propagated the worship of the five gods, 'Panchatantra': Ganesha, Surya, Vishnu, Shiva, and Devi. However, he insisted that all these were but names and that there is only one God, Brahman, the supreme, invisible, and indivisible ultimate being. A God that is formless and without attributes is a 'Nirgunan.' God can thus be understood only through negation, and when all is negated, we would be left with the inevitable conclusion that God is within me; that is why he accepted the Upanishad saying, 'Neti, neti, aham Brahma.' One of the great achievements of Sankara was to have brought the philosophical concepts of the Upanishads, which were known only to a small elite, to be argued and debated in public fora until they became known to a much wider group of people and finally became part of the religious philosophy of ordinary temple devotion and worship. The followers of Advaita were not all Shaivites, even though there is a continuing misconception that Sankara advocated only Shaivism, which is reinforced by the propagation of the belief that Sankara was an incarnation of Lord Shiva.

Sankara was perhaps one of the greatest thinkers that India has produced. However, his philosophy was far too abstract for the normal Indian, who is so terribly rooted in the flesh, to appreciate his otherworldliness. Sankara, in his brutal honesty and need for truth, realized the absurdity of caste distinctions before a universal God, but most Indians do not even notice the scorn with which he rejects such ideas. His philosophy was beyond morals and ethics and thus did not lead to a new way of life or a change of heart. He was too deeply immersed in deep metaphysical ideas to even notice the injustice of the social system, much less to change it. Despite the almost reverential awe with which his name is mentioned, he has made no impact on the vast majority of Indians who prefer the God at Tirupati, who can be bribed with gifts, or the many Godmen who claim to be able to perform miracles.

Ramanuja (1017-1137)

Ramanuja may not have been the most acute religious thinker, but he was perhaps the most influential. He represents all that modern Hinduism has become, with conscious temple worship at the core of its belief. This has also led to devotion to a personal God and belief in the reality of human life and the world of the senses. He justified Bhakti devotions and, in the process, justified the multi-billion-rupee industry that institutionalized temple worship that Indians have largely taken to. He is the patron philosopher of the Temple at Tirupati, where devotees gift millions in gold, diamonds, and cash for the protection, help, and favor of their personal God, Lord Venkateshwara, or Lord Vishnu. The unfortunate aspect of this belief in a personal God who is approachable to all and who seems to grant personal favors is that it leads to an avoidance of any deep thinking about God and the meaning of faith, which should be at the core of any religion.

His Life And Times

Like most ancient Indians, little is authentically known about Ramanuja and his life. Even though, as in the case of Sankara, many biographies have been written, most of them were written after the split in the Vaishnavite community into the Tenkala and Vadakalai fractions sometime between the 17th and 18th centuries and are therefore biased. Tradition has it that he was born to Brahmin parents sometime around 1017 C.E., near the modern-day town of Sriperumbudur, between Chennai and Kanchipuram. However, many scholars place him much later, closer to 1077 C.E. Tradition claims that he was a child prodigy who read the Vedas by the time he was eight and that in later life, he was almost constantly in direct communion with God. What is known is that, like a traditional man of his time, he must have married, and then the story goes that he went to Kanchipuram for further studies. At Kanchipuram, his teacher was the famous Advaita philosopher, Yadava Prakasa. He soon outgrew his teacher and began questioning his interpretations of the Vedic texts, leading to their parting of ways. He is then supposed to have sought out the Vaishnavite scholar, Yamunacharya, but before he could meet him, Yamunacharya had passed away. Tradition has it that Yamunacharya then awoke from his death to anoint Ramanuja as his successor to the Sri Vaishnava sect, of which he was the head. At this stage, Ramanuja renounced his marriage, took up sanyas, and then became the priest at the Varadaraja Srirangam temple in Kanchipuram.

Ramanuja lived in the Chola age in Tamilnadu when all religions, including Buddhism and Jainism, were popular, and even the Hindu tradition was pluralistic, with Vaishnavism, Shaivism, and many other religious traditions, including a strong presence of old local traditions coexisting without too much violence and the authorities being quite tolerant towards all of them. However, the Advaita of Sankara was clearly the dominant force.

His Religious and Philosophical Background

Ramanuja was supposed to have been a student of the great Advaita scholar Yadava Prakasa, and when he found he could not agree with his interpretations, he left him and started 'Vaishnava Advaita.' The truth, however, is that a strong tradition of Vaishnava Dvaita philosophy was already in existence as part of the offshoot of the Bhakti movement, where philosophy had stepped in to justify Bhakti devotion as valid and theologically correct. Nathamuni (perhaps 824–924 C.E., even though some traditions make him much older at around 582 C.E.), who was contemporaneous with the Alvar poet Madukarkavi Alvar and was of his 'parampara,' was born close to modern-day Tirunelveli and was the real founder of Vaishnava Dvaita. Tradition even talks of Kambar releasing his major work, 'Rama Katha,' in the Srirangam temple, in the presence of Nathamuni. His grandson, Yamunacharya, was supposed to have been the one who took the tradition forward and made it a theology to be reckoned with. However, because he had, at a very young age, challenged the high priest of the Chola court to a debate, he was scornfully called 'alavandar,' which stuck, and he was thereafter called 'Alavander.' Where Ramanuja contributed was in the introduction of his unique brand of Advaita, which he called 'Vishita Advaita' or modified monism, distinct from both the Advaita of Sankara and the Dvaita of Madavachari.

Ramanuja justified Bhakti devotion to a personal God, Lord Vishnu. While he asserted the duality of the Atman and the Brahman and insisted that they were two distinct entities, he claimed that the individual soul has the capacity to find eternal oneness with the Brahman. His philosophy was the result of his years as a priest in the Srirangam temple at Kanchipuram, where he witnessed the intense devotion of the Bhakti poets and their followers. Seeing this intense devotion, he was forced to reject that only the 'Nirguna Brahman' was real and assert that the 'saguna Brahman' was as real. In his manifestation, as 'saguna,' Vishnu could legitimately be regarded as a personal God. With this realization, he announced his brand of philosophy, and then he went on an extensive tour all over the country to propagate his philosophy. He is supposed to have, like Sankara, debated with scholars from all religions and with the proponents of other sectarian traditions. He is also supposed to have performed many miracles. The 'Sri Vaishnava' tradition claims that he wrote many books, including commentaries on the Vedas, his major work being 'Sri Bhashya,' a commentary on the Brahma Sutras. He also wrote a commentary on the Bhagavad Gita and many other texts. Like Sankara, he is supposed to have established many temples and mutts exclusively devoted to the worship of Vishnu and Devi or Lakshmi.

His Religious Philosophy

When Ramanuja began as a student under Yadava Prakasa, he was taught the Advaita philosophy of Adi Sankara, which was a philosophy of 'monism' or the oneness of God. As has been told, he broke away from that tradition and accepted the tradition of the likes of Nathamuni and Sri Vaishnavism, adding to it the element of a halfway house between Advaita and the Dvaita of Madhvacharya, which has since been called qualified monism. Like the leaders of the orthodox Hindu tradition, he accepted the authority of the Vedas and only claimed that others were wrongly interpreting the Vedas. Like Sankara, he claimed that others were merely cherry-picking from the Vedas to justify their line of thinking. He demanded a holistic understanding of the Vedas and all other sacred texts taken together as a corpus of ideas and to select only those that fit into a consistent philosophy. He claimed that an unbiased reading of the Vedas would show that it supported both views, of dualism and monism, and therefore the correct interpretation would be to accept both views as part of a unified theology, which he claimed is what he had done with the creation of qualified monism, modified dualism, or as he called it, 'Visishta Dvaita.' While Ramanuja seems to merely insist on a compromise or a dialectic approach, Sankara had demanded it be put to the test of his six principles of validity, including purpose, conclusion, emphasis, repetition, and uniqueness, as he insisted that all statements or ideas are not of equal importance.

Beyond the metaphysical nit-picking, the import of Ramanuja's philosophy was his defense of worship and devotion to a personal God, which was at the core of the Bhakti movement. In defending Bhakti, he took elements from the philosophy of Madavacharya's Dvaita. Where Ramanuja defers is only in his claim that the individual soul can achieve oneness with Brahman, while Madavacharya insisted on the separateness of the individual soul. Further, while Sankara saw Brahman as the only reality and divinity as 'Nirguna,' without form or attributes, Ramanuja accepted the reality of manifestation that was to Sankara, 'Maya,' as real, and claimed that it was only part of the 'Saguna' attribute of divinity, the Brahman of all qualities. In fact, Ramanuja went on to assert that even God has both body and soul, as matter is, after all, a part of God and his creations, therefore, part of the totality of the glory of God. The body and soul are both real and important. He advocated Bhakti for a personal God, in his case, Vishnu, where the contemplation of his goodness and beauty, which human beings can intuitively perceive, will lead to the realization of the infinite and indescribable, even the 'Nirguna' aspect of God.

Legacy and History

The Sri Vaishnava tradition that Ramanuja inherited was a mix of philosophies. With Sankara, the worship of the five gods had been authorized, but what the Sri Vaishnava tradition did was claim superiority for Lord Vishnu. And in the same way that Shaivism had incorporated Shakti or Goddess Durga as part of the concept of Shiva-Shakti, the Vaishnavites added Sri to Vaishnavism to incorporate Goddess Lakshmi into the Godhead of Vishnu. While Shiva-Shakti was a single concept where Shiva was almost powerless without Shakti, even though Shakti and Kali were gods in their own right, Lakshmi was only a part of Vishnu and was more like the Madonna of Catholic belief, a mediator between men and God. To this, Ramanuja added his unique philosophy of qualified monism. Vaishnavism has had a long history and has always been strong in the south, tracing its roots to Tamil Prabandham, which they claim only saw its culmination in the songs of the Alwars. In fact, Nathamuni is supposed to have collected the songs of Nammalvar and accommodated them within the framework of Vedic musical cannons and called it divine music, and through the tradition of 'Arigars' or Gurus, he kept this tradition of this music alive. Nathamuni was also supposed to have written 'Nyaya Tattva,' which has not survived but was a treatise on epistemology, where he asserted that the 'I' in humans is not their true self and only by abandoning that 'I,' which men are more afraid to contemplate than death itself, is the true knowing-self awakened.

This long tradition was to break in the 17th century with the division of the Sri Vaishnava order into two, led by the two great temple centers of Vaishnavism, Srirangam and Kanchipuram. They broke into the Thenkalai and Vadakalai fractions. The Thenkalai fraction represented the southern tradition propagated by the scholars attached to the Srirangam temple, while the northern tradition was advocated by the scholars attached to the Kanchipuram temple. The theological debate centered around the nature of God's intervention in human affairs. The southern tradition (Thenkalai) believed, like St. Paul, that God's protection and love were totally undeserved and the result of grace. For them, the analogy was that of a mother cat who carries her kittens by the scruff of their necks, with no aid from the kittens. The Thenkalai sect saw salvation only in total surrender to God, with faith in his grace. The Vadakalai tradition (northern) emphasized the need for devotion and faith. Thus, their analogy was that of a mother monkey who carries her young, but the baby monkey has to cling to her if she is not to fall. They expected men to seek God before God could help. Another major difference that separated them was the emphasis on their traditional roots. While the Northern Vadakalai sect was rooted in Vedic texts and beliefs, the Thenkalai sect was privileged to have a very strong local tradition that had culminated in the Bhakti movement. They had, therefore, incorporated the theology of the Bhakti poets into their beliefs and practices. They also pressed for a greater role for Tamil in the religious liturgy and practices.

Basava (12th Century)

Popular tradition holds that Basava was the founder of the Lingayat tradition, but historical research suggests that he refined an existing tradition. The Lingayat tradition is significant in the history of Hindu thought because it vehemently opposed superstitions, rituals, caste, and gender distinctions. It also marked the birth of religious violence and a fundamental belief that recognized only Shiva as a deity worth worshiping and was antagonistic to all other sects. It was the first sect to emphasize the need for a distinct identity. Similar to the Sikhs later on, Basava insisted that his followers carry a Linga, smear their foreheads with Vibhuti, and wear a rudraksha necklace.

Born around 1105 C.E. to upper-class Brahmin parents in North Karnataka, not much of Basava's life is properly documented. The first attempt to recount his life was made by the Kannada poet Harihara, born around 1180 C.E., making him a near contemporary of Basava. His account is based on close-to-first-hand knowledge. In the 13th century, the poet Pulkurika Somanatha wrote an epic poem on Basava's life called 'Basava Purana,' later edited by Bhima Kavi in 1369 and now part of the Lingayat sacred literature. The recognition of Basava's greatness reflects the extent and power of his personality and social contributions. Basava was not just a religious leader; he became an icon for all Kannadigas, providing them with identity and pride.

Coming from an influential family with ties to the court, Basava married Gargaminka, the daughter of the prime minister of a small kingdom in Karnataka (Kalachuri). When his father-in-law passed away, the king asked Basava to take his place, which he did remarkably. Basava was renowned for numerous social reforms, but he is most remembered for reviving Shaivism and establishing institutions for meditation and learning. He was also a poet of considerable merit, using his poetic abilities to spread his message through poetry and songs. His collection of poetry is popularly known as 'Vachanas.'

His Philosophy

By birth and tradition, Basava was a Shaivite, but what he propagated was an inspirational form of devotion to Lord Shiva, resulting in the creation of a new sect of Shiva devotees called 'Veera Shivas,' or ardent and heroic worshippers of Shiva, which eventually evolved into 'warriors of Shiva.' It is claimed that he and his sect borrowed much from the Nayanar tradition of Shiva devotion, which marked the beginnings of the Bhakti movement in Tamilnadu. However, he diverged from that tradition when it came to the question of temple worship, rejecting it as a farce propagated by interested Brahmins. Instead, he advocated for the personalization of worship within the individual, rejecting the worship of idols but encouraging the carrying of a small Linga icon to remind devotees of their loyalties. He asserted that temples and sacred texts were merely dead institutions, emphasizing that the body and soul of individuals were the dynamic elements that needed to seek God. In one of his poems, he asks:

"The rich
Will make temples for Shiva
What will I
A poor man do?
My legs are the pillars
My body the shrine
Things standing shall fall
But the moving shall ever stay."

The essence of his philosophy was that we are the temples of God, and like Tolstoy, he insisted that God is within us and not in any stone temple. While he continued to respect the authority of the Vedas and other sacred texts, he vehemently opposed what the Brahmins had created—a religion of rituals and empty worship. He also saw the continued use and reverence of Sanskrit as a hurdle in the understanding of God, considering it a dead language incapable of igniting the soul. He perceived temples as an attempt to limit the omnipresence of God.

In the 'Basava Purana,' there is a lengthy debate between Basava and his father, who supports rituals and temple worship, while Basava insists that every person has the right to directly approach God.

While he viewed the body as the temple of God and God as a presence within, not without, his metaphysics took the form of qualified dualism. Although he is said to have accepted the Advaita of Sankara and saw the Atma as God within, no different from the supreme Lord Shiva, there were instances when he appeared to make a distinction between the two. This sometimes ambiguous position led scholars to claim that his stance was closer to the qualified dualism of Ramanuja than the crystal-clear position of Sankara. He acknowledged the authority of the Vedas but insisted that they were neither God-given nor eternal.

Basava spread the teachings of Advaita in his unique way, asserting that true immersion in the glory of God involves a long process consisting of six stages, where the devotee progresses from religious discipline to devotion, to being a recipient of grace, to the awareness of God within, and finally to union with God. Unlike the Bhakti poets, who saw their ecstatic contemplation of God as an end in itself, Basava considered it a gradual ascent toward something akin to the Buddhist concept of Nirvana.

An aspect of Basava's religion, or what it became, was influenced by his insistence on identifying his followers. Although he opposed idols and temple worship, he insisted that each devotee carry a small 'Ishta Linga' or Linga pendant to remind them of their faith. Similar to the Sikhs later on, he desired a distinctive identity for his followers, requiring them to smear their foreheads and bodies with Vibhuti as a reminder of God and wear necklaces of Rudraksha beads. He encouraged the chanting of mantras, especially 'Shiva mamaya' and 'Om namah Shivaya.' This inevitably led to the creation of a clear new brand of followers, who eventually became 'Veera Shivas' or 'warriors of Shiva,' representing something martial rather than merely religious.

Basava, the Social Reformer

The core of Basava's belief was that all people were equal before God and that there should be no caste or gender distinctions. As he famously said, it is behavior, not caste, that distinguishes a Brahmin. He also advocated respect and reverence for manual labor, asserting that we are all laborers, with some engaging in mental labor while others in physical labor, and that one is not greater than the other. As a former public servant, he was keen on instilling a sense of discipline and rigor in all human endeavors. He fought to cultivate an attitude of hard work and cleanliness.

The tragedy is that these core values have been forgotten, and the sect is now no different from others. It has not made any impact on the detrimental practices of the caste system. Instead, it has created and perpetuated a group of 'Veerashivas' who have become the militant arm of the sect. History records significant instances of violence against members of other religions and their institutions. Yet, as a social and political force, they have become preeminent, at least in Karnataka.

Madhvacharya (13th Century)

The direct opposition to Sankara's Advaita came from Madhavacharya, who claimed that his philosophy of Dvaita was the realistic position. He recognized the inherent nihilism in Sankara's Advaita and criticized it for what it was, even referring to Sankara as a Buddhist parading as a Hindu teacher. He perceived Atman, the individual soul, and Brahman, the universal and divine, as two clearly separate entities. He viewed human life as determined by Karma and other universal forces over which humans have almost no control, and thus, human salvation was entirely dependent and possible only with the grace of God. There is nothing that man can do to attain his own salvation.

Madhavacharya was born in northern coastal Karnataka, probably close to modern-day Udupi, to Vaishnavite parents, sometime between 1199 and 1238 C.E. He was named Vasudeva. He is said to have taken up sanyasa at a very early age, possibly as early as the age of seven. He then joined an Advaita monastery in Dwaraka. Soon, he found that he disagreed with the Advaita philosophy, leading to many arguments with his teachers and his eventual departure from the monastery. In the meantime, he had studied all the ancient sacred texts. He is said to have been a prolific writer, producing commentaries on many of them and his own work, 'Bashya,' on the Dharmashastras. More than thirty works are attributed to him, written in Sanskrit, with most of them in verse form. His works are noted for their brevity and density of meaning.

After this, he was ready to propagate the Dvaita philosophy. He traveled widely, reaching places as far as Varanasi and even Bengal. His journeys aimed to spread his message, for which he became a teacher and debater, engaging with scholars from all schools of thought. A distinctive feature of Madhavacharya, compared to other religious leaders, was his claim to be the son of Vayu, the wind God. In fact, he asserted to be the third avatar of Vishnu through the wind God, with the first being Bhima, the next Hanuman, and claimed that his philosophy was the result of his direct communion with Lord Vishnu himself.

His Philosophy

Madhavacharya was a very intriguing religious philosopher. He observed the inherent nihilism in the Advaita philosophy and realized that a religion based on such a philosophy would never attract devotion. Furthermore, a 'Nirguna' God was of no use to people in distress. It is now difficult to fathom how he arrived at his religious beliefs, but what is surprising are the many similarities to Christian theology. Similar to Christianity, where Jesus claimed to be the son of God, Madhavacharya also asserted to be the son of God and created a theology that required individuals to approach God through his son. Moreover, echoing the core of Christian belief that man cannot do anything to attain salvation, Madhavacharya claimed that only through God's grace could man ever attain salvation. He fully endorsed the Bhakti option and categorically stated that any attempt at salvation based on individual human merit or effort, especially through Jnana Marga, the way of knowledge, was doomed to failure. This was a clear departure from traditional wisdom, as the 'Jnana Marga' was always considered one of the exalted paths to self-realization in Indian philosophy. His summary dismissal of such an option was, therefore, revolutionary.

Yet Madhavacharya's philosophy was based on rigorous logic. Like the Greek philosophers, he started with epistemology and identified three important ways in which knowledge is gained, which he called 'Pramanas':

1. Perception, including sensual perception (external perception) and internal perception, involves the connections the mind makes from sensual perceptions.

2. Inference, akin to Western philosophers, accepts the validity of analysis and deductions.

3. Authority, where he departed from most rationalistic philosophy by insisting on the validity of authority, including that of the Vedas and all sacred texts. He defended the recourse to authority by stating that human life is too short to personally experience everything, and it is therefore necessary to accept the findings of experts that have been tested and found true.

Yet, Madhavacharya was clear that knowledge of God, who for him was Krishna, Hari, Vishnu, Vasudeva, and Narayana, was possible only through a spiritual connection and not through knowledge. While knowledge, as in Mimamsa, of Jnana-kanda and Karma-kanda, was intrinsically valid, the truths of the Vedas were equally valid but did not naturally lead men to communion with God. That was possible only through the grace of God.

Madhavacharya's philosophy was essentially pluralistic. He claimed that there were two 'Tattvas': those with independent existence and those with only dependent existence. Only God, or Krishna, is an independent reality; all others are dependent on God for their existence. Human beings are made up of 'Jiva' and 'Jada' or soul and matter. While matter is dead and non-cognizable, Jiva is a sentient entity that causes desire and action. In his pluralistic philosophy, he divided all things into five main categories.

1. The difference between material things.
2. The difference between matter and soul.
3. The difference between matter and God.
4. The difference between the many souls.
5. The difference between the soul and God.

These differences, he said, are permanent and intrinsic. Each object is unique, and each soul is unique. In fact, Madhava maintains that due to the uniqueness of each soul, each soul encounters bliss in different ways, grades, colors, depth, and so on. Krishna lives in bliss, surrounded by chaos. He manifests himself in many ways, but all his manifestations are part of his infinity. Man cannot seek God through knowledge, as no knowledge can comprehend the infinite and eternal. Only through divine affinity, a natural attraction to God, and a total surrender to his immensity, is salvation possible. Finally, only the grace of God will allow humans to glimpse the bliss of the eternal one. In man's search for grace, only total faith in the son of God, Vayu, is of any use. Only a faith that surrenders itself totally to God would lead man to the path of possible grace because all man's individual effort would only bring him face to face with Maya, the delusion that is part of human suffering and bondage to desire and past karma.

God is all good, and evil is entirely the creation of man. Man, Madhava asserts, has free will, but his will is also influenced by his innate nature and past Karma. While only grace can save man, Madhava insists that there are ethical and moral values that lead man nearer to God, and only those that are closest to God have the chance of benefiting from God's grace.

While Madhava's philosophy was largely gentle and logical, his hatred of other sects and religions was sometimes violent. He hated Sankara and his Advaita philosophy and called its propagators 'deceitful demons' and accused them of being Buddhist agents in disguise. While Advaita believes in the oneness of God and the individual soul, Madhava asserts that they are different and distinct. Advaita, however, takes its belief from a very old tradition that has its roots in the Upanishads, where there is the saying, 'Tat tvam asi,' which has always been interpreted to mean, 'Thou art that.' Madhava, however, asserted that there is no grammatical or logical reason why it cannot mean, 'Thou art not that.' He therefore claimed the Upanishads also supported his contention of dualism. So adamant was he about dualism that he also flatly refused to accept the possibility of Ramanuja's qualified dualism, where human souls, as they rise in consciousness, would ultimately merge with the Brahman. Since such a merger is possible only if the Brahman and the souls of individuals are of the same substance, Madhava ruled out such a possibility and maintained that they were different and distinct. He ruled out the possibility of any merger of the human soul into the bliss of the almighty.

The Legacy that Remains

The philosophies of Sankara, Ramanuja, and others, which one must believe were the foundation on which the Bhakti movement was built, are far too arid to explain the outpouring of devotion and piety they released. Sankara may have initiated it with his approval of the worship of five gods. This allowed local religious practices and devotional traditions, distinct from the Vedic and Brahmanical systems of rituals, to be incorporated into mainstream Hinduism, leading to the liberty to worship with abandon. Yet Sankara's philosophy was neither a religion of consolation nor of piety and devotion. His God, as 'Nirguna,' was not a religious or even humanistic idea but a cold realism of a scientific principle. Worshiping such a God was pointless, as he was nothing human. The universe that Sankara perceived was also only 'Maya.' Consequently, human life was merely a mirage, a delusion. Such a world can have no intrinsic value. In the end, even the 'Moksha' that Sankara offers is nothing more than the 'Nirvana' of Buddha, where human souls merely dissolve into nothingness. Such a philosophy could hardly inspire humans to emotion, far less to piety and devotion.

Even the qualified dualism of Ramanuja offered nothing more. The world was still only a manifestation and only Maya, and all he offered was that instead of a move from nothingness to nothingness, we could bring our individual souls with us as we proceeded to nothingness. He offered the consolation that our individual souls, if prepared well, will be entitled to enter into the nothingness of Brahman. Only with Madhava does the individual soul have a separate existence, but he falls into the trap of having to explain how there can be anything that is not God, for then there must be a separate power operating in the universe. He does not explain. He, however, makes devotion possible by providing God with a human face, that of the Son of God. Yet, he does not give any hope for man to achieve salvation through his own efforts. What is worse is that, even with grace, all that one can hope for is one's immersion in the eternal bliss of God, again into nothingness.

Piety and devotion cannot be based on Sankara's Nirguna God but on the 'saguna' aspect of God. God, who is all things and all attributes. Goodness and beauty are merely reflections of God's beauty and goodness, which are part of his 'saguna' aspect. While Sankara persists that true knowledge leads only to the realization of the 'Nirguna' aspect of God, formless and without attributes, the concept of 'saguna Brahman' opens the door to a meaningful life. Even if life is an illusion, it is an illusion created and proceeding from the ultimate reality of God. Even this idea should not normally prompt man to the exaggerated piety and devotion that we see in the Bhakti poets, as there was nowhere, in any philosophy, the possibility of Karma being wiped away or that God could possibly be concerned with human life.

The Epics speak of gods who take human form as avatars, fight against adharma, and teach humans the right path. While there are stories that speak of God's concern for human suffering, there is no philosophy that is built on such a premise. There is no explanation as to why God should care, nor is there any concept of judgment or paradise that is integral to religions like Islam and Christianity. Thus, while the Bhakti poets, in their ecstatic devotion, reach a state of delirious unconsciousness, the state is no different from that which is attained through deep meditation, yogic practices, and even from drugs and alcohol. They, therefore, do not create any hope that there is anything to look for beyond the present experience. Why then the devotion?

Even today, it is difficult to isolate the causes that triggered the rise of the Bhakti movement. The evangelizing zeal of Sankara must have had much to do with it, as Sankara did not merely spread a special teaching but was also raising the fear that the Hindu tradition itself was under threat from Sramana religions, like Buddhism and Jainism and even from Islam and Christianity. Thus, even though the philosophy of his religion was extremely arid, he seems to have woken, at least among the educated and thinking few, to a concern, if not an introspection, about what was happening. Sankara's approval of the worship of the five gods may have triggered a new sense of personal attachment and fervent devotion. While the reasons for the sudden awakening may remain confusing, the results were clear and historically very important. The Bhakti movement was the one single religious movement in Indian history that forever changed the religious consciousness of the nation. While the cultural tradition of India was one of tolerance, with an attitude of 'live and let live,' a greater concern for customs and practices, the Bhakti movement wiped all such attitudes away, ushering in a new religious fever and the creation of a religious identity.

The Bhakti movement, which started merely as an ecstatic devotion to God expressed in poetry and song aimed at leading men to a total surrender to God, almost immediately became polarized into Shiva worship by the Nayanars and specifically Vishnu-oriented worship by the Alwars. This trend kept repeating itself with the break of the Vaishnava tradition into the Tenkala and Varkala sects and the birth of a new kind of Shiva worship propagated by Basava. What it did was make religion a social idea, with the mass also being part of worship. It was the personal involvement of individuals in religion that led to sectarian tendencies, as each person took positions regarding his beliefs. This taking of definite positions led to a sense of loyalty to particular beliefs, which in time led to the hardening of attitudes and the inability to compromise. First, a religious identity was created, then polarization took place with the inevitable hardening of ideas and beliefs. In the next stage, it led to militancy and the creation of the 'other,' a pagan, a non-believer, and that the 'other' is not like us.

The great contribution of the Bhakti movement was the awakening of the people, in general, to the idea of religion. With initial opposition to caste and gender, the Bhakti poets, especially the 'Veera Shivas' of Basava, galvanized the people to a greater affinity for religion. While reformers and poets continued to emerge from the Brahmin elite, as was inevitable due to their education, a feeling was created that religion was for all and not the exclusive domain of Brahmins and priests.

The significant emphasis that the Tenkala sect and the Basava sect gave to local languages as the medium of worship and debate made it possible for a much larger audience to participate. However, the greatest contribution of the Bhakti movement was that it transformed Hindu culture into a religion with a personal God, a creed, and the support of a consistent philosophy. Without a personal God, Vedic rituals were empty gestures to a silent universe. Still, with God being humanized by the Bhakti poets, they became tangible ideas and a basis for concrete hopes. This transformation turned Hindu culture into a belief system that slowly solidified, not just around its philosophical principles but around its social and political imperatives.

Bhakti Goes North: Ramananda (1400-1476)

Little is known about Ramananda, the first great devotional poet in the northern part of the country. While many biographies have been written, little is known with authentic certainty. He was born sometime in the 14th century along the Ganges, perhaps at Allahabad in North India. He was born to Brahmin parents, and a tradition even suggests that they were of South Indian origin. He spent most of his life in Varanasi. Tradition has it that he was influenced by the Bhakti movement in the south and that he might have also traveled to the south for his education, with Raghavendra initiating him into the Varkala school of South Indian Vaishnavism. There are others who claim that he actually started as a believer in Sankara's Advaita philosophy and changed when he met Raghavendra. What is known is that he preached a form of Vaishnavism with a philosophy similar to Ramanuja's qualified dualism. Yet there is a tradition in Sikhism that he was a worshiper of Sankara's Nirguna aspect of Brahman. Ramananda was also supposed to have been a practitioner of Yoga. He was a Bhakti poet, and many songs of devotion are attributed to him. Works like 'Ghayn Lilla' and 'Yog Chintamani' are also said to have been written by him.

His Philosophy

His philosophy was clearly based on the teachings of Ramanuja, with some influence from the Yoga school of philosophy. It would appear that, due to his exposure to Sankara's Advaita and Ramanuja's Vaishnavism, his philosophy was an attempt to be a bridge between the two traditions. Ramananda seems to accept both the Nirguna and Suguna aspects of Brahman as real, and his Bhakti is directed at both. However, he was not a believer in institutions of religion or in the concept of renunciation. He argued against a life of sanyas, austerity, and the torture of the body, seeing human life as one to be lived and insisting that enlightenment is possible only through life. He insisted that God is within, and it is the purpose of Bhakti to realize that 'Hari' is within us. He was also against mantras and rituals. As the first important Bhakti saint in North

India, he created what was later called the 'Sant Parampara,' or the tradition of Bhakti saints.

Being brought up on the banks of the Ganga, he inevitably came into contact with Islam and the impact of Muslim rule. He must have felt a need to personalize Hinduism in the face of Islamic culture, which was dominant, to keep the people tied to their religion. He had to make the common people feel more a part of the great tradition of Hinduism. To bring his message to the masses, he realized that caste prejudices would only stand in the way. Thus, he accepted disciples from all castes and preached against caste intolerance. Tradition has it that even Kabir, Ravidas, and many others from different castes were his disciples. His openness about caste made even some Muslims very close to him. He was also clear that gender bias was harming the country and allowed women to join his mutt. He was known to have had many close female disciples. His tradition also had a great impact on Sikhism, and some of his verses have been incorporated into the 'Adi Granth.' To attract the masses, he wrote in Hindi and taught in the local language. As a result, the 'Ramananda Sampradaya' is today perhaps the largest monastic order in India.

The Social Reformer

While he was first and foremost a Bhakti poet and religious teacher, he was also a social reformer. His main focus was on education, which he saw as the single most important need. Like Protestants everywhere, he was skeptical of temples and priests and spoke of the need for direct communion with God. In fact, his response to a demand that he worship at a temple was a poem that asks:

"Why should I go,
I am happy at home.
I have searched the Vedas and the Puranas,
You go there only if Brahman were not here."

He was also against all caste intolerance and famously said, "Don't ask a sadhu his caste or ask about his knowledge." The Bhakti tradition, brought from South India and perhaps by men of South Indian origin, was forced, when confronted with the growing power of Islam, to shed its orthodoxy and become a people's movement. In doing so, it was forced to look inward, especially at the injustice of caste and the suppression of women. All Bhakti-related movements were thus also social movements. To that extent, they did transform society and bring a greater number into the religious fold. What it most dramatically did was change the way the country looked at religion and its gods forever.

Tulsidas (1497 - 1623)

Tulsidas, also known as Goswami Tulsidas, was from a tradition that worshiped Ram as the supreme God. He transformed the Sanskrit Ramayana, inaccessible to most common people except in the oral tradition, into a personal and national epic with his rendering of it as 'Ramacharitamanas' in the local Awadhi Hindi. So great was the impact of his epic that he was regarded by many as the reincarnation of Valmiki himself. Apart from its clear religious impact, it also made him one of the greatest Hindi poets. To a large extent, the unity of religious beliefs in Northern India is almost entirely due to Tulsidas and his version of the Ramayana. From the concept of Dharma to all Indian ideas of womanhood, brotherhood, and loyalty, all are rooted in the story of Lord Ram.

Despite the fact that he lived in the 16th century, very little is known of him with certainty. He himself tells us very little about himself in his works. Yet Nabhadas is supposed to have composed a biography of him in the 17th century. He is supposed to have been born on the banks of the Yamuna in Rajapur or Chittracott, between present-day U.P. and M.P. His parents were Brahmins, and the most probable date of his birth is 1497 C.E. There is so much doubt about the real dates that all the dates are suspect. As usual, there are supernatural stories about his birth: that he was twelve months old in the womb and born with all his teeth, looking like a five-year-old boy. Legend has it that at his birth itself, he uttered the name of Ram. Because astrologers felt that his birth portended harm for his father, he was abandoned to a female servant who looked after him for the next five years, after which he was adopted by the Naharidass Sect of Ramananda's order, and there he settled with them in their monastery. It was at the monastery that he was given the name Tulsidas. He was also initiated at the Varaha Vishnu temple, where Naharidass narrated to him the Ramayana.

When he grew older, he gravitated toward the holy city of Varanasi to study Sanskrit and the Vedas. Tradition has it that he spent the next sixteen years studying before returning to Rajapur. As was customary, he might have gotten married somewhere along the way, but he soon renounced the householder's life and took up sanyas. He then traveled to all the holy places, from Dwaraka to Rameswaram and from Badrinath to the Himalayas. Tulsidas is also supposed to have performed many miracles, including raising a person from the dead. His fame spread so far that Akbar demanded his presence before him. Tulsidas, however, refused to perform any miracles, claiming that all he knew was the name of Ram. However, when he chanted a song in praise of Lord Ram, an army of monkeys descended on the city. The legend claims that Akbar was so impressed that he accepted Tulsidas as a man of God and even ordered that the Ram and Hanuman sects were not to be harassed.

His Literary Life

Tulsidas began composing Sanskrit poetry when he was at Varanasi, and the story goes that whatever he wrote during the day would disappear at night. One day, he had a dream that Shiva had visited him and ordered him to write in the vernacular. That is how he took to writing in Awadhi Hindi, the local language of the people. 'Ramacharitamanas' took him two years to complete (1575-1577). After completing it, he took it to Varanasi and recited it, dedicating it to Lord Shiva. Legend has it that the priests were not happy with his having written in the local language, and to test the value of the work, they put it under many sacred Sanskrit texts and locked the door. When they opened the door the next morning, they found Tulsidas's 'Ramacharitamanas' on top with the words 'satyam, shivam, sundaram' written and signed by Lord Shiva. However, the orthodox priests continued to doubt the value of his work and tried to get it destroyed. Fearing harm, Tulsidas finally donated it to Rai Todar Mal, the treasurer of Emperor Akbar. In 1607, he was afflicted by pains all over his body, and then he wrote 'Hanuman Bahuk,' a devotional work praising the devotion of Hanuman. His pain disappeared. His last work was 'Vinayapatrika,' an ardent plea to Lord Ram to instill devotion so badly needed in the Kali Yug. He is supposed to have died on the banks of the Ganga in 1623.

Ramcharitmanas

Ramacharitamanas is a long epic poem telling of the heroic deeds of Lord Ram. The work is in verse form and contains 1073 stanzas. Over the years, it has become the greatest devotional text in the Hindi language and the supreme religious text of the people of North India. Tulsidas wrote many other works, but his fame and greatness rest on this one work. In 'Ramacharitamanas,' Tulsidas propagated a religion of total devotion to Lord Ram and the efficacy of chanting his name continually. He claimed that the name Ram was the only antidote in the vicious world of the Kali Yug. He even makes Ram greater than Vishnu. In fact, he makes Sita see Shiva, Brahma, and Vishnu worshiping Lord Ram. According to him, what can be seen is merely a small part of Ram. Sita, according to him, was earlier born as Lakshmi, Parvathi, and Saraswati. For Tulsidas, Lord Ram was not merely an avatar but the very embodiment of the cosmic principle, the supreme Brahma, in whom Shiva is his consciousness, Brahman his reason, and Vishnu his intelligence. He is the sufficient cause for all the universe. Everything that we see is a manifestation of Ram. The greatness of his work is best attested by Surdas, a Krishna devotee and contemporary, who said he 'was the breath of life of the saints, and his work is similar to the Vedas for the Hindus and the Koran for the Muslims.'

His Philosophy

To the extent that Ram is responsible for all manifestations, Tulsidas accepts that the world is real. Yet, there are also places in his writings where he compares life to a dream, which seems more in tune with Sankara's concept of Maya. A compromise position that many critics advocate is that Tulsidas saw life as neither real nor unreal but as a 'Lila' of Ram, a play that Ram allows us to see and participate in. In narrating the story of the marriage of the princesses of Ayodhya to Mithila, he describes them as awake, sleeping, sleeping and dreaming, and conscious, thus indicating the many states in which we perceive reality. To Tulsidas, Maya is Sita, the Shakti of Ram. Yet he claimed that even Maya is made up of Vidya and Avidya, where Vidya is the source of all creation and final liberation, while Avidya is the source of all delusion and bondage to mortal flesh. While Tulsidas exalts Ram to the supreme position, this is not done by reducing or denigrating the supreme position of Lord Shiva in any way. Tulsidas accepted Sankara's worship of five gods.

Tulsidas had an interesting theology. He starts by asserting that the 'Nirguna' and 'Saguna' aspects of Brahman are one, the same, and inseparable. In the natural state, Brahman is formless; it is the devotion of human beings that results in the revelation of the Saguna aspect of Brahman. It forces the formless to take shape, as it were. He uses the analogy of water, which can take many forms, such as vapor, ice, and running water. Similarly, God, he claimed, is formed by human need. While the Nirguna and Saguna aspects are equally real, he prefers the Saguna aspect, represented in the life of Lord Ram. He saw the integration of Nirguna and Saguna aspects in Lord Ram. He then says that only by chanting the name of Ram can man move towards God. Bhakti is so important, he says, in the Kali Yug because meditation and Jnana, useful in a better age, have been so corrupted and can no longer be depended upon. Only in total devotion to Lord Ram and surrender to him is salvation possible.

The Legacy

Tulsidas has been called, even by a historian of the eminence of Vincent Smith, 'the greatest man of his age,' and others have called him the greatest religious leader after Buddha. His Ramacharitamanas have also been called by many the Bible of North India. Many simply regard it as the single greatest piece of devotional literature ever written. These are high praises that are not misplaced. It is difficult to make a comparative analysis of the poetic merits of works from different languages, as poetry is greatly prone to becoming a matter of cultural biases. Yet, based on the impact of his work, there is no doubt that his work was not only a monumental exercise but one that changed the perception of Hinduism from within, forever. To most Indians in North India, there is really no other text that defines their beliefs and unites them as Hindus.

Chaitanya Mahaprabhu (1488-1534)

While the Bhakti philosophers, starting with Sankara, all went all over the country preaching their respective gospels, it is not clear how they were received. It also took time for those ideas to germinate, and as was to be expected, the first fruits were seen in Bengal. Chaitanya Mahaprabhu, as he was called, meaning the great lord of wisdom, founded his own form of Vaishnavite dualism called Gaudiya Vaishnavism because Chaitanya was very fair and beautiful, and he transformed Krishna into the supreme God. Chaitanya was also pivotal in what became known as the Bengal renaissance and, more importantly, in Krishna worship and Krishna consciousness, making it an international phenomenon.

Chaitanya was born to Brahmin parents in what is present-day Bangladesh, close to or in Dhaka. It is claimed that he was born on a full moon on February 18, 1488. His brilliance was noticed early, and tradition has it that even as a child, he was constantly chanting the name of Krishna. He showed a great inclination for religious studies and soon decided on a life of scholarship. When his father died and he had to go with the ashes to Gaya, he met his guru, Ishwara Puri, who taught the Gopala Krishna Mantra. This changed his life, and when he returned to Bengal, he decided to take up sanyas. He then traveled widely all over the country but stayed most of his time in Puri. He became the leader of the Vaishnavite movement. In his constant chanting of the name of Krishna, he became lost in devotion, reaching moments of ecstasy similar to the ecstatic devotion of the Bhakti poets. In his ecstatic devotion, he took on the role of Radha. As he grew older and more famous, his biographers claim that he revealed to his close associates that he was God incarnate; consequently, even in his own lifetime, he was worshiped as Krishna reborn.

His Philosophy

Chaitanya did not write much; in fact, he is supposed to have written only eight verses in which all his philosophy was contained. He left it to his trusted disciples to write his message in full, which they did and which has become the sacred corpus of the Gaudiya Vaishnava sect. The Goswamis, who transformed his eight verses into a complete theological corpus, include Rupa Goswami, Sanatana Goswami, Goballa Batta Goswami, Ragunatha Goswami, and Jiva Goswami. The great success of the tradition was that they were fortunate to have, in each generation, great exponents of the philosophy, especially Narattoma, in the next generation, to carry forward his message and to create an ever-growing following. Initially, the religion spread mainly in Bengal and Odisha and then to the rest of the country. The core of his teaching is that Krishna is, all in all, the image of him that he shared with Arjun in the Geetha. His philosophy was clearly part of the Advaita tradition in which he was brought up. He saw individual souls as essentially part of the Lord but as separate entities because of the mortal coil that surrounds the soul. Surrounded by flesh, the soul is bound to the desires of the flesh yet the moment the soul frees itself from its bondage, it becomes capable of union with the Lord. He insisted that the individual soul was of the same substance as that of Brahman and therefore capable of union with the Lord. The purpose of human life was to love and worship God with devotion and see in Krishna all the lovable aspects of God.

Chaitanya started in the Sankara tradition of Advaita but soon converted to Madhava's dualism. His teachings first appealed to the upper castes and are not much different from those of Buddhism. He maintained that this life was not meant for happiness, as men will invariably grow old, become sick, and die. We are merely fugitives in this world, imprisoned in our mortal bodies. Krishna consciousness is about love and peace. We all seek peace, but the means may be different; it may be through Bhakti, Mukti, or Yoga. While Bhakti followers think that material things and sensations would give them happiness, the Mukti followers think that renunciation would bring them closer to God, while the Yogi thinks that meditation would give him peace. Against these expectations, the Krishna bhakta does not ask for anything except to be close to the Lord, always in his presence. This is Krishna consciousness, the peace and love that God gives freely and unconditionally. Krishna is within; we start by chanting his name but soon even the chant will go inward, reverberating from within. Chaitanya did not stop there but insisted that after one has found peace, one then has a duty to serve humanity and not merely to sit back.

History and Impact

In keeping with his philosophy of service, with the arrival of Kalachand Vidyalankar in the 18th century, Gaudiya Vaishnavism made a great leap into social reform. As Kalachand traveled across rural India, he came across the great crime of caste intolerance. He then made it his mission to fight untouchability and to insist on social reform and justice, emphasizing the importance of education. This moved a large number of members of the Dalit community to embrace his teachings. His disciples were thus called the 'Kalachandi Sampradhy.' This attitude of Kalachand was the forerunner to the birth of rationalism in Bengal in the later part of the century. Yet, this was not extraordinary, as the general attitude of Chaitanya's philosophy was tolerance. In fact, the story goes that his closest disciples, Rupa and Sanatana, were so infused with Islamic studies that they were almost Muslims, but their continued adherence to the teachings of Chaitanya only made it stronger and more tolerant. Tolerance also broke the religion into different sects. To try to patch up the differences within the group, Nithyanda and his wife, Tauranin Mishra, organized a festival at Khetri to bring all the sects together. While there was some success, it also led to the creation of a family domination of the sect and the propagation of a Vamhsa with his son Advaita Mishra and his followers, making it a family tradition. While this led to the narrowing of the tradition to a family, its values also led to a greater break with tradition, for it resulted in the spread of the tradition among the Dalits and the rise of teachers like Haridass Thakur and the Bhakti movement among the followers. This was the tolerant and all-embracing religion that Ramakrishna Paramahamsa was to adopt later. In the 20th century, the teachings of Chaitanya were also taken by Swami Prabhupad (1896–1977) to Europe and the U.S.A., which turned it into 'The International Society for Krishna Consciousness.' The religion also spread widely among the educated class and attracted westerners to the chant of 'Hari Krishna, Hari Ram.'

Kabir (1448-1518)

In both the life and works of Kabir, we have the first attempt to create a bridge between Hinduism and Islam, not by accepting either but by putting both to the acid test of rationality. The fact that history has proved him to have been an ineffectual messiah is the tragedy of Indian religiosity and human credulity. Instead, like Spinoza in Inquisition Spain, he was hounded by both Hindus and Muslims. Yet, like Tulsidas, the hero to most Hindus, he reiterated that the way to heaven was by chanting the name of Ram, Rama, Rama. Only in death did he achieve a modicum of respect, with both Hindus and Muslims claiming him as their own. His life and works exemplify the Indian attitude to religion most explicitly; all revere the saints, the renouncer, the sage, and the holy man, but very few look deeper into the content of their philosophy.

Like everything in Indian history, we know very little, with certainty, about the life of Kabir. Legend has it that he was born to an unwed Brahmin woman who had to abandon him and was adopted by a poor Muslim family of weavers who brought him up. He may have been born sometime between 1395 and 1448 C.E., even though there are historians who place his birth around 1440 to 1518 C.E. Biographers claim that his adopted parents may have been recently converted Muslims and were practicing a very loose form of Islam. It is, however, a persistent belief that sometime in his youth, he joined Ramananda's group of Bhakti devotees. His marital status is also disputed, with some claiming that he was married, while others claim he was celibate. However, most agree that he lived and preached mainly in Varanasi and the nearby areas.

Kabir the Poet

Even if Kabir was not a religious man, he would still have been regarded as one of the greatest Hindi poets of India. He wrote almost entirely in verse, with an ironic twist to everything he said. In Tagore's translation of his poems, he says,

"All the gods—Vishnu, Saraswati, and Krishna—all look in awe and with folded hands, where, Spring, the lord of seasons, reigneth; there unstuck music sounds itself. There, the stream of light flows in all directions."

However, this acceptance of nature in itself did not prevent his followers from claiming that his poems propound religious truths. They are thought to be so religious that the Sikhs have compiled a great number of them in their 'Adi Granth.'

Kabir the Philosopher

Kabir, benefiting from an Islamic background and a deep knowledge of Hindu philosophies through his association with the Ramananda group, was clearly well-placed to view both religions from a subjective and objective perspective. Thus, he was a stern critic of both religions for their reliance on rituals and symbols, such as the sacred thread among Hindus and circumcision among Muslims. Kabir asserted that God would always be with a person who is righteous and reveres all life. Yet, like a true Bhakti poet, he stated that salvation is possible only in the chanting of the name of Ram, Rama, Rama. Again, like the Bhakti poets, he scorned the way of Jnana and said,

"Reading book after book, the whole world died,
and none ever became learned."

Yet, at the heart of his message was the duplicity of all organized religions, the farce of fasts and rituals, where the heart remains unchanged. He laughed at the idea of a God who can be contained in a mosque or temple and asked, "If God is in a mosque, then to whom does the world belong?" Instead, he asserted that God dwells within,

"Look into your hearts, for there you will find,
Karim and Ram."

While Kabir makes no attempt to create a systematic philosophy, he accepts the tradition that saw God as formless and without attributes, as Nirguna. Yet tradition has it that Kabir did not see bliss in merging with God but in being in union with God. What he wanted to say most was about the stupidity of intolerance and the importance of dissent. Thus, he said,

"Keep the slanderer near you,
Build him a hut in your courtyard.
Without soap or water,
He will scrub your character clean."

He knew that religion was a taboo subject and that intolerance was emblematic of faith. He said,

"Saints see the world as mad.
If I tell the truth, they rush to beat me.
If I lie, they trust me."

His Legacy

There is little doubt that Sikhism was greatly influenced by the teachings of Kabir. They have acknowledged it by including many of his verses in the Adi Granth. That alone would have secured him a place among the great religious leaders of India. He was also greatly influenced by the Sufi tradition in Islam, for whom he is a saint. Yet, the lasting impact of Kabir is in the group that calls themselves the 'Kabir Panthis' and their organization, the 'Kabir Panth,' that has spread all over the country and to many parts of the world. His religion stresses the similarities that exist in all religions and fights against the stupidity of idol worship and the injustice of the caste system. Yet, feminists would object to his lines that say,

"Women ruin everything when they come near men,
Devotion, liberation, and divine knowledge no longer enter his soul."

However, he was only echoing a persistent theme in Bhakti philosophy that the sensual pleasures of the world are the creation of 'avidya,' a delusion that blinds the devotee to the reality of God.

Guru Nanak (1469-1539)

Guru Nanak, the founder of Sikhism, was born to middle-class Hindu parents from the trading community in a village close to Lahore on April 15, 1469. While later biographers have tried to show that he was born with many signs foretelling his future greatness and that, from an early age, he had shown clear signs of a religious teacher, the actual details of his early life are rare. We know that he was educated by his elder sister, whose husband was working for Daulat Khan Lodi. Thus, very early in his life, he came into contact with Muslim life and practices, realizing that there was nothing evil about Islam. In fact, the affection he received must have had a lifelong impact on his thinking. Consequently, his religion was at first only an attempt to reconcile Islamic ideas with Hindu beliefs and foster a bridge of understanding between the two religions. It was only much later, as a result of the persecution that the Sikhs faced with courage and pride, that the religion took on a martial façade, with distinctive attire that forced each Sikh to stand up for his religion and its beliefs. It was this open defiance in the face of persecution that created our distinctive identity as a group and as a religion.

In 1487, Guru Nanak married Mata Sulakhami, the daughter of Mul Chand, and had two sons. Mul Chand was also one of the first to accept the new religion preached by Guru Nanak and later became the head of the Udasi sect. Rai Bular, the local landlord, was another who saw divine qualities in the young Guru Nanak and supported him in his studies. As the story goes, one day Nanak went for a bath in the local river and did not return. When he finally returned, three days later, he was a changed man. He was silent for a whole day, and when he finally opened his mouth, he said, "There is neither Hindu nor Muslim, but only man. So, whose path should I follow? I will follow God's path. God is neither Hindu nor Musalman, and the path I follow is God's." He claimed that during the time he was away, he was taken up to the presence of God, where he was given a cup to drink that contained Amrita. He was blessed and commanded to teach the message of God.

Guru Nanak never claimed to be God, a prophet, or even a messenger of God; he was only an ordinary man entrusted to teach. The Sikhs do not believe in reincarnation, and thus the Guru is not some Avatar of God but only a Guru. The basic message was a simple one: to spread kindness, to create peace among the people and not to return evil for evil. Like the Protestants, the Guru emphasized that men do not need any intermediary to approach God; no priests are required, as God is accessible to all men. He also insisted that God was only one, even if people called him by many names. Like the Buddha, he asserted that all human conflict arises from the idea of 'I' and 'mine,' of the self and of everyone else and everything else, as the 'other.' Only in the abandonment of the self and the duality of seeing all others as 'other,' will men find peace and salvation.

Guru Nanak arrived on the scene when the Bhakti movement was at its height and he was also moved by the power of the idea of Bhakti and by the comfort of a caring and personal God. The Guru shunned metaphysical ideas and accepted the world of the senses as both real and valid. He said, What we see is very clear, even if only a part of the infinite reality, the true reality that God allows us to see. He also, like the later Vedantists, saw God as 'nirguni' or formless. His message was that, within this rather limited vision given to men, greater spiritual awareness leads to a more meaningful interaction with the world. Life is therefore to be lived with truthfulness and with faith and self-control, seeking purity of heart and never abandoning the world of people, for the good life must be an active life, lived for the benefit of all mankind. Men must participate in life and try to impact it with one's actions.

Guru Nanak preached the gospel of the brotherhood of men and the fatherhood of God. The basic creed involved the equality of all men before God and men, in which he asserted that it was the breaking of people into castes and religions and the creation of social distinctions that was the cause of all corruption. His religion involved active involvement in society and the community, and he lauded the idea of hard work and a concern for the poorest of people. In fact, when he finally returned from his tours, he actually settled as a farmer, actively cultivating the land. In very simplistic terms, the Guru's message can be said to be:

- Help and share with those who are less fortunate.
- Be honest in life and at work.
- Meditate on God so as to overcome the five weaknesses of the body.

To the Guru, the problems of hunger and poverty were very real and remained major concerns. That is why he came up with the idea of a langar where everyone could share food. It was an attempt not only to ensure the sharing of food but also to ensure the intermixing of all castes. He was always insistent that religion had an important social mandate; he insisted that all good men must actively resist evil and fight against injustice. Apart from social justice, he also insisted that, to God, there was no male or female—all were equal. Thus, Sikhism was the first religion in India to preach equality between the sexes and to permit women to participate in all matters related to the religion.

After attaining enlightenment, the Guru started on a journey to spread the message he had received. It is said that he undertook five extensive journeys, traveling to all parts of India, not only teaching but also talking to the religious leaders of all faiths. In his tours, he made it a point to shun the hospitality of the rich and make it a point to eat with the poor. It was also while on his tours that he composed many of the hymns that now form the 'Granth Sahib.' It is also claimed that he traveled a great deal outside the country and visited Mecca, Jerusalem, and even the Vatican. In the end, his followers claim, he just disappeared. His death is normally reckoned as September 22, 1539. Sikhism is, however, not only the religion that Guru Nanak taught but also contains the teachings of the ten Sikh Gurus, who are revered equally. Their sacred text, 'The Granth Sahib,' is also a compilation of the hymns composed by the many gurus. Guru Nanak is credited with composing as many as 974 of the hymns in 'The Granth Sahib.'

The History of Sikhism

The irony of the religion that started as a bridge between Islam and Hinduism was that it was subjected to the maximum amount of persecution from the Islamic rulers, especially from the Mughal rulers, from 1566 to 1707. This led to the militarization of the Sikh community to resist Mughal oppression. It finally led to the establishment of a Sikh empire under the leadership of their Maharaja, Raja Ranjit Singh. The Sikhs had a very turbulent history, and their faith has therefore to be judged, to a great extent, in the context of how they evolved and yet retained a great deal of their ideals.

It was in the time of their fourth Guru, Guru Arjan, that 'the Granth Sahib' was installed as their holy book in 1604. As persecution became intolerable, it was Guru Har Govind who started the martial institution that has now become synonymous with Sikh identity. He carried two swords, saying that one represented the temporal and the other the spiritual, accepting the fact that no religion can survive without accepting the reality of social and political compulsions. He thus inculcated the belief in the need to fight for the religion. He started by maintaining an armed group of warriors whom he called saint warriors. His grandson, Guru Har Krishna, who was a much gentler soul and preached peace, did not disband the armed warriors, thus making them, from then on, a permanent part of the Sikh institution.

Guru Teg Bahadur was the first Guru to be martyred when he refused Aurangzeb's demand that the Sikhs convert to Islam. Guru Govind Singh Jr., the 10th Guru and son of Teg Bahadur, saw in his father's martyrdom the need for even greater heroism. It was he who created 'The Khalsa Panth,' a separate and specially initiated group of Sikhs who were to be leaders and executors of the Sikh community. The Khalsa also meant 'the pure.' It was with the creation of the Khalsa that the Sikhs got a distinctive identity with the five 'Ks':

- Kesh (uncut hair)— symbolizes spirituality.

- Kangha (wooden comb)— represents cleanliness and orderliness.
- Kara (iron bracelet)— signifies restraint from evil deeds.
- Kachera (cotton undergarments)— a symbol of modesty.
- Kirpan (ceremonial sword)— signifies the defense of the truth and the weak.

The Khalsa was also prohibited from fornication, eating halal meat, the use of tobacco, and cutting of hair. It was the duty of the Khalsa to bear arms and to defend the faith. The great social impact that the creation of the Khalsa had was that it was open to the lowest castes, thus making it possible for them to actually rule over and lord over some of the higher castes, by their courage and general merit. In keeping with the social aims of the Sikh faith, when Guru Bandar Singh came to power, he abolished the Zamindari system and created a farmer's proprietorship over land. He was, however, constantly at war with the Mughals and was finally captured and martyred on June 6, 1716. This forced the Sikhs into hiding from where they resorted to guerrilla warfare. When the Mughals, despite all their efforts, could not suppress the Sikhs, they changed tactics and tried to woo them with sops and offers of friendship. Yet, all the Mughals could offer was a subordinate role that the Sikhs refused to accept. From then on, there was continuous fighting between the Sikhs and the Muslim rulers, leading to episodes when thousands of Sikhs were massacred in battles, including what is called Chota Ghalinghara, near Gurdaspur in 1746 and 'Wadda Ghalinghara' near Ludhiana in 1762. In 1783, the Sikhs captured Delhi, defeating the Mughals; at last, they had won, and its culmination was the crowning of Ranjit Singh as Maharaja on April 12, 1801. The Sikh Empire lasted from 1801 to 1849, till the British defeated them in the Anglo-Sikh war of 1845, after which there was a rapid decline. The importance of Sikhism as an Indian religion is due to the fact that it was the first religion to emerge out of India for two thousand years after the appearance of Buddhism and Jainism. It had, therefore, to remain distinct and immune to the enormous power of Hinduism that had submerged all new religions and to fight against the possibility of being absorbed into the larger Hindu religious identity. It was also important because it was the first attempt to bridge what appeared to be the huge divide between Hinduism and Islam. It also carried forward the reformist ideas of the many religious reformers who fought against the evils of caste oppression and the need to create a more equal society. In fact, Sikhism is perhaps the religion that most succeeded, even if skeptics would point to the lingering distinctions that may still prevail. It has to be said, to the credit of Sikhism, that whatever the lingering social failures, Sikhism, in its official stance, has never compromised on the idea of equality for all. While many of the finer humanistic thinking of the early Gurus had to be sacrificed when they became a militaristic organization, their concern for the brotherhood of men and their abiding concern for the less fortunate and their genuine concern and commitment to look after them have set them apart, in a way even the Christian community has not been able to do.

CHAPTER 13

ISLAM IN INDIA

The impact of Islam on Indian consciousness cannot be exaggerated. It is what distinguishes 'the other' and, by differentiation, defines the true Indian. Islam came to India almost as soon as Muhammad the Prophet first preached his new doctrine. The early converts quickly brought it with them in their trading vessels and spread it among their brother Arabs, who had already been in India for centuries on the Malabar coast. In fact, as early as 629 C.E., the Chera King of Kerala had given permission and land to the Muslims to build their first Mosque. Thus, the Muslims had a mosque in India even in the lifetime of the Prophet. There is also a tradition that claims that one of the Chera kings actually converted to Islam and even went on a hajj to Mecca. Yet, the impact of Islam is part of a troubled legacy. It is also a fact that despite more than 14 percent of the Indian population being made up of Muslims and India perhaps being the second-largest Muslim country in the world by population, the theology of Islam has made very little impact on the consciousness of non-Muslim Indians. In fact, it can be said that Islam has been more influenced by Indian thinking than the other way around. What Islam gave to India was not just a religion but the culture of the Muslim rulers, the culture of Persia, and the culture of the Arabs.

The History

It was the Arab traders who first brought Islam to India. There was already a large Arab population on the Malabar coast who had been engaged in trade with the Middle East since the first millennium B.C. The Arabs had also settled along the Konkan coast and the long Gujarat coastline. Islam came to India almost as soon as it was preached in Arabia itself, and the new Muslims built their own mosque as early as 629 C.E., with the full support of the Chera king. The mosque was called 'Cheram Jumma Masjid.' In time, many locals converted to Islam, and their numbers were augmented by intermarriages with the local people. The persistent belief that one of the Chera kings himself became a Muslim only shows how attractive the new religion was. Islam came to the Malabar coast peacefully and was happily accepted by the local people. However, this was to be the exception, as Islam was to come to the rest of the country on the bandwagon of conquering armies and thrusting down with the might of the sword.

In the 8th century, the province of Sindh was conquered by an Arab army led by Mohamed of Qassim. Then, in the 10th century, Mohammad of Ghazni conquered Punjab, and this was followed in the 12th century by the conquests of Muhammad of Ghor. But unlike the earlier raiding parties, Muhammad of Ghor stayed on to create a Muslim empire in India. He created what was called the Delhi Sultanate, which slowly extended its reach all the way to Bengal in the east and to Hyderabad and Bijapur in the South. The Delhi Sultanate, from 1206–1526, was led by men of Turkish origin and descended from the following dynasties: Mamluk, 1206–1290; Khilji, 1290–1320; Tugluq, 1320–1414; Sayyid, 1414–1457; and the Lodhis, who were Afghans. From the 14th century, the Muslims moved towards the east, conquered Bengal, and started a separate Sultanate in A.D. 1352 under Ilyas Shah, which lasted till the 16th century with minor interruptions. Similarly, Gujarat came under a sultanate in the 16th century. They also extended southwards to create sultanates in Bijapur, Golkonda, Ahmednagar, Bidar, and Berar, which all lasted till Aurangzeb added them to the Mughal Empire. It was the Mughals who came in the 16th century and created an empire that spread almost throughout the length and breadth of the country. Much has been written about their splendor and greatness. From the Peacock throne to the Kohinoor diamond, they exemplified the world of luxury and opulence, with the Taj Mahal standing as their defining monument. Their empire lasted until the arrival of the British. The story of the Mughals, along with the story of Muslim conquests, the destruction of Buddhist and Hindu temples, and the forcible conversion of many to Islam, is well-documented and part of every schoolboy's knowledge of Indian history and needs no repeating. What is important is the nature and extent of the Islamic legacy.

The Spectrum of Islam in India

India is one of the largest Islamic nations in the world, with a population of more than 180 million Muslims. Worldwide, with the exception of Iran, the majority of Indian Muslims are Sunni Muslims, comprising perhaps three-quarters of the total Muslim population. The Shias number about 40 million and account for about twenty percent of the Muslim population. However, what is interesting is the many other hues of Islamic faith that the people of India adhere to.

The Sunnis

Sunni, the word, comes from the term Sunnah, which refers to the words and acts of the prophet. However, the first division within the faith was the result of the fact that the Prophet did not specifically designate a successor. While there was a claim made by those who supported the succession of Ali, the prophet's son-in-law, the majority, however, believed that the companions of the prophet were the best suited to succeed and selected Abu-Bakr, the father-in-law of the prophet, claiming that Muhammad himself had said, 'the best people are of my generation.' That generation is also revered because they compiled the Quran. They saw Abu-Bakr as the 'Rashidin' or the rightly guided one. Umar was the second, and he is credited with establishing the Islamic calendar; the third was Uthman, followed by Ali, who became the fourth caliph. Sunni is also the short form of 'sunnah wa al mecum,' meaning those who follow the Sunnah. With the ascension of Ali to the caliphate, the schism in the faith became open, with his supporters claiming that the succession of the caliphate should only be through the bloodline of the prophet. Thus, when, at Ali's death, they tried to install Hussein, his son, as the next Caliph, there was an open war in which Hussein was killed, and the caliphate passed on to the Sunni majority.

Eighty-seven percent of Muslims are Sunnis, forming the largest single denomination of faith in the world, followed by Catholics. Sunnah also means tradition and custom, and thus, the Sunni faith is often also called the orthodox faith. However, it would be wrong to assume that the Sunnis were the original Muslims, as the divergence of thinking had existed from the beginning. While there are many schools of thought in Sunni Islam, their main creed can be summed up as what they call the 'Tahawi,' which consists of the following absolute beliefs:

- The reality of the one true God.
- The existence of angels.
- The authority of sacred books, including the Torah, the Psalms, the Epistles, and the Quran.
- Following the sayings and practices of the prophet.
- Preparing for the day of judgment.
- The supremacy of God's will.

The Shias

The Shias form the largest minority of Muslims in India, as they do all over the world. In India, they may number about 40 million. In fact, there are some towns and villages where the Shias actually predominate. The history of Shia Islam in India is very old, dating back to the tenth century, when there was a Sayyid migration consequent on their loss of power and the resultant persecution in much of the Middle East. While most Shias were the 'Ithna Ashari,' or the Twelver, the smaller groups included the Kojas and the

Bhoras, who were part of a larger Ismailis group. There are also others, like the Ahmadis. 'Ithna Ashari' translates as the Twelver, which is the number of Imams they accept as their spiritual heads. They are regarded as the spiritual successors of Muhammad, the prophet. While it is on the 'Sunnah,' the words of the prophet, that even the Imams propounded the 'Shariah,' the law, the Shias believe that the Imams were also infallible and that their words were to be accepted as part of divine revelation. Their faith is thus called 'Ismah.' However, the Ismaili Shias have their own twelve imams. The sanctity given to the twelve Imams is based on their direct descendants from the Prophet. In fact, the cardinal principle of their faith is the acceptance only of the direct descendants of the prophet as true Imams, and their line of Imams starts with Ali, Muhammad's cousin and son-in-law. They believe in succession only through the bloodline of the prophet and trace their first Imam to Ali, the husband of Fatimah, the prophet's daughter, and the prophet's cousin. While the Sunnis see Ali only as the fourth Imam, the Shias see him as the first legitimate Imam. The Shia faith is also built on the martyrdom of Hussein, Ali's son, whose fight is seen as a crusade against a corrupt caliphate. Hussein's death is, therefore, a defining moment in the history of the Shias.

The History

It was in 1501 that the Shias first tasted political power after their initial attempts at power were squashed by the majority Sunni community with the death and martyrdom of Hussein. In 1501, the Sayyid Dynasty came to power in Iran and declared Shia Islam as the official religion, despite the fact that the majority were Sunnis. As a result of their use of political power, by the time the Dynasty was overthrown in 1736, Iran, at least, was largely a Shia country, and the sect had spread itself to many other parts of the world. However, the most important development was the setting up of seminaries and schools that taught the tenets of the religion and became centers of learning. These remained even after they lost power, becoming the theological base for its further expansion.

To India, their migration started from Iran and the Middle East around the 10th century A.D. In time, there were Shia rulers who gave impetus to the spread and propagation of the religion. The first Shia rulers were in Awadh, U.P., and later there were rulers in Multan and Sindh. After the martyrdom of Hussein, many Shias chose to migrate to India from Iran, and many came from other parts of the Arab world. The Shias, however, began to face persecution with the arrival of the Mughals and the setting up of the Mughal Empire, as they were staunch Sunnis. They were also persecuted in Kashmir from the very beginning, and it has continued down the centuries. Officially, however, India is one of the few countries that has recognized the Shias and their faith. In fact, India has the second-largest Shia population in the world, second only to Iran.

Their Theology

As far as the basic tenets are concerned, there is little difference. They all believe in the five basic principles of Islamic faith, the 'Tawhid,' which comprise the following:

- God is one.
- God is unique in essence, and Allah is neither begotten nor created.
- The reality of God is beyond human comprehension; he is all and nothing.
- There is no other creator but God.
- God alone is the Lord of the universe.

The Tawhid further emphasizes that God is just, creation has a purpose, and all that God has created is good. They also believe that justice requires the separation of the good from the evil and that God will finally judge all people. They believe that through good deeds and faith, men can approach God. The Shias accept the reality of free will but insist that all creation is the work of God alone and that it is man's duty to attune his will to the will of God. An area where their belief is at variance with the Sunnis is marriage, where they permit temporary marriages for a specific period of time. The Sunnis consider such marriages to be haram.

The Ismailis

The Fatimid Dynasty pushed Shia Islam into India during the years when it was being persecuted in Yemen. It came to India in the form of Dawoodi Bohra Ismailis. It was in Gujarat that they found their largest number of converts, and there were also others who were called Khojas and those who are called Nizari Ismailis. Their head is the Aga Khan, considered the 46th Imam of the Nizari Ismaili Muslims. The Ismailis, as a whole, are the second-largest Shia sect in India and comprise many sub-sects. They believe in human reason, pluralism, and social justice. In reasoning, they accept Aristotelian logic and Platonic reasoning. Their religion is peace-loving and moderate. Azim Premji, the head of Wipro, is a Nizari Muslim. Like the many splits in the history of Shia Islam, the history of the Nizari sect is also full of bloodshed and betrayal that resulted in the further splitting of the sect. Like the concept of Nirguna, the Ismaili Muslims claim that God can be understood only through negation, for God is formless and limitless. It is not possible for human reason to fathom the nature or totality of God. They accept the seven pillars of Islam, which are pure love and attachment to God, purity, prayer, charity, fasting, Hajj, and jihad against vices like envy, wrath, intolerance, and greed. Their places of worship are called Jamat Khana, homes for prayer and study. Marriage, to them, is merely a legal contract and not a sacrament, and they also tolerate inter-religious marriage.

The Dawoodi Bohras

The Dawoodi Bohras are Shias who split from the main Ismaili group and are mainly found in Gujarat. Even the language of their religion is a mix of Gujarati and Arabic. They are believers in the hidden Imam. Their belief is that the true Imam will only reveal himself when needed and when the time is ripe. In the meantime, they accept a mortal head from among them to lead them. After a further split in the sect in 1657, Ismail Badurudin became the first Gujarati Dal, or head of the community. The community is, however, small and may not exceed 1 million. They wear distinctive three-piece attire, and their women, even though they wear a burqa, are not required to veil their faces. They are active in the field of education, having established many schools and institutes of higher learning.

The Khojas

The Khojas in India are also located in Gujarat and in the city of Hyderabad. They adhere to the Shia beliefs of the Ismaili sect of Nizari. The Ismailis and the 'Twelvers' split over the succession of Jaffer al Sadig, the nominated heir of Ismail al Jaffer, as the Twelvers preferred his younger brother, Muas al Kadhim. Their spiritual guru is the Aga Khan. The Aga Khan is a title given to the 46th Imam by the Persian King. Each Imam is considered the living and divine word. Thus, they believe that it is not the words of a text but the guidance of the Imam that is all important. Their sect stresses the need for love and devotion to the Aga Khan and adheres to the seven pillars of the faith. They practice a very ethnic Islam and have retained a great deal of their local heritage.

The Ahmadiyyars

The Ahmadiyyars are followers of Mirza Ghulam Ahmad (1833–1908) of Qadian, who claimed to be the awaited messiah, the incarnation of Moses, and the Mahdi. There may be about 1 million Ahmadiyyars in India, mostly in Rajasthan, Haryana, Delhi, and Bihar. The religion was founded in Punjab by Ghulam Ahmad, who claimed to be the final prophet, delivering the last revelation of God. They preach a peaceful Islam. They have a worldwide population of about 20 million, with a large following in Pakistan, where it originated, and where they have continuously faced persecution. In fact, in Pakistan, where more than 5 million Ahmadiyyars live, the sect has been officially declared a non-Muslim sect. It is a fact that there are many non-Muslim beliefs in their creed. For example, they accept the sanctity of books other than the Quran, including the Torah and the Psalms, and even acknowledge that the Vedas and the Avesta are divinely inspired texts. The Nobel laureate Abdus Salam was an Ahmadiyyar, and his claim to be a Muslim was erased even from his tombstone. To them, Jihad means the fight against the vices of the flesh like lust, greed, envy, and anger, and actual violence is permitted only under extreme provocation and only in self-defense. However, they are targeted for persecution in almost all Muslim countries, including Saudi Arabia, Palestine, and Bangladesh.

Sufism

Sufism was one of the anomalies created by Islam in its contact with other religions and perhaps as a result of its past. Islam, being a highly power-centered religion, allowed very little scope for interpretation and dissent but was yet forced to accept the infiltration of dissent in the form of Sufism, through the back door, as it were. It was a form of intense mysticism, a frantic devotion to God, that appeared like the ecstasy of the Bhakti saints. Consequently, their actual theology was never put under a microscope and critically examined. Mysticism was not really an Islamic characteristic, as Muhammad preached a religion of reason, where even the scientific method was accepted as an essential component of reasoning. While Islamic scholars would like to claim that Sufism was an internal development, it was much more likely to have been a harping back to an older mystic tradition and a borrowing from the Jewish mystics. In India, they met the proponents of the Bhakti movement and must have been greatly influenced by them, as well as by the general mysticism that pervades all religions in India, with its magic and its mantras.

While mainstream Islam came with the sword, as it were, Sufism followed and came peacefully with the Arab and Persian traders, and their religion was never forced down anybody's throat but was freely accepted, cherished, and allowed to evolve. Sufism made the often harsh and uncompromising religion of Islam soft and compromising and into a caring and devotional religion, where believers had merely to throw themselves at the feet of a caring and loving God. Sufism was born in modern-day Iraq, in places like Baghdad. It then spread to Persia and then to Afghanistan, from where it entered India. To claim to be part of the establishment of

Islam, the Sufis claim that their mawlas, or spiritual leaders, were people who descended directly from Muhammad, the Prophet. To buttress their claim even more firmly, they claim that their patron saint was Ali, the son-in-law of the prophet. The original Sufis were those who left all they had and sacrificed all to serve the prophet full time, and Muhammad is supposed to have said "I am the city of knowledge and Ali is the gate." However, it was also, in many ways, a revolt against the worldly and luxurious lifestyle of the caliphate once they became rich and powerful. The irony is that the term Sufi was coined by British orientalists. In Arabic, the tradition was called 'tasawwuf,' which is best translated as the inner dimension of Islam. The word Sufi, as used by the orientalists, is from the root word 'saf,' which means to purify or to be pure. At first, Sufism was nothing but an attempt to internalize Islam as something akin to personal faith, and through devotion to its prophet, the believers would have direct access to God. The first Mawla to be called a Sufi was Abdullah ibn Muhammad Ibn al Hanafiyya, who died in 716 C.E.

While most people tend to call Sufism a sect of Islam, to the Sufi, they are not a sect but an integral part of the Sunni Islamic faith. They claim that while the Shariah dictates the outward practices of Islam, Sufism deals with the inner requirements of the same faith. In this tradition, even by the 10th century, a number of tracts had already been written, formalizing the tenets of Sufism. One of them was called 'the revival of religious science.' These tracts were at pains to show how all the tenets of Sufism were taken from the Quran and that their beliefs were not in contradiction with the Shariah. In fact, even as recently as 2005, a number of Islamic organizations got together to issue the 'Amman declaration,' saying that Sufism was very much an integral part of Islam. Whatever the apology for it, it was Sufism that led to the peaceful adoption of Islam in many parts of the world, especially in Sudan, Libya, Turkey, and many parts of Central Asia and Southeast Asia. It also definitely led to the intellectual growth of Islam.

The Theology

While Islam believes in the day of final judgment, when all will be judged and the Lord will decide who will go to heaven and who to hell, the aim of Sufism is to bring heaven down to Earth. Through total surrender to Allah, humans can attain a state of bliss that is like heaven, for it is the presence of the divine on Earth. While Islam is a religion of rules and strict compliance with laid-down practices, Sufism is about sin, redemption, atonement, and repentance, demanding that a person make continuous efforts to become a better human being by purging human vices like greed, envy, hatred, lust, and so on.

One of the most important concepts in Sufism is the concept of 'Insan al Kamil,' the perfect man. Only the Prophet was perfect, but it should be the aim of all Muslims to imitate the Prophet and aim for perfection. It is their belief that only through Muhammad can man even glimpse the perfection of God. Like all mystics, they claim that human reason can only get us to a point, but for any true understanding of God, one must be prepared to make that leap of faith, and only in total surrender to God is illumination possible. They also see in Muhammad an intercessor for man before God and claim that Muhammad is even today listening to the prayers of the faithful and interceding with God on their behalf.

Their devotional practices are varied, but one of the important ones is the practice of 'Dhikr,' or remembrance of God, which is commanded in the Koran. This can take many forms and includes the repetition of the many names of God and constant prayers. Another important way is to remember God through meditation, which they call 'Muragaba.' They also encourage the visiting of pilgrimage centers.

Sufism in India

Sufism came along with the Muslim invaders and more peacefully with the Arab, Afghan, and Persian traders. The early Muslim dynasties welcomed them as scholars. Islamic scholars, however, were divided into two classes: one was the 'Ulema,' who were basically jurists rooted in the study of the Shariah, while the other was the Sufis, who were more interested in the inner soul of man and were also called fakirs, as they tended to be like ascetics, traveling like vagabond monks.

The major reason for the spread of Sufism in India was their practice of building the 'Khanqah,' a sort of hospice and lodge that also served as a community center and as a place for worship and study. The poor and the depressed, especially from the lowest castes, were welcomed and fed in these Khanqahs. This resulted in them becoming places where all castes, races, and religious groups could meet and learn from each other. These places served as outreach posts for Islam, where the religion was passed on in an atmosphere of charity and goodwill. This could not but affect the lower classes, as they were not used to such treatment. The obvious saintliness of many of the Sufi saints must have also made a great impression on them, leading to a great number being converted to Islam. To them, Islam was not the religion of the invaders, cold and rigid, but the religion of social reform and of a loving and caring God.

The Different Sufi Sects

Sufism was enriched by the teachings of many Sufi saints, and this, in time, led to the formation of different sects owing allegiance to separate saints. The Shadhili sect, founded by Abdul Hassan Ali ash Shadhili, has followers called 'murids' or the seekers. In India, the 'Fassiya' branch of the Shadhili sect was brought by Sheik Abubacker Miskeen and Sheik Mir Ahmed Ibrahim, who settled down in Madurai in Tamil Nadu to preach the religion. It grew from there, and there are presently more than 70 branches of this sect all over India.

The Chistiya version of Sufism, originally from Central Asia, was brought to India by Abu Ishag Shamin (died 941 C.E). Abu Ishag Shamin first established his order in Afghanistan and called it 'Chishti-I-Sharif.' In India, it became the most popular form of Sufism due to the work of their saint, Moinudeen Chisti. Moinudeen Chisti, originally from Iran, came to India in 1193 C.E. and worked mostly in and around the city of Ajmer. It is claimed that he came to India as a result of a dream in which he saw the prophet blessing his idea of going to India. He built a khanqah to reach out to the people. His selfless work and his charities soon attracted people to his khanqah, and many were converted to Islam. Their practices were based on the renunciation of all worldly goods and strict discipline, prayer, and meditation. In fact, Moinudeen saw in Islam a specific social mandate, which he expressed as the need to develop 'a river-like generosity, a sun-like affection, and an Earth-like hospitality,' through the sharing of all wealth and food and tolerance for all religions. Consequently, even today, a large percentage of pilgrims who visit his shrine in Ajmer are Hindus. He made it clear that the role of religion was to feed the poor and to care for the distressed and the helpless. Even by the 16th century, his fame was so great that it is said that Emperor Akbar had gone barefoot to his shrine. His shrine is called 'Ajmer Sharif Dargah' or simply 'Ajmer Sharif.' Shaykh Nizamudin, another Sufi, was mainly famous around Delhi and died in 1325.

The beliefs of the Sufis are varied. The Jabriya sect denies free will, while the Qudrariyya group rejects predestination. Like the Nirguna concept, many asserted that God was formless and without attributes. While scholars tried to rationalize the nature of the 'necessary being,' the Sufis were more interested in the inner realization of the divine. The Suhrawardiyya sect grew around Delhi on the fame of Shaykh Sama-u-d-Din, who died in 1496. His work was carried forward by his disciple, who called himself Jamali and was an eminent poet.

Persecution

Despite all that has been said, there is a deep undercurrent of thought among some Muslims who see Sufism as un-Islamic, and Sufis have been subject to persecution throughout history. Even today, important Sufi shrines are attacked and vandalized on a regular basis. In Turkey, Sufism was banned by Atatürk, and in Pakistan, there is a continuing persecution and vandalization of Sufi shrines. In Somalia, all forms of Sufi worship and ceremonies are banned; in Mali, their shrines are regularly attacked, and in 2010, Egypt banned most Sufi forms of worship. There have been reports of persecution, attacks, and vandalism of shrines in Russia, Tunisia, Libya, and even from Iran. Yet what is most terrifying is not state-sponsored terrorism, as most states put up a veneer of civilized behavior, but the fringe groups who claim orthodoxy and the terrorists who attack Sufi shrines and Sufi believers on a regular basis.

Caste among Indian Muslims

One of the great anomalies of Islam in India is the presence of the caste system among Indian Muslims. Muslims in India are divided into Ashrafs and Ajlats. The Ashrafs claim to be of a superior class, and many of them assert foreign origins, often contending noble blood or asserting that they were part of the ruling class in India, even if they were once slaves. This claim to nobility is similar to that of the Indian upper castes who converted to Islam. On the other hand, the non-Ashrafs are the converts from the lower classes of Indian society. The ignominy is that these converts were further divided along the lines of their original caste status in Indian society. This stratification was upheld even by the Ulema (Islamic law). Similar to Manu for the Hindus, there was Zalauddin Barani, a Turk who wrote a definitive book on the Muslim caste system called 'Fatwa-i-Jahandari.'

This resulted in Muslims having their own version of untouchability, where certain castes were labeled Azaral castes. Dealing with these castes required the upper castes to purify themselves. The upper castes were referred to as 'onchi zat,' while the lower castes were 'neechi zat,' and their relationship was to be that of a patron and client. Although the application of caste was not as rigid as in Hindu society, a high-caste Muslim was supposed to have a bath after any dealings with a low-caste Muslim. While this practice blatantly violates Koranic rules, its prevalence in India is justified as socially inevitable.

Alberuni's India
Translated by Dr. Edward Sachau
A Muslim (outsider's) perspective

Alberuni's India presents the best outsider's perception of India and its people, as well as the best critical review of its heritage and learning. It offers an outsider's view of India during the initial years of Muslim rule. His work is primarily a critical appreciation of the culture, science, mathematics, and philosophy of India, but it also provides a depiction of how India and Indians appear to an outsider. Alberuni arrived in India in 1017 at the behest of the Sultan of Persia, Sultan Mohamed, and stayed for thirteen years, extensively traveling throughout the country and engaging with scientists, philosophers, and religious pandits, especially astronomers and astrologers. He also studied all available books, particularly the ancient religious and scientific texts. By the time he left the country, he had become the foremost authority on India and its heritage outside the country. His writings were, as he puts it, only intended to present the cultural heritage of the country, not to comment on it. However, his prejudices surface despite his best intentions, and he cannot help but compare Indian learning with the superior Islamic traditions and, in his view, the pinnacle of classical Greece.

Alberuni came to India at the court of Mahmud of Ghazni (977–1030), which was then the center of art and literature in the region, attracting many intellectuals like Firdausi and other Persian poets. Abu Raihan, as Alberuni was called, was already a reputed student of literature when he arrived in India. When Mahmud of Ghazni conquered his homeland, he was taken prisoner along with many other nobles of his country. As a result, he did not hold much regard for the conquering exploits of Mahmud. Even while praising Mahmud's exploits, he says, "He utterly ruined the prosperity of the country. Hindus became like atoms of dust scattered in all directions." He, however, claims that it was God's punishment for the enemies of God. Yet he genuinely loved and admired Indian philosophy, stating that Indians were excellent philosophers, mathematicians, and astrologers. However, he couldn't suppress his pride in the achievements of the Islamic tradition, leading him to look down on everything Indian. He asserts that Indian philosophy was truly great, expounding a monistic theology of God, but laments that Indians have since descended into idolatry. He praises the 'pure action' theory of the Gita and was so struck by the greatness and depth of ancient Indian thought that he openly admitted that the Vedic Indians 'enjoyed the help of God.'

Alberuni made a deep and sustained study of Indian astronomy, science, mathematics, and philosophy, becoming the first to translate Indian works into a foreign language, Persian. He was also the first outsider to study the Puranas. Alberuni was already an acknowledged authority on many areas of knowledge even before he came to India. By the time he died, he had written more than 100 books—as the Arab saying goes, "The maximum a donkey can carry."

Alberuni begins his comprehensive work on India by explaining why he came, asserting that an eyewitness account is always superior to hearsay. Despite his apparent humility, he starts with an indictment of the Indian attitude, which he claims has persisted to this day. He observes, "They fight with words, but they will never stake their soul or body or their prosperity on religious controversy; on the contrary, all their fanaticism is directed against those who do not belong to them. They consider all foreigners as the devil's breed, and their presence would pollute a pure Indian." Consequently, he argues, Indian science has failed to grow and has receded, 'running away from the approach of the Muslim conquerors to where our hands cannot reach.'

Alberuni's enduring impression of the Indian attitude is that they believe "there is no country like theirs, no science like theirs, no religion like theirs." He characterizes them as haughty, foolishly vain, self-centered, and niggardly in communication, withholding knowledge from those of other castes. He acknowledges that their ancestors were not as narrow-minded. When he discussed new discoveries in science with them, they became abusive and spoke of him as acidic as the sea, stating, "Water is so acidic that vinegar, in comparison, is sweet." Conclusively, he describes Hindus as knowledgeable but not open in character like the Greeks, lacking figures of Socratic stature to bring Indian science to classical perfection.

Alberuni gracefully accepts that ancient Indians were different, emphasizing their belief in a single God who is eternal, all-wise, beyond likeness, and unattainable to thought. He cites the Gita, expressing the universe's unending nature and the concept that desire leads most people to seek refuge with God for their wants. He also indicates his understanding of the concepts of Atma and creation as manifestation.

As Alberuni understands it, karma is the core of Hinduism, and he expresses it thus: "There is no God but Allah and Muhammad is the last messenger.' is the shibboleth of Islam, the trinity is the shibboleth of the Christians, and the institute of the Sabbath is the shibboleth of Judaism, so metamorphosis is the shibboleth of the Hindu religion." According to Alberuni, humans need to be born again and again because, at first, they do not understand the totality of life and must, through many births, learn the true meaning of life. The purpose of migration through many lives, with rewards, is to direct the soul's attention to the good. The many births are due to gross desires, and as a result of these births, the soul is guided to attach itself to proper desires, desiring only the right things. Only when the soul turns away from the desires of the flesh does it break the connecting links to the cycle of endless life. Alberuni cautions readers with what Vasudeva tells Arjun: "The soul is immortal; you must know that what is born must die, and all that dies returns to another existence." He explains the difference between human souls and those of God, stating that God knows, while the human soul, clad in gross matter, cannot.

Alberuni then surveys the history of how the Hindu gods evolved and how even the concepts of heaven and hell came to be believed in. He reviews the moral code of Manu and Kautilya and how it became imprinted on the Hindu mind. Similar to Dante's Divine Comedy, he claims that the Vishnu Puranas record 88,000 hells, each specific to a particular sin. For example, those who connive in the shame of their wives or commit adultery with a sister would go to 'Mahajwala,' while those who take honey from a honeycomb would go to 'Vaitaram.' He also explains that in Hindu thinking, it is not the consequences of an act but the intention that matters. To escape the possibility of going to hell, one must always remember the Lord Vishnu in thought and in prayers. Alberuni continuously cites his knowledge of Greek philosophy, especially that of Socrates and Plato, while analyzing Hindu thinking. The soul is Earth-bound because it is clad in matter and has inherent ignorance. Only a man who has reached a Godlike state will want the good of all creation to lift his soul upwards. At this stage, a man would realize that all differences only hide a greater commonality. All human senses and organs of the body are provided only for men to acquire knowledge, and pleasure is the reward for learning. Men are created to know, but the body in which it is embedded is bent on action, and thus the soul, too often, descends to the body's level to do its bidding. That is how the body continually drags the soul into more and more births.

In a passage that is perhaps the best in his book, Alberuni explains Indian metaphysics and epistemology, showing how the ancient Indians had thought past Plato and Descartes and had reached the level of Kant's thinking. He explains how the Hindus considered the organs of the senses as the first receptacles of knowledge. At the next stage, the heart reflects on what the senses had perceived, taking into account both the present and past, and, as he puts it, 'prepares to wrestle with the future.' Reflection clears thought of errors that the senses may have made, and then it hands over the resultant knowledge to the power of reason. Reason then transforms what was merely particular into something universal and communicates that knowledge to the soul.

He explains that learning to be Hindu included revelation, learning from teachers, and the maturation of one's own intellect. The Hindus saw knowledge as a form of liberation, accompanied by the abolition of all evil in the mind. Lust and greed are impediments to the achievement of real knowledge. As he puts it, 'only when the heart quietly rests on one thing' would knowledge be possible. The reduction of 'feverish desire' sharpens the senses. He then says,

"All that which is the object of meditation is stamped upon him, so that he is even unconsciously guided by it."

Alberuni points out that the Hindu was practical enough to say that all the needs of the body and what is done merely for sustenance and life are never evil in themselves; in fact, "all things besides the necessities of life are in reality only pains." He claims that the Gita says, "Men err in the things he orders and the things he forbids." He then explains why Hindu philosophy advises fasting to discipline the body, and this, along with reciting the holy scriptures, would train the voice to do and say what is good. He compares this to what Pythagoras said: "How can you hope for detachment as long as you are clad in bodies?" He shows how Greek and Indian thinking were the same, as they both saw intelligence as 'the light the creator allows.'

In a final summation, he says that the Hindu believes "The Brahman is the upper root of the tree, its trunk is the Veda, and its branches are the different doctrines and schools." He tries to convey the subtlety of Indian thought when he says, "Patanjali says, 'as long as you can point to something, you are not a monist'" and concludes by saying, "Between man and God, there are a thousand shades of light and darkness."

The next chapter is on Sanskrit grammar, vyakarana, then about chanda, meter, and poetry. Next, he deals with Indian literature, the sciences, and especially astronomy and astrology. He deals at length with grammar and mathematics, especially the Hindu concepts in geometry. These form the major part of his work, but they are not the subjects that concern us. He also goes into details about social obligations and the rules of conduct that he culls out from Indian authorities. These include the rules for Brahmins, their rites and customs, as well as the customs of the other castes, sacrifices and pilgrimages, and the rules of charity and almsgiving. Additionally, he discusses the food that is forbidden and permitted, the role of women and their periods of uncleanness, law suits, punishments and expiations, inheritance, death, and the ceremonies associated with death, fasting and fast days, and festivals. In fact, he leaves out nothing important.

Alberuni's account of India and his survey of the knowledge of Indians and their customs are both exhaustive and, by and large, accurate. It also shows that the concerns of the outsider have remained the same almost through the ages: astonishment and genuine admiration of the knowledge and attitude of the ancient Indians and the acuteness of their perception. There is also great admiration for the level of knowledge of the Vedic people, which even Alberuni accepts was equal to, if not greater than, that of the Greeks. Then comes the dismay at what they have become—the descent into idolatry, from an open and questioning religion to a religion with its thousands of gods—a plethora of gods in place of monism, which was the norm. The greatness of their philosophy had descended to chanting rote things they did not understand. Then the dismay at the continuing arrogance of a people whose time had passed by without even realizing how low they had become but still holding on to their outdated knowledge as though others would steal it if they only slackened their guard.

The Impact of Islam

It is easy to forget that large parts of India were under Muslim rule for more than half of recorded history. In fact, history was first written by the Muslims. That India still remains so predominantly a Hindu nation indicates the depth of the Indian heritage, even though it is difficult to pinpoint where it exists among the poor and lower castes in India. One is, therefore, more inclined to say that India remained a Hindu nation because the Muslims did not try hard enough. The strict caste system that the Turks and Afghan invaders insisted on installing in India indicates the disdain—in fact, aversion—with which they dealt with the lower classes of Muslims in India. Perhaps they did not want to further soil their hands and hearts with more low-class converts and left it to the wandering Fakirs and Sufi saints to deal with them as best as they could, happy that someone else was dealing with their religious duty. They might have been happy to get more high-caste converts but with them they failed miserably, for to the educated Indian, no religion offered more than what could be found in the numerous philosophical traditions of India.

Abraham Eraly, in his book 'The Age of Wrath,' quotes John Marshall as saying, "Seldom in the history of mankind have two vast civilizations confronted each other as it happened when the Muslims invaded India. The very contrasts between them and the wide divergence in their cultures make their impact peculiarly instructive." Yet nothing happened, as 'they co-existed but did not react.' This, Eraly suggests, was because India was, by then, 'culturally quite barren.' There was no bold or deep reaction to the intellectual domination of Muslims, mainly because the institutions of higher learning in India were by then in decay. The Buddhists had more or less been driven out and Jain centers were weak and feeble at best. With the death of Buddhism, the fervor of persecution and the threatening presence of an enemy that needed to be defeated had been taken away, leading to complaisance, resulting in the decay of Hindu centers of learning with only Varanasi remaining, where the emphasis was only on rote learning. The initial wonder and genuine admiration of the

Muslim intellectuals for Hindu learning represented by people like Alberuni soon gave way to benign contempt. Thus, after the initial efforts, the next wave of interest was only in the reign of Firuz Shah Tugluq (1332), who acquired 1300 books of Indian texts and asked his translation bureau to translate them. The only other show of interest was in Akbar's court, where a gigantic effort was made to translate and study the important Indian texts like the Mahabharata, the Ramayana, and the Yoga Vasistha. Individual interest, as in the case of Dara Sukkoth, saw the translation of the Upanishads during the reign of Jahangir. While there were exceptional individuals like Dara and Amir Khusrou who showed interest in India's Hindu past, the rest of the Muslim intelligentsia soon forgot about them, almost as things that did not exist.

Muslim rule, with its concentration of power in their capital cities, led to a great thrust towards urbanization. In building new cities, they taught us to plan and to build on a large scale. Urbanization also meant the dissipation of education and culture among a much larger group of people. Thus, while Hindu culture, which was available only to the elite, created only an elite culture with its unique manners and rules of civilized behavior, the Muslims changed all that. By bringing in a culture rooted in the ancient civilizations of Egypt, Persia, Turkey, and Syria, they introduced a template for civilized behavior. Urbanization meant that such behavior had to be copied by even the lower classes. In time, Indian civilized behavior became what the Muslims taught us through their behavior and priorities. That is perhaps their greatest contribution to the Indian consciousness.

They introduced their architecture, painting, and crafts and changed our ideas of aesthetics. While Islamic architecture and art have been copied in all aspects of Indian life, we still tend to claim that we had our own greater art and talk of the Gandhari school of art and the Indo-Grecian and other schools, but the fact remains that our art today is largely Islamic. Yet, there is one area where their contribution is undisputed: the tradition of Hindustani music. In fact, so as not to acknowledge the debt, we claim it as our own creation, which is true to some extent, that it was born and had evolved in India. Another area is poetry, especially lyric and religious poetry. The ghazal and the qawwali we now assume to be Indian, and that is the extent of the Muslim contribution to our artistic life. The great betrayal, as far as any sympathizer of Islam is concerned, would be the fact that Islam in India, due to the arrogance of its rulers and the superiority complex of its upper classes, resulted in their losing sight of the cardinal principle of Islam, the brotherhood of man. Instead of accepting the rightness of the Prophet, they allowed their prejudices and their natural aversion to the dirt and squalor of the Indian poor to blind them to the great need for social reform, the care of the poor, and the general welfare of the people. Unlike the British after them, even though they came as invaders, they stayed on as Indians, with a stake in the future of the country. Their shortsightedness is, therefore, baffling, as nothing spectacular was demanded, only the application of a basic Islamic command, the brotherhood of men.

CHAPTER 14

REFORMATION IN THE BRITISH ERA

The next stage of religious and social reform had to wait for the impact of British rule to scare the conscience of the Indian psyche. Yet, it is difficult to say that Hinduism's reaction to Islam has exhausted itself. In fact, the problem was that too many unresolved issues were still sticking to the throat, neither assimilated nor disgorged. In some sense, the withdrawal inwards should have intensified with British rule—a more totally alien rule and culture. Yet what it did was the reverse. It was perhaps the result of English education and all other forms of education in general that resulted, not in a withdrawal but a sudden appearance of confidence. Indians were forced to examine themselves as a society and to relook at their religious beliefs. British curiosity in wanting to understand Indian culture and religion led to a great deal of effort in systematizing Indian languages, which, in the process, led to groups of scholars delving into their own languages and starting a process of self-education. At the other end, the literate Indian was being asked to explain his religion and social customs to English aliens. This resulted in a certain level of introspection and the placing of the sacred texts under the scrutiny of a class of people not exposed to them earlier. A combination of these factors led to a form of renaissance, a rediscovery of their ancient roots, and a questioning of their beliefs. The result was what is now called the 'Bengal Renaissance.' In some ways, it was also a culmination of the Bhakti movement in the North, which started with the Bhakti of Ramakrishna and meandered through the reformist movements of Raja Ram Mohan Roy, the Brahmo Samaj, Arya Samaj, and the independence movement.

The Bengal Renaissance

When delving into the Bengal Renaissance, we must consider various indologists, starting with Warren Hastings himself and individuals like Nathaniel Halhed (1751–1830), the linguist. Charles Wilkins, who translated the Bhagavad Gita, and William James (1746–1794), the great indologist responsible for the creation of the Asiatic Society, also played crucial roles. Other illustrious figures include Henry Thomas Colebrooke, a Sanskrit scholar and interpreter of the Vedantas, among many others, who sparked an interest in Indian studies and fueled the minds of young Bengalis during the Bengal Renaissance. Additionally, notable institutions like La Martiniere (established in 1836), St. Xavier's (established in 1835), Hindu College (founded in 1817 and later becoming Presidency College), and Bethune College for Women (established in 1849) contributed to the educational landscape.

Before these institutions, missionaries such as William Carey (1761–1834), who founded the Baptist Mission in Serampore, made significant contributions. Carey, who mastered Bengali and translated the Bible into the language, preceded Warren Hastings' gathering of Indian pundits and oriental scholars at Fort William. Pundits like Tarinicharan Mishra (1772-1838), Ramram Basu (1751-1813), and Mrtyunjay Vidyalankar (1762-1819) taught individuals like Carey to read Sanskrit. The Serampore mission also introduced the printing press on a significant scale. Alongside the mission, Sanskrit pundits, and the printing press, dedicated Indologists like Halhed elevated Bengali, previously considered barbaric by Muslim rulers, to a language of respect. This transformation brought many newly educated individuals into the fold of education and facilitated participation in discussions on philosophy and religion. The contribution of these indologists was so profound that some claim Carey was the first Bengali prose writer, and he indeed holds the distinction of being the first to translate the Ramayana into Bengali.

Charismatic Teachers

The Bengal Renaissance owes much of its success to the presence of dedicated and charismatic teachers in schools and colleges. Individuals such as Henry Derozio (1809–1831) at Hindu College, David Drummond at Dharamshala College, and David Hare played pivotal roles.

Henry Derozio, an Eurasian with deep roots in his Indian heritage, emerged as one of the first and greatest Indian poets to write in English. His poignant poems, such as 'The Harp of India,' lament the loss of the Indian literary tradition.

"The music once was sweet, who hears it now?
Neglected, mute and desolate thou art,
Like ruined monuments in a desert plain."

And in, 'To India my native land,' he bemoans the loss of its faith,

"My country, in the day of glory past,
A glorious halo circled around thy brow,
And worshiped as a deity thou wast.
Where is the glory, where is the reverence now?"

His best was when he cries for the departed glories of his country,

"And growling in the lowly dust thou art,
Thy minstrel hath no wreath to weave for thee,
Save the sad story of thy misery."

While he was perpetually endeavoring to rediscover the past glories of his beloved country, he was also an unapologetic rationalist, and Drummond was an even more fervent advocate of rationality. In his book, 'Objections to Phrenology,' he wrote, "He who will not reason is a bigot, he who cannot is a fool, and he who will not is a coward." Yet, when Derozio began questioning Hindu orthodoxy, he lost his job at Hindu College, with orthodox Hindus voting against him. However, at his death, one of his former students had this to say: "He used to impress upon us the sacred duty of thinking for ourselves—to live and die for the truth." Such teachings by dedicated and inspirational teachers were what created the ethos in which a Renaissance was possible.

Raja Ram Mohan Roy (1772-1833)

Among the Indians, the foremost names are the Tagores of Jorasanko, Dwarakanath, and Rabindranath, and then we have the great poet, Madu Sudan Datta. Yet in some way, the turning point was the arrival on the scene of Raja Ram Mohan Roy, a Brahmin and a Persian scholar, more at home in the world of Islamic literature and culture. However, Raja Ram Mohan Roy started like the rest of the debauched aristocracy, as a money lender with many wives and with a leaning towards Islamic studies and Persian verse.

Raja Ram Mohan Roy was born in the Bengal Presidency on May 22, 1772. His father was a Brahmin who followed the Vaishnavite tradition, while his mother was from a Shivite family. This itself was very unusual and a departure from the normal custom. This must have been the mole, as it were, that entered into the traditional Indian home and created the wedge that split open the entire Hindu traditional edifice. From an early age, it was recognized that Raja Ram Mohan Roy was intended for a life of speculation, the life of a scholar. He started his education in his village, learning Bengali and Sanskrit, and then is supposed to have gone to a madrasa in Patna to study Persian and Arabic, the official languages of the Mughal empire. His final stage of education was in Varanasi, where he studied the Vedas, Upanishads, and all other sacred Hindu texts. He was not meant to be a compliant student but a revolutionary and a reformer, and his first debates were with his father on the absurdity of idol worship.

He then turned to Buddhism, which took him all the way to Tibet. On his return, he took up a job as a teacher of the Vedantas, stressing the monism of God, almost in the vein of Sankaracharya. He also became a writer, and his first work in Arabic was 'A Gift of Monotheism.' His great work in Bengali was 'Vedanta Grantha' in 1815. His first work in English was 'Abridgment of the Vedant.' Between 1815 and 1819, he translated many Upanishads into Bengali. While remaining a pundit, he also took up a job with the

East India Company. It was through his association with the East India Company that he came into contact with William Carey, who had come to India as a missionary to convert Indians to Christianity.

Ram Mohan, however, used his contacts with Carey to learn and master the English language. In trying to understand Hinduism, Carey had befriended a Tantric Pundit by the name of Hariharandra Vidyabagish, and they soon became a triumvirate, trying to create new approaches to the understanding of Hinduism. The result was, on Carey's side, to claim that God was one and that Christ was the Brahman that the Hindus worshiped. Carey, whatever his religion, had a profound impact on Ram Mohan, and there was a time when it appeared that he would convert to Christianity. If he had done so, he would not have been the first, as, in fact, a large number of the young Bengalis, fired by the spirit of Derozio and Drummond, had converted to Christianity. The great poet Madhu Sudan Datta had converted and was called Michael, and of his conversion, he wrote:

"Long sunk in superstition's night
By sin and Satan driven
I saw not, cared not for light
That leads the blind to heaven."

While he did not convert, Raja Ram Mohan Roy became a fierce critic of orthodox Hinduism. He attacked the practice of Sati and fought for the remarriage of widows. At this time, he also formed the Amitya Sabba to debate Hindu philosophy. This made him clearly an apostate in the eyes of orthodox Hindus. His involvement in such heresy estranged him from his family, and there was even a plea to debar him from acting as a Zamindar, to which he was born. In the end, he also turned against his English mentor and denounced Christianity, especially what he saw as the absurdity of the concept of the Trinity. Having antagonized both the orthodox Hindus and the Christians and with nowhere to go, he created his own religious society called 'The Brahmo Samaj.' The Samaj worshiped not a particular God but a universal principle and also introduced the Christian idea of congregational worship. Yet, it was never smooth sailing, and Raja Ram Mohan Roy finally left for

England, where he passed away in 1833.

Brahmo Samaj

The Brahmo Samaj was essentially a reform movement within Hinduism that took as its basic belief the monism of God as Brahma. However, they refused to accept the authority of any sacred texts, including the Vedas, and refuted the concept of avatars, strongly opposing idol worship. It was also a social and reformist organization that vehemently opposed the practice of Sati and advocated for the remarriage of widows. Additionally, it was strongly opposed to the caste system. It was formed on August 20, 1828, by Raja Ram Mohan Roy and Debendranath Tagore to reform the Brahmanical traditions of the Hindu community. When Raja Ram Mohan Roy left for England in 1830, the leadership passed on to Dwarkanath Tagore and Raja Chandra Vidyasagar. Thereafter, the Samaj had a checkered history, with Keshub Chandra Sen introducing many changes to make it more like Christianity.

The Legacy

To a large extent, it is to Raja Ram Mohan Roy that we owe the spread of English education. Warren Hastings and his pundits, enamored with Sanskrit and other Indian languages, wanted to reverse the earlier decision to introduce English education, claiming that Indians would be best educated in their own languages. Raja Ram Mohan Roy saw through this as both an attempt to deny Indians the benefits of Western education and an effort to put education in the hands of Indian pundits who would drag everyone back to the Middle Ages. It is also to Raja Ram Mohan Roy that we owe the penetration of the utilitarian economic philosophy of the greatest benefit to the largest number. He was also the first to realize that the economic policy that the East India Company was following was draining India of its valuable assets for the benefit of England. To him, we also owe the establishment of Hindu College in 1815, along with David Hare. He also founded the Anglo-Indian School in 1822. We regularly talk about Hinduism as a religion, but it was Raja Ram Mohan Roy who first coined the term 'Hinduism.' His greater legacy was his attempt to drag the country out of its medieval mindset, to do away with some of the horrible aspects of Indian social customs, and to rationalize the Hindu religion. While some reformation did take place, almost in spite of itself, his attempts at meddling with Hinduism resulted in an immediate backlash in the form of the Arya Samaj, a return to the Vedas.

Other Voices

Ishwar Chandra Vidyasagar (1820–1891) was a product of Sanskrit College and was born Ishwar Chandra Bandopathya, but was later commonly called Vidyasagar, an ocean of knowledge. He was, in a sense, the first great polymath of modern India. He was also the first great Bengali prose writer to introduce prose writing to Bengali literature. Like Raja Ram Mohan Roy, he too was taken up by the need for social reform. He saw the plight of young widows who had nowhere to go and were forced into prostitution, and he made the remarriage of widows one of his reform goals. While many men, including figures like Keshub Chandra Sen, illuminated the Bengali literary landscape, it was the emergence of women from the hidden rooms of orthodox India that marked one of the great transformations of the Bengali renaissance.

A young woman begins the story of her life by saying, "A young girl wakes up one morning all decked in her bridal finery, in a boat taking her to an alien land, that of her in-laws." That young woman was Rassundari (1810–?), whose attempt to tell her own story opened the door to the possibility of the emancipation of women. This was possible because John Elliot Drinkwater had started a school for women in 1849 called 'Hindu Balika Vidyalaya.' Annette Arkroyd and Mary Carpenter then started the 'Banga Mahila Vidyalya,' the Bengali Women's College. These institutions made possible the writings of the great female poet Taro Dutt (1856–1877), the sister of Madhusudan, who was also the first woman novelist to write in English. She had a brief life but, in a short time, became a linguist, having learned Bengali, French, English, and later Sanskrit. She wrote novels in both French and English. She is famous for her poem 'The Casuarina Tree,' which looks back nostalgically at her childhood, and after her death, they found the manuscript of 'Ancient Indian Ballads,' the result of her later attempts to master Sanskrit and the resultant knowledge she gained.

The Bengal renaissance was a multifaceted revolution that, in many ways, produced the best that India is capable of, and it also released the natural sense of justice in all human beings against the brutal practices of intolerant Hinduism, vestiges of a tradition that was badly in need of change. That this sense of liberation and virtuous hope died so soon is the tragedy of this great awakening.

Ramakrishna Paramahamsa (1836-1886)

Ramakrishna Paramahamsa represents all the complexity and contradictions of the Hindu religion as understood and practiced. He came to the religious scene after the end of the Bhakti movement but was clearly moved by the general fervor and emotions behind the movement. He was born to poor Brahmin parents but in life he was taught the need to encompass all castes and all faiths. He seemed to have been epileptic all his life and had many episodes of seizures. However, he never admitted that he was epileptic or that his religious visions were caused by epileptic seizures. He maintained that his unusual behavior was the result of divine visions. He also had clear psychological problems that were exhibited in his ambivalence toward the nature of his sexuality. He admitted to being attracted to feminine clothes and, on many occasions, dressed in female clothes. He also admitted to being attracted to the idea of being a woman. While he was essentially a devotee of Goddess Kali, he was also, in many phases, a devotee of Lord Ram, Lord Krishna, and Lord Shiva, all of whom he worshiped in the way a woman would approach her lover. In fact, Ramakrishna was in his youth and early manhood so obviously unbalanced that his parents and brother sought help and, in the end, decided to get him married, hoping to ground him to the realities of human life. They chose a five-year-old bride, and happily for Ramakrishna, by the time she was fourteen, he had already become a sanyasi, and so the marriage remained unconsummated.

His religious journey was also like a tempestuous tour through all the known religious systems of Hinduism. For such a great journey, he did not have much of a formal education; he did not have much faith either and he dismissed most religiosity as mere money-making. Even his knowledge of the sacred texts, he admitted, he got only from listening to wandering monks. Yet, his future greatness was supposed to have been foretold even before his birth, with both his father and mother claiming to have had visions. His entry into religious life was, however, the result of his brother, who became the priest in a Dakshineswar temple built on the contribution of a rich woman, Rani Rashmoni. When his brother died in 1856, he was forced to take over the functions of the presiding priest. He thus started as a devotee of Goddess Kali, whom he worshiped as the divine mother. He saw in being a woman the conquest of sexuality that would otherwise corrupt the worship of the mother. Yet he was also aware of his ignorance of the deeper religious philosophies and started to seek a teacher to teach him Vedanta, Vaishnavism, and even Tantra. Despite all his later studies, he remained a devotee of the Bhakti mode of worship.

Ramakrishna's Religious Journey

The remarkable thing about Ramakrishna was that he was not rooted in any particular tradition, nor did he allow any Guru to force him into any dogmatic belief. Instead, he experimented and immersed himself in all forms of beliefs and practices to find out for himself what was the best. He started as a Bhakti devotee and took Ram as his personal God, whom he worshiped in the way of the devotion that Hanuman had for Lord Ram. In 1861, he took tutelage under a female sannyasin who introduced him to the worship of Ram and the Vaishnava pantheon of gods, as well as to the practice of Tantra.

Ramakrishna's initiation into Tantra practices was a very important phase in his religious development and spiritual journey, especially because, by nature, Ramakrishna was not a tantric. However, he was forced to realize that in this world, the knowledge of the high and the low, the spiritual and the carnal, were all parts of the total reality. To forgo any would be to be perpetually crippled. He was led mainly through the worship of Kali as Shakti and went through the major Tantric practices, which also involved what was called 'the left-hand practices'—things that are normally considered bad and included drinking, meat eating, and sex. Apologists, however, insist that Ramakrishna did not actually indulge in those practices but only understood the nature of the practices. These Tantric practices, however, clearly left a lasting impression on him, and he advised his disciples not to take up such practices unless fully prepared spiritually.

In 1865, he took his vows, as it were, to become a sannyasi. It was then that he was introduced to 'Vatsalya Bhava,' the worship of the mother Goddess, and then to 'Madura Bhava,' which was an imitation of the worship of the Gopis for Lord Krishna. During this phase, he worshiped Lord Krishna as a woman and as a lover, in total submission, like a bride to her beloved. He claimed that at the end of his worship, he felt, in a vision, Lord Krishna actually entering his body, uniting him with the Lord. It was only after this phase that Ramakrishna began to delve deeply into the sacred texts, especially the Advaita Vedanta, for which he had a teacher called Totapuri. He accepted the Advaita philosophy, which believed that all that we see is only the manifestation of Brahma and that there was no intrinsic reality—all was Maya.

While his devotion, learning, and meditations set him on the path of oneness with Brahman, he was called back, he claims, by Goddess Kali to be a teacher to humanity. The next stage of his spiritual journey involved the study of other religions, starting with Islam. He got immersed in the Sufi form of worship until he claimed he had a vision of the prophet merging with him in a union. He was so immersed in Islam at this stage that he claimed all Hindu religious practices had been erased from his consciousness. From 1873 onwards, he then took up the study of Christianity and was led to read the Bible by Kesheb Chandra Sen. In the end, he accepted the worship of the Madonna as a mother after seeing a vision of the mother merging with him.

The Gospel of Ramakrishna

At the end of such a journey, the message that he preached was one of universal peace and love for all. It was one of his disciples, Mahendranath Gupta, who put together the teachings of Ramakrishna in book form, as 'Sri Ramakrishna Kathamrita,' which was translated by another disciple, Swami Nikhilananda, as 'The Gospel of Sri Ramakrishna.' As a teacher, Ramakrishna was a talker who told stories in his rustic Bengali, explaining the Vedas, the Puranas, and the Tantras in a manner to attract the least educated. He preached the realization of the divine as the goal of human life. However, at the center of his teaching was the belief in what he called 'Kamini Kanchan,' literally translated as 'woman and gold,' as the greatest hurdles to the realization of God. His apologists have tried to claim that it was not an anti-feminist ideology in any way and that he was only trying to convey that the lust of the flesh and the greed for material wealth were at the heart of human decadence and are the greatest hurdles to the realization of the divine.

At another level, Ramakrishna's ideas on psychology predate both Freud and Jung when he talks about the universal consciousness from which human beings can tap for knowledge. He also saw subject-object duality as only the apparent difference between things; as in the case of milk and the whiteness of milk, one cannot exist without the other. The personal and the impersonal are also thus inextricably linked in a dance that creates what we know as life. While all life is only a manifestation and therefore essentially a form of Maya, to Ramakrishna, there were, however, two forms of Maya: the dark Maya that causes delusions and attracts the soul to evil, sexual excesses, and selfish desires, and the good Maya, which leads to selflessness, purity, love, and the path of enlightenment. The cornerstone of his philosophy was 'Jatra jiv tatra shiv,' meaning wherever there is life, there is Shiva, and therefore all life is sacred, and kindness and reverence are due to all life.

Legacy and Impact

The importance of Ramakrishna in the study of Hindu consciousness lies in the pivotal role he played in its creation. He happened to be in the right place at the right time and was born when the Bengali Renaissance was beginning to flourish. His association with Keshub Chandra Sen led to his being identified as the guru of the Brahmo Samaj and the source of their philosophy. He was also a friend of Tagore's father, Debendranath Tagore, and Ishwar Chandra Vidyasagar, the social reformer. Thus, he is also seen as the face of social reform, but his greatest legacy was his successor, Vivekananda. Vivekananda may not have fully agreed with all that Ramakrishna stood for, but as his successor and propagator of Hinduism to the rest of the world, he became the face of Hinduism. What he spoke of became the intellectual base of the new Hinduism that harmonized Tantra, Yoga, and Advaita Vedanta and presented it to the rest of the world as a homogeneous and unified religious belief. For good or ill, it was the direction that Hinduism took and became frozen into in the 20th century, refusing to accept dissent or compromise. Yet, because of the mixing of incompatibles, no one now knows what it all means. If earlier man worshiped as he believed, today all worship in the same way without any idea as to beliefs, except the conviction that what one does is what a good Hindu must do.

Reformation outside Bengal

The sense of betrayal that the Bengal Renaissance evokes is because it promised so much and then fizzled out almost without a trace. What started as a bright light in the late 18th century and burned brightly in the early years of the 19th century became a dim light in the dark by the end of the 19th century. The story of the Bengal Renaissance illustrates what happens to all attempts to reform Hinduism and all efforts at social justice at the cost of the caste system. The power of Hindu orthodoxy merely returns with even greater force to crush all opposition. In the case of the Bengal Renaissance, it was also the result of the British distancing themselves from all reformist and revolutionary movements and preferring peace with the Hindu hardliners over justice, as they slowly took the attitude that the issues of Indian society are best left to Indians. The consequent result was that, despite the proliferation of British education in Madras and Bombay later, all revolutionary ideas were successfully nipped in the bud.

The Arya Samaj

The Arya Samaj was a development that took place outside Bengal but must have been a reaction to the formation of the Brahmo Samaj. The credit for the creation of the Arya Samaj is usually given to Dayananda Saraswati (1824–1833) in 1860 in Gujarat. The movement was clearly a reaction to the forsaking of the Vedas by the Brahmo Samaj, and thus one of the most important tenets of the Arya Samaj was a return to the sanctity of the Vedas and its absolute primacy. It was not really a reactionary movement but was like all earlier reform movements, against idolatry, animal sacrifices, child marriage, and caste discrimination, for the equality of the sexes, and against all superstitions, especially astrology. It was, in fact, a movement that returned to the skepticism inherent in the Vedas. It preached the brotherhood of men, and like the Bhakti saints, it advocated devotion to God. It was a return to justice, as in the concept of Dharma. It taught respect for all life and saw in the human body the temple of God, preaching that one's service to society is to be held in greater esteem than the mere pursuit of Moksha. While it had an element of a reaction to the strident and revolutionary ideas of the Brahmo Samaj, idealizing Christianity, it could not escape the flavor of the times that were truly revolutionary and reformist.

Swami Vivekananda (1863-1902)

Vivekananda is the face of modern Hinduism. Having spoken at the World Conference of Religions in Chicago in 1893, he also became the face of Hinduism in the western world. To a large extent, it was the Indologists who rediscovered India's ancient religious texts and ignited an interest in these texts that led to an awareness of the Vedas and the Vedantas outside the narrow confines of priests and Sanskrit scholars. However, it was Vivekananda who made it known to the greater world outside India. Yet he was only part of the greater tradition of the Bhakti movement in Bengal, as he was the heir of Ramakrishna and his religious organization. As in the case of all Bhakti movements, he was also part of the reform movement within Hinduism that was acutely aware of the urgent need for large-scale social reforms.

Life and Times

He was born as Narendra Dutta, in Calcutta on January 12, 1863. His parents were Bengali Kayasthas with a long tradition of learning. Even his grandfather was a Persian and Sanskrit scholar who renounced family life to become a Sannyasi. His father, however, was a lawyer rooted in rationality and the here and now, while his mother was a Bhakti devotee who reveled in spirituality and mysticism. Narendra thus had two sides to his character: a rational and logical philosophical side and a mystical, transcendent side. In 1871, he joined the Iswar Chandra Vidyasagar school and then went on to study at the Presidency College (Hindu College). Both of these institutions must have instilled in him a certain degree of radicalism. In college, he studied Western philosophy and logic while pursuing his interests in Indian philosophy, the Vedas, Vedantas, and the Epics and the Puranas. He was also quite taken in by Mill's utilitarianism, like many in the Brahmo Samaj. At this time, he was especially drawn to Herbert Spencer's ideas of evolution, and he even translated Spencer's book, 'Education' into Bengali. Even in college, he had already gained a reputation for being a genius and a polymath.

In 1880, Narendra joined Keshub Chandra Sen's Nava Vidhan, an institution started by Sen after he came into contact with Ramakrishna and had reconverted to Hinduism from Christianity. At this time, Narendra was also drawn to the theology of the Brahmo Samaj, which he joined in 1881 and remained with until 1884. His religious beliefs at this time were in tune with those of the Brahmo Samaj, and he believed in the Monism of God and was against all forms of idol worship. However, it appears that his thirst for knowledge and conviction were not satisfied by these theories.

He needed to experience God personally. He thus kept asking people if they knew God personally. Even Debendranath Tagore, who had taken over the leadership of the Brahmo Samaj, would only say that he was a true yogi and had a yogi's eyes. It was Ramakrishna who finally told him that he had actually experienced God personally.

Meeting Ramakrishna was the turning point in his life because, until then, he was more of a rationalist follower of the Brahmo Samaj school of thought. Yet, it took Narendra time to commit himself to the discipleship of Ramakrishna. As a fellow Brahmo Samaji, he opposed all idol worship and all forms of polytheism and thus found Ramakrishna's devotion to Goddess Kali difficult to accept. Narendra also found it difficult to accept Sankara's idea that Brahman and the souls of men are one; such a radical Monism did not appear true to him. In 1884, his father died, leaving the family in poverty. The only solace that Narendra found was in Ramakrishna's ashram. When he requested that Ramakrishna pray to Goddess Kali to ease his family situation, Ramakrishna advised him to do so himself. The plight of the family being grave, he went to the Kali temple, but despite three visits, he was unable to pray and ask merely for material comforts. He was finally able to pray when he settled for knowledge, for which he was able to pray. In the process, he grew closer and closer to Ramakrishna.

He had first met Ramakrishna in 1881 and was initially quite skeptical about Ramakrishna's mystical visions; however, as they grew closer, the saint's unstinting love made them closer day by day. By 1885, Ramakrishna had become very sick, and in his most vulnerable state, he requested that Narendra be a guide and leader to his disciples. Then he also asked his disciples to also treat him as their leader, clearly passing his mantle to Vivekananda. When Ramakrishna died in 1886, Vivekananda, along with Ramakrishna's disciples, formed the Ramakrishna monastic order. In the same year, he decided to take monastic vows and became Vivekananda. After that, he traveled all over India and also to many parts of the world. He visited the U.S. and U.K., then Japan, Canada, and many other countries. His final triumph was to address the World Congress of Religions in Chicago in 1893. A large number of westerners were attracted to him personally and to the philosophy he preached. As he traveled, he carried only two books with him: the. 'Bhagavad Gita' and 'The Imitation of Christ,' which he had himself translated in 1889. As he traveled, he visited all the great centers of learning to absorb and assimilate their teachings. He made no distinction between people of different faiths and was happy to eat with untouchables. He finally settled on Belur Math. Towards the end, he was plagued by many illnesses and finally passed away on July 4, 1904.

His Philosophy

While Vivekananda proclaimed that Sankaracharya's concept of Advaita was the essence of Hinduism, he was actually closer to Ramanuja's position of 'qualified dualism,' which was what Ramakrishna also believed. He saw God as both transcendent and immanent, not merely a concept about which Sankara proclaims as 'Nirguna,' but as a daily presence in human life. Like Ramanuja, he also claimed that all human souls have divine potential. While he claimed no original philosophy, what sets him apart is that he was present when India was coming to terms with its own slavery and was wanting to break free of its foreign yoke. Vivekananda could not help but be moved by the nationalistic fervor in the air. He wanted nationalism to be a movement that would purge the nation of its own darkness and come out on the side of purity and truth. He stressed the importance of education and the need for all Indians to be beneficiaries of the noblest and best education.

The importance of Vivekananda is that he is the face of modern India and modern Hinduism. Hinduism, not of the new Vedanta that he preached but as an interpreter of India's intellectual and cultural heritage, included yoga and transcendental meditation. Yet, like all reformers, what he wanted most was to draw attention to the widespread poverty, dirt, and illiteracy in the country. Yet Gandhi said of him that 'he maintained the face of Hinduism in a state of splendor by cutting down the deadwood.' He was so much the face of modern Hinduism that Romain Rolland said that anyone who wants to know or understand India needs to only read the works of Vivekananda. He wrote an impassioned essay entitled 'Bartaman Bharat,' meaning today's India, where he emphasized the utmost importance of the brotherhood of men and the need to treat all Indians as brothers.

The proponents of Hinduism take shelter under the wings of Vivekananda by citing his call for reigniting the faith of people in their religion and in their cultural heritage. Seeing the sectarian trends in Hinduism, he also called for unity and a common base for Hindu religious beliefs. Yet, at the heart of what appears to be jingoism is the call to lift the country out of darkness and poverty and from the injustice of caste intolerance. His greatest emphasis was on the need for universal education. He said, "So long as millions live in hunger and ignorance, I hold every man a traitor who, having been educated at their expense, pays no heed to them." However, caste has remained, and education is still only a distant dream for too many Indians.

Narayana Guru (1856-1928)

Sri Narayana Guru is a curious case of a reformer who has since been almost deified by his own caste and was the only reformer to come out of Kerala. Despite the fact that Kerala was mythically famous as the land created by Parasurama and peopled with Brahmins selected by Parasurama himself, despite the fact that the core of Hindu intellectualism was started by Sankara, a child of Kerala, despite the fact that the people of Kerala were more literate than the people in the rest of the country, despite the fact that caste atrocities were almost at unbelievable levels in Kerala, and despite the presence of a sizable Christian and Muslim population that believed in love for all mankind, no other reformer, not even an orthodox religious leader, was to emerge out of Kerala. The tragedy of Narayana Guru was the terrible blandness of his reform and the fact that, in the end, it was neither religious nor social.

Narayana Guru was born most probably in 1856 to Ezhava (an Avarna caste) parents in Chempazhanthy, near Trivandrum. It appears that he had an elementary education, thanks to some Nair teachers, and it is said that he was immediately attracted to the philosophy of the Vedantas. In the process, he picked up Sanskrit and practiced Yoga. With these basic elements of education, he became a restless wanderer in search of enlightenment. In his search, he reached Aruvipuram, where later his disciples were to build a temple in open defiance of Brahmanical prohibition. He was then supposed to have lived the life of an ascetic. However, there is no indication that he ever received enlightenment.

Yet a phase of his life was over. After that, he worked as a teacher and became a self-proclaimed reformer. After this phase of active work, he decided to settle down in Sivagiri to take up Shadana or spiritual discipline. He was also supposed to have opened a school in Varkala where he taught Sanskrit and admitted students from all castes. In 1913, he founded the Advaita Ashram at Aluva, dedicating it to universal brotherhood. If Narayana Guru preached any religion, it was the brotherhood of all men and worship based on education, cleanliness, and devotion to God. He also encouraged the development of skills among craftsmen. In 1922, Rabindranath Tagore met him and declared that there was no greater spiritual leader than Narayana Guru.

The impact of Narayana Guru's mission was great; it propelled his people, the Ezhavas, into education, and they consequently became a powerful social and political force. Yet, the irony is that the Ezhavas, who were at the forefront of the temple entry satyagraha when they built their own temples, refused entry to those lower than them in the caste hierarchy, like the Puliahs and Pariahs. More ironic was the Guru's encouragement of Sanskrit studies and the study of Vedic and other orthodox texts, which were prohibited for the Avarna castes. In fact, the Guru made no attempt to reform the Hindu religion or its sacred texts but retained all its Brahmanical rituals and practices. What he thus achieved was the adoption of Brahmanical Hindu practices by his Avarna caste followers in temples that resembled the Brahmanical temples and, in open defiance of Brahmanical prohibition, continued to practice Hinduism, almost as a parody of the Brahmanical version. The Guru thus created caste Hindu traditions among his Avarna caste followers, in imitation of Brahmanical Hinduism. Yet, one unique legacy is owed to him: the Kerala villages are now dotted with temples, vibrant in color, and flowing with religious music, all belonging to the Ezhava caste, with no approval from the Brahmins.

Periyar (E.V. Ramaswamy) (1879-1973)

Periyar is perhaps the greatest social reformer that South India has produced. While on the surface, he appears to be a political failure and a forgotten social reformer, the changes he helped bring about, especially in Tamil Nadu, were so revolutionary that they have changed the very ethos of the state. In fact, the greatest aspect of his revolution was the silence and, in the end, the non-violent manner in which the epoch-making changes took place. With little resistance and almost no victory celebrations or fanfare, changes took place both socially and politically, so much so that if there is any failure in the complete revamping of society and of creating a more just society, it was not the lack of political power but a lack of political will and conviction. In some ways, Periyar and the movement he unleashed, which he called the self-respect movement, were the culmination of centuries of the Bhakti movement that slowly eroded the pillars of orthodoxy and made it possible to question, but more importantly, to demand change.

Life and Times

The man the world knows as Periyar was born in Erode, in Tamil Nadu, on September 17, 1879, to rich parents of the Naiker community, who named him Ramaswamy Naiker. His mother tongue was actually Kannada but he was to grow up speaking all the southern languages equally fluently. Because his father was rich, he had important gurus come to his house to espouse the intricacies of Vaishnavism, to which he belonged. This led him to question the veracity of much of the mythology that passed off as religious truths. In time, this led to the belief that religions were only a devious business to deceive the common people for the benefit of priests and temples. Yet, in 1904, he undertook a pilgrimage to Kasi, as Varanasi is called, and visited the Shiva Temple there, something like the holy of holies for Shaivism. What he saw there were only half-burnt bodies floating on the Ganges, dirt, and poverty. What really awakened his sense of injustice was that when he was very hungry and he saw that the temple authorities were giving free meals, he also stood in line only to be refused because he was not a Brahmin. Coming from a wealthy family, he had not been personally affected by the blatant abuse of caste discrimination before, but when he saw it and was personally affected, his attitude toward caste changed. At Kasi, the man who had listened to the sacred texts in the comfort of his home but had questioned them was still a believer in God but his experience turned him into an atheist, a position he was never to forsake in his life.

In 1917, he joined the Indian National Congress, fired by the nobility of the Gandhian movement and the propagation of Khadi, but mostly because he thought that the Congress was also for the eradication of the caste system. He went to jail a few times as part of the civil disobedience movement. At this time, he also came up with the idea of reservation in government jobs for the untouchables and lower castes, but his proposal was voted out by the upper caste lobby within the party. This led him to leave the party in 1925. He also participated in the Vaikom temple entry satyagraha and for his zealous participation, he was honored with the title of 'Vaikom Veeran.' All these injustices created in Periyar a burning zeal to create a more equal society. When his demands for social equality and justice fell on deaf ears, he started his own forum called 'The Self-Respect Movement.' The aim of the movement was to spread education, and it preached the brotherhood of men, the eradication of untouchability, and superstition. In 1937, when Rajaji, as chief minister of the Madras Province, tried to impose compulsory learning of Hindi in schools, Periyar found an ideal issue on which to unite all the Tamil people by creating the impression that it meant the death of the Dravidian culture and Tamil as a language.

Even while raising the fear of Hindi domination, the issue that Periyar continued to harp on was the dominance of Brahmins in all the affairs of the state. He linked Brahmanism to the imposition of Aryan language and values and to the essentially Dravidian culture of which Tamils were an important part. To create a united front in the fight against Brahmanism, he came up with the concept of equality for all non-Brahmins, a revolutionary idea considering the fact that the caste system survived by creating differences and a feeling of superiority among castes. To isolate Brahmins and fight all forms of Brahmanism, he created the 'South Indian Liberation Federation,' in 1916. With this shift towards anti-Hindi and all forms of Aryan domination, his party soon acquired a distinctly Dravidian flavor. In 1944, he renamed his party the 'Dravida Kazhagam.' This, however, led to a split in the party, with many of the old guards preferring to remain with the Justice Party, which was what his self-respect party was called when it became a political outfit. The new party stood for the negation of all Brahmanical institutions and Aryan cultural dominance, and a very important part of its aim was the abolition of caste, especially untouchability. The party was an immediate hit among the rural population and especially with students, for whom the imposition of Hindi was a very emotive issue.

With the increase in membership and support, different views came to the fore, the most important one being the need to become a political party with the aim of winning elections. Periyar, however, saw his main aim as social change, which he thought should be pursued with full-hearted vigor, and therefore thought that becoming a political party would invariably lead to compromises that would finally sideline the social agenda. One of his closest aides, Annadurai, disagreed and broke away to form the 'Dravida Munnetra Kazhagam,' in 1949. In fact, so convinced was Periyar about the diabolical hold of Brahmanical religion on social conditions that he took a procession to Marina Beach and burned the pictures of Hindu gods against the advice of many of his own associates. This led to his imprisonment and the alienation of a significant group of his supporters. What happened thereafter has been the content of Tamil Nadu's history for the next seventy years. Periyar lost support and the beneficiary was DMK, which came to power in a landslide victory in 1966. As anticipated, the social agenda got a backseat, and Periyar soon became a father figure for the party, respected but not listened to, until, in the end, he became just that senile old man.

Impact and Legacy

The impact of Periyar was to create awareness of the Dravidian roots of the South Indian people, along with pride in their glorious heritage. This united the bulk of the Tamilians behind the banner of the Dravidian movement, resulting in a landslide victory in the elections of 1966. Since then, one or another of the Dravidian parties, D.M.K. or A.I.D.M.K., has been ruling in Tamil Nadu. In the process, they transformed T.N. from an upper-class-dominated society to one run by the people. A silent revolution has taken place in the execution of power that was firmly held by the Brahmins and the upper castes, to one run almost entirely by the Avarna castes. The reservation that Periyar had fought for in government jobs has been implemented, not only for untouchables but also for all the Avarna castes, to the extent of 69%, in educational institutions and in government jobs. This was done as early as the late '60s, so when the Mandela Commission crisis hit North India, there was not a ripple in T.N. This led to a sea change in the power equation of power and power brokerage, which has shifted clearly in favor of the Avarna castes.

However, as Periyar feared, despite absolute power, the Dravidian parties had neither the political will nor the courage nor the philosophical conviction to push through the social reforms that they had originally stood for. Thus, in no time, the A.I.D.M.K. chief minister was an upper caste from Kerala, and the state was ruled by a Brahmin lady from Karnataka until her death. While Periyar demanded equality along with the questioning of the rationality of Brahmanical practices, a loosening of the Brahmanical power has only meant that the Avarna castes are now permitted in temples. What is ironic is that those who were denied entry into temples are the same ones who throng temples today, while the Brahmins are happy to stay at home. The worst is that caste violence continues unabated, especially in rural T.N., where scheduled castes continue to be the butt of violence, and the Avarna castes at the lowest level are the perpetrators. In fact, society has become so intolerant that writers have to fear personal violence for any negative portrayal of the continuing barbaric, tribal, and religious practices.

Mahatma Gandhi

There is no doubt that Mahatma Gandhi was the most important personality of 20th-century India, and there is a pervasive feeling that he means a great deal to Indians and Indian history. Yet, this may not be true. Gandhi was, in many senses, one of the most contradictory public figures of all time. The fact that, apart from his fads like satyagraha, non-violence, the propagation of the cottage industry, the spinning wheel, and so on, there is no Gandhism as such, with a consistent philosophy, is proof of his transitory importance. The mistake that most people make is to think that Gandhi was a great philosopher or religious thinker; he was neither. He was first and always a politician, and all that he said and did has to be understood only in the context in which he made them. The Ghanaian government has decided to remove a statue of Gandhi from their national university on the premise that they have finally understood him. Yet they are wrong. Gandhi was a politician who, over the span of his life, took up certain issues that were then close to his heart to fight for or against, and in the fight, all that mattered was victory, not the subtle nuances of philosophical detail. To understand him, one has to understand the philosophy of his favorite text, the Gita. Yet Gandhi was first and foremost a politician, then a public figure, and lastly a thinker of any kind, philosophical or religious. Yet, this is not to belittle the religiosity that permeated his being. He was religious most of the time in an unthinking way, enveloped as it were by his mother's religion and the religion of his society, which had become so much a part of his essential being. It also meant that he was rigid, prejudiced, and often terribly wrong. His greatness was his capacity to change and a willingness to reflect, at least after the rush of action had abated. However, this also meant that at each moment of his life, based on what he wanted to achieve, he was doing the right thing—that is, what was needed to succeed.

When he went to England, he almost starved himself to death because of the promise he made to his mother not to eat meat. Vegetarianism was for him a fetish, as he did not necessarily link it to Ahimsa, and therefore not part of his creed. Similarly, when he took up the cause of civil rights for his fellow Indians in South Africa, he was blind to the continued degradation of his own untouchable brothers and the plight of the Blacks, who in their own country were treated as animals with no rights whatsoever. When he finally agreed to mediate over the Vaikom temple entry agitation, he was floored by the logic of the Namboothiri priests at the temple, who asked him if he was a believer in the Vedas and the Shastras, to which he said yes, only to be asked to indicate where in those sacred texts it says that the Avarna castes can be permitted into temples. Thus, even when he later accepted that the totally inhuman treatment of untouchables was unwarranted, his main focus was only to abolish untouchability within Hinduism and not against the caste system in general. At each stage, there was a political battle to be won where collateral damage was acceptable. In South Africa, it was the rights of upper-caste Indians and Muslim merchants; later, it was the vote bank of Dalits. In fact, he refused to allow the Dalits to decide for themselves, claiming that he alone knew best what was good for them. How he assumed to usurp such rights and by what logic, he never said, except to claim a paternalistic interest in their welfare.

Satyagraha, bandhs, and hartals were clearly weapons against an occupying colonial power; used in a modern democracy, they only create huge national loss and public chaos. Yet, people justify it as Gandhian, not realizing that for Gandhi, it was only a useful tool at a time when he needed such tools but was never meant to denote a philosophical or ethically virtuous action. In fact, when he tried to think philosophically, as in his interpretation of the Gita, where Lord Krishna explains that action without hope of reward absolves one of Karmic taint, Gandhi made it into a debate on means and ends, claiming that the Gita does not justify the use of bad means to achieve good ends. He forgets that the crux of the Gita is that the need for action, good or bad, is a meaningless concept, as in the divine scheme of things there is no morality and even men, when they act for the sake of action alone with no regard for the consequences, are merely God's agents and exempt from the taint of Karma. Yet this realization was part of Gandhi's psyche; he acted in what he thought was for the good, with no idea of personal gain and therefore saw his actions as beyond good and evil.

The Mahatma in himself and in his life was a living analogy of what happens to Hinduism when it is forced to meet the western world, not on its terms but as an underdog. The response of Gandhi was to go into a shell, as he first reached England, and to think that in his strict vegetarianism he was somehow being true to his Hindu roots and beliefs. He refused to explore the philosophy, if there was any, that explained vegetarianism as something intrinsic to Hindu beliefs. Similarly, when he was forced to deal with Dalits, he continued to see them through his own tainted glasses of Varna and therefore failed to see the terrible injustice that was apparent to every Westerner. This also blinded him to the totally unjust treatment of the African blacks in their own country, always used to a differential treatment that he thought was inherent in all social activity. Only as a result of continued exposure was his thinking affected and only by an act of will was he able to overcome his natural aversions. Thus, he makes much of the fact that he cleaned toilets, proud that he had broken some sacred code of conduct—something every westerner does every day—as a matter of basic cleanliness. Thus was his submission to Brahmin pundits when it came to the interpretations of the Vedas and the Shastras, never once questioning the premises of Hindu ritualism or the theory of Karma.

The Hindu religion is so rooted in rituals devoid of any philosophical base that it is both difficult to defend and equally difficult to discard. Thus, when Gandhi discarded some rituals, he merely added new ones, like the spinning wheel. He realized that Hinduism was a religion of rituals, not of philosophy, and that it was a religion to be practiced, not a faith that was to change the thinking of men. The reluctance to let go is also something very Hindu. Thus, while he was persuaded by the theology of Christianity, he was also so proud of his heritage that he resisted his natural inclination to convert. Not only his own conversion, but he was aghast at the possibility that the Dalits, who were never even considered human by orthodox Hinduism, never allowed into temples, and never allowed any rituals, may consider conversion to any other religion.

He called them Harijans and refused to allow them to be converted. Not only that, he, in fact, maintained that he alone had a right to speak on their behalf, refusing to give them even an unfettered voice.

More importantly, despite all of Gandhi's international exposure, he refused to comment on the validity or logic of Hindu practices and Vedic rituals or the horrible practice of caste. Instead, he bends backward to say that the Gita does not justify the use of bad means to achieve good ends. He refuses to see that what the Gita really says is that morals are merely a human idea and that action is tainted only by desire. Once a man becomes God-like and is beyond the pull of desire, there are no morals, only the actions of an unthinking, uncaring, and impervious God. The problem is that too many people think they are gods.

CHAPTER 15

BRITISH INDIA

The British rule in India had something entirely transformative about it. The Muslim rulers accelerated the process of urbanization in India and were able to influence, to some extent, the history of urban life and manners. They were too disdainful of the villages to even go there, much less to stay, leaving even the tax collection to the Hindus. They had, at best, a benign contempt for all things Indian and Indians in general, and at worst, they persecuted the Hindus and all their institutions. Their mindset was that of the conqueror in possession of a much greater religion, so great that he was squeamish about spreading it among the lower classes of Indians. They were even reluctant to deal with the lower-class converts, who were invariably their servants and their menials. Thus, their impact on Indian society was, at best, marginal.

The British were a different breed. There was something about the Britisher, especially the Victorian Englishman, that was touched by a sense of perfection. As Kipling makes the character in 'The Man Who Would Be King' say when asked if he was a God, he replies, "No, but I am the next best thing, an Englishman." The British may have come as traders but stayed on as conquerors and then as saviors of the Indian people, taking on what has since been scornfully called 'the white man's burden' — the call to civilize a barbaric and heathen people. The conquerors turned into missionaries, even though the literal variety was also plentiful.

The Britishers came with their missionaries and the Indologists. They came not as conquerors but as transformers. Thus, while the Muslims stayed in the towns and cities, the ruling class of Englishmen worked as collectors and as police heads, right up to the district level and below. Where they were not required to go, the missionary went—from the mountains of Tibet to Land's End at Kanyakumari and to villages and tribal areas that few Indians had even heard about. They not only went but stayed on and mastered the local languages, systematized them, wrote dictionaries, and translated the Bible into those languages. They learned the local customs and the religion of the people and rebelled at the cruelty of child marriages and the practice of Sati in the name of religion. They were also horrified by the rigidity and cruelty of the caste system, leading to a consciousness about them and a slow revolt against such customs. So much so that it was the Indians themselves who took up cudgels against them. They spread education through the countless institutions they created and taught the need for compassion, along with the health and medical institutions they built. The Indologists dug, literally, and plowed through all the ancient texts they could lay their hands on to reveal the forgotten heritage and learning of ancient India, bringing to light a tradition only dimly remembered, even by the Brahmins, who chanted the verses by heart. India's past was exposed, and its traditions were brought out into the public's glare. With it, much that could not be justified in the light of later-day humanism was also exposed. This drove the orthodoxy into a shell, shimmering with hatred and waiting for the day of revenge.

British rule, unlike Muslim rule, was almost total. Where they did not rule, they coerced. They linked the entire country through a network of railway lines, creating for the first time, the possibility of a single nation called India. Yet, it was the common subjugation to British rule that created a sense of nationalism—the fraternity of the enslaved. This was fed by the nationalists and freedom fighters who represented, at least initially, only the rich and the educated but became a national movement through the genius of Mahatma Gandhi.

The Creation of British India

The challenge with any assessment of the impact of British rule in India is that it would force us to deal with exceptions rather than what they actually achieved. Modern India and Indians are so irretrievably entwined with what the British brought to India that it is difficult to approach them dispassionately. Educated Indians, by and large, still speak English, and all the institutions of power—from the Parliament and the Judiciary to the Executive—are clear creations of the British Raj and replicas of British models. The systems of trade, business, and even the banking system adopted by Indians are largely copies of those that the British initiated. The sports we play and the entertainment we watch are also largely acquired habits introduced by the British. In fact, there is hardly anything about India or Indians that is not at least partly influenced by the British.

Our national character has been shaped by consciously accepting or rejecting British models. Mahatma Gandhi, for instance, rejected British clothing and wore a Khadi loincloth, enduring even the British winter, but he spoke with his Gujarati accent. Nehru, on the other hand, wore a Sherwani, a garment neither Indian nor British, and spoke Queen's English with an Oxford accent. This rebellion against English influence has defined our response to it. For example, Chidambaram wears a dhoti and speaks with a clipped version of American English, while many Indians wear three-piece suits and speak like Lalu Prasad, with a pan mixed with saliva dripping down the corners of their mouth. We claim to support Kabaddi but watch only cricket, making the BCCI the richest cricket association in the world. In fact, the Indian sari and the North Indian salwar-kameez are the only traditional Indian dresses that have survived, possibly because Indian women were more restrained, as evident by the significant number of jean-clad women disembarking suburban trains at ChurchGate and V.T. stations.

The Indian character is thus schizophrenic, never sure whether to be Indian or Western, as we often fail to think deeply enough to recognize the intrinsic value of things and make rational decisions. Our decisions are emotional and complicated by an inherent sense of inferiority, resulting in anger and guilt. Indians dislike imitating the West but are invariably drawn to Western models, leaving them conflicted with both anger and guilt. Forced by poverty to live the life of an Indian peasant, one dreams of the day when their children will attend English-medium schools, and they themselves will wear trousers and terry-cotton shirts. While these are personal choices, the acceptance of British institutions of justice and the values attached to them is merely pragmatic. Indians accept them but may not truly believe in the values they represent. These institutions are seen as inevitable facets of modern life, sustained by power, which is what all Indians seek—the power to flaunt all the rules and be above all institutions.

The British Historical Perspective

All the problems of historical perspective are laid at the door of the British. It is claimed that they did not understand the ethos of the country, were arrogant and presumptuous, and created history to justify themselves, distorting it in the process. Perhaps the most important piece of writing dealing with the entire problem of what colonial historians have done is by the historian and social scientist Edward Said. He was perhaps not the first to call the colonial historians 'Orientalist,' but he certainly made it a byword of scorn, at least in the Middle East and India. Therefore, to both understand and deal with the issue, the best way would be to look critically at the contents of the book 'Orientalism.'

Orientalism: A Critical Look

'Orientalism' by Edward Said, said to be the definitive work on the subject, is a challenging read. It is not because it propounds difficult ideas or uses intricate words; yet, it is often beyond comprehension. There is nothing inherently wrong with the language; in fact, taken sentence by sentence, it appears like a well-written treatise. However, taken as a whole paragraph or page, it almost makes no sense. The problem is that Edward Said seems confused. He does not write with any accepted or stated premises but jumps to make logical and critical conclusions. Perhaps, by the very nature of the subject, such an attempt from the first premises would have been difficult, if not impossible, as he is trying to create the ground rules while criticizing the contents of his study. Consequently, there is no flow in the narrative and no logical collection of facts to support a thesis. Instead, the premises, facts, and narrative are so mixed together into a blob of paragraphs that the result is an incomprehensible mix of all these elements. Yet, it must be admitted that continuous reading soon allows the reader to discern the drift of the argument; however, it is never clear and always opaque and difficult. In the end, the greatest indictment is that he only presents trite truths that could have been said with much more clarity, without the need for pretentious obscurity.

Edward Said's main arguments are fair enough. It is that the Orientalists, unEarthing the literature, religion, and culture of the past, were trying to present them anew to a new generation, long after they were relevant. It had inevitably to be a little artificial yet presented as something living and true for all time. In thus presenting their findings, they made the cardinal mistake of not taking into account the archaeology, as Foucault would say, from which these texts originate. In the case of the Orient, they had actually to 'unEarth' the past, while the historical and archaeological finds in Greece and Rome were a resurfacing and the confirmation of a living tradition. In the case of India, it was the unEarthing of a history and tradition that was dead, buried, and had become alien and totally unfamiliar, not only to the Orientalists but to Indians themselves. Consequently, the archaeology and context in which they were written and to whom they pertained clearly mattered and were things that the Orientalists should have taken much greater pains to understand. The Vedas and the other sacred texts were presented by them as the fountainhead of all Indian knowledge, as though from them we could postulate the state of society and the trajectory of its growth.

The second argument is that the Orientalists were presenting their findings to an audience with its own expectations, interests, beliefs, and value systems. Without realizing it, they catered to their beliefs and ways of thinking, which they were also part of. Thus, from the plethora of artifacts and texts they had collected, they used only what interested them and was in line with whatever theory they were attempting to prove. A large part of the literature and culture were thus left unedited and unaccounted. The result was biased and based on a very limited understanding of the much larger context of the works in which they existed. While what they presented was merely a small part of the whole, it was taken to be all that mattered. This resulted in a lopsided and even perverted picture of the past. This initial effort then became a self-fulfilling type of study or 'bias confirmation' for further research, which was done only to prove their views correct. While a good statistician would have made allowance for the paucity of the samples, the Orientalists lacked the humility to accept the limitations of their study.

The third argument is related to the basic problem of knowledge itself. Edward Said's complaint is that the Orientalists looked at the oriental past as an 'object,' not as a living and growing organism, which had its own identity, an 'I' as it were, when it spoke of itself. In fact, the Orientalists looked at the whole of the East as an object of study, not as part of a living civilization and consequently could see it only in the context of their western biases and through a western sensibility. What was even more damaging was the fact that they had to actually translate all the works of the East into their own languages before they could interpret them, adding the biases of language to their cultural and religious biases. This is a problem as old as Plato himself, who said we cannot know anything unless we already know them. The process of knowing is an attempt by the knower to force his own knowledge onto an object to make it knowable, which inevitably makes the object more in the image of the knower, thereby losing its uniqueness. This aspect is true of all attempts to know and is therefore inevitable.

The final argument is that the Orientalists were truly exceptional men. They went where literally no men had gone before. They dug, they studied, and they persevered where most men would have given up. They studied dead and foreign languages until they became the living authorities on the subject. They studied the texts, annotated them, discussed them, and expanded their knowledge until Orientalism became a study in itself. The depth of their knowledge, their commitment to their study, and their hermit-like obsession with their task made them saints. The consequence was that while we could argue with opponents, enemies, friends, and other intellectuals, how could we argue with the saints? Thus, all that later Orientalists could do was become disciples and followers, not original thinkers. They could only build on the religion created by the pioneers, make it larger, and even create a dogma and build a religion with its strict beliefs and rituals. Where then was the possibility of dissent or a new approach?

The subsidiary arguments are based more on the narrative itself than on substantive questions of philosophy. Edward Said correctly points out that their work and working style were more like that of an invading army with a project and a time frame than that of cool and thought-out research by intellectuals. Be it the army of intellectuals that Napoleon took with him to Egypt or the fervor with which the Indologists competed with each other to complete the translation of the Gita, the approach was the same: a sense of urgency and hurry. Consequently, they looked at the Orient as a mystery to be solved, not as something to be understood, as a living culture, or as the relationship of the people to their forgotten past. They thus ended up exposing only segments of the past with no sense of context, and sufficient effort was not made to see it within the larger context of the ocean of undiscovered knowledge. The project-like attitude also created a sense of accomplishment, as in the successful launch of a space shuttle when the limited task taken up was completed, leading to a feeling that some problem had been solved for good and therefore again buried as solved.

The more problematic issue was the character of the Orientalists. They were invariably part of a colonial and imperialist group that saw the East as inferior and barbaric and were therefore arrogant of their own worth and power. They looked at the East as weak, defeated, effeminate, and decaying. The general attitude was thus one of mild contempt. They saw the East as steeped in darkness and superstition, having to be awakened from a long slumber. Even though many of the Orientalists were men of exemplary character with great wisdom and warm hearts, they could not help but be touched by the glow of warm condescension.

Finally, while most of the Orientalists tended to praise the Indian past, as anyone who spends an inordinate part of their life discovering and interpreting such works invariably does, they were really unsuited to see the Indian past, except by comparing it with their own culture. Thus, they saw the Mahabharata as infinitely greater than the Iliad and the Odyssey but could not see it in the context of Indian culture alone. The Orientalists' greatest fault was the judgmental attitude they brought to all that they studied. Their work was invariably tinted by their prejudices and hidden value systems.

Most of these criticisms are not even contested by any serious historian, and, in fact, the Indologists and Orientalists themselves would agree with them. Almost all the better Indologists accepted that they came with long-held prejudices and tried very hard to make allowances for them. Like Alberuni earlier, they tried to describe what they studied and tried hard not to be judgmental. Our antipathy toward the Indologists has less to do with their scholarship than with the fact that they were part of an imperial past when we were a subject nation and thus cannot find the grace to accept them for what they did. In the case of Indians, the problems are even greater, as we would have had no history without the effort of the Indologists. As a nation, we have never written history and have shown little, if any, respect for the past.

We are totally dependent on the research, archaeological findings, and interpretations of artifacts found by them, and we are even indebted to them for deciphering our ancient languages and for dating the past. Such total dependence can only create hatred, not gratitude.

The British Perspective

The problem with the Orientalists was actually a question of perspective. All the historians, without exception, could only see Indian history through the prism of nationalism. They could not understand how to deal with history without upscaling events to national importance. In a sense, this was inevitable, as history is inevitably an attempt to see patterns and large trends within, at best, an amalgamation of micro-events. Further, as outsiders looking at the history of another country and people, they did not have the ability to see the inevitable differences and had to make more of the larger picture, as they thought they saw it, and to see all things from the perspective of some larger narrative. Every event thus had to be of national importance and create a national emotional impact even where it had no real physical significance. The British, as a result of their slow conquest of most of the country, had, towards the end of their rule, a government that could be said to have ruled India as a nation. Thus, the idea, if not the reality, of India as a single country was created. This was taken up by the Nationalists during the freedom struggle to bring the whole population within the struggle, which was then accepted as a given truth. Yet, the truth was that India was never a single state at any time in its history. Even the name 'India' was merely a designation of the land beyond the Sindhu river.

Consequently, when the British came to write Indian history, mostly sitting in London, as James Mill and Thomas Babington Macaulay did, they had to presume that they knew the history of 'India,' not of the little, fragmented, and disjointed history of some parts of the sub-continent, mainly in the northwest. The result has been that the history of India, to most people, has meant the story of a few dynasties that ruled over northern India, which starts with the Nandas, followed by the Mauryas, and then there is a long silence followed by the golden age of the Guptas, followed by many more silent periods with claims of raiding tribes like the Sakas, the Yueh Ti, a Chinese tribe, followed by the Hunans, the Yunans, and the Mongols, all claiming to have started empires in the north and northeastern parts of the country. No attempt was made to tell us what was happening to the rest of the country, especially South India. It was left to later Indian historians, like Neelakanta Shastri, to give us a glimpse of what may have been happening in that part of the country. We have no idea what eastern India was like until the extension of the Mauryan empire eastwards. In fact, we learn that Buddha's mother was of the Licchiva tribe but we do not know if they were Aryans or some tribals from across the Himalayas. All Tamilians talk of their golden age as that of the Sangam period, but we have absolutely no idea of the people or the region it pertained to. We know that the people of Kerala were trading with the West even as early as the 6th century B.C., but we have no idea of the people or their history. This is true for most of the country.

While this made Indian history, by its very nature, fragmented and a minute part of the real history of the sub-continent, the presumption that it was 'the history of India' generated an attitude toward Indian history that has caused many subsequent problems. The enforced nationalism picked up by the nationalists during the freedom struggle has now become part of the national historical ethos that refuses to die. Thus, the intrusion of the Greek army of Alexander into the northwestern part of the country is treated as an invasion of India so that Chandra Gupta can be made a national hero, while the later invasions of the Persians, the Huns, the Chinese, the Sakas, and the Mongols who stayed on and created small empires were never treated as invasions. Thus, even the raids of Mohamed of Ghazni and the rest of the incursions by Muslims from Persia and Afghanistan, right up to the raid of Babur, the Mughal, were only local raids that were the norm among the many small states with common borders. However, nationalism has made them into attacks on India and their subsequent rule: the subjugation of the Indian people by dastardly foreigners, even though it was no different from the rule of the Sakas or Kanishka, who were from a Chinese tribe, the Yueh Ti, or of the Rajputs, who were tribals from across the border.

The attack on the Somnath temple complex did not cause any ripples in the rest of the country. In fact, there is no mention of it in any historical texts, not even in the large amount of religious literature written after that period, not even in the copious writings of Sankaracharya, who had traveled widely throughout the country. It was no different from the Marathas or Rajputs attacking and plundering nearby, weaker states. Yet the British historians made it out as though it was an attack on the sovereignty of the Indian state, something that did not exist even in the minds of the Indian people. Similarly, the three battles at Plassey were nothing more than local battles that were transformed by British historians into the Rubicons of Indian history, epoch-making battles for the soul of India. Even the Mughals came as local raiders, not as national conquerors, as is evident from the fact that even Babur went home after his first raid. It was only the weakness of the petty kingdoms of north India that gave the Mughals the opportunity to expand and become something close to a national government. In doing so, they used local support and local armies made up of Rajputs and Marathas, among many others. The Mughals did not conquer India; a government headed by the Mughals with very huge contributions from local armies and people helped create the unified empire called the Mughal Empire, administered largely by turncoat Kshatriyas who became Kayasthas.

In fact, it was the Mughals who helped create the idea of India as a state ruled by a unified Mughal government. This idea was taken over by the British, to whom all natives from Afghanistan and Punjab to Tamil Nadu and Burma were merely natives and thus lumped into a single category. Our Indianness is thus a forced identity, the common identity of slaves or enslaved people subjected to the same slave masters, not some noble ideal represented by a common history, culture, or heritage. It was a creation of British historiography, a legacy that allows us to be a single nation with our different languages and cultural realities, leading to a continuing conflict as to who we are, Indian or something else.

The Continuing Discourse

While none of the points raised by Edward Said are disputed by any serious historian, they were not really knowingly done, for they were in the nature, not of intellectual failures, but the result of the inherent nature of any investigative study when a foreigner tries to probe the history and culture of an alien people. The outsider has to come to the investigation with his own value system and language. While they may be able to suppress, at least momentarily, their prejudices and refuse to judge based on their own value system, their language gets the better of them as it is invariably loaded with emotive words and a value system. This problem is impossible to bypass except, as Derrida said, by using a language devoid of cultural, social, and political overtones. The answer to the indologists is therefore not to merely abuse them but to do our own research and place our findings on the table as an alternative view. The problem has been the dEarth of native scholars and the poor level of native scholarship. Our cries are thus only the moaning of a crybaby who refuses to rise up to the challenge by raising the level of our scholarship to a higher level.

As more natives began to read and study their own history, culture, and religion, what started as a criticism of Orientalism became an assertion of national pride. Many native scholars took to this bandwagon. In India, the notable voice has been Pankaj Mishra, who, in his interesting book, 'From the Ruins of Empire,' makes the case that there were stirrings of rebellion, genuine new departures, and true inventiveness before the colonial period, during, and after the imperial period. He gives many accounts of brilliant works and cases of deep and extensive scholarship that could be seen as shoots of a new spring, with new thinking that was progressive and radical. There is no need to deny that great work must have been done even in the darkest part of our history; however, it was clearly too little and perhaps too late, as the Westerners did overpower us with their knowledge and their superior technology. In fact, the fact that they ruled over us for so long is clear proof of the feebleness of our intellectual abilities and the weakness of our social structures.

With the shifting of the intellectual power base from Europe to the U.S.A., there has been a change in the tone of scholarship, with America being the land of the free; their scholars imply that their studies were devoid of the biases of the Orientalists. An Indian American, Rajiv Malhotra, however, warns that they are no different and takes the fight to them in his book, 'The Battle for Sanskrit.' He calls American scholars of Sanskrit 'American-orientalists,' and their brand of scholarship, 'post-orientalism.' While they were not colonists, they came with the mentality of those who annihilated the native American population and forced the opening of the West to white settlements. They played the typical 'good cop, bad cop' psychological game, where a group learned the native ways and their language and befriended them, only to let them down in the end, with claims that they were powerless in the face of the superior might of the 'bad cop' group. That, warns Malhotra, is the attitude of some American scholars; they pretend great love for India and its past and back such sentiments with hard work and extensive knowledge of Sanskrit, with which they lull most Indians to sleep, while their real intention is to destroy the glories of the Indian heritage and to defame it.

Saving Sanskrit

Malhotra has a problem with the way Sheldon Pollock and many American academics view India, Hinduism, and Sanskrit. He sees them as trying to counter the Hindutva thrust by making it appear that everything about ancient India—its religion, language, science, and culture—was superlative. While Malhotra himself does not claim to be a Hindutva advocate, he detests the other extreme that Pollock represents. This is fair enough, but despite writing a book that runs to more than 400 pages, he is not able to make out a coherent charge sheet, much less make it stick.

Malhotra's book, 'The Battle for Sanskrit,' like Edward Said before him, is not so difficult to read as it is confusing. Like Said, he forms his premises as he goes along, and thus there is neither thrust nor clarity. Malhotra accuses Pollock and others like him of treating Sanskrit as a dead language and harps on the continuing corpus of

Sanskrit writings from Sankara to the end of the 16th century as evidence of its robust continuing life. While his facts are true, it is also a fact that all such writing was only for the initiated and the elite and did not make any impression on the masses. It was merely the continuation of the work of a very elite and closed society.

The second point he makes is that Pollock and his ilk insist on secularizing Sanskrit. Even if this were true, it would be futile for them to try, as Sanskrit was nothing if not the vehicle of the sacred. Pollock cannot change that, as then Sanskrit would be left with nothing. Pollock, Malhotra says, claims that there is no transcendental element in Sanskrit; this is again absurd, for not to recognize the transcendental in Indian philosophy would be to miss the point altogether. What can be said is that after the Vedas, it gradually became, with the Bhagavata cult, more of a material philosophy. Vedic Indian philosophy is nothing if not transcendental, from its concept of Maya to its idea of Nirguna.

Pollock also seems to deny the existence of secular Sanskrit and brushes aside the claims of Sanskrit poetry. The fact that Sanskrit has a rich poetic tradition cannot be wished away, however much Pollock tries. The fact that all poetry and, in fact, all the arts have thrived on royal patronage, on power and money, is also an accepted fact. That cannot be the basis on which Sanskrit poetry is denied its rightful place. By such logic, all poetry is compromised. Pollock's arguments do not take away from the greatness of Sanskrit literature, mathematics, science, astronomy, dance, and music. While this is true, it is also true that it was Buddhism and Jainism that brought Sanskrit to the common man. In fact, it was the systematic persecution of the Buddhists that killed a thriving tradition of Sanskrit writing, along with their later preference for local languages as a tool for their religious work.

However, it is Pollock's insistence that Sanskrit was a language of oppression that irks Malhotra most. While Malhotra makes a distinction between language and policy to defend it from the accusation of being oppressive, he fails to understand the power of language to create stereotypes and to cause emotional stirrings. It may be accepted that Sanskrit by itself was not overtly oppressive, but it was the tool used by the 'establishment' to deny access to 'the other.' Thus, Sanskrit learning was limited to certain castes and Vedic learning, treated as sacrosanct, was also permitted only to certain castes. Shudras were not only not permitted to perform rituals or sacrifices; they were not even allowed to be present when they were performed. Sanskrit learning thus became the tool of the elite to retain power. Malhotra fails to grasp the fact that language has everywhere been used as a tool to retain power, be it English, Latin, or Sanskrit. Languages come loaded with emotion, prejudices, and a built-in value system. All linguists, from Wittgenstein to Chomsky, attest to this fact. Consequently, Malhotra is, in this case, barking up the wrong tree.

Pollock sees the Sanskritization of India as no different from the work of colonizers and their subsequent subjugation of the native people by an oppressive regime. In trying to deny this accusation, Malhotra tries to dismiss the Aryanization of the country as a myth, pretending that it was an internal movement. While an Aryan invasion of the country is now being taught as unlikely, the fact that a separate people who called themselves 'Arya' did enter the country and spread from the north-west of the country along the Gangetic plain to the east and crossing the Vindhyas came to the south is part of the Vedas itself and cannot be denied. To pretend that Aryanization was merely the extension of the Harappan civilization is also not factually tenable. The language of the Harappans has yet to be deciphered and seems to bear no resemblance to Sanskrit; the only good statue or stone relief from the ruins of Mohenjo-Daro appears to be of a king or noble, does not resemble the Aryan at all and has the features of a Negroid or Australoid. Further, Dravidian culture claims them as their ancestors, and even Vedic literature accepts Agastya, a non-Brahmin, as the father of the Tamil people.

The aryanization of the subcontinent has already been dealt with, along with the compromises it entailed. It was clearly a give-and-take, but what is important is the eventual dominance of Brahminical Hinduism along with Vedic rituals and the paramount importance of Sanskrit in the scheme of things. The religion that emerged, despite the vociferous rebellion of the natives and despite the attempts of reformers to moderate, has been one that made caste rigid and thereby oppressed the lower castes, denied them any avenue for progress, and demeaned their lives. The vast majority of Indians were thus denied equality and justice in the name of religion. This is a fact and therefore Pollock is not wrong to see the spread of Sanskrit as an oppression and as the work of a set of internal colonizers. Pollock's assertion that the Ramayana was redone in the 15th and 16th centuries to fight 'the other,' the Muslim, and that while the other was a brother in the Mahabharata, in the Ramayana 'the other' is evil and to be destroyed is less tenable. This is a poor reading of the Epics, as in both, the focus is the battle between dharma and adharma. While it can be argued that the difference very often gets blurred, there is no doubt that what is being attempted is a definition of Dharma. While the depiction of Southerners as monkeys could be resented by the Dravidians, what is interesting is that it is in the North that Hanuman is most worshiped as a God. Thus, even if the original intention was to demean the natives, it backfired, making Hanuman a powerful God. This trend is also seen in the Puranas. Ravan is only the common depiction of Asuras as 'the other,' not eternally evil, as most of them were great Tapsis who gained powerful boons from the same gods. They were only the 'other,' but also seen as the elder brothers of the gods.

The claim that racism and Nazism came from India through Sanskrit is also nothing but an attempt to pass on the blame. The European tradition had enough examples, from slavery and the barbarians that the Greeks and Romans so thoroughly despised to the philosophy of Nietzsche and Heidegger and the music of Wagner, if anything more was required, to feed their anti-Semitism and rank racism. The Aryan sense of superiority merely gave them the needed sense of legitimacy.

CHAPTER 16

THE THIRD MILLENNIUM

As in past ages, Indian consciousness kept evolving, with traumatic events pushing it in new directions. Thus, during the Axial age, the collision with the thinking of the upstart Aryan created the glorious religions of Buddhism and Jainism, filling the landscape with all the philosophies from Stoicism to Epicureanism. Since we have so little idea of the Harappan civilization, we may never know the base from which all the thinking started. The axial age was thus also the first known fracture in Indian thinking.

The Second Millennium saw the newly cemented thinking that adopted Buddhist and Jain ideas into Indian thinking and rituals being assaulted by prophetic religions like Christianity and Islam. The response to their presence resulted in some unrest but was largely met with silent withdrawal. The arrival of the British and their final domination, in a way never experienced before, caused an implosion created by access to education and global ideas. While the Bengal renaissance and the many reform movements were the result, it also led to the independence movement.

In 1947, when India became independent, the consciousness of the nation was very splintered, with even political ideologies like Marxism making inroads. No great religious idea or reform movement captured the imagination of the Indian people. Yet Vivekananda had made it appear that there was something called 'Hinduism.' This idea was latched on to, not so much as a truth but as a political need to unite us in our independence struggle. The reality of the presence of Islam and other religions meant that few really believed in it and fewer saw any need to do anything. However, the partition and the creation of an Islamic Pakistan made the idea of Hindu India a possibility.

The last century of the second Millennium thus saw an attempt to visualize such a possibility and to work towards it. The attempt to crush the almost infinite beliefs in Indian religions and to force conformity in practice has thus been crude and non-intellectual. The results have been mixed and troubling because they have also meant an intolerance of free thinking.

Unlike the earlier epochs, when the Axial Age produced a plethora of philosophical and religious ideas and the second millennium was the culmination of the Bhakti movement, which saw great thinkers like Sankara and Ramanuja produce great works of thought, the last years of the second millennium and the new one saw nothing of worth being produced in philosophy or religion. Indian consciousness was instead wrung through the mill of imperialism and the independence movement, and partition created a new consciousness that was basically non-religious and political. It was politics that shaped the new consciousness.

While Vivekananda came from the Ramakrishna tradition, which accepted the plurality of faiths, in trying to present Hinduism to the outside world, he had to mutilate, compress, and generalize. Nationalism then demanded an unquestioned acceptance of our religious past, whitewashing its aberrations and denying its plurality, where Indians were Shaivites, Lingayats, Vaishnavites, Vokkalingas, Krishna worshippers, and Ram bhakts. All were called Hindus to describe the Indian consciousness, which actually described nothing real or existing.

The Discovery of Hinduism

Hinduism had long been buried in the debris of its battles with Buddhism and Jainism and in its many conflicts with insistent reformers. It had changed almost unrecognizably, with compromises that had to be made to stoop to conquer. Centuries went by, with Hinduism being practiced in its many different forms and ways across the country—from the worship of Murugan and Meenakshi in the south, Kali in the east, Ganesh in the west, and Hanuman in the north. No effort was made to seek conformity, as all were allowed, and no claim was made that the practices were of the same religion. Only the officiating priests were Brahmins and the mantras and Vedic chants remained the same throughout India. Yet, Sanskrit as a language had been forgotten, and even the priests did not know what they were chanting.

It was the indologists from France, Germany, and Britain who rediscovered Sanskrit and its past and then deciphered the edicts of Ashoka and the splendors of classical Sanskrit. This led to translations of the ancient texts, including the Vedas, the Epics, and the Puranas. As they translated and published their findings to the world, they could not resist making comparisons to Western philosophy and their own civilization and religion. Very often, even without meaning to comment, India's past, especially its religious evolution, appeared puerile, and its beliefs and practices were barbaric.

To the elite and the officiating priests, this was an affront that needed to be answered. Yet the general reaction was a hidden sense of shame and the creation of an inferiority complex. However, such shame was accompanied by the inevitable hatred of those who exposed their nakedness. From this emerged a solidarity cemented by shame. Like the common identity of slaves who gang up against their masters, Indians closed ranks to protect their beliefs, decry the exposers, and create a new Hinduism that would stand the glare of modern thinking. Thus was born the idea of 'Sanatana Dharma,' something like the core of Hinduism that was pure and true. The impossible diversity of beliefs and practices that all grew up on the subcontinent were then made to appear like a single religion. The hidden anger at their shame then turned it into a militant religion, proselytizing and demanding conformity. Thus was born the concept of 'Hindutva.'

This was a new Hindu identity, made of two parts: a pseudo-intellectual part that claimed that there was a 'Sanatana Dharma,' an eternal religion, that was being merely polished to make it shine again, and a second part made up of majoritarian chauvinism, what the brute majority could claim as their right. In its initial reaction, it created the 'Arya Samaj' and the missionary zeal of Vivekananda. In time, it was to produce 'The Hindu Maha Sabha,' the R.S.S., and 'Hindutva.' It also produced the slogan that all Indians are Hindus and the reverse, that only Hindus are Indians. While a Hindu can be defined as a person who lives in Hindustan, it is much more difficult to define Hinduism. Pushed to the wall, the apologist calls it 'Sanatana Dharma.'

Sanatana Dharma

A historical search for Sanatana Dharma is less definitive. As we trace the evolution of Hinduism from the Vedas to the present, the hope of finding a core slowly recedes. The Vedas began as a religion of sacrifices, where not the gods but the power of sacrifices sustained the universe. It was a religion of the individual with a specific set of sacrifices. It was not temple-based and had no concept of salvation but was a religion that saw man's role as that of being in harmony with the rest of creation and to sustain the world. God was merely the ultimate principle and seen as 'Brahma.' The universe was merely a manifestation of Brahma, and therefore merely 'Maya.' One did not pray to the gods, as the God was 'Nirguna,' without qualities. There was no concept of morals or ethics. It was Jainism and Buddhism that created an awareness of the sacredness of life and, with it, the concept of 'Ahimsa.' They, with their four truths and the eightfold path, created the idea of a moral life. With the concept of 'Nirvana,' they created a goal for life, and the concept of 'Karma,' despite the endless cycle of births and deaths, was an emphasis on the moral life, creating with it the idea that some invisible agency was calculating and adding merits and demerits to each person's life to determine his future.

At the stage of the Puranas, the gods were deified without adding much to the concept of ethics. Thus, from the Vedas to the time of the writing of the Puranas, there was nothing like a core ethic or even the flesh and bones that could be taken to stand for a religion. All that we had was the smallness of man in the face of the immensity of the universe. With the Atharva Veda, we see the beginnings of a religion of personal needs, which were to be attained by the power of mantras and magic and with Tantra. Men were then tempted to undertake strange and convoluted sacrifices and elaborate rituals to achieve personal ends related to wealth, lust, and power. The gods became a simpler way to achieve their carnal needs: just pray to some God, who was all-powerful.

While there was no ethical base, the Vedic religion, by the time of 'Manusmrithis,' had created a cultural prototype by the division of life into four stages with clear duties in each phase of life. These duties became the core of what was to evolve as Hinduism. With the separation of people into four different Varnas or castes, a further set of rules were made applicable to each caste. The varna segregation was the first set of rules for society; they were meant to regulate the intercourse within society and soon became rigid with a religious flavor. It was then boldly said that it is better to do one's caste duties badly than to attempt to do, however well, the duties of another caste. To justify the Varna system, the concept of karma was made into a sort of reward and punishment for work done in a life. Based on the merits and demerits accumulated in life, the nature and condition of the next life were decided, along with those accumulated over many lives. This explained why one was born a Brahmin, another a Shudra, and some as untouchables; why one was rich, another poor, and so on. This justified the caste system and allowed the rich to flaunt their wealth, as each was merely enjoying the rewards and retributions of past lives. Duties were caste-based and thus totally relative. The core of Hindu ethics was the caste duties of each caste, and stage-wise duties were an add-on for the twice-born. While killing and stealing are considered intrinsically bad, the punishment was caste-based, where almost invariably, the lower castes were punished more severely while the Brahmin was almost always let off very lightly and physical punishment was prohibited.

No attempt was made to define right and wrong on a universal basis or state the principles of law. Further, with no specific goal to life, no judgment, and no end, except an endless cycle of births and deaths, no moral law made any sense. Consequently, the Hindu response to life was to live and to live it abundantly, if possible. They saw Artha, Kama, and Dharma as equally important, even if they kept saying that Dharma was supreme. Dharma was, however, always caste Dharma, and there are no universal laws. It was with the Epics that the rules of conduct and ethics were laid. It was not so much stated as to be discerned from the conduct of the heroes and heroines of the Ramayana and the Mahabharata. The problem is that these epics tell us stories so full of ambiguity that it is difficult to find a clear set of laws. Thus, Ram kills Vali by shooting him in the back; the God of Dharma himself, Yudhistra, actually lies. Even if he were punished for that sin, it suggests that lying is often inevitable and that in life, nothing is absolute. The great guru Dronacharya demands the thumb of Eklavya as guru Darshana; Rama insists that Sita undergo a test even though he knows that she is virtuous; Kunti absent-mindedly allows polyandry; and many of the heroes of the Mahabharata use underhand methods in the war at Kurukshetra, including Arjun and Lord Krishna himself. However, it is with the Bhagavad Gita that we reach the pinnacle of Hindu Ethics. Yet Lord Krishna's advice has to be seen only in the context of the Karma theory, and what Lord Krishna says is that, since man must act, for that is his dharma and the purpose of his birth, if he acts without hope of reward and without desire, such acts are washed of karmic stain. While this leads to a better life the next time, it is still an appeal to rewards, but on a different plane; the real problem is that it is not possible to act without desire. In fact, no action is possible without an incentive, motive, or desire. The ancient Vedic sages had actually denied the possibility of a creator God for that reason—for what possible motive or desire would have prompted an all-powerful, all-knowing God to create the universe? Since action without desire is not possible, the morality of the Gita was filed along with other sacred texts. Further, Krishna continuously appeals to Arjun's duty as a Kshatriya; is his advice then applicable to other castes?

What then is 'Sanatana Dharma?' As we look back from the Vedas to the present, the things that have not changed are the Vedas themselves, the division of life into four stages, the division of society into four Varnas, and a belief in karma. All the rest have been part of an evolution and compromises based on the demands of the times. The division of society into Varnas and life into stages is more social in nature, and thus the only perennial philosophy that has come down, almost from time immemorial, has been the belief in Karma and in the cycle of births and deaths. Yet that does not explain the present texture of Hinduism. The concept of Ahimsa, borrowed from the Jains and the Buddhists, has led to the fetish of Vegetarianism, and the old Aryan totem animal, the cow, has become more than a taboo and has become sacred. However, the actual basis of Vegetarianism, which was 'Ahimsa,' tolerance, and love for all creatures, has been forgotten. Finally, the real constant has been the Vedas; even as practices and beliefs have changed, the Vedas have remained supreme, regarded as divine revelation, never questioned, except by rebels, who have invariably been banished from Hindu society.

Hindi, Hindu, and Hindustan

Akshaya Mukul has written a very interesting book called 'The Gita Press and the Making of Hindu India.' In it, he tells the story of how Hinduism has been associated with nationalism and with organizations like the Hindu Maha Sabha and the R.S.S., propagated and popularized by the 'Gita Press' and its founding editor, Hanuman Poddar. The potent and heady mix of Hindi, Hinduism, and nationalism was all given voice by the birth of such organizations. While the H.M.S. was born in 1915, the R.S.S. in 1925, and the Hindi Sahitya Sammelan in 1910, the Gita Press was founded in 1923. The fact that the journals of the Gita Press have a circulation of two lakhs in Hindi and one lakh in English speaks volumes for their reach and power. More importantly, it was the special organ of an entire brand of intellectual nationalism, inextricably permeated with Hinduism. It propagated the idea of Sanatana Dharma, the eternal values of Hinduism, and embraced the slogans 'Hindi, Hindu, and Hindustan.'

In many ways, the Gita Press, which started publishing in 1923, was the mother and architect of modern Hindi and must be given credit for making Hindi the national language of the country and the language of religion, selling more than 6 million copies of the Ramayana, a similar number of Bhagavad Gitas and millions of copies of the many Puranas. The memories of Muslim rule, the suppression of Indian nationalism by the British, and their religion, Christianity, made the Indian nationalist, by definition, Hindu. The 'others' were the Muslims and Christians. Insisting on making Hindi the national language, against the grain of the sentiments of the people of South and North Eastern India, was possible because of the confidence of the H.M.S. and the R.S.S. and the reach and clout of the Gita Press.

The success of the Gita Press and its supporters in creating a pseudo-intellectual identity based on religion was achieved despite their reactionary attitude toward reform and change. Thus, in defining Sanatana Dharma, they still saw the four stages of life, the four varnas, and Karma as fundamental. Since the Epics and

Puranas refused to be strait-laced into a simple philosophy with basic principles and internal consistency, they stood for no real philosophy but for everything that was perceived as Hinduism, accepting contradictions and fantastic mythology. There was no attempt to explain or justify caste, the Hindu view, or the place of women. They almost never spoke of the philosophy of the Vedas or of the deeper ideas of Sankara or Ramanuja. While their intellectual credentials may be suspect, the reason they succeeded to the extent they did was that the Gita Press and its founder editor, Hanuman Podder, were and remained 'unbuyable,' and many of the R.S.S. men were selfless men devoted and dedicated to what they believed in. The founders of the Hindu Maha Sabha, including men like Madan Mohan Malaviya, P.D. Tandon, and K.M. Munshi, and many leaders of the R.S.S. and many others who worked tirelessly to create Hindu nationalism, were also Arya Samaj members who believed in the sacredness of the cow and propagated cow protection and Shuddhi, a return to the basic tenets of Hinduism. Along with these political leaders, the Gita Press also got the best Hindi poets and writers to write for them, thereby not only creating modern Hindi but also making it appear that such men, including Gandhi, were supporters of the values of the Gita Press. To this was added the clout of wealth, as it was created and supported by Marwari businessmen, including the Brilas, the Dalmias, and later the Jains, of the Times Group.

The Gita Press, with the support it got from religious leaders, rich businessmen, intellectuals, including writers and poets, and political leaders at the forefront of the independence struggle, including Gandhi and many others, helped define Sanatana Dharma as made up of the caste system, the protection of women (which meant that women must stay at home and never be allowed independence), the sanctity of the cow, and nationalism with a Hindu complexion. To the definers of Hinduism, in this manner, the 20th century has been a nightmare. In 1928, the Kerala Royal family allowed the entry of lower castes into the roads leading to the temples after a long and protracted agitation; in 1956, the Kerala Government opened the doors of the temple itself to the lower castes. From 1932 onwards, temple after temple in Bombay Presidency was opened to the lower castes. Untouchability was banned, widow remarriage was allowed, sati was prohibited, and sweeping changes took place in society. Even a man like Gandhi was initially ambivalent about the correctness of temple entry by the lower castes, the status of women, and the abolishment of caste.

Then came independence, partition, and the subsequent bloodbath. While the H.M.S., the R.S.S., and the Gita Press would later claim that they had valiantly fought against partition, detective novels would make us ask the question, who had the most to benefit from partition, and the answer would be obvious: the Hindu fundamentalists. The rise of a militant Muslim League and the arrogance and ambition of Jinnah, who was reluctant to play second fiddle to Nehru, may have had much to do with it, but it was the communal riots from 1920 to 1950 that left the Muslims feeling that they had no place in India that really brought about partition. These riots were clearly fanned by the H.M.S. and the R.S.S., even if they did not start them on purpose. Having forced the Muslims out of the country, accompanied by the demonization of the Muslims, the partition led to an unprecedented bloodbath. What mere demonization could not do—the bloodbath, the lasting memories of cruelty and hatred, the long journeys of relocation, and the long periods of suffering—made Muslims the enemy without any redeeming features. Forgotten were the long periods of friendship and mutual respect; only hatred remained. This made it possible to polarize the Hindus against 'the other' and to create an identity of the 'Hindu' along much narrower lines, making it possible to see the Muslim as the enemy within and without. This was most essential as Sanatana Dharma had been compromised by the national government, and a new identity and a rear-guard action were now absolutely necessary.

State Religion

While we claim to be a secular republic, the fact that the state has inevitably acted in religious matters, be it in temple entry, the abolition of untouchability, allowing all castes in some states to become priests, and finally allowing women entry into Sabarimala temple, means that the state assumes that religion is subject to the fundamental principles of the constitution. The state has thus been assuming the role of the Pope or the final religious body, to decide on faith and religious practices. The fact that Hinduism does not have a supreme head or a supreme body to decide on doctrine and practice makes the secular judiciary assume such a role. While the nationalistic Hinduism of Vivekananda tried to project a homogeneous, omnibus type of Hinduism, the state has legislated on issues like caste, so central to Hinduism, and on other beliefs specific to certain sects, so that both the validity of the larger issues of Hinduism and the specific issues that make certain sects unique have been destroyed. What religious consciousness can an Indian have when his faith is actually subject to the dictates of the secular state? This nebulous uncertainty is another schizophrenic fracture in the psyche of Indian consciousness.

While the judiciary may justify its intervention on the plea that all modern states separate the secular from the spiritual and that, as far as the law is concerned, the secular constitution must prevail, it is also an infringement of the explicit understanding that, as far as faith goes, every man is entitled to his beliefs. Thus, conscience is not to be a matter on which the law can adjudicate. While the separation of the spiritual from the secular was supposed to have been a great advancement in the idea of freedom of thought and speech, it has begun to show its limitations. The Nazi regime in Germany exposed it for what it is worth—an insidious idea to kill the conscience in matters of state. This led to blind obedience to the state. The problem is now gaining international proportions as the whole world is divided into states, each with its own laws, citizenship rights, and prohibitions on free entry. What then happens to a stateless person? Does he have no rights? This is where Karl Marx, the German thinker, rose to protest when the Nazis forced all Germans to be only loyal to the state. He claimed that the laws of God and the transcendental idea of morality cannot be reduced merely to the needs or priorities of a state. There must be a higher morality that respects the divinity of each individual, his person, and his spiritual being.

Inclusive Hinduism

While Vedic Hinduism was meant only in the region of Aryavasta and only applicable to the Aryan, a separate race of noble and pure warriors, these same people, when they entered India, were faced with many levels of opposition and forced to compromise their standards and beliefs to penetrate and to conquer. Compromises were thus first seen merely as temporary adjustments in the pursuit of the higher goal of domination. Thus, a slow process of dilution and changing emphasis took place. The Vedic people, who believed in no specific God and saw in sacrifice the ultimate obeisance for the sustenance of the universe, soon accepted many gods and idol worship. The people who saw God as an ultimate principle beyond comprehension and approachable only through negation, as 'Nirguna,' became bhakti exponents. This journey has already been traced and needs no repeating. While Hinduism became inclusive, it also retained in its psyche the anger at their own treachery and the weakness that forced them to compromise. That sense of sliminess that gets attached to the weak and devious tends to build to become what Dr. Radhakrishnan calls 'the tyranny of the weak.' The apparent unity that was created was at the cost of fragmentation, becoming an entity at war with itself. It had no common ethos and was ready to explode at every new stage of evolution or compromise. We have already seen this in the case of the rise of the 'Veerashaivas' and even in the militancy of a Sankara. Yet, the general trend was clear: a final capitulation to the needs of political compulsions with continued rear-guard resistance until a new crisis demands new resolve.

From the agnosticism of the Vedas to the accommodation of the Atharva Veda to the acceptance of Yoga, Tantra, and all forms of magic, the capitulation to the common herd saw personal gods, idol worship, magic, and the boon-giving gods all being accepted. All along, the importance of 'jnana' was never questioned, even though, with every compromise, the place of knowledge in religion continued to be demeaned. Yet, all along, there was an upper end of religious thought that still saw in the way of Jnana not only a way but the ultimate path to spiritual realization. The rise of

Bhakti, however, saw it as an impediment to a religious life and condemned the Jnani as irreligious and an atheist. This led to the closing of the Hindu mind, the rise of unthinking belligerence and the creation of a bigoted and self-righteous religion. While the Bhakti of the Epics still allowed Arjuna to question the Lord, the later Bhakti movement wanted the total annihilation of the self; only unquestioning love mattered. Indian identity, including the Hindu identity, continued to evolve despite the arrival of other religions from the West and the annihilation of Indian religions like Buddhism and the near annihilation of Jainism. While new sects were created, the only lasting one has been Sikhism. Islam, while retaining a sizable population of Muslims, has not been able to affect the psyche of Indians in any significant way. Instead, the caste system and the belief in Karma have penetrated deeply into Islam and Christianity, as they are practiced in India. The caste system is a study in itself, but we cannot run away from its deep impact on the Indian soul.

A Summation

As the Aryans entered the subcontinent, they were hunters and herders of cattle. Their only wealth was their cattle and horses. As they subdued the native people, they settled into what were very fertile river-fed lands, where almost anything grew. While they started as a tribal group with an ethnic identity, the need to subdue large and powerful opposing forces led invariably to the centralization of leadership and the emergence of kings. With kings came specialization, a standing army, administrative machinery, and a royal priesthood.

The Aryan religion was both very open, questioning, and personal. It was a religion of personal duties that amounted to a religious ritual. Yet, it demanded that each man do his duty to ensure harmony with what appeared to be divine powers. This led to the worship of the sun, the sacredness of fire, and the cleansing power of water. respect for learning, elders, ancestors, and most importantly, guests. As specialization took place, there was an inevitable conflict between the warrior class and the priests. Religion became more complex to ensure that only the priestly class could decipher the rites and the mantras.

The initial division into Varnas was merely an occupational division that did not presume any hierarchy and was only limited to the three Varnas. The conflict with the natives meant the taking of prisoners, who became slaves, and there was also a need to accommodate the non-fighting class of people who merely lived in areas subdued by the Aryan. They were ethnically different and were mostly peasants. To accommodate them in society, the Shudra class was formed.

As the Aryans settled into fertile lands, the king was initially the owner of all conquered lands, but almost immediately, it was necessary to reward his generals with land. Soon, the king was handing out land as gifts and grants and finally as leases with tenant rights. As the landholdings were initially too large for self-cultivation, there was an urgent need for agricultural labor. That was where the Shudra was used, as indentured labor, as serfs, and perhaps as slaves. The slave women were already doing most of the domestic chores of the wealthy warriors and priests.

At first, chariot makers and makers of arms, armor, and fighting equipment were of select Aryan ancestry, but as the Aryans settled down, these functions, being manual and labor-intensive, were slowly siphoned off to slave labor and the Shudra. This was both the curse and the lifeline extended to the Shudra, as he was soon identified with all manner of labor, including artisans, craftsmen, blacksmiths, metal workers, glassblowers, and jewelry makers. It gave them a route to wealth while also branding them as inferior manual workers.

As society grew, trade and agriculture also grew, leading to a surplus economy, allowing for freedom and social possibilities, as clearly brought out in Arthashastra. This also meant a loosening of social bonds and a questioning of religious beliefs. Consequently, all forms of philosophy grew, mainly materialistic and agnostic. Along with these grew a more refined idea of humanness and moral duty. This led to Jainism and Buddhism.

Initially, the Vedic religion stood no chance against their onslaught that questioned meaningless rituals and emphasized a deeper philosophical and moral basis for religion. These religions consequently swept through the land and enthralled even great kings like Asoka, who spread the teaching throughout India and helped make it an international religion. That Vedic Brahmanism not only survived but drove out all other religions is a testimony to the religion's capacity to absorb and renew itself and, more importantly, the tenacity of the Brahmin intellectual class that lay low in times of trouble only to return with greater power and force. With each setback, Brahmanism returned with more rules and a greater regimentation of society. Their tactic was always to stoop to conquer.

To counter the force of Buddhism and Jainism, which mainly attracted the Vaisyas and Shudras, Vedic religion gradually changed from being a sacrificial religion to a 'puja' religion and accepted Ahimsa and vegetarianism as integral to their faith. It then opened the doors of Vedic religion to the Shudra through Vaishnavism and Bhakti. However, with each concession to the Shudra, the rules of caste became even more rigid.

When the Shudra was outside the scope of religion, there were no rules; however, with their acceptance into the fold, Brahmanical customs and behavior became an ideal to be followed. The great change, however, was brought about by the Epics, the hearing of which was permitted to the Shudra. Thus, playacting and storytelling of the epics became a national pastime and the basic form of entertainment. At every village and town, the same story was repeated and acted out, creating a national consciousness and a sense of a common heritage. Yet, the more it spread, the more the caste system became a noose around the people of India. Where earlier, local rebellions against the Brahmanical caste order were possible, now it meant a national rebellion, which the Shudra could not attempt as he was neither economically nor intellectually equipped to challenge the ruling class. The control of education ensured that Shudra was kept illiterate and submissive. Yet, it also meant that the intellectual and creative abilities of a huge portion of the population were locked up with contempt.

The Shudra became a stakeholder in the Varna system by allowing them to lord over tribals and untouchables. The Shudra now had someone to look down upon and thus had a stake in upholding the caste system. The more untouchables the system accepted, the more important the Shudra became. While Manu lists only 16 groups of untouchables, by the time of the Puranas, it had grown to hundreds. The more menial tasks were then thrust on the untouchables, thus elevating the Shudra in the hierarchy of labor. At all stages, compulsion and ideology played their part. While Kautilya and Manu could resort to the king to ensure the caste system, in later years, it was more the result of religious and ideological pressure to conform. Through religious inclusion and ideological theories, especially the karma theory, the Brahmin had control over the rest of society, preventing upward mobility and the resultant conflicts. The division of the lower castes into Shudras and untouchables was a masterstroke, as it prevented two of the largest groups from forming an alliance, and the animosity between them was fostered by religious exclusion and a false sense of superiority. The tragedy of all religious reformations, from Jainism and Buddhism to Vaishnavism, Shaivism, Bhakti, and Tantra, was that they all started as reform movements against Brahminical Hinduism and especially caste injustices, but all of them inevitably got engulfed by orthodoxy and soon merged with mainstream Hinduism, accepting caste and social segregation.

Hindu Nationalism

As new identity is created, the old is totally forgotten, and the distant past has almost no hold. Even when we, imaginatively, nostalgically, or in anger, look back at our past, it is always with the confidence that the past is dead and buried. We realize that even in the near future, things that happened less than a hundred years ago are unreal and have no impact on our thinking or lifestyle. Consequently, to understand the Indian of today, nothing more than the history of the last hundred years would suffice.

While some of these events have been etched in memory and imprinted on the psyche, most have only a passing impact and have gone with the wind, as it were. Thus, being Indian is not a return to our Vedic past, the glories of the Guptas, or even Muslim rule, but to the most recent experience of British rule. Our memory is, however, not jolted afresh every morning when we read the newspaper to realize that we can read, thanks to the printing press and the idea of 'The Press' that the British brought to the country. Every time we take a train or fly, we are not reminded that it was the British who brought us the industrial revolution.

Institutions that the British brought surround us everywhere, even the languages we speak, from English to Bengali and Malayalam to Assamese. We owe something to the British. From the judiciary to the Lok Sabha, from the police force to the Indian Army, we owe them to the British. Our character is thus nothing but our reactions to British rule and the institutions they implanted on our soil.

A negative reaction to British rule was called nationalism, and the upsurge of Indian pride was based on the claim to historical greatness and therefore was a return to and a glorification of our ancient roots. However, when Hinduism became nationalism, the truth was not enough.

A lingering memory that is not allowed to die is of Muslim rule and the suppression of Hinduism in their time, added to which were the fresh memories of partition and the consequent bloodbath, which were very real and horrifying to a large percentage of Indians. The last hundred years have also seen the partial emancipation of the depressed classes, with laws against untouchability, rights to temple entry, the opening of education for all, and most importantly, the policy of reservation and affirmative action in support of the depressed classes.

Caste has become more an identity of victimhood than ever before, with all Shudra communities seeking reservation and affirmative action on their behalf, when only years ago, they were the foot soldiers of the caste system, enforcing the system and helping to put the uppity Dalit in his place with violence and general contempt. These emotional events were fortunately accompanied by a substantial increase in literacy among the people, which tempered the otherwise volatile situations that these events could have created.

The growth of literacy has been truly phenomenal. When the British arrived at our shores, we had less than one percent of our population literate. When they left, we could claim that about fifteen percent of our people were literate. Today, many states like Goa, Kerala, and Tamil Nadu can claim close to one hundred percent literacy, and the country as a whole has about 75 percent literacy. Merely mythological and emotional appeals can no longer suffice; a new matrix of appeal had to be developed. While nationalism created a single identity for a captive people, the effort was to use that identity to create an inclusive culture and then to redefine it.

The Indian Character

It is said that character is fate; if so, what is the Indian character? Nirad Chaudhuri laments the fact that this question is not taken seriously, as the Indian is a living paradox, living in a world that even Freud would not be able to unravel. He claims that the British ruled India for 250 years, but after the initial exasperation at the contradictions of Indian behavior, they stopped even trying to understand. They lost their temper at the impossible Indian attitude and became incapable of objective understanding. Instead, they called Indians 'degraded, perverse, grotesque, and effeminate.' Even Alberuni, a very objective observer, said that the Indian mind was 'particularly difficult to penetrate' and added, "I find many traits in the Hindu character very trying." Chaudhuri claims that the Orientalists tried to disregard what they saw before their eyes by trying to create a Hindu character from the Sanskrit texts, from the Vedas to the Puranas. Thereby, they created a literary fiction of the Hindu character. Even the Hindu spirituality that the study revealed was a Western myth, not to be found in the real Indian. His final verdict is that our civilization was at the point of exhaustion, and the sterility of our people was clearly apparent. The truth was that India was dying, and its culture was creating a decay that was there for all to see. Thus, there was no European who came to India who did not leave the country with a poorer opinion. To them, we appeared irrational, inconsistent, and unholy, with an unnatural insistence on chastity accompanied by a sex obsession, a morbid respect for animal life, and an insensitivity to cruelty to living creatures, like untouchables. Our sense of time measured in Yugas and cycles seemed to make all sense of values absurd.

Every Indian is a person divided against himself, says Chaudhuri; he is in 'solidarity with the uncontrollable tendency towards disunity within the Hindu order, collective megalomania with self-abasement, extreme xenophobia with xenolatry, authoritarianism with anarchic individualism, violence with non-violence, militarism with pacifism, cleverness with stupidity.' Chaudhuri insists that we are violent people, and our obsession with Ahimsa is only like the repentance of Asoka after the massive killing of his Kalinga enemies. He claims that it is merely a panic reaction to extreme violence—a recoil reaction. Non-violence is as irrational as violence, says Chaudhuri. He then passes his final judgment, saying to Polonius, "I will be brief; your noble son is mad." He claims that his long observation of Indians has convinced him that there is a streak of insanity in Indians, including dementia, praecox, and paranoia, and that we survive as a nation only because ninety percent of our people are totally inert.

To explain the Indian psyche, Nirad Chaudhuri uses the problems faced by the Englishman when he had to rule India. He claims that the Englishman, who is generally temperate, slow to anger, and compassionate, when taken out of his temperate home and cast into a burning furnace of the tropical climate, literally and figuratively loses his cool. In this climate, where everything seems to be at odds and nature seems to be waiting to cut his throat, he had to be ruthless to survive. That, says Chaudhuri, was what the Aryan faced when he entered India. His behavior was the result of his inability to cope with the climate that was forced upon him and of his need to defend himself against the overwhelming numbers against him. The result was a fragmented character—a person with the intention to do good but forced to employ needless cruelty to defend himself. Chaudhuri says words like 'tribulations' and 'ordeal' are insufficient to describe what the Aryans went through. Further, since he had decided to stay, his tribulations were endless, and the unending experience hardened him into his bad behavior. However, when his period of dominance was turned into subjugation under the Muslims and the British, he turned to diabolical cunning to hide his own weakness, making capital out of his weaknesses and even more on the decencies of others. This became the national character: 'weak when not degraded.'

Indian Thinking

Nirad Chaudhuri has a very interesting and deeply intuitive idea about the Indian character and its consequent philosophy. He says that it is the response of the white man, cast into the inferno that is India, where he is hot, irritated, and endlessly in pain. This torture defined his philosophy. Thus, while western philosophy bemoans the lack of spiritual and rational absolutes, Indian philosophy is merely a response to human pain—pain of the flesh. The typical response is, therefore, that of the Buddha, a philosophy that merely reacts to seeing a poor man, a sick man, and a dying man. Is there any more pitiable failure of courage and a collapse of the will than that, asks Chaudhuri? What kind of philosophy can a man who faints at every pain of the flesh have but that of a frightened coward, asks Chaudhuri. Consequently, the Vaisesika philosophy starts by saying, "Seeing the world sunk in the mire of sorrow, the compassionate sage composed his philosophy in order to rescue it." Samkhya philosophy, perhaps the most typical of Indian philosophies, claims as it aims the reduction of sorrow arising out of three sources: oneself, others, and the acts of God. These are then enumerated: those caused by oneself are anger, hatred, fear, envy, sadness, lust, and greed, and those caused by others are beasts, snakes, spirits, yakshas, and so on, while God is responsible for all the natural calamities. Thus, all the problems of life are merely related to the flesh. There is no idea of universal suffering or innocent suffering, of evil, or of the emptiness of the soul bereft of God. Hindu philosophy thus cannot fathom the sorrows of St. Augustine or of Kierkegaard. They cannot see life as Kafka saw it or cry in pain like Nietzsche for glory, courage, and honor. Most Indian philosophies, especially yoga, speak more of the disciplines of the body than of the soul.

The only saving grace is that, in their concern for human suffering, they raised the mundane to a level of grandeur. Thus, "the philosophical systems lose none of their passionate character by being dryly argumentative," says Chaudhuri and adds, "the suffering of the Hindu in everyday life was so drab and even sordid and was so continuous and irritating that no man, if he knew that he was condemned to live with it forever, could hope to save himself from utter degradation except by raising suffering to a level at which it could be borne without shame and where it would not be cowardly, squalid, and repulsive, as it was in life." However, the resulting consequence of Indian philosophy was, at best, an attempt to redeem human suffering from the inferno of life and take it to a purgatory. Their only solution was to separate the human being into Purusha and Prakriti and give primacy to the soul, thus taking away everything that makes him human. Consequently, even the Hindu Nirvana is only the death of the body and the death of the world. Even in the Nyaya philosophy, the best that is offered is the dreamless sleep of one who never wakes up. Only the Advaita Vedanta of Sankaracharya offers something different, as he advises us to treat the world as Maya, an illusion, a manifestation created by a magician that the soul can negate as unreal and thereby be freed from any attachment to life. Indians, for that very reason, do not love their philosophy, as it offers no relief to the sufferings of the flesh. They prefer the sadhus, who claim to have the power to change and improve their worldly condition with the power of their mantras. A philosophy that deals with abstract things like knowledge has no fascination for the Indian, who prefers the religion of power.

Chaudhuri then claims that everything about Indian religious practices is a reaction to the harsh conditions he had to face. The result is two diametrically opposite reactions. The first is the Brahmanical reaction, which was the quest for cleanliness; the opposite reaction was that of the hermit, who seemed to say, "Since we can do nothing about the filth, let us wallow in it." The hermit and Sadhu throw ash on his body, refuse to have a bath, refuse to clean himself, defy the summer heat and sit naked in Himalayan snow. To the ordinary Indian, for whom neither option is open, life can be most painful. He is forever refraining himself, while the heat makes him irritable and tense; his tolerance is always just minutes away from an explosion. The final distinguishing feature of the Aryan in Indian thinking is the perverse and ingrained adoration of fair skin, the one feature that sets them apart from the dark-skinned natives of their wretched new home.

The encounter with the British, as rulers and as propagators of Christianity, was a convulsive moment. The Portuguese, the French, and the Dutch had come and gone without much of an impact, except in their strongholds in Goa, Kerala, and Pondicherry, leaving the rest of the country untouched. The British were different; not only did they become the rulers of the entire country, directly or indirectly, but they also brought with them the industrial revolution. Society was changed; education was universalized and made available to everyone and to all castes; they introduced a more egalitarian judicial system and brought to the country modern medicine, the banking system, the printing press, and 'The Press.' This alone would have revolutionized social and political thinking, but they added to that with the insidious infiltration of Christian missions and missionaries who spread their religion, Christianity. The impact of Christianity was much more than the content of their beliefs; it was in fact that most of the institutions they introduced into the country were based on an implicit acceptance of the tenets of Christianity. Modern Europe was created by the agricultural revolution, the industrial revolution, and the political revolutions in France and the faraway U.S.A. on the basis of an underlying belief in the values implicit in Christianity. Consequently, modern Indians who grew up in British institutions were naturally drawn to Christian ideas.

Many Indians converted; in fact, many of the best. Since it started in Bengal and Calcutta, the headquarters of British rule in India, it was there that the reaction also began. At first, it was the benign creation of the Brahmo-Samaj into which Christian ideas were incorporated, including the aversion to idol worship and the caste system while seeing God as the ultimate principle, Brahman. Such compromises led to a backlash with the creation of the Arya Samaj and a return to the Vedas and, what they considered, the eternal values of Hinduism. It also resulted in the missionary zeal of men like Vivekananda, who felt the need to explain Hinduism to the world.

Indian Culture

All our claims to being a great civilization and culture have to answer the reality of the almost total illiteracy in the country. When the British came to the country, we had less than 1% of our country that could read and write, and the illiteracy among women was almost total. Even when they left, only 15% of our population was literate. When the British and, before them, the other Europeans came to the country, most of our regional languages had no known grammar, and no effort had been made to define the meaning of words in a dictionary. It fell on these European missionaries and scholars to develop grammars and to write dictionaries for most of the languages. This is a nation that boasts of the first great grammar in Sanskrit by the great Panini and languages like Tamil claim an antiquity dating back beyond the Aryans. In a nation that had perhaps the oldest university in the world at Taxila and in a nation where the Buddhists had created a university at Nalanda to which scholars from all over Asia used to come, we became a country with destroyed universities and without any culture of learning. Our culture is merely what is enjoyed by less than 1% of the country. In fact, the only common bond that held all Indians together was their ignorance. It is this feature of Indian society that answers what we have become as a people.

In classical times, when the Vedas were composed and there was a fervent churning of ideas, we were equal, and our society, if not greater than the Ancient Greeks, was equal to the best in the world. All the philosophies, from Stoicism to Epicureanism, were propounded, and there was a healthy respect for intellectual freedom. This led to the Upanishads and the evolution of religious thinking, culminating in religions like Buddhism and Jainism. At this stage, the evolution of knowledge was taking the natural path that led to greater and greater refinement of knowledge and progress in society. However, like some ice age that killed everything, Indian society suddenly turned inwards, closed the door, and became paranoid, forcing society into a time capsule, frozen in time, closed to new ideas, and imprisoning society from all change.

It was only in the glorious years of Buddhism and Jainism that there was that great sense of intellectual adventure—some forgotten past to be looked back on with nostalgic yearning. A time when thinking was free and men were not locked up in the prison of caste. In their heyday, these religions were the only time when knowledge was free, and attempts were made to educate people and lead them to a higher level of consciousness. It was not the content of their philosophy but their attitude and the general equality of opportunity that were unique. They became mass religions because of their social philosophy rather than their religious content. For the first and perhaps the last time, leaders believed that they had a social mandate—to educate and to care. Thus, mutts, monasteries, and sangas where monks congregated became centers of learning from where the monks went out to teach the people. The lay people were encouraged to study and to contribute to the creation of knowledge. This golden age of freedom was trampled under by orthodoxy; the monasteries were destroyed and the temples desecrated, all in the name of religion.

Vedic Hinduism was initially not a temple-oriented religion, but with the resurgence of Brahmanical Hinduism consequent on the persecution of Buddhists and Jains along with the destruction of their temples and mutts, the Brahmins realized the power of institutions like temples. The greatest crime of orthodox Hinduism was not its suppression of Buddhism but that it did not learn or perhaps did not want to imitate the success that the Buddhists achieved through their temples and through their idea of communal living. They destroyed what was good and saw no reason to build anything new. It took many centuries for Hindu temples to do even a small percentage of what the Buddhist temples were doing in the 3rd and 4th centuries. Hinduism's greatest failure was its refusal to teach. Its worst attitude was a fear of knowledge. Thus, from Manu to Kautilya, the intent was to keep the people in ignorance so that the Brahmanical class could claim all knowledge and thereby rule over an ignorant mass of people. Not only did they not create educational institutions, they also created draconian laws against the leakage of knowledge to the lower castes. Like the Grecian gods, who withheld fire from humans, they felt that by denying the lower castes the power of knowledge, they could keep them eternally dependent on them. The result was the perpetuation of ignorance until it became the defining nature of the Indian consciousness.

Education then became the privilege of the elite, and knowledge was handed down only from father to son in a closed loop that excluded everyone else. When more educated men were required for their narrow purpose of dominance, they created mutts and gurukuls where only Brahmins could be taught. In time, the thirst for knowledge and the hunger for the truth were extinguished, and no attempt was made to create educational institutions until the 19th century. Since there were no educational institutions, Indians ceased to feel any sense of loss or of deprivation. That was perhaps the greatest tragedy because, with such an attitude, there was no attempt to rebel and no urge to know; all curiosity was literally extinguished. The sense of curiosity so vital to learning is yet to be rekindled in our society.

India Today

Indian civilization, said Dr. Radhakrishnan, is characterized by its spiritualism. The other feature associated with Indian thinking is 'Ahimsa,' made synonymous with non-violence by Mahatma Gandhi when he made it into a revolutionary idea in the struggle for independence. In popular perception, India is the land of 'Karma' and the caste system, at a purely economic and social level, is seen as a poor, illiterate, and dirty country. Our review has shown that despite strong opposition and many attempts at reformation, Indian society has held firm to the sanctity of the Vedas, a belief in Karma, and a society ordered on the basis of caste stratification. Philosophy and spiritualism, so prominent in nascent Indian thinking, slowly settled into their place as a refuge for the Jnana Yogi. The idea of Jnana itself has been devalued over the years with the overpowering influence of the Bhakti movement and has lost its hold on the Indian imagination.

Spiritualism

Indian philosophy was initially so great that its success became its greatest stumbling block. Instead of looking for a God or a creation story, they started with the bold declaration, 'who knows.' This created a philosophical climate of scientific inquiry instead of dogma. The result was almost immediate, for they realized that only what the mind visualizes is what is apparent. There is no objective reality. All we have are our own minds that create everything else. We are Brahman. Consequently, the world is only 'Maya,' a creation of the mind. To explain the commonality of perception, they declared that it is all a 'manifestation' of Brahma. With the world as a manifestation and we as the creators of our universe, Indian thinking reached an abyss. God could only be 'Nirguna' and impossible to worship. Thus, there was only apparent existence with no refuge and no purpose, and only the continuous operation of karma that may have its own purpose. We knew so much that there was nothing more to know, and our intellectual abilities seemed thereafter to atrophy.

The reason Western philosophy has such a large corpus of

thought is that it took them 2000 years to reach where the Indians reached, even at the time of the writing of the Upanishads. Western philosophy started with Plato, who explained reality as a mix of 'form' and 'essence.' Plato started by claiming that all we perceive is a shadow of the real thing. This idealism allowed them to believe that there was something beyond human perception. Descartes said it is all in the mind, while Hume asserted that it is all about sense perception. Since human perception can be faulty, the West developed the scientific method of experimentation and instrumentation to remove subjective fallacies. Only in the collision of these ideas did Western philosophy realize that all is 'Maya.' Then came 'Existentialism' and the questioning of language itself for it to realize that we may be part of a magic show limited by our perception and chained by our language ability. The greatness of Western philosophy was the respect for the way of Jnana that the ancient Indians had exalted; it was not necessarily the attainment of final truth that was important, but the search itself. It was the arduous search, the difficulties on the way, and the little things we learned that strengthened character and deepened knowledge. The greatest crime against the intellect is to sit back and pretend that all knowledge has been found. The mind then becomes lazy and no effort is made to look deeper, creating a complacency that kills the intellect. It is like the body of a person who does no exercise; it becomes weak and anemic, with neither strength nor stamina.

That is what happened to the Indian mind. Having reached the pinnacle of thinking so soon, Indian thinking could only descend. It started with the logical alternative that as God is 'Nirguna,' he can also be 'saguna,' the fountain of all qualities. Thus, while the Shaivite Advaita was nihilistic, the Vaishnavite dualism allowed for value to be attached to human life. After that, it was not logic but human need that forced the gods to be created, who became avatars engaged in human affairs. This led to personal gods, temples, and, soon, the representation of gods as idols to be worshiped. It was the importance of existentialism that forced Indian thinking into its new materialism. With that, Indian thinking lost most of its spiritualism while remaining transcendental, where gods merely catered to human needs. Religion became materialistic and even the purpose of Bhakti, which was initially an immersion in God, as in Yoga, became all about personal needs and desires.

The other problem faced by Indian thinking was the tendency to immediately create dogma around new intellectual ideas. Like Sanskrit and the Vedas, all the Upanishads and the Puranas became sacrosanct. They were then beyond critical review and were seen as some treasure to be protected, instead of treating them as merely working hypotheses that needed refinement. What Dr. Radhakrishnan claimed as India's good fortune was only true till the arrival of the Aryan, after which India was almost forever at war with some invading intruder or other and finally, internally. Thus, the Aryan, with his thinking, challenged the beliefs of the local people and new religions like Jainism and Buddhism vied with each other for patronage and mass support. Then came the Muslims and finally the British. The siege mentality that the locals exhibited to the intrusion of Aryan thought was just getting stabilized when Jainism and Buddhism erupted as an cxplosion, leading Orthodoxy to retreat into their shells. When finally the ideas of Jainism and Buddhism had been assimilated, came the Muslims, not only as a religion but as conquerors. This forced the Indians to take cover, lick their wounds, and regroup so as not to disintegrate.

The greatest weakness of the Indian intellectual tradition is that it was exclusive and the vast majority of the people were not allowed to participate. The caste system effectively excluded all the Shudras from any intellectual pursuit, while the untouchables remained totally illiterate. Most Indians therefore had no idea of the philosophical base of their religious beliefs, while Jainism and Buddhism were able to galvanize the people by making it open to them. This sent a shiver down the back of the orthodoxy and then they tried to include the Shudra and permit the hearing of the Epics to them. Once they came to the fold, more compromises were made to accommodate their crude beliefs, and the system collapsed when they began pandering to their vulgar requirements. Instead of making an effort to educate the people, they stooped to conquer, not realizing that it would soon drown them in the quagmire of their own duplicity. The second was ambiguity. From the idea of

'Nirvana' to 'Maya' and the idea that the gods may be a creation of man, Indian thought confuses the common man. The final nail in the coffin of intellectual thought was the pervasive acceptance of 'Bhakti' as the way. While Jnana continued for some time to be given some importance, in time, it became the way of the atheist, who was considered a greater threat to society than terrorists. Thus came the hatred for the rationalist. We have become misologues, haters of knowledge—the very thing that Dr. Radhakrishnan boastfully claimed we were not.

The Vedas

The one perennial and sacred text has been the Vedas. Their authority may have been questioned, but those who questioned them have all been silenced. Through the turmoil of religious debates and the uncertainties of Indian history, the Vedas alone have remained untouched. Untouched also in the sense of not being read. It is repeated in chants every morning and in every Hindu ritual and ceremony, in the same words and the same intonation, as it was done thousands of years ago. Yet, few have read it and few can understand the old Sanskrit in which it is written. The Sanskrit of the Vedas is dead, and so is the spirit behind the great hymns. What is left is the empty repetition of parrots. In fact, what is worse is that even as the Epics are read every day in pious households, their message of the brotherhood of men has little impact. While Ram is Mariyada Purusothom and gives up his kingdom to his brother, the idea of sacrifice is not what is followed by most Indians but the way of Ravan, to grab all that one can and never share if possible.

Religion Without Philosophy

The Vedic religion was so philosophical that it was often seen as agnostic. However, with every compromise, Hinduism became a religion full of outward signs and symbols, with mantras and rituals, while the underlying philosophy kept leeching away. Philosophy just could not deal with the plethora of new gods. Idols with temples as their abode imprisoned gods, where once they roamed free all over the universe and permeated all nature. Temples, pilgrimage centers, and birthplaces of gods became cages where the faithful worshiped. With a total surrender to contingency, it was difficult for philosophy to justify all compromises. The writing of the Puranas made the mythical, divine, and all critical examination disrespectful and profane. With no philosophy to support beliefs, there was a divorce between belief and practice. While the Sankaras and the Ramanujas continued to preach a God, who is 'Nirguna' or 'Saguna,' and that we live in a universe that is 'Maya,' a manifestation of Brahma, an eternal principle, their philosophy is revered and attracts students and researchers but has ceased to mean much in the practices of Hinduism. Indian philosophy is revered and presented as Hindu thought to indicate the depth of its philosophy. It is, however, an impossible thought, akin to the higher reaches of algebra, certainly true and consistent but beyond the intellectual grasp of ordinary men. What started as a fracture in the thinking of Hindu scholars became a clean break, where thinking and practice deviated so much that they could no longer be recognized as the same religion.

This nebulous, weak, and anti-intellectual approach was continually opposed by the brightest and the best. Their rebellion, in most cases, was against brainless ritualism and the segregation of people into a rigid caste system, where certain castes were never allowed to participate in any religious function, debarred from education, and condemned to a life of degradation. The later rebellions of Ramanuja against Basava and Guru Nanak were against the proliferation of rituals and the continued oppression of the people in the name of caste. This trend has continued into the 20th century with Ramakrishna, Narayana Guru, and Mahatma Gandhi, all demanding a more open religion and the inclusion of the lower castes, to no avail.

Ahimsa

The Indian intellectual tradition's greatest contribution to human culture is perhaps the concept of 'Ahimsa.' It took on a modern form when Gandhi equated it with non-violence. The idea of Ahimsa is not merely non-violence but a reverence for all life. Unfortunately, this idea has been found to be too demanding and the offshoot of the belief vegetarianism, an avoidance of meat eating, as though that meant Ahimsa. This convoluted understanding of such a noble concept appears comical when, in the later versions of the Ramayana, Ram and Lakshman happily hunt animals, almost as a sport, but decline to eat the meat. This justified violence, demanded vegetarianism, and reduced Ahimsa to a fetish. Ahimsa, which required men to treat life as sacred, made the caste system barbaric. It had inevitably opened one's eyes to inequality, poverty, and the total cultural exclusion of large chunks of humanity as totally unacceptable. Thus, the Indian intellectual tradition preferred instead to turn a blind eye to such problems and live in a make-believe world of Maya.

Intolerance

From the beginning, one characteristic of the response has remained unchanged. The violence with which all new philosophies were opposed, tooth and nail, hides an inferiority and an implicit acceptance that the new philosophies were better. While we have accepted new gods and the various ways in which a God may be worshiped, it was not without violence. The sanctity of the Vedas and the caste system have remained non-negotiable, along with the right of the Brahmin to officiate in all ceremonies. The Jains and the Buddhists were persecuted, their temples destroyed or usurped, and their nuns raped and degraded, yet in the end, the Buddha became the ninth Avatar of Lord Vishnu. The sword of Islam posed a greater challenge than Mohammed or Allah. The result was mutual disdain; while the educated Indian looked away with contempt, the aristocratic Muslim saw in the Indian attitude only the stupidity of the ostrich. Thus, the clash of civilizations ended with nothing more than a whimper.

The Impact of Caste

While the gods have come and gone, the caste system has been a constant. While Buddha and Ramanuja and reformers from Basava to Guru Nanak and Ramakrishna continued to rail against the caste system and the need to purify the religion, the system resisted all change, and reformers were often chased out of the main body of believers and forced to create their own cults and sects, which in time, inevitably, got submerged into the ocean called Hinduism. Even more than the Vedas, the caste system has been the most defining aspect of Indian consciousness. It has so impacted all aspects of life that it can be said that Indian consciousness is synonymous with caste consciousness. A man is born into a caste, not a state or even a village. His caste determines his life, his occupation, and the level of his knowledge. In fact, as someone pointed out, India is a federation of castes, more than of states. Each caste has both opted for and been cajoled and forced into joining the union. Each caste has its own village, its own occupation, its own guilds, and its own customs and rituals. From Manu to Kautilya, Indian law-givers have seen caste as paramount. While this, in a sense, gave each some autonomy and a sense of relative freedom, it also meant that interaction between castes was limited and strictly mandated by social prohibitions. It also meant a small world where no man could look beyond his caste or hope to know beyond his caste needs.

Apart from the brutalization of certain sections of society, it also thrust down a sense of inevitability, leading to lethargy, as it was futile to aim at anything beyond one's caste. Without access to education, most Indians were doomed to a life of repetitive futility. This bred an attitude toward life that accepted the stifling of dissent and the death of the critical spirit, along with an apathy to growth, improvement, and even hope. Perhaps more disastrous has been its impact on art, literature, and culture in general. In the Axial age and the early years of the rise of Buddhism and Jainism, when people were not excluded from all religious and cultural activities, Sanskrit literature attained a certain degree of greatness, especially during the age of Kalidasa. Thereafter, not only did we not produce a Shakespeare or a Cervantes, we could not produce a Tolstoy or even an Elliot. In fact, the corpus of Indian literature atrophied to almost nothing. So much so that most Indian languages, including Bengali, had no prose tradition until the arrival of the British. Even Tamil, after the Sangam period, saw an arid phase that lasted to the 19th century, with the Bhakti poets in the 7th to the 10th centuries being the exceptions. In the Vedangas, treatises were written in music and dance but being in Sanskrit, they remained on the shelves of the educated till the 19th century, when dance, nurtured in the womb of the Devadasi caste, was usurped by the Brahmins as a cultural showpiece for the 20th century. Castes and guilds that developed and preserved art forms like Kathakali and Theyyam in Kerala, the Ram Leela of U.P., and the theater groups of Tamil Nadu, as part of the worship of local gods and festivals, are now appropriated as national culture. After the initial years of Grecian and other foreign influences, India has almost no traditional painting or sculpture. Their being merely artisan-based with no intellectual inputs, Indian art and even literature became repetitive, where all that was done was to endlessly copy accepted works of art. Be it the sculptures that adorn temples or the Chola bronzes, it was the handiwork of artisans who could only imitate, and that too from a very limited range.

While huge changes have taken place at the insistence of the state, even these changes have been modulated by caste consciousness. The idea of the Brahmin at the top of the system has meant that the aim of all Indians is to become Brahmins. This desire is also religious, as it is claimed in Karma theory that, if one does enough good, one may be reborn a Brahmin. With it came the degradation of all manual labor. While the Brahmin-dominated education system produces good mathematicians and scientists, it does not produce good engineers who are prepared to work with their hands. Good engineers are mostly seen in the field of information technology. Worse, it reduced ambition to the climbing of the caste hierarchy. For however good one may be as a mason or carpenter, one is never given the respect due to a Brahmin. The other way to see it is through the attitude that says, now that I am the boss, treat me like a Brahmin. Touch my feet and like Kautilya said, as I am now a Brahmin, I am now above the law of mere secular kings.

In the End

The modern Indian is the result of many cultural and religious movements, always determined by caste, the level of education, and wealth and position. Consequently, it has been caste and the abject levels of literacy, poverty, heat, and dirt that have determined what the Indian would become. For more than 70% of the population excluded from culture and education, it was poverty, not the Vedas, that was the determining factor. Even for the educated few and the twice-born, the sacred texts have meant less than they are made out to be, as most did not know them in any detail, and the philosophy of the Upanishads was meant only for those who had dedicated their lives to learning, a group that, history shows, has been diminishing with the greater hold of the material world.

Uncertainty about our origins and the blanks in our history make any linear account of how we became what we are almost impossible. A full study of Indian history does not prepare us for the reality of the present-day Indian or the shape of his thinking. We are forced to the conclusion that Jung may be wrong; there is no such thing as 'racial memory' or 'universal unconsciousness.' Modern men are merely the sum of their immediate past and do not carry with them any 'racial memory' nor do they come, as Wordsworth claimed, 'with trailing clouds of glory.'

The modern Indian has almost no memory of his Vedic past; he had forgotten Ashoka and even the Buddha until the Indologists unEarthed them again. Even the philosophies of Sankara, Ramanuja, and Basava are only available to serious students of religion, and to others, they are long-forgotten, irrelevant, obscure, and too arid to be a guide for modern life. The fact that the Nairs and the Ezhavas, who had a matrilineal system until about a hundred years ago and whose women went where they liked and loved whom they liked, are today as prudish as Victorian matrons, confirms the irrelevance of history. The Nairs, who, to show their status, carried two swords and had a life devoted totally to the martial arts, like the Samurai, till about two hundred years ago, are today no more martial than a railway clerk. The Mappila Muslim women who went where they liked but are today all covered up, dressed in black, and told to stay at home make us wonder what happened to their special brand of Indian Islam.

While India had a rich religious and philosophical past that made historians call it a place of spiritual refuge, the truth is that such a heritage was available to too few, and even that has been eroded by the culture of the literate and the poor, trumping the merely spiritual. The modern Indian is more of a philistine and a hedonist who lives for the present. Yet he can be easily moved by emotions, especially any call to religion. It must be his guilt at being so removed from true spirituality and from any claim to knowledge that he rages like a headstrong juvenile, as though somebody were beating his dear mother, whom he never visits, whenever there is a perception of sacrilege.

Since he knows practically nothing about his religion, any demagogue can inflame him into an irrational rage at the mere whisper that his religion is threatened. Even the materialistic Indian who has forsaken his homeland for greener pastures in the U.S.A., Europe, and the rest of the West is moved to rage at every real and imagined slight to his religion, a religion he knows next to nothing about. Everything becomes Hinduism, from the bindi to the cow, from Ganga to naked sadhus, from idol worship to all forms of Tantric practices, from mantras to magic. Out of these, an identity has been formed, difficult to define except by negation—not Christian, not Muslim, not even Sikh, perhaps everything else.

Yet religion is the mold out of which the modern Indian is created. The mold is a mixture of unreasoned beliefs, the inferiority of a defeated people, combined with the hauteur of a people who think theirs is a superior culture, groping for meaning in Western institutions without any belief in their underlying logic. The terrible handicaps of caste discrimination leave 70% of Indians burdened with feelings of victimhood, rarely able to rise above their cultural limitations. The centuries of cultural malnutrition, along with the real and apparent physical malnutrition, make the Indian weak, lacking stamina for the long haul, easily depressed, and too easily satisfied. It is not any intellectual belief that determines the attitude of an Indian but the inferiority bred in our bones through centuries of oppression, not of any foreignnation, but of our own people and our brand of social thinking. Our very bodies bear the testimony of our oppression.

BIBLIOGRAPHY

1. Discovery of India by Jawaharlal Nehru
2. India by Alberuni
3. Hindu History by A.K Mazumdar
4. Oxford History of India by A. Vincent Smith
5. The Wonder That Was India by A.L Basham
6. Part 2 by S.A.A Razvi
7. Early Indian History by Romila Thapar
8. History and Beyond by Romila Thapar
9. India: A Short History by David Luddem
10. Ashoka by Charles Allen
11. Coromandal by Charles Allen
12. The Hindus: An Alternate History by Doniger Wendy
13. The Rig Veda by Doniger Wendy
14. The Laws of Manu by Doniger Wendy
15. India Discovered by John Keay
16. The Honorable Company by John Keay

17. The Last Crusade by Nigel Cliff

18. A History of South India by N. Shastri

19. Awakening by Subrato Das Gupta

20. India: A Religious Geography by Diana L. Eck

21. Indian Philosophy by S. Radhakrisnan

22. Principles of the Upanishad by S. Radhakrisnan

23. The Upanishads by S. Radhakrisnan

24. The Mahabharatha by C. Rajagobalachari

25. The Ramayana by C. Rajagobalachari

26. The Mahabharatha by Kamala Subramaniam

27. The Ramayana by R.K Narayanan

28. The Philosophies of India by Heinrick Zimmer

29. The Indian Heritage by Beni Madab Barua

30. Buddhism by Bimala Churn Law

31. Hinduism Reconstructed by Gunther Diaz Sonthemer/ Herman Kulke

32. The Rise of Civilization in India and Pakistan by Briget and Raymond

33. To Uphold the World by Bruce Rich

34. 1492 by Filipe Fernandez Armesto

35. History of India by Percival Spear

36. Bagavat-gita by Barbara Stoner Miller

37. Bagavat-gita by M.K Gandhi

38. My Experiments with Truth by M.K Gandhi

39. The Age of Wrath by M.K Gandhi
40. The First Spring by M.K Gandhi
41. The Peacock Throne by M.K Gandhi
42. Continent of Circe by Nirad Choudhri
43. Scholar Extraordinary by Nirad Choudhri
44. Clive of India by Nirad Choudhri
45. Caste by M.N Srinivas
46. Socio-Economic Philosophy of Ambedkar by P.V Rathnam
47. Doctrine of Karma by Swami Abdedananda
48. Panchatantra by Arthur.W. Ryder
49. The Last Nizam by John Zubrzycki
50. Ambedkar by Gail Omvedt
51. From Plassey to Partition by Sekher Bandyopadhya
52. Annihilation of Caste by B.R Ambedkar
53. The Proudest Day by Anthony Read/David Fisher
54. Man Before Mahatma by Charles Di Salva
55. India After Gandhi by Ramchandra Guha
56. Post Hindu India by Kanchi Ilaiah
57. Wicked Women of the Raj by Coralie Younger
58. India Unbound by Gurucharan Das
59. A History of India by John Keay
60. White Mughals by William Darymple
61. The Last Mughal by William Darymple

62. Flaws in the Jewel by Roderick Mathew

63. Getting to Know Hinduism by Mark W. Muesee

64. The Men Who Ruled India by Philip Mason

65. The Gazetteer of India: History and Culture by Philip Mason

66. India and the Apostle Thomas by A.E Medlycott

67. Survey of Kerala History by A. Sreedhra Menon

68. The Ivory Throne by Manu.S. Pillai

69. The Battle for Sanskrit by Rajiv Malhotra

70. Breaking India by Rajiv Malhotra

71. Being Different by Rajiv Malhotra

72. Gita Press and the Making of Hindu India by Akshaya Mukul

73. The Land of the Seven Rivers by Sanjeev Sanyal

74. The Ocean of Churn by Sanjeev Sanyal

75. Know the Puranas by Ramanuj Prasad

76. The Transformation by Karen Armstrong

77. Creation by Gore Vidal

78. The Indians by Sudhir Kakar

79. The Indian Identity by Sudhir Kakar

80. Intimate Relations by Sudhir Kakar

81. Shiva to Sankara by Devdutt Pattanaik

82. Shyam: Bhagavata by Devdutt Pattanaik

83. Seven Secrets of Vishnu by Devdutt Pattanaik

84. Sita: Ramayana by Devdutt Pattanaik